MEDIA STUDIES

Media Content and
Media Audiences

MEDIA STUDIES

VOLUME 3

Media Content and Media Audiences

First Edition
Revised Reprint

Pieter J Fourie (Editor)

This volume is part of a four-volume series.

Media Studies Volume 3
Media Content and Media Audiences

First published 2009
Revised reprint 2018

Juta and Company (Pty) Ltd
PO Box 14373, Lansdowne, 7779, Cape Town, South Africa

© 2018 Juta and Company (Pty) Ltd

ISBN 978 1 48512 550 1
WEB PDF ISBN 978 1 48512 551 8

All rights reserved. No part of this publication may be reproduced or transmitted in any form or by any means, electronic or mechanical, including photocopying, recording, or any information storage or retrieval system, without prior permission in writing from the publisher. Subject to any applicable licensing terms and conditions in the case of electronically supplied publications, a person may engage in fair dealing with a copy of this publication for his or her personal or private use, or his or her research or private study. See Section 12(1)(a) of the Copyright Act 98 of 1978.

Project Manager: Sharon Steyn/Seshni Kazadi
Editor: Alfred LeMaitre
Proofreader: Lee-Ann Ashcroft
Cover designer: Genevieve Simpson
Typesetter: Mckore Graphics
Indexer: Jennifer Stern
Illustrations by Mckore Graphics

Typeset in 10.5 pt on 14 pt Minion Pro

Print Administration by DJE Flexible Print Solutions

The author and the publisher believe on the strength of due diligence exercised that this work does not contain any material that is the subject of copyright held by another person. In the alternative, they believe that any protected pre-existing material that may be comprised in it has been used with appropriate authority or has been used in circumstances that make such use permissible under the law.

This book has been independently peer-reviewed by academics who are experts in the field.

SERIES CONTENTS

1 MEDIA STUDIES VOLUME 1: MEDIA HISTORY, MEDIA AND SOCIETY

Part 1: History
Chapter 1: History of the South African media — *David Wigston*
Chapter 2: The media in Africa — *Fackson Banda*

Part 2: Media and Society
Chapter 3: Approaches to the study of mass communication — *Pieter J Fourie*
Chapter 4: The role and functions of the media in society — *Pieter J Fourie*
Chapter 5: The effects of mass communication — *Pieter J Fourie*
Chapter 6: Media culture — *Magriet Pitout*
Chapter 7: The ideological power of the media — *Stefan Sonderling*
Chapter 8: The public sphere in contemporary society — *Pieter Duvenage*
Chapter 9: Globalisation, information communication, technology and the media — *Pieter J Fourie*

2 MEDIA STUDIES VOLUME 2: POLICY, MANAGEMENT AND MEDIA REPRESENTATION

Part 1: Media Policy
Chapter 1: The nature of media and communications policy — *Jo Bardoel and Jan van Cuilenburg*
Chapter 2: External media regulation in South Africa — *Pieter J Fourie*
Chapter 3: Internal media regulation in South Africa — *Marié van Heerden*

Part 2: Media Management
Chapter 4: Media and communication markets — *Jo Bardoel and Jan van Cuilenburg*
Chapter 5: Strategic media management — *Jo Bardoel and Jan van Cuilenburg*

Part 3: Representation
Chapter 6: Representation defined — *Julie Reid*
Chapter 7: News as representation — *Arnold S de Beer and Nicolene Botha*
Chapter 8: Media and the construction of identity — *Herman Wasserman*
Chapter 9: Media and race — *Lynette Steenveld*
Chapter 10: Gender and the media — *Beschara Karam*
Chapter 11: Media and sexual orientation: The portrayal of gays and lesbians — *Christo Cilliers*
Chapter 12: Media and the environment — *Ian Glenn*
Chapter 13: Media and HIV/AIDS — *Corrie Faure*
Chapter 14: Media and violence — *Magriet Pitout*
Chapter 15: Media and terrorism — *Gysbert M Kirsten*

3 MEDIA STUDIES VOLUME 3: MEDIA CONTENT AND MEDIA AUDIENCES

Part 1: Media Content and Content Analysis
Section A: Quantitative content analysis
Chapter 1:   Quantitative content analysis — *David Wigston*
Section B: Qualitative content analysis
Chapter 2:   Media semiotics — *Pieter J Fourie*
Chapter 3:   Media, language and discourse — *Stefan Sonderling*
Chapter 4:   Media and visual literacy — *Trudie du Plooy*
Chapter 5:   Visual text analysis — *Trudie du Plooy*
Chapter 6:   Textual analysis: Narrative and argument — *Jeanne Prinsloo*
Chapter 7:   Narrative analysis — *David Wigston*
Chapter 8:   Film theory and criticism — *Pieter J Fourie*

Part 2: Media Audiences
Chapter 9:   Media audience theory — *Magriet Pitout*
Chapter 10: Questionnaire surveys in media research — *Elirea Bornman*
Chapter 11: Field research in media studies — *Magriet Pitout*
Chapter 12: Measuring media audiences — *Elirea Bornman*
Chapter 13: Psychoanalysis and television — *Stefan Sonderling*

4 MEDIA STUDIES VOLUME 4: SOCIAL (NEW) MEDIA AND MEDIATED COMMUNICATION TODAY

Chapter 1:   Social media and mediated communication in postmodern society — *Pieter J Fourie*
Chapter 2:   What are social media? Introductory definitions — *Tanja Bosch*
Chapter 3:   Researching audiences in the age of social media — *Tanja Bosch*
Chapter 4:   Social media and globalisation — *Gabriël J Botma*
Chapter 5:   Thinking about the public sphere and new (social) media — *Marc Caldwell*
Chapter 6:   Identity 2.0: Negotiating identity and the politics of belonging in cyberspace — *viola candice milton and Winston Mano*
Chapter 7:   Social media: Freedom of expression, and media regulation and policy — *Julie Reid*
Chapter 8:   Social media policy in Africa — *Monica B Chibita and Wilson Ugangu*
Chapter 9:   The impact of social media on journalism — *Ylva Rodny-Gumede*
Chapter 10: Journalism and new (social) media in South Africa — *Nicola Jane Jones*
Chapter 11: The ethics of social media in South African journalism — *Herman Wasserman*
Chapter 12: Using social media for branding — *Charmaine du Plessis*
Chapter 13: Participation in the digital age: Public self-expression and public identity 'work' — *Mariekie Burger*

CONTENTS

List of Figures and Tables	xiii
Acknowledgements	xvii
About the authors	xviii
Introduction to the 2018 Revised Reprint	xx

PART 1: MEDIA CONTENT   **1**

Chapter 1: Quantitative Content Analysis   **3**

David Wigston

1.1	Introduction	4
1.2	What is content analysis?	5
1.3	Uses of content analysis	6
	1.3.1 Descriptive research	8
	1.3.2 Explanatory research	8
1.4	Steps in doing a content analysis	10
	1.4.1 Contextualising the research	11
	1.4.2 The literature review	13
	1.4.3 The method	13
	1.4.4 Findings	24
	1.4.5 Interpretation and conclusion	29
1.5	Analysing content on the internet	30
	1.5.1 Formulating the research problem	31
	1.5.2 Selecting the sample	31
	1.5.3 Defining the categories	32
	1.5.4 Coding the units of analysis	32
	1.5.5 Analysing and interpreting the data	33
	1.5.6 In conclusion	33
1.6	An evaluation of content analysis as a method	33
	1.6.1 Advantages	33
	1.6.2 Limitations	34
1.7	Ethical issues	35

Chapter 2: Communication and Media Semiotics   **39**

Pieter J Fourie

2.1	Introduction: the field of semiotics	40
2.2	The history of semiotics	42
	2.2.1 Structuralism	42
	2.2.2 Founding fathers of modern semiotics: de Saussure and Peirce	47

Media Studies: Volume 3

2.3	The sign	50
	2.3.1 The characteristics of a sign	50
	2.3.2 The components of a sign	51
	2.3.3 Kinds of signs on the basis of the signifier/referent relationship	51
	2.3.4 Sign functions	53
2.4	Sign system	57
2.5	Code	57
	2.5.1 Code typology	58
	2.5.2 Characteristics of codes	62
2.6	The paradigmatic-syntagmatic system	65
2.7	Meaning	66
	2.7.1 Denotation and connotation	67
	2.7.2 Encoding and decoding	68
	2.7.3 Ideological meaning	70
	2.7.4 Social semiotics	71
2.8	A basic semiotic analysis	75

Chapter 3: Media, Language and Discourse — 83

Stefan Sonderling

3.1	Introduction	84
3.2	Language in society and society in language	85
3.3	Approaches to the study and analysis of language	88
3.4	Language of the text	91
3.5	Discursive practice: Rules and convention for the use of language and production of text	102
3.6	Discourse as social interaction and social orders of discourse	105
3.7	Language and political discourse	107
3.8	Orders of discourse	110
3.9	Language, power and ideology	111

Chapter 4: Media and Visual Literacy — 116

Gertruida M du Plooy

4.1	Introduction	117
4.2	The meaning(s) of media/visual literacy	118
	4.2.1 Verbal and visual language – an analogy	118
4.3	Levels of media and visual literacy	121
	4.3.1 Media content literacy	121

Contents

	4.3.2 Media grammar literacy	122
	4.3.3 Medium literacy	124
4.4	Ontological and epistemological assumptions	126
4.5	Perceptual approach to visual communication	127
	4.5.1 The semiotic approach	128
	4.5.2 The cognitive approach	132
4.6	Research	135
4.7	Future developments	137
4.8	Case study	139

Chapter 5: Visual Text Analysis   147
Gertruida M du Plooy

5.1	Introduction	148
5.2	Pictorial codes in a static filmic shot and photograph	149
	5.2.1 Lighting as a code of content	150
	5.2.2 Colour as a code of content	152
	5.2.3 Field forces within the shot, or frame	153
	5.2.4 Balance as a code of content	162
	5.2.5 Depth and volume as content codes	162
	5.2.6 Area orientation as a code of form	165
	5.2.7 Lenses and focus as codes of form	166
	5.2.8 Basic camera shots as visual codes of form	169
	5.2.9 Building screen space – camera viewpoint	170
5.3	Picturisation through movement in film and television	173
	5.3.1 Objective versus subjective time	173
	5.3.2 Picturisation through primary movement	174
	5.3.3 Picturisation through secondary movement	175
	5.3.4 Picturisation through tertiary movement	176
5.4	Auditory codes and the combination of audiovisual codes	186
	5.4.1 Auditory codes	186
	5.4.2 The combination of auditory and visual codes	190
5.5	Research	195
5.6	Future developments	197
5.7	Case study	198

Chapter 6: Textual Analysis: Narrative and Argument   204
Jeanne Prinsloo

6.1	Introduction	206
6.2	Discourse and ideology	206

ix

Media Studies: Volume 3

	6.2.1 Discourse	206
	6.2.2 Ideology	209
6.3	Media texts: Mediation and rhetoric	211
	6.3.1 Organisation of media texts	212
6.4	Structuralist approaches	214
	6.4.1 Syntagmatic theories	215
	6.4.2 Paradigmatic theories	235
6.5	Narrative and genre	242
6.6	Argumentation	243
6.7	Argument as narrative and narrative as argument	250

Chapter 7: Narrative Analysis 254
David Wigston

7.1	Introduction	255
7.2	The basic narrative paradigm	260
7.3	Roland Barthes's theory of narrative	266
7.4	The role of binary opposition in a narrative	276
7.5	Todorov's model of narrative	278
7.6	Vladimir Propp's narrative model	281
7.7	Umberto Eco's narrative model	290
	7.7.1 Level one: binary oppositions	291
	7.7.2 Level two: play situations	291
	7.7.3 Level three: a Manichean ideology	293
	7.7.4 Eco's narrative model and television	294
7.8	Postmodern narrative	297
	7.8.1 The contribution of Jean Baudrillard	298
	7.8.2 The contribution of Frederic Jameson	299
	7.8.3 The contribution of Jean-François Lyotard	300
	7.8.4 Postmodern television	302
7.9	An evaluation of narrative analysis	306

Chapter 8: Film Theory and Criticism 312
Pieter J Fourie

8.1	Introduction	313
8.2	What is film theory?	314
	8.2.1 Establishment, medium and close-up theories	315
	8.2.2 Normative and descriptive film theory	317
	8.2.3 Film history, film criticism, film analysis and film theory	317
	8.2.4 Why film theory?	325

Contents

8.3	Classic film theory	326
	8.3.1 Introduction	326
	8.3.2 Expressionist film theory	330
	8.3.3 Formalist film theory	332
	8.3.4 Realist film theory	339
	8.3.5 Auteur theory	349
	8.3.6 Genre theory	351
8.4	Film semiotics	355
	8.4.1 Film as a sign	356
	8.4.2 Film, denotation and connotation	357
	8.4.3 Codes in film	358
	8.4.4 The paradigmatic–syntagmatic nature of film	359
	8.4.5 Communicative possibilities of film	361
	8.4.6 Communication functions in an image	362
8.5	Contemporary film theory	364
	8.5.1 Introduction	364
	8.5.2 Ideological criticism	366
	8.5.3 Psychoanalysis	369
	8.5.4 Film theory and identity: Feminist criticism, queer theory, film and race, postcolonial theory	380

PART 2: MEDIA AUDIENCES — 387

Chapter 9: Media Audience Theory — 389

Magriet Pitout

9.1	Introduction	390
9.2	The active audience paradigm	390
9.3	The uses and gratifications theory	391
	9.3.1 Theoretical assumptions	392
	9.3.2 Typology (categories) of needs	392
	9.3.3 The dimension of 'gratifications sought and obtained'	395
	9.3.4 Ritualised and instrumental media use	396
9.4	Reception theory	398
	9.4.1 Assumptions of reception theory	398
	9.4.2 Application of reception theory to popular culture: The soap opera genre	402
	9.4.3 Structural model for the analysis of the soap opera genre	403
	9.4.4 Viewers' pleasures: Rituals and the social dimension of television viewing	408

xi

Media Studies: Volume 3

9.5 Ethnography	411
9.5.1 Assumptions of ethnography	412

Chapter 10: Questionnaire Surveys in Media Research 421

Elirea Bornman

10.1 Introduction	422
10.2 Brief historical overview of survey research	423
10.3 What is a survey?	425
10.4 Research topics appropriate for questionnaire surveys	426
10.5 Steps in survey research	428
10.6 Sampling	433
10.6.1 Important concepts in sampling	434
10.6.2 Probability sampling	438
10.6.3 Non-probability sampling	443
10.7 Types of questionnaire surveys	449
10.7.1 Self-administered surveys	449
10.7.2 Postal surveys	450
10.7.3 Group-administered surveys	451
10.7.4 Computer surveys	452
10.7.5 Face-to-face interviews	452
10.7.6 Telephone interviews	454
10.7.7 New technological developments and survey interviewing	456
10.8 Questionnaire design: The art of asking questions	457
10.8.1 Open-ended versus closed-ended questions	459
10.8.2 Compiling closed-ended questions	461
10.8.3 Quantity questions	464
10.8.4 Multichoice type and checklist questions	464
10.8.5 Contingency questions	465
10.8.6 Rank–order questions	466
10.8.7 Intensity measures	467
10.8.8 Overall structure of a questionnaire	472
10.9 Quality measures for evaluating surveys: Reliability and validity	473
10.9.1 Reliability	474
10.9.2 Validity	475
10.10 Sources of error or bias in questionnaire surveys	477
10.10.1 Sampling error	477
10.10.2 Non-response error	478
10.10.3 Interviewer effects	479
10.10.4 Response bias	479
10.11 Case study	480

Contents

Chapter 11: Field Research in Media Studies   484
Magriet Pitout

11.1	Introduction	485
11.2	Field research techniques	486
	11.2.1 Participant observation	487
	11.2.2 In-depth interview	494
	11.2.3 Document analysis	497
	11.2.4 The focus group interview	498
11.3	Transcribing, analysing and interpreting field research data	504
11.4	Reception research and media ethnography	507
11.5	Case study: Audience ethnographic research	510

Chapter 12: Measuring Media Audiences   515
Elirea Bornman

12.1	Introduction	516
12.2	Who needs information on audiences?	518
12.3	Which questions are addressed in audience research?	519
	12.3.1 How many people are there in the audience?	519
	12.3.2 How often do people show up in the audience?	519
	12.3.3 Who are the members of the audience?	520
12.4	Key concepts in audience measurement	521
	12.4.1 The concepts of 'watching', 'listening', 'reading' and/or 'visiting'	521
	12.4.2 Coverage or reach	522
	12.4.3 Audience share	523
	12.4.4 Audience ratings	524
	12.4.5 Frequency	526
12.5	Estimating the audience	526
12.6	Sources of error in audience measurement	528
	12.6.1 Sampling error	528
	12.6.2 Non-response error	528
	12.6.3 Response errors	529
	12.6.4 Interviewer error	529
	12.6.5 Sources of error external to the research process	529
12.7	Instruments for capturing data on audiences	530
	12.7.1 Social surveys	531
	12.7.2 Diaries	533
	12.7.3 Metering devices	537

xiii

Media Studies: Volume 3

12.8	Measuring the audiences for particular media	546
	12.8.1 Measuring television audiences	546
	12.8.2 Measuring radio audiences	549
	12.8.3 Measuring the audience of print media: newspapers and magazines	552
	12.8.4 Measuring cinema audiences	556
	12.8.5 Measuring outdoor media	558
	12.8.6 Measuring internet audiences	560
12.9	Audience measurement in South Africa	562
	12.9.1 The South African Advertising Research Foundation	564
	12.9.2 SAARF All Media and Products Survey	565
	12.9.3 SAARF Radio Audience Measurement Survey	567
	12.9.4 SAARF Television Audience Measurement Survey	568
	12.9.5 SAARF Out of Home Media Survey	570
	12.9.6 SAARF Universal Living Standards Measure	571
	12.9.7 The SAARF Media Groups Measure	572
12.10	Case study: Peoplemeters detect potential disciplinary problems in South African schools	574
12.11	Problems, limitations and criticism of audience measurement	576

Chapter 13: Psychoanalysis and Television — 580
Stefan Sonderling

13.1	Introduction	581
13.2	Psychoanalytic theory: Freud and Lacan	583
13.3	Psychoanalysis and the study of television	588
13.4	Model for the analysis of the television viewer's involvement	590
	13.4.1 Desire and pleasure	590
	13.4.2 Regression	591
	13.4.3 Mirror identification	593
	13.4.4 Modes of enunciation	594
13.5	Critical evaluation	596

References	600
Index	627

LIST OF FIGURES AND TABLES

Figure 1.1 Simplified communication research model compared with Shannon and Weaver's mathematical model of communication 6
Figure 1.2 The position of content analysis in the communication process 7
Figure 1.3 The research process when using content analysis as the method 10
Figure 1.4 When coding, a unit should only be allocated to one category 19
Figure 1.5 Although the golfer places the golf ball in the same place each time (reliability), he is not achieving his objective, a hole-in-one (validity). (Adapted from Moore, Nuttall & Willmott, 1974:30) 23
Figure 1.6 In this case, the golfer drives the golf ball in every direction but where it should go. His aim is neither reliable nor valid. (Adapted from Moore, Nuttall & Willmott, 1974:30) 23
Figure 1.7 This golfer gets a hole-in-one each time. His shots are both reliable and valid. (Adapted from Moore, Nuttall & Willmott, 1974:30) 24
Figure 1.8 A pie chart is ideal for displaying categories graphically, for example the various categories of South African news (as a variable) as presented by a particular radio station 26
Figure 1.9 By using a bar chart we can easily compare the amount of South African news as presented longitudinally by four different radio stations over a five-year period 27
Figure 1.10 By using a stacked bar chart we can easily compare the amount of South African news (variable 1) with that of the rest of the world (variable 2). The length of the bar then represents the total number of items in each news bulletin. 27
Figure 1.11 Changing the size of a geographic area to represent the coverage gives us an immediate overview of how the world was covered by Radio A during the sample period (Wigston, 1987:55) 28
Figure 1.12 By using a scatter graph we can establish the relationship between two variables, in this case the number of items in a bulletin with the total duration of the bulletin 29
Figure 2.1 Jakobson's communication model (functions) 54
Figure 5.1 Notan lighting 151
Figure 5.2 Rembrandt lighting 151
Figure 5.3 Cameo lighting 151
Figure 5.4 Silhouette lighting 151
Figure 5.5 Horizontal balance, conveying calmness 153

Figure 5.6 Vertical balance, conveying high energy 154
Figure 5.7 A tilted horizon 154
Figure 5.8 A comfortable space between the people and the frame 155
Figure 5.9 Magnetism of the sides of the frame 155
Figure 5.10 Up-diagonal 156
Figure 5.11 Down-diagonal 156
Figure 5.12 Challenging the down-diagonal 156
Figure 5.13 Figure and ground (adapted from McDermott [sa]) 156
Figure 5.14 Woman-and-building as figure–ground 157
Figure 5.15 Mug-and-woman as figure–ground 157
Figure 5.16 Proximity as a principle of psychological closure 158
Figure 5.17 Pointing and looking as index vectors 159
Figure 5.18 Graphic and index vectors combined 159
Figure 5.19 Continuing (index) vectors 160
Figure 5.20 Diverging vectors 161
Figure 5.21 Index vectors structured as indirect focus 161
Figure 5.22 Labile balance 162
Figure 5.23 Overlapping planes and relative sizes 163
Figure 5.24 Height in plane, relative sizes and linear perspective 164
Figure 5.25 Narrow-angle shot 167
Figure 5.26 Normal lens position 167
Figure 5.27 Wide-angle shot 167
Figure 5.28 Focus on the foreground 167
Figure 5.29 Focus on the background 168
Figure 5.30 Extreme close-up (or big close-up) shot 169
Figure 5.31 Close-up shot 169
Figure 5.32 Medium close-up shot 169
Figure 5.33 Medium shot 170
Figure 5.34 Medium-long shot 170
Figure 5.35 Long shot 170
Figure 5.36 Objective camera 171
Figure 5.37 Subjective camera 171
Figure 5.38 Positioning a camera on eye level 172
Figure 5.39 Positioning a camera above eye level 172
Figure 5.40 A political rally as event 181
Figure 5.41 Sectional analytical montage 181
Figure 5.42 Idea-associative montage based on comparison 183
Figure 5.43 Idea-associative montage based on collision 184
Figure 6.1 The rhetorical triangle 245

xvi

List of figures and tables

Figure 7.1 Timeline showing development of structuralist and postmodern narrative analysis 257
Figure 7.2 The elements that are responsible for the chain effect in a narrative (adapted from Gillespie, 2006:91–96) 261
Figure 7.3 Narrative showing a linear progress 262
Figure 7.4 Narrative showing a non-linear progress 262
Figure 7.5 Aristotle's three-act narrative model 264
Figure 7.6 A structuralist model of a narrative (adapted from Chatman, 1978:26) 267
Figure 7.7 Graphic illustration of the position of cardinal and catalyser functions in a narrative (adapted from Chatman, 1978:54) 271
Figure 7.8 Binary oppositions found in *Hart to Hart* (adapted from Fiske, 1987b:132) 278
Figure 7.9 Similarities between the narrative models of Todorov and Propp (based on a discussion by Lacey, 2000:48) 282
Figure 7.10 Binary oppositions found in Umberto Eco's narrative model 292
Figure 7.11 A generic overview of Umberto Eco's narrative model, specifically showing the interaction between the three levels for the move labelled 'A'. Each of the nine moves will have a similar interaction. 295
Figure 8.1 The Russian director and film theorist, Sergei Eisenstein, directs a scene from his film *October*, 1928. 316
Figure 8.2 Expressionism: a scene from the 'Odessa Steps' sequence in Sergei Eisenstein's film, *The Battleship Potemkin*, 1925 333
Figure 8.3 Expressionism: Vera Baranovskaia and Nikolai Batalov in V.I. Pudovkin's *Mother*, 1926 337
Figure 8.4 Expressionism: Max Schreck as the vampire Nosferatu in Friderich Murnau's film *Nosferatu*, 1922 339
Figure 8.5 (Neo)realism: a scene from Vittorio de Sica's film *Miracle in Milan*, 1950 341
Figure 8.6 Realism: Orson Welles as Kane in his film *Citizen Kane*, 1941 346
Figure 8.7 Realism: a scene from D.W. Griffith's film, *The Birth of a Nation*, 1915 348
Figure 12.1 Section of the diary employed by SAARF 534
Figure 12.2 Handset and display unit of a peoplemeter used in South Africa ... 539

Tables
Table 1.1 The possible uses of content analysis 9
Table 1.2: Elements of a message as unit of analysis (adapted from Singleton, Straits, Straits & McAllister, 1988:349; Berg, 1989:112–113) 15

xvii

Media Studies: Volume 3

Table 1.3 Charts to use for presenting data and when to use them (adapted from Berman Brown & Saunders, 2008:42–43, 47) 25
Table 4.1 Examples of visual 'language' variables: print media versus film/television 123
Table 5.1 Examples of auditory variations and typical associations 186
Table 6.1 Two narrative possibilities of a workers' strike 220
Table 6.2 Two narrative possibilities for 'Bargain hunting' (Ndaba, 2008:11) .. 222
Table 6.3 Propp's seven character functions (adapted from 1968:79–80, Wigston 2001) (see also Table 7.4 in the next chapter) 227
Table 6.4 Propp's 31 narrative functions (see also Table 7.3 in the next chapter) 228
Table 6.5 Propp and Todorov: Two narrative stages compared 232
Table 6.6 Applying Todorov's five-stage model to 'Some say success …' 233
Table 6.7 Applying Propp's narrative model to 'Some say success …' 234
Table 6.8 Omitted events in 'Some say success …' 235
Table 6.9 Binary oppositions in relation to the hero, 'you', in the UCT ad 239
Table 6.10 Binary oppositions: the donor/dispatcher in 'Some say success …' 240
Table 6.11 Rhetorical argumentation (Richardson, 2007:158) 246
Table 7.1 Cardinal functions and catalysers found in the *MacGyver* episode entitled 'The Lost Amadeus' 273
Table 7.2 Folk tale scenarios according to Vladimir Propp 281
Table 7.3 Functions of characters in Russian folk tales according to Vladimir Propp (adapted from Lacey, 2000:47; Berger, 1997:26) 283
Table 7.4 Propp's *dramatis personae* categories (adapted from Tilley, 1991:58; Watson, 1998:141; and Lacey, 2000:51) 285
Table 7.5 *Dramatis personae* found in television narratives (adapted from Kozloff, 1987:50) 287
Table 7.6 Binary opposition of Diane and Carla in the pilot episode of *Cheers* (adapted from Berger, 1989:95) 288
Table 7.7 Binary opposition of main characters from the pilot episode of *Cheers* (adapted from Berger, 1989:96) 288
Table 7.8 Proppian functions in the pilot episode of *Cheers* (adapted from Berger, 1989:99) 289
Table 7.9 Baudrillard's three orders of simulation (adapted from Laughey, 2007:149) 298
Table 7.10 Categories of postmodern motifs found in television programmes 304
Table 12.1 South African programme ratings: average from 1 January 2008 to 22 May 2008 (SAARF TAMS®) 525
Table 12.2 Variables included in development of SAARF LSM™ groups 572

ACKNOWLEDGEMENTS

As editor, I would like to thank the authors of this volume for their contributions and commitment throughout the process of getting this book published. I also would like to thank the lecturers of the Department of Communication Science at the University of South Africa for their valuable inputs in the writing of study material that enriches the content of this and the preceding two volumes of this book. I would like to acknowledge and thank the many individuals and institutions who have graciously allowed the use of illustrative material.

This volume has been reviewed by independent critical readers. I would like to thank Dr Mariekie Burger, Department of Communication, University of Johannesburg, and Dr Elsabé Pepler, Department of Communication and Information Studies, University of the Free State, for their scrupulous critical reading of the manuscript and their valuable comments and advice. Their work and knowledge in the field of media studies are highly appreciated.

Finally, I would like to thank Juta's Rainhardt Genis and Sharon Steyn for managing the project, and Alfred LeMaitre for his outstanding language editing.

Pieter J Fourie

ABOUT THE AUTHORS FROM THE FIRST EDITION

Elirea Bornman is associate professor in the Department of Communication Science of the University of South Africa (Unisa). She holds a DLitt et Phil in Psychology from the same university. She was chief researcher at the Human Sciences Research Council (HSRC) for 17 years before she joined Unisa. Her main research focus is social identification and processes related to ethnic, racial, national and other forms of social identification. She has also conducted research into globalisation, issues related to international communication and global news flows. She is furthermore interested in metatheoretical issues concerning research methodology and, in particular, in the methodology of questionnaire surveys and the complexities and intricacies of the world of audience measurement.

GM (Trudie) du Plooy is a professor in the Department of Communication Science, University of South Africa, where she was appointed in 1977. Her Master's and Doctoral studies focused on the use of music as a communication code in television, and guidelines for improved visual literacy through an understanding of television. In addition to publications on communication research methodology and a bilingual communication dictionary, her research interests and publications address areas such as genre analysis, organisational research, educational television and the communication challenges facing higher and distance education.

Pieter J Fourie is professor in the Department of Communication Science, University of South Africa where he was also head of the department for 17 years. He is the author and editor of a number of key works in the field of South African media studies, including the first publication in South Africa in the field of visual communication and semiotics, *Beeldkommunikasie: Kultuurkritiek, Ideologiese Kritiek en 'n Inleiding tot die Beeldsemiologie* (McGraw-Hill, 1983) and *Aspects of Film and Television Communication* (Juta, 1988). He is the editor of the accredited research journal *Communicatio: South African Journal for Communication Theory and Research* (jointly published by Unisa Press & Routledge) and on the editorial boards of a number of research journals in the field of communication science. In 2003 the South African Academy of Science

About The authors

and Arts honoured him with their Stals Award for his contribution to the development of communication science in South Africa. In 2007 he was elected fellow of the International Communicology Institute. His research interest continues to be critical media studies and media semiotics.

Before her retirement, **Magriet Pitout** was an associate professor in the Department of Communication Science of the University of South Africa. Her major areas of specialisation are audience studies, popular culture and research methodology, on which she has published a number of research articles and chapters in textbooks. She currently teaches media studies on a part-time basis at a number of tertiary colleges.

Jeanne Prinsloo is a professor in the School of Journalism and Media Studies at Rhodes University in Grahamstown. She pursued her postgraduate studies in the field of cultural and media studies at the universities of Natal, London and the Witwatersrand, where she obtained a Ph.D. that focused on critical literacies and was informed by a Foucauldian framework. She teaches and researches in the broad fields of media, identity and critical literacies.

Stefan Sonderling is a senior lecturer in the Department of Communication Science at the University of South Africa. He lectures in communication theory, postcolonial and Afro-centric communication theory, media studies, language and society and development communication. He has also worked as photojournalist on a number of South African newspapers and as a television camera reporter for SABC television news.

David Wigston is a senior lecturer in the Department of Communication Science at the University of South Africa. He specialises in teaching research methodology and media studies, particularly broadcasting. He is a regular contributor to the department's highly successful annual Winter School in research methodology for postgraduate students.

INTRODUCTION TO THE 2018 REVISED REPRINT

Pieter J Fourie

Volume 3 is the third book in the four-part Media Studies Series. In this Volume, the emphasis is on media content and media audiences. The academic and practical value of the authors' discussions and explanations of both the theory and techniques of content and audience analysis are reaffirmed with the publication of the revised reprint. The chapters remain a sound foundation in the methodology of content and audience analysis and can still serve as an important guide for how to do content and audience analysis. Some of the research theory and techniques discussed in Volume 3 are expanded on in Volume 4 with its emphasis on new (social) media and the digital media landscape.

REVIEW AND CONTEXT

In *Media Studies, Volume 1: Media History, Media and Society*, it is argued that media studies is the systematic, critical, and analytical study of the media (television, radio, press, video, film, internet and new media) as one of the most important producers and disseminators of symbolic meanings to a public, group, organisation and/or individual. Critical media studies investigates the owners of the media, the producers of media content, the media content itself, and the users (readers, listeners, viewers) of media. It investigates the (power) relationships between the media and politics, media and culture, media and economy, media and society, and between the media and the public, as well as the relationship(s) between media and democracy and freedom of expression as a prerequisite for democracy.

The following topics are dealt with in the consecutive chapters of Volume 1: South African media history; a brief history of media in Africa; media theory and theoretical approaches to the study of the media; the functions of the media in society; the effects of the media; media and culture; media and ideology; the media as public sphere; and globalisation, the development and rise of information and communication technology and the media.

The above topics deal with questions, theories and research about the nature of the media as a seminal and powerful institution in democratic society and about the media as a producer and disseminator of meaning. By 'disseminator

Introduction to the 2018 Revised Reprint

of meaning' we mean that we try to understand how the media portray reality or aspects thereof in different ways with different forms of expression in different genres and with different content, and how the media through such portrayals give (specific) meanings and understandings of and to reality or an aspect thereof.

In Volume 2, the focus is on the political economy of the media, media policy and management and on the media as a representation of a topic, a person, a group, etc – *the content of the media*. *Media Studies, Volume 2: Policy, Management and Media Representation* consequently deals in three parts and fifteen chapters with the following: the nature of media and communications policy; external media regulation in South Africa; internal media regulation (self-regulation) in South Africa; media and communication markets; and, strategic media management.

The part on media representation (and media content) has chapters on representation as a concept; news as representation; media and the construction of identity; and on how the media represent (portray) race, gender, sexual orientation, the environment; HIV/AIDS, violence and terrorism.

Besides the academic content, meaning and importance of these chapters, the chapters in their treatment of the topics consequently also deal with questions about the nature of media portrayal and coverage. All of them deal in one way or another with various aspects of the media's ability or inability to capture or represent reality or an aspect thereof in an accurate and objective way. In the case of media entertainment and fiction, questions related to representation concern the quality of media content.

While Volumes 1 and 2 deal with the media as an institution and media content in terms of representation, the focus in Volume 3 is exclusively on the analysis of media content and media audiences.

VOLUME 3

Media content

Media Studies, Volume 3: Media Content and Media Audiences is divided in two parts. Part one deals with media content and part two with media audiences.

The content of the media is perhaps the most researched field in communication and media studies. It varies from quantitative content analyses of almost every topic covered by the media (eg crime, war, violence, human interest, politics, economics, etc) to the qualitative analyses of how the media produce meaning. This is done, for instance, in semiotic, discourse, semantic and linguistic

xxiii

analyses of media content. Not only is the language or verbal content analysed, but also visual content.

Quantitative content analysis

The eight chapters dealing with content vary in terms of theoretical emphasis and practical analysis.

In Chapter 1, *Quantitative content analysis*, by David Wigston, the emphasis is on the technique (and practice) of quantitative content analysis. By the end of this chapter the reader should be able to define the concept of content analysis, coding, categories and units of analysis, list some of the uses of content analysis, describe the methodology used in content analysis, explain how one would establish and improve the reliability and validity of content analysis, identify the advantages and limitations of content analysis, and undertake a content analysis on a small scale.

Communication and media semiotics

In Chapter 2, *Media semiotics*, Pieter J Fourie discusses semiotics as an important theoretical paradigm in communication and media studies. He sees semiotics as a prominent theory and method in communication science to describe and understand the media as a symbolic form of expression. Put differently, he sees semiotics as one of the most important ways to describe and understand media communication primarily as a producer, carrier and dispenser of meaning in and about society, its people, their activities, their sense-making of the world, and so on. He substantiates semiotic theory with a framework for a practical semiotic analysis. The reader is introduced to the origin of semiotics, the theoretical basics of semiotics, meaning, social semiotics, and a framework for semiotic analysis.

Media, language and discourse

An additional mainly theoretical chapter in the discussion of media content is Chapter 3, *Media, language and discourse*, by Stefan Sonderling. The point of departure is that media content is made up and consists of the skilful use and manipulation of language – language which is the most powerful communication tool. Sonderling aims to create an awareness of the role and power of language in society. The focus is on the formal aspects of language as text, language as social interaction, and the social context for the use of language in and by the media.

Introduction to the 2018 Revised Reprint

Media and visual literacy

GM (Trudie) du Plooy introduces the reader in Chapter 4, *Media and visual literacy*, to the different meanings, levels and the ongoing development of media and visual literacy in the context of media studies. Emphasising theory, the most important topics she deals with are the conceptual and theoretical debates about the notion of literacy as they apply to media and visual literacy, three levels of media literacy based on how researchers view the mass media, ontological and epistemological assumptions in and about media and visual literacy, and the perceptual, including semiotic and cognitive, approaches to visual communication. She also deals with past research in this field, as well as future challenges.

Visual text analysis

Chapter 5, *Visual text analysis*, also by Trudie du Plooy, is of a more practical nature, showing the reader how to do a practical analysis of, for example, pictorial codes in film shots and photographs, picturisation through movement in film and television, auditory codes and the combination of audio-visual codes, and the use of signs and codes in photographs, films and television to produce and influence meaning(s) presented. This chapter closely links, but from a more practical perspective, with semiotics dealt with in Chapter 2.

Textual analysis: Narrative and argument

Another example of qualitative content analysis compared to quantitative content analysis (Chapter 1) is Jeanne Prinsloo's Chapter 6, *Textual analysis: Narrative and argument*. The most important topics dealt with in this chapter are the discursive nature of media texts, narrative and argument as forms of textual organisation, narrative theories, and forms of arguments. The aim of the chapter is to allow the reader to understand and discuss media texts in terms of their mediating and rhetorical roles, outline the narrative theories of Propp, Todorov and Levi-Strauss and describe their value for critical analysis, outline the approach to argumentation informed by Aristotelian ideas, and to undertake textual analysis.

Narrative analysis (2)

Closely related to Chapter 6, David Wigston gives in Chapter 7, *Narrative analysis*, a systematic, almost tabularised, discussion of narrative analysis as it is done in and applied to media texts.

Media Studies: Volume 3

Why two chapters on narrative analysis? The main reason is that media and media content is primarily about *storytelling*. All media content are presented as narratives, be it news, documentary, human interest, education, or even sport. Becoming acquainted with theory and techniques of narrative analysis is thus crucial in critical media studies.

Wigston sets out to investigate how stories (narratives) are constructed and how we interpret them in order to gain meaning from them. He deals with the syntagmatic arrangement of the narrative through the work of Tzvetan Todorov and Vladimir Propp, the paradigmatic arrangement through the work of Umberto Eco, and he introduces the theories of Seymour Chatman, Roland Barthes and Claude Levi-Strauss.

Film theory and criticism

To conclude Part One of the book, and thus the focus on media content, a chapter on film theory is included. Film theory and criticism is a discipline on its own. A single chapter on it in a book in the field of critical media studies can hardly do justice to the topic. Nevertheless, the inclusion is justified by the argument that no other form of content analysis better illustrates the difference between media content, media form and media substance or emphasises the ways in which content, form and substance independently but also in relationship to each other contribute to the production of meaning. In Chapter 8, *Film theory and criticism*, Pieter J Fourie introduces the field of film theory, looks at different kinds of film theory, the difference between film history, film criticism, film analysis and film theory, and the value of film theory. Departing from the distinction between content, form and substance, he offers an explanation of the difference between expressionist, formalist and realist film theories (and theorists) and concludes this section on classic film theory with an introduction to auteur theory and genre theory. The emphasis then moves to film semiotics. The chapter concludes with contemporary film theory's emphasis on, amongst other approaches, ideological criticism, feminist criticism, and the psychoanalytical approach.

Media audiences

The five last chapters of the book are concerned with media audiences.

As made clear in Volume 1, critical media studies focuses on three areas or segments of the media as an object of enquiry. The first is the media as an institution. Who are the media? Who produce media and what media are produced how and with what intentions? What are the relationships of the

media with other institutions in society? In short, studying the media as an institution concerns the politics, economics and sociology of the media. This was the topic of Volume 1 and the first part of Volume 2.

The second main area of investigation is the content of the media. This is studied in Part 3 of Volume 2 and in Part 1 of this Volume. The main questions are: What are the media about and how do the media select and form their content in order to tell the stories of the world and its people (usually with specific purposes and agendas)?

In the final part of this book we deal with the third main area of critical media studies, namely the audience (readers, listeners, viewers, also referred to as the subjects of the media and/or as media users). Again, we distinguish between quantitative and qualitative approaches as well as between theory and practice.

Media audience theory

In Chapter 9, *Media audience theory*, Magriet Pitout's point of departure is that theorising about audiences is a critical and intellectual activity involving different questions about the nature of audiences, their needs, how they interpret media messages, and about the social and cultural contexts of media consumption. In this chapter, she introduces three of the most popular and prominent audience theories in media studies, namely uses and gratifications theory, reception theory, and ethnography.

Questionnaire surveys in media research

In Chapter 10, *Questionnaire surveys in media surveys in media research*, Elirea Bornman gives an overview of the theory and practices associated with questionnaire surveys as a quantitative methodology in media audience research. The most important topics dealt with are the historical development of the use of questionnaire surveys in the social sciences and other applied disciplines; research topics appropriate for questionnaire surveys; steps in questionnaire surveys; probability and non-probability sampling; types of surveys; the design of questionnaires; reliability and validity as yardsticks of quality for questionnaire surveys; and, sources of error in questionnaire surveys.

Field research in media studies

Magriet Pitout deals with *Field research in media studies* in Chapter 11. She specifically looks at ethnographic research and reception research. She explains the processes of participant observation, the structured interview, focus group

Media Studies: Volume 3

interviews and document analysis in ethnographic media audience analysis, with the purpose of understanding the behavioural and cultural impacts on media audiences and their uses and understandings of the media.

Measuring media audiences

In *Measuring media audiences*, Chapter 12, Elirea Bornman explains the methodologies and techniques employed in measuring the audiences of different broadcasting, print and outdoor media, the cinema as well as new media such as the internet. She also introduces the problems associated with and criticism on audience measurement (or as often referred to, media market research). The most important topics dealt with in this chapter are, amongst others, the reasons for audience measurement, key concepts in audience measurement, research questions in audience measurement, methodologies and techniques in measuring audiences, and audience measurement in South Africa.

Psychoanalysis and television

Whereas the previous four chapters introduce and lead the reader to do 'practical' audience research and to apply the most frequently used forms of audience analysis, the final chapter in this part of the book is an illustration of a pure 'qualitative' if not a pure theoretical approach to the audience. In this case, the focus is on the television user. The approach (psychoanalysis) seeks to understand one of the psychological processes involved in looking, enjoying and understanding television (or a television programme), or the act of watching/looking. (Also, refer to the discussion of the psychoanalytical approach in film theory (Chapter 8)). For Stefan Sonderling the aim of Chapter 13, *Psychoanalysis and television*, is to provide us with an understanding of the role of conscious and unconscious structures in the understanding of the viewing experience of film and television.

THEORY AND METHOD

Throughout the book there is a mixture of theory and method. In some chapters, the focus and aim is on practice and research skills for applied content and audience research. In others, the focus is on theory and communication philosophy as ways of understanding media content and audiences. In some chapters, as should ideally be the case, we have both. All the same, the overall aim of the volume is to introduce the reader to the main paradigms and research techniques prevailing at this stage in critical media studies' investigation of media content and audiences.

Introduction to the 2018 Revised Reprint

New research methods and techniques are necessary for audience analysis in the digital media culture. This is especially true for the analysis of the audience (and user) of and in the context of the new social media. This is dealt with in Volume 4, and particularly in Chapter 2 *What are social media? Introductory definitions* and Chapter 3 *Researching audiences in the age of social media* both written by Tanja Bosch.

Pieter J Fourie

June 2017

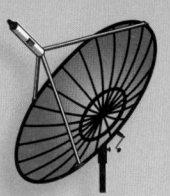

PART I

Media Content

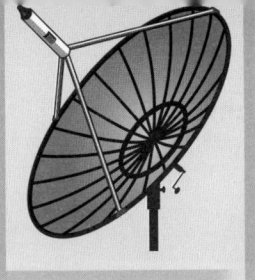

chapter one

QUANTITATIVE CONTENT ANALYSIS

David Wigston

LEARNING OUTCOMES

At the end of this chapter, you should be able to:
- define the concepts of content analysis, coding, categories and unit of analysis;
- list some of the uses of content analysis;
- describe the methodology used in content analysis;
- explain how you would establish and improve on the reliability and validity of content analysis;
- identify the advantages and limitations of content analysis;
- undertake content analysis on a small scale.

Media Studies: Volume 3

THIS CHAPTER

In this chapter, we present a brief debate concerning the definition of content analysis, followed by a description of possible uses. We look at the procedures for undertaking a content analysis within the broader research process. Included are aspects such as what gets counted, the slotting of these items into appropriate frames or categories, and how to ensure that our analysis is reliable and valid. We then turn to the application of content analysis to new media technologies and the implications this holds for research. Finally, we consider ethical issues and look at the advantages and limitations of this particular research method. Although this chapter is intended for the novice researcher, at the same time the assumption is made that you are familiar with the more common concepts associated with scientific research.

1.1 INTRODUCTION

Why bother with media content? After all, is it not the most obvious part of the communication process?

We are interested in the content of mass communication in its own right, but that content contains numerous clues about many of the other hidden forces that helped to shape that message. By analysing the content we can make a number of inferences about the people and organisations and even the environment that helped to produce that content. If we, for a moment, consider two newspapers, the *Sun* and *The Star*, and consider their content, it will very quickly become obvious that they are designed for very different audiences. If we piggyback this idea onto the assumption that media is responsible for establishing our view of reality, then it becomes important that we know what messages are being sent out into our society. Content analysis on its own is not sufficient to explain the causes or effects of the media, but it is a good starting point.

quantitative and qualitative content analysis

There are two basic types of content analysis: quantitative and qualitative. The quantitative approach involves some form of counting, and applies the scientific method rigourously. Qualitative content analysis follows a somewhat different procedure, since no physical counting of data is involved. It tends to be more critical in nature and can be used when we need to penetrate the deeper layers of a message, such as in a semiological or narrative analysis. Qualitative content analysis is

Quantitative Content Analysis

discussed further on in this book. Quantitative content analysis proves more useful for examining manifest messages, while qualitative content analysis is preferred for analysing latent messages. In this chapter, we concern ourselves only with quantitative content analysis, as qualitative content analysis will be dealt with in a later course.

1.2 WHAT IS CONTENT ANALYSIS?

If we study the various manuals available on research, we find as many definitions of content analysis. Although the definitions may vary, the concept remains the same. Let us look at two definitions of content analysis:

| definition

> Content analysis is a research method for the objective, systematic and quantitative description of the manifest content of communication. (Berelson 1952:18)

> Content analysis is a research method based on measuring the amount of something (e.g. violence, negative portrayal of women, or whatever) found in a representative sample of a mass-mediated popular art form. (Berger 1991:25)

What emerges from these definitions is a method that focuses on the message, which is reduced to a set of categories representative of the research problem, in order to discover the meanings contained in these messages, in a systematic way. Three key concepts emerge from these definitions: a content analysis must be systematic, objective and quantitative. What do these concepts mean?

- *Systematic* means that the organisation of the study follows precise rules and a set procedure and is applied to the sample being analysed.
- *Objective* means the study should be easily duplicated by others. Objectivity is achieved by defining the methodology precisely, so that another researcher can apply it to the same content and get the same results. Objectivity is the opposite of subjectivity. If content analysis were subjective then each researcher would produce a unique analysis, as in the case of qualitative content analysis. Being objective means that the results are dependent on the procedure and not on the interpretation of the researcher.
- *Quantitative* means that the analysis should give precise and accurate results. Quantitative data are always either numerical values or frequencies.

5

Media Studies: Volume 3

generality

Now let us look at the definition given by Holsti (1969:3–5). He says content analysis must be systematic, objective and have *generality*. Why does Holsti substitute the concept of *generality* for *quantitative*? He argues that findings about communication content are meaningless unless they are related to at least one other datum, the link being some form of theory, which in turn determines the type of comparison being made. The term 'quantitative' is too restrictive as a definition of the method. Although quantification offers a research project a degree of precision, statistics by themselves say nothing. The information revealed by statistics needs to be interpreted before the meaning becomes clear. And this is basically what Holsti means when he says that content analysis must have generality. Purely descriptive information about the content of a message, related neither to the attributes of the material studied nor to the communicator or recipient, is of little value.

1.3 USES OF CONTENT ANALYSIS

communication process

To understand the uses of content analysis we need to know where it fits into the communication process. To find out, let us look at a model shown in Figure 1.1.

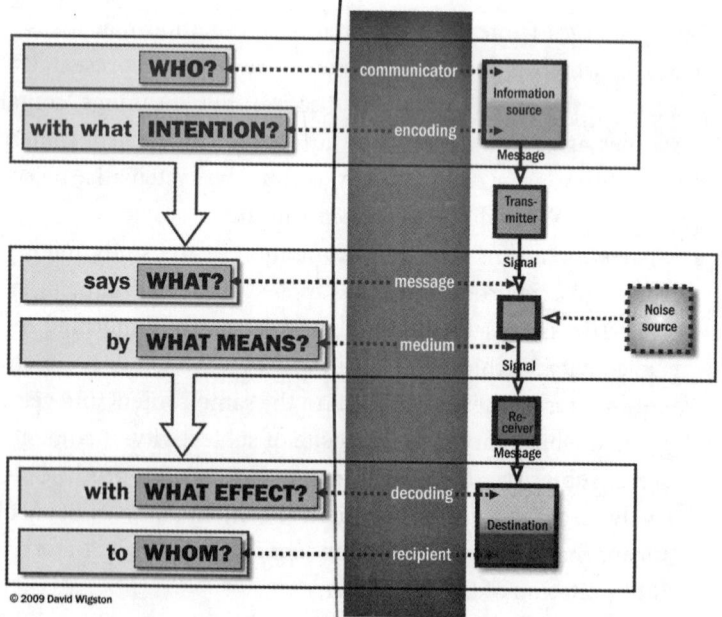

Figure 1.1 Simplified communication research model compared with Shannon and Weaver's mathematical model of communication

Quantitative Content Analysis

Babbie (1989:294) considers content analysis 'particularly well suited to the study of communication' and to answer the question posed in Figure 1.1. However, the method does not deal directly with all these aspects. Figure 1.2 illustrates the relationship of content analysis to the communication process. Do you see how content analysis is specifically linked to the message part of the communication process? However, content analysis is not limited to the message component only. The method makes a basic assumption that an investigation into messages will also give us insight into the communicator's intention and the recipient's interpretation of the message.

basic assumption

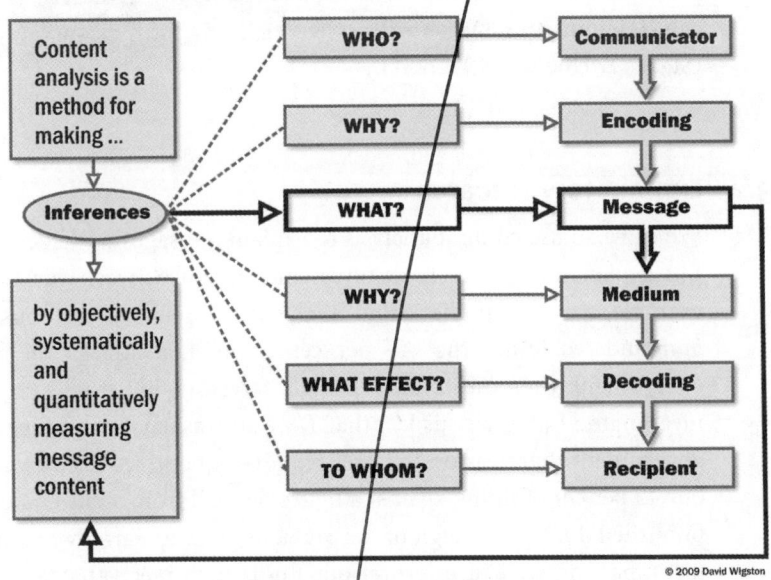

Figure 1.2 The position of content analysis in the communication process

Content analysis only allows us to make inferences about the communicator's intention and the recipient's interpretation. At best, such inferences are based on the researcher's interpretation of the content, and findings should be treated with a large degree of circumspection as such inferences are bordering on guess work. However, what content analysis will allow us to do is to identify and evaluate various relationships between the variables in the message, which may otherwise not be apparent (Wurtzel 1985:8–9). As a result, content analysis is particularly well suited to descriptive and explanatory research.

1.3.1 Descriptive research

descriptive research

In field research we observe behaviour and then write down what we observe. Similarly, we can observe messages so that we can describe a certain event. If we are interested in the way Nelson Mandela's speeches, while president, contributed to the democratisation of South Africa, then a content analysis of those speeches will tell us what topics Mandela spoke about, the frequency of selected topics and the persuasive appeals he used. By drawing inferences, we can consider whom he addressed and his motives. Content analysis, as a descriptive method, is a starting point for establishing the effects of a particular set of messages, and we can link content analysis with other methods, such as survey research (Stacks & Hocking 1992:251).

1.3.2 Explanatory research

explanatory research

We can also use content analysis to explain messages we have observed. But explanatory research requires comparison between variables. For example, if we (hypothetically) analysed the political cartoons in *The Star* and we found that 45 per cent contained attacks on the new government, then on its own this is interesting, but it tells us nothing meaningful. But, if we suspect that *The Star* was harsher on the previous government than it is on the present government, we need to compare our 45 per cent finding against a figure derived from analysing cartoons published during the reign of the previous government. By making such a comparison we can interpret our findings to mean that some of the cartoons observed are biased. We can use this bias to help explain the percentage of political cartoons that attack the government in power (Stacks & Hocking 1992:252).

We can also compare competing genres in similar media – for example, articles in two magazines such as *Cosmopolitan* and *Fairlady* – or we can make comparisons between the news on a commercial versus a public radio station, between a morning newspaper and an afternoon one, such as *Business Day* and *The Star,* or between liberal and conservative media like Radio Sonder Grense and Radio Pretoria. From the differences revealed by such comparisons we can infer what emphasis has been placed on the message. From any emphasis we find, we can deduce certain things about the communicator and the recipient, since these

Quantitative Content Analysis

components of the communication process are not the direct objects of our study. For example, the differences that emerged in a 1987 content analysis of the news on Radio 702 and Radio Highveld were used to infer that the SABC was consensus-orientated, supportive of the status quo and avoided controversy or conflict in its news broadcasts (Wigston 1987:37–67).

Table 1.1 gives us a breakdown of some of the uses of content analysis (Holsti 1969:26). Keep in mind that content analysis focuses on the message, but what we find in that message can be used to draw inferences about the reason for the message and its effects.

Table 1.1 The possible uses of content analysis

QUESTION	RESEARCH PROBLEM	COMPARISON	PURPOSE
Who? **Why?** (what intention?)	• Resolve disputed authorship • Gather political and military intelligence • Analyse traits of individuals • Determine intellectual differences • Measure cultural change	• Message compared to behaviour	To make inferences regarding **encoding** of messages by the communicator
What? **How?** (what means?)	• Describe trends in message content • Relate known aspects of communicator to the message • Audit messages • Analyse techniques of persuasion • Analyse style	• Message variable X across time • Message variable X across situations • Message variable X and Y in the same population • Message A with message B • Message with certain standards	To **describe** and/or explain characteristics of messages

QUESTION	RESEARCH PROBLEM	COMPARISON	PURPOSE
With what effect?	• Measure readability • Analyse flow of information • Assess responses to messages	• Communicator's message(s) with recipient's message(s) • Communicator's message(s) with recipient's behaviour	To make **inferences** regarding the effects of **decoding** of messages by the recipients
To whom?	• Relate known aspects of the recipient to the message	• Message variable X across recipients	

1.4 STEPS IN DOING A CONTENT ANALYSIS

The fact that research is a multi-stage procedure causes it to appear complex and perplexing. Figure 1.3 summarises the research process where quantitative content analysis is the method used.

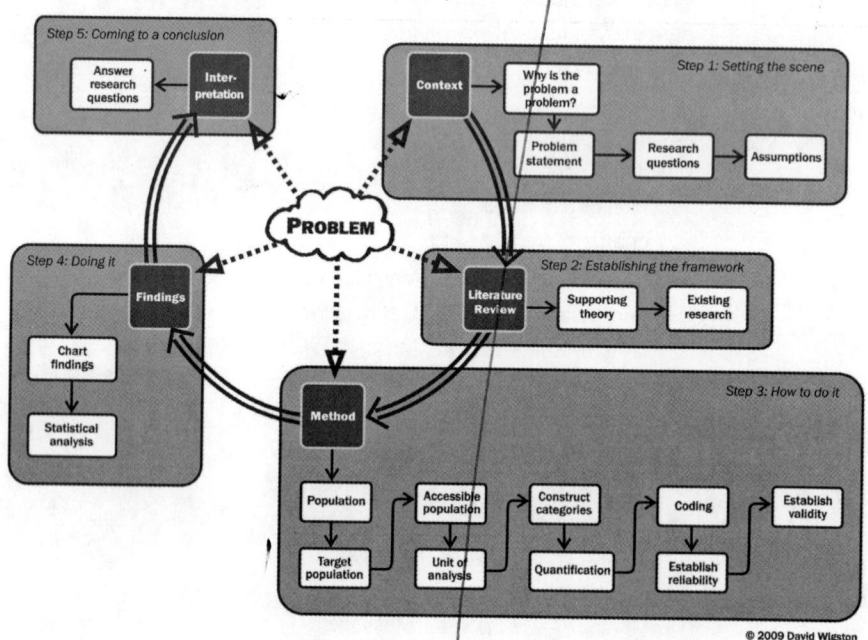

Figure 1.3 The research process when using content analysis as the method

1.4.1 Contextualising the research

This is the most crucial phase of our research, since if we are not too sure what our problem is or why it is a problem then our research is doomed to failure. Getting the research problem clearly defined is so important that it is worth repeating what Leedy (1980:50) has to say on the matter.

> At the heart of every research project is the problem. It is paramount in importance to the success of the research effort, and it should be considered by every researcher. The situation is quite simple: no problem, no research. To see the problem with unwavering clarity and to be able to state it in precise and unmistakable terms is the first requirement in the research process.

contextualisation

Research is, unfortunately, not merely a case of 'doing something', like finding a correlation, gathering data, making notes, etc. (Leedy, 1980:51). None of these activities qualifies as research. In order to become research we need to engage with the facts and then synthesise the meaning to emerge from those facts in order to resolve our problem. Leedy (1980:51) says that it is easier to describe what research is not than what it actually is. Thus, the following aspects do not make up research:

- a means of achieving self-enlightenment;
- to compare two sets of data;
- finding a relationship between two elements or factors;
- questions that result in a yes or no answer;
- a simply gathering of information.

This means that our starting point is to construct a statement of the problem that we want to resolve. Let us consider an example:

research problem

> Radio news about South Africa

Very succinctly, Leedy (1980:53) calls this a 'mere verbal blob', which only hints at the problem and does not actually state it. Rewritten as a problem statement, the example becomes the following:

> The purpose of this research is to establish the amount and type of news about South Africa that is presented by Radio A compared with that of Radio B in their 18:00 news bulletins, over a three-week period, in order to determine the differences in terms of the topics covered, position in the bulletin and duration.

This statement tells you considerably more about what we are going to do. So, then, what are the key elements that make up a statement of the problem? They are as follows:

- The problem statement must be written as a single, grammatically correct sentence.
- There must be an indication that interpretation of the data will take place.
- Have you said precisely what you mean?

Once we are happy with the research problem, we can move on and establish the research questions, state our assumptions and express the limitations of our research. If our statement of the problem contains any jargon, then we also need to provide definitions of those words.

research question

assumptions

While we can use any recorded message for a content analysis, we must have a good reason to do so. Our research must answer an important research question or validate a hypothesis. The research question helps us further to delimit exactly what we will be studying. A literature review helps formulate our research question or hypothesis, since this formally presents the logic behind the theory and previous research on the topic we are going to study (Stacks & Hocking 1992:251, 367). Below is an example of a research question and a hypothesis.

- Research question: 'Are toy-linked cartoons (on television) more violent than non toy-linked cartoons?' (Eaton & Dominick 1991:68)
- Hypothesis: 'The number of commercials (on television) using an emotional appeal will be larger than the number using an informational appeal.' (Ramaprasad & Hasegawa 1990:1028)

We must always keep the research question(s) or hypothesis/es in mind while doing our content analysis as this usually results in increased accuracy of our work.

If we were to investigate the research question mentioned above, how many programmes would we have to examine? Make use of television schedules published in the press or magazines and scan the programmes listed for a period of one week. How many toy-linked programmes can you identify? Eaton and Dominick (1991:68), for example, found over 40 toy-linked children's television programmes. This leads us to establishing the population, which we will return to in section 1.5.3.

1.4.2 The literature review

The purpose of the literature review is often overlooked; its prime purpose is to help us construct a framework in which we can then conduct our research in order to resolve the problem. In order to fulfil this purpose we need to look for theories and existing research that relate to our problem, as this provides us with a deeper insight into resolving the problem. Leedy (1980:64–65) cites the following as the benefits of a literature review:

- It reveals past research relevant to our own, which then shows how other researchers handled their research.
- It can suggest methods and techniques of dealing with problematic aspects related to our research and provides us with ways of dealing with these situations. See section 1.6 of this chapter for an example.
- It can reveal sources of data that you did not know about.
- It introduces you to other researchers with interests in similar problems.
- It helps you to see your research problem in a historical context.
- It can provide you with new ideas and approaches that may not have occurred to you.
- it can assist you in evaluating your own research by comparing it with similar efforts done by others.

literature review

1.4.3 The method

The first thing we need to do in this step is to establish the boundaries that will limit our research. For example, we need to ask ourselves, what period of time do we wish to cover? We need to base our decision on the resources at our disposal, such as coders, time and message content.

time frame

In the study of televised violence that we discussed earlier we may have discovered that it is impossible to view everything. As Babbie (1992:314) says, 'your brain would probably short-circuit ..' So we have to be selective. However, before we decide on our *sample*, we need to establish our target population and accessibility. For example, which channels will we observe? Over what period of time? During which hours of the day? How many programmes? Having made decisions on these aspects, we can select our sample.

population

sampling

There are several ways in which we can select our sample from the population. The method selected will depend on our research problem and can be one of those indicated below. We will not go into the intricacies of drawing a probability or non-probability sample in this chapter, but refer you to the various texts indicated at the end of this chapter.

- simple random sampling
- systematic sampling
- stratified random sampling
- cluster random sampling

} Probability sampling methods

- purposive sampling
- snowball sampling
- quota sampling

} Non-probability sampling methods

unit of analysis

The unit of analysis is what we actually categorise and count. It is a measurable unit, which provides us with a standard method of analysing the data. If we want to analyse cartoon strips, the frame can be considered as the standard unit. On a newspaper page with ten cartoon strips consisting of four frames each, there will be 40 frames to analyse (Berger 1991:27–28).

The unit of analysis we select will depend on what we want to study. As an example, we want to analyse television coverage of strike action by comparing news stories that show labour's point of view against management's point of view. We may use the number of stories as our unit of analysis, but this will not always give us a complete picture. In one week we might find that 15 stories gave the labour point of view and 15 stories were devoted to management. However, if we count the amount of time allocated to each story, we might find that labour received only 37 minutes of news and management 49 minutes, making coverage not as fair as originally suggested. The important point is that both units (the number of news stories and amount of time given to each story) are correct, but using more than one measure offers us a safeguard against the problem illustrated here. Remember that the unit of analysis selected should always reflect the research question. Table 1.2 indicates six major elements of a message that we can use as units of analysis.

Quantitative Content Analysis

Table 1.2: Elements of a message as unit of analysis (adapted from Singleton, Straits, Straits & McAllister 1988:349; Berg 1989:112–113)

UNIT	COMMENT	EXAMPLE
Words	Words are the smallest element we can use to establish a frequency distribution of specific words or terms. Can be used for propaganda analysis	Nouns, proper names
Themes/ concepts	Themes and concepts are more useful, but we need to specify where to search since themes can be found, for example, in sentences or phrases. Can be used to study propaganda, attitudes, images and values	Ideas like self-esteem, positive views, democracy, etc.
Characters	Here we count the number of persons, or characters, portrayed rather than words or themes	Gender, occupation, race, culture, stereotypes, etc.
Sentences/ paragraphs	Not a good choice because of the difficulty in coding the various aspects that can be contained in a sentence or paragraph. Much depends on the initial problem to be resolved.	Ideas, themes, concepts, attitudes
Items	Useful for news stories which can be classified by either subject or geographical location or people involved	The whole message can be used, such as an entire book, letter, speech, interview, or it can include symbols, plots, or a frame-by-frame analysis (in film and television)
Time/space	Can be used for frequency, such as the number of violent incidents per hour in television programmes or the amount of space occupied in a newspaper	Column centimetres, type size, airtime

As a general rule, the more obvious and clear-cut the unit of analysis, the easier the coding and the more reliable the results. While smaller units are usually coded more reliably than larger units because they contain less information, units as small as words may contain insufficient information for us to code successfully. It all depends on our research question and what we are looking for.

categories

Categories are the meaningful groups into which we allocate our units of analysis. They are probably the most important part of our content analysis. Take, for example, a content analysis to establish the amount of violence on television. Our first step is to establish what is meant and understood by violence. We need to make certain decisions concerning the concept of violence. For instance, will we consider *cartoon violence* as violence? Are *accidents* resulting in physical injury to be considered as violence?

Some of the many concepts of violence we need to consider are indicated in the list given below:
- physical violence aimed at someone else, which results in that person's death;
- physical violence aimed at someone else, which does not result in death (e.g. assault, rape);
- physical violence aimed at objects (e.g. destroying a building or car);
- violence involving the use of a weapon versus violence where no weapon is involved.

These form some of the categories we could include in our analysis of televised violence. But which of these will we include in our analysis, and why? The answers to these questions will largely depend on the nature of our research problem and purpose.

We also need to distinguish between violent acts actually shown on screen and implied violence which is not actually shown. For example, the discovery of a corpse by Jessica Fletcher in *Murder, She Wrote* is not a violent act in itself, but the visualisation of the discovery of the corpse obviously implies that a murder has been committed.

Thus, the definition of our categories is crucial to the success of our content analysis. How do we define violence? In this regard a thorough literature study becomes important. There is a great deal of difference amongst researchers about what violence is and how it should be defined. If our definition of violence includes the intent to commit harm, then we are going to find more violence on television than if our definition limits the concept to actual physical harm. What about unsuccessful attempts at committing harm? What about verbal abuse? And what about self-inflicted violence such as suicide? It is clear then that we must provide an *operational definition* of the concept or subject we intend investigating. Our operational definition should be composed of the attributes included in the concept and these should be mutually exclusive and exhaustive (Babbie, 1992:3, 19). Berger (1991:27) offers us just such a definition for an investigation into televised violence: 'violence will be taken to cover the actions and threats involving bodily harm done purposefully'.

If we use this definition, it means that we cannot include accidental injury as one of our categories. What then of the slapstick violence found in cartoons? Such violence falls within the ambit of the definition given above. If we include 'pie-in-the-face' slapstick as well as aggressive violent behaviour we will produce a totally different analysis of a television action drama like *Tropical Heat* to that of a researcher who excludes slapstick horseplay.

By asking these sorts of questions we bring to light the difficulties of conceptualising exactly what it is we are seeking to analyse. If we define *violence* very narrowly, it will be difficult to find a suitable sample to analyse. On the other hand, if we define it broadly and loosely, then examples will be found everywhere. Where do we draw the line? This is why a detailed and precise explanation of the concepts we intend to use is essential. The next question we need to ask is, how detailed do our definitions need to be? The answer here would be determined by the problem you are trying to resolve, but we can generally say that the more detailed the definition the easier it will ultimately be to code the units of analysis. As an example, if we are going to analyse broadcast news about South Africa, then merely listing the categories is not good enough. We need to give our coders guidance regarding which unit of analysis belongs in what category, such as in the definition below for the category 'economics'.

| definitions

Economics
Agreement of trade; tariffs; international trade; imports; exports; trade balance; capital investment; stock issues; state investments; loans; credit facilities (excluding international aid or grants, which should be classified under 'international relations'; banking; the stock exchange; share prices; profits and losses; economic performance; gold price; cost of living; unemployment statistics (hardships caused as a result of unemployment should be classified under 'social'); inflation (similarly, hardships as a result of inflation should be classified under 'social'); turnkey projects; establishment

and expansion of factories, dams, transport; harvest yields; foreign exchange rates; taxation; disinvestment; foreign investment; money supply and price control.

You will surely agree that the above definition leaves you in no doubt as to what aspects a category labelled 'economics' would include. You would need to do the same for each category you include in your analysis.

There are three essential criteria with which categories must comply (Frey, Botan, Friedman & Kreps 1992:196–197):

- *Exhaustivity.* All the units should fit into the categories – there should be no units left over when coding is finished. However Wimmer and Dominick (1994:173) have a neat trick that we can use to mop up any unit that will just not fit neatly into the categories we have. They suggest that we always include an 'others' category to cover all possibilities, but Wimmer and Dominick warn that if more than 10 percent of our sample is placed in the 'others' category then we need to revise our coding scheme and consider adding extra categories.
- *Mutual exclusivity.* Every unit of analysis should fit into only **one** category. If not, then it means there is something wrong with our set of categories and we need to restructure or redefine these. As an example, if we are establishing the various types of news and have a news item about government interference in a particular sport, do we classify it as politics or sport? There is no hard-and-fast answer to this type of question: it is one that you need to think about carefully and write into your definition of the category. Hopefully a pilot study will highlight such problems before you begin your actual coding.
- *Equivalence.* Each category should carry equal weight – one category should not be superior to any other. However, this depends largely on how we decide to quantify our data and the nature of the problem we want to resolve.

pilot study

How many categories should our coding scheme contain? Stempel and Westley (1989:129) merely advise 'keep it manageable', but anything more than 10–20 categories would be cumbersome to work with. Too few categories, such as two, on the other hand, can make categorisation easy. But how meaningful would our result be? We have to tread a fine line between too many categories (resulting in a very fine distinction being made) or too few (producing little distinction). We need to pre-test our categories with a pilot study in order 'to get a feel for the content and the appropriate number of categories necessary to answer the research questions adequately' (Stacks & Hocking 1992:259). Having successfully allocated all units of analysis to appropriate categories, we simply count the number of units in each category.

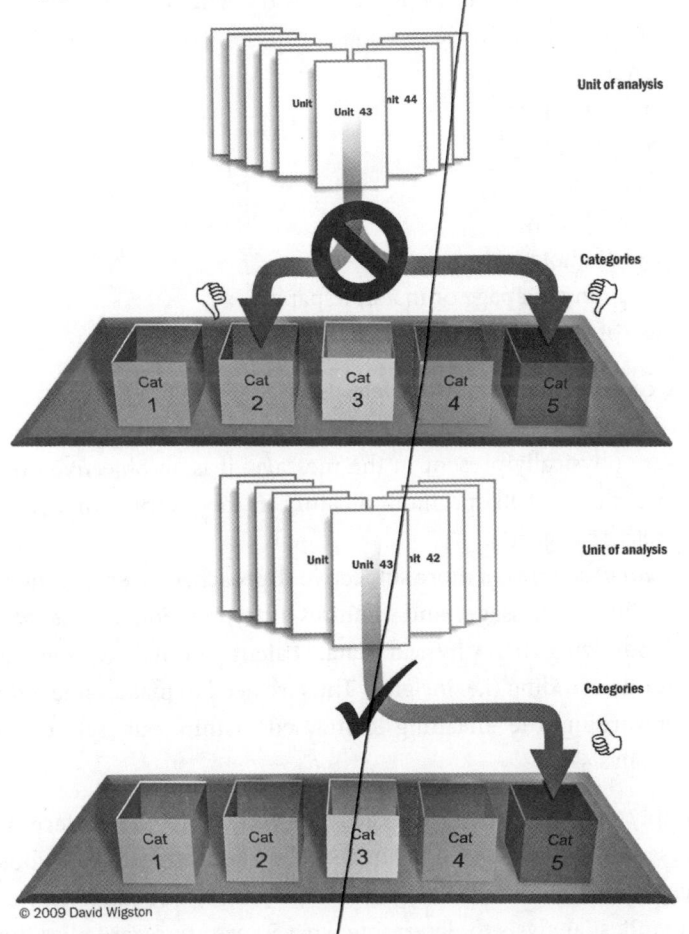

Figure 1.4 When coding, a unit should only be allocated to one category

Coding is the process of transforming raw data into a form suitable for analysis. Generally we use a team to code our data. Teamwork helps speed up the process while eliminating individual bias. Coders have to be trained and a comparison of their coding made in order to establish reliability. Differences that emerge between coders in the allocation of units of analysis to categories need to be resolved before the study is conducted (Wurtzel 1985:13). We shall discuss this further below, under

coding

'reliability'. Although it is ideal to have a team do the coding, this is not a must, as an individual can do the job just as easily. Much depends on the physical size of the sample.

When coding, we need to consider ways of coding and levels of coding. We can code data in a number of ways. The following is a list of the many ways in which we can code print news (Lemert 1989:48):
- length;
- subject matter;
- readability;
- structure;
- possible bias;
- use of quotations;
- location on a page or in a newspaper;
- use of value-laden terms.

We can code data on two levels.
- *Manifest coding* is an actual physical count of those elements that are physically present in the message. It is an objective exercise for which we need specific indicators in the message that will help us select categories.
- *Latent coding* is a more subjective approach, concerning the meaning within a message, and requires interpretation of the symbolism underlying the physical data. Latent coding requires depth of understanding (i.e. insight). Thus we need to make value judgements regarding the meaning contained within our selected unit of analysis.

deep structures

Simply stated, a manifest analysis is limited to the surface structure present in the message, or *what is said*, while a latent analysis looks at the deep structure of the message, or *how it is said*. For example, we can use a manifest analysis to determine what issues are regarded as important by political candidates in their election speeches, simply by counting references made to specifically mentioned issues. But this does not tell us anything about the attitude taken by the candidate towards those issues. To establish attitude, we need to undertake a latent analysis of those same speeches we used to establish the issues that were considered important. We could examine aspects such as intonation and inflection of voice used by the candidates to describe the particular issue they were talking about. We could even include nonverbal communication as an indicator of how the politician felt about a certain issue. However, our findings would be strongly influenced by how we individually interpreted the various symbols used by politicians in the speech-making process.

Babbie (1989:298–299) raises a problem with the two levels of coding discussed here. He says that specificity and insight (or depth of understanding) are actually in conflict. Specificity requires objectivity, in which case only those symbols that we actually see in the message may be recorded. Specificity limits us to recording only those items. Depth of understanding (insight) is subjective and requires us to read between the lines, where we have to use our intuition in order to make meaningful inferences from the data. Latent coding is better for revealing the underlying meaning of the message, but at the cost of reliability. Someone else, in replicating our study, might interpret the message in a very different way and hence come to a conclusion that differs from ours.

specificity

insight

Holsti (1969:14) resolves this debate by saying that 'inferences about the latent meanings of messages are therefore permitted but ... they require corroboration by independent evidence'. Such evidence can be provided by referring to appropriate examples from the message being analysed.

There are three ways in which we can attach numerical values to the data in our units of analysis (Stacks & Hocking, 1992:263–264). Listed below are the ways in which we can quantify data in a content analysis:

quantification

- *Nominal level*: this is the division of data into separate categories by means of naming or labelling. This is the method that will be most commonly used in content analysis.
- *Ordinal level*: this is a measurement of a variable when you rank-order along some predetermined dimension.
- *Interval level*: this is similar to the ordinal level except that it uses an equal unit of measurement, such as degrees Celsius to measure temperature.

If content analysis is to satisfy one of the tenets of scientific methodology, then the procedure we follow must be reliable. Reliability means that if our study were repeated it would produce the same results as the first time. One way of establishing reliability is to test the correlation (or degree of agreement) between coders' decisions on allocating units of analysis to categories. The higher the agreement, the better the

reliability

reliability. Thus if other researchers, using the same criteria as we did, examined the same material, they should reach the same conclusion about the nature of the message. If there is a marked difference, then our study should be regarded as unreliable and would need to be reviewed. However, what if the two sets of data are markedly similar?

Take, as an example, a content analysis of 100 news items in order to discover the emphasis placed on bad news. One coder categorised 40 items as bad news. A second coder, categorising the same 100 items, agreed with the first coder on only 35 items. This means our two coders differed in opinion on 5 news items, which represents an error of $5/40$ or 12.5 percent, giving an accuracy of 87.5 percent. This sounds fairly satisfactory, since it is almost impossible to agree 100 percent on coding decisions. But we need to exercise caution as the possibility exists that our two coders allocated some news items to the same categories merely by chance. We need to adjust our reliability score of 87.5 percent in some way in order to eliminate agreement by coincidence (Singletary & Stone, 1988:175). The score can be adjusted by using a statistical formula such as Scott's pi index (Wimmer & Dominick 1994:179–180), which produces a correlation coefficient that ranges from 0 (where there is no agreement at all) to 1 (perfect agreement). The higher the better, but 0.7 is considered as being the minimum score necessary in order to call a study reliable.

In the example above, the pi score is 0.77 (or 77 percent). This tells us that the reliability of the coding was considerably more modest than the 87.5 percent agreement originally observed. If our pi score is low, we should interpret our results with a certain amount of caution or disregard the data altogether and try again with a new set of categories and coding scheme. However, if the operational definitions of the concepts in our study are not easily quantifiable then our reliability will be low and our research still acceptable. Ways in which we can enhance our reliability are indicated below:

- Ensure all coders understand and can use our categories.
- Conduct a pilot study. Carefully examine all disagreements about coding. We might need to redefine some categories.
- Establish procedures for resolving disagreement.
- Use standardised coding forms.

Figure 1.5 Although the golfer places the golf ball in the same place each time (reliability), he is not achieving his objective, a hole-in-one (validity). (Adapted from Moore, Nuttall & Willmott, 1974:30)

Figure 1.6 In this case, the golfer drives the golf ball in every direction but where it should go. His aim is neither reliable nor valid. (Adapted from Moore, Nuttall & Willmott 1974:30)

In addition to being reliable, our research should also be valid. Validity means that we have measured what we intended to measure. For example, if we want to determine the stand taken by a local newspaper on the environment, our study would not be valid if we analysed only the type size of the headlines. Here we need to ask ourselves, what does headline size tell us about the position of the newspaper on environmental issues? The answer here is not very much. Headline size can, however, be used to gauge the importance of a news report. In order to infer the position of a newspaper on the environment we need to examine the text for positive, negative and neutral coverage of environmental issues. If we find a predominance of positive articles then we can deduce that the newspaper is favourably predisposed towards a healthy environment.

Problems of validity can be resolved by using logical reasoning and replication (Babbie, 1992:332–4). Our research is based on the assumption that positive reporting on environmental issues implies a 'green' orientation. Such findings can be replicated if we measure the

| validity

amount of space devoted to environmental news with the premise that greater environmental coverage implies a higher level of concern by that newspaper. We can confirm our findings by giving attention to additional aspects, such as position of articles within the newspaper, inclusion of photographs, references in editorials, cartoons, and so on. Possible sources of a lack of validity in content analysis are indicated below.

- Our definition of categories and concepts is crucial to the success of our content analysis, since these create the boundaries within which we work.
- Allied to our definitions is our coding scheme. Such schemes should be mutually exclusive and exhaustive.
- Our sample must reflect the research problem. For example, if we are concerned with the whole message, we should select a systematic random rather than a cluster sample.

Figure 1.7 This golfer gets a hole-in-one each time. His shots are both reliable and valid. (Adapted from Moore, Nuttall & Willmott 1974:30)

1.4.4 Findings

This is the point where we need to set out the data we gathered from our sample in a manner in which we can start to interpret the meanings

Quantitative Content Analysis

contained in that data. Because we are dealing with quantitative content analysis, our key tool is going to be statistical analysis. Obviously, the limitations of this chapter prevent us from delving into the vast realm of statistical analysis, so we are only going to look at a few basic ways of presenting your data.

There are two basic ways in which you can represent your findings: you can list figures in a table or you can plot them on a chart. Tables and charts allow us to describe, compare and contrast the variables we have been working with. Tables and charts also allow us to show any relationships between the variables and to present a 'picture' of what we have found (Berman Brown & Saunders, 2008:39)

Tables make use of rows and columns to present the data, and are best used if we want to summarise the information in a concise way. But the use of a table is limited by the amount of data you have to insert. It can occur that you will not be able to get all the information into a table on a single page, in which case you will either have to break up the table into clusters or think about using charts. *tables*

The advantage of using charts is that you can see patterns that emerge from the data much more easily than from a list of numbers. There are a number of different charts that we can use. The charts that are most frequently used are summarised in Table 1.3. *charts*

Table 1.3 Charts to use for presenting data and when to use them (adapted from Berman Brown & Saunders, 2008:42–43, 47)

CHART	USE
Bar chart	- show frequency of occurrence of a variable - emphasise the highest and lowest categories of a variable - show the trend for a variable over time
Line chart	- show trends for one variable at a time
Multiple line chart	- compare trends for two or more variables over time
Pie chart	- emphasise proportions in each category for a variable
Multiple bar chart	- compare the frequency of occurrence for two or more variables - emphasise the highest and lowest categories - compare the trends for two or more variables over time

Media Studies: Volume 3

CHART	USE
Stacked bar chart	• compare the frequency of occurrence for two or more variables • emphasise the variables' totals
Scatter chart	• show the relationship between the individual case for two variables

We illustrate some examples of these charts in Figures 1.8, 1.9 and 1.10. Today we are at a considerable advantage in that we no longer have to draw charts by hand using pen, ink and a ruler on graph paper. A number of computer programs such as SmartDraw, Corel Presentations and SPSS will produce readily usable charts once we have typed in the data. In fact, the charts that are illustrated here were produced in MS Word 2007 and are more than adequate for our needs.

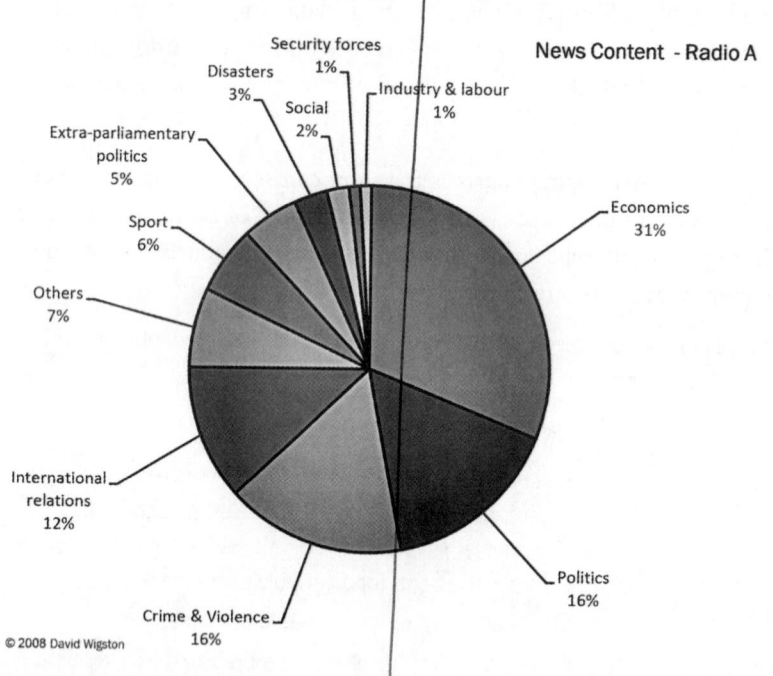

News Content - Radio A

- Security forces 1%
- Disasters 3%
- Social 2%
- Industry & labour 1%
- Extra-parliamentary politics 5%
- Sport 6%
- Others 7%
- International relations 12%
- Crime & Violence 16%
- Politics 16%
- Economics 31%

© 2008 David Wigston

Figure 1.8 A pie chart is ideal for displaying categories graphically, for example the various categories of South African news (as a variable) as presented by a particular radio station

Quantitative Content Analysis

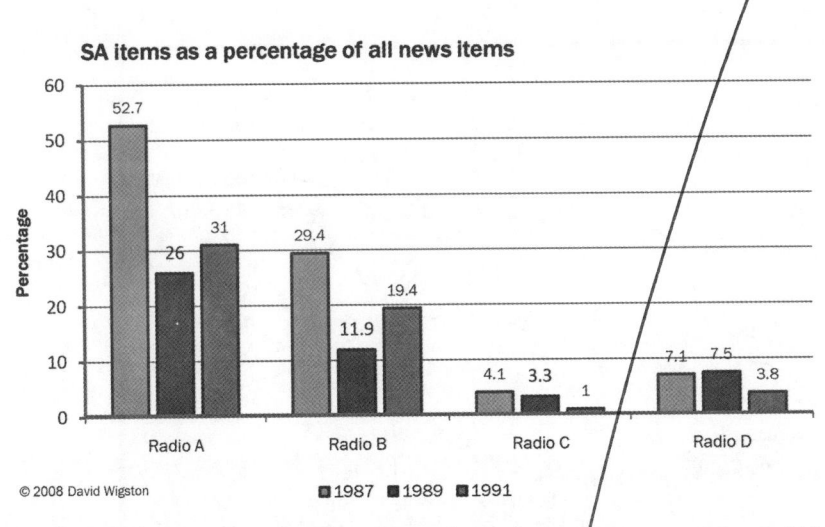

SA items as a percentage of all news items

(Bar chart showing percentages for Radio A, Radio B, Radio C, Radio D across 1987, 1989, 1991)

- Radio A: 52.7 (1987), 26 (1989), 31 (1991)
- Radio B: 29.4 (1987), 11.9 (1989), 19.4 (1991)
- Radio C: 4.1 (1987), 3.3 (1989), 1 (1991)
- Radio D: 7.1 (1987), 7.5 (1989), 3.8 (1991)

© 2008 David Wigston

Figure 1.9 By using a bar chart we can easily compare the amount of South African news as presented longitudinally by four different radio stations over a five-year period

The number of items per bulletin

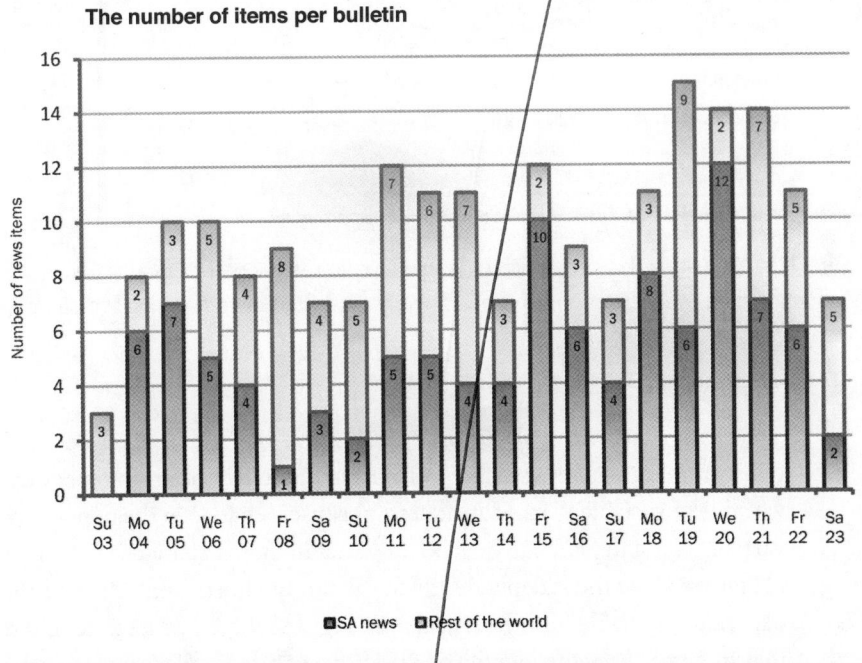

(Stacked bar chart showing SA news and Rest of the world for each day from Su 03 to Sa 23)

Figure 1.10 By using a stacked bar chart we can easily compare the amount of South African news (variable 1) with that of the rest of the world (variable 2). The length of the bar then represents the total number of items in each news bulletin.

Media Studies: Volume 3

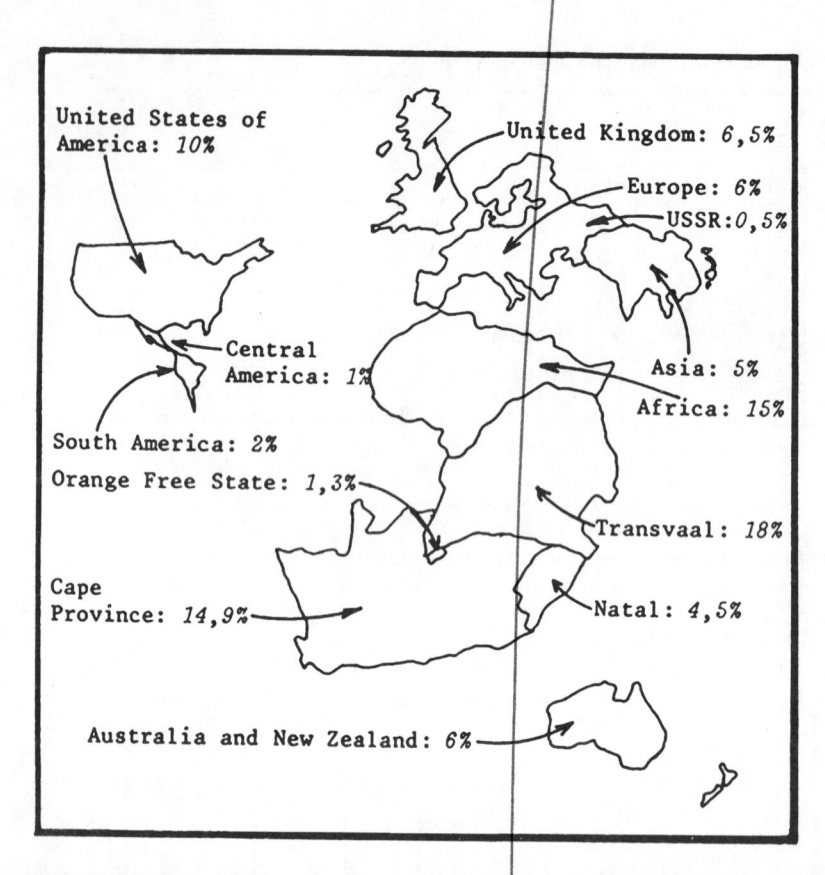

```
United States of                    United Kingdom: 6,5%
America: 10%                        Europe: 6%
                                    USSR: 0,5%

            Central
            America: 1%             Asia: 5%
                                    Africa: 15%
South America: 2%
Orange Free State: 1,3%
                                    Transvaal: 18%
Cape
Province: 14,9%                     Natal: 4,5%

     Australia and New Zealand: 6%
```

Figure 1.11 Changing the size of a geographic area to represent the coverage gives us an immediate overview of how the world was covered by Radio A during the sample period (Wigston 1987:55)

scatter chart

The scatter chart is a useful tool to establish the relationship between two variables, where we want to find out the effect of an independent variable (a variable that is considered to cause a change in the dependent variable) on a dependent variable (a variable that is changed). The rule is that we show the independent variable on the horizontal axis and the dependent variable on the vertical axis. Figure 1.12 shows a scatter chart that indicates how the length (or duration) of a radio news bulletin (the dependent variable) affects the number of items in that bulletin (the dependent variable).

Quantitative Content Analysis

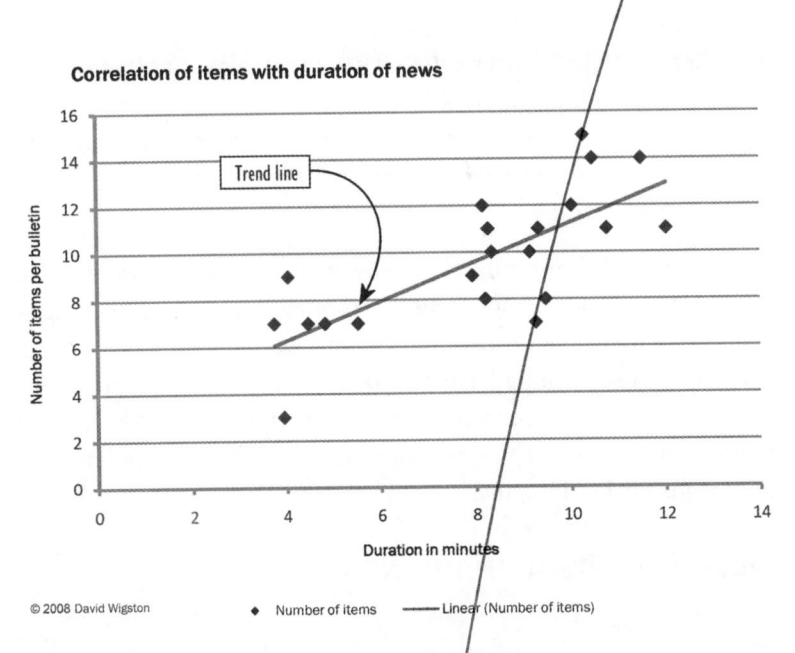

Correlation of items with duration of news

© 2008 David Wigston

Figure 1.12 By using a scatter graph we can establish the relationship between two variables, in this case the number of items in a bulletin with the total duration of the bulletin

On the chart each diamond shape represents one news bulletin. From the pattern produced when we have plotted all our data we can see that in this case there is a relationship between the duration of the news and the number of items included, although that relationship is not a very strong one. So, we can then say that the longer the duration of a bulletin, the more items are included. The closer the diamond shapes are aligned to the trend line, the stronger the relationship between the two variables.

To end this section, we hope that you have noticed that we have not used any 3D charts. There is a good reason why we avoid using 3D charts. While 3D charts look more attractive in a presentation, from a scientific point of view it is much more difficult to interpret the data on a 3D chart because of the visual distortion. As a result an element of bias can enter into your research.

3D charts

1.4.5 Interpretation and conclusion

Our research does not end once we have obtained results from our analysis. Suppose we found that 30 percent of advertising in children's programmes on television was for sweets and snacks. On its own this statistic means nothing (the 'so what?' factor). Thirty percent may be a high figure in comparison to other television genres or dayparts. We need to compare our findings against the figures for primetime television, as an example.

We need to discover meaningful patterns in what we have observed and measured. Our findings have to be interpreted in order for us to draw conclusions and, in the process, rethink our work. Was there anything we did wrong? What could have been done better? If we did the project again, what would be changed? How can our findings be used? Most research, while answering our initial question, should generate new problems for further investigation.

1.5 ANALYSING CONTENT ON THE INTERNET

internet

The emergence of new media technologies over the past 20 years has dramatically changed the media environment that many of us have been familiar with. For example, the coming of the internet has changed the way in which most of us work and live. A common trend evident in new media technology is that of rapid evolution and constant change. While most consider these changes for the better, they have presented us with new challenges when it comes to analysing the content presented by such media, according to McMillan (2000:80). The question we need to ask is, does the internet require any special treatment when we use content analysis to assess internet content?

If we look at the advantages of content analysis (to be discussed in more detail in the following section), then the methodology would seem ideally suited to the analysis of internet content, in that content analysis:
- accepts unstructured material;
- is context-sensitive;
- can cope with large volumes of data.

We will look at each step in conducting a content analysis in turn in order to assess what problems exist and what we can do about resolving those problems. The problems emerge from the fact that traditional media such as the press and broadcasting assume a linear sequence of messaging. This is not the case with the internet as hypertext defies this assumption. As a user, we interact with the internet in a very different

Quantitative Content Analysis

way to traditional media, in that the internet combines text, audio, video, still and animated images all at the same time.

This section is based on the findings of McMillan (2000) in her analysis of 19 studies that assessed internet content.

1.5.1 Formulating the research problem

How should we structure the research problem?

As we explained earlier, the fact that the problem we wish to resolve is the crux of any research project is equally as important here. Here we need to define our problem and research questions as specifically and narrowly as we possibly can. At this stage of development, content analysis of the internet is best suited to descriptive research where we want to describe the characteristics of internet content. In this case, the research process remains similar to that used for traditional media.

1.5.2 Selecting the sample

How do we identify and select our sample?

This is a challenging area, particularly if we want to make use of probability sampling. Selecting a true random sample is almost impossible, given the vast number of internet sites and that they change constantly (McMillan, 2000:81). When using random sampling, the challenge is ensuring that each unit has the same chance of being selected as all units in the population. Why do we say this is a challenge?

The answer here lies in establishing the target population, as this proves to be an extremely difficult task. How can we establish a list of all the websites that fulfil the requirements of resolving our problem? McMillan (2000:91) says that offline sources are always going to be out of date and that online sources, such as search engines like Google and Yahoo, are a better proposition to use in identifying sites. But online sources still remain problematic. Different search engines will produce differing lists, while slightly differing keywords can render vastly differing lists. Also, search engines present us with sub-menus, meaning that we will end up with duplicate material. Here the problem lies in eliminating the sub-menus so that we can avoid the duplication and then allocate numbers to sites to facilitate the random sampling process. If the target population is small this task can be done manually, but once we start looking at populations that run into hundreds, or even thousands, then this task becomes impossible. The implication is that we have to seriously consider making use of non-probability sampling techniques in order to select our sample, which then challenges the ability to generalise our findings.

1.5.3 Defining the categories

When looking at an internet site, what is our unit of analysis?

In most cases, researchers will answer 'the website'. But what does this mean? Websites are made up of a large number of elements and the unit of analysis can include any of the following:
- the 'home page' or screen seen on entering a website;
- all the pages in a site, which can be limited to a few or as many as 50,000;
- the key features of a site or page;
- website content, although here no standard list of categories has yet emerged as with conventional content analysis (McMillan 2000:87);
- elements such as links, animations, video, sound, text or illustrations;
- demographic parameters such as country of origin, type of institution, purpose of the site and so on.

Ultimately, the unit of analysis that we are going to use should be determined by the problem we wish to resolve and we need to specify exactly how much of a website is going to be used, such as, for example, the home page plus the first three levels.

1.5.4 Coding the units of analysis

How are we going to establish the reliability of our coding if internet content is constantly changing?

The answer here is simple – fast! The challenge lies in making sure that identical data is being cross-coded. But, the dynamic nature of the internet means data must be collected as quickly as possible so that all coders can analyse the same content. A solution is to download the sites and then archive them. But this solution can present us with new problems. Firstly, we need to establish if the duplication of a website is prohibited by copyright laws. Secondly, if the sample is big, having a large enough storage space could be very problematic. The solution will be determined by the needs for resolving the problem.

1.5.5 Analysing and interpreting the data

What statistical tools can we use to analysis the data that we have gathered?

This depends largely on what type of data we have gathered and the initial problem we want to resolve. But having got to this point we can revert back to the various forms of statistical analysis that are used for data collected from traditional media.

1.5.6 In conclusion

Despite the numerous challenges presented to us, as researchers, by the internet, we can say that content analysis as a research method can be successfully applied to a dynamic communication environment, such as that presented by the internet, but we do need to be aware of the potential problems that the new media technologies bring with them. McMillan (2000:93) concludes that it is essential to build rigour into our research design. For a more detailed discussion on analysing the content of the World Wide Web, you can go to the article by Weare and Lin (2000).

1.6 AN EVALUATION OF CONTENT ANALYSIS AS A METHOD

1.6.1 Advantages

The most important advantage of content analysis is its unobtrusive and non-reactive nature. People act differently when they know they are being observed. This is known as the Hawthorne effect (Babbie 1992:240). Experiments and certain surveys place subjects and their behaviour in a highly artificial situation and this can alter their responses, giving false results, which makes replication difficult.

unobtrusive

non-reactive

In content analysis our influence as researchers is indirect, since we are studying mediated messages and not the behaviour of people. It allows us to study social life from afar, without any effect on the subject being studied. According to Berg (1989:125) 'no one needs to be interviewed, no one needs to fill out lengthy questionnaires, no one must enter a laboratory. Rather, newspaper accounts, public addresses, libraries, archives, and similar sources' allow us to conduct an analytical study. These sources will not always provide us with structured material, as do questionnaires, interviews and experiments, which give respondents predetermined choices the meanings of which are easily coded. However, this is no problem as content analysis readily accepts unstructured material.

context-sensitive

In addition, content analysis is sensitive to context and symbolic forms. For example, in experiments, symbolic meaning is often separated from the data being analysed. Content analysis allows us to research situational, semantic and political aspects of messages. Content analysis combines well with other methods. For example, we can use content analysis to evaluate interview data or responses to open-ended questions in a survey. Yet, compared with the other methods, content analysis is cost-effective. The materials we need for conducting a content analysis can be easily and inexpensively accessed. Even you, as an individual student, can effectively undertake content analysis, whereas a survey, for instance, might require more staff, time and financial costs.

Content analysis is flexible. It can be used for a longitudinal study if we want to study changes over a long period of time, such as the changing image of women in the media from 1995 to 2005; or we could take a slice of time and use content analysis for a cross-sectional study, such as a comparison of the images of women in advertisements in contemporary men's and women's magazines.

Finally, content analysis can cope with large volumes of data. However, the data generated by content analysis can easily exceed what you, as an individual researcher, can cope with. Then additional workers will have to be hired and/or processing will have to be spread over a longer period of time.

1.6.2 Limitations

Perhaps the most serious limitation of content analysis is locating unobtrusive messages relevant to our particular research question (Berg, 1989:125). And do the messages represent or measure values in the society where the message originated? The method is limited to examining material that has been recorded in some or other retrievable format. While the messages may be oral, written, graphic or electronic, they must be recorded in some manner in order that we may analyse them. Another possible limitation lies in the problem of using the method for a latent analysis of messages with a high degree of reliability.

Quantitative Content Analysis

More of a weakness than a limitation is the ineffective nature of content analysis in testing causal relationships between variables. We must exercise care that we do not infer any such relationship when interpreting a content analysis. Content analysis cannot tell us how an audience interacts with a message. The method cannot tell us how a message affects the attitudes or behaviour of an audience. We cannot say that since television news devotes more time to domestic events than foreign, viewers will automatically have less knowledge about international affairs. Similarly, we cannot say that viewers of a television action drama with a high content of violence will behave more aggressively than those who don't watch. 'All that content analysis can do is tell us what messages exist and how often they appear, and to provide some systematic and objective way to evaluate the individual elements that together comprise a total communication' (Wurtzel, 1985:9). Statistical findings in content analysis can be used to indicate the magnitude of certain responses. The findings cannot be used to determine the cause of those responses. Before we begin any research project we need to weigh up the advantages of content analysis against the advantages and limitations of alternative methods. If we want to evaluate the impact of messages on an audience we need a different research method. Content analysis will not always be the most appropriate method, but can be useful if we want to study events or processes in a particular society or group where messages are a matter of public record. Content analysis is beneficial if we wish to do an explanatory or descriptive study, but will be of no value if we wish to undertake experimental research (Berg 1989:125–126).

> causal relationships

1.7 ETHICAL ISSUES

Ethics in research takes two forms. First, ethics deals with giving credit where credit is due. Second, ethics deals with the treatment of people (Stacks & Hickson 1991:355) we are studying. Since content analysis deals specifically with the message, we are not as concerned with the ethical problems regarding people in our research. Stacks and Hocking (1992:42–63) indicate some ethical issues we should consider.

> ethics

- Are the basic rules of research being followed?
- Has the source of original ideas been acknowledged?
- Is conflicting evidence reported?
- Is credit given for work done in a group? By other researchers? Are coders acknowledged?

35

Media Studies: Volume 3

- Are any flaws or limitations in the research described?
- Have participants been informed of the procedures involved? Will participants be debriefed when the research is concluded? (Where messages are a matter of public record this is not necessary.)
- Is deception appropriate to the research?
- Is the topic ethically appropriate?

Consider the situation where we wish to determine the changes that have occurred in conversation topics as a result of hairdressing salons and barber shops being changed from single-sex to cross-sex institutions. In order to analyse topics of conversation, it will be necessary to have those conversations recorded in some form. It is only ethical that the participants involved in our study are aware of our research, otherwise we could be guilty not only of eavesdropping, which is socially unacceptable, but also of an invasion of individual privacy (Stacks & Hickson 1991:356).

SUMMARY

This chapter is concerned with the multi-stage method known as content analysis. We started with the definition and possible uses of content analysis and then moved on to describe the procedures to be followed in doing an actual analysis within the broader research process. We considered the problems to emerge from efforts to analysis content on the internet and possible solutions. We concluded this chapter by looking at the advantages and limitations of the method and possible ethical issues.

LEARNING ACTIVITIES

1. A radio station broadcasting in your area has been accused of biased reporting on a strike/protest action. You have been asked to justify or repudiate this claim. Draw up a research plan for a content analysis of the accused radio station's news. Make use of the model given in figure 1.3 as a guide. Remember this will be an explanatory study, so you need to make a comparison of at least two radio stations. Draw up a list of the advantages of using content analysis as a method for this particular study. Then identify the limitations. Compare your two lists. What conclusion(s) do you come to regarding the suitability of content analysis as an appropriate method for this research project?

2. Briefly describe the function of the unit of analysis in a content analysis. List the unit(s) of analysis you would select in order to validate the hypothesis.
3. Distinguish between manifest and latent coding. Indicate what problems could possibly emerge from using latent or manifest coding in a content analysis and how you could possibly resolve those problems.
4. Consider the concept of televised violence and list incidents and acts depicted in action drama television programmes you consider as violent. From this list construct a set of categories that can be used to analyse violence in television programmes.
5. Explain why it is necessary to give very close attention to the definition of categories before doing a content analysis.
6. You are interested in finding out the geographical distribution of television news. While watching a news programme on television, write down the possible units of analysis and categories that you can use. Indicate why, if you use only two categories – say 'national news' and 'international news' – your findings will not be very meaningful. On the other hand, why would we not have a category for every country in the world?
7. Using the coding scheme and unit of analysis you devised for discovering the geographical distribution of the news, ask members of your family or friends to code a news programme for you. Check on the reliability of your categories by comparing how many units of analysis were identified and how everyone allocated the various items. If you have a video recorder, it might be a good idea to record the news you are analysing so that you can replay any item where there was a dispute. How will you handle any differences that emerge during the coding? How can you improve on the reliability and validity of your findings? Expect a fair amount of disagreement during your first few attempts at coding.
8. You want to discover the values currently expressed in popular songs. Write down an operational definition of the concept 'popular songs'. Then ask a friend or family member what they understand and interpret from your definition. How similar was their understanding and interpretation of your definition to what you actually intended? How would you change your definition to correct the differences that emerged? Based on your revised definition, how would you go about selecting a suitable sample?

FURTHER READING

Babbie, E. & Mouton, J. 2001. *The practice of social research*. South African edition. Cape Town: Oxford University Press.

Holsti, O.R. 1969. *Content analysis for the social sciences and humanities*. Reading, Mass: Addison-Wesley.

Kranzler, J.H. 2007. *Statistics for the terrified*. Upper Saddle River, New Jersey: Pearson.

Krippendorf, K. 1980. *Content analysis: An introduction to its methodology*. Beverly Hills, Calif: Sage.

Neuendorf, K.A. 2002. *The content analysis guidebook*. Thousand Oaks, Calif: Sage.

Riffe, D., Lacy, S. & Fico, F.G. 2005. *Analyzing media messages: Using quantitative content analysis in research*. Mahwah, New Jersey: Lawrence Erlbaum.

Wimmer, R.D. & Dominick, J.R. 2006. *Mass media research: An introduction*. 8th edition. Belmont, Calif: Wadsworth.

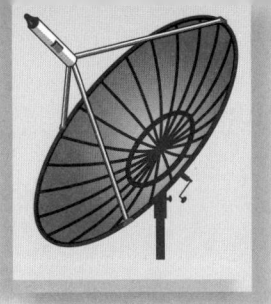

chapter two

COMMUNICATION AND MEDIA SEMIOTICS

Pieter J. Fourie

LEARNING OUTCOMES

At the end of this chapter, you should be able to explain the following with your own examples taken from media content:
- what semiotics is;
- the history of semiotics and structuralism;
- the distinction between the concepts 'signifier' and *signifié*/'signified', and between the concepts *langue* and *parole*;
- the characteristics of a sign;
- the arbitrary, iconic, symbolic and indexical sign;
- the functions of signs;
- different kinds of codes;
- the characteristics of codes;
- the concepts denotation, connotation, ideology and the polysemic nature of television;
- the nature and goals of social semiotics;
- how you would go about doing a basic semiotic analysis.

THIS CHAPTER

In this chapter, you are introduced to the following:
- a definition of semiotics;
- structuralism as the origin of semiotics;
- the founding fathers of semiotics and the distinction between the concepts 'signifier' and *signifié*/'signified' and between the concepts *langue* and *parole*;
- the characteristics of a sign;
- different kinds of signs;
- the functions of signs;
- different kinds of codes;
- the characteristics of codes;
- different kinds of meaning;
- social semiotics;
- a framework for semiotic analysis.

2.1 INTRODUCTION: THE FIELD OF SEMIOTICS

media semiotics

symbolic form of expression

How do the media communicate? In semiotics it is argued that we, including the media, communicate with signs. Signs are combined according to the rules of codes. With the use of signs and codes we convey meanings. Semiotics is thus the science of signs and codes and the meanings they convey. The point of departure in media semiotics is that media content is not reality itself, but a representation and an imitation of reality. In these representations, signs and codes are combined in a structured way to convey specific meanings the media wish to distribute about reality. The media are thus a symbolic form of expression similar to other forms of symbolic expression such as drama, theatre, dance, myth, literature, music, and so on.

But the media are also a very specific sign system in the sense that media accommodate numerous other sign systems. By this we mean that the media include linguistic sign systems (language), nonverbal sign systems such as clothing (costumes), body language, visual (pictorial/imagery) sign systems such as moving and digital images (film, television, the internet) photographs, graphics, verbal sign systems (voice, articulation, register), and so on.

The aim of media semiotics is to sharpen our critical awareness of the ways in which the media reflect, represent and imitate reality or aspects of reality with the purpose of conveying a specific meaning, usually in support of an underlying ideology, point of view, ideal, argument and attitude.

Semiotics embraces four principal areas of study:

- The *sign*: this involves the study of the sign itself. What does a sign consist of? Which different types of signs are there? How are signs related to reality? How are signs related to the users? For example, what is a linguistic sign (words) and how does it differ from a pictorial or visual sign (such as a photograph)?
- *Sign systems*: this involves the study of how signs collectively form a sign system. Language is an example of a sign system; television (which consists mainly of audiovisual signs) is a sign system; nonverbal communication (gestures, facial expressions) is a sign system. Further variants are found within a particular sign system. For example, Zulu, Xhosa, Afrikaans, English and Sotho are variants of language as a sign system. The national costumes belonging to different cultures and peoples are variants of clothing as a nonverbal sign system; the different culinary styles of various peoples and cultures are variants of culinary practices as a sign system.
- *Codes*: this involves the study of how signs are related to one another by means of codes that are understood by the users, and how the various sign systems are related to one another by means of various codes. For example, how are words (verbal signs) related to one another in a language by means of grammatical sentence constructions (codes) to form sentences? How are the words (for example, the dialogue in a film) and images of a film related to one another through the use of the camera and editing techniques (codes)? How do these codes develop and what is the role of culture and cultural conventions in the creation, use and comprehension of codes?
- *Meaning*: what is meaning, and are there different kinds of meaning?

In the following parts of this chapter we will return to each of these areas of study in more detail. The purpose is to acquaint you with the basics of semiotic concepts and instruments. You will also note that semiotic concepts will be referred to and used in many of the chapters of this and other volumes of this book. This is because semiotics is, to a certain extent, an underlying point of departure in our critical approach to the study of media.

Before we take a more detailed look at signs, sign systems, codes and meaning, here are some brief notes about the history of semiotics.

2.2 THE HISTORY OF SEMIOTICS

Since Greek antiquity, philosophers have been interested in the concept 'sign' and the fact that a sign represents something to someone in some respect or capacity. The fact that a sign is not reality as such, but replaces reality or an aspect or a concept of reality, so that it is a substitute for the original, has raised searching questions throughout history about the anatomy of reality and even about the existence of reality.

The hypothesis that the entire universe is perfused with signs – if it is not composed exclusively of signs – forms, for example, the basis of a period in German philosophy known as Idealism, and specifically conceptual idealism. An eminent representative of this school was the German philosopher Immanuel Kant (1724–1804), who held that our view of reality, namely our *Umwelt*, entails an essential reference to mind (*Gemüt*) in its constitution. Based on this point of view it is argued that raw experience is unattainable. Before we can apprehend experience it must first be steeped in, strained through and seasoned by 'a soup of signs' (Sebeok, 1991:20).

Taking the preceding paragraphs as an indication of how far back people's thinking on the sign and the relationship between the sign and reality really goes, we shall next proceed to examine 20th-century structuralism, which is the origin of modern and postmodern semiotics.

2.2.1 Structuralism

It is generally accepted that present-day semiotics had its origin in structuralism. But what is structuralism?

Defined in its simplest form, structuralism is:

> ... an intellectual enterprise characterised by attention to the systems, relations and forms – the structures – that make meaning possible in any cultural activity or artefact. (O'Sullivan, Hartley, Saunders, Montgomery & Fiske 1994:225)

In other words, structuralism is about describing and explaining in detail the different components of, for example, a human body, a building, a machine, an organisation, a government, etc. In our case (media

Communication and Media Semiotics

studies), structuralism mainly seeks to explain a text (a newspaper story, a television programme, a film, a novel, a photograph) and how each component of such a text looks and works in relation to the other components of the text.

Structuralism as a philosophy and as a paradigm

Throughout the centuries, the practice of science has been influenced by the thinking and models of the 'dominant' science of the period. For example, medieval thinking about man, society, politics, ethics, aesthetics and the like was mainly dominated by theological concepts and thinking. Consequently, one could say that theology was the dominant paradigm in medieval 'science' practice.

In the 19th century, it was mainly the natural and medical sciences that influenced human beings' way of thinking about their existence and reality. The practice of the humanities and social sciences – sociology and psychology, for example – was therefore heavily influenced by the natural sciences, which accounts for the intensely behaviouristic nature of the social sciences in the 19th century. (See the discussion of positivism in Chapter 3 of Volume 1.)

It can be argued that language and the study of language (especially structural linguistics) became a dominant paradigm in the 20th century. Structural linguistics, and particularly the work of the Swiss linguist Ferdinand de Saussure (1857–1913), directed for the greater part of the 20th century most of the humanitarian and social scientific thought about humankind.

> Ferdinand de Saussure

Ferdinand de Saussure is acknowledged as the father of modern linguistics. He was born in Geneva, Switzerland. In 1916, his influential work, *Course in General Linguistics* (*Course de linguistique générale*), was published posthumously by two of his former students. In this work, the formal system of different elements of language is explained, beginning with the differentiation between the linguistic sign, signifier, signified and referent. This differentiation between different elements of an object (in Saussure's case, language) became a model (paradigm) for the analysis of almost all phenomena, be it the study of religion, medicine, law, economy, the psyche of the human being, etc.

langue

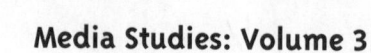

parole

Thus, structuralism (as defined by and practised in linguistics) was, at least for part of the last century, one of the main and dominant paradigms in the human and social sciences. With his distinction between *langue* and *parole*, de Saussure points to the underlying structure (langue, a code or grammar) on which language usage (parole) is based. The ordinary user of a language is hardly aware of this underlying structure. The structure becomes visible only through linguistic analysis and description; only through such an analysis and description can one gain knowledge about the nature, working, power and possibilities of language. Likewise, it is argued, an underlying structure directs and supports a person's thinking, behaviour and values, as well as the functioning of society.

According to the philosophy of structuralism, the purpose of scientific analysis should then be to lay bare these underlying structures. Only through knowledge of how these structures are constituted and how they work can people obtain knowledge about their own ways of thinking and behaviour and about the functioning of society.

Thus, structuralism could be applied to various disciplines:
- Psychoanalysis: to lay bare the underlying structure that dictates behaviour – the unconsciousness is then seen as the underlying structure of behaviour.
- Economics: to lay bare the underlying objectives and modes of production of capitalism or socialism.
- Sociology: to lay bare the underlying structures of power and control and to show how these structures dictate and direct the functioning and/or disfunctioning of society.
- Anthropology: to lay bare the ways in which social taboos, archetypes and myths direct the behaviour of a person as a social being as well as the collective unconsciousness of a society.
- Media studies: mainly to lay bare the underlying structures of media production and its resultant messages; the relation between these messages and other power, social, cultural and economic structures in society; the way the media represent and reflect all the above-mentioned structures, and how all this is manifested in media content.

deep structure

To put it another way: according to structuralism, the surface structure (in other words, what we see and hear) of literature, the fine arts, film, television, radio, the press, myths, politics, the administration of justice, the economy, society, the human psyche, is based on a *deep structure*. Therefore, Karl Marx's economic, political and social theories are a structuralist exposure of the deep structure of capitalism. In this case, the deep structure is based on class difference, dispute and conflict. Sigmund Freud's psychoanalysis is a structuralist analysis of the unconscious mind, which forms the deep structure of human behaviour and the mind.

As a philosophy, structuralism differs radically from, for instance, existentialism. Existentialism emphasises the individual and his or her freedom to determine his or her own fate and identity. In contrast to existentialism, structuralism depicts the individual (humans) as no more than another structural component of reality: an object among other objects. Even a person's thinking is only regarded as one object among various others in reality, and is actually nothing more than the result of the collective unconsciousness or deep structure of society.

Structuralism as a method

Apart from its underlying philosophy, structuralism also refers to all those methods applied to investigate, describe and explain the underlying or deep structures of different sign systems.

We distinguish the following stages (cf. Dethier 1993:490) in the history of the development of structuralism as a method:

- Linguistic structuralism and the origin of semiotics: Ferdinand de Saussure and the publication of his book, *Course de Linguistique Genéralé* (1916), and the American philosopher, Charles Sanders Peirce (1839–1914). Although Peirce had been theorising about the sign around the end of the previous century, it was not until 1931 that his writings were published as the *Collected Papers of Charles Sanders Peirce* (produced by Hartshorne & Weiss). See our subsequent discussion of de Saussure and Peirce.
- Russian formalism (between 1910 and 1920): the leading proponents include Tomasjevskij, Sklovskij and Eichenbaum. Formalism is concerned with the formulation of a distinct literary and aesthetic theory. A work of art (such as a novel) is regarded as an autonomous text and analysed as such. The sociological and psychological context of the work, and biographical data about the artist (writer), his or her world and philosophy, are not considered relevant. Russian

formalism laid the foundation for the structural narrative analysis of, for instance, Vladimir Propp (1895–1970) (see Chapter 6 on narrative analysis). Even today, Propp's work can be regarded as one of the influences that shaped narratology – narrative analysis as applied to the analysis of narrative in, for instance, cinematic art, the analysis of television programmes, and so forth. Propp also had a strong influence on the work of Claude Lévi-Strauss (born 1908) and Roland Barthes (1915–1980) (see subsequent discussion).

- The Prague circle: founded around 1930 by well-known figures such as Roman Jakobson (1896–1982). The aesthetic isolation of Russian formalism was interrupted and the work of art (literary text) was seen and studied in its social context.
- Parisian structuralism: structuralist activity was extended to anthropology (Lévi-Strauss), philosophy (Foucault, 1926–1984), sociology (Bourdieu, 1930–2002), and psychoanalysis (Lacan, 1901–1981).

The first stage was important for communication and media semiotics in the sense that it formed the basis for semiotic theory/theories on meaning. Russian formalism and the Prague circle were especially important for the development of literary theory and its application to literature and later to film and television. The last stage, and its influence on modern thinking on the media as a symbolic form of expression, is especially important in communication science and semiotics.

rules of structuralism

What is important as far as structuralism *as a method* is concerned are the rules that developed out of structuralism for the analysis of a structure of something, be it the structure of an organisation, a group, a text like a newspaper story or a soap opera, a drama, a documentary, a news bulletin, etc. To put this in another way, in the application of structuralism as a research method the principal concern is the discovery of one or more of the following rules in a sign system. Here we mention only some of these rules:

- the rule of *immanence or peculiarity*: the discovery of whatever is peculiar to a specific structure; for instance, what is peculiar to the structure of an organisation, or a newspaper, or a recipe or a novel – what makes it different from other organisations, novels, newspapers, and so on;
- the rule of *pertinence*: whatever is striking in a structure (stands out);

- the rule of *displacement*: what happens when one structural element in a structure is replaced by another? For instance, if a central character is left out of a soap opera or replaced by another character, how would it change the structure of the soap opera?
- the rule of *compatibility*: which structural elements in a structure are compatible?
- the rule of *linkage*: how are structural elements in a structure linked?
- the rule of *synchronism* and *diachronism*: what is the nature of a structure at a given moment and how does it change?
- the rule of *functioning*: how does a structure function?

These rules can be made applicable to literally all structures: the press, broadcasting, political structures, the social and health structures of a country, education as a structure, the structure of interpersonal communication, organisational structures, and so on. In the case of media studies the structuralist researcher will, for example, look for and describe the peculiar qualities of crime reporting in a specific newspaper, the pertinence of crime reporting in a specific newspaper, the displacements in crime reporting (what is left out in comparison with other newspapers' crime reporting), the relationships between different crime reports in a newspaper and different newspapers (compatibility), how different crime reports are related (linkage) to each other, how the above rules are applied or occur over a period of time (rules of synchronism and diachronism), and how all or one of these rules contribute to the functioning of a newspaper (e.g. its popularity or not with readers).

From the above it is clear that semiotics originated out of structural philosophy and method in the sense of semiotics' emphasis on signs and codes as structural elements of sign systems, and their role in the production of meaning within a given sign system or its combination with other sign systems. Let us now turn to the origin of modern semiotics.

2.2.2 Founding fathers of modern semiotics: de Saussure and Peirce

The Swiss linguist Ferdinand de Saussure and the American philosopher Charles Sanders Peirce are regarded as the founders of modern semiotics.

One of de Saussure's premises was that language should be studied as a system of signs. He was intimating at the same time that he did not consider linguistic signs to be the only kind. In fact, in de Saussure's view, linguistics is the study of a particular kind of sign (language), which is subordinate to the study of a general theory of signs, or semiology.

signifiant/ signifier

signifié/ signified

langue

parole

His most important contribution was to describe the distinction between:

- *signifiant/signifier* (SA), and *signifié/signified* (Sé) (see the later discussion of the sign);
- *langue* (linguistic system/sign system) and *parole* (language usage/ use of signs), to which we shall return at a later stage.

It was not until several years later, after the publication of *Cours de Linguistique Générale* (1916), that his proposal regarding a general theory of signs was followed up by linguists. The result was a form of semiology that was strongly influenced by linguistics.

Between 1931 and 1935 the first six parts of Peirce's work, *Collected Papers of Charles Sanders Peirce* (Peirce 1960) were published posthumously. His conclusion – that people think in signs – is rooted in his knowledge of, and work in, the field of logic. He became increasingly convinced that everything could be reduced to signs. In consequence, it became important for him to establish the function(s) of a sign/signs. He argued that the essential function of a sign is to make 'ineffective' relations 'effective' – whether this means communicating with others by means of signs, or using signs to improve our thinking about, and understanding of, the world.

According to Peirce, communication and an improvement in our understanding of the world take place through what we (invisibly) believe (think) and visibly capture or express. The capture of (invisible) beliefs/thought takes place through verbalisation and visualisation (including cognitive visualisation) with the aid of signs. For example: I am thinking of my mother. My thinking about my mother is determined by (i) the mental and cognitive image (sign) I have of her; and (ii) the expression of this image in a linguistic sign, indicated in Afrikaans by the letters 'ma', in English by 'mother', in Zulu by 'úmama', in Sotho by 'Mme' and in Xhosa by 'Umame'. The use of signs such as these is destined to create mutual understanding of the world (effective relation). If I had not had a sign (whether visual or

Communication and Media Semiotics

verbal) for the concept 'mother', I would not have been able to capture/express my feelings, thoughts and comprehension of 'mother' or communicate these to anyone else.

For Peirce, the value of semiotic concepts such as 'sign' and 'code' lies in the fact that they make us more aware of our own habitual beliefs (the way we use signs to verbalise and visualise the invisible – that which we know and believe) and the beliefs of others, and in consequence make us more aware of our conduct and thinking, and that of others. This is related to Peirce's view of the three approaches to our comprehension of the world (cf. Van Zoest 1978:17–20).

Peirce refers to these three approaches by means of the concepts 'Firstness', 'Secondness' and 'Thirdness':

- *Firstness* is related to concepts such as 'property', 'feeling', 'probability character', 'essence'. Firstness is the conception of what is, without referring to anything else. This is the conception of the possible and potential;
- *Secondness* is related to concepts such as 'confrontation with reality', 'the outside world', 'what happens'. Secondness is the conception of the way things are in terms of another or a Second, but without reference to a possible Third. This is the conception of what exists;
- *Thirdness* is related to concepts such as 'a rule', 'a law', 'a pattern of behaviour', 'an element of generality in our collective and individual experience'. Thirdness is the conception we arrive at by relating what has been brought about by a Second to a Third. It is the conception of the generally valid.

> Firstness
> Secondness
> Thirdness

(For a further valuable introductory discussion of Peirce's contribution, see the recommended reading *Images: A Reader* (Manghani, Piper & Simons 2006)).

Various developments have taken place in semiotics since the time of de Saussure and Peirce and various streams or movements have emerged. The following is a concise account of the most important of these:

- the 'communication' semiology of thinkers such as Buyssens (1967), Preito Mounin (1970) and especially Umberto Eco (1976), with the emphasis on the literal meaning of a sign and on formalism (the description of the visible relationship between the signifier and the signified);
- connotative semiotics, of which Roland Barthes (1967) is a leading

proponent, with the emphasis on the social and ideological relationship of and between signs and codes;
- the expansive semiotics of Julia Kristeva (1974), for example, in which the emphasis falls on the production of meaning, semantic practices and ideology, and which relies largely on Marxist and psychoanalytical theory.

For a more in-depth discussion of some of the theorists referred to above, see chapters 3 and 5 of Volume 1 of this book (Fourie 2007). Under key poststructuralist/postmodern thinkers, we introduced the main tenets of Roland Barthes (1915–1980), Michel Foucault (1926–1984), Jacques Derrida (1930–2004), Pierre Bourdieu (1930–2002) and Jean Baudrillard (1929–2007). Also see section 2.7.4 for a discussion of Roland Barthes.

With this brief introduction to the history of semiotics, we return to the four areas of study in semiotics, namely the study of the sign, sign systems, codes and meaning. In the remainder of this chapter we will look at each of them separately.

2.3 THE SIGN

sign

Semiology distinguishes between different kinds of signs. A *sign* is never the real object. It is not reality, but represents and serves as a means of referring to reality. In their daily communication people use linguistic signs in order to refer to things, and to express their feelings, desires, thoughts and attitudes. How could one refer to something like a dog, for example, unless one knew the linguistic sign D-O-G? One could draw a dog, but that would simply be to use a pictorial or iconic sign as opposed to a linguistic one. In short, without signs it is impossible to communicate. Imagine a situation without the linguistic and/or nonverbal means of referring to something.

2.3.1 The characteristics of a sign

Basing our analysis on Peirce's work (see Peters 1974; Van Zoest 1978; Fourie 1983; Leeds-Hurwitz, 1993), we can identify a number of characteristics of the sign:
- If it is to function as such, a sign must be *physically perceptible*, that is to say it must in some degree be visible, audible or tangible, or we must be able to smell or taste it.

- A sign always refers to something, and therefore it has a *representative character*.
- The representative character of a sign is indissolubly linked to its *interpretive character*. A sign is always interpreted. This interpretation gives rise to a second sign in the mind of the interpreter.

To sum up: three elements determine the presence of a sign. These are the perceptible sign itself, what the sign refers to and the other sign that is created in the mind of the recipient when he or she is confronted with a sign – in other words, one's interpretation of a sign. There is a relationship between the sign and the referent; that is, the sign has a representative character. A sign is followed by interpretation; it must be interpreted if its meaning is to be understood. Perceptibility, representation and interpretation therefore characterise the sign (see Van Zoest 1978:23).

2.3.2 The components of a sign

For the purpose of this chapter we only focus on de Saussure's distinction between *signifier*, *referent* and *signified*. For de Saussure, a sign consists of three components: a signifier, a referent and a signified. The signifier is the physical quality of a sign, such as a word, a traffic light, a cloud, a crucifix, a photograph or a television image. These signs are physically observable, often tangible and concrete. The signifier stands in the place of, refers to and/or represents something, which is called the referent. The referent is the object/concept/idea the sign is referring to. Between the signifier and the referent there can be different relations, on the basis of which different groups and kinds of signs can be distinguished, as will be discussed later on. The signified is the meaning attached to the signifier by the recipient; it is abstract, impalpable and may vary from one person to the next. This distinction is made clear below, in our explanation of the different kinds of signs.

| signifier
| referent
| signified

2.3.3 Kinds of signs on the basis of the signifier/referent relationship

On the basis of the relationship between the signifier (sign) and its referent, one can differentiate between various kinds of signs. We confine ourselves to *arbitrary, iconic, symbolic* and *indexical* signs.

- *Arbitrary sign*: the best example of an arbitrary sign is a linguistic sign, such as a word. Here there is no resemblance between the signifier

| arbitrary sign

(sign) and the referent. The sign D-O-G ('dog') bears no resemblance to a real dog. In order to understand the sign D-O-G, users of that language have to agree to attach a certain meaning to it – they have to *learn* the meaning of the word. To a Frenchman the sign D-O-G will mean nothing; he will not spontaneously attach the same meaning to it that an English speaker would, unless he knows English as a sign system.

- *Iconic signs*: the best examples of iconic signs are pictorial images or visual images (paintings, film images, photography, and the like). Here the signifier (sign) resembles that to which it refers (the referent) in the sense of corresponding with it visually. A photograph (or television image) (sign) of a dog looks like a dog. It is immediately recognisable and the recipient does not need any special knowledge to interpret the sign. Speakers of all languages will attach the same literal (denotative) meaning to the iconic sign. Because of the directly identifiable resemblance between an iconic sign and its referent, it is possible that the recipient will treat the iconic sign as the real thing, especially in film and television. This might explain the power of television and film. People believe television news more readily than press bulletins, lending fresh significance to the old adage, 'seeing is believing'.

- *Symbolic signs*: as in language there is no outward correspondence or correlation between the sign (signifier) and its referent. This applies to linguistic and literary symbols no less than to pictorial symbols. To many people a picture of a cross symbolises Christianity; a picture of a skull symbolises danger. Whence do these meanings derive? The answer is that the meanings of symbols are culturally determined and that people belonging to a particular culture learn these meanings.

- *Indexical signs*: in the case of indexical signs, there is a causal (cause–effect) relation between the sign and its referent. Natural signs are the best examples: clouds signify rain; smoke signifies fire, thunder signifies a storm.

It is important to remember that the referent (that is, whatever the sign refers to) need not be a concrete object (such as a person, a house, a garment, food); it may well be abstract (such as thoughts, ideas). The referent may be something that existed in the past (take the example of a deceased person), or something that does not yet exist (e.g. an object in science fiction or a sketch of an unborn baby). The referent may be conceivable (such as life) or inconceivable (such as death). According to Van Zoest (1978:30), any imaginable or unimaginable thing could possibly become the referent of a sign.

Collectively, the distinction between these four kinds of signs forms the basis of semiotics and embraces more or less all the signs available to human beings for the purposes of communication. In practice, however, it is not always possible to draw rigid distinctions between the signs. Furthermore, the same sign can have different meanings in different cultures and more than one type of sign can operate in a sign system. For example, in television, film and on the internet iconic signs (the images), indexical signs (the actions) and symbolic and arbitrary signs (the dialogue and text, but remember that an image – icon – may also be symbolic) occur at the same time and interact with each other to convey meaning. What is more, the same sign could be an index, a symbol or an icon in different circumstances. Take the example of religious relics (a body part of a saint or an object which has been in contact with a saint's body and which is worshipped or venerated). The significance of such a relic would depend on a person's beliefs and culture; it would be seen as a different kind of sign in different religions and different cultures. In some cases it would be an icon, in others a symbol and in yet others an index – or all three.

2.3.4 Sign functions

For the purpose of this discussion, one of the last questions to be asked about the sign is the following: what are the functions of signs? Here we cite the structuralist model of the Russian-American linguist, Roman Jakobson (1896–1984), who distinguished six linguistic functions, or in other words contended that language (as a sign system) has six functions. Today these functions are generally cited as the functions of signs and sign systems and are organised into a systematic communication model. That is to say, signs have the following functions, or we communicate by means of signs because signs enable us to:
- refer to something (referential function);
- express and communicate our attitudes/views/ways of understanding about something or someone (expressive function);
- express something in a *specific way* (poetic function);
- find particular ways of shedding further light or explaining what we have expressed (metalinguistic function);

- persuade or convince others (conative function);
- make contact with others (phatic function).

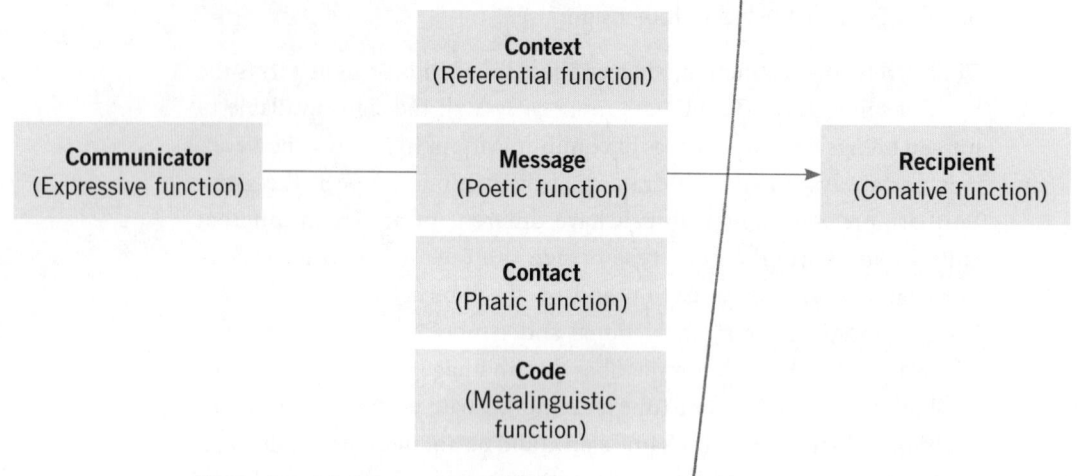

```
                    Context
                    (Referential function)

Communicator        Message                        Recipient
(Expressive         (Poetic function)    ───▶      (Conative function)
function)
                    Contact
                    (Phatic function)

                    Code
                    (Metalinguistic
                    function)
```

Figure 2.1 Jakobson's communication model (functions)

referential function

The *referential function* relates to the content and context of the communication. This is what the communication is about, the *subject*. One could also see this function as relating to the observed and imaginary world to which both the communicator and the recipient are able to refer. The key word is content. The question is, which signs are used to represent the content of the message?

expressive function

The *expressive function* refers to the *communicator*. The expressive function embodies the expression of the subject and incorporates the attitude, thinking, values and/or feelings of the communicator regarding the subject of the communication. In a political report, the expressive function would be what a politician had to say about a topic such as provincial boundaries, for example, as well as the journalist's opinion on the matter. The keyword is *attitude* or *thinking* or *feeling*. What signs does the communicator use to convey his or her attitude about the matter in question?

conative function

The *conative function* refers to the message that is intended to influence the recipient and persuade him or her to adopt a particular point of view. In what form is the message intended to reach the recipient? What signs in the message are specifically intended to persuade the viewer, to catch him or her? In an advertisement intended to convert people to a particular brand or product, these signs usually take the form of attractive models (male or female), attractive settings, and so on. However, it is not only in advertisements (which openly set out to persuade) that signs have conative functions. Political communication, in the form of speeches and reports on speeches, newspaper editorials, or political commentaries on radio, television, internet, personal and group blogs on the internet, and so on, also contain built-in rhetorical techniques, which may be consciously or unconsciously used, and are intended to persuade the recipient. When it comes to the conative function, the keywords are *persuade, influence/convince*. The question is always, what signs in the message play a conative role? Dethier (1985:85) points out that the expressive and conative functions are directly related to the *I/you* binary opposition. *I think and feel this away about something, someone, a topic, and I want you to feel/think the same.*

The *poetic function* relates to the *form* or the 'how' of a message. Which signs are used and how are they used to express the content of the communication in a p*articular way*? The poetic function of signs is generally directly related to the *nature* of the medium. Each medium has its own way of expressing a particular message; the message might be the same but it would take on a different form in television as opposed to the printed media. As recipients of messages we are seldom primarily aware of the way the message is shaped, or the poetic functions. This aspect becomes apparent in a field such as art photography, where we are explicitly aware of the communicator's use of camera techniques, camera angles and lenses; or in art films, where there is a deliberate and visible use of camera and editing techniques to express a particular point of view; and frequently also in film, television and (lately) internet advertisements. But since most mass media messages aim to reflect reality as faithfully as possible, there is no attempt to make the recipient aware of the poetic functions. In television news broadcasts, which are intended to be as 'slick' as possible, the viewer is not intended to see the deliberate creative and structuring processes that are fundamental to news broadcasting. The key word is *form*. (For a more in-depth discussion of the distinction between content and form, see chapter 8 on film theory and criticism.) How are the signs, by means of which we communicate, created, selected and combined (given a particular form) so that they can embody a specific meaning?

| poetic function

The *phatic function* refers to those signs in the message that are specifically intended to establish *contact* with the recipient. In visual communication, the phatic function would refer to the things in an

| phatic function

image that immediately attract the attention of the viewer. In the printed media, such signs would be the layout and typography, such as the letter type and the size of the headings, the placement of a report on a specific page and at a specific point on a page; in language, we would be referring to usages such as cries of joy, exclamations of astonishment, shock, greeting or anything else intended to draw the attention of the listener or reader to something specific. The key word is *contact* and the question is, which signs in the message are specifically intended to attract the attention of the recipient?

metalinguistic function

The *metalinguistic function* refers, in simple terms, to those signs in the message that are intended to throw further light on, explain or emphasise the subject matter that is communicated. In visual communication (photographs, television images, film images, internet images, etc.) such signs would be the linguistic text – for example, captions to photographs and commentary on the content of television or film, or other images. The intention is to make certain that the viewer understands the photograph or television image. In language, some examples of metalinguistic signs would be aspects such as intonation, articulation, projection, and also gestures, physical attitudes, and so on. The key word is *illumination* (or clarification/explanation) and the question is, which signs in the message are principally intended to explain the message and make it more accessible to the viewers?

It is important to remember that these sign functions do not occur in isolation. Although a sign may have a specific and/or dominant function in a message, it could also have more than one function. For example, the tropical scene in a holiday advertisement may be referential, expressive, phatic and conative at the same time. Furthermore, the same sign could be seen by different recipients as having different functions in a message.

In any event, Jakobson's six-function classification is a valuable model, the uses of which extend beyond semiological analysis. It is also a valuable aid in the planning and practical formulation of professional communication messages (advertisements, film images, television images, newspaper reports and articles, internet sites, blogs and chat rooms) and in communication campaigns. How effectively do you as a communicator use signs in terms of their functions in the message you are formulating? The questions set (above) at the end of the discussion

Communication and Media Semiotics

of each function should serve as a yardstick. If you are able to use signs effectively in terms of their functions, then you have made considerable progress on the road to effective communication.

2.4 SIGN SYSTEM

Apart from the individual signs, one can also distinguish between different types of *sign systems*. A sign system is a group of signs with much the same character, integrated by the same rules or grammar. Examples include language, style of dress, traffic signs, mathematics, music, physical movements (kinaesthetics and proxemics), television, film and photography (the electronic, internet and digital visual media). Based on their similar iconic nature, film, television and photography can be described as a unique visual sign system. The newspaper, using symbols (language) and icons (photographs), is a sign system, just as nonverbal communication, a particular language, maths and music are unique sign systems, each with its own rules, grammar, syntax or codes.

sign system

Note that in communication we seldom use a sign system in isolation. In communicating we generally use several sign systems simultaneously. During a conversation we use not only language as a sign system, but also gestures, facial expressions, and metalinguistic components such as intonation, articulation and projection. People also communicate by the way they dress (another sign system); for example, the clothes someone is wearing would probably say something about the communication situation – whether it is formal or informal – and might also provide an indication of the profession or group the person belongs to. Television communicates by means of language, images, nonverbal communication, sound and music, and often by all of these simultaneously, as do film and the internet.

2.5 CODE

Like 'sign', 'code' is a central concept in semiotics.

A *code* is the 'recipe' or technique according to which signs are combined in order to convey meaning – that is, the grammar we use in our everyday linguistic formulations (written or spoken), the rhetorical techniques in public communication, the camera and editing techniques in film and television, all the codes in printing, designing, architecture, theatre, poetry, prose, music and culture in general.

code

57

Meaning is generated not only from the raw material of signs and the relationship between a signifier and the signified, but also from the relationship between various signs. The relationship between signs is determined and directed by codes. A code is therefore a group of signs and the rules for their use.

2.5.1 Code typology

Based on the work of numerous scholars, Fiske (1982:68–89) provides a rather comprehensive typology of communication codes. The following paragraphs are based on this typology, as well as on previous work on codes done by Fourie (1983:1988).

Codes of behaviour

codes of behaviour

Almost every aspect of our social behaviour is codified. Behavioural codes govern behaviour such as table manners, the way we dress for various occasions, the way we conduct ourselves at social occasions, the way we behave towards our superiors and inferiors, the way we obey traffic signs, the way we queue in an orderly fashion at a bus stop or box office, the way we behave at a soccer match or a tennis tournament, at a pop concert, a wedding, a funeral or in church, and so on.

Such behaviour is governed by what we call *codes of behaviour*, which are the result of the prevailing norms and values in a society and of cultural traditions and customs. These are handed down from one generation to the next, but are modified over time in response to political, economic, social and cultural changes. In a society, we agree to behave in a certain way in terms of these codes of behaviour in given social situations. Without such codes of behaviour there would be social chaos. In the case of the media, internal policy and codes of conduct (cf. Chapter 3, Volume 2 of this book) can be seen as codes of behaviour – 'the way things are done' at a certain newspaper, radio station or television network, and so on.

Signifying codes

signifying codes

In contrast, *signifying codes* are codes that are specific to specific sign systems, such as codes of grammar in language and camera and editing codes in electronic and digital visual communication (film, television, the internet, etc.). These codes are specifically intended to fulfil a particular communication function, in the sense that they have and convey a specific meaning. Examples of signifying codes in, for example, visual communication include the editing techniques of fade, dissolve and cut in film and television – each has its own quality and meaning and can give a specific meaning to a scene, depending on how it is used by the communicator (see chapters 4 and 5 on visual literacy and analysis). The tenses in a grammatical system are another example of a signifying code. The use of tenses differs from one language to another. Tenses have specific meanings, and when used incorrectly they turn language into a grammatical chaos.

Analogue and digital codes

The best illustration of a *digital code* is provided by comparing a digital watch with an analogue watch. A digital watch tells the seconds and minutes one by one, whereas a conventional watch does not indicate each second and each minute. Clear distinctions are a feature of digital codes, like digital watches. In the case of digital codes, the distinction is between the signifier and the signified. Language provides a good example of digital codes – there is a clear distinction between sign and meaning. Arbitrary codes (based on convention, consent and agreement) are digital and therefore easy to record (like music and mathematics).

| digital code

The dance, on the other hand, is an example of an *analogue code*. The dance functions through gestures, posture and distance, and these are continually changing and are therefore more difficult to record. Whereas culture is principally a digital code, nature, which changes continually without any intervention on the part of humans is an analogue code.

| analogue code

Presentational and representational codes

A further important distinction is that between *presentational* and *representational* codes. Texts (a newspaper article, a television programme, film, a radio programme, a legal document, a novel, a play, a cartoon strip, internet site, and so on) may be considered to be inherently representational codes. They stand for something else; they were created with a specific purpose, to convey something specific in a controlled and orderly fashion, to comment on something or express something. Representational codes are usually iconic and symbolic. By contrast, presentational codes function in and for the thing itself, and they are related to the communicator's present social situation.

| presentational code
| representational code

59

Presentational codes are indexical. Nonverbal communication is a good example of a presentational code; it depends on gestures, eye movements, vocal quality, and so forth. Another feature of presentational codes is that they function in the present (here and now), with the object of controlling and directing interaction. For example, my tone of voice or facial expression may reveal the way I feel about something at that particular moment, but they cannot send a message about what my feelings were last week. Presentational codes are restricted to face-to-face communication or communication when the communicator is present (see Fiske 1982:68–89).

Elaborated and restricted codes

elaborated code
restricted code

We can also distinguish between *restricted* and *elaborated codes*. In the area of language it has been found that people from a lower socioeconomic class have more limited linguistic abilities (vocabulary, powers of expression and comprehension) than those from higher socioeconomic classes (although exceptions will always be found). This may be ascribed to educational opportunities and social factors. The former group is considered to be people with a restricted language code; and the latter group as people with an elaborated language code.

This distinction may be extended to almost all social phenomena. In semiotics it is used mainly to distinguish between the restricted codes of particular organisations/occupations/bodies/people and explain their influence on meaning. For example, the accepted rules in a subcultural group such as the skinheads constitute a restricted code. The same applies to the legal profession; if one is not familiar with the rules and regulations (restricted code) that govern court procedures, one is excluded from that world. This is equally true of the restricted codes of the army, parliament, journalism with its codes of behaviour, the medical and health care professions, and so on. The purpose of semiotic investigation is to determine the exact nature of these restricted codes and how they ultimately determine and direct the behaviour of these groups/people and the content and meaning of their communication.

One could also argue that apartheid, with its laws, rules and regulations, was a restricted social code, and that since the demise of apartheid South African society has tended to function in terms of elaborated codes such as the Universal Declaration of Human Rights.

Logical, aesthetic and social codes

The best examples of these three codes are:
- *logical codes* (science): for example, mathematics, Morse code, the alphabet, road signs;
- *aesthetic codes* (art and symbolic forms of expression such as the media): for example, drama, opera, prose, poetry, fine art, sculpture, architecture, television, film, radio;
- *social codes* (society): for example, clothing, foods and cookery, objects, social conduct, conventions, rituals, sport, furniture, games.

logical code

aesthetic code

social code

These codes do not occur in isolation. For example, we cannot speak of the media as merely an aesthetic code; they also constitute a social code and, frequently, a logical one as well. But because the media's representation of the world includes a deliberate and structured creative process, the media are regarded as principally operating and functioning in terms of an aesthetic code.

Codes of content and codes of form

The distinction between codes of content and codes of form embraces all the above codes, which may be either codes of content or codes of form, or both.

The distinction between *codes of content* and *codes of form* can readily be illustrated by referring to examples from the visual media. The techniques that are used to unite the components of an image to enable them to convey meaning jointly may be described as codes of content. These include aspects such as composition (levels and lines in the image), the combination of colours, costume, the actors and their acting techniques, and objects in the image, such as people, furniture, props, scenery, buildings and streets. All of these could be described as codes of content.

code of content

code of form

Codes of form, on the other hand, are the aspects associated with the way the camera looks at the content and the manner in which the various shots are combined in editing. Take as an example a battle scene in a film/television drama. Before the 'shoot', that is the recording of the shot on film, the director composes the sequence of shots. He or she might decide to arrange the actors on horseback with a hill in the background, for example. They would be wearing uniforms and a great variety of people, colours, sounds, trees, weapons and other objects typical of a battle scene would be visible. In one shot the camera would focus on the hero. The next shot would show the wounded hero falling off his horse. In the following shot the horse would be falling on top of the hero, and so on and so forth. All the above represent codes of content. These codes may be logical, aesthetic and/or behavioural.

The content of these shots is *viewed* in a particular way by the camera or group of cameras. The director or photographer may now decide to capture the whole scene in a *wide-angle shot*, show the pain on the hero's face in a *close-up*, show the horse's hooves in another *close-up*, add a *bird's-eye-view* of the scene from the air, and so on. The *way* (or *ways*) in which the content is reproduced by the camera constitutes the codes of form.

Similarly, the director may decide to link the various shots in different ways. In battle scenes, film producers often use a rapid succession of shots, but the shots may overlap (dissolve). The way in which the shots are *linked* is also a code of form.

The same distinction between codes of content and codes of form may be found in language and other sign systems. If a writer were to describe the same battle scene in a newspaper article for instance, the soldiers, the battlefield, the weapons, the horses, and so on would be the content of the article and therefore the subject. The codes of form would be the way in which the writer gave the content form: he or she might decide to tell the story in *verse* or to use other *stylistic techniques* to give expression (form) to the content.

2.5.2 Characteristics of codes

Codes have certain typical features (see Fiske 1982; 1987; Leeds-Hurwitz 1993), of which the following are singled out for mention:

codes in use

Codes exist only in and through the way people *use* them. They have no existence outside someone's head. Unlike signs, which have an objective existence outside the human mind (take as an example the sign 'tree' for something with leaves and branches and roots, which has a meaning that can be recorded in a dictionary), codes do not exist as objective phenomena. Only when one uses a code such as the camera point of view is it and can it be described as a code. What, for instance, is a close-up? You can't touch it, or see it as an independent object; it has no inherent meaning, you can't read, smell or hear it. It has no sensory existence. Only when it is used does it acquire a meaning. The same applies to grammatical, stylistic and social codes. On the subject of social codes, a code (which we could just as well call a custom or convention) such as a man rising when a woman enters a room, or in other cultures of remaining seated when a woman enters a room, has no objective existence. It is merely a custom that exists and acquires a meaning through the fact that it is used.

By implication, codes are *linked to culture and context*. The above example of rising when a woman enters a room is relevant here. In some cultures this is the acceptable social code but exactly the same code is considered unacceptable in other cultures. Similarly, every language employs grammatical codes in a unique way. Even the codes related to the use of technology may differ from one culture to another. To cite one example, there are often distinct differences in the ways in which Easterners, Africans and Westerners make films. The use of codes in various cultures bears a relationship to those cultures' prevailing attitudes and views on matters such as reality, family relations, relations between the sexes, ancestors, religion, time and space.

<small>codes, culture and context</small>

Codes function *intertextually*. One learns to understand and interpret a code through other codes that are used in other media, behavioural forms, cultures, and so on. For example, if I were to drive a car in Kuala Lumpur, the local traffic safety practices (traffic code, also an example of a digital code) would not be entirely unfamiliar to me, and I would soon learn this code by comparing it with my own (South African) traffic code.

<small>intertextuality</small>

Codes act as *filters* for our perceptions of and about the world, people, things and events. Codes form what may be called the skeleton of our cognitive comprehension of something, and allow us to condense and understand an enormous amount of data and information. Fiske (1987:4) speaks of *encoding* and *decoding* information. (See also the discussion of meaning further on and the reference to the work of Stuart Hall.) For example, my comprehension and understanding of and/or attitude towards someone are filtered by a social code. For example, we are taught (codified) to treat handicapped people in a certain way, and think about and behave towards them in a particular way. This is a code in terms of which people think and behave when they come into contact with a handicapped person. (See our discussion of stereotypes in

<small>filter</small>

63

Chapter 5 of Volume 1; Fourie 2007.) The same applies to our thinking and actions regarding race, gender, homosexuality, ethnic groups, countries and political systems. One can also argue that the media as such, and the codes operative in the media, are filters of our experience of reality. They provide us with specific interpretations of reality and in the process filter how we think about reality.

marker

In accordance with their culture-relatedness and their function as filters in our structuring of reality, codes function as *markers* for social classes, groups, cultural groups and subcultural groups. (See previous discussion of restricted and elaborated codes.) By using codes in a particular way and creating new codes, a sign or group of signs can undergo a change of meaning in a particular subgroup, for instance in a subculture like the punks or tsotsis. By transforming (codifying) the signs associated with Christianity to fit in with their own views, satanists give radical new meanings to Christian symbols. When different garments are combined (codified) in a certain way, they become associated with particular subcultural groups, such as the hippies. The Nazis provide a further example. One could argue that the genocide for which they were responsible was a direct result of their codes of behaviour, which also formed the basis for their view of humankind, and which differed radically from accepted social norms and views of humankind. A last example of a code as marker is to be found in, for instance, Ndebele art. As soon as we see the symmetrical patterns and characteristically bright colours painted on a house we immediately associate them with the Ndebele people and their culture. These decorations become markers of Ndebele culture.

changing codes

A last, and an important, characteristic of codes is that they *change*. This is evidence of the fact that some or our customs and conventions differ from those of our ancestors. In many cases we also think differently from the way they did. For example, people are less critical of divorce these days; they are less rigid in their ideas about marriage; views on birth control have changed, as have views on women's place in society. It is frequently argued that the media are responsible for and in the forefront of the changes in codes and perceptions. For example, the more liberal way of thinking about divorce or sex is often ascribed to the media's liberal attitude towards these issues. Another example would be apartheid and all the customs, conventions and ways of thinking that went with it. Since 1994 there has clearly been an entirely new set of codes in South Africa, both in terms of people's thinking and in terms of the way in which they behave towards one another.

Having now looked at the sign, sign system and codes as three of the main areas of semiotic study, there are also other semiotic aspects that can be discussed, such as paradigms and syntagms, and synchronic and diachronic semiotic analysis. However, for the purpose of this introductory chapter on semiotics we now continue with the fourth main area of semiotic study, namely, the study of different kinds of meaning and how signs and codes constitute meaning. Before this, however, we need to look briefly at the so-called paradigmatic–syntagmatic system.

2.6 THE PARADIGMATIC–SYNTAGMATIC SYSTEM

A *paradigm* represents the choices at the communicator's disposal when formulating a message. The *syntagm* is the formulated message/statement/text. In language, the smallest semantic unit is the word. To be able to conduct a conversation, words have to be combined into sentences according to certain grammatical rules. Sentences are in turn combined into larger units to form paragraphs, and so on.

> paradigm
> syntagm
> choice

In film (or television, video or the internet), for instance, the smallest unit of meaning is the (single) shot. In order to tell a story, single shots are combined into scenes and scenes into sequences by means of editing techniques to tell the eventual story. The single shot, as the smallest semantic unit, is only one component of a series of semantic units that conveys the eventual meaning of the film. In 'formulating' a shot, the communicator (director/photographer) has a choice of paradigms offering different options. The director who, for example, wants to take a shot of a man walking down a street has such options as the following: camera distance (e.g. a close-up, a medium shot, a long shot); camera movement (e.g. panning, crane, dolly); filter; and speed.

Choice is therefore a key factor, without which communication would not be possible. People are constantly choosing, albeit often unwittingly, in their daily spoken and written communication. Depending on their communication need(s) – to inform, tell a story, persuade, express emotions, etc. – they choose from a range of words and syntactic constructions. The same thing happens in other media, for instance film and television, where the communicator's means of expression include not only words but also images.

The decisions taken or made by a communicator between alternatives, antonyms, synonyms, and/or binary oppositions – such as, for example, black versus white, hot versus cold, red versus pink, love versus hate, and so on – determine the eventual meaning conveyed in and by a text. A paradigm thus consists of numerous alternatives between signs, within sign systems and within codes. The selection of one word (sign) instead of another within the same paradigm, and the selection of a particular grammatical way or structure of presenting the word (sign) to form a syntagm, all contribute to the eventual meaning conveyed by the text. (See Chapter 8 for a further discussion of the paradigmatic–syntagmatic system.)

2.7 MEANING

Since the earliest times, scholars from various academic disciplines have been intrigued by the complex issue of how people attribute and understand meaning. In language studies, for example, a 'classic' distinction used to be made between seven varieties of meaning (cf. Leech 1974:10–27). Here we only briefly mention them:

> language – seven varieties of meaning

- *conceptual meaning* (sometimes called 'denotative' or 'cognitive' meaning): the basic and central meaning in linguistic communication;
- *connotative meaning*: the communicative value that an expression has by virtue of what it refers to, over and above its purely conceptual content;
- *stylistic meaning*: that which a piece of language conveys about the social circumstances of its use;
- *affective meaning*: language reflecting the personal feelings of the speaker, including his or her attitude to the listener or attitude towards something he or she is talking about. It is explicitly conveyed through the conceptual or connotative contents of the word used. For example, the sentence 'you're a vicious tyrant and a villainous reprobate and I hate you for it' (Leech 1974:18), leaves little doubt as to the feelings of the speaker towards the recipient. Keep in mind that there are less direct ways of disclosing attitude. Examples in the media are numerous, especially on television where not only language is used but also all other forms of nonverbal communication;
- *reflective meaning*: the meaning that arises in cases of multiple conceptual meaning, when one sense of a word forms part of our response to another sense. 'On hearing, in a church service, the synonymous expressions "The Comforter" and "The Holy Ghost",

both referring to the Third Person of the Trinity, I find my reactions to these terms conditioned by the everyday non-religious meanings of *comfort* and *ghost*' (Leech 1974:19);
- *collocative meaning*: consists of the associations a word acquires on account of the meanings of words that tend to occur in its environment. *Pretty* and *handsome* share common ground in the meaning 'good-looking', but may be distinguished by the range of nouns with which they are likely to co-occur: girl = pretty/boy = handsome; village is pretty/typewriter is handsome (Leech, 1974:20);
- *thematic meaning*: what is communicated by the way in which the speaker or writer organises the message, in terms of ordering, focus and emphasis. It is often felt, for example, that an active sentence such as 'Mrs Bessie Smith donated the first prize' has a different meaning from its passive equivalent (where the subject undergoes the action of the verb) 'The first prize was donated by Mrs Bessie Smith', although in conceptual content they seem to be the same.

See Chapter 3 for a more in-depth discussion of language and the role of language in the media.

In semiotics, the main distinction is between *denotative* and *connotative* meaning. In addition, present-day media semiotics emphasises *ideological meaning*.

2.7.1 Denotation and connotation

Denotation is the literal or dictionary meaning (conceptual meaning) attached to a sign. For instance, the linguistic or verbal sign D-O-G means 'any four-legged flesh-eating animal of the genus *Canis*, of many breeds domesticated and wild, kept as pets or for work or sport'. Without being able to attach a denotative meaning to, for instance, the colour red, or a table, or a facial expression, or a uniform, or to the visual signs (representations) of these signs, meaning and communication would be impossible.

denotation

In contrast to denotation, *connotation* is the communicative value a sign and/or code has by virtue of what it refers to over and above its denotative meaning or conceptual content. Connotation is the subjectively personal meaning assigned to a sign/code. It is the 'real world' (Leech 1974:15) experience one associates with a sign when one hears, reads or sees it. The linguistic sign D-O-G now not only means

connotation

'any four-legged animal ...' but the user of the sign also attaches to and brings to the sign his or her own experience and cognition of a dog based on his or her experience with a dog as either a pet, a flesh-eating, biting and/or working animal.

The same distinction applies to other kinds of signs, such as visual signs. A photographic, television or internet image (sign) of a dog will be identified by all viewers as a dog, but in addition to this denotative meaning (and despite the iconic nature of the visual sign – the fact that one can recognise a dog as a dog when one sees one), each viewer will attach a subjective, personal meaning to it. One can therefore state categorically that a television programme, advertisement, internet site, news flash and/or a film – despite the fact that they are all visual and usually iconic presentations and representations – will not necessarily convey the same meaning to all viewers. Viewers assign different meaning to images (signs) and experience them in terms of their own knowledge, background and experience.

Therefore, and for the purpose of this discussion, one can conclude that connotative meanings are relatively unstable: they can vary considerably according to culture, historical period and the experience of the individual. It was exactly this acknowledgement that brought about a change from formalist semiotics in the tradition of structuralism to poststructuralist interpretations with people such as Roland Barthes and Jacques Derrida taking the lead in emphasising the openness of meaning, or as Derrida has formulated it, the signifier as a floating signifier to which numerous meanings can be attached.

2.7.2 Encoding and decoding

encoding and decoding

Before continuing with a discussion of *ideological meaning* (as a third kind of meaning after denotation and connotation), this may be the appropriate place to again refer to the concepts of *encoding* and *decoding*, both being central in semiotics and especially in contemporary semiotics, with its emphasis on the role of the reader/viewer/listener in the production of meaning.

Chandler (2006) writes that after Roman Jakobson's formulation of the six sign functions described above, and the influential role this model played in the semiotic analysis of sign systems, the British cultural theorist Stuart Hall's emphasis of the importance of active interpretation in mass communication marks another milepost in semiotics' understanding of meaning.

Hall's (1932–) work on media audiences illustrates a move in semiotics from structuralism to post-structuralism in the sense that he emphasised the role of the recipient (reader/viewer, listener) in the interpretation of texts. His model of *decoding/encoding* (see his influential article 'Encoding and decoding in television discourse', 1973) serves the purpose of showing how media texts and discourses are not only the product of media producers but also of media users who may consume and understand media texts differently from the producer's intended way. In short he emphasised the *active audience* and differentiated between three ways in which media users may interpret a text: the so-called dominant reading of a text, the negotiated reading and the oppositional reading. Like other poststructuralists, Hall highlighted the importance of active interpretation and rejected textual determinism. (See Chapter 6 in Volume 1, Fourie 2007, on media culture for a more in-depth discussion of Hall's theory.)

> Stuart Hall

According to Chandler (2006, who also refers to John Connor's (1983) interpretation of Hall's work), Hall also distinguished between various phases or moments in the encoding/decoding model:
- *The moment of encoding*: the formulation of the message in which mass media practices play a very important role, in other words, as the story is written or programme produced in a *particular way* using 'standardised' media codes (technique);
- *The moment of the text*: the content and form that comes together in a text;
- *The moment of decoding*: the moment when a reader or a viewer is confronted with a text and applies his or her own understanding to it, in which, according to Hall, the role of social positioning is cardinal. It is in this moment that different readings can take place, as mentioned above:
  - *the dominant or hegemonic reading* in which the recipient simply accepts the meaning as produced in the text (by a journalist/ programme maker, etc.);
  - *a negotiated reading* in which the recipient accepts the meaning of the text partially but also applies his own interpretation against the background of his own knowledge, culture, social background, and so on;

- *the oppositional or counter-hegemonic reading* in which the recipient disagrees with the meaning as presented in the text against the background of his own knowledge, culture, social background, and so on.

The fact that media audiences (and the individual reader/viewer/listener) are not passive but active in the production of meaning has also been emphasised by other key media semiologists, such as Umberto Eco. Eco emphasises that a recipient does not need to accept the code and its meanings in terms of which a message has been constructed and the preferred meaning it intends to convey. Eco (probably best known for his work as a novelist) contends that recipients would probably disagree or attach a different meaning to texts if their background differs from that of the encoder of the message. He uses the term *aberrant decoding*. Furthermore, he distinguishes between *open and closed texts*. Open texts are those that by nature are open to different interpretations, or lend themselves to different interpretations, and are explicitly produced to encourage the production of different interpretations and meanings. Closed texts mean those texts that are deliberately produced to have a restricted or single and focused meaning. One may cite advertisements as closed texts in the sense that they have the specific intention of producing a specific meaning (usually with the purpose of persuading the recipient towards something), whereas films and novels of a higher literary merit are more than often open texts, lending themselves to different interpretations.

2.7.3 Ideological meaning

The emphasis on the social background, knowledge, culture and education of the recipient in the process of assigning meaning to a text brings us to the concept of *ideological meaning*. (See also chapters 3 and 7 in Volume 1, Fourie 2007, for a discussion of ideology and ideological meaning.) Here, we present just a few notes about the concept's importance in media semiotics.

Media semiotics is concerned not only with the denotative and/or connotative meaning of a sign/code, but also with the way in which the meaning of a sign/code is shaped and determined by the media to produce, convey, support and uphold an ideology.

Communication and Media Semiotics

More specifically, the focus in media semiotics is on:

- the ideological functioning of the media as a symbolic form of expression and thus on media texts (or media content). Text in this context refers to newspaper reports (or a newspaper in its entirety), films, television programmes, structured speeches (such as radio talks), speeches, radio programmes, news bulletins, soap operas or sportscasts, to give a few examples. In brief, *text* is taken to mean media texts. How do these texts produce, reproduce and disseminate ideologies?

- the ideological functioning of the media as a social institution. This is what is known as the institutional approach. By this, we mean the study of the media as an institution of power similar to the schools, the state and the church – the media as the *Fourth Estate*. (See the discussion of the political economy of the media in Chapter 3, Fourie 2007.) For example, how do certain sectors of the media in this country or the South African media as a whole go about establishing, reproducing and maintaining, or adopting a critical stance towards, an ideology or ideologies? (See the chapters on policy and media management in Volume 2, Fourie 2008.)

- the public's interpretation of and contact with ideology as produced and reproduced by the media and media texts. In recent semiotic investigations the emphasis has shifted from an analysis of signs and codes as such to a description of the relationship between the user/recipient of signs/codes or the relationship between subject and text and the meaning that is generated by this relationship. (See Chapter 9 on media audience theory and especially on reception theory and ethnography as examples of the importance of the subject (or recipient/media user) of media messages.)

ideology and ideological meaning

media text

institutional approach

Fourth Estate

2.7.4 Social semiotics

The above three areas of investigation of the media and ideology and/or the media as an ideological instrument also constitute the terrain of social semiotics.

social semiotics

Social semiotics is the most recent and present development (after structuralist and poststructuralist approaches) to the semiotic study of the media and of how the media produce meaning. This section looks at some of the basic tenets of social semiotics.

Firstly, although a basic understanding of the 'technical' working of a sign system – and thus of the formal qualities (signs and codes) of a sign system (such as television) – is still necessary, the emphasis should be on how a subject (the viewer/reader/listener) produces meaning. Put in another way, and in the tradition of poststructuralism, media semiotics has accepted that meaning is not at all the stable relationship between a signifier and a signified presumed by de Saussure. What *fixes* meaning is the punctuation of the signifying chain by the *action of the subject* – in other words, how the media user (the subject) subscribes meaning to a media text.

subject

This 'new' insight has forced semioticians to re-evaluate their former writings on the formal nature of a sign, code and sign system and to follow Julia Kristeva (1974) in her call for a theory of the *speaking subject* constituted within a text.

The emphasis is thus: how do I (as the reader/subject) interpret, for example, the newspaper story I'm reading, the television programme I'm watching or the website I'm browsing?

Secondly, and after the emphasis on the role of the subject, social semiotics emphasises the *power of the text* (content and form) to determine the subject's response. In other words, which properties in, for example, a newspaper story or television programme are responsible for the fact that I may interpret (and understand) the newspaper story or television programme in a specific way?

power of the text

Watching a film, reading a newspaper, looking at television, listening to radio, browsing the internet, necessarily entails adopting the spectator (subject) position that is *inscribed* in the text. In accordance with this dictum, social semiotics is concerned with the following question: how do the codes in a sign system (for instance, the use of the camera and montage in film and television) *position* the subject? To answer this question semiotic analysis has shifted away from the text as a *system* towards the text as a *process*; away from the 'object media' and towards the 'operation media'. (See also Lapsley & Westlake 1988.)

A third tenet or emphasis of social semiotics is that formalist semiotics itself ran the risk of becoming an obstacle rather than the road to the analysis of the text's ideological functioning. To circumvent this danger, a conception of communication and media as a *specific signifying*

signifying practice

practice is proposed. *Signifying* indicates the recognition of media as a system or series of systems of meaning – of media as an articulation of an aspect of reality. The term *practice* entails that a medium (such as television, or a radio station, or a newspaper or the internet) is not a neutral medium transmitting a pre-ordained ideology, but is the active production of meaning. The term also carries the further implication that, since media produces meanings, the question of the positioning of the spectator enters into the analysis of media.

How do mainstream media contribute to maintaining the existing social structure? What is the appropriate form for an alternative media that will break the ideological hold of mainstream media and transform media from a commodity to an instrument for social change? By means of questions such as these, social semiotics can be fully situated within the realm of critical theory (see Chapter 3, Volume 1, Fourie 2007) as practised in media studies, its main point of reference being Althusser's ideological theory.

As a specific signifying practice, media is now (in social semiotics) not only studied in terms of *langue* and *parole* but also of *discourse*, thereby implying a subject. Under such a conception, media is furthermore viewed as one of a number of 'machines' generating ideology and as a work of *semiosis,* in other words a work that produces effects of meaning and perception, self-images and subject positions for all those involved, both communicators and recipients.

<aside>discourse
semiosis</aside>

With the above as some of the main tenets of social semiotics, Chandler (2008) formulates, for instance, the following as some of the questions that can be raised in a semiotic analysis of media texts:
- What does a purely structural (formalist) analysis of the text downplay or ignore?
- Who created the sign?
- Whose realities does the text represent and whose does it exclude?
- For whom was the text intended?

These questions are exactly the kind raised by the famous French social critic, semiologist and leading figure in structuralism and poststructuralism, Roland Barthes, during the 1960s and 1970s. In our earlier discussion of Barthes (see chapters 3 and 5 in Volume 1, Fourie 2007) we wrote that Barthes argued that meaning does not derive from an author's intention and structured representation of something, but from

<aside>Roland Barthes
obtuse meaning</aside>

the reader's interpretation, which is open and can differ from reader to reader. We referred to Barthes' analyses of ordinary objects, gestures and practices in order to show how the meaning of things that surround us in our everyday lives are myths (beliefs and ways of thinking that masquerade as social truths) and how we accept these truths as being natural whilst they are actually or in fact an illusory reality constructed in order to mask the real structures of power. Mass culture (its icons, stars, fads, objects), of which the media and its products are the flagship, constructs this illusory reality and encourages conformity to the values of the *petit bourgeoisie* who control the media and who are part of a bigger power elite (cf. McNeil 2006). We strongly suggest that the reader revisit the sections on Roland Barthes in Volumes 1 and 2, Fourie 2007 and 2008 respectively.)

What social semiotics sets out to do, in the tradition of Barthes, is to uncover and describe what Barthes called the *obtuse meaning* of a text. Remembering that Barthes distinguished between the informational level of a sign and the symbolic level of a sign, which he equated with the level of communication and the level of signification, obtuse meaning refers to that meaning that goes beyond the obvious meaning of a text; that goes beyond communication and signification and constitutes the level of signifying (*signifiance*) – meaning that moment of giving meaning to something by a subject in the process of signification. For example, we attach meaning to a photo of a dog on two levels, brought into action by the signifier (the dog as sign) and the level of signification, namely attaching to the signifier the meaning that this is a four-legged animal or a resemblance of my dog Basjan or my dog Elsie, a dog with certain characteristics. But in addition to these meanings we also decide (attach a meaning) that this is a 'silly' dog, a 'funny' dog, a 'lovable' dog or a 'fierce' dog. What are the qualities in the signifiers of this image in the processes of its signification that leads me to attach these (additional) meanings to the signifier? The subjective additional 'quality' we attach to a signifier is what Barthes calls the obtuse meaning.

Barthes explains obtuse or third meaning as being 'in excess, as a supplement one's intellection cannot quite absorb, a meaning both persistent and fugitive, apparent and evasive' (Barthes in Manghani, Piper & Simons 2006:109–14).

Apart from analysing the social and ideological meanings of media texts

Communication and Media Semiotics

and of media discourses, social semiotics also seeks to analyse, or at least describe, what can thus be called the obtuse meaning of a text or a discourse.

2.8 A BASIC SEMIOTIC ANALYSIS

We conclude this chapter with a guide for a basic semiotic analysis of a text. The outline is based on the preceding discussion of the sign, codes and meaning. It is also based on and with reference to the do-it-yourself model of Daniel Chandler (2008). In this regard, we present, as Chandler does, the outline in the form of questions that can be asked to guide a semiotic analysis, including some of Chandler's questions. See the topics and questions below as incentives or stimuli for numerous other and/or related questions that can be raised in terms of meaning.

We suggest that you focus on the following seven stages of a semiotic analysis:

1 *Select and identify a text*
   - Being a first analysis we suggest that you choose a text that lends itself to an 'easy' semiotic analysis: for example, a photograph, a published advertisement, a postcard, a poster. (Keep in mind that electronic and/or digital images or moving images such as film and television images are far more complex to analyse given their multiple levels of signification and the inclusion of different sign systems.)
   - Select different texts of the same sort (genre) in order to be able to compare them. In other words, if you select a family photo (as a genre), collect a number but at least two family photos to compare them with each other on the different levels of your analysis.
   - Identify the text:
     - Briefly describe the medium: photography, television, internet, film or whatever, and its basic characteristics.
     - Briefly describe the genre: nature photography, food advertisements, travel advertisements, sports photography, fashion photography, crime drama, social documentary, or whatever.
     - Briefly describe the institution from which the text originates: for instance, a newspaper and/or magazine group such as Media24 or Independent Media, a private television station or public television station, an individual photographer

or a photographer working for a group, and so on. Such knowledge is necessary for an analysis of the ideology and social meaning of the text when you get to the description of how the political economy of an institution from which a text emanates may impact on the meaning of the text.
- Is the text individually produced or by a group? If it is individually produced, how would your knowledge of the producer (communicator/artist) and his or her personal circumstances, historical period, and so on, affect your interpretation of the signs, codes and meanings? In other words, briefly identify and describe the communicator.

2   *Describe the purpose of your analysis*
   - What do you want to prove with the analysis? Formulate clear reasons for the analysis and what you intend to prove. Is it to expose the ideology of, for instance, a magazine, or the communicator, or is it to unravel the way in which a genre creates meaning, or to learn something about the subject's (reader/viewer) interpretation of the text?

3   *Describe the signs (signifiers) in the text*
   - This concerns a description of the content of the text, in your case the content of the photograph. What do you see in the photograph? Give a detailed description of, for instance, the setting, people, objects, animals, buildings or whatever may be in the photograph. See section 2.3 for an explanation of the sign, the components of the sign, the different kinds of signs, the functions of signs, etc. In a semiotic analysis all this needs to be covered in your description of the signs in a text.

4   *Describe the sign system*
   - In a single photograph, only one sign system may be present. Identify the sign system (for example, visual image as a sign system), as well as, if present, other sign systems. For example, the photo may be accompanied by a written text (language as a sign system). See section 2.4 for an explanation of sign system.

5   *Describe the codes in the text*
   - This concerns the form of the text and how the communicator presents the content. See section 2.5 for a description of the code and different kinds of codes of form, such as camera techniques, social codes and codes of behavior, and try to answer the following questions by Chandler (2008):

- Do the codes have double, single or no articulations?
- Are the codes analogue or digital?
- Which conventions of its genre are most obvious in the text?
- Which codes are specific to the medium?
- Which codes are shared with other media?
- How do the codes involved relate to each other (e.g. words and images)?
- Which codes are notable by their absence?
- What relationships does the text seek to establish with its readers through the codes?
- How direct is the mode of address and what is the significance of this?
- How else would you describe the mode of address?
- What cultural assumptions are called upon?
- To whom would these codes be most familiar?
- What seems to be the preferred reading?
- How far does this reflect or depart from dominant cultural values?
- How 'open' to interpretation does the code seem to be?
- As far as *modality* is concerned:
    * Does the image convey itself as being the reality or a fictitious reality?
    * Does it come over as fact or fiction?
    * What references are there to the everyday known world or circumstances of the viewer?
    * What exactly is it in the image that leads you to explain the modality as you do? In other words, what are the modality markers?
    * How do you use the markers to draw conclusions or make judgments about what you see and the meaning it conveys to you?
    * To *whom* may the picture appear real? (Chandler 2006:2)
    * What, according to you, is not visible or obscured about the signifiers and codes in the text?

6   *Describe the paradigmatic and syntagmatic system in the text*
   - This concerns the choices out of alternatives that the communicator has made and how such choices affect the

meaning of the text. The choices relate to content and form, in other words *what* the communicator has chosen and how he presents it. In the case of a photograph, a description of the paradigmatic–syntagmatic system of or in the photograph will concern the *what* the photographer has chosen to show us and how he or she shows it. See section 2.6 for an explanation of paradigm and syntagm.

Chandler (2008) lists the following questions:
- To which class of paradigms (medium/genre/substance) does the text belong?
- How might a change of medium affect the meanings generated?
- What might the text have been like if it formed part of a different genre?
- What different paradigms can be analysed: composition/shot/colour/clothing, etc.?
- Why do you think each signifier was chosen from the possible alternatives within the same paradigm set? What value does the choice of each particular signifier connote?
- What signifiers from the same paradigm set are noticeably absent?
- What are the binary oppositions in the different set of paradigms, e.g. black/white (in colour), close/far (in distance), close-up/long shot (in cinematography), and the meanings conveyed by these oppositions?
- Is there a central opposition in the text: for example, nature/culture, good/bad?
- What are the syntagmatic structures: for instance, the level of the subject/the level of the representation of the subject, the level of the expression of the subject?
- How do the different signifiers relate to each other (on the different syntagmatic levels)?
- How do the spatial arrangements (composition) of the different signifiers contribute to meaning?
- What are characteristic of the syntagmatic levels in a comparison between different texts of the same genre?
- Apply the commutation test in order to identify distinctive signifiers and to define their significance. This involves an

imagined substitution of one signifier for another of your own, and an assessment of the effect.

7   *Describe the meanings in the text*
- Finally, you need to describe the meaning of the text. First focus on the literal or denotative meaning, and then on the subjective meaning or the connotative meaning. Finally, describe the social meaning that would probably be associated with an ideology or the ideological meaning of the text. Thereafter you can focus on specific 'techniques' of establishing a specific meaning such as the following:

Rhetorical tropes
- Describe the metaphors and metonyms used in the text (if any) and their meaning(s).
- How are they used to influence a preferred reading?

Intertextuality
- Does the text include recognisable elements of other texts? In other words, does the text allude or bring into mind other texts?
- Does the text allude or bring into mind another genre?
- How are similar themes (subjects) recognisably and in an obvious way (that clearly spring to mind) dealt with in other genres?
- How are different sign systems used in the same text to explain or clarify each other (metalinguistic functions)?

- Describe the ideological meaning conveyed: 'what kind of reality does the text construct: and how does it do so? How does the text seek to naturalise its own perspectives? What assumptions does the text make about its readers?' (Chandler 2006:2)
- Social semiotics
  - What does a purely structural analysis of the text downplay or ignore?
  - Who created the sign? Try to consider all of those involved in the process.
  - Whose realities does it represent and whose does it exclude?
  - For whom was the text intended? Look carefully at the clues and try to be as detailed as you can.
  - How do people differ in their interpretation of the sign? Clearly, this needs direct investigation.

- On what do their interpretations seem to depend?
- Illustrate, where possible, dominant, negotiated and oppositional readings.
- How might a change of context influence interpretation?

SUMMARY

In this chapter we focused on the media as symbolic forms of expression. The point made was that the media offer a treatment of reality and not reality itself. This premise is investigated in media semiotics by focusing on the media as a sign and a combination of sign systems that communicate according to different kinds of codes in order to convey specific meanings. Media semiotics is furthermore interested in the relationship between media users and media content and the ways in which media content is structured in order to obtain a specific effect.

We looked at a definition of semiotics and structuralism as the origin of semiotics. We considered the founding fathers of semiotics and the distinction between the concepts 'signifier' and 'signified' and between the concepts 'langue' and 'parole'. Next we examined the characteristics of a sign, different kinds of signs and their functions. We briefly introduced the study of codes, the paradigmatic–syntagmatic system of a text and different kinds of meaning. We concluded with an introduction to social semiotics and a guideline for a basic semiotic analysis.

LEARNING ACTIVITIES

1. Write a paragraph in which you explain semiotics and its emphasis on the use of signs in your own life-world. In other words, what is the importance of signs in your own life and interests?
2. Write a paragraph in which you explain how the media articulate meaning: for example, in a story about a political speech, or a fashion show.
3. Explain the origin of semiotics as a structuralist development.
4. Explain with your own examples the following concepts: signifier, signified, langue and parole.
5. Explain the characteristics of a sign with your own examples taken from media content.
6. Provide an example for each of the different kinds of signs, namely the

Communication and Media Semiotics

arbitrary sign, the iconic sign, the symbolic sign and the indexical sign. Select your examples from media content to explain the relationship between the signifier and the signified in each case.

7   Explain sign functions. We suggest that you look for an artistic and imaginative advertisement in a magazine that will lend itself to the identification and description of the referential, the expressive, the conative, poetic, phatic and metalinguistic functioning of signs. For the sake of clarity concentrate on visual (iconic) signs, except for the description of the metalinguistic function.

8   Compare this advertisement with a less artistic and imaginative advertisement in which the sign functions have not been used to their full, or may even be absent.

9   Explain each of the following codes with an example from media content:
    - codes of behaviour and signifying codes;
    - analogue and digital codes;
    - presentational and representational codes;
    - elaborated and restricted codes;
    - logical, aesthetic and social codes;
    - codes of content and codes of form.

10 Briefly explain the characteristics of codes by providing an example for each of the following:
    - codes exist only in and through the way people use them;
    - codes are linked to culture and context;
    - codes function intertextually;
    - codes act as filters for our perceptions of and about the world, people, things and events;
    - codes function as markers for social classes, groups, cultural groups and subcultures;
    - codes change.

11 Give explanations of the following concepts, using examples from media content: denotation, connotation, ideology and obtuse meaning.

12 Briefly explain with an example your understanding of social semiotics.

FURTHER READING

Barthes, R. 1967. *Elements of semiology.* New York: Hill & Wang.
Chandler, D. 2002. *Semiotics: the basics.* London: Routledge.
Eco, U. 1976. *A theory of semiotics.* Bloomington: Indiana University Press.
Fairclough, N. 1995. *Media discourse.* London: Arnold.
Hawkes, T. 1977. *Structuralism and semiotics.* London: Methuen.
Hodge, R. & Kress, G. 1988. *Social semiotics.* Cambridge: Polity Press.
Leeds-Hurwitz, W. 1993. *Semiotics and communication: Signs, codes, cultures.* Hillsdale, New Jersey: Lawrence Erlbaum.
Manghani, S., Piper, A. & J. Simons. 2006. *Images: A reader.* London: Sage.
Peters, J. 1974. *Pictorial communication.* Cape Town: David Philip.
Rice, P. & Waugh, P. (eds) 1989. *Modern literary theory: A reader.* London: Arnold.
Sebeok, T. 1991. *A sign is just a sign.* Bloomington: Indiana University Press.
Sturrock, J. 1979. *Structuralism and since: From Lévi-Strauss to Derrida.* Oxford: Oxford University Press.

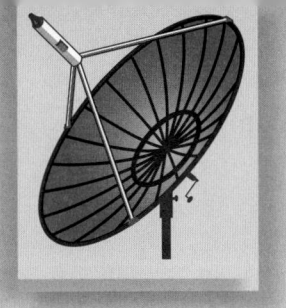

chapter three

MEDIA, LANGUAGE AND DISCOURSE

Stefan Sonderling

LEARNING OUTCOMES

At the end of this chapter, you should be able to:
- provide definitions of language;
- explain the role of language in society;
- describe the relationship between language and thought;
- recognise levels of language analysis;
- identify the main elements of a text, the rules of discursive practice and the social context of language;
- describe the relationship between language, politics and social power.

THIS CHAPTER

The aim of this chapter is to provide you with an awareness of the role of language in society. You will gain knowledge about the role of language in society and in your own life, definitions about the formal aspects of language as text, language as social interaction and the social context for the use of language. We also pay attention to a critical evaluation of the use of language by the mass media.

3.1 INTRODUCTION

language
verbal communication
speech
writing

The concept 'language' is most generally used to describe any system of signs used for communication. In this chapter it is used more specifically to describe a system of verbal signs. Verbal communication takes two main forms: speech and writing, which are our most common and important means for *oral* and *literary* communication. To understand the nature of language it is useful to describe how verbal language is used for signification and communication. The distinction between signification and communication indicates that language is a complex phenomenon in its own right and as a social phenomenon. By 'signification' we mean how language as a sign system produces and creates meaning, while the concept 'communication' refers to the social relationships and the way language is used to communicate and transmit meaning in social context. In other words, such a perspective indicates that language exists in society as a means of communication, and at the same time it is much more than a means or medium of communication because language creates meanings or representations (such as images and ideas) of the society in language. What is meant by this is that language and society mutually influence each other: language is created by society, but it also creates or re-creates society. In short, in this chapter our perspective is not on language as a technical or neutral means of communication (e.g. language as a practical instrument to write a letter), but a critical understanding of its complex communicational, social and ideological aspects when we encounter its use by the mass media. What this difference suggests is that understanding language as a technical means of communication can simply tell us how people communicate but a critical approach shows how people and media can manipulate language to persuade, inform and misinform, and use language to construct and communicate ideology and support or oppose political power.

3.2 LANGUAGE IN SOCIETY AND SOCIETY IN LANGUAGE

Language is the most highly developed and most frequently used medium of communication that we possess, yet language is more than a simple means of communication. We encounter language as spoken (oral) and as written (literary) forms of communication. Language is important and central in all aspects of our lives, from face-to-face situations to communication through the mass media. Our lives depend on language: understanding the language spoken in our society makes us acceptable to our friends, our ability to speak persuasively earns the respect of our peers, and speaking the right way at a job interview gets us the job we desire.

The language we speak and the way we speak it can sometimes be a matter of life and death. An example is found in a story in the Hebrew Bible in the book of Judges, Chapter 12, which narrates a story of the victory of the tribe of Gilead over the tribe of Ephraim. The defeated Ephraimites tried to cross the Jordan River back into their home territory but the Gileadites secured the river crossings to stop them. To identify and kill these disguised refugees, the Gileadites used a simple *language test*: whenever an Ephraimite fugitive attempted to cross the river the men of Gilead would ask, 'Are you an Ephraimite?' If he answered 'no' he was put to a further test and asked to say the word '*shibboleth*'. Because the Ephraimites had no 'sh' sound in their language they pronounced the 'sh' sound as an 's', so by pronouncing 'sibboleth', they betrayed themselves and were killed by the Gileadites. Forty-two thousand Ephraimites were slaughtered by the use of such a simple linguistic test.

While questions of life and death are still decided in language, these issues have moved onto the economic field. In modern societies the mass media have become important industries producing linguistic goods, such as text, books, newspapers and television programmes, and employing a large number of people, such as journalists, editors and advertising copywriters who earn their living almost exclusively by working with language. The introduction of new information and communication technologies, such as the computer, internet and mobile telephone into all aspects of society has resulted in language gaining more importance, demanding efficient communication and linguistic skills.

linguistic goods

Language has also become a target for planning and changes that are political rather than linguistic in nature: examples of the enforcement of *political correctness* are the demand to use 'non-sexist' and 'non-racist' language, and eradication of freedom of speech under the pretence of eradicating 'hate speech' and 'verbal aggression'. For example, a European Union commissioner suggests the imposition of internet censorship 'to prevent people from using or searching dangerous words like "bomb", "kill", "genocide" or "terrorism" as part of anti-terrorism security measures' (cf. Melander 2007). Such legislation would make the use of certain words and ideas a thought crime. Therefore, like George Orwell's idea of the fictitious language called Newspeak, the eradication of the words 'bomb', 'kill' or 'genocide' would prevent people from thinking about such acts.

words and meanings

In a fundamental way language makes it possible for us to understand and make sense of the world by providing us with words and meanings to name things and interpret the world, to represent it to our mind, talk about it and exchange information with other people. Our knowledge and experience of the world are words and meanings mediated by language. The way we organise and articulate our experiences is an interpretative process that takes place mainly in, and through, language. Stated differently, language stands between us and our world; by using words to describe objects in our world we re-present the world to our mind and such representation influences, shapes and also distorts our view of the world. Thoughts do not exist independently of language; on the contrary, language makes our thoughts possible. This means that the existing social institutions and procedures and ways of solving social issues, such as conducting political debates and the art of governance, provide the basis for our mode of thinking and reasoning.

symbolic universe

For example, we know what things in the world are because they have *names* and are *meaningful*. Indeed, philosophers have always suggested that language is our environment – a symbolic universe in which human beings live. The American linguist Edward Sapir (1957:69) said that we cannot grasp our world directly but are dependent on a *symbolic universe* of meanings provided by language. It is also only through *language* that all other forms of nonverbal communication can be understood, interpreted and made meaningful. For example, the French literary scholar Roland Barthes (1982:28) explains that our ability to understand visual images, such as drawings, photographs and the cinema, is dependent on our ability to *verbalise* them. What he means is that we only notice or see the things for which we have words to name and describe.

Media, Language and Discourse

Learning how to use language is part of a socialisation process through which we become members of society. It is through such a process that we acquire words and their meanings, and obtain the values, attitudes and *ideology* of our culture. As Sapir (1957:69) put it, we are at the mercy of the particular language that has become the medium of expression for our society and we see, hear and experience the world as we do because the language habits of our community provide us with certain choices of interpretation and meanings. This is known as the Sapir–Whorf hypothesis. Moreover, Canadian communications scholar Marshall McLuhan (1969) even goes so far as to suggest that the dominant forms of linguistic communication, such as speech, the invention of printing and later the introduction of the electronic media, have each in turn created distinct cultures. For example, our dependence on reading written or printed communication forced us to view one letter after another in a sequence, which made us develop a literate mentality or *logic* that is different from the ways of thinking of oral societies that only use speech.

| Sapir–Whorf hypothesis |

Research done in the US by Kochman (1974:92), seems to confirms the view that there is a distinct difference between the behaviour and ways of thinking of people whose communication is predominantly through spoken language (*orality*) as against those who have been socialised through prolonged education and are accustomed to written communication (*literary*), and that such differences are the main causes of many intercultural misunderstandings and conflicts.

| spoken language (orality) |
| written communication (literary) |

Yet for most of us, language is like water for the fish, or like the air we breathe: we are surrounded by language but do not pay much attention and think that it is a transparent and natural means for communication. In particular, this is evident in the societies of the Third World or the postcolonial part of today's global information society, where the English language has become almost a universal means of communication. For most people in non-English speaking societies, the English language is considered as a means of communication and the acquisition of English as a technical language is essential to be able to operate a computer and other forms of communication technology. Most of these people use English as technical language without much knowledge about the subtle and ideological aspects of the language. When a language such as English is used as a technical language the result can sometimes be strange, jarring or funny; for example, newspaper headlines that state

| postcolonial |
| information society |
| technical language |

the obvious, as in *'Official: Only Rain Will Cure Drought'* and *'Heat Wave Linked to Temperatures'*, or government officials who proclaim the importance of *'this point in time'* and that *'at the end of the day'* someone will do something.

polysemy
levels of meaning

Even the correct use of grammar and syntax, but ignorance of the many possible meanings of a word (polysemy) or different levels of meaning, can produce strange results, such as the following headline, *'Tiger Woods Plays With Own Balls, Nike Says'* or an advertisement that says *'For sale: antique desk suitable for lady with thick legs and large drawers'* (cf. Journalism.co.za; littlecalamity.tripod.com). To make the point, novelist James Joyce describes the discovery of an unspoilt natural place as the place where the *hand of man never set foot* (cf. McLuhan 1969). It is the subtleties of language and social knowledge that make it possible to use it in different and playful or critical ways: for example, a newspaper columnist refers to a drunken *'cabinet'* minister, as the *'cabernet'* minister (cf. Hogarth 2007).

Indeed, we only take notice of language when it seems strange, when we have problems communicating or expressing ourselves, misunderstand what someone said, or struggle to write letters and reports. From such experiences it becomes clear that language is not a simple medium for communication but is a powerful and complex social communication system that requires better understanding.

3.3 APPROACHES TO THE STUDY AND ANALYSIS OF LANGUAGE

Approaches to the study and analysis of language have changed over the centuries. In ancient times it was believed that language was given to people by the gods and had magical powers. For example, it was believed that if we use a correct word to name an object we would have power to control it, or if we could guess a person's true name, it would put that person under our control. Even today there are people who still believe in the magic power of words: for example, people avoid talking about certain illnesses, or misfortunes in fear that such talk may cause an illness or bad luck. In Africa the use of language in magic and sorcery is common.

There are a number of competing ways to define and analyse language. Philosophers, psychologists, linguists, sociolinguists and communication scholars study language from different perspectives and focus on different

aspects that they consider important. Lewis and Slade (1994:26–7), classify the different definitions and approaches to language into two main categories:
- Language is defined as a system of signs for the communication of meaning. From this perspective language is described as a code or rule-governed system of signs. The aim of study is to focus on signification and meaning construction.
- Language is defined as a social phenomenon and is studied as a form of social interaction.

These definitions are reflected in the traditional division in linguistics, where the study of language proceeds from the smallest units such as sounds and words and grammar, the meaning of words, and the use of language in the wider context of society. These aspects are studied respectively by *semiotics*, *semantics* and *pragmatics*.

Semiotics considers language as a system of signs, rules and conventions and explains how such signs are used for signification or how meaning can be constructed. Semantics is concerned with the study of meaning of words and sentences. Both are interested in the study of language as a sign system. On the other hand, pragmatics is concerned with the study of the functions of language and how it is used to do things in social context.

semiotics
semantics
pragmatics

While such division is useful for linguists, for the study of language as a communication system we need a wider and more comprehensive communication framework. For the purpose of our study we need to consider language as a system of signs, such as sounds, words, sentences and texts, that is used according to specific rules or grammars that provide people with resources to give meanings to the language used in social interaction.

In other words, the language we encounter in our verbal communication is not simply the *raw* material such as sounds or single words; communication takes place through articulated language, that is, language organised into the form of verbal messages. A verbal message can be a single word such as 'stop!', a sentence or a longer segment of text with a single message. Therefore, we can consider *verbal messages* as our basic units that are created, exchanged and interpreted during any communication encounter (cf. Kress 1983:3; Kress 1988:86). Messages are made up of linguistic *signs* – such as spoken or written words – that have already been selected and organised into meaningful sentences and

articulated language
verbal messages

paragraphs. In verbal communication people usually do not interpret the meaning of single words or even individual sentences but look for the message that is communicated in sentences, paragraphs or the overall story in a newspaper article. Similarly, when we speak or write we usually have a message that we want to communicate.

The verbal messages can be analysed on three dimensions or levels that are usually described as text, discourse and social context (cf. Kress 1983:3; Hodge & Kress 1988:5–6; Fairclough 1990:20–25; Fairclough 1992a:3; Fairclough 1992b:10; Fairclough 1997; Van Dijk 1997):

- *Text*: the linguistic and formal aspects of the verbal message; the text of a message is constructed from *written* or *spoken* language signs, such as sounds, spoken or written words, sentences, paragraphs and whole segments of texts (also known as extended discourse). At this level the study focuses on these significant sounds, letters, words and sentences. Methods from both *semiotics* and *semantics* are used for such analysis. The text is directly linked to the group of people, institutions and rules and conventions that are involved in producing the text. In other words, the text is the product of a discursive practice.

- *Discursive practice* or *discourse*: the people, institutions, rules and conventions that are used to produce the text of verbal messages determine the linguistic interaction between people and the type of text they produce. Discursive practice refers to the fact that the use of language is a practical social action or practice. For example, conversation or dialogue between two people involves much more than the simple use of language; it determines *who may speak or may not speak* to whom, how, where and when. Discursive practice also refers to specialised and formal styles of speaking and writing that produce specific types of text; for example, the discursive practice of literature produces prose writing such as novels or the more regulated and measured language of poetry; while the study of literature produces commentary texts, academic books and articles, and so on. The study of discursive practice draws on the insights of *pragmatics*, sociolinguistics and social sciences studies. For our purpose we use the concept *discursive practice* (or discourse) to refer to the specific types of identifiable social groups and their rules and behaviour and the specific texts (speech and writing) they produce. For example, discursive practice can refer to the speech of youth gangs (*tsotsi taal*), various professional groups such as poets, literature writers, journalists, lawyers, academics, and so on.

- *Social context of the use of language, or orders of discourse*: both text and discursive practice are situated in a wider social context – they are communicative acts of specific professional groups that take place in different social settings within a society. The social contexts of text and discursive practice are the social conditions, such as the class and power relations within a society, that influence and organise the production, circulation and interpretation of texts, determine who may speak and who must remain silent and listen, and where and when one may speak and determine the values to be placed on a person's speech. Here both pragmatics and a variety of social analyses inform the study of language in social context. Interest in social power means that we pay attention to the institutions that produce discourse: for example, in most democracies the discourse (judgements) of the Supreme Court or Constitutional Court is more powerful than that of politicians.

margin: orders of discourse; power relations

Important: Please note that in this chapter we use the words 'text' and 'discourse' in a specific way and we would like to suggest that you do not use the dictionary to look up the definitions of these words. In daily use, in the study of linguistics, sociolinguistics and the social sciences, the word 'discourse' is used in a great number of ways and has acquired meanings that are often contradictory and confusing (cf. Georgakopoulou & Goutsos 1997:1–5). For example, you may pick up two books with a title 'discourse analysis' that have no relation to each other (compare, for example, the views on 'discourse' in the following: Fairclough 1990; Van Dijk 1997; Torfing 1999; and Wodak & Chilton 2005). In this chapter we follow on the work of social semiotics and critical language analysis (CLA) or critical discourse analysis (CDA) rather than on the purely linguistic or sociolinguistic perspectives.

margin: critical language analysis (CLA); critical discourse analysis (CDA)

3.4 LANGUAGE OF THE TEXT

The text is the first encounter in a communication process: it is the message that has significance, which is exchanged in the process of communication.

The text of verbal messages is composed of many signs and has a formal structure, coherence and organisation. The word *text* comes from the

Latin *textus*, meaning something woven together (cf. Hodge & Kress 1988:6). For example, a look at any printed page such as a newspaper or a book creates the impression of a tapestry made from words. Texts can be *spoken* or *written* segments of language; such extended segments of text are also known as *discourse*.

We consider texts as the *material product* of a particular *discursive practice*. Different discursive practices produce different and distinct types (or *genre*) of text (cf. Fairclough 1990:20). For example, the discourse of literature produces *prose*, such as novels and literary criticism, while the discourse of journalism produces news reports. One type of text may be used for different purposes; for example, the text of the Bible can be used as a document of divine revelation within religious discursive practice, while for literary criticism it is an example of poetic style. The formal structure of a text reflects the process of its production. For example, the text of a newspaper is characterised by a particular *style* of presenting the information.

inverted pyramid

The text of the news story printed in a newspaper has a particular form, traditionally known as the inverted pyramid. Text written according to the inverted pyramid format begins with the climax of the story and presents all the important facts in the first paragraph. The following is an example of a first paragraph of a news report:

> *Rude South African police officers have cost the country's safety and security minister R30 000, after a judge ruled they had humiliated a law professor, a newspaper said on Wednesday.* (News 24.com, September 2007)

In such a paragraph the facts are arranged to satisfy the readers' curiosity regarding the *whom, what, when, where, why* and *how* of a newsworthy occurrence. While such a formal presentation is considered self-evident today, it originated in the American Civil War period when journalists used the telegraph for the first time. Fearing that their stories would not be transmitted all at once, the journalists crowded as much information as possible into the first paragraph. Subsequently, such a practice became institutionalised and accepted as a formal requirement for journalistic writing (cf. MacDougall 1969:50). Indeed, the form of presentation or style is an important aspect of media news reporting.

Media, Language and Discourse

Media news reporting is considered as an objective re-presentation of facts, as if the reporter allows the facts to *speak for themselves*. Such a mode of writing is thought to have a zero-degree signification by itself, as if language was a transparent *form* that did not influence the *content* it communicated (cf. Barthes 1984:5–6). The belief in the objectivity of language is still common among journalists and television reporters, and their viewing publics, who believe that the medium can re-present reality without *mediation*. However, *content* and *form* or the techniques of presentation are interrelated and do not exist independently. There is no escape from the distortions imposed by language, and *realistic* writing is still a form of mediation or re-presentation, or staging of reality through language.

| zero-degree signification

Some of the important elements of language in texts that we need to know and understand how they communicate are: *sounds, words and vocabulary, sentences, rules and grammar, cohesion* and *text structure* (cf. Fairclough 1992a:75; Van Dijk 1988:170).

Sounds and words

The basic elements of spoken language consist of *sounds*, while written language consists of graphic *signs* such as the *letters* of the alphabet and *words*. The basic element of spoken language that makes a significant difference is a phoneme: for example, we notice that the sound 'p' is different from the sound 'b'. Morphemes are sounds or combinations of sounds that are meaningful, such as words or parts of words. The Swiss linguist Ferdinand de Saussure, who introduced the science of *semiotics*, considered language as a system of *signs* such as words and the *rules* or *conventions* for using them. The material aspect of the word as a sign, such as the *sound* of a spoken word or the *graphic* marks on a piece of paper of a written word, is termed the *signifier* and the corresponding mental image or concept called the *signified*. For example, for me to communicate an idea that I have in my mind, I need to express it in a linguistic sound or written mark (such as a word) with which it is associated. When I address my message to you, the sound of the word will evoke a concept in your mind that corresponds to my idea. In this way signs do not refer to things in reality but rather to ideas or concepts of such a reality in our mind. The way people pronounce words or the ways they speak are also indicators of social class and position. This means that language can be used to classify people.

| phoneme
| morphemes

93

Words, vocabulary and jargon

In order to communicate, the writer or speaker of language needs words and a vocabulary before he or she can represent reality. A vocabulary consists of words for *naming* things. There are also specific vocabularies such as *technical terminology*, the *key concepts*, or jargon that has specific meaning and value within a certain type of formal and specialised discursive practice. The meaning of a concept is related to, and is dependent on, other concepts and their use, thus forming a network of related concepts. For example, in the discourse of geography we cannot use the word *north* without reference to the corresponding words *south*, *east* and *west* (cf. Williams 1993:345).

Words or concepts represent categorisation of the world from a particular point of view, as they exist within a system organised by ideological assumptions (cf. Kress 1984:124–5). Put differently, the vocabulary of a language or a particular discursive practice is a *map* of objects, concepts, processes and relationships about which the members of the culture or discursive community need to communicate (cf. Fowler 1991:80). All writing, from personal letters to news reporting in the mass media, is an act of *mediation*.

schemata

That is, an event is mediated through language from perceiver (communicator) to someone who did not witness the event (recipient). However, perception is selective and directed by a framework of ideas or schemata about what is important (cf. Kress 1984:120). The writer or speaker looks at the world and notices only those things that correspond with the schemata. A writer would only write what he or she already knows and interprets everything according to such knowledge (cf. Gombrich 1986:73). Words or concepts can be considered as *labels* that structure perception by classifying objects, people and situations. Such a classification depends upon the ideological assumptions of the writer and not on any quality of the object, situation or behaviour being classified. For example, imagine that you are a psychologist and you are having a conversation with a person when suddenly you notice that he or she is getting agitated. You could interpret and describe the agitation as an indication that the person gets *angry* or gets *aggressive*. Each description refers to the same event but implies a different evaluation and classification, which carry different meanings and justification for subsequent responses. For example, if the person you are talking to is a friend you would probably say that he *gets angry* but if the person is a mental patient you would say that he *gets aggressive* (cf. Edelman 1974:300). Indeed, such classification of activities and categorisation of people are performed by the practice, talk and writing of psychiatrists and other members of the *helping professions* who have constructed a vocabulary of concepts such as *mental illness, deviance, help* and *therapy* to label certain common activities as demanding professional intervention. Edelman (1974:297) shows the logic behind the use of the concept *therapy* by psychiatrists. In psychiatrists' discourse, ordinary people may simply go dancing, but mental patients have *dance therapy*; engaging in sport is *recreation therapy*; group discussion is *group therapy*, and reading activity is *bibliotherapy*. The use of such a vocabulary has political implications, as Edelman (1974:297) puts it: 'To label a common activity as though it were a medical one is to establish superior and subordinate roles, to make it clear who gives orders and who takes them, and to justify in advance the inhibitions placed upon the subordinate classes'. According to Edelman (1974:295) psychiatrists often ignore the demands and requests made by mental patients because granting them would not be in line with *helping* but would rather *reinforce deviant behaviour*; in line with the helping ideology, demanding mental patients are sometimes *punished*. Is the psychiatrist's action punishment or help? Or, for example, how should one interpret the following description of the treatment of mental patients, recommended by psychiatric textbooks?

> *Deprivation of food, bed, walks in open air, visitors, mail, or telephone calls; solitary confinement; deprivation of reading or entertainment material; immobilizing people by tying them into wet sheets and then exhibiting them to staff and other patients; other physical restraints on body movement; drugging the mind against the client's will; incarceration in locked wards; a range of public humiliations such as the prominent posting of alleged intentions to escape or commit suicide, the requirement of public confessions of misconduct or guilt, and public announcement of individual misdeeds and abnormalities.* (Edelman 1974:300)

Depending on the specific professional ideological perspective, psychiatric treatment could be described as either *help* and *therapy* or *punishment* and *sadism*. For persons not trained in the perspective of the discourse of psychiatry such language would evoke the horror of torture and repression, while for the trained professionals subscribing to the accepted ideology these are necessary means to achieve rehabilitation.

The professional and non-political classification and language of the *helping professions* fulfils a political function. As society has become more complex and more people have become discontented, more types of behaviour have been labelled as *deviant* by psychiatrists, and so medical doctors and social workers gained authority and the power to apply such labels. These 'professionals create and reinforce popular beliefs about which kinds of people are worthy and which are unworthy: about who should be rewarded through government action and who controlled or repressed' (Edelman 1974:297). The mass media are important in promoting labels that become the 'official vocabulary' by being constantly repeated in general usage. The use of such *technical labels* prevents discussion and critical thought as it authoritatively defines *good and evil* and communicates decisions, dictums and commands that must be unquestionably accepted (cf. Marcuse 1970:89). Increasingly, the uses of technical vocabularies of *experts* in the service of government agencies comes to dominate the political decision-making process.

bureaucratic domination

bureaucratic language

Such a *scientisation of politics* (Habermas 1972:62), or the *rationalisation* and *programming* of society through the *medical, psychiatric, carceral, etc, techniques* of intervention (cf. Foucault 1980, 1988), eliminates the open public debate on social policy that is characteristic of democratic politics, and replaces it with bureaucratic domination (cf. Habermas 1972:62–80) by the use of seemingly neutral and authoritative bureaucratic language (cf. Edelman 1977:98).

The use of such vocabulary makes it easy to accept without question the increasing number of legitimate political activities that are criminalised. For example, consider the concept *unemployment*. If, in a large city, one man or a woman is unemployed, we would consider this to be the individual's *personal trouble* resulting from some personal failing. But in a nation of 50 million people, if 15 million are unemployed and living in poverty, then this is no longer individual trouble but a *public issue* requiring economic and political solution (cf. Mills 1978:15). Indeed, attempts by individuals to make political statements can be easily subverted by the use of professional vocabulary: for example, a woman whose poverty makes her angry or despondent becomes a symbol of individual sickness rather than a victim of a malfunctioning economy after a psychiatrist defines her as *hysteric* (cf. Edelman, in Fourie 1991:4). In this way, *public issues of social structure* over which the individual has no control are transformed by definition into personal *troubles* attributed to the private faults of the individual (cf. Mills 1978:14). Indeed, political opposition from the powerless classes in South Africa during the era of apartheid was often classified as *deviance,* justifying violent reaction from the state. The *helping professions* have become part of the new *social science police* – effective agents of social control – and through their professional language they help 'manipulate the discontented into conformity and docility and to isolate or incarcerate those who refuse to be "rehabilitated"' (Edelman 1974:310).

Metaphors

In the most general way, words and concepts are essentially metaphors that translate sense experience into vocal and visual symbols (cf. McLuhan 1969:67). Metaphors are concepts that allow us to understand and experience one kind of thing in terms of another and are useful means for understanding a new or problematic situation in terms of situations that are already familiar. As ideas and concepts become more abstract metaphors are used to translate them into more concrete basic domains that are already understood. Metaphors influence and structure the way we think and behave. Lakoff and Johnson (1980:4) show how the metaphor *argument is war* influences our understanding and conduct of everyday arguments. In our everyday language the metaphor *argument is war* is commonly encountered:

- Your claims are *indefensible.*
- He *attacked* my arguments.
- Her criticism was right *on target*.
- I *demolished* her argument.
- He *shot down* my arguments.
- I have never *won* an argument with him.

Of course, arguments and war are different kinds of actions, but because of the prevalence of the metaphor in our everyday language we tend to think of, and argue as if, we were conducting war. The metaphor provides a limited perspective, through the related framework of concepts, on the activity and has the ability to highlight one aspect while concealing other ways of thinking about it. As a result we do not only use the war metaphor to talk about arguments in terms of war and we

metaphor

actually conduct our arguments as if we were engaged in real combat. The war metaphor is a favourite in mass media discourse to describe politics (cf. So 1987:624; Chilton & Ilyin 1993:10).

Identifying various metaphors should make us aware of their influence on our thinking and acting. For example, the use of the metaphor of the 'Dark Continent' to describe Africa still exerts its ideological power, as it did during the 19th century. This metaphor reaffirms Western dominance and reveals racist valuations of Africa.

Another favourite metaphor used by mass media is to describe the *economy* in terms of an organic metaphor, as if it was a plant: the 'economy is growing'. The choice of metaphor is not coincidental but reflects an ideological position: the capitalist economy is the *natural* order of things. There are, of course, other metaphors for presenting the economy such as a *building structure*, or a *performance* (cf. Nelson 1990:18–20). Indeed, in the financial and business sections of media the economy is presented in terms of the metaphors for *war* or a *boxing match* (Pretoria News Business Report, 2 & 3 July 1998); for example:

- Fight for full payout on your endowment policy
- Big guns help Rand claw back
- Double blow puts rand on the canvas

Sentences and grammar

sentence

Traditionally, grammar is considered as 'the art of speaking and writing correctly', and the grammarian's task is to identify 'good usage' of language. Most often we think of grammar as rules to construct clear, meaningful sentences. For example, a sentence such as 'the cat sat on the mat' is a simple illustration. But it is also possible to use correct grammar to produce a meaningless sentence, for example: 'The green ideas sleep furiously'. Consider the following example of a letter published in the *Los Angeles Times* (cf. Hospers 1992:11):

Mr Baggage Man

American Airlines

Gentlemen Dear Sir

I dam seldom where my suitcases are.

She no fly.

You no more fit to baggage master than for crysake that's all I hope.

What's the matter you?

In the above example, the sentence and grammar may be defective but the intended message and meaning can be understood by most people who have had their baggage misplaced by an airline.

These examples show that the correct use of grammar does not guarantee the production of meaningful sentences, and indicates that grammar involves more than the use of technical rules.

Grammar does much more than dictate good usage of language; grammar provides a theory of reality for a culture, as it provides categories for distinction between *subject* and *object* for constructing a sentence, and also provides explanations for events by linking a *deed* to a *doer*. In the production of text the writer or speaker makes choices and selects words and grammatical constructions. Each choice affects the meaning communicated by presenting a different perspective of the world. For example, in reporting on an action a writer can present it from various perspectives by using *transitive* or *intransitive* verbs or using the *active* voice or *passive* voice. Each choice *transforms* the meanings and presents a different perspective that usually reflects an ideological commitment (cf. Fowler 1991:70–8). For example, consider the following sentences:

- Police kill prisoner in a cell.
- Prisoner found dead in a police cell.

active voice

passive voice

While the two sentences have similar meanings, they imply different perspectives on the situation. In the first sentence the focus is on an *actor/agent* ('police') who performs a transitive action affecting someone or something; here the action ('kill') is performed on someone – the *affected participant/object* of the sentence ('prisoner'). The sentence focuses attention on the actor/agent, providing an explanation and placing the responsibility for the action on the actor. In the second sentence the point of view is that of the affected participant/object and the emphasis is no longer on the action or actor but on a *state of affairs* ('prisoner found dead'). Such a transformation displaces the responsibility from the actor to the object. A similar transformation is done by a change from *active* to *passive* voice. Compare the following two newspaper headlines:

- Police shoot 11 dead in Harare riot.
- Rioting protesters shot dead by police.

In the first headline the emphasis is squarely on the agent performing the action, identifying the police as responsible for the deaths. The use of the passive in the second headline places the emphasis not on those who did the act of shooting but on those on the receiving end. The change of emphasis displaces the responsibility for the action from the police to their victims (cf. Montgomery 1986:186–7; Kress 1984:127; Fowler 1991:78).

The grammatical choices made by the mass media could be explained if linked to the discursive practice of the particular newspapers, their assumptions about society, and their professional or institutional ideology (cf. McQuail 1980:174–82). We may discover, for example, that second headline above is derived from a pro-government publication while the first headline from an opposition newspaper. Such examples of grammatical manipulation motivated by ideological assumptions could be found in the use of language by the South African Broadcasting Corporation (SABC) television news broadcasts during the apartheid era. Because South African television was controlled by the regime, all news reports on police activity were actively manipulated, and reporting on police shooting of protesters were almost exclusively in the passive voice: for example, 'nine people died and almost 200 injured' or 'countrywide unrest cost the lives of two rioters last night' (cf. Posel 1989:264). By removing the grammatical acting agents of the sentence, the television viewer was prevented from considering the police as the agents who were responsible for the death of protesters, and attention was directed to the abstract concept *unrest* as being responsible for death, and the protesters presented as *rioters* who *paid* with their lives.

Texts produced by scientists are also characterised by the passive voice and the absence of the reporting subject. For example, scientists report that 'it was decided to use this method ...' rather than 'we decided to use this method ...', or 'the test indicates there is a significant difference ...' and not 'based on the test, we concluded ...' (cf. Gusfield 1976:20). The choice of the passive voice is a convention of the discourse of science and 'implies that to be scientific is to exercise a definite form over language in use and to write in a particular way which shows the audience that the writer is *doing science*' (Gusfield 1976:17). *The impersonal style of scientific discourse combined with a technical vocabulary serves to establish a position of superiority and power for the scientist.*

Structures of text segment

Text structure refers to larger segments of the text, such as the *topics, themes, perspectives* and overall *meaning* of the text (cf. Fairclough 1992a:75; Van Dijk 1988:170). Words, individual sentences or sequences of sentences are organised into a coherent unity and form the particular text. Such a framework or *text structure* gives us the overall *topic* or theme represented in the text. Selection of particular topics and the avoidance of others give an insight into assumptions, beliefs and systems of knowledge and ideologies of the discursive practice. For example, a newspaper reports on an increase in the number of children imprisoned by the police; however, a government-aligned newspaper will not report on such matters but will instead deflect attention by constructing a new *social problem* by discovering a new form of sexual abuse of children (cf. Sonderling 1993).

| theme

Simple cohesive devices such as the conjunctions *since, if, and,* etc., can be used to create coherence and explain connections between different and unrelated things or situations that we would not usually perceive as being related. Such a method is commonly found in advertising text (cf. Fairclough 1992a:77, 176), as in the following example: 'The road through life is full of bumps and unexpected twists and turns. Toyota has always been committed to making the journey as smooth as possible' (*Sunday Times,* 1995:17). The advertisement makes a connection between life and a motorcar journey by using a metaphor to describe life as a bumpy road, followed by a statement that the car manufacturer is committed to making the journey through life as smooth as possible.

Arguments and persuasion

Rhetorical devices such as argumentative structure are another means to provide cohesion and an insight into the assumptions and ideologies of the communicator. One way to understand argument is to study the way it is produced and structured in language. Toulmin developed a model that can be used for such a study. According to Toulmin (cf. Borchers 2006:100–1), in presenting an argument a person makes a *claim* about reality or proposes a political plan for action. The claim is based on a

| rhetorical devices

| argumentative structure

conclusion based on some *data* or appeals to facts that are linguistic statements: for example, citations of research reports or reference to proclamations by some authoritative institution. To make the argument more persuasive, the person making the claim explains how he or she interpreted the data; such an explanation is termed a *warrant*. Of course, the more data and warrants that are produced, the more the argument may sound persuasive and will defeat a weaker argument presented by someone else.

Having discussed the main elements of the text, we can turn to the rules and conventions used to produce the text (discursive practice) and to the use of language as part of social interaction.

3.5 DISCURSIVE PRACTICE: RULES AND CONVENTION FOR THE USE OF LANGUAGE AND PRODUCTION OF TEXT

discursive practices

In the discussion of the texts above we have already noticed that there are different types of texts: for example, texts that are classified as poetry, prose literature, newspaper texts, etc. Each such text is produced according to certain rules and conventions and by a group of people that specialise in producing such texts. Such groups of people, the conventions they use and the texts they produce are known as discursive practices.

Language is not homogeneous and uniformly used by the entire linguistic community; rather, language is used in various ways. For example, the English spoken by South Africans is a particular national variety of the English language. Within any large linguistic community there are different regional dialects, slang and formal discourses of social groups. Culture also provides specific rules to a discursive practice. For example, there are distinctive differences in the communicative behaviours between social class or subcultures that are less educated and predominantly use *oral* communication as against the more educated and *literate*, for whom writing and printed texts have more importance. Such differences are acquired by different socialisation and education (cf. Botha 1991; Kochman 1974; McLuhan 1969; Ong 1982).

Besides national and regional varieties in language use, there are also specialised discursive practices such as science, law, religion, journalism, art, etc., regulated by formal rules, conventions and institutional constraints. These determine what qualifications a person should have before he or she may speak as an expert, who may speak with authority, who is excluded, how a person may or may not speak, and what should or should not be said.

Scientific writing is a clear example of a discursive practice that has many formal rules and conventions for producing text. Whenever a scientist has something to say about his subject of study, his or her way of saying it is determined by conventions laid down in style manuals. Such conventions are learned during the process of entering the scientific community. The specific rules and conventions determine the grammatical constructions, vocabulary and the general layout of the text. Thus, a scientist wanting to publish an article in an academic journal needs to conform to the conventions and style that the editorial board believes is appropriate (cf. Crystal 1974:29). Orwell (1975:149) provides an example of how to transform everyday language into scientific text. Orwell takes the following biblical text: 'I returned and saw under the sun, that the race is not to the swift, nor the battle to the strong, neither yet the bread to the wise, nor yet riches to men of understanding, nor yet favour to men of skill; but time and chance happeneth to all' (Orwell 1975:149). The biblical writer provides important observations on social phenomena but the personal style and details do not conform to the requirements of scientific writing. For example, the author describes how an element of unpredictability comes into play in competitive activity, warfare and earning a livelihood. For such an observation to be accepted as a scientific report it needs to be transformed and given an abstract style of scientific language, as Orwell shows by rewriting the sentence: 'Objective considerations of contemporary phenomena compel the conclusion that success or failure in competitive activities exhibits no tendency to be commensurate with innate capacity, but that a considerable element of the unpredictable must invariably be taken into account' (Orwell 1975:149).

By changing the personal style into an impersonal and abstract style and transforming concrete examples into generalisations, the Biblical text is easily translated into the language of scientific discourse. Today the mass media, social psychology and other helping professions conduct similar translations and rhetorical re-codification of popular superstitions into scientific vocabulary (cf. Harré 1985:141). In other words, the central activity consists in *translating* from the vocabulary and style of one discursive practice to another. Another good example of a discursive practice is journalism.

Discursive practice of journalism

The discursive practice of journalism in particular, with its formal and informal rules, has become important for constructing and communicating ideology in contemporary society. To understand how such ideological work is performed we can examine how journalists construct texts.

A news article that appears in the newspaper confirms the institutional assumptions and professional ideologies of the journalists (cf. McQuail 1980:174–82). The selection of the topic is the result of assumptions regarding what is considered newsworthy. Events do not make their way into the news simply because they happen but because they are recognised as fitting in with a category predefined or 'framed' by the media as *news*. To be accepted within such a category, the event must fulfil certain criteria of *news values* before it is selected by the media. For example, for a topic to be considered newsworthy it needs to occur frequently, take a short time to unfold and its meaning should be quickly discerned. In addition, the newsworthy event also needs to be dramatic and involve celebrities such as film stars or a large number of people; for example, a neighbour's argument is less newsworthy than an argument between two famous film stars or a war (cf. Hartley 1982:76).

Once the topic of the news article has been acknowledged as newsworthy there is a further complex process of reporting, writing and rewriting. For example, a press statement from a government department is delivered to the news editor. The news editor assigns a journalist to the story. After reading the press release the journalist may consult other related reports on the issue to become familiar with the background. The journalist then sets up interviews with the people involved to gain more information and will then write a report. The journalist's report is in turn handed to the news editor, who may make some corrections or changes. The text is then delivered to a subeditor for 'cutting', tightening, clarifying and making the text conform to the official style and policy of the newspaper. The edited version of the original story may again be read by the newspaper editor, who may suggest additional changes. Should there be some legal issues involved, the editor may obtain legal advice and make the appropriate changes to the story. The final version is sent to the printers and, once printed, the newspaper is delivered to the public. Thus a newspaper article is the result of a collective effort by the journalist, editors, managers, technical personnel, etc., working within a complex institution.

Media, Language and Discourse

A particular distinction in made in journalistic text production between news stories and editorial opinion. The type of text or genre known as an editorial opinion can be contrasted with a news report, which is considered factual and objective and has its own particular formal structures. An editorial opinion clearly presents the newspaper's own view of reality and the newspaper's ideology. That is, most editorial opinion takes the form of moralising as it puts forward what the newspaper thinks reality *ought to be* rather than *what it is* (cf. Braham 1982:269–70). Characteristically, such opinion is presented in the authoritative style of a lecture, claiming to represent social consensus, exhibiting definitive knowledge regarding what is good or right as well as common-sense wisdom, and offering rebuttal of other people's ideas (cf. Fowler 1991:211, 221). The editorial text also reflects self-serving interest: by claiming the moral high ground, the media substitute themselves for the democratically elected politicians who are the true representatives of the public (cf. Braham 1982:269–71). An interesting difference has been noted in the way editorials and news stories present social conflict. The text of news reports is considered dramatic and interesting when involving conflict. It also fits within the media's binary mode of thinking, which always sees conflict as having opposing and clashing views, or *two sides to a story*. As against the news stories, the texts of the editorial opinion columns present a different image. If news reports claim to present *news as it is* – based on conflict and drama – the editorial opinion texts present *news as they would like it to be*, an image of a calm consensus devoid of conflict (cf. Braham 1982:270). Thus, the media claim to represent the wisdom of the *common-sense* view in society; they claim to represent *consensus* that is supposedly beyond and above politics; they represent a supposedly *rational discourse* of *cool-headed*, practical men pronouncing the *truth* to politicians and other lesser mortals (cf. Fowler 1991:49, 212).

3.6 DISCOURSE AS SOCIAL INTERACTION AND SOCIAL ORDERS OF DISCOURSE

The linguist Roman Jakobson (1964) explains that language can function for a variety of purposes, and lists these as follows (see also Chapter 2 for a discussion on Jakobson's functions):

- *Referential function* – refers to our ability to use language to provide information to people about things of which they did not know, and

| functions of language

to talk about things in our world. For example, to inform and describe are referential uses of language.

- *Expressive function* – refers to our ability to express our emotions, beliefs and opinions. For example, to apologise for a mistake or to praise someone.
- *Conative function* – refers to our ability to use language to influence people, to direct them to follow our wishes or orders.
- *Phatic function* – refers to our use of language to make and maintain contact with other people: for example, small talk, idle chatter and greetings such as 'how are you?' 'hello' and 'it's a nice day' show other people that we take notice of them and welcome their communication.
- *Poetic function* – refers to our ability to use language for the pleasure of such use. For example, we enjoy the sound of words rhyming in a poem, or find delight in the sound of a particular word.
- *Metalinguistic function* – refers to our ability to use language in order to talk about language, or other aspects of our verbal communication. For example, when we say 'I don't follow what you are saying' or 'what do you mean?' we are talking about the use of language and communication.

speech act

If we follow on Jakobson's emphasis on the way language functions or is used in society, the conclusion we reach is that the use of language is a social activity. Indeed, as the philosophers John Austin (1984) and John Searle suggest, the use of language is a *practical activity* or a social performance called a speech act. For example, in the first place when we speak or write we are doing something, and by speaking we also attempt to do something, such as to make statements, to ask questions or to give orders.

It is clear that the use of language, which we call *discursive practice*, is a distinct form of social activity that involves social interaction in the production of texts. As such, we can consider the use of language a distinct social activity, one that can be distinguished from non-linguistic activities such as production of goods and action.

An example that shows that the act of speaking, rather than what is said, can have an important social significance, is illustrated by the following newspaper report:

Media, Language and Discourse

History was made in Parliament yesterday when a deaf MP addressed the National Assembly in sign language. ANC MP Wilma Newhoudt-Druchen drew a respectful silence from members in the House as they listened attentively to her maiden speech, delivered through an interpreter. The whole Assembly and the public gallery broke into applause once she had completed her address, made during debate on the communication budget vote. (Pretoria News, 10 May 2000)

The most significant aspect of the report above is the fact that the person made a speech – not what was said, as you may note there is not a single word that tells us what the Member of Parliament said in her speech. Indeed, politics mostly consists of verbal acts: speaking, writing, arguing, persuading and giving commands; it consists of the use of symbols and interpretation (cf. Graber 1976).

| verbal acts

3.7 LANGUAGE AND POLITICAL DISCOURSE

The world of politics is mostly constituted by the word 'politics', which may be better considered as a form of communication, and defined as 'who says what to whom with what effect'.

| political action
| speaking action

Politics is largely a word game. Politicians rise to power because they can talk persuasively to voters and political elites. Once in power, the daily activities are largely verbal – commands, dialogues, debates, formulation of proposals, laws, orders, decisions and legal opinions. The skills with which they wield the tools of political discourse, adapting them to the needs of various audiences and the goals to be achieved, determine their success. (Graber 1981:195)

Indeed, any quick survey of mass media reporting on politics would confirm this observation. Newspapers, radio and television political news consists mainly of reports about what politicians have said and what others say about their sayings, while very little is reported about what politicians actually do. You are welcome to do such a brief analysis yourself while reading the daily newspaper: How many reports begin with the words: Politician or Minister X said the following …? and what other politicians said in reaction to the original statement. In politics, if there is any 'action', it is usually minimal and becomes the centre of verbal interpretation and comments, as Edelman (2001:1) puts it: 'public officials normally exercise little initiative … [and] … established institutions ensure that little change will occur; that such change as does take place will be superficial, making little difference in people's lives'. Political action consists mainly of 'speaking action'.

Indeed, affirmation that in politics *action* should be avoided or minimised, and speaking promoted to the level of primary activity, can be seen in the example of former President Thabo Mbeki in explaining why he removed Deputy Minister of Health, Nozizwe Madlala-Routledge from her job. President Mbeki alluded to her excessive activities, such as her unauthorised surprise visit to a dilapidated hospital in the Eastern Cape and an unauthorised trip to attend an Aids conference overseas. It seemed that too much activity by the Deputy Minister of Health had begun to embarrass her boss, the vocal but inactive Minister of Health, Manto Tshabalala-Msimang. As President Mbeki put it in his explanation for removing the Deputy Minister from her post (Mbeki 2007):

> *None of the members of the ANC deployed in government will be treated by our movement as heroes and heroines on the basis of 'lone ranger' behaviour, so-called because of their defiance of agreed positions and procedures of our movement and government ... At the same time, throughout its history, to date, our movement has insisted on the need to respect the right of every member freely to express his or her view within our constitutional structures.* (emphasis added – author)

This is an example of how an incompetent politician can be made to look good by the verbal pronouncement of a man of power and points to the central importance of language in politics. As one newspaper analyst says:

> *Unlike Mbeki and his loyalists, Madlala-Routledge responded to public health crises, Aids as well as Frere Hospital, by promising to do something about them, not by denying they exist. Her dismissal, and Mbeki's subsequent attacks on her, say that a minister's job is not to acknowledge and promise to fix problems but to back leaders who deny them.* (Friedman 2007)

Indeed, from a modern and postmodern linguistics perspective politics can be considered as consisting almost entirely of verbal action or a language game. As Bayart (2005:109) puts it, both speaking and listening to political discourse are forms of political action and participation.

Media, Language and Discourse

In politics, as in social life, it is usually the powerful elite who speak and command while the less powerful are reduced to the position of listeners. Indeed as Nietzsche and Foucault remind us, originally the pronouncements of the powerful members of society defined the world and laid down the law. In other words, it has always been acknowledged that facts do not speak for themselves, but need to be interpreted. And interpretations of facts are never uniform; there is always a variety of interpretations and conflict over the meaning and interpretation of reality. If one particular interpretation becomes dominant, then it is power that allows someone to impose that particular interpretation of the world and have that interpretation accepted as legitimate. With the spread of democracy and parliamentary politics, politicians have had to become eloquent speakers, interpreters and masters in persuasive speaking (rhetoric) if they desire power and success in politics. In today's world, dominated by the mass media, language is the central aspect of reporting on politics. Language is not simply a communication medium about the world; *language constructs images of the world* and constructing such images and interpreting reality is the essence of political activity. Language as political activity also means that the images and interpretations of the world often contain misinterpretation and misrepresentations that are calculated to serve the interest of politicians. As George Orwell (1975) puts it: 'political language ... is designed to make lies sound truthful and murder respectable, and give an appearance of solidity to pure wind'. While Orwell (1975) and Edelman (2001) highlight the way misinformation and lies are promoted in the world dominated by the mass media, the American philosopher Harry Frankfurt (2005:22) identifies another important category – verbal *nonsense* – as increasingly dominating political discourse. For Frankfurt, *nonsense* (he calls it *bullshit*) is meaningless speech. It is produced when politicians and other celebrities are called upon to express their opinion in public even if they do not have an opinion to express. The result is that these people speak on issues on which they do not have knowledge but believe that they need to have an opinion on everything. In the age of the mass media public visibility and being heard to speak is all-important – even meaningless pronouncements keep a politician in the news. And by being seen and heard, politicians are able to *create favourable perceptions or images* of themselves among the electorate, even if the language and messages have no real content. As Edelman (2001:6) reminds us: 'reality is

misinterpretation

misrepresentations

dependent on epistemology rather than ontology'. It is not a matter of being, but rather of being seen and known.

3.8 ORDERS OF DISCOURSE

orders of discourse

discursive practice

As we saw above, language and discourse have their own rules and conventions. However, the use of language is also influenced by the social situations or context within which it is used. Texts and discursive practices are socially determined, through the various formal conventions that influence the way we communicate. For example, the manner in which we conduct interpersonal conversations with close friends or family members differs greatly from the manner we communicate in formal contexts such as delivering a speech in public. Within a particular society, the different and distinct *types of discursive practices* and the texts produced by them are given different values, prestige and authority. Such differences in values of discourses are termed orders of discourse (cf. Fairclough 1992a:69). For example, *slang* is considered inferior to the *official* and *correct* language; the discursive practice of the law courts and judges are given greater prestige, value and power than the discursive practices of poetry.

The authority of an individual to speak socially and to be taken seriously is institutionalised throughout society according to membership in different discursive practices. For example, in our society particular professional discursive practices have acquired a privileged position, and people such as doctors and psychologists are authorised to define health and illness, as Foucault (1986:51) puts it: 'Medical statements cannot come from anybody; their value, efficacy, even their therapeutic powers, and, generally speaking, their existence as medical statements cannot be dissociated from the statutorily defined person who has the right to make them, and to claim for them the power to overcome suffering and death'. It is evident that to speak meaningfully and to be taken seriously in any society is limited and not everyone has the right to speak everywhere or on any topic; some people in society speak with authority while some are silent and only listen. Such a hierarchy of roles is determined by the culture of a society. For example, gender in many societies determines that the words of men are taken more seriously than those of women because women are considered inferior to men. Consider the meaning of the word *professional* in the following two sentences:

Media, Language and Discourse

- He is a professional.
- She is a professional.

The word *professional* should have the same meaning in both sentences. However, it is not so. Most speakers of English would conclude that in the first sentence *he* refers to someone who is a doctor or lawyer while in the second sentence *she* is a prostitute (cf. Spender 1980:19).

In addition to ascribing value to people according to their sex or gender, other important valuation criteria include membership of social class, ethnic group and race. For example, in South Africa the mass media have labelled black minibus taxi drivers as *Third World drivers*; such a label implies that they are *bad, reckless, murderous* drivers responsible for most road deaths because as inferior drivers they are unable to master *First World* driving conditions (cf. Sonderling 1992). The use of such First World/Third World dichotomy conceals an underlying racist evaluation and devaluation (cf. Janks & Ivanič 1992:326–9).

The social hierarchy of discursive practices – or *orders of discourse* – is the result of a long history of social and political struggles. From such struggles, particular types of discourses and the people authorised to use them are given privilege and authority to define social reality.

3.9 LANGUAGE, POWER AND IDEOLOGY

The ability of certain discursive practices to define our reality should make us aware of the close relationship between language and social relations of power and *ideology*. Ideology can be considered as *meaning in the service of power* (cf. Thompson 1992:7), and refers to the ways in which particular meanings or significations serve to establish and maintain relations of social domination (see Chapter 7 in Volume 1 of this book (Fourie 2007)). Such meanings are constructed and communicated through the social use of language – from our everyday conversations to the complex texts of the various discursive practices (cf. Thompson 1990:5; 1992:7). Ideology operates most effectively when it becomes naturalised and achieves the status of a common-sense explanation for the ways the world and society operate. The use of language by the powerful social groups is a strategy for *symbolic violence* – the exercise of power and social control through the manipulation of language (cf. Bourdieu 1992:51).

Many examples of ideological assumptions are found in discursive practice of the mass media. For example, from a journalist's point of view, a good interview is one that contains interesting opinion. To make the interview more interesting for the readers of a newspaper or viewer of a television show, a good journalist will attempt to introduce personal aspects or a *human factor* of the people being interviewed by asking for the interviewee's first name, having them say something about themselves and asking for their opinion on the current topic of the interview (cf. Mey 1985:68-9). This is evident in particular when journalists interview striking workers or their families, and questions such as the following are considered *interesting*:

> *Tell me what you feel about this situation, how does it affect you and your family, is there anything in it for you, why are you doing this, how come you and your children put up with all these hardships, what does your wife/husband say about it, how do you relate to the other people here, how about this particular strike and the union, do they help you at all, what do the bosses say, do you think the strike is going to be a success, etc.* (Mey 1985:69)

However, while such questions are taken for granted by the discursive practice of journalism, they, nevertheless, reflect the ideology of individualism of our Western society. By adding such a *personal touch* the journalist manipulates and distorts the situation because the workers' decision to go on strike and their motives are not the individual worker's alone, but express the motives of the labour community as a whole and are based on collective consciousness of the labour situation (cf. Mey 1985:69-70). Asking striking workers for their personal opinion is inappropriate, but such an individualist perspective is enforced by the mass media and propagated as the only legitimate position regarding labour disputes. This is further motivated by the rules of journalistic discursive practices that perpetuate such a perspective for news reporting on labour relations. Reporters are often ignorant about labour issues (cf. Burton 1987:192). Trade unions consider *an injury to one as an injury to all*, therefore, the dismissal of one worker is protested by all workers. Furthermore, most reporting on labour disputes is biased in favour of big business, as the media usually strive not to offend the economic sector that pays good advertising money. The media's insistence on quoting *authoritative sources* who are easy to reach for comment results in representatives of big business, employers and management being the first to be contacted by the media. By the time the media interview the workers, the story angle has already been fixed (cf. Burton 1987:193; Tomaselli & Tomaselli 1987:68). Story angles favoured by the media to represent labour disputes present them as *unnatural* activities that are not in the *national interest* (cf. Burton 1987:191), because it is usually claimed that investors will become fearful and withdraw their money from the country. With such underlying bias it is not unusual to find traces of managerial persuasive communication reproduced by the media: for example, statements by management that combine two or more imperatives connecting and purposefully conflating unrelated issues, such as: 'the employment, housing, health and feeding schemes are specifically for you, so why strike?', or the use of unanswerable negative questions such as 'isn't the security of employment and a pension fund more important than questioning new appointments?' (cf. Du Plooy 1995:25).

SUMMARY

In this chapter we examined the importance of language in society and ways we can analyse the language used by the mass media. We suggested that verbal messages were the basic units of linguistic communication and analysed messages on three levels: the formal structure of the text and the elements that make such text, the discursive practice that determines the rules and conventions for the use of language and the social context of language in society.

LEARNING ACTIVITIES

1. Do you think that it is possible to think without the help of language? Can you think about any situation in your life where you do not use language?
2. Read the first paragraph of a number of newspaper articles. Is every article structured according to the inverted pyramid?
3. Select a number of newspaper articles on topics such as political protest or labour disputes and identify the words that are used to describe these activities. Can you find instances where political protest and labour dispute are described as criminal activities? Is such a description justified?
4. Describe an argument using the 'argument is a dance' metaphor. Does

this metaphor provide a different perspective from the 'argument is war' metaphor?

5. Read a number of newspaper articles and identify instances of the use of passive and active voice. Rewrite the passive voice sentence into active voice and the active voice into passive voice. Can you notice the change of meaning?

6. Observe the organisation where you work or study or any other organisation you belong to and identify the rules that determine where and how people may talk to each other.

7. In your workplace or in your family, can everyone express his or her opinion on any issue? In the above situation, identify the people who have authority to speak and express their views and those who remain silent, and explain the reasons why some people have the right to speak while others must remain silent.

8. Select a number of newspaper articles on labour disputes. Identify how the workers are represented in the articles. What words are used to describe the dispute? What ideology is represented in the article?

9. Select a newspaper article and conduct your own case study on the use of language by the media. Your study should be guided by the following questions:
   - What type or genre does the text represent?
   - What are the main concepts, words or jargon that you can identify in the text?
   - What metaphors are used and to what effect?
   - How are the arguments structured?
   - What grammatical structures are used?
   - What type of discursive practice produced the text?
   - Who is the audience for the text?
   - What ideology is evident in the text?
   - How does the text relate to other media text on the particular topic?

FURTHER READING

Austin, J.L. 1984. *How to do things with words.* 2nd edition. New York: Oxford University Press.

Bourdieu, P. 1992. *Language and symbolic power.* Cambridge: Polity Press.

Fairclough, N. 1990. *Language and power.* London: Longman.

Fairclough, N. (ed) 1992. *Critical language awareness*. London: Longman.

Fairclough N. & Wodak R. 1997. Critical discourse analysis, in: *Discourse as social interaction, discourse studies: A multidisciplinary introduction. Volume 2*, edited by T.A. van Dijk. London: Sage.

Fowler, R. 1991. *Language in the news: Discourse and ideology in the press*. London: Routledge.

Lakoff, G. & Johnson, M. 1980. *Metaphors we live by*. Chicago: University of Chicago Press.

Montgomery, M. 1986. *An introduction to language and society*. London: Methuen.

Pinker, S. 2007. *The stuff of thought: Language as a window into human nature*. London: Allen Lane.

Van Dijk T.A. (ed). 1999. *Discourse as social interaction, discourse studies: A multidisciplinary introduction. Volume 2*. London: Sage.

Philips, L. & Jorgensen, M. 2002. *Discourse analysis as theory and method*. London: Sage.

Wodak, R. & Chilton P. 2005. *A new agenda in (critical) discourse analysis: Theory, methodology and interdisciplinarity*. Philadelphia: John Benjamins.

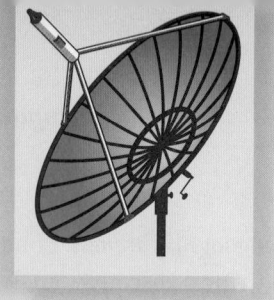

chapter four

MEDIA AND VISUAL LITERACY

Gertruida (Trudie) M. du Plooy

LEARNING OUTCOMES

At the end of this chapter, you should be able to apply recognition, recall and formulate inferences and judgements in the analyses of media texts to research the following:
- visual signs as mediated codes;
- implied narrative of the content of visual images;
- functions of visual images in relation to verbal messages;
- content, grammar and medium levels of visual literacy;
- denotative, connotative and cultural/ideological meanings of media texts.

Media and Visual Literacy

THIS CHAPTER

This chapter deals with the different meanings, levels and especially the importance of the ongoing development of media and visual literacy in the context of media studies.

The most important topics dealt with in this chapter are:
- the conceptual and theoretical debates about the notion of literacy as they apply to media and visual literacy;
- three levels of media literacy, based on how researchers view the mass media;
- ontological and epistemological assumptions;
- the perceptual, including semiotic and cognitive, approaches to visual communication;
- past research in media literacy and future challenges.

4.1 INTRODUCTION

Media and visual literacy represents an eclectic field, historically rooted in the philosophy of art, design, architecture and aesthetics, cinema studies, semiotics, television and mass-media studies, the theory of photography, graphic design and typography, and verbal–visual relationships in literary, aesthetic and rhetorical theory. Media literacy is also linked to the development of visual technologies, including digitisation and virtual realities, plus the physiology and psychology of visual perception.

> media literacy

This chapter addresses media literacy with a conscious focus on visual communication. This bias towards visual communication is based on the argument that the most important subcategories of media studies research, such as public opinion and attitude research, content analyses, ratings research, uses and gratifications studies, agenda-setting research, readership studies, political communication, effects studies, advertising and marketing research, should include an analysis of visual forms and content, and their role in mass communication processes.

> visual communication

The next section deals with the conceptual issues and theoretical debates about the notion of literacy as it applies to visual and media literacy.

4.2 THE MEANING(S) OF MEDIA/VISUAL LITERACY

The term 'visual literacy' was first used by John L. Debes (1969) with reference to the use of pictures and photography as educational aids by teachers, librarians and media experts. It was his enthusiasm for the use of visual aids in education that led to the first National Conference on Visual Literacy in America in 1969, where visual literacy was described as follows:

> *A group of vision competencies a human being can develop by seeing and at the same time having and interpreting other sensory experiences ... When developed they enable a visually literate person to discriminate and interpret the visual actions, objects, and symbols, natural or man-made, that he encounters in his environment. Through the appreciative use of these competencies he is able to comprehend and enjoy the masterworks of communication.* (Debes 1969:25)

Since the 1960s visual literacy has been defined as 'a result ... and effect ... a belief ... a condition' (Schiller 1976:5–6) and media literacy as an ability to become 'mentally skilled' (Winn 1982:4) in the creation, manipulation, use and interpretation of imagery in the mass media. A scrutiny of definitions related to media literacy yields constructs as visual learning, television literacy, media–linguistic literacy, and 'cineliteracy' (Eidsvik 1978). More recently, media literacy has been described as an 'understanding [of] how mass media work, how they create reality and produce meaning, how the media are organised, and knowing how to use them wisely' (Carlsson 2007:227). The above constructs and definitions illustrate the theoretical and conceptual diversity associated with the topic of media and visual literacy.

4.2.1 Verbal and visual language – an analogy

The question arises whether or not one can speak of a visual language and, if so, whether it is analogous to verbal (written or spoken) language. These questions are answered below by briefly considering the nature of verbal and visual language, with specific reference to similarities and differences, and by looking at the construction and interpretation of meaning.

Media and Visual Literacy

Ontology deals with questions about the nature of communication phenomena. The ontological assumptions of a visual language theory are that in order to understand the construction and interpretation of visual illusions, visual images need to be read in terms of visual elements (such as lines, shapes and movements). These assumptions are analogous to verbal language in that visual communication has an innate grammar, which is comparable in some respects to the grammar of verbal communication. For example, the syntactical units of television programmes or films, which deal with the visual arrangement of shots or frames into scenes and sequences, are compared with words, sentences and paragraphs in written communication. Accordingly, it is not strange to read about 'the "grammar" of acting' (Eidsvik 1978:80), the syntax of visual language and visual thinking (Arnheim 1969). Although proceeding from an art rather than a linguistic perspective, Dondis (1973:11) puts visual literacy on a par with verbal literacy by arguing that because the basic elements (such as shape and colour), together with compositional and manipulative techniques, may be learnt and used 'to create clear visual messages' one may arrive at a 'clearer comprehension of visual messages'.

| ontology |
| syntactical units |

From the point of view of semiology, these basic elements include visual signs, codes and conventions that are characteristic of a mass medium and accepted by the community of readers (listeners, readers, viewers as recipients of mass communication) and in terms of which signification occurs. A convention in this context refers to the rules, regulations or practices that are shared by different texts. Ferdinand de Saussure (1959), a pioneer of semiology, made a distinction between signifier, which expresses the shape, sound or texture of a sign, and signification, the connection between expression and concept. The relationship between signifier and signified is a central concern in an analogy between verbal and visual language.

| readers |
| conventions |

In verbal communication the arbitrary nature of signs is obvious, because it is based on random choice – there is no reason why the graphemes D-O-G should signify a four-legged animal. Due to the arbitrary nature of words in terms of a literal relationship between signifier and signified, the system of concepts, meanings or signified acquires a functional degree of socialisation through continued use. In contrast, the majority of pictorial images consist of conventional pictorial signs that rely to some degree on realistic resemblance. With regard to a

| arbitrary signs |

referential relation between signifier and signified, the arbitrariness in visual communication is relative and may be less or more motivated depending on the nature of the pictorial codes used. On a continuum from less to more motivated, the following order may be distinguished: a stylised drawing < a realistic drawing < a black and white photograph < a colour photograph < an image which portrays colour and movement. The motivated nature of visual signs, in contrast with verbal signs, means that they are more dependent on associative learning and more concrete as references. This dichotomy, or contrast, between arbitrary and motivated signs in verbal and visual communication is aptly summarised by Monaco (1977:128) when he states that 'the power of language systems is that there is a very great difference between the signifier and the signified; the power of film is that there is not'.

> dichotomy
> motivated signs

The word 'literacy' is essentially metaphoric and not literally applicable as there is no evidence that readers' understanding of, for example, television is analogous to their understanding of printed words. Printed letters have no intrinsic meaning but during the reading process they are translated into sounds, concepts, feelings and mental pictures. In contrast, television and filmic images are less abstract and more representational or more direct. Ontologically, visual communication is always coded. Visual communication appears to be transparent because readers passively know the codes. However this transparency is a myth – a popular but unfounded belief – which is demonstrated when attempting to understand the meanings of the stylised art of other cultures. One may interpret such art as mysterious, beautiful or decorative, but unless one is a member of such cultures, these art forms are not understood as forms of communication.

> metaphoric
> myth

The diversity of arguments about the meaning of the term literacy, especially as it applies to the mass media, have since the 1980s given rise to the following kinds of questions: is it a skill? Is it an accumulation of knowledge? Is it a particular cultural perspective of the world? Is it the ability to critically analyse media texts as creators of a view of the world? Or is it an understanding of how media texts reduce readers to becoming consumers of social and other values? Any attempt to debate and reach meaningful conclusions about these diverse questions and issues within the confines of one chapter would be superficial. Instead, and with reference to works published by scholars such as Messaris (1994, 1998), Zettl (1998, 2008) and Meyrowitz (1998), as well as Evans and Hall (1999), we first deal with different types or levels of media literacy, followed by the most important assumptions on which media literacy is based.

4.3 LEVELS OF MEDIA AND VISUAL LITERACY

According to Meyrowitz (1998:96–108), three types (or levels) of media literacy can be distinguished on the basis of how researchers and analysts view the mass media. Each of these three views will lead to different research questions being asked that guide systematic investigations of the media, will lead to different methods used when doing media research, and consequently will lead to different ways of defining media literacy. These three views of the mass media focus on the content, the form (or grammar), and the medium on a micro level, as well as in a macro or societal context.

levels of literacy
research questions

4.3.1 Media content literacy

Content literacy is not necessarily limited to specific communication media, because it focuses on those message elements that can be found in settings that involve interpersonal communication, small-group communication, as well as mass communication, including the internet. These content elements refer to the subject matter dealt with in media texts, such as the topics, themes, values, ideologies, settings, objects, characters, narratives and genres found in different texts. Genres in this context refer to categories, types or styles, such as a television drama versus a television advertisement. Accordingly, basic media content literacy requires a scholar and critic to be able to access and analyse the content of messages in a variety of media.

content
genre

The kind of research questions that can be asked when undertaking a text analysis, based on this view of media literacy, include the following: what is the overt (manifest, open, clear or explicit) message and what is the covert (hidden, latent or concealed) message being communicated? How do different content genres influence the construction of content in certain ways? How can the same content (text) be read differently by different individuals? (These last two questions are briefly addressed below and from different perspectives in other chapters in this book.)

overt message
covert message

Religious leaders, politicians and media critics who address issues such as violence, bias, stereotyping – conforming to standardised mental

stereotyping

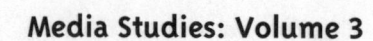

impressions – as well as the manifest (overt) and latent (covert) content of news, are essentially viewing media texts in terms of their content. This is understandably a popular approach to text analysis, for the following reasons:

1. The content is manifestly accessible and can be broken down into smaller manageable units of analysis, which – for the purpose of both quantitative and qualitative text analyses – can be coded, in some instances counted by quantitatively calculating quantities, as well as qualitatively analysed, using categories such as paragraphs, sentences and verbal phrases, or using categories such as television sequences, scenes and individual camera shots.
2. Content that deals with themes and behaviours (e.g. related to sexism, racism and ideological bias) is not limited to a particular communication medium. For example, evidence of stereotyping may be found in the way in which a character is visually depicted in a film or how a politician's visual image is portrayed in news reportage.
3. A text analysis that focuses on media literacy in terms of the content of messages therefore enables critics to formulate research questions and hypotheses, which are propositions based on reasoning and investigate any aspect of social life, such as overt and covert forms of persuasion in advertising.

By concentrating only on the content of messages, researchers deny the relevance of the encoding characteristics of different media. Therefore the second level of media literacy is concerned with how these characteristics contribute to the construction of texts, as well as the construction of meaning.

4.3.2 Media grammar literacy

The use of the term 'grammar' in the above subheading suggests that this type of media literacy regards communication media as each having its own so-called language, which distinguishes between codes of content and codes of form – or what Zettl (1998:84) prefers to refer to as 'the basic elements of contextual media aesthetics'.

Table 4.1, below contains examples of these encoding variables as they apply to the visual languages that are used in print media and film/television.

Table 4.1 Examples of visual 'language' variables: print media versus film/television

Print media	Film/television
• page size and shape	• sequence, scene, shot
• paper: colour, thickness, texture	• still vs. moving camera
• typeface: designs, size(s), colours	• focus vs. defocus
• column widths	• objective vs. subjective shots
• spacing	• zoom vs. dolly
• paragraph breaks	• pan vs. track
• blank spaces	• tilt up vs. tilt down
• page layout	• fade in vs. fade out
• graphics	• cuts vs. dissolves
• cropping of photographs	• single screen vs. split-screens
• size and shape of images	• single image vs. multiple images

typeface

camera shots

Table 4.1 illustrates how each medium has a unique combination of encoding and production variables. Yet some variables can operate in more than one medium. For example, when designing the opening titles for a film or television programme, the attributes of the typeface (size and style of printing font) would have to be considered. Or when selecting a photograph for the front page of a newspaper, variables such as whether it should be a close-up camera shot versus a long shot, or objective camera shot versus subjective shot, as well as camera angles, have to be considered.

media grammar-literate

Readers and critics are media grammar-literate if they are able to analyse how the encoding characteristics of a particular medium are manipulated to convey a particular perception of the message content. Even if a message's (overt) content is kept constant (e.g. *bomb blast in city centre*), readers' perception of the event, as well as the causes and consequences of the event, would differ depending on whether it is shown from the perspective of the victims, the perpetrator, the eyewitnesses, the rescue team or even from the perspective of a local politician.

mise-en-scène

Media grammar literacy is based on assumptions that the mass media (film, radio, print, television, the internet) use specific languages. The encoding and production aspects of media are studied using the structural and semiological approach. Chapter 5 deals with the basic assumptions and some practical applications of this level of literacy. Accordingly, the meaning(s) produced by each element or code, such as lighting and colour, sound and visual narrative structures, mise-en-scène (which is French for the scenery, properties and surroundings

of a setting) and montage (how the sequences of shots are structured through editing) are analysed in that chapter.

montage

In addition to understanding the language of each medium, this level of literacy also requires readers to be able to analyse genres within each medium, such as advertising, news and soap operas in the case of television. Without entering the ideological level of meaning, readers deal with signs, symbols, stereotypes, metaphor, metonymy, denotative and connotative levels of meaning. The aesthetic and ethical significance of media productions are studied based on the assumption that mass media messages are subjective presentations (not representations) of reality.

According to Meyrowitz (1998:102) media grammar has in the past not received as much attention as in the case of media content. One of the main reasons is that the analysis of the grammar of media texts requires an understanding of the workings of the medium, as well as the vocabulary unique to that medium, as listed in Table 4.1. For example, in the absence of being educated to recognise and name the different camera shots, television viewers are not only unaware of their uses but cannot be expected to describe or analyse how these shots influence their perceptions of particular content.

The above represents an ironic situation, because if the encoding characteristics of a particular text have been used effectively, they will be less noticeable to readers or researchers and will inadvertently shift their attention and analyses to the content. The learning outcomes for this chapter are precisely aimed at counteracting the latter tendency.

4.3.3. Medium literacy

Medium literacy – 'medium' being used in the singular form – deals with how the nature of a medium influences communication on a micro and macro level. Although an in-depth discussion of this approach to media literacy is beyond the scope of this chapter, some of its concerns and questions are addressed below.

micro level

On a micro or small-scale level, questions are prompted as to why certain interactions (e.g. selling a house) work differently depending on the medium of communication used (e.g. an advertisement that is printed, versus one disseminated via the internet). Based on a social semiotic theory of communication, visual communication has to serve several requirements in order to function as a system of communication. Kress and Van Leeuwen (2000:40–2) address these requirements as ideational, interpersonal and textual metafunctions. Metafunctions refer to forms or types of functions that are used to talk about particular functions fulfilled by means of communication. The ideational metafunctions refer to the assumptions that any semiotic system (e.g. a television programme) has to represent (refer to) aspects of the experiential world that surrounds that system. The interpersonal metafunctions are fulfilled when a semiotic system projects a particular relation between the communicators (producers of a sign or sign system), readers (recipients or re-producers), and the sign. The textual metafunctions refer to a semiotic system having the capacity to establish or form texts consisting of signs that are integrated both internally and with the context in and for which they were produced. Each of these metafunctions can be fulfilled by an array of choices within one semiotic system, such as the combination of photographs and printed language in the layout of newspapers. Another example is found in an interpersonal relation of interaction that is (artificially) created when a person on television addresses viewers by looking directly at the camera. In contrast, when not facing the camera, a discontinuation or absence of interaction with viewers can be depicted.

metafunctions

On a macro or societal level, medium literacy requires the reader or critic to consider how social forces, including political and economic forces, contribute to the development of certain media, as well as their effects. For example: how does the increasing use of the internet influence the organisational structures of corporations and other institutions? How is the promotion of globalisation through the use of the World Wide Web changing the function and role of the mass media, for example, with reference to information, economic and cultural exchanges on a worldwide scale? Or, what effects is the internet having on individual users' language and social skills?

macro level

globalisation

These questions address broad social changes and are clearly more abstract than the 'content' and 'grammar' of texts. However, as Zettl (1998:81–95) argues, one can obtain access to these intellectual and cultural frameworks of media criticism by starting with analyses of the encoding characteristics in relation to the content (and therefore context) of message texts.

4.4 ONTOLOGICAL AND EPISTEMOLOGICAL ASSUMPTIONS

ontology
epistemology

Against the background of the above brief overview of three types or levels of media literacy (content, grammar and medium literacy), this subsection summarises the ontological and epistemological assumptions on which media literacy, and especially visual media literacy, are based. Ontology addresses questions about the nature of communication phenomena, whereas epistemology addresses questions about knowledge – how we know what we claim to know.

conventions

A familiarity with the codes and conventions of a particular mass medium is a prerequisite for analysing media texts. When considering visual communication (e.g. photographs and films) it is argued that making sense of visual images comes naturally – unlike having to be taught how to read and write verbal texts. In other words, the average television viewer ascribes meanings to visual images, without having learnt to differentiate between different camera shots or editing techniques. In contrast to the above assumption, the argument that visual images have an arbitrary relationship with appearances in reality, implies, as Gombrich (1982) argues, that if someone has not previously been exposed to a visual image, such as a photograph, he or she may not necessarily make sense of it.

cognitive consequences
formative research

Media literacy may have general (or wider) cognitive consequences related to both the knowledge and awareness of the reader as scholar and researcher. According to this assumption, and in terms of development that occurs as a form of life-long learning, the cognitive knowledge acquired from analysing one type of media text (e.g. television) can contribute to a reader's sensitivity and awareness of how meaning is produced in other texts and settings. These wider cognitive consequences may in addition contribute to the ability to make informed decisions when applying audiovisual codes in formative research of media texts, that is, the continuous measurement of effectiveness during the planning and production stages when producing messages.

Media literacy contributes to readers' awareness of how meaning is produced by the media and consequently minimises the manipulative effects of these media. In other words, by acquiring an increased awareness of the manipulation of codes in the construction (production and interpretation) of meaning, this assumption is based on the argument that readers will be less vulnerable when receiving messages with a persuasive or propagandistic intent.

The above three assumptions (knowledge of codes and conventions, cognitive development and increased awareness) are prerequisites for an aesthetic evaluation of the content and form of texts, as well as an analysis of mass media on a macro or societal level.

In order to develop a critical level of media literacy the most advanced and simultaneously the most complex degree of such a literacy is visual literacy. The complexity lies in deconstructing the (hidden) ideologies of mass communication, where constructs such as ideology, myth, alienation and hegemony play a role. Hegemony in this context refers to the assumption that mass communication exercises a dominating or controlling influence on readers. Simultaneously, readers are social beings with their own identities whose interpretations are mediated by peers, parents, expectations, cultural values and social contexts. Hegemony is therefore not limited to economic control or power, but includes other forms of capital, such as symbolic forms (e.g. status, gender), cultural forms (e.g. education) and social forms (e.g. family).

| hegemony

According to Howells (2003:71) ideology 'is simply the study of ideas, systems of thought and systems of belief', and the study thereof requires investigating how meaning is constructed and conveyed by symbolic means, including visual images. However, concentrating mainly on the qualities of visual texts is a restrictive methodological emphasis that does not incorporate the social, economical, cultural and historical conditions in which texts are produced. The underlying aim of critical analyses would therefore be to reveal how the apparently informative and neutral texts, such as in news reportage, may convey ideological attitudes, as do advertising, propaganda (persuasive) discourses and other texts usually classified as entertainment.

| ideology

The conceptual issues about the notion of literacy, especially media literacy, can also be debated from different theoretical perspectives or approaches. In the next section we deal with one such approach.

4.5 PERCEPTUAL APPROACH TO VISUAL COMMUNICATION

Sensation is the elementary process of sensing and is something that readers experience when stimuli from the outside world, such as hearing a dog bark, activate the nerve cells in their sense organs. Perception is the second stage of observing the world, involving understanding and knowing objects/events, which refer to the meanings readers almost

| sensation
| perception

Media Studies: Volume 3

perceptual approach

instantaneously ascribe to the noises, smells, temperatures, or sights – as raw stimuli. For example, the barking dog can be perceived as a warning of a threat to someone's safety. When considering a perceptual approach to visual communication, a distinction can be made between the semiotic approach and the cognitive approach. Both approaches, according to Lester (1995:61), share two assumptions, namely that meaning is influenced by the nature of sensual stimuli (such as the content of a visual image); and, secondly, that readers have the ability to assign complex meanings to such images.

4.5.1 The semiotic approach

During the Rugby World Cup in France during 2007, television viewers throughout the world were greeted by images of different rugby attire, flags and anthems representing different countries, as well as roaring crowds and referees' gestures during the matches. Each of these sounds, objects, actions or images is a sign if it has meaning beyond the sound, object, action or image. For example, one gesture by a referee is a sign that a try has been scored, whereas another gesture signifies that a penalty has been awarded.

media semiotics

As the ontological and epistemological assumptions of media semiotics – the science and study of the meaning of signs in auditory and visual messages – are dealt with in greater detail in Chapter 2, we briefly mention some of the main points and assumptions on which this approach to visual communication is based.

Three types of visual signs used to communicate

iconic sign

The meaning of all signs must be learnt; an iconic sign (or icon) is probably the easiest, because it most closely resembles the 'thing' that it represents. An iconic sign is a sign that is in common with what it signifies, such as an identity photograph, because it contains a direct resemblance to the person's face and therefore forms a representational connection with that person.

indexical sign

Indexical signs, however, do not have a direct resemblance to the object or idea being represented, as they are signs or indicators of something else, and therefore have to be learned through everyday experiences. The connection between an indexical sign and that which it represents is often based on logic or common-sense. Footprints of a wild animal in the sand are indexical signs that the animal has recently walked through that area. However, in order to assign these meanings to the footprints, readers would have had to experience previously these signs and their meanings.

The meanings conveyed by symbolic signs, because they are more abstract and rooted in our social and cultural past, have to be taught, and usually represent stronger emotional meanings than do iconic or indexical signs. The colours and symbols that appear on the national flags of different countries are examples of symbolic signs that represent the heritages of those nations. In other words, these signs involve the use of symbols to represent propositions and/or express (abstract) ideas. In view of the powerful effect created by the symbolism of flags and the loyalties they stimulate, we attribute an almost spiritual quality to flags – a national flag becomes the people.

| symbolic sign |

Relationships between a sign and meaning communicated

Different relationships exist between a sign and the meaning that it communicates. An understanding of these relationships is essential if we are to critically analyse visual media texts.

The denotative meaning conveyed by a sign refers to its common-sense meaning. It is the literal, everyday, shared meaning of a sign. For example, an image of books on a table denotes, as iconic signs, the meanings *books* and *table*. In contrast, connotative meaning is deduced by the individual reader, which may result in many different meanings – due to factors such as age, past experience, gender and cultural background. For example, this image of books on a table can have connotations, such as *learning*, *authority* and *high culture*. A table is usually found in the centre of many television dramas, such as the gaming table in a Western, or the operating table in a hospital series. However, when carrying books, as in above example, the table can on a connotative level (for some readers) represent a symbol of *intellectual life.*

| denotative meaning |
| connotative meaning |

Connotative meanings are very often described as mythical meanings because they are meanings constructed by society in support of a particular viewpoint, approach, culture or ideology. Mythical meanings are conventional expressions based on fictitious things, persons or ideas.

| mythical meaning |

The portrayal of women in advertisements as (brainless) sex objects is an example of a stereotypical myth. Because photographs, films and television are visual media, they tell their mythic stories of good versus evil, or social order versus lawlessness, or group dependence versus individual freedom, by means of visual symbolism. Examples of the ideological values and beliefs of a particular culture are very often be found in comic books and cartoons, such as *Madam & Eve* (Francis, Dugmore & Schacherl 2000), or the editorial cartoons of *Zapiro* (Shapiro 2007), which comment on pre- and post-apartheid myths in South Africa by means of both visual and verbal symbols.

| aberrant decoding |

Based on the above distinction between denotation and connotation, it becomes clear that if a reader interprets a sign differently from the meaning as intended by the communicator, the message will be misunderstood. When such poor or ineffective communication takes place, a relationship of aberrant decoding has taken place.

Signs used as codes

| narrative |

In verbal (spoken or written) texts, one word follows the previous words in a particular order, which means that the narrative is linear. In visual texts, however, the narrative refers to the structure, components, order and organisation of a story and is created by combining and presenting signs in different ways – usually called codes. Visual communication therefore enables communicators to combine signs (as codes) in different ways to communicate complicated and often abstract ideas. Berger (1991a:20–7) suggests that two types of codes can be distinguished, namely metonymic and analogic codes.

| metonymic code |

A metonymic code consists of a collection of signs that prompt the reader to interpret meanings on the basis of their associations or assumptions. For example, a character who, in a local soapie, is portrayed in a living room with expensive paintings and furniture would communicate that she is an upper-class citizen. If the same character is situated in a dirty backstreet setting, a different image would be communicated – based on readers' assumptions and associations. In other words, a metonymic code implies that the code (e.g. expensive furniture equals upper-class citizenship) already exists in readers' minds, which enables them to make the intended connection. A common form of metonymy, called synecdoche, is often used in visual communication. This is created when a part (or partial image) represents a whole – a crown is a metonym for a king. For example, a close-up shot of a hand holding a gun represents the person as a whole, as well as the action that is about to take place. A news item that shows the destruction caused by a street bomb in Cape Town functions as a metonym for crime in South African society. A documentary television programme that deals with the problems experienced by two black children during integration in a previously whites-only school in a particular town, serves as a metonymic code – the two children stand for the whole local black community.

An analogic code is an equal counterpart for something else and consists of a collection of signs that prompts the reader to make mental comparisons. These codes are usually applied, either as metaphors or similes. A metaphor is based on a relationship between two things, which is suggested through the use of analogy and an imaginative or symbolic comparison. A metaphor transposes characteristics of one thing onto another; by suggesting equivalence, it *symbolically stands for something else*. For example, a cowboy hat has become a metaphor for the American Wild West; *Coca-Cola* has become a metaphor for enjoyment; and an umbrella used as a logo by a South African insurance firm has become a metaphor for protection. A simile creates meaning by suggesting that a sign is 'as' or 'like' something else and is therefore a comparison based on coinciding characteristics. *Granny is like an angel* is a verbal example, whereas a picture of pencils bundled together can serve as a simile for a crowd of people. Through personification, human qualities are attributed in this example to the inanimate objects (the pencils). In other words, a simile suggests that the two signs have similar characteristics, namely the *togetherness* of the pencils visually representing and suggesting the *cohesion* of a group of people.

_{analogic code}

_{metaphor}

_{simile}

These two types of codes can further be used and analysed, depending on whether or not they are displaced codes and condensed codes. Displaced codes include those codes that are used to transfer meaning from one sign, or collection of signs, to another and in so doing taking the place of something else (of which above pencils are an example). Advertisements for cigarettes, bottles of liquor and lipstick, as well as certain cover designs of sex magazines, often displace images of penises with other phallic symbols, based on the assumption that readers will make the link between the product and sexual regeneration.

displaced codes

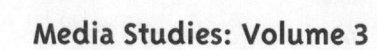

condensed codes

Condensed codes are more concentrated, intense and complex and are produced by combining several signs, in so doing creating a new collective sign. Television advertisements and music videos, in which multiple images are portrayed, often combined with fast cuts, graphics and flashing colours, are examples of condensed codes being used to produce complex messages such as the *American Dream* of democracy and freedom.

The above subsection contained a brief overview of the semiotic approach, as part of a perceptual approach to visual communication. In the next section we consider the cognitive approach, which is also closely related to the perceptual approach.

4.5.2 The cognitive approach

cognitive approach

The cognitive approach to visual perception treats perception as a process involving mental events or actions, related to knowledge and awareness. According to this approach, readers perceive and ascribe meanings to that which they perceive (e.g. see or hear) on the basis of association. Such associations can be based on past experiences (learned behaviour) or assumptions. For example, some readers may interpret the meaning of an image of a pipe with security and authority, based on their association with father-figures in their past, whereas others may interpret the same image to mean complacency and peace, based on an association with traditions of smoking a peace pipe.

visual perception

As no two people have experienced exactly the same lives, it stands to reason that visual perception is personalised and subjective. However, the argument advanced in section 4.3 is that such differences are minimised as readers grow older because they are exposed to the same mass-media texts. In other words, those memories and associations that are based on readers' experiences via mass-media texts may be different, but will not necessarily be highly personalised or uniquely subjective. The relevance of mental activities to textual analysis has to be emphasised. These activities show that meaning is not only situated in the manipulation of visual and other codes, but that meaning is also situated in what (e.g. selective perception) readers bring to the mediated experience.

In addition to memory, projection, expectations, selectivity, habituation, salience, dissonance, cultural influences and words are other mental activities, which – according to the cognitive approach – can influence visual perception. These mental activities are briefly dealt with below.

Psychologists use (Rorschach) ink-blot tests to uncover an individual's personality traits, based on the assumption that we project something of ourselves (e.g. state of mind, characteristics or ways of perceiving the world or behaving in it) onto these oddly shaped ink blots. This mental activity – called projection – means that some readers make sense and ascribe meanings to vague, ambiguous and unstructured objects or images, whereas others find the same objects or images meaningless. (This explains why some people can read a person's *fortune* on the basis of tea leaves in a cup, whereas others perceive nothing more than tea leaves.) While watching a card game being played in a television programme, one viewer may read the cards as being a king, queen or knave, while another viewer may read them as representing the father, mother and the ego. Projection as a research technique, which requires subjects to respond freely to complete a story or picture, or which involves a series of pictures about which a subject must tell a story, or various forms of play, involving objects, such as a doll's house, are often used in formative mass-media research. Such techniques are also sometimes used when conducting research, such as during the concept testing – in which subjects arrange images or ideas in rank order – for advertisements and educational television programmes.

projection as a research technique

concept testing as a research technique

Readers' visual perception can also be impaired if their preconceived expectations and/or selectivity in perceiving result in focusing only on details or events of a visual message that are of interest and/or confirm their expectations and prejudices and ignoring others. For example, television viewers have a preconceived expectation of how a news presenter should conventionally be dressed. Therefore, unless that expectation is contradicted, viewers do not really notice the dress worn each evening. Most of our visual perception is an unconscious act that takes place automatically. It is therefore not an uncommon experience, while travelling to work, to selectively concentrate on the traffic and road signs without processing other visual images. This selectivity, of focusing only on important details, is also reinforced by a mental activity called habituation. In other words, readers develop habits, which through prolonged practice become activities and behaviour that become relatively automatic and which are repeated unconsciously.

selective perception

habituation

salience

People who are trained as graphic artists or engineers may read more meanings into graphic drawings and other visual designs than the average person. For example, only someone with training in architecture will be able to differentiate among the different structural parts of a drawing or picture of a church, such as the flying buttress, clerestory, triforium, spandrel and nave. This example illustrates how salience – the degree to which something is prominent or important – can affect our perception, because a stimulus that has meaning for a particular person will be noticed more by that person.

dissonance

Dissonance, which is a disagreeable combination of sounds, printed words and/or visual images, is a term that originated in music, and refers to an unpleasant noise created when two notes are sounded together that do not form a harmonious sound. When applied to perception, dissonance is created when two or more stimuli compete for our attention, such as following a television programme and reading the evening newspaper at the same time. Visual messages, in which condensed codes are used, are apt to minimise our perceptual abilities, because they have the potential of causing dissonance.

random meanings

idiosyncratic meanings

shared meanings

Cultural influences, as manifested in the ways we talk, eat, dress, behave socially and practise different religious beliefs, also influence our visual perception. Random, idiosyncratic and shared meanings are three possible ways in which we can ascribe different meanings to visual codes. Random meanings are assigned to communication that takes place without conscious choice, aim or purpose and therefore does not necessarily convey any specific meaning, such as the physical contact being shown between a dentist and a patient in a television drama. Idiosyncratic communication is normally unique to an individual, such as stroking something to relieve tension. Despite the fact that actions, such as rubbing one's nose or scratching one's head, are performed unintentionally, when observed and analysed by a critic, they can be assigned highly individualised and idiosyncratic meanings and be incorrectly interpreted as signs of stress, discomfort or irritation. Shared meanings are often culture-specific. Examples are found in proxemics (especially the distance between two people while they are conversing) and haptics (e.g. physical contact as part of greeting rituals). If unaware of these shared meanings in another culture, readers could easily misinterpret such behaviour in filmic texts as *distant and aloof*, or as *too close for comfort*.

Media and Visual Literacy

Although visual perception concentrates on ascribing meaning to visual images, most of our thoughts are actually formulated in verbal language. Therefore, when words are combined with visual images, they may directly influence the meaning ascribed and remembered of mediated images (i.e. communicated by means of an intervening medium or text).

| mediated images

Based on above overview, we need to remind ourselves that the following are research questions that we may not ignore, whilst analysing details found in both the content, and especially in the encoding characteristics of a text: does the text (overtly or covertly) make provision for or even manipulate the influence which culture and previously learned behaviour may have on a reader's perception? For example, is the association between certain objects (e.g. expensive jewellery) and certain meanings (e.g. an elite social status) perpetuated? To what extent do words support, accentuate and therefore complement and elaborate on the visual communication; or to what extent do words regulate or even contradict the visual communication?

| research questions

We are continuously surrounded by a visual environment, which could vary from clothes, furniture, buildings, people and moving vehicles to the plants, birds and other animals found in nature. Being surrounded by visually perceivable artefacts in almost every aspect of our lives implies that they can reflect and affect our attitudes towards happiness, politics, health, success, culture, business and whatever else may be significant in our lives. The meanings that we ascribe to perceptions of our visual environment may range from a condition or state, an action or an event, to a quality. However, to ensure that effective communication takes place requires us (as readers and analysts) to make the same transfer, from the visual image to the intended meaning, as premeditated by the communicator. The nature of this transfer process is dependent on many variables, such as our perceptual abilities, cognitive thought, memory, emotions, expectations, attitudes, involvement, the context in which communication occurs and our past experiences.

| effective communication

4.6 RESEARCH

The foundations of mass media, such as television, are found in the ontology and epistemology of photography and cinema (film). Since the 19th century, scholars of photography have debated whether it is an art or a science; whether it is a visual expression or a mechanical

| foundations of past research

record; whether it is a technique that creates a particular viewpoint or a reflection of reality (cf. Sontag 1977). This debate between whether pictorial images should be regarded as windows that create and structure readers' views versus mirrors (or copies) of reality has been addressed extensively in film theories, which serve as important foundations for past research and understanding current visual communication. Realist theorists, such as Kracauer (1960) and Bazin (1967) argued that there is a direct and natural relation between everyday life and visual images, whereas formalist theorists, such as Münsterberg (1970), Arnheim (1957), Pudovkin (1954) and Eisenstein (1949), considered filmic presentations as visual expressions through camera and editing techniques.

windows versus mirrors

The research conducted of visual communication, as a subdiscipline of media studies, therefore reiterated the historical (windows versus mirrors) issues of film and photography, but also became evident in schools of communication, art and journalism. According to Griffin (1992) and Barnhurst (1994) traditional educational programmes that concentrated on mass communication and related fields, such as news reporting, public speaking, advertising and entertainment, could no longer ignore learning and researching the visual imagery as an integral part of these presentations. So, for example, Raymond Williams (1974) researched the forms and practices of media production and representation as part of cultural studies.

diverse research issues

The following are examples of issues that have been researched to illustrate both the diverse and continued scholarly attention since the 1990s. Craig (1992) researched the reliance of image association in advertisements. Intrinsic conflict between accepted myths of original realism and the actual deception of image construction in television news and photojournalism was investigated by, for example, Banks (1992), Linton (1992) and Schwartz (1992). How visual manipulations can affect responses to visual images was one of several issues investigated by Messaris (1992). He highlighted ontological and epistemological questions about the distinctive nature of visual images as communicative signs and the extent to which visual interpretation depends on media-specific schemata or learned cultural conventions. Although empirical evidence was found for cultural differences in areas such as linear perspectives and figure–ground perspectives, many of the iconic qualities of visual images, according to Messaris (1994), are the same visual and informational cues that mimic real-world visual experiences, or human perception. His studies drew on a wide range of research in the psychology of perception, cognitive theories of spatial learning and film analyses.

Based on research conducted and theoretical models developed by British, Canadian and Australian scholars, the Media Literacy National Leadership Conference in the United States of America concluded that the following concepts ought to be included and considered in the textual analysis of media messages (Aufderheide 1993:2)

concepts in textual analyses

- Media messages are constructed.
- Media messages are produced within economic, social, political, historical and aesthetic contexts.
- The interpretive meaning-making process involved in message reception consists of an interaction between the reader, the text and the culture.
- Media have unique 'languages', characteristics which typify various forms, genres and symbol systems of communication.
- Media representations play a role in people's understanding of social reality.

The introduction and expansion of each new mass medium brought with it concern from governments, educators, religious leaders and parents who feared the expansion of popular culture, with its sex, violence, stereotypes and antisocial effects. In order to develop the critical awareness to discriminate between similarities and differences in mass media, according to Martinez-de-Toda (2002:15), such readers need to know: 'how the mass media function as institutions; which are the production processes of the media industry; which are the media interests, especially those commercial and political; and how [the] audience is treated'. These four concerns highlight the multidimensional and diverse nature of variables that past research has addressed in equating media and visual literacy with a critically aware reader.

multi-dimensional and diverse variables

4.7 FUTURE DEVELOPMENTS

The role of the mass media, particularly news genres, in the promotion of democracy can be reduced to a normative requirement, namely the quality of materials on which media base their enquiries (e.g. about abuses of power by politicians). According to Asp (2007:38–9), four demands could be made of such information: firstly, the information

normative principles

must be true; secondly, the person responsible for the actions and the actual behaviour or event must be relevant to the readers (general public); thirdly, the media's enquiry and reportage must be independent from those in power positions; and lastly, the presentation of facts must be fair (impartial). In order to validate the hypothesis that the promotion of principles of democracy is one of the most important outcomes of improving visual and media literacy, it stands to reason that the choice of (normative) premises will determine which functions media are required to perform, plus which criteria are to be applied when conducting future visual media research.

internal validity

In addition, research that deals with the measurement of readers' levels of media and visual literacy is challenged by several variables. For example, in future readership and interpretative studies, in order to secure proof of propositions and assumptions the internal validity of questionnaires will require tests and re-tests to ensure that researchers (interviewers) and readers (interviewees) ascribe the same meaning to abstract constructs and connotative meanings.

research questions

Research questions that can guide future research (especially related to the macro level of medium literacy) include whether users of the mass media know their rights, whether they know how the mass media function as industries and subsystems of a particular society, and whether they know how to deal with antisocial content (e.g. bias, sex and violence). Additional research questions that could fruitfully guide future research include the following: do the messages received from certain mass media (e.g. newspapers) correspond with the values and information received from other sources (e.g. television), and how do those messages correlate with readers' own identities, values and cultures? How are hegemony and ideology cloaked in visual texts? How can the analyses of visual texts make hidden ideologies explicit and visible?

domains of public communication

Visual communication has entered many domains of public communication where verbal language was previously the dominant mode of communication. The role of visual communication in society should therefore be understood in the context of the range of modes of public communication available in a particular society and their uses, which Kress and Van Leeuwen (2000:33) refer to as 'the semiotic landscape'. This metaphor suggests that visual mass media have to be seen in their environment, in relation to other modes of mass communication that surrounds them, plus the histories, values of a society and their cultures. The surroundings in the southern African context clearly include the recognition of linguistic and cultural diversity, economic enhancement, the fading of national borders and developments in global technologies.

Cultural values have been high on the agenda of the South African government in the post-apartheid era. Future research therefore ought to focus on explaining the transformative nature of cultural values. How are cultural values re-constituted, and what are the consequences of cultural fluidity for the contemporary mediated society? How, for example, are worship, sexual mores, social sanctions, social identity, rituals, and customs symbolically (and visually) re-constructed via the mass media?

transformation

In the case of television, it is argued that some viewing experiences can draw near the status of direct experiences by viewers. However, in a multicultural society such as South Africa, a fruitful area of future research would be to investigate how, and why, mediated experiences are (can be) regarded as potent as direct experiences. The issue of the form (rather than content) of visual media poses challenges for future visual communication researchers. This is particularly relevant in the era of virtual realism, with the digital textualisation of images in cyberspace – especially when the issue of referentiality is revisited in the quest of promoting equality and democracy.

mediated experiences

The following argument by Griffin (2001:452) offers an apt synopsis of challenges that face future research, namely that the 'relationships between the natural (and perhaps universal) characteristics of human image perception and the culture-bound aspects of representational schemata and connotative discernment are complex, ambiguous and still at the heart of visual communication studies'.

4.8 CASE STUDY

This case study, by Howells (2003:112–13), addresses a semiotic analysis of an advertisement, as an example of popular culture, progressing from the overt and covert to the underlying (ideological) meaning of a television advertisement for microwave pizza.

The scene is a suburban dining-room in which a handsome father and two good-looking children are seated at an informal but well-presented table. There is a good-natured expectation in the air, which is affably rewarded as mother appears in the doorway with a tray full of hot and appetizing microwave pizza. The family dig in: this pizza is clearly delicious. The kids smile at each other, father smiles at mother, and mother smiles at us, knowingly. She has made a wise consumer decision, and she is rewarded with domestic bliss. The commercial closes with a close-up of the box and the slogan 'Potterton's Pizza Puts the Mmmm in the Microwave'. At first level, the commercial openly tells us something about the product: it's made by Potterton's, you cook it in the microwave, here's what the packaging looks like and it tastes good, too. But at the second level, we discover that what this commercial is really selling is a happy family life, and it suggests, covertly, that the way to obtain it is by buying this particular brand of pizza. It does this by the association of the two. Who would not want the lifestyle that Potterton's Pizza implies? The family are healthy and attractive, and they eat together as a wholesome domestic unit. The kids are not fighting or wandering the street, and father is neither philandering nor spending his nights in bars. What's more, they all appreciate mother for her loving care in feeding them so wisely and deliciously. The signifier that is Potterton's Pizza has now been made to signify the family idyll. But what, at the third level, 'goes without saying' here? Does it go without saying that all happy families comprise a mother, a father and two children? Does it go without saying that happiness and material comfort are inseparable? And does it go without saying that in the ideal family, it is the mother who should buy, cook, serve and (presumably) clear away the family meal? What about dad? This is not the place to try and reach any conclusions over the nature versus history in gender roles in twenty-first century culture. All this seeks to accomplish is to call into question that which contemporary visual culture seems to present as natural. It reminds us, further, that even the most seemingly trivial visual text may have a deep yet unintended ideological content which structured and intelligent analysis will help to expose.

Comments on the case study

This case study demonstrates that visual and media texts are symbolic forms that should not be taken at face value. This is why the analysis of the culture and ideological meanings cannot be based on a positivist or experimental research designs in search of laws, but an interpretive one in search of meaning. (Positivist research is conventionally based on observations to explain communication by referring to an objective world, whereas experimental research tests hypotheses in controlled conditions by assessing relationships between independent and dependent variables.) It is therefore argued that because visually mediated texts are riddled with ambiguity, and because a visual text can mean several things at the same time, an interpretative research approach is more appropriate. In other words, from a semiological perspective the connotative and especially mythic layers of meanings consist of coded or symbolic meanings which are communicated by convention. Readers would, therefore, have to be part of the particular culture in order to interpret the coded and symbolic meanings of signs.

| positivist research |
| experimental research |
| interpretive research |

The assumption is made that ideology is constructed by the mass media, which determines the interpretation of mass-mediated messages. However, authors such as Fiske (1987b) argue that criticism need not only be derived from an analysis and discussion of ideology, but from other elements, such as a reader's identity. In other words, the concern for a reader's identity is important because of the relation between that identity and the preferred reading of a text. The construct 'identity' is not intended to be limited to individuals in a physiological sense, but rather as social subjects whose social context, including the comprehension of mass-mediated meanings, contribute to their formation of identity. Therefore an additional point to be debated in terms of this case study is that ideology is not limited to texts, or limited to textual analyses, but is an integral part of both the production and reception processes.

| ideology |

The above comments highlight the concern for the historical and cultural visual forms and content of mass media, such as television, and how they have evolved in particular industrial and commercial systems that inevitably delimit the nature of mediated discourse. For example, instead of portraying realist styles of production techniques, production costs are cut in genres such as sitcoms through artificially created locations and sets. Furthermore, modern-day media institutions represent a paradox of diverse elements (e.g. economical and technological) that

| mass media as systems |

can and do change, yet continue to apply standard procedures, news values, narratives and genre options.

SUMMARY AND CONCLUSION

The discord between the realist and formative approaches to visual communication continues today, between those who believe the ultimate aim of visual communication is the representation of natural perceptions and those who regard visual media as reflexive tools that provide new ways of perceiving the world and – more importantly – commenting on it.

visual codes and meaning

A premise of this chapter is that perception, or the reception of visual sensory data, is an active process, which involves the processes of searching, selecting and comparing. It is therefore acknowledged that the transference of meaning by means of visual codes can be influenced by the reader's attitude and expectations; how selectively he or she perceives, which may be linked to defence mechanisms; and his or her projections, which can be linked to fantasy and gratifications sought. It is against this background that the relevance of aspects such as figure–ground perception and psychological closure, together with the properties (or characteristics) of the mediated codes by means of which the mass media communicate, are dealt with in greater detail in Chapter 5.

visual literacy and education

The central argument proposed in this chapter is that the promotion of media and visual literacy can be equated with the development of readers' consciousness through education. The continual development of media and visual literacy is important because it can raise readers' awareness of the priorities and needs of specific regions, such as southern Africa, and of the development of ethical principles and democratic values. Developing more informed and responsible citizens has several implications: it can promote the social dimension of the process of globalisation and greater participation and active production and use of new media, such as the internet; it can ideally also bring about a creative dimension, whereby readers reconstruct messages and/or create new messages using different visual and other mediated languages, such as by means of community newspapers.

ontological and epistemological questions

Because visual images simulate reality, communication scholars tasked to promote media and visual literacy will continue to be challenged by the ontological questions regarding the nature of images, together with

Media and Visual Literacy

the epistemological questions of 'the validity of images as evidence' (Griffin 2001:453). These blurred boundaries are highlighted by changes to the traditional documentary film genre in the form of edutainment or infotainment programmes, so-called reality television and docudramas. With the growing convergence of traditional mass media with computer technologies, media literacy of the future will require the development of new competencies and skills that will increasingly relate to issues of active citizenship and democracy. 'We need to better understand how media and communication may be used, both as tools and as a way of articulating processes of development and social change, improving everyday lives and empowering people to influence their own lives and those of the fellow community members' (Carlsson 2007:227).

One of the challenges and opportunities that faces communication scholars in the 21st century is to deal with the interdependent independence that is being established by means of global technological innovations. If the road to achieving the dream of global peace is via effective communication and mutual understanding, then every endeavour to improve readers' level of media literacy can contribute to them becoming active builders of that road.

challenging innovations

LEARNING ACTIVITIES

1 Research question: What is the implied narrative conveyed by the content of a static visual image – what do you see? Select a visual image that includes one or more persons, such as the cover of a magazine, a CD cover, a visual advertisement, a press or any other photograph, such as captured in Figures 5.5, 5.8 or 5.14 in Chapter 5. Do this learning activity with a member of your family, a friend or fellow scholar. Compare what you see with what the other person sees by answering the following questions:

1.1 What is the central or basic subject matter? Are the people men or women, young or old, which ethnic group do they represent, and do they look proud, friendly or sad? Look at their clothing: can you make an educated guess as to their lifestyle, social class and type of job? Are they sitting, standing or which actions are they performing? What artefacts (props) are they holding or carrying?

1.2 What is the background and location of the scene? Is it in a showroom for motorcars, on a boat, in a southern African kraal, in the desert or on top of Table Mountain? What does the background and location communicate (for example, a hobby, a fashion statement, a profession, a leisure activity or a specific event)?

1.3 What is the historical period depicted? Do the clothing worn, hairstyles and make-up represent a past time period (for example, the 1960s)? Are other visual clues found to represent a particular historical period – nature of the buildings, roads, transport (type of cars), street lights, billboards, power lines or parking meters?

1.4 What is the season or time of the year? Does the clothing worn (e.g. a swimsuit), natural elements (e.g. snow or leafless trees) or activities (e.g. harvesting wheat) provide clues about the time of the year?

1.5 What is the time of day? If it is an outdoor scene, is it light or dark; what are the length of shadows; are street lights switched on? What activities are the people performing (e.g. enjoying breakfast), or what clothes are they wearing (e.g. tuxedos)?

1.6 What is the particular instant captured by the photograph? This question can be answered by looking at the subjects, props, background, location and time of day individually or collectively, and by considering whether the instant would have been different if the photograph had been taken moments earlier or later.

1.7 Does the text (overtly or covertly) make provision for or even manipulate the influence that culture and previously learned behaviour may have on your and your co-analyst's perception? For example, is the association between certain objects (e.g. clothing) and certain meanings (e.g. an elite social status) perpetuated?

1.8 How do your interpretations correspond with or differ from those of your co-analyst?

2 Research question: Do the visual mass media favour or discount a specific politician?

Select a politician in your country and monitor specific news media (newspapers, or television news) over a period of two weeks. On the basis of deductive reasoning (making inferences from particular instances based on an initial general premise or assumption) determine whether or not, how and how frequently the politician is favoured (or discounted) by means of positive, neutral or negative meanings conveyed in relation to the following: the visual image of the politician as an actor; how an issue (phenomenon, or context) is visually presented to the readers; and how the politician's visual image is presented in relation to the issue (phenomenon or context) being reported in the verbal text.

3. Research question: How do visual images in television newscasts or newspapers contribute to the agenda-setting function of the mass media? (Agenda-setting refers to the mass media activating ideas, feelings or values that focus readers' attention.)

Select an issue that is currently on the agenda in the news media, such as the dismissal of a member of parliament, or a controversy involving a well-known celebrity. Do a qualitative content analysis of the visual images that appear in television newscasts or newspapers over a period of two weeks, by answering the following questions:

  3.1 Does each image fulfil an anchorage function? In other words, does it focus on one specific factual element (who? what? when? where?) of the issue being reported in the news and/or does it represent facts or rationales that underlie the argument presented?

  3.2 In contrast, does each image fulfil a complementary or relay function by expanding on the news item? In other words, does the visual image represent occurrences prior to, during or after (consequences) the newsworthy event – the why and how. Do the images serve as an amplification of actions, conditions, causes or effects of the news item?

  3.3 To what extent do words support, accentuate and therefore complement and elaborate on the visual communication; or to what extent do words regulate or even contradict the visual communication?

4. Apply the above research activity to a cross-sectional qualitative content analysis of the front pages of all the newspapers distributed in your neighbourhood on a particular day. Are differences in terms of anchorage versus complementary functions found when comparing the lead photographs on the front pages of tabloid versus broadsheet newspapers? (Tabloid newspapers are half-size pages of broadsheet newspapers, with bold headlines and large photographs.)

5. Research question: What denotative, connotative, and cultural/ideological meanings are conveyed by visual images of an advertisement for one of South Africa's top brands (or top brands in any other country)?

> Select a visual advertisement from one of South Africa's top brands (e.g. *Coca-Cola, Vodacom, Nike, Toyota, Clover* or *Nokia*). With reference to the first learning activity and the case study above, describe how and which denotative, connotative and cultural/ideological meanings are conveyed by the visual image.

FURTHER READING

Carlsson, U. & Helland, K. (eds) 2007. Media structures and practices. As time goes by ... *Nordicom Review, Jubilee Issue,* 28. Göteborg: Nordic Information Centre for Media and Communication Research.

Evans, J. & Hall, S. (eds) 1999. *Visual culture: The reader.* London: Sage, in association with the Open University.

Griffin, M. 2001. Camera as witness, image as sign: The study of visual communication in communication research, in: *Communication Yearbook 24,* edited by William B. Gudykunst. Thousand Oaks, Calif: Sage Publications, 433–63.

Kress, G. & Van Leeuwen, T. 2000. *Reading images. The grammar of visual design.* London: Routledge.

Kubey, R. (ed) 1997. *Media literacy in the information age: Current perspectives.* New Brunswick, New Jersey: Transaction.

Lester, P.M. 1995 (or later edition). *Visual communication: Images with messages.* Belmont, Calif: Wadsworth.

Messaris, P. 1994. *Visual 'literacy'. Image, mind & reality.* Boulder, Colorado: Westview.

Meyrowitz, J. 1998. Multiple media literacies. *Journal of Communication* 48(1):96–108.

Zettl, H. 1998. Contextual media aesthetics as the basis for media literacy. *Journal of Communication* 48(1):81–95.

Zettl, H. 2008. *Sight, sound, motion: Applied media aesthetics.* 5th edition. Belmont, Calif: Thomson Wadsworth.

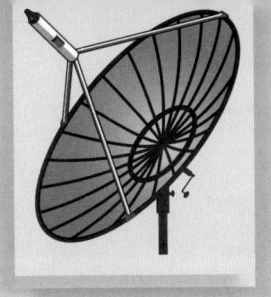

chapter five

VISUAL TEXT ANALYSIS

Gertruida (Trudie) M. du Plooy

LEARNING OUTCOMES

At the end of this chapter, you should be able to conduct research by doing a textual analysis of the signs and codes that are used to create meaning in:
- static filmic shots and photographs;
- filmic or television extracts.

THIS CHAPTER

This chapter deals with the analysis of mass-media content and forms, with specific emphasis on visual and audiovisual texts communicated by means of photographs, films and television.

The most important topics dealt with in this chapter are:
- pictorial codes in static filmic shots and photographs;
- picturisation through movement in film and television;
- auditory codes and the combination of audiovisual codes;
- how signs and codes are used in photographs, films and television to produce and influence meaning(s) presented.

5.1 INTRODUCTION

The central point of the argument presented in this chapter is that an understanding of the use of audiovisual codes contributes to an increased awareness of their manipulation in the construction of meaning; and that such an understanding contributes to an informed aesthetic appreciation of the content and form of photographic, filmic and television texts.

text

readers

The word 'text' can take on different meanings. On the one hand it refers to mass-media messages as experienced by readers. For example, a television soap opera becomes a text when it is watched and enjoyed by the viewers. However, for the purpose of this chapter, the word 'text' refers to the form and content of the message itself, which could be in oral, written or graphic languages, using still and moving images, or using multimedia, including computers. In other words, a text has a physical existence of its own and stands detached or separate from the communicator and from the mass-media readers. 'Readers' in this context refers to listeners, readers or viewers as recipients of mass communication.

codes

applied media aesthetics

This chapter deals specifically with the application of the basic codes of applied media aesthetics, namely lighting, colour, two- and three-dimensional space, time and movement and sound. Codes therefore refer to the rules and conventions that govern the interplay between the equations of the signifier and signified. Applied media aesthetics, according to Zettl (2008:389), deals with 'sense perceptions and how to influence them' with the specific focus on 'video, film, and other electronic audiovisual media'. Although these codes influence the encoding of the content of messages, the focus in this chapter is on the analysis (not the production) of these codes. The semiotic approach (see Chapter 2) is regarded as an integral part of media aesthetics, as addressed in this chapter. This chapter therefore has to be read against the background provided in Chapter 4, which discusses conceptual issues related to the notions of media content literacy, media grammar literacy, and medium literacy on a micro level, as well as on a macro-societal level, plus the perceptual approach to visual communication, and the assumptions of the semiotic and the cognitive approaches to visual perception and interpretation.

5.2 PICTORIAL CODES IN A STATIC FILMIC SHOT AND PHOTOGRAPH

In this section, the following codes are dealt with in terms of the conceptual (not technical) aspects of production, with the primary focus on their meaning construction when conducting a text analysis: lighting, colour, field forces within the shot or frame (main directions, magnetism of the frame and attraction of mass, asymmetry of the shot or frame, figure–ground perception, psychological closure, vectors), balance, depth and volume, area orientation (aspect ratio, size of the object), lenses and focus, basic camera shots and camera viewpoint.

| meaning construction

A single shot or photograph of a person is an icon that represents the person according to the principle of *similitude*. In other words, a *similarity* exists between the sign and the person. However, from a semiotic perspective, the meaning created, even by a single, static shot, is governed by a complex set of rules and codes.

| similitude

Codes organise our perceptions and create structures of meaning, which sometimes means that film and television producers draw on meaning systems that already exist among their mass audiences. Because of the existence of shared-meaning systems, and because mediated messages draw on codes found in other similar messages, certain rules that guide interpretation have been established over the years. Communicators who use a camera as a medium can and do convert existing meaning systems into modified meanings to suit their particular intentions. The production of meanings (sign values) is best illustrated in advertising, where it is the communicator's intention to create or reinforce an association between a product or service and abstract meanings (e.g.

| mediated codes

between a particular beer and friendship). In other words, mediated visual codes sell moods, feelings, lifestyles and shape readers' self-concepts.

mise-en-scène

In this discussion, and with reference to Fourie (1988:32–4), we make an artificial distinction between codes of represented form and codes of visual representation, or codes of content. The most important visual code of form – in the case of a static shot or photograph – is that of the camera point of view. Content codes include thematic, *mise-en-scène* (French for the scenery, properties, and surroundings of a setting), and colour and lighting codes – in addition to nonverbal behavioural codes such as kinesics and proxemics.

5.2.1 Lighting as a code of content

When thinking about light and darkness, we often associate light with clarity, warmth and/or security, whereas darkness can be associated with resting, coldness, unpredictability and/or tension. When considering lighting as a visual code of content, we exclude internal light sources, such as the electronic television beam, which makes the perception of projected impulses possible, and we deal specifically with the light captured by the lens.

key light
back light
fill light
low-key lighting
high-key lighting

When key lights (the main source of light, usually a directional spotlight), back lights (usually a directional spotlight, which separates a figure from the background) or fill lights (a flood or soft spotlight, which minimises harsh shadows) are used to create artificial lighting effects, this may be done for various reasons: for example, to distinguish the actual shape of an object, contours and/or texture. The tonality of a film is also determined by the proportions of *light and dark* in a scene. The latter is an important code in creating emotional connotations, atmosphere and suspense. For example, a simplistic distinction may be made between low-key lighting (e.g. using lights to create a dark or dramatic scene) versus high-key lighting (e.g. using lights to create a bright scene, such as in a comedy, a musical or in news broadcasts).

notan lighting

Notan and chiaroscuro are traditionally distinguished (Zettl 2008:39) as two types of external lighting. Notan lighting is flat lighting, which is characteristically low in contrast, with all the areas captured by the shot being equally bright, including the background (see Figure 5.1 for an illustration). Due to the non-selectiveness of notan lighting, visual

Visual Text Analysis

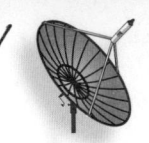

images and settings portrayed in this manner are usually associated with neutrality and objectivity, such as a television news studio.

Chiaroscuro lighting, on the other hand, refers to *selectively* lighting certain areas of the content. 'Chiaroscuro' is Italian for light–dark (*chiaro* = light; *oscuro* = dark). Three types can be distinguished. The first is Rembrandt lighting, named after the Dutch painter Rembrandt's (1606–69) dramatic and compositional use of contrasts of light, shadows and half tones. When Rembrandt lighting is used, it means that certain areas are illuminated, whereas others are left either in semi- or complete darkness (see Figure 5.2 for an illustration).

| chiaroscuro lighting
| Rembrandt lighting

The second type of chiaroscuro lighting is called cameo lighting, which means that a figure or object in the foreground is well lit – like a cameo – against a dark background (see Figure 5.3 for an illustration). Just as gestures are frequently used as indexical signs, so too are Rembrandt

| cameo lighting

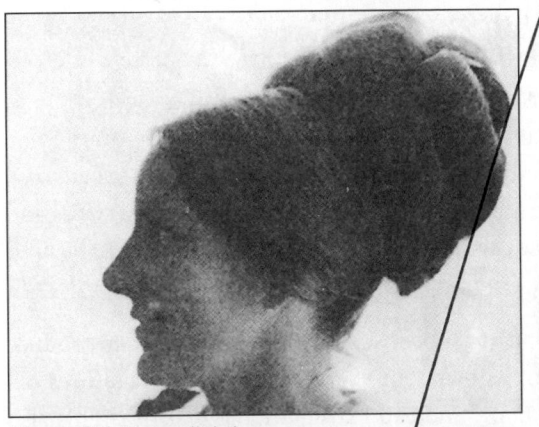

Figure 5.1 Notan lighting

Figure 5.2 Rembrandt lighting

Figure 5.3 Cameo lighting

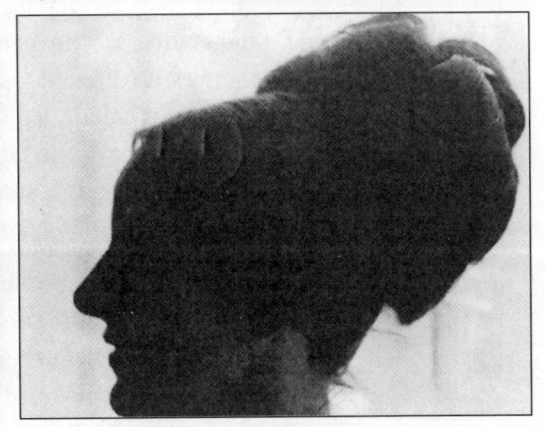

Figure 5.4 Silhouette lighting

151

and cameo lighting – pointing to and focusing attention on selective elements of the content within the frame.

silhouette lighting

The third type is called silhouette lighting, whereby the frame or contours of a figure or shape are made visible against a brighter background (see Figure 5.4 for an illustration).

Unlike the objectivity and neutrality associated with content depicted by means of notan lighting, chiaroscuro lighting tends to draw the audience's attention to the thematic or emotive meaning of the content. Compare for example Figure 5.1 (notan lighting) with Figure 5.4 (silhouette lighting). Because the content is *not* evenly lit, chiaroscuro lighting can be used to make a scene appear more realistic and/or it can be used to add to a compositional orientation by balancing the different visual elements in relation to one another and/or can contribute a dramatic emotion to the content.

5.2.2 Colour as a code of content

information

Colour is part of our daily life-world. For example, according to international road traffic sign systems, *yellow* signifies temporary signs such as those used at roadworks and to indicate changes in the roadways, while *brown* signifies tourism signs that deal with facilities, services and tourist attractions. These examples clearly show that colours can be used to convey and clarify *information*.

hue

saturation

However, colours work on our subconscious and each colour can produce an emotional reaction of its own. For example, in Western cultures *red* usually attracts attention and indicates strength and warmth. This also shows that colours are associated with temperatures (such as warmth and coldness). Our perception of colours and their meanings (moods, energies or dramatic qualities) is influenced by attributes such as hue (the actual colour, e.g. blue versus red) and saturation (the richness of the colour), as well as factors such as surface reflection, surrounding colours and lighting techniques (Zettl 1990:55–68).

Preferences for certain colours are also influenced by demographics, such as gender, age, social group and past experiences. It has been said that lower social classes prefer stronger or brighter colours, whereas upper classes prefer lighter colours. Particularly in advertising (in Western cultures) it is assumed that the use of certain colours can influence consumers' reactions to the product being advertised, as well as their

Visual Text Analysis

perceptions of symbolic meanings (abstract concepts) such as quality, value and purity. Studies have shown (Russell & Verrill 1986:516) that coffee is perceived to be *mild*, a *weaker blend*, *too strong* and *rich and full-bodied*, depending on whether the coffee is brewed and poured from a blue, a yellow, a brown or a red pot, respectively. These examples, however, refer to the symbolic meanings that we learn to associate with certain colours. Because the meanings have to be *learned*, they are subject to traditions – traditions that may vary from one context, period or culture to another.

5.2.3 Field forces within the shot, or frame

Whether the purpose is to clarify and/or to intensify the meaning visualised in a single shot, according to Zettl (1990;101–27), six field forces influence the way in which visual codes are used: main directions; magnetism of the frame and attraction of mass; the asymmetry of the frame; figure–ground perception; psychological closure; and vectors.

Main directions

The main directions within a single shot or photograph are horizontal (X-axis) and vertical (Y-axis). If the content stresses one direction, such as horizontal, calmness can be conveyed (see Figure 5.5), in contrast to the high energy, dynamism, power and/or excitement suggested by the vertical directions, as illustrated in Figure 5.6.

horizontal (X-axis)

vertical (Y-axis)

Figure 5.5 Horizontal balance, conveying calmness

If we were to tilt the horizontal axis or plane, this could convey meanings such as energy, progress, failure or even a feeling of discomfort. (Compare Figure 5.7, which, due to the tilted *horizon*, conveys a feeling of greater instability than Figure 5.6.)

Figure 5.6 Vertical balance, conveying high energy

Figure 5.7 A tilted horizon

Magnetism of the frame and attraction of mass

The top and side edges, as well as the corners, of a frame, tend to exert a *magnetic pull* on elements positioned closest. For example, in Figure 5.8 the wedding couple are standing at a comfortable distance (proxemics) from one another, *because* space has been left on the sides, and especially because *looking room* (or nose room) has been included on the left-hand side (that is, the direction in which they are looking).

However, by moving to a closer shot (and in so doing *removing* the spaces on the sides), the magnetism of the side edges is increased, as shown in Figure 5.9, almost pulling the couple apart. The magnetism of the left-hand side is particularly prominent, because of the limited looking room (or space) in front of the bridegroom. The magnetism of the frame is a significant force when doing a text analysis of camera shots and is further discussed below.

magnetic pull

nose room

Visual Text Analysis

Figure 5.8 A comfortable space between the people and the frame

Figure 5.9 Magnetism of the sides of the frame

Asymmetry of the shot or screen

In cultures where pictures are read from left to right, then, according to Zettl (2008:109), Figure 5.10 represents a graphic up-diagonal, and Figure 5.11 a graphic down-diagonal.

up-diagonal

down-diagonal

In other words, if communicators want to reflect the power and stamina that a mountaineer requires, or the effort and struggle that a refugee experiences while pushing all his belongings on a home-made wagon, they would reflect the climber or refugee moving and facing *against* the down-diagonal (see Figure 5.12). By having to work against or having to overcome the down-diagonal, the meaning conveyed is that the person

155

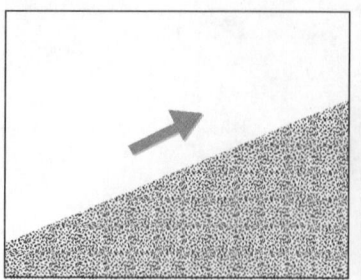

Media Studies: Volume 3

Figure 5.10 Up-diagonal 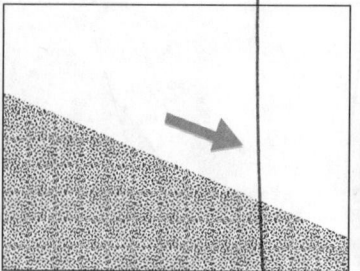 **Figure 5.11** Down-diagonal 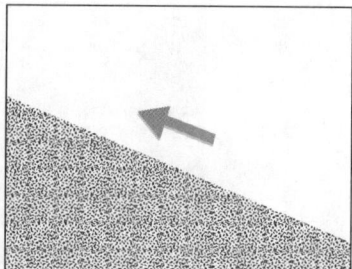 **Figure 5.12** Challenging the down-diagonal

depicted as moving from right-to-left *uphill*, requires strength, effort or courage.

Figure–ground perception

figure versus ground

Look at Figure 5.13; are these stone pillars or are they the outlines of nude figures? This is an illustration of the figure–ground phenomenon of perception and interpretation, which means that we tend to see (perceive) a figure as if it appears in front of a background. Therefore, in Figure 5.13, what we regard as the *figure* and what we regard as the *ground* (or background) will determine whether we see stone pillars (as the figures) or whether we see nude figures (as the figures).

Figure 5.13 Figure and ground (Adapted from McDermott [sa])

shift in focus

When interpreting Figure 5.14 the woman is perceived as the figure and the building as the background. However, a closer shot changes the figure and background relationship. Figure 5.15, for example, shows that the woman (who was previously the figure) now becomes the background, with the mug as the figure. The change in figure–ground

Visual Text Analysis

Figure 5.14 Woman-and-building as figure–ground

Figure 5.15 Mug-and-woman as figure–ground

relations created by Figure 5.15 alters the meaning presented because the focus shifts to a new figure.

Psychological closure

When presented with visual information that contains gaps or missing details, we tend to fill in the missing parts to obtain a complete image. This perceptual activity is called psychological closure, which is based on the Gestalt principle, in terms of which our eyes naturally tend to organise, for example, a series of dots into a coherent pattern, or to create a whole image that is more than the sum of the parts shown or seen. According to Lester (1995:53–7), psychological closure is based on

Gestalt principle

157

the principles of proximity, similarity and continuity. According to these principles, we will combine those elements that appear closer to one another (*proximity*); we will group similarly shaped elements together (*similarity*); and we will try to make connections between letters or symbols to create a dominant line, shape or pattern (a *continuity*), rather than detached sections. In Figure 5.16, for example, we see four narrow columns, rather than three fat columns, due to the proximity of the lines (and attraction of mass). In Figure 5.9, for example, readers would fill in the missing information of priest or person conducting the wedding ceremony, plus a large gathering in the background, although they are not shown.

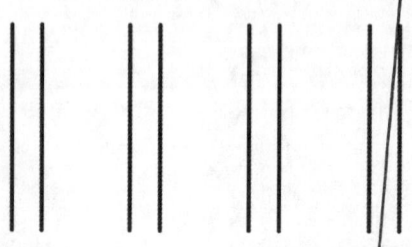

Figure 5.16 Proximity as a principle of psychological closure

Vectors

Vectors are directional forces, such as objects, people, lines or movements that point or move (or are perceived to point or move) in a particular direction. They are placed within the frame in such a way that readers' eyes are led from one point to another; or to some directional orientation, inside or outside the frame. Zettl (2008:119–23) distinguishes between three main types of vectors: graphic, index and motion.

graphic vectors

index vectors

Graphic vectors are created by lines or objects. For example, the pole in Figure 5.7 represents a graphic vector, which guides readers' eyes upwards to the sky or downwards to the person in the foreground. Index vectors are created by something (e.g. an arrow) or someone pointing (or looking) in a specific direction. In Figure 5.17, the direction in which the man is looking and pointing leads readers' eyes beyond the frame to the left. According to the Peircean typology of signs (icon, index and symbol), such index vectors are indexical signs, because through contiguity the thing or person pointing relates to the person or object that is being looked at or pointed at.

Visual Text Analysis

Figure 5.17 Pointing and looking as index vectors

Figure 5.18 Graphic and index vectors combined

In Figure 5.18 the rifle (graphic vector) leads readers' eyes to the space above. The lines of the wall tiles, paper towel, curtains and open oven door (more graphic vectors) lead our eyes horizontally to the woman, and the direction in which she is looking (index vector) returns our attention to the rifle.

A motion vector cannot be illustrated by means of a still picture, and is created by something or someone actually moving in front of a camera and/or by the camera's movement (discussed in section 5.3 below).

motion vectors

The meanings that readers ascribe to vectors can differ, depending on what types of vectors are used (graphic, index or motion) and, in the case of index and motion vectors, whether their *directions* continue, converge or diverge.

Continuing vectors are graphic, index and/or motion vectors that point or move (or are perceived to point or move) in the same direction. Figure 5.19 illustrates *continuing* index vectors, as both people are *looking* (index vector) in the *same* direction. Continuous index vectors are also displayed in Figure 5.17 because the directions in which the man points and looks are the same. Continuing vectors, as found in these two

continuing vectors

Media Studies: Volume 3

examples, emphasise the importance of what is being looked at, even if the object or person is outside the frame. In the case of film/television, that object or person (outside of the frame) would in all likelihood be shown in the subsequent shot.

Figure 5.19 Continuing (index) vectors

converging vectors

Converging vectors are graphic, index and/or motion vectors that point or move (or are perceived to point or move) towards one another. Converging vectors are best illustrated by a shot of two people facing one another whilst conversing, because the fact that they are looking *towards* one another means that the index vectors point at each other. The use of converging vectors can contribute to creating closure, or conveying a feeling of togetherness. However, if the context is confrontational then converging vectors can contribute to the fact that conflict between the elements or people is heightened.

diverging vectors

In contrast to converging vectors are graphic, index and/or motion vectors that point or move (or are perceived to point or move) in *opposite directions*. For example, in Figure 5.20, the woman sitting on the ground is looking (index vector) in the *opposite* direction from the women who appear behind her. Depending on the context in which such diverging vectors are used, they could emphasise separation, opposition or disagreement between the elements or parties depicted.

direct focus
indirect focus

Two or more index vectors can be structured or positioned in such a way so as to create vector structures, which are referred to as *direct focus* or *indirect focus*. A shot of two or more people (who appear in the same shot) looking at the same object or person, is an example of direct focus.

160

Visual Text Analysis

For example, the wedding couples in Figure 5.8, who are all looking at the person conducting the wedding ceremony, represent direct focus. In the case of indirect focus, one or more index vectors are *redirected* by an intermediary before reaching the target object or target person. For example, in Figure 5.21 the two women on the left are looking at the woman on the right (intermediary), who is looking at the ballot paper (target object).

Direct focus is used to guide a reader's eyes to the target person, or object, such as a product in an advertisement. Indirect focus, although it could be used for the same purpose (to focus attention on the target object), can also contribute to prolonging conflict or to increasing tension between the individuals depicted, especially in films and television.

Figure 5.20 Diverging vectors

Figure 5.21 Index vectors structured as indirect focus

161

Media Studies: Volume 3

5.2.4 Balance as a code of content

stabile balance
neutral balance
labile balance

The changes in lighting, colour and the shape and location of the content of a shot in relation to factors such as main directions, magnetism of the frame and attraction of mass, the asymmetry of the frame, figure–ground perception, psychological closure, and vectors, all contribute to structuring the balance. Stabile, neutral and labile are three categories of balance that can be created and distinguished. For example, Figure 5.5 illustrates what Zettl (1990:155) calls 'stabile balance', because the graphic elements are structured symmetrically and the balance is stable. On the other hand, Figures 5.18, 5.20, 5.21 and 5.23 illustrate a neutral balance, because the elements are to a certain degree arranged asymmetrically, yet quite ordinarily, in the frame. However, in the third type of balance (labile) the elements of the content are extremely tilted, irregular, unstable and/or unbalanced, such as illustrated in Figures 5.7 and 5.22.

Figure 5.22 Labile balance

The balance created by the framing of a shot must correspond with the particular visual moment in a particular context. The choice of one of these three types of balance would therefore be motivated by whether the communicator wants to convey stability, neutrality or instability.

5.2.5 Depth and volume as content codes

depth (Z-axis)

In contrast with television and film, a photograph represents a *static* event (people and artefacts). When considering the codes of content, a number of codes can be manipulated to artificially create a feeling of depth (Z-axis) and volume on a surface that is two-dimensional (without any depth), namely volume duality and graphic depth factors.

Volume duality

When reconsidering Figure 5.14, the woman and building represent *positive* volume in that their appearance has substance – it can be

Visual Text Analysis

touched – whereas the cloudless sky in the background represents *negative* space. Volume duality refers to the visual contrast between positive and negative volumes or spaces and therefore refers to the way in which positive and negative volumes are combined, with the intention of creating the illusion of depth.

Graphic depth factors

Factors that create the illusion of depth (without movement) on a two-dimensional surface, for example a photograph, are referred to as graphic depth factors. The most obvious graphic factor contributing to the creation of depth is the positioning of elements so that they overlap one another: the element that is partially covered is interpreted as being behind the one in front. A second factor, closely related to the overlapping of planes, is the relative size of the elements or images. If the normal size of an element is known (such as that of the human body), those images that appear smaller will be perceived to be further away, while those that are larger will seem to be closer. Figure 5.23 illustrates how both these graphic factors contribute to our perception of depth. Notice how the drum majorettes' bodies overlap and how their relative sizes differ.

illusion of depth

overlapping planes

relative sizes

Figure 5.23 Overlapping planes and relative sizes

163

height in plane
linear perspective
vanishing point
bird's-eye view
worm's-eye view

aerial perspective

Height in plane is the third graphic factor that contributes to readers' depth perception, and refers to an interpretation of an object or element as being further away, or more distant, the higher it is positioned in the picture in relation to the horizon. Figure 5.24 illustrates this graphic factor: the positioning of the mounds of earth high in the picture field makes them appear to be distant and also helps to emphasise the difference in size compared with the railway trucks. The fourth factor, linear perspective, is shown by the way in which the vertical and horizontal lines converge and seem to move closer to one another in the distance (as in Figure 5.24). The point where these lines converge is called the vanishing point. This vanishing point will be either below the horizon, where the camera is positioned above eye level and is tilted downwards (bird's-eye view), or above the horizon, where the camera's position and angle is below eye level and is tilted upwards (worm's-eye view).

Look at Figure 5.24 again, and observe how much more detail we can see in the foreground (e.g. the patterns on the dunes and the texture of the trucks); this clarity diminishes and becomes greyer as we look into the distance. These differences in the clarity of detail and in brightness (called aerial perspective) can also enhance the illusion of depth when skilfully manipulated.

Figure 5.24 Height in plane, relative sizes and linear perspective

Visual Text Analysis

In addition to the manipulation of colours – such as using less saturated colours to signify distance – light and shadows are very often used to create the illusion of depth. In Figure 5.1, for example, the absence of any shadows minimises the volume or depth. It makes the picture look 'flat' (which is another way to describe notan lighting). In Figure 5.23, the shadows are attached to the people depicted, which adds to readers' perception of depth. (Notice how the shadows are attached to their feet.) The cast shadows in Figure 5.14, on the other hand, give greater prominence to volume and depth. (Notice, in Figure 5.14, how far removed the figure's cast shadow is from her body, when compared with the attached shadows in Figure 5.23.)

attached shadows

cast shadows

Lastly, one other graphic code needs to be considered, namely adding graphic lines and lettering to a photograph. In news reportage and advertising, for example, it is particularly important to realise that the headline, slogan or caption that is added to a static shot can signify and define different relationships between the images of the event depicted or product being advertised, and the meanings conveyed. (These relationships are further discussed in section 5.4.2 in this chapter.)

graphic lines and lettering

5.2.6 Area orientation as a code of form

A still photographer can exercise a number of choices in the orientation of a single shot or image, including two structural codes, namely aspect ratio and size of the object.

Aspect ratio

Aspect ratio refers to the height and width of a photograph, film or television screen. The form or shape of a photograph, in addition to its aspect ratio (the height and width), could be square, vertical, horizontal, round or even irregular. The shape or frame in Figure 5.5, for example, is horizontal in order to accommodate the horizontal orientation of the buildings, in contrast to the vertical shape or frame used in Figure 5.6 to accommodate the vertical nature of the content.

aspect ratio

Size of the object

When interpreting the size of visualised objects, readers use previous knowledge of the object (e.g. the size of a normal chair), such as the clues reflected by the environment that surrounds the object and, more particularly, by the human body. For example, we know the normal size of a petrol pump. It is only when a human hand clasps the pump and a child is shown looking down at the pump that we are able to interpret the real size of the object. The size of a person or object is also directly influenced by the use of different lenses, and by changing the focus and the framing of the actual shot, which are discussed below.

5.2.7 Lenses and focus as codes of form

narrow-angle lens

In addition to the graphic depth factors discussed above, the use of a camera lens in a normal, narrow-angle or wide-angle position also influences our perception of positive and negative volumes and, more particularly, our perception of depth. The narrow-angled lens position (long focal-length lens) reflected in Figure 5.25, tends to intensify the close proximity of the stables, thereby suggesting cramped conditions.

The normal lens position used in Figure 5.26, on the other hand, reflects the perspective and relative sizes of the stables and horses as we would normally see them.

wide-angle lens

In contrast, a wide-angle (short focal length) lens distorts readers' normal depth perception by placing more emphasis on elements or people in the foreground (as shown in Figure 5.27).

selective focus

As discussed above, when analysing a photograph according to the principles of aerial perspective (whereby the brightness and clarity of detail diminishes in the background), we may find that selective focus has been used to counteract the natural aerial perspective. In other words, the communicator can use the camera's focus to place emphasis on or isolate the foreground (as in Figure 5.28), the middle ground or the background (as in Figure 5.29).

codes of form and content combined

In Figure 5.28 the camera focus differentiates the person and rifles in the foreground from the persons behind. Despite the fact that they all share the same proximity, this camera technique differentiates between the person in the foreground and the others and, depending on the context in which this shot is used, could (in addition) signify that the person in focus is the most important. However, Figure 5.28 also contains an interesting combination of codes of form and codes of content. The focus (code of form) on the person in the foreground is not obvious at first glance, because it is counteracted by the selective lighting (code

Visual Text Analysis

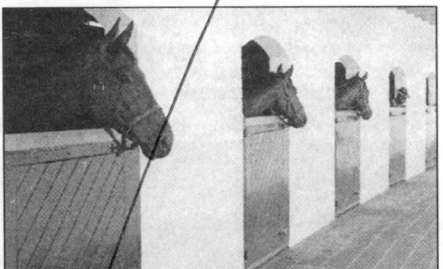

Figure 5.25 Narrow-angle shot

Figure 5.26 Normal lens position

Figure 5.27 Wide-angle shot

Figure 5.28 Focus on the foreground

167

of content) of one of the people in the background, and because of the vertical graphic vectors created by the rifles – pointing at the person in the background (another code of content). Consequently, despite the camera's focus on the person in the foreground, readers' attention is initially drawn to the person (out of focus) in the background.

Selective focus is also used in Figure 5.29, but to create a different effect. The focus is on the person in the background, the aim of which – depending on the context – could be to:
- differentiate between the person focused on in the background and the two people who appear in the foreground;
- signify the importance, conflict or superiority of the person in the background.

focus as metaphor

From a semiotic perspective, we could say that focus (in contrast to out-of-focus) is a spatial (symbolic) metaphor for significance. Nevertheless, our interpretations cannot solely be determined by camera focus, because – as illustrated in Figure 5.29 – the denotative, connotative and symbolic meanings conveyed would depend on the indexical and symbolic meanings that readers assign to these signs. In the post-apartheid era in South Africa, the icons of a white man in

Figure 5.29 Focus on the background

Visual Text Analysis

uniform and a black man (with a clenched fist) still convey symbolic meanings, such as oppression and liberation, for some readers.

From the above discussion and illustrations it becomes clear that lighting, colour, field forces within the frame, balance, depth and volume, area orientation, as well as camera lenses and focus, are all codes of content and form, which can be used to differentiate between elements or sections of a shot or to connect the content and form into a whole.

5.2.8 Basic camera shots as visual codes of form

Figures 5.30–5.35 illustrate the names and characteristics of basic camera shots used when framing shots (and which are conventionally also used in film and television productions). The *closer* shots (see Figures 5.30, 5.31 and 5.32) convey meaning according to the principle of synecdoche, in terms of which the whole, whether it be a person, an object or scene, is represented by a part (i.e. a part is used to represent the whole).

| synecdoche

ECU – An extreme close-up shot (also called *BCU*, or big close-up) shows a person's lips, nose and eyes; or a logo in an advertisement; or a small section of an artefact, such as a door handle. This shot is used mainly for impact and/or to show detail.

Figure 5.30 Extreme close-up (or big close-up) shot

CU – A close-up shot is a tight shot that shows a person's face, including the shoulder line and the top of the head; or the whole product in an advertisement; or a larger section of an artefact, such as a door. Based on the assumption that the eyes reflect the emotions of the soul, this shot is often used to convey emotion. As every blemish on the skin is clearly perceptible, it can also be a cruel shot.

Figure 5.31 Close-up shot

MCU – A medium close-up shot frames a person from about the chest level with room above the head; or shows the whole product with some background, in an advertisement; or shows a still larger section of an artefact, such as the door and adjacent window of a building. When used to frame a person on television, it is frequently referred to as a *talking-head shot*.

Figure 5.32 Medium close-up shot

Media Studies: Volume 3

Figure 5.33 Medium shot

Figure 5.34 Medium-long shot

Figure 5.35 Long shot

MS – A medium shot usually shows a person from the waist upwards and shows more details of the setting or background than in the case of an MCU. Since this shot combines someone's facial expression with the background, it should allow for *looking room* (also called *nose room*).

MLS – In a medium-long shot, a person's head is placed in the hypothetical upper third, without touching the upper edge of the frame, with the lowest point of the frame being above or below the knees. This shot includes more visual information about the setting and allows room or space for the person to move.

LS – A long shot (also known as the *far shot*) shows the full length of a person; or shows a product in an advertisement from a distance; or an artefact such as a house as a whole. This shot (or *XLS – extra-long shot*) is normally used to establish the location, hence the label of *establishing shot*.

5.2.9 Building screen space – camera viewpoint

When building screen space, we are dealing with a particular *viewpoint*, which can be influenced by the actual shot or frame (e.g. a close-up shot versus a long shot) and by the event or context of the particular shot. In other words, the camera viewpoint can vary according to the field view and the amount of visual information that is in/excluded in the shot and the *positioning* of the camera in relation to objects, and/or person(s) and/or scene being filmed.

objective camera

By adjusting the camera's viewpoint, a variety of angles can be created, which not only provides a particular point of view but also intensifies the emotive qualities of the visual event. Objective camera refers to the camera's viewpoint that looks at a scene (something or someone) with neutrality and detachment. For example, Figure 5.36 reflects an objective camera viewpoint that enables readers to 'look at' the people.

subjective camera

In contrast, subjective camera is applied when the camera's viewpoint reflects participation in an event, such as assuming the viewpoint of one of the persons who are involved in the scene. For example, in Figure 5.37 readers no longer look at the people, but, due to the camera's position, they feel as if they actively participate in what the people in the shot are doing (subjective camera). A subjective camera view means that the content (that which appears in front of the camera) is shown from

Visual Text Analysis

Figure 5.36 Objective camera

Figure 5.37 Subjective camera

one (or more) of the character's point of view. This camera position is frequently used for instructional and marketing purposes (e.g. in demonstrations of how a machine works), or to increase the tension in a dramatic scene, because it increases the readers' involvement.

Qualities such as superiority and inferiority can also be suggested by placing the camera *below* or *above* the eye-level position in relation to the subject that is being filmed. For example, Figure 5.38 shows a shot of two people at eye level, while in Figure 5.39 the same people are depicted far above eye level, literally looking down on them. The importance,

camera's eye-level positions

171

Figure 5.38 Positioning a camera on eye level

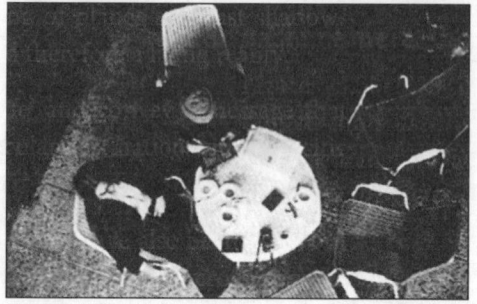

Figure 5.39 Positioning a camera above eye level

golden ratio

power or authority of objects, persons or events can be diminished by positioning the camera *above* eye level (bird's-eye view) and by looking down with the camera. On the other hand, the reverse impression or emotive qualities can be created when positioning the camera *below* the eye-level position (worm's-eye view).

When comparing Figure 5.38 with Figure 5.39, it is clear how a change in camera angle and position – as codes of form – enables the communicator to manipulate the meanings conveyed by the represented content.

The codes and conventions that are particularly important in television news are the selection of particular camera shots, and the syntagmatic combination of shots and sequences. By, for example, selecting an eye-level camera position when recording an interview with a national leader, the camera conveys the impression of being a passive onlooker, which in turn implies 'objectivity'. Nevertheless, the mere selection of a particular shot means that an element of subjectivity enters the news report, because other visual information that is excluded from the framed shot (and which is not seen or known by the viewer) could have been more relevant.

Both codes of content and of form contribute to the composition of a single shot and, unless its purpose is to convey disequilibrium or incoherence, *unity* and *balance* are two of the most important compositional codes. A bisymmetric *formal* (but static) *balance* is usually created by framing the shot in such a way that elements on the right-hand side are matched in size, shape, intensity of colour and/or dark–light contrasts with those on the left-hand side. *Informal balance*, which is more imaginative and distinctive, is created by arranging elements according to the *golden ratio*. The golden ratio is determined by dividing a framed area (e.g. one shot or a photograph) into two parts, whereby the ratio of the small part to the large part is equal to the ratio of the large part to the whole shot or photograph. The optical centre of the shot differs from the mathematical centre and is based on the *see-saw principle*, in terms of which a lighter weight on a see-saw can easily balance a heavier weight if the lighter weight is further away from the fulcrum, as illustrated in Figures 5.24 and 5.37. (Weight, in this compositional sense, refers to any of the codes of content and of form discussed above.)

5.3 PICTURISATION THROUGH MOVEMENT IN FILM AND TELEVISION

In addition to the codes of content and form dealt with in section 5.2, visual codes in film and television not only deal with the visual image as a spatial field, but also more specifically with a *space–time (moving) image*.

5.3.1 Objective versus subjective time

The relevance of time in film and television becomes obvious when we consider the distinction between objective and subjective time. Objective time refers to time as measured by a clock. Zettl (1990:278–95) distinguishes between the following types of objective time:

- *spot* time – the actual time when a television programme is broadcast;
- *running* time – the duration of a film or television programme;
- *story* time – the time span of an event, such as 75 years, if the story deals with the life of an important figure.

Suspense in detective and police genres, for example, relies characteristically on a double temporal tension; that is, the time/story of the crime and the time/story of the investigation, together with the temporal process of the programme itself. However, running time (e.g. 28 minutes) and story time (e.g. 75 years) are seldom identical. Running time can also be divided into *sequence* time, *scene* time and smaller units, namely *shot time*. In a film, a single frame is often regarded as the smallest unit, whereas in television the smallest visual unit is represented by a shot, namely the interval between two distinct visual transitions, such as between one cut and another cut/wipe/dissolve. (These editing techniques are discussed below in section 5.3.4.) A *scene* represents a combination of several shots to create a part of an event or action, whereas *sequence* consists of a combination of several scenes that create an organised whole.

> shot
> scene
> sequence

subjective time

cliff-hanger endings

Subjective time, however, cannot be measured or subdivided into different types because it is dependent on a number of contextual variables, such as whether or not the message is interesting, funny or dull. As the duration of subjective time by readers while interpreting mass-media messages depends on their personal experiences, it is also called psychological time. For example, the central themes in soap operas, such as births, marriages, divorces and deaths, are usually treated in multiple plot-structures and the narrative structures are characteristically open-ended (that is, open to different interpretations, including that of subjective time, by mass audiences). On the other hand, despite cliffhanger endings in soap operas, which are suspenseful and unresolved endings to each episode, the passage of time generally seems to keep pace with the passage of 'real' time.

5.3.2 Picturisation through primary movement

primary movement

If the film or television camera remains stationary and merely records what happens in front of it (that is, the camera is objective and passive), readers are observing primary movement, which occurs along any one or more of the X- (horizontal), Y- (vertical), or Z- (depth) axes. Primary movement therefore refers to motion that takes place in front of the camera. Movement, or the creation of a motion vector, along the Z-axis, by a person or object moving towards or away from a passive camera, is one of the strongest indexical signs of depth.

kinesics

Takalani Sesame

The meanings that can be conveyed by a person who challenges the down-diagonal are discussed above with reference to Figure 5.12. It would make for an interesting textual analysis if we were to research how often the meanings of binary opposition, such as the fight for integrity (versus corruption), humanity (versus savagery), freedom (versus restriction) and equal rights (versus domination) are depicted in film/television by shots of people whose primary movements are shown to challenge such a down-diagonal. The significance of primary movements as motion vectors has been revealed in a study (Sammur 1990:81–92) investigating preschoolers' viewing patterns of 19 *Sesame Street* pre-reading and pre-science segments. (*Takalani Sesame*, the South African adaptation of the American educational television programme *Sesame Street*, has been broadcast on SABC since 2000.) The study revealed that the use of kinesics (gestures and other primary movements of the body, hands or head) by the Muppets (puppet characters) behind or below printed

Visual Text Analysis

letters on the television screen is one of the most effective visual codes to encourage left-to-right reading.

5.3.3 Picturisation through secondary movement

Secondary movement refers to the movements made by the camera *lens* (zoom in or out); or made by the *camera head*, usually while its tripod or base remains stationary (pan left/right; tilt or crane up/down); or made by the *camera together with its base* (dolly and track in/out/left/right/around).

| secondary movement |

The zoom – a lens movement – is normally used as a transition from a long shot to a close-up shot (zoom in), or from a close-up shot to a long shot (zoom out). A series of studies (Salomon 1974:499–511; Comstock 1978:22) that investigated the relationship between television viewing and the stimulation and development of children's skills in doing cognitive tasks, showed, for example, that zoom-in lens movements (to isolate sections of artworks) increase children's abilities to undertake such tasks on their own. Zooming in/out creates a motion vector along the Z-axis, which, in addition, reinforces the illusion of depth on a two-dimensional screen.

| zooming in or out |

To *pan left* or *right* means that the camera head moves along the X-axis on a horizontal plane. This secondary movement is often used to follow the primary movement of an object or person. However, if no primary movement occurs, a horizontal pan can also be used to reveal a contrast, similarity or relation between two objects, persons or actions.

| panning left or right |

The camera head can *tilt upwards* or *downwards* (e.g. the downward tilt can be used to frame something at a level lower than the horizon). On the other hand, when using a *crane* movement, the framed shot remains at the same horizontal level of the person or object being framed. For example, while an actor proceeds to climb down a flight of stairs, a crane down means that the framed shots remain at the same horizontal level as the actor's face or body. If a tilt down is used, the camera will also follow the actor's primary movements, but will ultimately be positioned above eye level in relation to the actor.

| tilting upwards or downwards |

The *dolly* or *track* means that the camera in its entirety (on a tripod, track or some form of mounting such as on a vehicle or aircraft) changes position completely. To *dolly in* means moving the camera towards the person or event and to *dolly out* means to move away in the opposite

| dolly or track |

175

direction. Moving the camera as a whole to the left or right is also sometimes called *to crab*, whereas a *dolly track* usually signifies that the camera moves parallel to the primary movement of the actor or object. As in the case of a lens movement (zooming in/out), the dolly in/out along the Z-axis is frequently used to create or to reinforce the illusion of depth by means of a motion vector.

5.3.4 Picturisation through tertiary movement

tertiary movement

Tertiary movement is motion that is produced by means of editing techniques that are used to combine two or more individual visual shots into scenes, and two or more scenes into sequences. *Instantaneous editing* occurs while an event occurs, such as during a direct television broadcast of a soccer game or a tennis match.

post-production

In contrast, postproduction editing means that the paradigmatic selection and syntagmatic sequencing of prerecorded filmed or videotaped material occurs after the event or scene has occurred.

cut
fade in/out
dissolve

The most common editing techniques used are cut, dissolve and fade (in or out). The cut is an instantaneous transition which, to a certain extent, corresponds with the way we look at something. Our eyes blink (or cut) rather than pan when we change field or focus. The fade is generally used either at the beginning (fade in) or at the end (fade out) of a film or television programme. When used between sequences, this could signify a long transition of time or place, or could be a marker for a commercial break. Emotionally, a fade out/fade in provides a moment of relief after a climax in a preceding scene or sequence. The dissolve (also known as mixing, cross-fade and lap-dissolve) is a transition in which elements or parts of two different shots are seen simultaneously on the screen. In other words, while one image is being faded out, another is gradually faded in *before* the first one disappears from the screen. The dissolve signifies a shorter lapse of time (than a fade out/fade in) and – depending on the context – can signify the introduction of the actor's thoughts or dreams. According to Zettl (1990:296), a dissolve can 'provide continuity, follow or establish a smooth event rhythm, bridge large space and time intervals, and show structural or thematic relationships'.

special visual effects

In addition to the cut, fade and dissolve, the following are techniques not only used for editing purposes, but also to create special effects.

The *wipe*, where one image is pushed off the screen, while another moves in, is a technique that can hardly occur unnoticed. It disrupts the reader's illusion of reality because it is so obvious. Other techniques are the *focus/defocus*, where one shot ends out of focus and the next comes into focus; the *wash*, where the screen seems to ripple as if water were washing over it; and *photographic effects*, where, for example, one shot ends in smoke and the subsequent one starts in smoke or steam. All these editing techniques focus the reader's attention directly on the technique itself. Special effects, such as slow-motion visuals, can, for example, convey meanings of softness, tenderness and freedom, because just like extended dissolves, a slow-motion visual involves the reader's kinaesthetic sense (i.e. a sensation and awareness of movement). For example, South African audiences frequently see this technique used in filmic advertisements for fabric softeners and in the sensory appeal made when margarine melts into porridge or slowly runs down a mealie.

The narrative of both fictional and factional films and television programmes is largely determined by building an iconographic (visual) event by means of different combinations of individual camera shots. Zettl (1990:299–330; 2008:289–329) distinguishes between two categories of editing (in which the above editing techniques are used), namely continuity and complexity editing.

| visual narrative

Continuity editing

The structuring of the vector field, in the case of film and television, is usually bigger than the screen area. If a target object is not visible in one shot, but followed up in the next shot, the vector field has been expanded into a syntagmatic combination of shots. For example, two people look screen-right in one shot (as in Figure 5.19), which is followed by a shot of the person or target object at which they are looking.

| syntagmatic combinations

Simultaneity, as a type of montage, developed from the Hollywood film tradition where two actions are developed simultaneously and the outcome of one depends on the outcome of the other. *Montage* refers to the combination of two or more separate images, which (when combined) form a more intense whole. Simultaneity is a temporal relation, sometimes also called parallel action, that involves cross-cutting between two scenes, which supposedly take place at the same time. For example, when applied in a chase scene in television police drama, this would mean cross-cutting between the police chasing the

| montage
| parallel action

criminals and the criminals being chased. When used for purposes of *elaboration*, the syntagmatic combination of shots can either enlarge the event (e.g. a close-up shot is followed by a long shot of the same action or event) or introduce concentration on detail (e.g. a long shot is followed by a close-up shot of something that appeared in the long shot). For example, if the shot depicted in Figure 5.15 is followed by the shot depicted in Figure 5.14, this combination would illustrate the latter form of concentrated elaboration. (This combination also illustrates a metonymic, or part–whole, relation.)

As vectors can be extended over several shots to form a total image, the use of tertiary movement lends itself to creating meanings such as continuity, convergence and divergence. (See vectors in section 5.2.3.) Tertiary movement (or editing) is used to clarify and intensify the screen event, with the main purpose being to establish *continuity* (e.g. between vector fields, positions of objects or persons within and off screen and between actions). In other words, when shots are combined to *clarify* an event, the *continuity* among the selected shots is an important filmic and television convention. Such continuity can be established by manipulating a number of iconographic (visual) codes, of which the following are three examples:

- The graphic, index and motion vectors continue from one to the next shot (e.g. a long shot of a character running screen right should be shown to continue running screen right in the following medium shot).
- A cut from one shot to the next occurs during the action (not before or after) to ensure visual action continuity (e.g. a subjective shot showing a person opening a door is cut – while the door is being opened – to an objective shot of the person who knocked on the door).
- A character's appearance, lighting, colour and other codes of content are preserved from shot to shot (e.g. when the production of a film occurs over a period of time, scenery such as furniture and curtains in a room must remain the same).

Complexity editing

Complexity editing is primarily, but not exclusively, concerned with *intensifying* an event, the purpose being to convey inner emotions, conflicts and/or confusions. Montage is the main convention that is manipulated in this type of editing.

Visual Text Analysis

In the early days of silent films, *visual conjunction* was conveyed explicitly (by means of verbal titles, such as *'meanwhile'* ... or *'later'* ...), whereas today visual conjunction is realised more implicitly by means of dissolves and cuts. In film theory and film aesthetics considerable attention has been devoted to the concept of editing (or montage), notably through the theories of Eisenstein, Pudovkin, Timoshenko, Bazin and Metz (Van Leeuwen 1991:76–113). Complexity editing is based on the artistic principle of montage, by means of which the juxtaposition of two or more separate images creates a more intense whole, or Gestalt.

Three types of montage can be distinguished (Zettl 1990:318–29), depending on *how* these separate images or shots are combined. *Metric montage* is created when a series of images is combined in approximately equally spaced intervals. In so doing, a tertiary motion rhythm is created, irrespective of whether the actual shots are related to the same event, or whether they are unrelated. | metric montage

Analytical montage is created when important (structural or thematic) elements of an event are selected and combined in order to intensify the screen event, for example: | analytical montage

Shot 1	A boy runs across a road (cut)	A motion vector – from screen left to screen right
Shot 2	A car approaches (cut)	A motion vector – from screen right to screen left, which is a converging vector in relation to above left-to-right motion vector
Shot 3	The same boy lies motionless in front of the same car	The implied result of the two converging vectors having collided

The above example illustrates *sequential analytical montage*, because details of an event are presented in different shots, in a cause-and-effect order. In the above example, the essential elements of the theme (an accident) are combined in their original cause-and-effect sequence. One of the conventions that characterises sequential analytical montage is that the main event is *implied* and not explicitly shown. (In the example above, viewers do not actually see the boy being hit by the car and therefore have to apply psychological closure to fill in the missing visual information.) | sequential analytical montage

Media Studies: Volume 3

Suspense does not depend only on the story line, as the manipulation of any *encoding techniques* must also be in keeping with the *content* (unless the purpose is to create comedy or satire). For example: suspense can be created or heightened through the manipulation and combination of different *camera shots*, as illustrated below.

Syntagmatic combination of shots	Creating/heightening suspense through a combination of camera shots
Shot 1	medium-long shot of a blind girl running (cut)
Shot 2	medium-long shot of girl's killer searching for her (cut)
Shot 3	medium shot of girl hiding zoom in to a close-up shot of girl's face (SFX – sound effects – of killer approaching) (cut)
Shot 4	close-up shot of killer's face

syntagmatic combination to heighten suspense

A textual analysis of a fictional television programme often reveals patterns of *action* → *reaction* → *action* being depicted. However, the gradual and progressive increase in conflict or suspense, and the development of a story line, which is characteristic of many films, has been altered by television. Mainly due to time limitations and competition from other stations, television must capture the interest and involve the emotions of the viewers at the beginning of the programme and maintain their interest throughout. Therefore, a textual analysis of fictional programmes will often reveal instances where *only reaction* is portrayed, in the *absence* of *action*, such as discovering a corpse without having witnessed the crime. In so doing, communicators rely on the principle of psychological closure (discussed above in section 5.2.3) and assume that readers will 'fill in' the criminal action.

sectional analytical montage

In contrast to condensing the progression of an event, *sectional analytical montage* is created when isolated moments or viewpoints from one event are selected for the purpose of focusing on the quality, detail and/or complexity of the moment. For example, the political rally as an event, which is reflected in Figure 5.40, can be reconstructed into a special event by isolating and focusing on different viewpoints. The montage of three shots in Figure 5.41 illustrates how the filmic version

Visual Text Analysis

Figure 5.40 A political rally as event

of an event can contribute to the complexity of an event, depending on the viewpoints selected and combined. With reference to the analysis in the table on the next page, note how the kinesics (gestures and facial expressions) in the first two shots convey jubilation, in contrast to the facial expression in the third shot. More importantly, notice how the way in which these three shots have been combined creates conflict or disagreement that is not reflected in the original event, in Figure 5.40.

Figure 5.41 Sectional analytical montage

In addition to field forces, other visual codes also reinforce the conflict or opposition created between the first two shots and the third shot in Figure 5.41. Let us analyse volume and camera shots as two of these visual codes:

- *Volume*: the positive volume in shot 3 is more prominent (than in the other two shots) and therefore emphasises the importance of the person.
- *Camera shots*: shot 3 is framed in a medium close-up shot, which

181

Media Studies: Volume 3

brings the person and his facial expression closer to the viewer than the medium shots in shot 1 and 2, which assign importance to both the people as well as the setting or background.

syntagmatic combination and field forces

Syntagmatic combination of shots – Figure 5.41	Examples of field forces within the shot	Meanings created
Shot 1	Continuing index vectors (screen right to left)	Challenging the down-diagonal and conveying jubilation
Shot 2	Continuing index vectors (screen right to left)	Supporting and reinforcing the jubilation in shot 1
Shot 3	Diverging index vector (screen left to right)	Opposing or disagreeing with shot 1 and shot 2
	Magnetism of the frame, attracting the mass to the right	Supporting the opposition created by the diverging index vector

idea-associative montage

The third type of montage that is conventionally used in complexity editing is called 'idea-associative montage' (Zettl 1990:324). In an idea-associative montage, two images that are seemingly unrelated are combined and, by means of this combination, a third idea or meaning is created. In other words, different visual ideas are combined to create, or reinforce, a new idea. However, this combination of unrelated visuals does not occur at random. The combination is conventionally guided by two criteria, namely *comparison* and *collision*.

comparison

The juxtaposition (combination) of two visual events that are unrelated, but which do relate to the same theme can, by means of comparison, reinforce that theme or idea. Figure 5.42, for example, illustrates idea-associative montage that is based on comparison, in that the combination of a deserted building and a derelict farm reinforces the idea or theme of decay.

The (third) idea of decay is further supported by the *absence* of people in both shots; an absence of normality and calmness is suggested by the vertical aspect ratio and vertical graphic vectors in both shots. The dominance of positive volume in the shot of the building suggests a confinement of movement and makes the reader experience a restricted feeling – perhaps a restriction on life. In contrast, the shot of the farm

Visual Text Analysis

and windmill reflects spaciousness and a cloudless sky and, although it differs from the overwhelming positive volume in the other shot, the spaciousness can also promote feelings of emptiness, of being isolated and lost – perhaps of lifelessness.

Figure 5.42 Idea-associative montage based on comparison

A second criterion that is conventionally applied in idea-associative montage is based on *collision*. The dialectic principle on which this montage is based (Flew 1984:94–5; Peters 1977:14) argues that by juxtaposing a thesis (e.g. a poor condition) with an antithesis (e.g. an opposite condition), a synthesis (e.g. a new idea) can be created. When editing is based on the selection of actions and reactions to construct a story, it also fulfils a structural function. However, as indicated above, editing can also be used to establish or to convey relational meanings: montage can contrast or convey simultaneity, and construct symbolic meanings. For example, when a shot shows a starving child, followed by an image of a well-to-do man wasting food, a collision is created through negative comparison, which can create a new Gestalt symbolising social injustice.

collision

Gestalt

When considering the two shots that are collided in Figure 5.43, the dialectic principle mentioned above can be analysed and explained as follows:

183

Media Studies: Volume 3

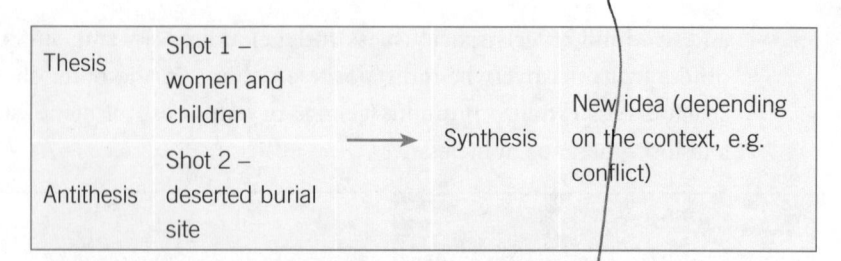

Thesis	Shot 1 – women and children	Synthesis	New idea (depending on the context, e.g. conflict)
Antithesis	Shot 2 – deserted burial site		

Figure 5.43 Idea-associative montage based on collision

The collision between these two shots becomes more meaningful if we do a text analysis with reference to the codes of content (that are dealt with above in section 5.2). In shot 1, the following are examples of codes of content that convey *life*:

- *Magnetism of the frame*: the frame attracts the people, especially on the left and right, thereby suggesting a wider setting in which other people (not seen) are present.

Visual Text Analysis

- *Figure–ground perception*: as the figures (positive volume) fill most of the frame, their presence dominates the shot.
- *Psychological closure*: the cast shadows that are projected onto the women and children signify that other people are watching the procession, and although they are not shown readers can fill in such missing visual information.
- *Index vectors*: the continuity created by everyone looking and pointing from screen left to right, suggests progress and implies movement from on-screen space to off-screen space on the right-hand side.
- *Graphic depth factors*: the overlapping of planes and cast shadows signify a three-dimensional depth and therefore a living reality.

All these codes reinforce the idea of 'life' and convey a message that these people are moving towards a particular destination with a specific purpose in mind.

In shot 2, on the other hand, the above codes have also been used, but produce meanings that contradict 'life'. Apart from the crosses in the foreground, which in Western culture symbolise death or a burial site, the following are examples of the codes of content that are presented:

- *Magnetism of the frame*: the frame does not exert any meaningful pull on the mass (crosses), thereby emphasising the isolation of the crosses from a world beyond the frame.
- *Figure–ground perception*: the background and sky (negative volume) fill most of the frame and, through this domination, contribute to an idea of emptiness.
- *Vectors*: graphic vectors that emphasise a vertical direction lead the readers' focus upward towards the emptiness of the sky.
- *Graphic depth factors*: aerial perspective is the most important graphic depth factor, which diminishes clarity as readers look into the distance.

The above codes therefore signify an absence of a future, of purpose – of life.

Having dealt with picturisation through primary, secondary and tertiary movement, in the next section we consider how auditory and audiovisual codes contribute to the construction of meaning via film and television.

5.4 AUDITORY CODES AND THE COMBINATION OF AUDIOVISUAL CODES

One of the easiest ways to experience the meanings conveyed by auditory codes is to view a television programme or a film without any sound. Whether it is a drama, the news, a documentary, sport or a children's programme, with the sound turned off the film or television programme will lack information and its essential dramatic quality will be greatly diminished.

5.4.1 Auditory codes

human voice
music
sound effects (SFX)

There are three auditory codes: the human voice, music and sound effects (SFX). Each of these codes consists of four basic elements that are manipulated to convey or elicit certain emotions or descriptive associations. The variations of these elements and their typical associations are given in Table 5.1:

Table 5.1 Examples of auditory variations and typical associations

Elements	Variations	Typical associated meanings
Pitch	high	lightness, excitement, tension, anger
	low	solemnity, depression, affection
Timbre	thin (e.g. flute)	purity
	percussion (e.g. drums)	drama, power
Volume	loud	definiteness, importance, energy, anger
	soft	weakness, calmness, tranquillity, affection
	sudden increase (fade up)	climax, impatience, suspense, aggressiveness, conflict
	sudden decrease (fade down)	defeat, lack of purpose, fear
	gradual increase (fade up)	pursuit, increased intensity, gathering strength
	gradual decrease (fade down)	reorientation, temporary defeat, casualness
Tempo	fast	excitement, instability, tension
	slow	peacefulness, stability, melancholy

Visual Text Analysis

From Table 5.1 it is clear that a particular variation of an element (e.g. loud volume) may express different descriptive associations, depending on the context and type of audiovisual text in which it is used. Timbre refers to the tone or quality of a sound, apart from its pitch, volume or tempo. When doing a text analysis, a direct relation may, therefore, be sought between the *nature* of the elements (irrespective of whether the codes used are voice, music or sound effects) and the *context* of the specific scene being analysed. For example, during a chase scene in a detective television drama, the voice, music and sound effects used will very likely have a fast tempo and a loud volume.

Human voice

Much of the research into the functions of vocal (paralanguage) variations of the human voice has been concerned with their expressive or emotive capacities. Paralanguage is also called prosodic features, such as pitch, intonation or emphasis. Tests regarding the emotional connotations attached to vocal features have found (Elam 1980:80), for example, that high pitch, moderately blaring timbre, loudness, a fast tempo and regular rhythm combine to connote 'joy'. Such research suggests that expressive or emotional connotative meanings conveyed are not arbitrary, and, when mediated, the expression of attitudes and emotions by means of paralanguage features appears to be rule-bound.

| paralanguage

Apart from manipulating the paralanguage elements of the human voice, this code is also used according to different *types of address*, namely direct address and indirect address:

| direct address
| indirect address

- *Direct address*: the communicator, via the text, addresses the readers directly by means of words such as 'you' and 'your'. Direct address is conventionally used in advertisements, political speeches, game shows and educational texts, with the purpose of involving the viewing audience by speaking to them directly.
- *Indirect address* is divided into three types of address. Dialogue takes place when two people address each other in the text. Mediated dialogue, in order to be natural, must be written to be heard (not to be read) and must characteristically consist of interruptions, and incomplete phrases and sentences. Soliloquy (also called monologue) takes place when a person or character muses to him- or herself – as if thinking out loud – and usually takes place while a character is alone. Narration refers to the delivery of verbal commentary, with

| dialogue
| soliloquy
| narration

the narrator appearing on-screen (e.g. television news) or off-screen (e.g. television commentary of a soccer game). Off-screen narration is also called voice-over commentary, during which the narrator is not seen. Verbal narration is the conventional type of address used in documentary genres, and as a convention is written for the ear (to be heard), is in the active (rather than the passive) voice, consists of short simple sentences, and does not repeat what is visually obvious to the viewer. The dialogue during a soapie, a soliloquy during a fictional film and/or the narration during a documentary programme, therefore, addresses the readers indirectly.

genre

The use of specific types of address is largely dictated by the communicator's objective and the genre. For example, in an advertisement broadcast by means of television, the primacy will alternate between the words and the visual images; hence the verbal speech and the visual action jointly assist the communicator's intention to persuade. (The combination of auditory and visual codes is further discussed below in section 5.4.2.)

Clarity of speech sounds and *economy of words* are two of the most important criteria when using the human voice – irrespective of the type of address used. In the case of dialogue, words must sound natural and spontaneous, whereas in soliloquy and narration the address is structured as a carefully planned, condensed form of the dialogue in real life.

Sound effects (SFX)

noise
literal sounds
descriptive SFX
transcodification

Sound effects (SFX) differ from noise (unwanted sounds) in that they are intentional and are used with a communicative purpose in mind. Sound effects can be produced by electronic or mechanical means and can consist of *literal* sounds that convey denotative meanings. Examples of sources of sound effects include animals (e.g. dogs barking), nature (e.g. the wind, thunder, crashing waves), artefacts created by humans (e.g. a clock ticking, the siren of an ambulance, a car crashing), an individual (e.g. coughing) or a group of people (e.g. an audience applauding).

Descriptive sound effects, on the other hand, do not have a literal meaning and include those sound effects that cannot be linked to the sound-emitting source, such as the 'boings', 'hisses' and 'bangs' that accompany cartoon characters' actions. Sound effects, as signs, are often used in a process that Elam (1980:15) calls 'transcodification', whereby one form of coded presentation is converted to another form. In other words, instead of verbalising '*I'm afraid*' in a dramatised children's programme, the message of fear can be signified by the sound of a howling wind, which in narrative terms means that sound effects can be manipulated to represent and symbolise an antagonist.

Music

Music as a communication code is often a recourse in periods of emotional stress, probably because it is simultaneously 'more nurturing of reverie and introspection, and also more emotionally stimulating' (Comstock 1978:31). From a semiotic perspective, the meaning of music is not sought on the first order of signification, or level of meaning, as a self-contained sign conveying representational meaning. When music is regarded as an iconic sign, it should exhibit the properties of the thing being represented, such as bird calls.

However, Merriam (1964:235) points out that the relation between the musical sound and that which it represents 'can only be made through ascription of meaning which is culturally defined'. As a connotative agent for the expression of moods, and other affective states, music is expressive of 'subjective rather than objective experience' (Fiske & Hartley 1978:44), within the framework of specific cultures. However, music is not only indicative of behaviour and myths in a particular culture. Through repetition via the mass-communication media, some of the symbolic meanings have become universally applicable. For example, a visual country scene recorded in England is accompanied by the sounds of African tribal drums; hence the viewers accept that the scene depicted is in fact in Africa. The latter example illustrates a musical cliché, which refers to music that is stereotypically associated with particular meanings. Other examples of such musical clichés that function as a short cut to express certain denotative information and simultaneously connote affective associations are also found in the traditional *Western* film, where the sound of a tom-tom drum signifies Native American Indians.

| musical clichés

Music can be divided into several structural elements, of which two – in addition to the elements identified in Table 5.1 above – are worthy of consideration, namely *mode* and *distinct melody*:

| mode

- *Mode*: in music, a melody can be composed in several modes, of which the major and minor modes are the best known. Modality can be described as the arrangements of eight diatonic tones (of an octave) according to certain intervals. In addition to tempo and volume, the major mode is usually equated with 'happiness', whereas the minor mode is usually associated with 'sadness'.

- *Melody*: a melody is composed of a succession of notes, for example by ascending (increasing in pitch) or by descending (going down in pitch). Any suggestion that music is the mere sum of structural elements, such as timbre, pitch, volume, tempo, mode and melody, would be erroneous. The functions that music fulfils as a communication code also depend on the objective of the message, for example the use of music in a historical documentary programme versus its use to stress the climax in a television drama. In a text analysis of advertisements, for example, the meanings conveyed could also vary, depending on whether a jingle is used (i.e. a musical tune, with or without words being sung), whether the music is readily identified with a particular brand, and whether lyrics are used to convey the message of the relevant product or service.

5.4.2 The combination of auditory and visual codes

All auditory and visual codes used to construct a screen event can be classified as 'operationalizing either *screen event density* or *viewer involvement density*' (Barbatsis & Guy 1991:73 – author's emphasis). The interrelatedness among various audiovisual codes (e.g. human voice, kinesics and aspect ratio) is well illustrated by the fact that the small screen space of television requires that action be expressed through kinesics (gestures and especially facial expressions). This is particularly relevant in television soapies, where action is constructed by means of dialogue, rather than through extensive physical movement.

Due to the 3:4 aspect ratio of a regular television screen, it is basically a medium in which close-up shots are used, as the screen is too small to convey extraneous details, which are more easily accommodated by motion picture screens (with aspect ratios that vary between 3:6 and 3:8). As a result, television advertisements frequently consist of a syntagmatic combination of close-up shots using a *predicament + solution = happiness* formula, with off-screen narration. A text analysis (Du Plooy 1981) of the use of music in South African television programmes showed that the use of music as a semiotic and structural code in documentaries differs significantly from the use of music in

Visual Text Analysis

other programmes, particularly dramas, children's programmes and situation comedies.

Furthermore, Grimes (1990:762) found that a translation process apparently occurs when television viewers confuse what they see on a television screen with what they actually hear. The two examples cited below illustrate how the *images* described in the *middle* column influenced the translated interpretation in the right-hand columns.

Auditory channel	Visual channel	Translated interpretation
Recent studies show that many people are susceptible to stress during dating. +	SHOT OF UNDERGRADUATE MEN SITTING ON A BENCH =	Recent studies show that many men are susceptible to stress during dating.
There are some groups that seem to be more successful with first dates. +	SHOT OF BLACK COUPLE WALKING HAND-IN-HAND DOWN A HALLWAY =	Blacks seem to be more successful with first dates.

Findings such as these, as well as arguments that recipients visualise the semantic content of sentences (Slack 1983:631–40), or that the imaging of words may be automatic and involuntary (Bagnara, Simion, Tagliabue & Ultima 1988:138–46), mean that when undertaking a text analysis, we should *not* treat the auditory and visual codes of film and television as two distinctive codes, but as *integrated* components of one information medium.

By way of illustrating how the auditory codes form an integral part of the visual content and form of film and television, we briefly deal with four communicative *functions* which the different auditory codes fulfill: to inform, to pace, to bridge and to create a mood.

To inform

- *Human voice*: any of the types of address is a more effective auditory code for transmitting information (than sound effects or music), be it about a locality, a place, a period, a time of day, a quality, a condition, an event or an action. The off-screen narration in a documentary, for example, gives information about the topic being presented visually, but, in addition, projects information beyond the confines of the visual images.

- *Sound effects*: sounds of heavy traffic in the city, or the cock's crow announcing a new dawn, are unseen sound effects that serve to inform readers of the locality or time of day.
- *Music*: the music that accompanies the opening and closing titles of regular television programmes informs viewers both of the commencement of their favourite programme and in fact also its nature. Compare, for example, the type of music used at the commencement of a news programme, versus a children's programme. Music is also used to fulfill a *leitmotiv* (German for 'lead' + 'motive') function, whereby the recurrence of a musical phrase is linked to a character, an event or an action, informing viewers (through a process of association) of what they can expect.

<!-- margin: leitmotiv -->

To pace

Tempo, as an element of sound, forms an integral part in the pacing function. However, when used, together with visual codes of content and form, the pacing function goes beyond the manipulation of tempo.

- *Human voice*: certain topics can be described more economically in words than visually, thus saving time. In fictional dramas, dialogue or soliloquy is often used to uncover or advance the plot, just as narration can accelerate the pace of certain sections or the whole of a documentary, game show or educational programme.
- *Sound effects*: sound effects are used more often to support than to create the pace or movement that already exists visually, such as the sounds of sirens and screeching tyres that accompany a car chase scene.
- *Music*: although every musical phrase has a certain pace (tempo) built into it, the most effective use of music as a pacer is when the text contains emotional movement (i.e. changes that are excitable, dramatic, romantic, spiritual and/or psychological). In other words, music can superimpose an emotional consistency or counterpoint, either in relation to the visual codes or to the other auditory codes used, or to a combination of both.

<!-- margin: emotional movement -->

To bridge

Any of the three auditory codes can be effectively used to link or bridge two or more visual shots or scenes, or to link other sounds into a cohesive whole. For example, music can bridge two scenes of a narrative structure, which visually represent a change of time (e.g. from morning to evening) or place (e.g. from workplace to home), so that they form a whole.

To create a mood

A mood has definite emotional connotations, such as happiness, fear, sadness, tension or shock.
- *Human voice*: dialogue can reveal the emotions that two people feel towards each other, and this type of address, just like soliloquy, can also be very expressive of emotions and internal conflicts that cannot readily be expressed visually.
- *Sound effects*: the ominous sounds of a howling wind or of dangerous animals, together with a dark scene in the woods, are examples of how sound effects can contribute to expressing the fear experienced by a young character in a children's programme.
- *Music*: as the meanings conveyed by music are not limited to the denotative meanings of words, it is used more effectively to establish, heighten, maintain or even change a mood. In the words of Stout, Leckenby and Hecker (1990:898): 'music augments pictures and colors words and can be a form of energy available through no other source'.

Although the above four functions have been dealt with separately, it is important to realise that all four functions are frequently fulfilled simultaneously. Let us take the music in a filmic advertisement for *Coca-Cola* as an example. The theme of the music and the song may be aimed primarily at identifying the product (information), but, simultaneously, the relatively fast tempo lends an energetic pace to the scenes portrayed, the visual shots are linked to form a whole and the mood created by the music intensifies an advertising slogan: *enjoy – the real thing*.

Ways in which to create an audiovisual Gestalt

From the above discussion it becomes clear that the combination of visual images and sound in film or television programmes does not imply the mere combination of separate parts. As the visual images and sounds are structured to form an audiovisual Gestalt, a text analysis will reveal that such a Gestalt – depending on the objective of the message and intended aesthetic impact – has been created in one of the following ways:

- *(V/a)*: the visuals dominate and the audio fulfils a supporting function (e.g. in a chase scene, a man runs along a deserted road and is chased by a speeding car, with fast music supporting the action).
- *(A/v)*: the audio dominates and the visuals fulfil a supporting function (e.g. a government spokesperson makes an important announcement during a news broadcast, and he is visualised by means of an MCU shot).
- *(Va/Av)*: the visuals and audio alternately dominate and support (e.g. visual images set the scene of a story by showing a couple walking in a park, together with music – *Va*; followed by a dialogue between the couple who introduce the initial conflict in the story – *Av*).
- *(V/A)*: the visuals and audio are independent of one another and yet, when combined, equally contribute to forming an audiovisual Gestalt (e.g. a slow-motion replay of a controversial moment in a cricket game, together with voice-over commentary interpreting the visual action).

Contextual variables

From the discussion and examples described above, it becomes clear that *context* plays a significant role when we ascribe meaning during a text analysis of films and television programmes. Context must be understood in two senses: firstly in terms of our different cultural roots; and secondly in terms of the immediate actualities as contained in observable content and mediated codes. In an investigation of the role of culture in the work of foreign correspondents, Starck and Villanueva (1993:27), for example, emphasise the importance of the cultural context, by concluding as follows:

> *Without a sensitive eye searching for cultural context, stories can result that convey invalid information or misguided meanings ... interpretations can be erroneous, possibly enforcing stereotypes and ethnocentrism.*

Therefore, when conducting a text analysis, meaning must be sought in terms of auditory and visual *codes in context*, or audiovisual *communication-in-use* relationships. In both film and television, the visualised setting and social space are two of the most important contextual variables. In soapies, living rooms and bedrooms are the main environments in which action takes place – as 'real' settings in which 'real-life' issues occur. The 'room', situated within the family's 'home', has become an index for everyday life. These settings, including *mise-en-scène*, reflect on the characters' social positions, almost as extensions of their lives, and function as metaphors for their personalities. The purposeful use of these settings and visual artefacts therefore contributes to conveying what Williams (1965:141) calls 'a whole way of life'.

5.5 RESEARCH

Contemporary semiotics (the science and study of the meaning of signs in auditory and visual messages) emerged from the work of two linguists, Ferdinand de Saussure (1959), a Swiss, and Charles Sanders Peirce (1931–58), an American, who concentrated on studying how words, through narrative structures, communicate meanings. Further studies of semiotics have since then also been undertaken by the American, Thomas Sebeok (1991b), the Italian, Umberto Eco (1982) and the French, Roland Barthes (1972; 1977b; 1999). The application of semiotics in research studies over the years has been diverse and varied, from the analysis of signs and symbols in theatrical performances and television advertisements to an analysis of cities as examples of social symbols. | semiotics

Past research has therefore focused on diverse issues related to the content and forms of mediated communication, and factors related to readers. For example Gerbner, Gross, Morgan and Signorielli (1980) claimed that the mass production of television messages creates dominant cultural messages that minimise differences of opinion among heavy viewers. In contrast, other researchers, such as Potter (1991) and Hoijer (1992) found that two readers can and do interpret the same mediated message in different ways. As Hoijer (1992:599) notes, readers' interpretation of the media is a dynamic interaction among 'content, structure and presentation, and the realism of social experience of the viewers'. | content and form

British cultural theorists, such as Berger (1972), Williamson (1978), Hebdige (1979) and Fiske and Hartley (1978) borrowed from the conceptual constructs provided by film studies. However they drew attention to the nature of visual symbol systems and processes of meaning construction. Visual analyses were incorporated in studies of meaning construction, ideology and representation. For example, reading images is a metaphor developed by Gombrich (1982) that made another contribution to the ontology of visual images, namely that they | meaning construction are junctures between art and the psychology of visual perception. He argued that visual texts are intertwined with cultural systems of language, and that visual communication is made possible because of the mutual support of language, which facilitates memory and interpretation. In contrast, perceptual psychologists, such as Gibson (1982), argued that visual meanings are not necessarily culturally learned, but that visual perception should be regarded as a natural, sensory, neurological and perceptual process.

The debate as to whether or not the nature of visual communication (in this instance, films) reflects attributes (codes and conventions) of the world-views, values and concerns of the cultural groups to which the filmmaker belongs, were extensively researched in the Navajo Filmmakers Project (Worth 1981). Students in Arizona produced 16-mm films, which were analysed not as records *about* their Navajo cultures, but as examples *of* Navajo culture (to determine what their vision was of their world). This research reopened the criticism of visual texts, such as film and photography, being treated as objective representations of reality.

strategies of analyses

In terms of text analyses, a fundamental objective of the structuralist theory that developed from works such as those of Barthes (1972) was to generate social movements as forms of resistance against ideology and manipulation (by the mass media). The application of Barthes's ideological semiotics tended to view the mass media as powerful and the readers as essentially passive recipients. In contrast Stuart Hall's (1977) critical reception theory ascribed a greater importance to the active reception and negotiation of readers. This was supported by Masterman's (1985) critical-reading model in England, according to which the ultimate aim of media education is not to be merely critical, but for readers to develop and apply a critical independence. Addressing the so-called cultural power of visual media, especially in advertising, Messaris (1997), for example, explored three strategies by means of which visual texts could be analysed, namely the use of iconic qualities to simulate reality, the use of images as evidence, and the use of editing and juxtaposition to construct implied propositions.

readers' active role

The active interpretation of mass-media messages also has theoretical roots in the cultural studies tradition represented by the works of, for example, Fiske (1987b) and Morley (1992). For example, instead of treating hegemony as governance through economic and/or political powers, Hall (1982), as director of the Centre for Contemporary Cultural Studies, at the University of Birmingham, treated hegemony as a discourse of meanings, whereby readers' interpretations could represent a range of preferred, negotiated or oppositional readings. Fiske (1987b:108–27) in the United States also emphasised the active role of readers in text analyses. Accordingly, the increased use of open-ended narrative in television, plus the polisemy of texts (irony, metaphor, incongruity, hyperbole) invite alternative interpretations of texts.

5.6 FUTURE DEVELOPMENTS

Future research would have to acknowledge that sophisticated readers will recognise that the people, artefacts, and events in visual texts, such as a films, are there, at least in part, because the communicator included them intentionally; that the sequence of events in the texts has been structured by the communicator's intention to say something by arranging them in that order (which may differ from the order in which they occurred in reality); and that the overall structure of texts reflects the use of established and new conventions to communicate to readers who are capable of drawing the appropriate inferences. For example, from a genre perspective, each category of media content has to meet the requirements of contractual agreements with industry, and simultaneously meet the readers' needs, expectations and understandings of conventions.

communicators and readers: two sides of the same coin?

However, and with specific reference to the distinction between form and content made in this chapter, one can expect that a direct correlation between developments in the internet and mobile technology, plus the acceptance and use thereof across all market segments in southern Africa will prompt new research enquiries. Visual codes as systems of references, signs and symbols will in future have to be studied as to how and in what contexts they change. The idea of mediated content will have to include analyses as to how messages are produced to tie in with the limitations and expressive possibilities of each medium. New platforms have been created by means of the internet (weblogs and wikis, net news and citizen reporting) that not only create new forms of public spheres, but also increase the number of people whose roles are changing from readers to communicators. In addition, more readers turn to the internet to view videos, films and television programmes, as well as

new technologies provoke new research

online and social networks, such as MySpace, Facebook and YouTube. South Africa's switchover from analogue to digital broadcasting not only makes provision for different language groups and regions but also for more channels, which translates into new content. The introduction of media platforms, such as Internet Protocol Television (IPTV), will revolutionise how, when and what television viewers will watch via their cellphones and computers. These changes in mediated communication and developments in the application of computers and communications technology suggest that future research involving text analysis will require new frames of reference.

Future data collection methods are also challenged to contribute to the development of awareness that different readers do give different interpretations of messages, especially in a culturally diverse country such as South Africa, and that such research techniques should ideally also promote readers' self-reflection. Examples of interview items that address the latter would be: *what do you like most when looking at a particular advertisement on your cellphone; and why?* The production of the same message in different media, changing the endings (climax resolution, denouement and catharsis) of films or television dramas, or producing advertisements in the form of digital texts, are all examples of how future text analyses can be extended to accommodate new forms of visual communication. How to produce a message using different media platforms would therefore be an ideal if incorporated as an integral part of future text research studies. The challenge that still faces visual communication scholars, according to Griffin (2001:455) is 'to clarify the processes of viewer reception and interpretation, and to analyze the social and cultural ramifications of the peculiar properties of the visual in contemporary media'. Future research would therefore have to investigate not only *how* visual images are produced by means of digital technologies, but also *for what purposes* such productions are used.

5.7 CASE STUDY

The photograph in Figure 5.40 is a shot taken during a political rally, and it is hypothetically assumed to be broadcast during a television news broadcast. The qualitative content analysis below is based on the signs and codes discussed in section 5.2 in this chapter.

The analysis is directed by three research questions, namely:
- Which visual signs and codes are used?

Visual Text Analysis

- How are these signs/codes used?
- What meaning(s) is/are produced?

Key to abbreviations used in the analysis:

A	=	4 people on the left
B	=	3 people on the right
L-H	=	left-hand side
R-H	=	right-hand side
3-D	=	three dimensional
F	=	Figure
G	=	Ground
Pos	=	Positive
Neg	=	Negative

Analytical scheme

Visual codes	How the code(s) is/are used in the shot	The meaning(s) produced
Lighting	Notan	A natural outside scene; neutrality and objectivity
Colour (or absence of colour)	Black-and-white (no colour)	Creates a documentary tone
Field forces:		
• Main directions	• Vertical (Y-axis) created by bodies, arms and tent (graphic vectors)	• High energy; power
• Magnetism of the frame and attraction of mass	• Magnetic pull at L-H and R-H	• Pulls A and B in opposite directions
• Asymmetry of the shot	• A challenges the down-diagonal B follows down-diagonal	• Strength, courage, jubilation B opposes, disagrees with A
• Figure–ground perception	• F = people G = tent	• The focus is on the group of people

Media Studies: Volume 3

Visual codes	How the code(s) is/are used in the shot	The meaning(s) produced
Psychological closure	• Missing detail: A and B's bodies; people outside of shot; rosettes represent political party	• Missing visual information filled in: peoples' bodies; crowd outside of shot; politician addressing meeting
Vectors	• Continuing index vectors A: R to L; B: L to R	• Draws attention outside of frame
	• Combined: diverging index vectors	• Contributes to asymmetry; disagreement
	• Graphic: tent lines; vertical poles	• Heightened excitement
Balance	Stabile	Stability; dependability
Depth and volume:		
• Volume duality	• Pos volume: people Neg space: tent	• Group is more important than background; 3-D depth
• Graphic depth factors	• Overlapping of planes; relative size of figures; height in plane; linear perspective	• 3-D depth
Lenses and focus	Normal lens position; normal focus	A realistic situation
Area orientation:		
• Aspect ratio	• Horizontal (3:4)	• To accommodate group; 3:4 = TV
• Size of the object(s)	• Normal sizes of human bodies; and tent	• Neutrality; normality
Camera shot	Medium shot	Shows facial expressions; looking room and places A & B in a setting (gathering of people in a tent)
Camera viewpoint	Objective camera shot; on eye-level position	Reader becomes a passive onlooker; implies neutrality; objectivity

Summary of main findings

icon

denotative meaning

connotative meaning

The iconic signs used (denotative level of meanings), are found in the direct resemblance between the content of the photograph and the people's faces and bodies, their clothing and rosettes. Formal clothing (connotative level of meaning) is an indexical sign of the serious nature of the meeting; clothing also makes this photograph 'dated' to the 1980s and represents conservatism, because people in the 21st century do not dress in this manner when attending a political rally.

indexical signs

Of greater importance are the different meanings conveyed by their facial expressions, together with the different index vectors – as indexical signs. Read sections 5.2.3 and 5.3.4 above for an analysis of continuing versus diverging index vectors, applicable specifically to this photograph. The emotions reflected by the man on the right can also be interpreted as being serious and pensive, which contrasts with the facial and bodily postures of jubilation by the rest of the group.

Taken collectively, the above signs represent a metonymic code, and in instances where the reader has to apply psychological closure to complete the visual image, such as a larger crowd and political speaker(s) outside of the frame, it is an example of synecdoche. (Synecdoche applies when a part is used to represent the whole, or vice versa.) A metonym is used when the intended meaning is substituted by an attribute, such as when a physical object signifies abstract concepts. The rosettes worn by the people are not only metonymic codes for the identification of a political party, but can extend to more abstract notions of the democracy, freedom of speech and party politics.

synecdoche

metonymy

The meanings produced by the symbolic signs will depend on the reader's social and cultural past. Nevertheless, a number of symbols can be distinguished; by regarding them as analogic codes, the reader makes mental comparisons to reach the meanings produced. In other words, each symbol individually and in combination is treated as a metaphor, as each symbolically *stands for something else*:

metaphors

- white shirts and dark jackets – symbols of formality and propriety;
- ties – essentially male articles of attire, symbolising bondage, submission to an institution – in this instance, a political party – and the idea of allegiance;
- rosettes – symbols for a political party and commitment to that party;
- V-sign – symbolic sign to denote 'victory'.

If one combines the above signs, codes and meanings, one can conclude that a condensed code has been created that addresses one central message, namely that these people support this political party, which will triumph.

condensed code

SUMMARY AND CONCLUSION

This chapter has dealt with audiovisual codes (of content and form) in terms of the conceptual aspects of production, with the primary focus on their meaning construction when conducting a text analysis. Pictorial codes in a static film shot and photograph were analysed, including lighting, colour, field forces, balance, depth and volume, area orientation, lenses and focus, basic camera shots and camera viewpoint. This discussion was extended to the visual codes that apply to television and filmic messages, with the emphasis placed on movement (primary, secondary and tertiary), as well as the human voice, types of address, sound effects and music as auditory codes. In addition to picturisation through movement in film and television, this chapter ended with a discussion of how auditory codes and the combination of audiovisual codes can be manipulated to create particular meanings.

An argument that recurs throughout this chapter is that the meanings readers ascribe to audiovisual signs and symbols can change, depending on the context and culture in which communication takes place. A central tenet is that a semiotic analysis of texts can reveal multi-dimensional and different levels of meanings. Therefore, although scholars look for signs and codes that represent immanent systems of meanings as objective qualities of a text, metonyms and metaphors point to double meanings and hidden messages that require *reading between the lines*.

LEARNING ACTIVITIES

If studying in a group, involve a fellow-scholar as co-analyst and report on the extent and why your text analyses in the learning activities below corresponded and/or differed.

1. Research question: How are visual codes used to produce and influence particular meaning(s) presented?

    Access a recording of a film or television programme and conduct a text analysis of an extract of at least one sequence, by following this procedure:
    - refer to and use the headings and subheadings in sections 5.2–5.3 as an analytical scheme;
    - identify the use of these codes in your analytical scheme in the sampled extract;
    - describe in approximately eight pages how these codes were used to produce and influence the meaning(s) presented.

2. Research question: How are the codes of content and of form used in visual reportage?

    Select a press photograph and do a text analysis by distinguishing between codes of content and code of form, as discussed in this chapter. Describe whether these codes were manipulated to clarify the visual information and/or to intensify the thematic or emotional meanings of the news topic (people, event) that is presented.

3   Research questions: Which communicative functions are fulfilled by the auditory codes in a television newscast or advertisement? How are the visual shots, scenes and/or sequences combined with auditory codes to produce an audiovisual Gestalt?

Record a television newscast or television advertisement. Analyse the types of address (human voice), sound effects and music in relation to the visual shots, scenes and/or sequences.

4   Research question: How are visual images used in the exposition of a specific television genre, such as sitcoms?

Exposition, development and resolution form the basic narrative structure in filmic and fictional television series and serials. Explore and answer the above research question by viewing a specific sitcom over a period of two or three weeks and describe how visual images are used: to establish the locality; convey the era and time (time period, seasonal time, the occasion, time of day); give a historical reminder of the main characters (e.g. hero, heroine or villain); draw attention to the cause and/or nature of underlying conflict; reintroduce one of the themes or subplots; highlight an event from a previous episode; remind viewers of a subplot; and/or focus on the essence of an unresolved conflict in a previous episode.

FURTHER READING

Burnett, R. 2004. *How images think*. Cambridge, Mass: MIT Press.

Gripsrud, J. 2006. Semiotics: Signs, codes and cultures, in: *Analysing media texts*, edited by M. Gillespie & J. Toynbee. Berkshire: Open University Press, 9–41.

Lester, P.M. 1995 (or later edition). *Visual communication: Images with messages*. Belmont, Calif: Wadsworth.

Messaris, P. 1994. *Visual 'literacy'. Image, mind and reality*. Boulder, Colorado: Westview.

Metallinos, N. 1996. *Television aesthetics*. Mahwah, New Jersey: Lawrence Erlbaum

Zettl, H. 1998. Contextual media aesthetics as the basis for media literacy. *Journal of Communication* 48(1):81–95.

Zettl, H. 2008. *Sight, sound, motion: Applied media aesthetics*. 5th edition. Belmont, Calif: Thomson Wadsworth.

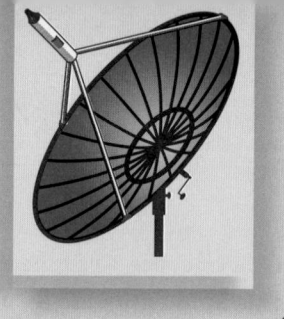

chapter six

TEXTUAL ANALYSIS: NARRATIVE AND ARGUMENT

Jeanne Prinsloo

LEARNING OUTCOMES

At the end of this chapter, you should be able to:
- explain what is meant by discourse and ideology;
- identify the central difference between a discursive and an ideological approach;
- discuss media texts in terms of their mediating and rhetorical roles;
- outline the narrative theories of Propp, Todorov and Lévi-Strauss and describe their value for critical analysis;
- outline the approach to argumentation informed by Aristotelian ideas;
- apply the theories around narrative and argument to both fiction and non-fiction texts in order to establish their discursive work;
- undertake textual analysis that views the text holistically as a mediating act.

Textual analysis: Narrative and Argument

THIS CHAPTER

This chapter is concerned with the analysis of media texts. Media studies is centrally concerned with understanding the complex relationship between the media and society, and media scholars have considered the three areas of production, text and audience as central to the field of study. While this remains the case, they now generally recognise that, firstly, these three areas always need be understood in relation to their contexts; and, secondly, they are not discrete areas but complex and interconnected. Each impacts on the other and they operate rather as a circuit. Production, text and audience are 'moments' within what was described as a 'circuit of culture' (Johnson 1986). Underpinned by this understanding, this chapter focuses on the crucial moment of 'text' and textual analysis.

The idea of media texts as mediations informs this chapter: the world we inhabit is constantly mediated and the media play a central and critical role in this process. Every media text or programme we encounter is made by someone or some group for other people and they mediate their social, political and cultural contexts, while the decision processes of selections and constructions are largely obscured and invisible. In other words, they make selections about what to include and how to construct the text within their specific context, and in so doing they *mediate* the events and ideas. Media scholars frequently refer to this process as 'representation' (Hall 1997). If you think of how any single event or story could be represented, it becomes clear that the possibilities are almost endless. Faced with a diversity of media texts it is necessary to develop approaches and strategies for textual analysis or, in other words, for analysing these mediations.

Two forms of analysis have become associated with media studies, and it is important that these analytic approaches and strategies should not be seen as working in isolation. Used together, they can enable and enrich the analyses you undertake. The one tends to focus on the minutiae of linguistic, visual and other kinds of textual detail, and is informed by semiotics in the first instance and more recently by critical linguistics (or critical discourse analysis). Semiotics is dealt with in Chapter 2. The other focuses on the text more broadly and sets out to understand the workings of the text as a whole.

This chapter sets out to develop analytic approaches to texts that are

Media Studies: Volume 3

useful for looking at the texts holistically and in terms of their discursive work.

The most important topics dealt with in this chapter are:
- the discursive nature of texts;
- discourse/discursive versus ideology/ideological;
- two forms of textual organisation: narrative and argument;
- narrative theories – syntagmatic approaches;
- Lévi-Strauss's paradigmatic contribution and binary oppositions;
- argumentation – forms of arguments and their modes;
- textual analysis using narrative and argument;

6.1 INTRODUCTION

What do texts do, or to start with, what do they not do? Texts, whether they are fiction or non-fiction, do not reflect the world or the 'real' in any kind of mechanistic way. They do, in contrast, produce particular versions of the world. Media texts need to be recognised as deliberate actions – they are the products of processes of selection and construction. To put this differently, media texts engage in discursive or ideological work; they mediate the realm of events, ideas and feelings and they frame events in relation to social contexts.

6.2 DISCOURSE AND IDEOLOGY

The previous statement introduces the idea of discursive and ideological effects. This chapter makes reference to discourse rather than ideology. Therefore, before discussing media textual analysis further, it is important to clarify what is meant here by discourse and ideology. Both are terms that have been employed to consider and problematise unequal power relations in society. Although at times they might even be used as though they are interchangeable, they emerge within different intellectual paradigms and offer different approaches. They also have different meanings depending on the field or discipline in which they are used.

6.2.1 Discourse

discourse
discursive work

What is meant here by *discourse* and *discursive* work is informed by Foucault's concept of discourse. This understanding of discourse is broader than the linguistic definition of discourse as a string of words,

Textual analysis: Narrative and Argument

groups of signs or text. Rather, texts provide us with instances where discourses are articulated. 'Discourse' refers not only to text and signs (as linguists have it) but also a multitude of institutions (for example, law, medicine, education, prisons) and practices in which particular knowledge is produced.

In the first instance, a discourse sets up parameters of what are permissible statements about a particular topic and thus it also defines what counts as appropriate forms of behaviour in relation to that discourse. It regulates both what can and cannot be said and done in relation to that field by proposing what counts as 'truth'. This can be illustrated by the following examples. Consider how people who have been stressed and experienced severe insomnia might seek help to deal with this problem. If one consulted an African healer, the treatment might include reference to ancestors accompanied by recourse to certain rituals of appeasement and be consistent with (African) traditional medical discourse. Such beliefs and behaviours are outside of Western medical discourse, which has its own set of knowledge and practices that are permissible, and it is possible that the prescribed treatment would include tranquilisers and sleeping pills. These two discourses draw on different sets of 'truth'. In the same way patriarchy as a discourse also has its knowledge that counts as 'truth'. Its initial premise is that biological sex differences result in different and unequal capacities for women and men. These differences are understood as essential or natural and, therefore, the idea of gender differences being the result of social or cultural processes is rejected as false. This concept of discourse includes not only ideas but the range of social practices that reinforce those ideas as knowledge and 'truth'.

This idea of discourse is concerned with knowledge (or what counts as 'truth' in a particular period and space) and power. This power works in such a way that it produces particular kinds of subjects who identify with this positioning. It achieves its status as truth through a range of strategies that legitimate it. Patriarchal discourse is legitimated by selective recourse to particular sets of ideas (including biological determinism) and it depends on a range of institutional and cultural practices for it to be enacted. It serves as 'truth' for the subjects, both female and male, who are constructed not merely as different but in a relationship of unequal status and power. This 'truth' then justifies ways of organising social life along gender lines, and the institutions of the family, religion, education, the judiciary and a host of others engage in this discursive work as well. The discursive power is evident in its effects – these different and unequal ways of being become understood as natural. One can understand this more fully by applying it to other sets of knowledges and circumstances. Consider how a racist discourse underpinned and legitimated unequal power relations and access to resources during apartheid South Africa with reference to both social Darwinism and selected biblical quotes and interpretations. They were enacted through producing subjects for whom these ideas constituted 'truth' and not prejudice.

Think about the people or occupations below as constituted in different orders of discourse and answer the questions in relation to each one of them. This will give you a sense of what counts as knowledge/truth and what practices bestow authority in that discursive order. In each case ask who is made 'powerful' by the language. How? Who is made powerless?

Rabbi, Tibetan monk or Catholic priest

Who speaks with authority?	To whom?	About what?	Where?	What is the authority derived from?	What topics would be excluded?

Traditional healer, physiotherapist, heart surgeon

Who speaks with authority?	To whom?	About what?	Where?	What is the authority derived from?	What topics would be excluded?

Banker or environmental activist

Who speaks with authority?	To whom?	About what?	Where?	What is the authority derived from?	What topics would be excluded?

Importantly, no discourse exists in isolation, for while a discourse may be dominant or hegemonic, there is always an opposing one in circulation. Certainly the South African constitution, with its authoritative and powerful assertions around gender equality, presents an opposing discourse to patriarchy and acts as a powerful counter to sexist ideas and practices. It contests the (arguably) dominant patriarchal discourse. When it comes to media texts in which particular events and ideas are mediated, for example around a high profile rape trial, either the discourses of gender equality or patriarchy might be articulated and priviledged within the media texts. Such media texts go beyond merely recounting events, for they carry out discursive work. They seek to position readers through the choices they make. Decisions are made about what content to include and how to organise it. In this way, media texts reinforce a particular discourse and sometimes explicitly counter another contesting discourse.

6.2.2 Ideology

Similarly, notions of ideology are concerned with power relations. The meanings attributed to ideology have varied over time and have been widely debated. Here, reference is made to Thompson's critical conceptualisation of ideology (1990), for it is has been influential and is frequently cited in the field of critical media studies. He discusses ideology in relation to the roles the media might play in the age of modernity or 'the way in which symbolic forms [media texts] intersect with relations of power' (1990:56). He identifies his conception of ideology as 'critical' rather than neutral because he wishes to retain the negative sense of ideology as relating to domination. (Thompson's discussion of ideology (1990) presents a history of the different approaches, and in doing this he differentiates between neutral and critical conceptions. A *neutral* conception views ideologies as circulating in society in a relationship of relativity rather than being judged as good or bad. In contrast a *negative* sense of ideology is driven by a concern for unequal power relations in society, or, in other words, social justice. It therefore foregrounds how unequal power relations are naturalised and sustained.)

> ideology

Thompson understands domination as referring to those circumstances in which established relations of power are unequal or 'systematically asymmetrical' and 'when particular agents or groups are endowed with power in a durable way which excludes, and to some significant degree remains inaccessible to, other agents or groups of agents, irrespective of the basis upon which such exclusion is carried out' (1990:59). The impulse for his study of the media therefore is 'ideological' and such ideological analysis focuses on 'the ways in which meaning serves to establish and sustain relations of domination' (1990:56). It should be clear from his emphasis that his concern is within a broader project concerned with social justice.

The value of Thompson's formulation is his insistence on the ideological work achieved by texts and his identification of a range of modes through which these work, which are not outlined here. Importantly, Thompson does not limit his conception of ideology to unequal class relations, which has been the concern of many Marxist or critical thinkers. He includes other relations of domination or inequality, such as race and gender. However, because he limits ideology to referring to dominant relations of power only, he does not consider positions that contest dominant power as ideological. Thus feminism is seen as outside of ideology because it attempts to counter domination and is viewed simply as 'incipient forms of the critique of ideology' (1990:68). On the same terms, socialism rather than capitalism, environmentalism rather than industrialism or revolutionary political movements rather than ruling party beliefs would be deemed outside of ideology.

Circumstances in the 21st century are marked by uncertainty and strongly contesting positions and ideas. Significant historical shifts have resulted in previously widely held views being challenged and, as a result, different sets of ideas, beliefs and attitudes jostle and contest with each other. The understanding of ideology as presented here does not adequately allow for complex social contexts that are characterised by a high degree of inconsistency of ideas and values and where it is difficult to be clear which position is dominant. It also does not address situations where formerly dominant ideas and practices have been partially or largely usurped but continue to operate.

The position taken in this chapter is that this notion of ideology is less productive than Foucault's ideas about discourse for dealing with textual analysis. The concept of discourse does provide an explanation for contesting positions and it is employed in this chapter because textual analysis needs to engage with competing sets of representation and account for the choices made.

Arguments and stories produced within media texts are relayed from different positions and are part of the ongoing contestation between societal discourses. One need think only of South Africa and the contested positions about where power does and should lie, about what

Textual analysis: Narrative and Argument

it is to be 'African', and the kinds of power relations and identities that are proposed in these debates. It is not suggested here that the discourses that circulate in society are merely equal and therefore relative. They engage in work to produce 'truth' and power, as Foucault suggested. Particular discourses in circulation do not merely entertain their audiences but propose ways of being in the world that are not merely benign. They have *mediating* and persuasive functions, and they work to maintain and legitimate dominant power and to contest it.

While the language used in this chapter refers to discourse and the discursive, the theories and strategies for textual analysis presented are relevant to the analysis of media texts, whether through the lens of ideology or discourse.

6.3 MEDIA TEXTS: MEDIATION AND RHETORIC

The word 'text' itself has its roots in Latin (the verb *tego*, with its past participle *textum*) and refers to weaving. If a text is viewed as a weaving or a tapestry it can be examined in terms of the strands that make it up: it is a complex weaving of the warp and the weft of ideas and discourses expressed in languages, whether print, visual, audio and/or moving, and is a result of the selections made in producing the weaving. Some strands have their roots in distant times and places. Racist discourses certainly draw threads from social Darwinism, the discourses of childhood as innocence that we encounter in so many advertisements are informed by Rousseau's Enlightenment construct of childhood, and so on. Texts also respond to other texts. They can draw on them intertextually and they can introduce them in order to counter them. A media text needs to be examined in terms of how it weaves these strands. It needs to be analysed as a social act that mediates the substance of the text, and is therefore also a rhetorical act.

mediation

rhetoric

Rhetoric is essentially an attempt at persuasion, and this is undertaken through the choices made in producing the text. The particular choices made to construct a text draw on the various social patterns or social orders of their time and place. These would include the institutional context of their production and reception. The choices both presuppose or assume the discourses at play in society and respond to them. They are acts of mediation. The social space in which texts are received is also at any time marked by social hierarchies. There are always those who have and those who have not (and the wealth, or 'capital' in Bourdieu's terms (1984), can be material, social or cultural); there are those who have authority and those who do not; and those who are in and those who are out. These hierarchies are of course fluid and contested. Texts play their role in mediating social actions in relation to inequalities. Media texts invite what Burke refers to as 'congregation' or 'segregation' (in Stillar 1998:59). The reader is invited to, symbolically, enter the inner sanctum of belonging by sharing the ideas and their orientation. The text is the product of a range of semiotic decisions that act to position the reader. It invites the reader to adopt one position and, at least implicitly, reject another.

When we analyse texts as rhetorical acts we are seeking to identify how the world of experience is constructed and orientated or positioned – for texts actively mediate and interpret the worlds of which they 'speak'. They propose and validate a way of knowing and being in the social spaces they and the readers inhabit. We therefore look at the patterns of selections and combinations of the various semiotic resources that are presented in the text. We are not looking for hidden meanings – we look at the text as 'a record of a series of social acts' (Stillar 1998:118).

When we look at these patterns of selections it is crucial that we engage with the textual detail and do not make judgments for which we can muster no compelling textual evidence. There is a tendency for some analyses to find what they are looking for, or to spot the stereotype regardless, and this must be avoided. This approach has been critiqued, for example by van Zoonen (1994). A text is not, for example, sexist or racist merely because it presents a black woman in a domestic space. One needs to probe what discourses are at play in that context and what position the reader is being invited to adopt.

6.3.1 Organisation of media texts

The approach presented here is unusual in one way. Unlike most textbooks, which address either narrative or argument, it includes narrative and argument and views them as interconnected. Narratives recount events with the purpose of influencing emotional, rational, aesthetic and other reactions. Arguments similarly seek to persuade the audience of their positioning through emotional, logical and ethical lines of reasoning that draw on narratival structures in the process.

Textual analysis: Narrative and Argument

These two forms of textual organisation, that is *narrative* and *argument*, are outlined to enable holistic analysis of media texts. These can be understood as the two major meta-genres that both producers and receivers employ to make sense of the world. Like language itself, we constantly use these sense-making mechanisms and they are so inherently and implicitly part of our ways of being that they seem to be there 'like life itself'. As they are the 'mechanics of mediation', by making their workings explicit we can consider how they, in Silverstone's words, seek to 'persuade, please and seduce us' (1999:30). Narrative has long been held to be part of the canon of media studies and is outlined in textbooks along with genre and semiotics in relation to textual analysis. However, the addition of argument is more recent and introduced by media theorists Roger Silverstone (1999) and John Richardson (2007).

narrative

argument

The analytic approaches introduced relate to all kinds of media texts, whether they are factual or fictional, although these two categories might seem to be un-alike and of a very different order. What they have in common is their role as mediation. Factual texts like news or documentaries set out to represent and interpret the events and circumstances that exist in the material world; they represent and mediate these events. In spite of the protestations by some journalists about their objectivity and truth claims, in Zelizer's words, they are 'an entanglement of narrative, authority, and rhetorical legitimation' (Zelizer 1993:191). Fictional texts similarly offer us numerous scenarios of people encountering and negotiating life. They also act as interpreters or guides, with scripts that tell us what counts as normal or good or bad. For this reason we are able to, and need to, ask the same set of broad questions for both kinds of media:

- What sense is being made of the event (or world) in a particular text or set of texts?
- How has the event or set of ideas been represented or mediated?
- What has been omitted in this instance?
- And, crucially, what is the political work of the text in relation to identity and power relations?

Why narrative?

The significance of narrative or story in the lives of all people has frequently been related to thinking and communication processes.

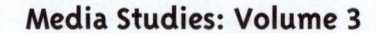

Humans have been described as 'storytelling animals' (Watson 2003:150). Narrative has also been identified, along with language, as the way we make sense of the world. British cultural and media studies theorist John Fiske wrote, 'Like language, narrative is a basic way of making sense of our experience of the real' (1987:128). In this way he acknowledges it as having particular significance in both thought and communication. It has also been described as essential to cognition and thought processes and so used to 'weigh events and interpret our lives' (Bruner 1986). Richard Bauman, author of *Story, Performance and Event*, sees narrative as one of the basic social practices used in social life: 'people telling stories to each other as a means of giving cognitive and emotional coherence to experience, constructing and negotiating social identity … investing the experiential landscape with moral significance' (1986:113).

If these ideas seem abstract, it is useful to illustrate them with your own experiences. Consider Bauman's statement above in relation to the kinds of personal narratives you tell to people you know. Think about how, when you meet with a friend or two, you interact with them; think about how you soon tell each other stories (both good and bad) of what has happened recently, or perhaps they are updates or instalments of stories. They might be premised with statements such as, 'Oh, I must tell you what happened' or 'Did you hear about …?' or 'So what has happened about (or to) … since we spoke last?' In this way you narrate and update your stories and so make sense of and judge your experiences. You seek to achieve the 'cognitive or emotional coherence' in relation to those experiences as Bauman suggests above.

In addition, the universality of narrative has been emphasised. It is recognised as crossing all social and cultural divides. The French theorist Roland Barthes describes narrative as follows: 'Like life itself, it is there, international, transhistorical, transcultural' (Barthes 1977:79). It is there, too, in the media texts we encounter.

6.4 STRUCTURALIST APPROACHES

structuralism

Structuralist theories were developed in order to make visible or expose the ideological or discursive character (the implicit power dimensions) of all social and cultural constructs. The narrative theories presented here can be described as structuralist because they were an attempt to identify and give an account of the laws that govern narrative structure. Early structuralists sought to identify a universal narrative structure,

Textual analysis: Narrative and Argument

and, while this intellectual phase has given over to and informed subsequent poststructural thought, the earlier work done on narrative has produced useful basic insights. Structuralism has, according to Fiske (1987:131), 'shown us that narratives have much in common and need to be studied in terms of their relationship to others'.

Structuralist approaches to narrative include both syntagmatic and paradigmatic approaches. The syntagmatic type of analysis identifies and describes the structure of the formal organisation of the text following the chronological order or the linear sequence of the narrative events. Todorov and Propp's models are examples of syntagmatic analysis. A paradigmatic type of analysis seeks to identify the deeper, latent patterns or organisations which underpin the story. Lévi-Strauss, with his concept of myth working through binary oppositions, is the principal theorist in this regard. Because syntagmatic and paradigmatic analyses are of a different order, in combination they enable deeper and more productive analysis of media texts. In the first instance they help us look at how they are structured. Using this understanding we can then consider the position the text has privileged or refuted and its relationship to other texts. In other words, we can examine its cultural and political work. The focus then is not on the judging the uniqueness of a single text as might be the intention of many literary studies, but on identifying its choices in organising the text, and so to consider the nature of the politics of mediation.

6.4.1 Syntagmatic theories

What actually is a narrative? How would you define narrative? Many people answer these questions by saying that it consists of a sequence of things that happen, while others say it has a beginning, a middle and an end. These definitions pick up on a significant characteristic of the syntagmatic dimension: in a narrative we encounter a chain of events. There are three characteristics of narrative that the syntagmatic dimension introduces. Firstly, narrative is characterised by its economy. Not all the events that occur during the time span that the narrative covers are included. Rather, the narrating of the story leaves out all the detail that is not relevant to moving the plot forward at some stage of the narrative. The material that is included is necessary either for comprehensibility of the story or to develop suspense and intrigue on the part of the audience. All other incidental details are ignored and

narrative

omitted. It is this tightly structured product that is addressed through structural approaches to narrative.

Secondly, the events are linked together causally so as to make their relationship meaningful rather than random. Film theorists Bordwell and Thompson (1986:83) define narrative as 'a chain of events in a cause–effect relationship occurring in time and space'. This relationship of causality links together selected events over a period of time in a way that makes each event of consequence in the overall plot. As Fiske (1987:129) suggests:

> *This refusal of randomness creates consequence out of sequence and in so doing provides the means of understanding that most elusive dimension – time.*

The third characteristic is linked to the second. While a narrative does consist of a chain of events, the narrating or telling of the narrative does not necessarily follow a chronological order. In fact many genres rely on withholding information about what occurred first until the end of the narrative. Crime fiction narratives in particular begin with a crime, while the events that occurred before the crime are only released gradually and the actual perpetrator is usually only revealed at the close of the story. In contrast, other genres follow the chronology of events faithfully – for example, the musical. We thus distinguish between the story and the plot, or the narrative and how it is narrated.

The *story* consists of all the events in a narrative, including those events actually presented and those you must infer. This might, for example, include inferring intimacy, as suggested by a passionate embrace before the movie scene fades to the next morning; or the scenario where a person packs a gun and follows another person, and then the corpse of the person who was followed is presented. (The audience have to engage and make meaning across the gaps.)

The *plot* is everything presented before us, or in other words, those selected moments of the story ordered and put before us so that we gradually piece together the story. The plot might present us with an enigma and gradually feed us information so we make sense by following the plot.

This idea of a chain of events introduces the syntagmatic element of narrative. A number of theorists have concerned themselves with the

Textual analysis: Narrative and Argument

flow of narrative or the syntagmatic dimension. Two of these, namely Todorov and Propp, are outlined here. (Other syntagmatic approaches have been taken up in different fields of study – for example, Barthes in literary analysis and Labov in sociolinguistics.)

Todorov

While a narrative can be identified as having a beginning, middle and an end, Tzvetan Todorov – a Bulgarian-born philosopher who has lived and worked in France since the 1960s – offers a more explicit model. He has engaged with literary and cultural theory and, in his work on narrative, developed a narrative model that offers a good point of entry into the task of textual analysis.

Todorov describes narrative as a causal transformation through five stages:

1. a state of equilibrium at the outset;
2. a disruption of the equilibrium by some action;
3. a recognition of that disruption;
4. an attempt to repair the disruption;
5. a restoration of the equilibrium.

> narrative stages

He describes the first stage of the model as a point of equilibrium. It constitutes and implies harmony or order. This state is then usually disrupted fairly early in the process (stage 2) as the result of some action, and this action can be on the part of another person, group of people, a creature (such as the shark in *Jaws*) or even a natural phenomenon (such as a tsunami or other natural disaster). The course of the narrative is then caught up with the attempt to set right the disequilibrium or deal with the disruption and its effects. This is dependent on there being a recognition that the disruption has occurred (stage 3), and a consequent action or set of actions (stage 4) – a quest, in other words, to address the disequilibrium. By stage 5, or the conclusion of the narrative, this disequilibrium has been rectified and there is restoration of a new state of equilibrium. Importantly, this second state of equilibrium is never identical to the initial equilibrium. Rather it is an altered or transformed state.

> equilibrium

If you apply this model to an example that relates to your own experience, it will become more obvious. Consider the following personal narrative and then construct your own scenario. Remember, to apply Todorov's model it is necessary to first put the events in chronological order if they have not been narrated in that order.

It's early on Monday morning when I wake up. I lie in bed until the alarm goes, running over in my mind what I'm going to do and how I need to get to the airport/taxi rank on time. The alarm rings and I leap up sharply. I shower, get dressed, and all is going well, that is, until I get to the kitchen. What, no coffee? I meant to get some more yesterday. I can't get going without my caffeine hit! How will I ever manage? There's no time to go to the shop and there's no chance of a cup on the way. I peep out the window at the neighbour's house. There's a light on. I put the kettle on and quickly run over and knock on the door. A sleepy neighbour peers at me. "What on earth …?" she starts. I try to look apologetic, explain my plight, and she grins. She comes back with some coffee powder in a cup. Great! I tear home, pour boiling water onto the coffee and savour the aroma. I gulp it down. I'm sure it's going to be a great day after all. Oh, and I must remember to stop at the shop this evening to buy coffee.

causality

transformation

Central to Todorov's approach are the two principles of causality and transformation. The causal principle refers to the way the events in the chain are in a relationship of cause and effect: one event or action causes another. For example, if a victim is discovered in crime fiction, this leads to an investigation. The investigation then has further consequences. As noted earlier, because of the causal relationship that underpins narrative, other incidental occurrences are omitted from the narrative as inconsequential. This explains the economy of detail characteristic of narrative.

Linked to the idea of causality is that of transformation. In the beginning there is always an act of violence, a violation or an interruption of the equilibrium that sets the narrative in motion; the remainder of the narrative is concerned with rectifying or transforming this disruption. When achieved, as the model above describes, the second equilibrium is never identical to the first one. Transformation has occurred, for the elements have been altered and refigured in some way.

Todorov's model is useful for identifying how a particular narrative has been structured, but this must be understood as the initial phase for more probing analytic work. If we are concerned with texts as mediations or the products of processes of selection and construction, the structure of the narrative as identified by Todorov's model lends itself to asking

Textual analysis: Narrative and Argument

about the choices made and the position that is privileged. The nature of transformation that is presented is what we are concerned about then – after all, the specific transformation validated in a text is one of many possible ways of framing. Therefore, we can ask the following questions:

- What counts as the initial equilibrium?
- What counts as the disruption?
- What is the nature of the quest (stage 4)?
- Who is the hero/actor who recognises and acts to resolve the disruption?

The decision as to what constitutes the first and final equilibrium establishes its discursive or ideological position, for this is considered a desirable state. By looking at the disruption we are able to identify what counts as a problem. The role of hero is attributed to some entity, and her or his actions and values are validated in this process. What we have to remember is that a narrative could be told differently by identifying a different disruption, a different hero and a different quest.

The table below provides two possible narratives arising from the events relating to a fictitious and generalised wage dispute. Consider what counts as an equilibrium and a disequilibrium on the part of the two opposing parties – the employers and the workers – on the timeline below. The events are presented in chronological order, in order to apply the model.

In mainstream news, the reporting on labour disputes tends to frame the narrative in the interests of capital and so articulates a discourse of capital. The disruption for such a story would be the strike action (event 6) that disrupts the working of the factory. The management would recognise and act through negotiating with the union (events 7, 8 and 9). What would constitute its re-equilibrium would be the restoration of the factory to full production (event 12) without increasing wages beyond a particular level; for management the concern for profit is central and is naturalised as appropriate. This narrative is in strong contrast to what constitutes the disruption within the narrative of labour. In this case the narratival disruption would be the issue of rising cost of living and low wages paid to workers (event 2). The recognition (event 3) and action (events 4, 6 and 8) would incorporate lobbying their union, which takes action on their behalf, including strike action

news

Table 6.1 Two narrative possibilities of a workers' strike

Events		Narrative 1 – a story of capital	Narrative 2 – a story of labour
1.	Workers labouring in factories and production is on target	initial equilibrium	
2.	The cost of living goes up		disequilibrium
3.	Workers are very conscious that they need more money to live on		recognition
4.	They task their union to negotiate with the management for their annual wage increase, which takes into account the increase in the cost of living		action 1
5.	The union engages with management, which offers a much lower increase, so the parties do not agree on the proposal		
6.	The workers embark on a strike and the factories are shut down, or rely on skeleton staff	disequilibrium	action 2
7.	The management become concerned at the loss of production and their ability to meet orders	recognition	
8.	The management and the union renegotiate	action 1	action 3
9.	A compromise is reached that includes a higher wage increase	action 2	re-equilibrium
10.	The workers return to work		
11.	The workers are not paid for the time they were on strike		
12.	The factory is in full production and makes a profit once again	re-equilibrium (not identical to first one)	

and renegotiation. For them the re-equilibrium would be a substantial increase in wages (event 9) rather than the factory in full swing. In this case, the concerns of management to retain a particular margin of profit are less relevant. While it would be mistaken to assume the labour discourse is automatically and totally excluded from mainstream publications, this narrative is more likely to be encountered in labour and trade union publications or certain tabloids with their higher working-class readership.

What should be striking is the difference in what counts as the

Textual analysis: Narrative and Argument

equilibrium, what counts as the disruption, and who are considered the heroes who take action. Identifying them enables us to establish the positioning of the text and to consider who and what is omitted from the story and consequently its discursive positioning.

When it comes to news stories, Todorov's model is extremely useful in explaining how news stories work as social and political narratives. In line with the example above, Fiske discusses how news tends to mediate what is often described as labour 'unrest'. He argues that:

news as social and political narratives

> ... the event conventionally selected as a cause of an industrial dispute is an action of a worker or a union, whereas the event selected to restore order is equally conventionally an act of management or government agency. In the narrative structure this puts unions into the roles of villains and management into that of heroes. Similarly, the disruption of the equilibrium will usually be in terms of the dispute's effects on the consumers, and rarely in terms of the hardships undergone by the striking unionists. This again serves to position the reader with the hero/victim (i.e. management–consumers) and in hostility to the villain (union). (1987:139)

News stories tend to focus on events that are disruptions of the equilibrium (bad news and negativity), or those that restore the equilibrium such as an achievement or completion of a task or quest (Fiske 1987:139). Consequently, because the initial state of equilibrium (things as usual) is not new or newsworthy, it is generally omitted. A cursory examination of news billboards or headlines will reveal this trend. Also, a news narrative often does not reach closure and the ending is still anticipated. Yet there is always a clear middle in some way, and what Todorov alerts us to is the most critical element of all: what sets off the middle section of the story is the issue of a disruption, disharmony or disequilibrium. Think for a moment about how news billboards and headlines constantly scream out the bad news. What they are picking up on is the disruption of social harmony. Consider how the headlines of two Sunday newspapers on one Sunday in 2008 do this:

- ANC abuses power (*City Press*)
- Wheels come off car sales (*City Press Business*)
- Cops push panic button on crime (*Sunday Times*)
- Rand will claw back – Manuel (*Sunday Times, Business Times*)

To extend this understanding of the selections in narrative, consider the following example of parallel events that relate to the global economic recession and its effect on the property market. In the column marked 'Distressed selling' are the events that tell the as yet incomplete narrative of people who are not very wealthy seeking to own their property. The column headed 'Vulture investors' provides the events that make up the narrative of the investors who buy up property cheaply to make profit.

Table 6.2. Two narrative possibilities for 'Bargain hunting' (Ndaba 2008:11)

	Distressed selling	Vulture investors
1.	Households desire to own their homes	Desire to make money through investing money
2.	Raise bonds/borrow money	
3.	Acquire property	'Wait' for opportunity
4.	Interest rates rise repeatedly	Recognise that distressed homeowners will be forced to sell soon
5.	'International property market meltdown'	
6.	Homeowners cannot meet payments	
7.	Sell at great loss	'[p]ounce: buy at lowest price possible; looking for 'value for money' 'discounted prices'
8.		Hold properties for a few years
9.	Perhaps buy at an even higher rate later	Sell to young people needing houses as result of population growth
10.		Make 20% interest year on year

Read the article, 'Bargain Hunter' and follow the steps listed below.

When applying Todorov's model, it is helpful to follow the following procedure:
1. Identify the events, including those that are implicit or that you must infer.
2. Order them chronologically.
3. Identify:
   - what has been selected as the disruption (and so the nature of the quest);
   - the hero/protagonist of the quest;
   - the actual or implied re-equilibrium;
   - the nature of the transformation.
4. Ask how it could be written from a different position and what the implications of this would be.

Textual analysis: Narrative and Argument

NEWS&INSIGHT

Bargain Hunting

New R100-million vulture fund seeks to benefit from international property market meltdown

DENNIS NDABA | SENIOR STAFF WRITER

A R100-million global property vulture fund has been launched and will enable South African investors to take advantage of the international property market meltdown.

The fund will target investors desiring medium- to long-term stable capital growth and a diversification of assets.

It will acquire properties at bargain prices from distressed sellers in different countries and resell them at a profit.

The sons of leading quantity surveyor CP de Leeuw, a former president of the South African Property Owners' Association, are the brains behind the vulture fund. Anton heads South African investment educationist and financial services provider YDL.

Mike is an Australia-based chartered accountant and CFO of a global privateequity firm with R10-billion under management, and provides financial, tax and structuring advice to the fund.

The third brother, Karl, is a quantity surveyor and full-time property investor in Dublin, Ireland.

"The rand is unusually strong because of the revival of the carry trade with mainly Japanese investors borrowing in yen at low interest rates and investing in the high interest rate rand markets.

"It is ideal to build investments in a foreign currency. We will hold investor money to invest over the next few years as opportunities arise," says Anton de Leeuw.

He adds that the first properties will probably be bought in the Republic of Ireland, followed by Belfast, Northern Ireland, and Warsaw, Poland.

The Irish housing market has fallen by 15% to 20% and is expected to stabilise around this mark.

It is expected to gradually pick up again later this year or next year, providing an extended period for bargain hunting.

YDL expects medium- to long-term growth in this market to be steady, especially on the back of expected high population growth, leading to increased demand for housing. Ireland has the youngest population in Europe and has the highest predicted population growth on that continent.

"Karl has already found apartments in central Belfast at half the average price. But we can probably do better if we wait a bit longer," says Anton de Leeuw.

"We may take up to two years to invest the full fund.

"It will need intensive research to get the timing right, and aggressive, sometimes protracted, negotiations to get the best opportunities. It's not possible to say what we will achieve but we have a target return in excess of 20% a year."

Anton de Leeuw cannot estimate the demand by South Africans for the fund.

"But we are having meetings with our investor base where we will be able to judge their appetite for vulture investment."

Given the slowdown in the global economy, precipitated by the credit crunch and attendant downturns in housing markets,

YDL believes that exceptional opportunities exist for purchasing properties in a buyer's market at value-for-money or discounted prices.

YDL provides expert access to selected markets for investors prepared to wait and then pounce when appropriate or distressed sales come along.

Such purchases will create a solid platform for growth once markets recover and the global economy picks up again.

ANTON DE LEEUW
It's ideal to build investments in a foreign currency

> Given the slowdown in the global economy, precipitated by the credit crunch and attendant downturns in housing markets, YDL believes that exceptional opportunities exist for purchasing properties in a buyer's market at value-for-money or discounted prices

Propp

Vladimir Propp, a Russian formalist who worked at the turn of the 20th century, is known for his study on the morphology of the Russian folk tale, first published in 1928 and translated into English only in 1958. His theory found its way into structural approaches to narrative and informed the burgeoning field of cultural studies from the 1960s in the English-speaking academic world. His approach is a more extreme example of a syntagmatic approach than that of Todorov, for it provides a more detailed breakdown of the range of events that might constitute the narrative.

His initial aim was a fairly modest one. He chose to analyse the Russian folk tale, more specifically fairy tales, in an attempt to establish a reliable system for their classification. Prior to his study, many researchers had classified the tales according to what might have been a more obvious criterion, namely theme, and with a clear focus on content. Propp considered this problematic in certain ways as themes would frequently overlap and, more importantly, this approach masked the similarities between those tales with dissimilar themes. Consequently, Propp deliberately ignored the actual content of the sample of 100 folk tales he analysed, and concentrated solely on their form. The narrative of these folk tales, he found, could be one of two kinds. It could be organised as a quest in which there is a seeker/hero, an object of the quest and possibly contestation with a villain; alternatively, it takes the form of a story in which a victim/hero acts to transform his (or her) circumstances.

narrative functions

In contrast to Todorov's five narrative stages, Propp broke down these tales into what he considered their essential 'narrative functions', of which there were 31 possibilities arranged sequentially (See Table 6.4). A function consisted of a single action, which was not related to a literal event, but served to describe the particular function that it performed in the overall development of a narrative. Accordingly, it is possible to find the same action having a different function in different narratives. An example of this is the action of a hero entering a city. The function could be:

- breaking an interdict or prohibition (function 3);
- leaving home (function 11);
- reaching the location of the object of his quest (function 15);
- solving a difficult task (function 26);
- preparing for his wedding (function 31).

Conversely, two different acts can serve the identical function. With reference to the tales that Propp examined, he invited his readers to compare the following:

- A tsar gives an eagle to a hero. The eagle carries the hero away to another kingdom.
- An old man gives Súčenko a horse. The horse carries Súčenko away to another kingdom.

Textual analysis: Narrative and Argument

- A sorcerer gives Ivan a little boat. The boat takes Ivan to another kingdom.
- A princess gives Ivan a ring. Young men appearing from out of the ring carry Ivan away into another kingdom (1968:19, 20). (See also Table 7.2 in the next chapter.)

Clearly there is something very similar going on in these examples, and this is what Propp was addressing. In these instances, the hero is being given a magical agent (function 9), which enables him to move forward in his quest. Consider how this can work in contemporary stories we encounter, such as in TV ads, as they provide a very economic way of telling stories:

- A housewife has a dirty toilet. A team with product X arrives and demonstrates how X cleans her toilet. Her problem is solved.
- A young mother is hanging her washing on the line and her white blouse rips. She tells her visiting grandmother that she does not know what to do as she tries her best to keep her whites white and uses bleach every time. The older woman tells her to use product Y as she always has. Later, the young mother (back at the washing line) tells the older woman that Y has worked wonders.
- A young teen looks at the mirror and his acne. An older sister tells him to use product Z. A week later he is getting ready to party.

What is apparent is that in these mini-narratives a hero(ine) experiences a lack and thus goes on a quest to resolve the lack. In each case there is a donor who gives the magical agent (function 10) and the initial lack is made right (function 19).

Propp arrived at four conclusions. These are described below.

> Propp's conclusions

- *Conclusion 1: functions of characters serve as stable constant elements in a tale, independent of how and by whom they are told. They constitute the fundamental components of a tale.*

  Propp established seven character functions in all: villain, donor, helper (to the hero or the villain), princess and father, dispatcher, hero or victim and, finally, false hero. While Propp places more emphasis on action than character, the characters enact the actions. He analyses the story according to the function of its characters. A character function 'is understood as an act of a character, defined from the point of view of its significance for the course of the action' (1968:21). Thus a character is defined in terms of their sphere of action in the narrative. Importantly, it is not their personal characteristics that are of significance here. The hero is not identifiable by his noble intentions or by signifiers such as his white cowboy hat or sheriff's badge, but by the sphere of action he inhabits in the narrative. A hero goes on a quest or a mission (see function 9). (Note that function 9 equates with Todorov's stages 3 and 4.) In spite of surface variability, as in the three advertisements described above, the actions of the characters play the identical role in how they move along the narrative.

As intended by the word 'function', in order to identify the character function it is necessary to identify the role the character plays in the overall narrative structure. It is also possible that one character can also serve two character functions. The dispatcher can also be the hero's helper, and the princess can also be donor, for example.

While Propp's hero is listed as a single character function, as mentioned above, there are two separate kinds of heroes. This is significant, for they reflect two different kinds of narratives. The hero as *seeker* is the one who goes on a quest which might include a contestation with the villain. The *victim* hero (or victimised hero) encounters some kind of adversity – possibly he or she is seized or banished – and the narrative is then linked to his or her fate. It is possible to think of countless examples of both kinds of heroes in contemporary popular culture. The seeker hero on a quest occurs most obviously in cowboy and gangster movies, crime fiction and action genres. We encounter the victim hero in those *bildungsroman*-type tales of overcoming personal adversity – the disadvantaged child or person who makes good against all odds, etc.. Think about news reporting of sportsmen or women who have experienced conditions of adversity and who become national heroes. The *Mail & Guardian*, for example, ran an article on Springbok rugby player Jongi Nokwe entitled 'Zero to hero'. His rise is constructed as similar to cricket player Makhaya Ntini's, as both 'come out of the [Eastern Cape] province's many small dusty villages' (Davie 5–11 September 2008).

Bildungsroman is a German term used to refer to a genre in which the plot recounts the incremental psychological, moral and social shaping of the personality of a (usually young) protagonist as he or she engages with life and reaches maturity. The following elements

Textual analysis: Narrative and Argument

Table 6.3 Propp's seven character functions (adapted from 1968:79–80, Wigston 2001) (see also Table 7.4 in the next chapter)

Character role	Sphere of action	Purpose	Function
Hero	Departs on a search, reacts to demands of donor, marries	Seeks to restore equilibrium	10, 13, 31,
Donor	Gives, or provides the hero with, the magical agent	Provides the objects that help to restore equilibrium	12, 14
Helper	Moves the hero, makes good a lack, rescues from pursuit, solves difficult tasks, transforms the hero	Helps hero to move the action towards resolution; (could be villain's helpers too)	15, 19, 22, 26, 29
Princess	A sought-after person who assigns difficult tasks, brands, exposes and recognises with her father, who punishes the false hero, marries	Leads to the climax of the narrative by being threatened by the villain; object of marriage (reward)	17, 25, 28, 30, 31
Dispatcher	Sends hero on mission/journey/quest	Sends the hero off	9
Villain	Causes harm or lack to member of 'family', fights/struggles with the hero	Blocks the action, so complicating the narrative	8, 16, 21
False hero	Like the hero, departs on search, reacts to donor, makes unfounded claims as hero	Appears good, but eventually revealed as flawed	10, 13, 24

might occur: the protagonist moves from childhood to maturity; the protagonist often has a reason to embark upon his or his journey and might need to leave the family setting; the process of maturation is generally long, arduous and gradual; eventually, the spirit and values of the social order become manifest in the protagonist, who is ultimately accommodated into the society. Dickens' *Great Expectations* is a literary example you might be familiar with.

Propp (1968:93) also allows for a dual hero function where two hero/seekers may part in the first move, act to resolve the lack or move the quest forward, and reunite before the end. This occurs in so-called buddy movies or other forms of crime fiction where partners work together to solve various crimes: for example, one of the early TV series of this kind was *Cagney & Lacey*; Batman and Robin or Mulder and Scully in *The X-Files* are further examples.

- *Conclusion 2: 'The number of functions of the folk tale is limited'.*

  Propp examined the body of 100 folk tales and reduced the narrative events to 31; function 8 was expanded to include 8a. These he organised into six stages.

Table 6.4 Propp's 31 narrative functions (see also Table 7.3 in the next chapter)

Stage 1: Preparation
1. a member of a family leaves home;
2. a prohibition or rule (interdiction) is imposed on the hero;
3. the prohibition is violated;
4. the villain makes an attempt at reconnaissance;
5. the villain gains information about his victim;
6. the villain attempts to deceive the victim to take possession of the victim or victim's belongings (trickery; villain disguised, tries to win confidence of victim);
7. the victim is taken in by deception, unwittingly helping the enemy;
Stage 2: Complication
8. the villain causes harm/injury to family member;
8a. alternatively, a member of the family lacks something or desires something (magical potion etc.);
9. this lack or misfortune is made known; the seeker hero is given a request or demand and he goes or is sent on a mission/quest; alternatively, the victim hero is sent away, freed from imprisonment;
10. the hero or seeker plans action against the villain;
Stage 3: Transference
11. the hero leaves home;
12. the hero is tested, attacked, interrogated, etc., preparing the way for his or her receiving a magical agent or helper;
13. the hero reacts to actions of future donor;
14. the hero uses a magical agent (directly transferred, located, purchased, prepared, spontaneously appears, eaten/drunk, help offered by other characters);
15. the hero is transferred or led to the location of the object of the search or quest;
Stage 4: Struggle
16. the hero and villain join in direct combat;
17. the hero is branded;
18. the villain is defeated;
19. the initial misfortune or lack is resolved;

Stage 5: Return
20. the hero returns;
21. the hero is pursued;
22. the hero is rescued from pursuit;
23. the hero arrives home or in another country and is not recognised;
24. a false hero makes false or unfounded claims;
25. a difficult task is set for the hero;
26. the task is accomplished;

Stage 6: Recognition
27. the hero is recognised;
28. the false hero or villain is exposed;
29. the hero is transformed (given a new appearance);
30. the villain is punished;
31. the hero marries and ascends the throne (is rewarded/promoted).

- *Conclusion 3: 'The sequence of events is always identical'*

    Propp identified six sequential stages, namely preparation, complication, transference, struggle, return and recognition. Here the syntagmatic dimension is clear in how he orders the functions, and his model insists on this chronology or sequence of events. Propp noted that certain kinds of functions always occur at the same stage of the narrative: for example, the interdiction always occurs near the beginning whereas the villain can only be punished towards the end.

    Three additional points relate to the issue of sequencing. Firstly, certain functions tend to occur in twos or threes: for example functions 8a, 9 and 10. Once a 'family member' lacks or desires something (8a), this is made known to the hero (9), who goes, or is sent on, a quest (10), who consequently plans action. This is a typical sequence of a quest narrative.

    Secondly, Propp allows for the omission of functions, and it is rare that a narrative would include all of the 31 functions. In contemporary media narratives, the preparation stage is frequently omitted completely, and the story begins at the complication stage. This is particularly clear in news reporting, as has been identified in the discussion of Todorov's model. Once again, look at the headlines from the two Sunday newspapers included above, which present narratives where the preparation stage has already occurred and the complication informs the headline.

Thirdly, narratives may, and often do, have more than one development or move to resolve the complication and to reach the resolution. If the story proceeds from an act of villainy or lack through to the resolution of the villainy or lack (and marriage), this often includes several trials. There might be a series of acts of villainy or lack, and each will need to be acted upon. This means there can be parallel movements where the hero has to deal with sets of obstacles and recurring movements. This model allows for the repetition of functions. Here again, we can look to popular media texts to illustrate this point. In a crime thriller, for example, the hero can face several acts of villainy in the form of several crimes and be tested repeatedly (function 8 and 12); he may join in direct combat with the criminal (function 16) several times before the task is accomplished. In James Bond movies, this scenario plays out with Bond receiving magical agents on several occasions, which he uses before defeating the villain.

Fourthly, consider how not all narratives are structured as a single account that reaches closure in one episode. The media include a range of genres that have their own sets of conventions and the narrative can be sustained over several episodes. A single episode may contribute to the larger narrative, as is the case in TV drama serials and reality shows like *Survivor* or *Big Brother* where the winner (hero) is established at the end of the season. This is also characteristic of the plotlines in soaps. News coverage of a lengthy court case of a prominent individual will also be constructed as a narrative that extends over the time period of the trial and will be presented episodically. Take the reporting of the Jacob Zuma rape trial as an extended narrative. It first made the news after a rape charge was laid in late 2005. The trial was set to commence in January 2006, but experienced several setbacks as the judiciary battled to appoint a judge. Once the trial began in March 2006, there were several breaks and recesses before judgement was passed on 9 May 2006.

- *Conclusion 4: 'All fairy tales are of one type in regard to structure'.*

Propp's final conclusion foregrounds the similarity of structure in the Russian folk tale. He took care to confine his judgements to the Russian folk tale while suggesting that these narrative forms, ostensibly stylised

Textual analysis: Narrative and Argument

and primitive, might have the same structure as other contemporary texts. Modern Anglo-American film theorists were quick to take up his ideas (Turner 1988). While Propp had worked from the folk tale material and proceeded to reach his conclusions, these theorists worked from the hypothesis that the structure suggested by Propp for the fairy tale is also present in the fiction film. They tested the hypothesis and claimed an easy fit; examples of this include Peter Wollen's close reading of Hitchcock's *North by Northwest* (1982) and Roger Silverstone's reading of TV fiction (1981).

Similarity between Propp and Todorov

The syntagmatic or linear models of Propp and Todorov, where the events are in a cause–effect relationship, have much in common. Todorov's model is more economical and Propp's contains much detail, but they both identify the same stages in essence, as the table below indicates.

The role of narrative as a sense-making mechanism that hinges on the occurrence of a disruption or a lack becomes increasingly clear when you apply the models to a range of media texts that you would not immediately consider a narrative. To undertake a narrative analysis using these structuralist approaches, the first and necessary step is to organise the story in chronological order precisely because they assume a passage of time. In the advertisement under consideration, it is necessary to consider how the advertisement is organised in order to plot the narrative. The second step requires that you identify the disruption – the disequilibrium, according to Todorov, and the complication stage for Propp. From there it is possible to get a sense of who the hero is who recognises the disruption and acts.

'Some say success …' is an advertisement that was placed in the September 2008 issue of *SL* magazine. It is a full-page portrait-format text that includes a dynamic visual in shades of green in the upper half and print with various typographies in the lower half. The University of Cape Town logo is included in the lower right-hand corner. In applying Propp and Todorov here, the focus is primarily on the printed text. Some attention is given to the visual signs when Lévi-Strauss's theories are used for analysis.

Table 6.5 Propp and Todorov to's narrative stages compared

Todorov's 5 stages		Propp's 31 narrative functions
1. Equilibrium	1.	Preparation
	2.	
	3.	
	4.	
	5.	
	6.	
	7.	
2. Disequilibrium	8.	Complication
a Upset	8a.	
b Recognition	9.	
	10.	
c Action	11.	Transference
	12.	
	13.	
	14.	
	15.	
	16.	Struggle
	17.	
	18.	
	19.	
	20.	Return
	21.	
	22.	
	23.	
	24.	
	25.	
	26.	
3. Equilibrium	27.	Recognition
	28.	
	29.	
	30.	
	31.	

Textual analysis: Narrative and Argument

Table 6.6 Applying Todorov's five-stage model to 'Some say success …'

1.	state of equilibrium at the outset	assumed: a time before you worried about career decisions and adult responsibilities
2.	disruption of the equilibrium by some action	you lack the wherewithal to achieve future success
3.	recognition of that disruption	you need the right 'degree' for your 'chosen career' from 'one of Africa's top universities', i.e. UCT
4.	an attempt to repair the disruption	you apply for admission and for financial help through one of the funding options; you 'learn from leading researchers and academics' with 'people from all over Africa'
5.	restoration	you graduate and are thus prepared 'to take centre stage and lead the way'

Applying Propp's narrative functions provides a more detailed linear account of the same small text.

Table 6.7 Applying Propp's narrative model to 'Some say success ...'

6.	the villain attempts to deceive the victim to take possession of victim or victim's belongings (trickery; villain disguised, tries to win confidence of victim)	'some say' that succcess is about who you know
8a.	a member of family lacks something or desires something (magical potion etc.);	you (hero) lack success and the strategies to achieve it in your chosen career – you desire 'to achieve great things', 'to take centre stage'
9.	this lack or misfortune is made known; the seeker hero is given a request or demand and he goes or is sent on a mission/quest	you recognise this lack and seek to do something about it
12.	the hero is tested, attacked, interrogated, etc., preparing the way for his or her receiving a magical agent or helper;	you don't know what to do. Should you believe the advice that 'success is about who you know'? You also read the UCT ad in SL magazine
13.	the hero reacts to actions of future donor;	'we' (UCT serves as donor and dispatcher) make known to you how to achieve by suggesting what path you follow to do this and you agree
14.	the hero uses a magical agent	you make an application to study at UCT
15.	the hero is transferred or led to the location of the object of the search or quest	you enrol
26.	the task is accomplished	you graduate (implied)
29.	the hero is transformed (given a new appearance)	you are given the status of a graduate
31.	the hero marries and ascends the throne (is rewarded/promoted)	career reward – you can 'take centre stage' and 'you can lead the way in your chosen career'

This is a story in the subjunctive – a story 'as if'. It is offered almost as a promise – *this* could happen. What is interesting about this story is that UCT is not constructed as the hero. This character function is attributed to 'you', the prospective student. UCT becomes both the dispatcher who tells you to go on this quest, and the donor who ensures access to all the hero's helpers, the leading 'researchers and academics' and fellow students, the 'people from all over Africa'.

What is also significant in this narrative is what is omitted from this quest, for it is constructed as one that equates the application and enrolment with the final success. It is possible to infer a range of other stages that will form part of a student's story. There will be many other tests, and below are possible functions to this narrative that one might infer. Their omission is important because the advertisement is a rhetorical act that chooses what to include, and here it is not the slog and study that is entailed. To acknowledge that would require the following three narrative functions be repeated for each academic year:

Table 6.8 Omitted events in 'Some say success …'

12. the hero is tested, attacked, interrogated, etc., preparing the way for his or her receiving a magical agent or helper	have to pass degree and work is complex
14. the hero uses a magical agent	attend lectures, read the writings of scholars, write assignments, etc.
25. a difficult task is set for the hero	you write final examinations

This is a narrative that serves a particular rhetorical function – to persuade or encourage 'you' to go to UCT, and it proposes a way for 'you' to transform yourself.

By applying these theories, we can identify what counts as the disruption, the quest and the resolution of the quest. We can work out what detail is omitted. The advertisement mounts an argument that rehearses particular discourses that appear to be common sense. This is taken up in the next section, which outlines and applies Lévi-Strauss's paradigmatic approach.

6.4.2 Paradigmatic theories

Lévi-Strauss

Claude Lévi-Strauss, a French anthropologist born in 1908, made highly valued contributions within his own field of anthropology. His approach is structural but, unlike those of the Propp and Todorov outlined above, it is not syntagmatic. Lévi-Strauss's paradigmatic approach can be seen as a riposte to those who have accused structural approaches to narrative analysis as being primarily formalist, and consequently 'largely unconcerned with questions about "content" and thus with political and ideological judgements' (Kozloff 1987:42).

Often students or analysts get caught up in applying the models of Todorov and Propp in a kind of 'spot the structure' exercise and neglect to probe the ideological positioning. However, Lévi-Strauss's focus on deeper meaning ensures a movement from the syntagmatic to the paradigmatic. It draws the attention of the analyst to the question, 'what is the meaning of the event?', and so goes beyond 'what happened?' Together, the syntagmatic and paradigmatic approaches enable questions of positioning and power to be posed.

binary oppositions

Lévi-Strauss's study of rituals, customs, myths and folk tales of particular tribes in Brazil was focused on not merely the surface content, but the meaning, or more specifically the underlying rules and codes that produce or construct meaning. He was concerned with identifying a deep structure of meanings in mythic narratives that can only be grasped by taking the characters, settings and actions out of the syntagmatic flow, and by analysing their relations of similarity and difference, usually in terms of *binary oppositions*. Thus the chain of events, or the surface structure, was of less significance than the deep structure that underpinned a myth or folk tale, a deep structure it shared with other myths and narratives.

This deeper structure, Lévi-Strauss proposed, was evidence of the underlying contradictions in society and is a symbolic way of negotiating such tensions. Myth for Lévi-Strauss functioned as 'an anxiety-reducing mechanism that deals with unresolvable contradictions in a culture and provides imaginative ways of living with them' (Fiske 1987:131–2). These unresolvable contradictions can be expressed as a tension that exists between two poles – for example, good and evil, wealth and poverty, or male and female. Lévi-Strauss, as a consequence of working with particular South American tribes, identified nature and culture as two opposing poles, which he also referred to as raw (in contrast to cooked), and humankind (in contrast to the gods).

It is important to note that these binary oppositions are large, abstract generalisations that underpin the myths he examined. Following his

Textual analysis: Narrative and Argument

approach, analysts look at how these generalisations are given concrete form in the narratives and texts of social groupings by identifying these oppositions. Lévi-Strauss refers to this as the 'logic of the concrete'. Thus, by examining the contradictions or oppositions that are worked over in a narrative, we can seek to identify the underlying tensions. It becomes possible to group together, in two opposing lists, the qualities that get structured into the story's conflict. Think for a moment about the oppositions that underpin crime fiction stories or news reports on crime: law and order versus crime and chaos; and good versus bad.

While Lévi-Strauss was attempting to establish a more essentialist meaning, poststructural approaches moved beyond myth as reflecting an essential societal or cultural structure to reading narratives as engaging in meaning-making that is contemporary, historically located and also fluid or changing. Consider how the political contestation that occurred in 2008 around the removal of the then president of the South Africa, Thabo Mbeki, was narrated by constructing oppositions in relation to Thabo Mbeki and Jacob Zuma, who was president of the African National Congress at the time. The qualities that constituted the oppositions included honour versus dishonour and public interest versus self-interest, and they were widely contested in political party structures and a range of media. The mediation of these circumstances through texts provides a clear illustration of the discourses in contestation at the time.

> poststructural

The role of texts as mediating social existence and ideas within specific social contexts was established above. Texts play a role in constituting our ways of knowing and being, and, most importantly, they work to privilege particular social orientations, attitudes and interests. The identification of binary oppositions in a text enables us to identify and probe the textual orientation as the binary construction does not merely present neutral opposites, but is linked to a social context and history that is marked by contestation. More regularly flagged oppositions with which we are all familiar include those of race (white/black), gender (male/female) and class (rich/poor).

Binary oppositions function through the process of classifying and distinguishing between the categories thus produced. They are the manifestation of a process of classification and evaluation. People are classified as male or female, as black or white. But this is not all. These categories are weighted. 'Male' is not only 'not female'; it is, within

237

patriarchal discourse, strong, rational, and so on, in contrast to being weak and emotional. Also, implicitly or explicitly, one is evaluated as superior while the other is rated inferior. Therefore, when we identify the binary oppositions within a text we are able to identify the way in which the 'real' is being defined and produced, and what and who is being valued and devalued. We are able to identify the discourses. One set of the opposition dominates and is validated over the other. The other term is constituted as negative or pejorative – it is expurgated in this process. The privileged side forms the 'truth' and knowledge of the discourse. The text thus rehearses shared schemes of understanding, and dominant discourses often appear as common-sense or as natural. This will become more evident when applying the theories.

Applying Lévi-Strauss's binary oppositions

The UCT advertisement was analysed earlier in order to identify the narrative structure and, by extension, what served as the equilibrium, the problem or disruption, and the nature of the quest. It is used in this section to extend the analysis and to probe its positioning further.

A central aspect of the rhetorical work that the UCT advert undertakes lies in its address, for it proposes that a UCT degree is desirable, and invites young people to spend at least three bookish years at its institution. The way it does this can be analysed in terms of its selections and the nature of its orientation. It is the image, the colour and font choice that propose an identity for the reader as trendy. There are two silhouetted figures, the larger (fairly androgynous) one on the left with a big Afro hairstyle sings or raps into a microphone with his hand pointing to an (intended) audience. The masculine figure on the right is smaller and similarly singing into a mike. They are performing against the backdrop of UCT's iconic and classically inspired architecture, including columns and steps and the silhouette of Table Mountain. The reader is thus hailed by this energetic and dynamic scene in a classy space. The large-font caption speaks directly to the reader, to 'you'. It rhymes, and the caption is presented as the rhythmic words of a rap song that is coupled with the singers' gestures – pointing and addressing you, the audience:

> Some say success is about who you know.
> We say it's about where you go.

Textual analysis: Narrative and Argument

In doing this it presents its first set of oppositions in the text, namely success based on competence (where you go) versus success through contacts (who you know). It also visually represents 'you' (a trendy young party-goer) in the place to go (UCT steps against the iconic mountain silhouette, that is Cape Town).

By offering a system of binaries, a text such as the UCT advertisement engages the readers and extends an invitation to them to make the same classifications and distinctions as the text does and invites them to identify with it. To put this differently, as Thompson (1990) argues, it deploys the strategy of unification that invites the reader to be unified as part of that 'in' group. By addressing the reader directly as 'you', it invites you to share in its project. The compliant or 'preferred' reader is asked to make the distinctions that are embodied in the social order that the advertisement draws on, reproduces and reinforces.

It also proposes that 'you' be the hero of your own narrative. The table below uses the words of the text (as textual evidence) and constructs the list of opposites that are implied to make explicit what position is valued.

Table 6.9 Binary oppositions in relation to the hero, 'you', in the UCT ad

hero/ 'you'	loser
achieve 'success'	fail
'take centre stage'	be marginal
'where you go' (good advice)	'who you know' (poor advice)
'lead the way'	follow others
'join people from all over Africa'	remain isolated from other African people
'learn'	remain ignorant
'achieve great things'	fail
'get the right degree'	get the wrong qualifications
attend the 'right university'	attend the wrong institution
'give back to the community and the environment'	take from/exploit the community and environment
'apply now' and act with determination	'delay'

At the same time as constructing 'you' as the hero of the narrative, it validates UCT in ways that can be made obvious in the oppositions that are implied and listed below. You must recall that UCT was identified above as the Proppian characters of dispatcher and donor.

Table 6.10 Binary oppositions: the donor/dispatcher in 'Some say success ...'

UCT	Other institutions
'we'	they
'leading researchers and academics'	inferior researchers and academics
'right university'	wrong university
'one of Africa's top universities'	second-rate/inferior university
have 'various [socially responsible] outreach programmes'	lack social responsibility edge
offer 'financial help through a range of ...'	offer limited forms of financial help
'changing minds'	reinforce existing ideas/mindsets
'changing futures'	entrenching the present and past
of value	worthless
good	bad

This advertisement works within the broader societal context and in particular repeats ideas about intellectual or mental work, which in turn assume and naturalise class relations. Consider the grid of binary oppositions that relate to the hero, 'you'. It emphasises personal or individual 'success' evident in what actions are attributed to 'you': 'you' will 'lead the way', 'achieve great things' and 'take centre stage'. This success implies leadership and its material rewards consistent with capitalist discourse.

This construction of what constitutes personal success is attributed to higher education, for here the product being advertised is a higher education qualification from one particular university. Higher education here delivers status and power (knowledge is not foregrounded), and is consistent with the powerful economic discourses that prevail. Intellectual achievement is constructed as the gateway to success; by implication, manual labour, which does not deliver similar access to power and material wealth, is devalued. The discourse of formal education as naturally valuable and ensuring social mobility prevails in modern societies.

If you consider the grid of binary oppositions relating to UCT, these constructions extend this idea with UCT's self-construction as a superior, while socially responsible, university that looks to the future. It constructs itself as socially aware by referring to their financial assistance

Textual analysis: Narrative and Argument

and outreach programmes and to 'changing futures'. This construction stands in contrast to the focus on fun and partying in the vibrant image. If there is a tension between these two constructions, another tension exists for the text to negotiate, namely that between personal (read material) success and the South African context of social inequalities. By including reference to its 'outreach programmes', poverty and community are implicitly acknowledged. But these initiatives are not termed 'charity', with the negative connotations that the word has acquired in recent times, but as reaching out, with its connotations of both generosity and effort. 'Outreach' becomes suitable and legitimate, approved in the way that 'charity' has become unacceptable. There is also silence around another form of social inequality related to academic achievement. Omitting to mention that entrance to university is exclusive and excluding by means of entrance requirements obscures this dimension. Instead, UCT serves as dispatcher/donor and seems to offer inclusion through financial support.

It is necessary to question the purpose of the inclusion of 'people from all over Africa' for its implied binary opposition in this context is 'the West'. By referring to them, this text reveals that the producers were mindful of powerful discourses that circulate around issues of African identity, the African Renaissance project and its contestation for African 'truths'. If there have been accusations that Western values have informed and been privileged in higher education, to the detriment of local knowledge and exclusionary practices in terms of enrolments, the inclusion of people who are African seeks to deflect it, and construct this diversity as valued.

Like any other text, this example mediates its ideas and proposes attitudes and values while seeking to hail its audience. As a contemporary narrative, it works metaphorically to negotiate current tensions or contradictions through concrete representations. What becomes evident from using all three sets of narrative theories is that the advert mediates a structure that relates to lack and fulfilment, poverty and wealth, failure and success. The way it does this does not resolve any of the insecurities permanently, but it engages in discursive work. It temporarily provides a structure for negotiating those tensions in relation to its specific purpose, and, in Fiske's words, 'the structure makes the contradictions conceptually and culturally capable of being handled and thus not dysfunctional' (1987:132-3) in this instance.

It is at the point of disruption identified in Todorov's model that the oppositions become evident and can be identified. In the UCT advertisement the quest is for success in personal and not communitarian terms. The narrative works to legitimate a way of individualistic acting in the world, one that relates to high status, that is, of being 'centre stage'. It is also an argument, an argument that says this behaviour is not only acceptable, but in fact admirable. This is more starkly obvious when you analyse the article, 'Bargain hunting', reproduced above.

Analyse the article, 'Bargain hunting'. There, the desire for great material wealth informs the quest; its opposition is poverty. It is wealth not humaneness that is validated, aggression not passivity; economic savvy not compassion. What would be represented as a tragic disaster for a property owner in one narrative becomes the golden opportunity for the aggressive buyers, who will achieve their wealth while causing poverty for the distressed sellers.

6.5 NARRATIVE AND GENRE

Media texts are conventionally categorised in relation to their genre (see Chapter 8 on film theory and criticism). Genres refer to 'kinds' of texts and serve as a categorisation that signals to the audience the nature of the texts. Particular media genres have been described as negotiating particular sets of prevailing tensions (Gledhill 1997). That particular genres rise and fall in popularity can be linked to the prevalence of particular discomforting issues in a particular time and place. That US film production saw a spate of films about Vietnam after the war can be argued to respond to the need for US citizens to symbolically engage with that tension – their powerful country fighting that war, and losing that war. South Africa has seen a spate of media productions, from novels to TV serials to films, that similarly engage with South African apartheid history, where the central opposition relates to race. Similarly, other South African films negotiate the concern with law and order, the conventional focus of crime fiction and gangster movies, now in relation to a contemporary South African context.

When we employ narrative theories, particular generic conventions can be anticipated. These serve as conventions that ensure similarity between the media texts in relation to the issues being negotiated, while ensuring sufficient difference to remain interesting and fresh. It is necessary to become familiar with the generic conventions and ordering

Textual analysis: Narrative and Argument

of the narrative in relation to the genre. It also enables the analysis to identify transgressing moments in relation to the genre, for no genre is static either.

6.6 ARGUMENTATION

If we have drawn on these 20th-century theories for analytic approaches to narrative, we go much further into the past when it comes to a model for analysing argument. We look back two millennia or so, to the idea of rhetoric. This work has been reintroduced into media studies more recently by Silverstone (1999) and Richardson (2007).

The term 'rhetoric' has had some bad press, and is often used disparagingly as 'mere rhetoric'. It has been reduced at times to refer to 'the artifice of the well-turned phrase or the stunning metaphor' (Silverstone 1999:31) or 'ornate oration' (Richardson 2007:156). This is not how classical thinkers like Aristotle or Cicero understood it, or how it is used here. Rather, rhetoric is essentially an attempt at persuasion; it refers to language oriented to action or influencing action, and, as was argued in terms of narrative, it is seen as an essential aspect of human existence, along with language and social organisation. This is how Burke describes it.

| rhetoric

> *Rhetoric is rooted in the essential function of language itself, a function that is wholly realistic and is continually born anew, the use of language as a symbolic means of inducing co-operation in beings that by nature respond to symbols. (Burke 1955:43 in Silverstone 1999:31)*

Rhetoric is consequently a dimension of the media as they too engage in selecting and organising ideas. Media language is thus rhetorical, and makes claims on the audience, seeking to persuade its readers of its position, ideas or values. While we are foregrounding the idea of the media as seeking to persuade, it would be misguided to confuse persuasion with manipulation. To the contrary, and it is important to link this to the ideas of discourse earlier in the chapter. Different discourses circulate in any social space and there is contestation between dominant and opposing discourses. Media texts are the vehicles of such contestation as they seek to shape readers' ideas and feelings. What rhetoric involves is classification and argument, and is central to both the exercise of power as well as to opposing power. There is no contradiction between rhetoric and democracy or between rhetoric and knowledge (Silverstone 1999).

argumentation

Argumentation can be defined as the 'verbal and social activity of reason aiming at increasing (or decreasing) the acceptability of a controversial standpoint for the listener or reader, by putting forward a constellation of propositions intended to justify (or refute) the standpoint before a rational judge' (Van Eemeren et al. 1996:5 in Richardson 2007:155). With reference to this definition, three characteristics of argumentation are identified.

- It is an active process as it aims in some way to change or modify an existing state of affairs or way of acting.
- It is a social practice as it engages in a process of communication that seeks to resolve a difference of opinion or persuade the listener to share an opinion.
- It is a joint process as it can only work if the listener is open to the argument and therefore persuasion.

Argumentation assumes that the listener can act as a 'rational judge', and this implies that there are rules by which an argument is deemed reasonable. Drawing on Aristotle, rhetoric has been defined as 'the faculty of observing in any given case the available means of persuasion'. It requires the arguer to identify first 'the persuasive facts in each case' (Richardson 2007:156), which can then be presented in such a way as to persuade the listeners. The rhetorical triangle he describes includes the argument, the audience and the arguer.

To explain this model more fully, three kinds of rhetorical practice are outlined, namely forensic, epideictic (or demonstrative) and deliberative. These categories can be distinguished by the subject the arguer addresses and the desired response of the audience. Each has its own goals, and for that reason they tend to focus on particular topics and use particular means to reach these goals. Knowledge of these divisions or practices enables the textual analyst to identify how the argument is working and so consider the form or forms of persuasion being used.

kinds of arguments

- *Forensic* (or judicial) argument focuses on past actions, and can be understood as the term suggests, as the practices in a court of law. It either seeks to defend or accuse someone (for example, a political leader) and it tends to focus on topics of justice and injustice. The main focus is proof and examination of evidence, through which it

Textual analysis: Narrative and Argument

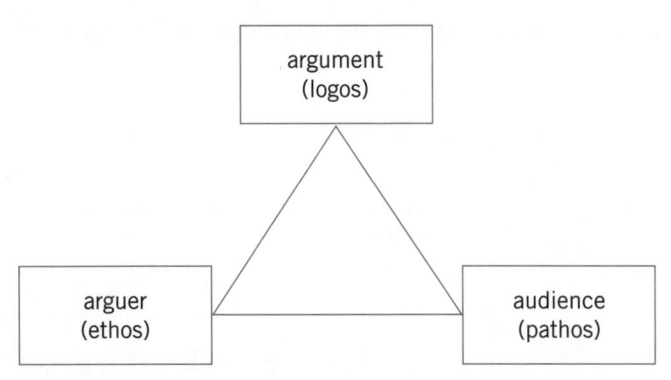

```
                argument
                 (logos)
                    △
        arguer          audience
        (ethos)          (pathos)
```

Figure 6.1 The rhetorical triangle

seeks to make the audience predisposed to the position and person it is attacking or defending.

- *Epideictic* (a Greek term) is also referred to as 'demonstrative' argument by Dixon. He notes that it arose out of public rituals where either gods or men were praised (1971:23). It came to include praise or defence as well as censure or denunciation. It focuses on the character or reputation of the person or persons and attempts to persuade the audience to admire them for their goodness or dislike and reject them for their dishonour.
- *Deliberative* argument encompasses deliberating about possible future actions in relation to their desirability or undesirability. It seeks to persuade or dissuade the audience in relation to a future course of action. An obvious example would be news reporting of American presidential election campaigns and the reasoning presented to persuade citizens about the direction of their vote. Similarly, an advertisement that seeks to encourage students to enrol at their institution, or a piece of investigative journalism that deliberates on an aspect of local government in an attempt to hold the authority to account and motivate a response on the part of the readers, are examples of deliberative argument. The arguer seeks to induce or dissuade the reader and in Aristotle's words: 'if he [for no doubt women had no place in public life at the time Aristotle was writing] urges its acceptance, he does so on the grounds it will do good; if he urges its rejection, he does so on the ground it will do harm' (1358b:22–4, in Richardson 2000:157).

Table 6.11 Rhetorical argumentation (Richardson 2007:158)

Division	Focus	Means	Special topics
Forensic	Past actions	Accusation or defence	Justice and injustice
Epideictic	Present character or reputation	Praise or censure	Honour and dishonour
Deliberative	Future actions	Inducement or dissuasion	The advantageous and the disadvantageous

This classification helps to identify the form of argument and is complemented by knowledge of the three modes of persuasion Aristotle identified. They include ethos, pathos and logos, with each relating to a different point of the rhetorical triangle.

An ethotic argument invokes the personal character and quality of the speaker. It is used to effect when both sides of the argument are reasonably convincing and so an appeal to the ethos of the speaker is useful. This is effective when the person has first-hand experience which works to persuade the audience, or where it is assumed that they are trustworthy. Thus in South Africa, particular figures lend credence to an argued position – for example, Archbishop Desmond Tutu or former president Nelson Mandela, whose stature as ethical statesmen lends credence in some way to positions they endorse. Similarly, newspaper campaigns such as the *Daily Sun*'s 'I am a man' campaign of 2007 used a range of celebrities to endorse the campaign against violent abuse of women – the argument being that if they are signing up the campaign is credible and valuable. Moreover, journalists resort to this form of proof by invoking the opinion of experts as evidence of the plausibility of their position by referring to 'research' and 'studies', and the authority of sources is invoked by referring to them as 'Professor', etc.. They might defer to Professor X's opinion, Richardson (2007:168) suggests, for an opinion about, say, the benefits of privatisation when the topic under consideration is completely unrelated to the academic's area of expertise – Egyptology, in the example he offers.

A pathotic argument seeks to induce a particular mindset among the audience. Through pathos or an appeal to emotion they can be moved to pity, fear, anger, even guilt as the arguer tries to get them into the kind of mindset that will make them open to the line of argument. Examples of pathotic arguments would include the construction of a group of people as less than deserving and therefore justifying harsh treatment of these people. Xenophobic examples abound, but perhaps the most horrific example might be the radio denunciation of Hutus as cockroaches deserving to be crunched underfoot, which was broadcast on Rwandan radio during the 1990s genocide in that country. Similarly, an audience can be swayed by emotions of love, pity, etc. to behave in new ways. By flattering the audience as reasonable and intelligent, too, the arguer can seek to put the audience in a receptive frame of mind to engage with the argument. Calls for patriotism and national loyalty are frequently used to call for particular behaviours. Think of the famous World War I slogan, 'Your country needs you'.

Finally, the logetic argument is dependent on the logic or proof provided. An appeal to logos relies on two kinds of arguments, either inductive or deductive. In a deductive argument an assertion is made by making a series of statements. From these statements a valid conclusion can be reached – for example:

deductive and inductive argumentation

- All South African sports bodies are racist.
- Rugby has a sports body.
- The rugby sports body is racist.

Thus in deductive argument, if the premises are valid the conclusion cannot be false. If one of the premises is invalid, so is the conclusion. Frequently, one of the premises is not stated and the audience has to fill in the missing step, making it in effect a more powerful argument. In the example above, because there are racist attitudes among all South African sports bodies, rugby is racist.

Inductive argument, on the other hand, draws on specific cases to present the argument. It can be a symptomatic argument, argument by analogy or argument of a causal relationship. In all cases, they relate to the particular context and propose that the argument is plausible. In a symptomatic argument an individual example is used to illustrate a wider example. Particular stereotypes can be invoked by reference, for example, to an individual of a particular social group who is convicted of a crime. This characteristic (criminality) is then generalised to all others with that identity. Terms like 'characteristic', 'typical', etc. indicate this form of inductive argument.

An argument by analogy draws on a comparison to make a point and will use words like 'similarly', 'and so also' or 'accordingly'. Describing a group of people as cockroaches dehumanises them and implies they should be treated as such.

An argument of causal relationship assumes a cause–effect relationship, and is the form of argument frequently used when attributing responsibility to 'the media' for some social problem. Thus violence and school shootings have been attributed to the media habits of schoolboys, as in the case of the Columbine massacre. In that case, it was established that one of the boys involved was a Marilyn Manson fan. Similarly, the murder of two-year-old James Bulger in the United Kingdom by two young boys was attributed to the so-called video nasty they had been watching in the first instance. (In these instances, chronology is confused with cause and effect and other factors are consequently ignored. In the case of the shootings, one might question the easy access to guns at home, being such good marksmen at a young age, and importantly, a particularly violent form of masculinity. These issues are raised in Michael Moore's 2002 film, *Bowling for Columbine*.)

Inductive forms of argument need in turn to be judged according to rules of reasonableness or plausibility (see Richardson 2007:165-7). Richardson provides a detailed account of such rules.

Application

We will now analyse the UCT advertisement as a particularly economic text to explicate the concepts. The advertisement presents us clearly with the three dimensions of the rhetorical triangle. Look at the second line of the caption, which reads, 'We say it's about where you go', posing an enigma that we quickly resolve. 'We' is UCT, the arguer, 'you' is the audience that are the readers of *SL*, and potential UCT students. This is a direct form of address using first and second person (we and you) and seeks to make direct contact with its reader. The third point of the rhetorical triangle is the argument made through the rest of the text. The advertisement constructs a simple but remarkably inclusive argument, for it calls upon all three modes of persuasion (ethos, pathos and logos) and all three forms of argument (forensic, epideictic or deliberative), at least to some extent.

The arguer in this case is UCT and, using an ethotic argument, attention

Textual analysis: Narrative and Argument

is drawn to the character and quality of UCT, which is presented as a 'top' and the 'right' university with 'leading researchers and academics'. It refers to its present character and reputation in order to argue its superior worth intellectually, its sense of social responsibility (in the form of outreach programmes), its sensitivity to its social context (its considerate awareness of potential financial obstacles students might encounter), and its inclusive approach in relation to the diversity of the student body. Its self-presentation constitutes an epideictic argument that serves as praise or, in this case, a self-eulogy (a strategy frequently employed in advertisements).

The extolling of its virtue is extended from the present to the past, both in relation to itself (UCT) and its past students, thereby constituting a forensic argument but of a fairly superficial nature. It is selective of what it presents about itself and is silent around its historical place as a white English-speaking university during the apartheid era. Rather, it elides this by referring merely to its role 'for decades' of preparing people for greatness. In a sense it defends itself implicitly and seeks to predispose the reader to UCT.

It also presents a deliberative argument as it deliberates on the desirability of the decision to attend UCT. It seeks to persuade the student to act in a particular way in the future – to enrol at UCT. To this end, it provides a litany of the advantages for the student, from leading the way, having a 'career', giving back to less advantaged people and engaging with fellow Africans. However, the central argument is one that proposes a future that is different to the present and where the reader will take 'centre stage' as a result of acquiring a UCT degree. It presents its logic or proof by means of a deductive argument: UCT has prepared successful people for decades and is a top university; it is socially concerned and responsive to its African context. If you go, you too will achieve this prestige and power.

The mode of persuasion in this deliberative argument is that of pathos or emotion. It seeks to move the reader ('you') from one emotional state to another. If the reader was indifferent or unsure about enrolling as a UCT student, it sets out to speak directly to the reader and to persuade the audience through an appeal to their sense of worth – 'people like you', that is, intelligent people who recognise it is 'not only who you know'. The arguer flatters and invites the reader to share the UCT position. It asks the student to recognise his or her place among the achievers: 'it's your turn'. It further addresses the reader not as a dull bookish student but as a trendy and dynamic party-goer – as the image, colours, font and caption propose. It leaves agency with 'you', as it is your decision – 'if you want to take centre stage and lead the way' – but clearly this is designed as an inducement.

The UCT logo and economical caption at the bottom of the page seek finally to sum up the argument: UCT constructs itself as the transformative agent, 'changing minds and changing futures', proffering this successful future to the hero/reader.

6.7 ARGUMENT AS NARRATIVE AND NARRATIVE AS ARGUMENT

In this chapter the two macro forms of textual organisation have been examined by drawing on theories relating to their structure and strategies. The purpose of the detailed discussion of these theories is to enable analysis that identifies how elements of media texts are constructed and organised for particular purposes. It seeks to enable analysis that charts the text holistically. This assists the analyst in probing the implications of the choices made in their construction to their discursive meaning. What discourses do they articulate? What knowledge do they seek to naturalise? What are the politics of their representations?

The chapter has been concerned to demonstrate approaches to unpacking the discourses at work in media texts. No representation, factual or fictional, is viewed as simply neutral, but as working with purpose and so rhetorically. Narrative theories have tended to be considered more relevant to media fiction, to Hollywood movies and entertainment rather than non-fiction texts. The view outlined in this chapter sees the division between a focus on storytelling in fiction on one hand and a focus on information for non-fiction on the other as misleading. We have used narrative theories (and theories about argument) to investigate non-fiction media texts as we analysed the stories that journalists and advertisers present to us, for as documentary film theorist Nichols suggests, the boundaries between documentary and fiction 'inescapably blur' (1994:1).

In the same way, theories about argument have been generally considered more relevant to non-fictional texts. Once again, this division overlooks the point that non-fiction and fiction texts equally articulate and privilege particular discursive positions. The analytic tools need to be able to investigate their arguments and positions whether implicit or explicit.

As a final example, we turn to a fictional narrative to make obvious the rhetorical and discursive work of story by referring to a story broadcast on TV for children. The choice is deliberate, as childhood and children's fiction is generally viewed as apolitical and benign rather than anything else. Below is the synopsis of episode 9 of *Magic Cellar* as it is recounted on the website which describes the series as celebrating 'Africa's cultures and traditions'. Each episode has a moral to the tale – an explicit indication of the story as a purposive rhetorical and discursive act.

> Episode 9
>
> The chief's bride
>
> A village woman has two daughters, one good and one naughty. The Chief decides to choose a bride, and summons both of them to meet him. The naughty daughter takes the wrong path and is not successful. The good daughter takes the right path and ends up with the Chief.
>
> The lesson: respecting and obedient behaviour is rewarded in the end. (http://www.sabceducation.co.za/magiccellar/Cellar.html)

Accepting that this story has a hero (the girl who gets the chief) and a false hero (the girl who lost out) and that the quest is for marriage to the chief, we can clearly identify the binary oppositions. Girls should be obedient, respectful and unadventurous. The reward is marriage to a chief in an arranged marriage. The binary oppositions of this construct would include girls being disobedient (questioning), disrespectful (challenging) and adventurous. The punishment would be failing to secure the arranged marriage. Clearly this is a patriarchal discourse that rehearses a particular kind of femininity that serves to complement dominant masculinity. The emphasis on the moral of the tale makes it clear that this narrative is producing a deliberative and deductive argument. By analogy, girls should seek to behave like the 'good' girl in order to live happily ever after.

As the story stands, its discursive work is to conserve patriarchal power relations and to validate a feminine role as passive and submissive.

Here then, in concluding this chapter, we have an example of story as argument, of a powerful discourse being rehearsed to naturalise a particular 'truth' and to construct subjects of that discourse.

FURTHER READING

Bauman, R. 1986. *Story, performance, and event: Contextual studies of oral narrative.* Cambridge: Cambridge University Press.

Kozloff, S.R. 1989. Narrative theory and television, in: *Channels of discourse*, edited by R.C. Allen. London: Routledge: 42–73.

Propp, V. 1968. *Morphology of the folktale.* Translated by L. Scott. 2nd edition. Austin: University of Texas Press.

Richardson, J. 2007. *Analysing newspapers. An approach from critical discourse analysis.* Basingstoke: Palgrave Macmillan.

Stillar, G.F. 1998. *Analyzing everyday texts. Discourse, rhetoric and social perspectives.* London: Sage.

Thompson, J.B. (1990). *Ideology and modern culture. Critical social theory in the era of mass communication.* Palo Alto, Calif: Stanford University Press.

Bauman, R. 1986. *Story, performance, and event: Contextual studies of oral narrative.* Cambridge: Cambridge University Press.

LEARNING ACTIVITIES

- Present a summary of the similarities and differences between the two concepts outlined in this chapter, namely discourse and ideology.
- 'Not a window on the world, nor a reflection of reality'. Discuss the role of the media as mediating or rhetorical.
- Outline the different narrative theories and apply them to the article, 'Bargain hunting'.
- Apply the theories introduced in the section on argumentation to either an editorial in a recent edition of a newspaper or a set of letters to the editor on a single topic.
- Rework the Magic Cellar story by constructing the adventurous girl as hero. This will result in a very different discourse. What Proppian character roles do the other characters take up in your version?
- Read the Fred Khumalo column, 'The green and gold in black and white' (7 September 2008). First apply all the narrative and argumentation strategies you have encountered in this chapter. Thereafter, present a detailed and structured critical analysis of the argument he presents.

Textual analysis: Narrative and Argument

he Fred Khumalo Page

SOMEWHAT SERIOUS
SOMEWHAT FUN

ecent successes of black Boks have only uncovered the
risy that has always hidden behind rugby's 'merit' badge

Fred wants to hear your comments about his column.
Send him an e-mail atkhumalof@sundaytimes.co.za.•
Read Fred's blog at http://blo.gs.thetimes.co.za/khumalo/

The green and gold in black and white

was a time when the
us rugby brigade
d hundreds of
per column centimetres
ining about players of
being drafted into our
al squad for all the wrong
s – to fill in racial quotas.
e opposing side, of
averred that rugby,
e rest of society, had to
sformed – not only at
inistrative level– and
of colour had to be
n opportunity to prove
ey deserved to don the
nd gold.
ne of them – including
s of Chester Williams,
n Paulse and Bryan
a – proved beyond doubt
ey were worthy of being
Boks.
ose waving the "merit"
e a talisman should be
ting that, at last, we are
ng more black players to
rt on merit.
s, this past week's events
that the chorus about
as but a smoke screen.
r sister newspaper, The
reported on Tuesday
gby fans who sat in the
tand at Ellis Park called
adio 702 to tell about
o of spectators who
d "kaffir" every time Bok
ngi Nokwe scored a try.
his doesn't tell you
about the state of mind
e of our rugby followers,
nsider an incident that
ed at the same game.
ingi Shibambo, 30, had
tting in the stands for the
on of the first half.
told The Times: "I
off during half-time

to the ladies', and on my way back one of the guys bumped into me.
When I confronted him he said: 'You bloody kaffirs, you took over what was the only exclusively white sport in South-Africa.' "

TRYING TIMES: Jongikhaya Nokwe is injured after scoring his fourth try at Ellis Park
Picture: SYDNEY SESHIBEDI

She said one of the three men
pushed her up against the wall and the other two kept tapping their fingers against her forehead, saying: "You have also taken our fathers' land."

This sparked memories of an eventful visit to a rugby game a couple of years ago.

I asked my childhood friend, Vika, to accompany me to a Bulls game at Loftus Versfeld.

"Since when are you a rugby follower?" asked my friend. "You guys are rushing to this reconciliation thing too fast, when the other side is not moving to the table with equal haste. *Nithanda uinto zabelungu* – you like white people's things."

I challenged him on the notion of rugby being a white man's game. Soccer was brought to this country by white people, but no one sees it as a white man's game. Cars first reached these shores via white people, but no darkie has told me not to use them because they are a white man's tool. So, generalisations such as these are dangerous.

In any case, because my friend was bored and didn't mind going for a drive, he decided to come with me.

No sooner had we parked, not far from the stadium, than we were confronted by a group of white guys who wanted to know what we were doing in the neighbourhood.

Giving them my best manure–eating grin, I told them we were here not to steal cars, but to watch rugby.

"What do you know about rugby?" one of them asked.

But we shrugged them off and continued to our suite.

Anyway, my friend Vika's words about whites protecting rugby with all that they have proved to be prophetic if you consider what those men said to Shibambo at the weekend.

Maybe, in our naivety as progressive South Africans, we always assume that everyone is moving at the same-pace as us, in the same direction, to the appointed destination of a true, shared, egalitarian and nonracial nationhood.

We assume too much.

Unfortunately for the bigots, however, you can't sit on the lid of a boiling pot forever, as the alleged poet Mzwakhe Mbuli once said.

I come from an era when our soccer was, through government edict, segregated" with whites and blacks having their own federations.

But the artificial walls collapsed under pressure, and white players such as Andy "Jesus" Karajinsky, Phil "Uyindoda" Venter, Noel "Mzala" Cousins, Basil Hollister, Neil "MokQko" Tovey, Dave Watterson,'Gordon Igesund and many others started gaining prominence at black clubs.

These players, and also the likes of Sulie "Bump Jive" Bhamjee and Deshi Bhaktawer, ruled the roost. Nobody complained about whites and Indians taking over a "black" sport.

That's why there has never been a need for quotas when it came to soccer; whites were always welcome. And the cream (an apt expression to refer to white players) always rose to the top.

Against this background, therefore, I must thank Nokwe for exposing the lie about merit for what it really is: a bigoted smoke screen.

Nokwe performs well but is still not wanted for the simple reason that he is black.

Many will say these are but isolated incidents; they might well be, but they speak eloquently about the resentment that is still there among whites who labour under the notion that some aspects of South African life and culture belong to them exclusively.

I am thoroughly pissed off at the righteous rugby hypocrites who will do anything including subterfuge, lies and violence – to keep black people away from a shared South African experience, on and off the field.

253

chapter seven

NARRATIVE ANALYSIS

David Wigston

LEARNING OUTCOMES

At the end of this chapter, you should be able to:
- identify in a text the basic components and elements that make up a narrative;
- describe Roland Barthes's narrative theory and identify elements of Barthes's theory in a text;
- identify binary oppositions within a text and determine the meanings generated by these oppositions;
- use Tzvetan Todorov's elementary narrative model to analyse a text;
- use Vladimir Propp's narrative model to analyse a text;
- use Umberto Eco's model to establish the world view in a particular text;
- explain the effect postmodernism has had on narrative.

Narrative Analysis

THIS CHAPTER

This chapter is about telling stories, particularly those we find in the media. We investigate how stories, or more correctly narratives, are constructed and how we interpret them in order to gain meaning from the text. Firstly, we look at the syntagmatic arrangement of the narrative, where we focus on what happens in the narrative in order to move the story forward. This concerns the linear arrangement of the narrative where the temporal chain–effect relationship between events in the narrative is important. This syntagmatic approach is represented by the models of Tzvetan Todorov and Vladimir Propp. Secondly, we consider the narrative structure paradigmatically, where we look at how meaning is generated by probing the various levels found within the narrative. This paradigmatic approach is represented by the narrative model of Umberto Eco. These models are supported and explained by the theoretical views of Seymour Chatman, Roland Barthes and Claude Lévi-Strauss. But, to start, we look at the characteristics of a narrative. Although the contents of this chapter are inclusive of all media messages, for the sake of convenience an emphasis has been placed on television narratives. However, this does not imply that all mediated narratives are synonymous in their construction as the nature of the medium can influence the structure of the discourse. The well-known sitcom *Cheers* is used in a case study to demonstrate how binary opposition and Propp's model can be used to analyse the narrative structure of a text. We conclude the chapter by taking a brief introductory look at the effect of postmodernism on the structure of a narrative, particularly that found in television.

7.1 INTRODUCTION

Why study narrative? Hobbs (1998:264) comments that, as individuals, we need no instruction in how to watch a film or television. We simply either like or dislike what we see. Chances are that we arrange our daily schedule around those television programmes we enjoy watching. It is also likely that we discuss some of those programmes with our friends, family or colleagues the next day. This points to the pervasive nature of the media and its unique powers, which go unnoticed because the media are such a part of our daily lives. But as students of communication, we need to think critically about what we read and see. A critical analysis of media content is not particularly easy, owing to the sheer omnipotence of the media. Because of its visual basis, we particularly tend to treat film and television as we do the rest of the world. Film and television have acquired so much power simply because they appear to be genuine, authentic and real. This has led to an 'as-seen-on-TV' syndrome, where, because it was seen on television, it must be so. Unlike our direct experiences, we have to remind ourselves that film and television are merely representations 'carefully and expensively designed for our consumption' (Hobbs 1998:264).

In this chapter, we are not going to enter the debate on whether film and television represent a window on the world or if they are a mirror of society. Instead we opt for the position where film and television are seen as skilfully manufactured products. Within the context of this discussion, the broad purpose of this chapter is then to develop our critical skills about the media so that we can function effectively and efficiently in the current information age. We consider ways in which we can analyse and deconstruct some of the messages put out by film and television, in particular the narrative contained in those messages.

Narrative is not limited to film and television, as it can be found in any text that contains language, images, gestures or aspects of these. The French literary philosopher, Roland Barthes (1977a:79), who provides us with the dominant thinking on narrative (which we discuss in more detail in a later section), indicates that narratives are not limited to the media, but exist in a variety of genres, such as myths, legends, fables, tales, novellas, epics, history, tragedy, comedy, mime, film, the news, and even in paintings and stained-glass windows. Basically, this comes down to the fact that, as humans, we all have narratives and we like sharing these with other people. Initially, stories were passed down through the ages by word-of-mouth as folk tales. Inventions such as the printing press and film have helped to preserve and record these tales for us. But with the development of the media there has been an increase in the number of stories at our disposal. This commonplace nature of storytelling often means that we are unaware of the fact that we are constantly surrounded by a variety of stories. Amongst many others, stories form part of the advertisements we see on breakfast-time television. We refer to items in news bulletins as stories. The cartoon strip we so avidly turn to in the newspaper tells a story. Of all the media, one of the most prodigious in the production of stories today must surely be that of television. It is for this reason that we emphasise television narratives in this chapter.

Narrative Analysis

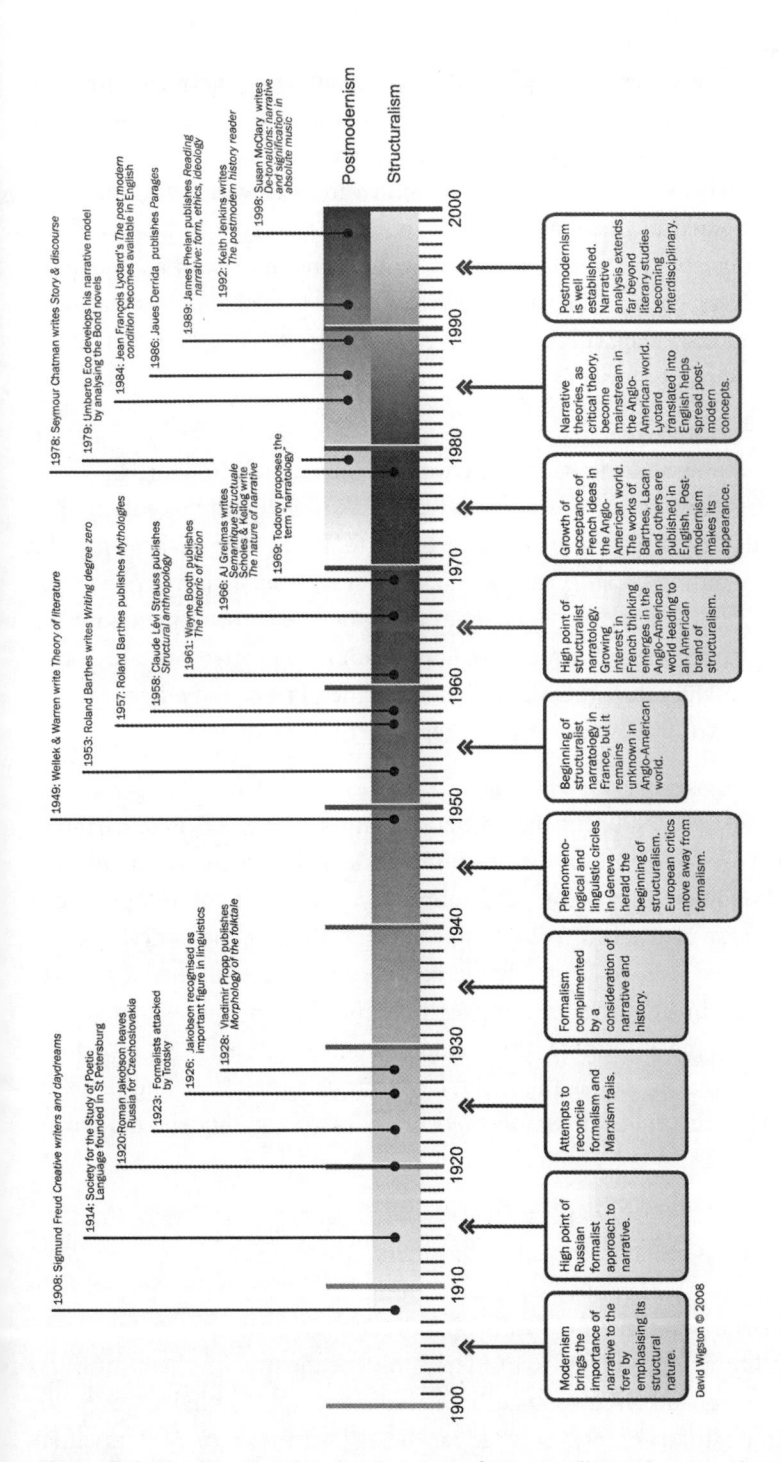

Figure 7.1 Timeline showing development of structuralist and postmodern narrative analysis

But how do stories work? Is there any similarity between the way television tells a story to that of a paperback novel? Although we know how an action drama series shown on television will end – the hero always wins so that he or she can return in next week's episode – we still sit glued to the edge of our seats. Why? In order to answer these questions about how television (as being representative of all mediated narratives) works, it 'becomes necessary for us to step out of its magnetic pull and take it apart piece by piece' (Kozloff 1987:45). This then is the gist of narrative analysis.

That narrative has a structure was first described in ancient Greece by Aristotle and Plato, a point we will come back to shortly. It was the development of the Critical School during the 20th century that provided us, over time, with some of the tools necessary to broaden our understanding of storytelling. Slowly a new field, known collectively as narrative theory, took shape, drawing on the work of many diverse scholars, beginning with the work of Vladimir Propp in the late 1920s. Structural literature theorists, such as Barthes, Propp and others, argued that all narratives share certain deep structural elements.

The notion of narrative having a structure gained renewed popularity as a critical concept during the mid-20th century. The vast field of narrative theory received input from different subjects such as linguistics, anthropology, film theory and semiology, where the common binding agent is structuralism. We attempt to bring all these theoretical strands together so that we can study the nature of narratives in mediated texts and explain how these narratives function. We introduce you to the work of some well-known structuralist scholars in this field, particularly the theoretical explanations of Seymour Chatman, Roland Barthes and Claude Lévi-Strauss, followed by the narrative models of Tzvetan Todorov and Vladimir Propp.

Perhaps, at this point, we need to consider a brief definition of structuralism. Pateman (2005) considers structuralism as 'an ahistorical, synchronic [concerned with something, especially a language, as it exists at a point in time – author] approach to the study of the products of cultural endeavour, considered independently of their authors, consumers and circumstances'. The reference to structuralism as being ahistorical is contentious, as it can be argued that history is essential to the shaping of a cultural product since the writer works within a specific context that has been determined by what went before. But, says Pateman (2005), the reader inevitably encounters cultural products ahistorically, since when they are consumed for pleasure it is done without regard to history.

However, these ideas began to recede when postmodernism, as proposed by Michel Foucault and Jacques Derrida, claimed that such widespread shared deep structures were logically impossible. Although we do touch on postmodern views of narrative, we place the emphasis on the structuralist approach to narrative analysis because of its historical dominance and effective application in revealing a particular narrative structure. Figure 7.1 gives you a historical overview of the development of narrative analysis so that you can place the various developments into perspective.

Our study of narrative is based on three important assumptions regarding messages in the media. These are (Hobbs 1998:266–269):

- *Media messages are constructions:* all media messages are created by a variety of people with distinct and varied purposes, which complicates the construction. Internal forces which can influence message construction include company policies, budgets and processes. The visual nature of film and television means that we, as the audience, find the content easy to interpret with little awareness of its constructed nature. We take the conventions used in that construction to be natural and normal.
- *Media messages have economic and political contexts:* the organisation of television as an institution has a large influence on the way in which the programme content is constructed. External forces at work include such bureaucratic aspects as regulation of the broadcasting environment, legislation and competition. We also have to take into account market forces, such as the role played by advertising, which are central to the operation of any broadcaster today. These forces are invariably covert and long-term in nature.
- *Individuals negotiate meaning in media texts:* we now recognise that meaning is result of the interaction between the individual and the content of media messages. The process governing this interaction is a complex one involving a number of variables unique to each individual. We bring to the text our own unique circumstances and knowledge when interpreting those messages. These circumstances and knowledge can either complement or contradict the information

| assumptions

in the message, so aiding in the construction of the final meaning. The implication of this point of view is that we can no longer assume a universal interpretation of any message.

Much of what we learn in this chapter is derived from linguistics, where some of the theories and models of narrative were initially developed. A peculiar convention that has carried over to media studies from the study of literature is our use of the term 'read' when we view, and subsequently interpret, a film or television programme, while we use 'text' when we refer to the content of that film or programme. As Hobbs (1998:260) elaborates, '"reading" a film or television program is not substantially different from reading a newspaper or a novel'. She substantiates her argument by saying that the visual images in film and television are symbolic, like those we use for representing the printed word. We, as the readers, have to learn those symbols in order to interpret the meaning of any particular image.

To conclude this introduction, we need to return to the question we posed at the beginning: why study narrative? A succinct answer to this would be so that we can appreciate how it was put together in the first place. Such an understanding would provide us with a competency in evaluating the relevance of mediated messages, and with such insight we can then start creating our own meaningful messages.

7.2 THE BASIC NARRATIVE PARADIGM

chain effect

What exactly, then, is a narrative? We can define a narrative as a 'sequence of events that are linked causally in time and space' (Gillespie 2006:91). The basic progress of a narrative is that of a linear cause–effect relationship; 'A' is the cause of 'B', which in turn is the cause of 'C', and so on (Butler 1994:20). This is also known as a chain effect, where one event causes the next, which in turn causes the next. There are exceptions to this rule, notably in postmodern narratives, which we will return to at the end of this chapter.

Before we can proceed, we need to look in a little more detail at the three elements that make up the chain effect in a narrative, and in so doing help us to make sense of that narrative. These are summarised in Figure 7.2 and then briefly discussed.

Narrative Analysis

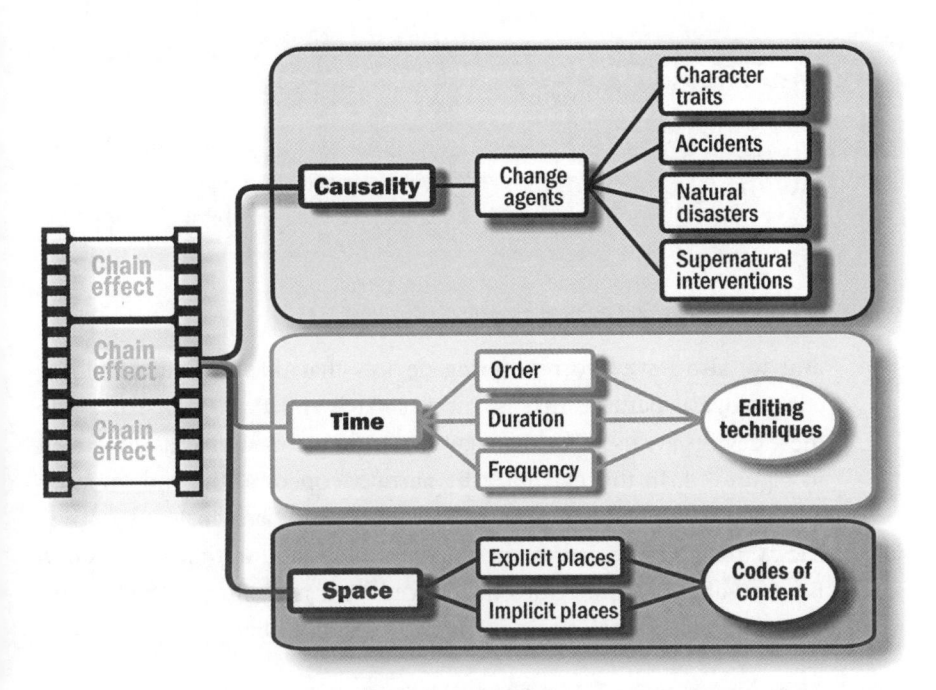

Figure 7.2 The elements that are responsible for the chain effect in a narrative (adapted from Gillespie 2006:91–96)

- *Causality:* change agents are essential for the chain effect to take place. We can identify four basic groups of change agents:
  - traits of characters (i.e. their attitudes, beliefs, values, abilities, etc.);
  - accidents;
  - natural disasters;
  - supernatural interventions.

  These change agents can work individually or in combination. It then becomes possible for us to analyse the different ways in which, for example, a character can set a particular chain of events into motion.

  | change agents

- *Time:* here we need to consider how time is structure and represented. We can identify three types of time relationship in a narrative (Gillispie 2006:93–95):
  - *order,* which is used to build dramatic tension and relates to the positioning of the climax and resolution (see Figure 7.5). To achieve this, use is made of a linear chronological sequence which is illustrated in Figure 7.3;

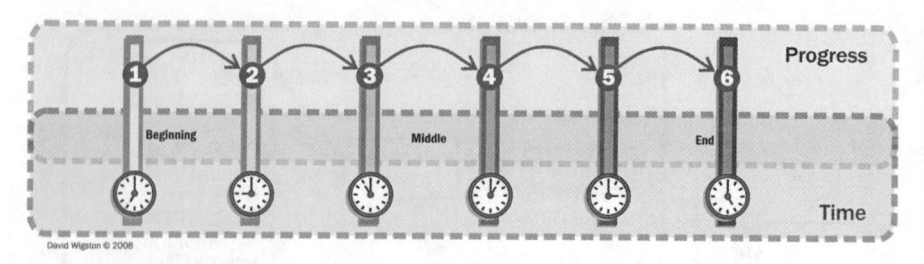

Figure 7.3 Narrative showing a linear progress

But we also have two reordering devices that do not follow a linear chronological pattern; that is, the flashback and flash-forward. When these devices are used, we then have a non-linear narrative, as illustrated in Figure 7.4. In this example, the narrative opens at the end (number 1 in Figure 7.4) and, by means of flashbacks and flash-forwards, moves backwards and forwards along the chronological duration of the story. Because of the complexities introduced by a non-linear narrative, we will continue to focus on linear narratives in this chapter.

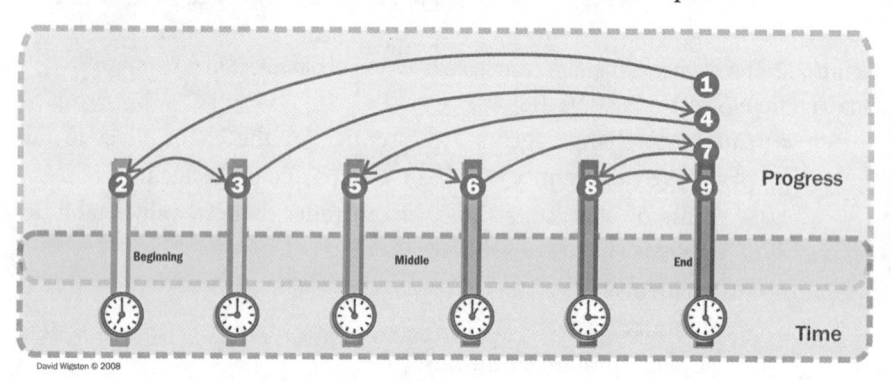

Figure 7.4 Narrative showing a non-linear progress

- *duration*, where we need to compare the screen time of the narrative with the time period covered by the story. For example, the screen time could be 115 minutes, while the story told in the narrative could cover a period of 12 years. Editing techniques are used to condense a 12-year period into 115 minutes by removing aspects irrelevant to the narrative;
- *frequency*, or the amount of times that any one event is presented to us. For example, the same event can occur several times in a narrative, with each occurrence presented from a different perspective, in so doing presenting us with additional information.

- *Space*: relates to the movement of objects and figures, since a narrative has to occur within a particular social setting and geographic place. We can determine two types of places:
  - *explicit places* are the places that are overt and manifest, in which action physically takes place. The sense of place is constructed by the codes of content that are used, that is, lighting, colour, décor, props, costumes, etc.;
  - *implicit places* are those talked, imagined or dreamt about by characters in the narrative.

  The codes of content [that which occurs in front of the camera – author] that are used to indicate space give, but also hold back, information about what is happening and what is about to happen. The representation of space is a very important part of the structure of a narrative as it is responsible for creating a relationship between us, as the readers of the narrative, in seeing and knowing.

The basic narrative paradigm that we are familiar with today was first described by Aristotle, who identified the classic three-act dramatic structure in his *Poetics*. This structure consists simply of a beginning–middle–end sequence, although each element is essential in order to form a narrative structure. No matter how you arrange or divide up the parts of the story, there will always be a beginning, a middle and an end – remove one and we no longer have a complete narrative structure. The soap opera, with its open-ended narrative, is just such an example. In addition, given the vast number of episodes that make up a soap opera, often running into several thousand, we can say that the narrative is also lacking a beginning. This, then, is the reason why it is so difficult to analyse the narrative of a soap opera; it is always missing a formal beginning and end.

| Aristotle

Within this beginning–middle–end structure, the narrative also undergoes a certain development as part of its linear progress, in which we can identify distinct phases. The generalised location of these within the duration of a narrative is illustrated in Figure 7.5.

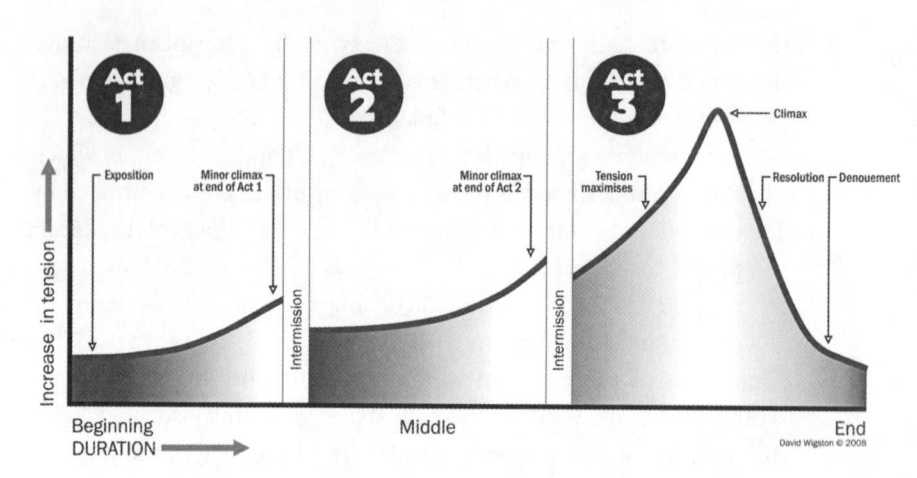

Figure 7.5 Aristotle's three-act narrative model

These various phases are explained below.

- *Exposition*: the exposition introduces the reader to the two basic components that make up the story, which are the principal characters and the space or environment that they occupy. Every narrative must have an exposition, but it is not necessarily always located at the beginning of the narrative as suggested in Figure 7.5 (Butler 1994:19). In television series, the constant recurring nature of certain characters means that the exposition phase of the narrative is usually very brief because it is assumed that we, as regular viewers, are already familiar with those characters. The usual technique is to reintroduce the characters as part of the title sequence. If the narrative opens with the action already in progress, then we say the narrative is *in media res* (Butler 1994:19). The enigma or problems to be resolved in the narrative are usually stated in the exposition.
- *Climax*: the climax occurs when conflict in the story reaches its peak. While the climax is considered to be the most concentrated moment of the entire narrative, its does not signal the end of that narrative (Butler 1994:21). In television programmes we usually find a number of smaller climaxes, where the plot peaks prior to cutting away for an advertising break. The purpose of these mini-climaxes is not to resolve tension, but rather the opposite: to heighten interest in the narrative so as to ensure that the audience returns to the programme following the break.
- *Resolution*: the resolution follows on from the climax, where the enigmas posed at the beginning of the narrative are resolved.

Narrative Analysis

- *Denouement*: the denouement brings about closure to the narrative by rounding out the story. If a narrative ends without a resolution and denouement then we have an open narrative. In this case we refer to the climax as a cliffhanger. This is a device used to attract the audience to the next episode by making use of a strong element of suspense. Open narratives abound in certain film and television genres, such as the soap opera, since this technique facilitates a continuance of the narrative at a later time, either as a sequel or as a continuing episode.

> cliffhanger

From the above discussion we can identify certain characteristics of a narrative structure:

- The boundaries of an act are in approximate known locations and can be made up of a single event or a sequence of events.
- Each act contains one climax, considered to be the most intense moment in the act. The climax occurs close to the end, if it is not the last dramatic event in the act.
- There is a short break, or interval, between acts in order to create boundaries for the act.
- The structure is established from the placement of various dramatic elements.
- The narrative structure is subject to variation.

When studying the narratives of mediated messages, we have to remember that, while the principles governing those messages remain the same, no two narratives are alike. We also need to keep in mind that narrative is closely allied with genre, and that television genres are constantly evolving. One of the relatively more recent developments in television genres is the introduction of multiple plots within the narrative. A ground-breaking programme in this field is considered to be the police drama *Hill Street Blues*, which aired for the first time in the United States on 15 January 1981 (Deming 1985:1). Up to five distinct plots can be identified in any episode of *Hill Street Blues*, where each plot has its own exposition, climax, resolution and denouement.

> multiple plots

In narrative analysis, the literary work of a text is not the object of the exercise. Barthes (1977a:79) succinctly phrases it as: 'caring nothing for the division between good and bad literature, narrative is international, transhistorical, transcultural: it is simply there like life itself'. To quote Chatman (1978:17), in narrative analysis the question we need to ask

265

is not 'what makes *Macbeth* great?' but rather 'what makes *Macbeth* a tragedy?' Narrative analysis does not concern itself with the empirical content, literary merits or quality of production and performances in a text. It does concern itself with the structure and functioning of a discourse in order to establish a grid of possibilities by identifying constant features. A grid is established and each text is plotted on the grid, not to adjust the text, but to adjust the grid (Chatman 1978:18–19). Structuralist theories of narrative thus seek to explain the laws that govern narrative structure, not the accuracy of its representation of reality (Fiske 1987b:131).

7.3 ROLAND BARTHES'S THEORY OF NARRATIVE

Where, then, does one start looking for the structure of a narrative? Obviously in the narrative itself. But the tools needed to analyse this structure are provided by a model; the findings are explained by a theory. In order to construct a suitable model and accompanying theory, the French structuralist Roland Barthes (1915–1980) suggests we look to linguistics, from which structuralism originally evolved (Barthes 1977a:82). Barthes's assumption was that language is made up of a system of signs that reflect the beliefs of a particular society at a particular time. Narratives found in media texts differ little, if at all, from those found in literature. Thus, we can begin our study of media narratives by looking at how narratives function in literary texts. Then we can make the necessary analogies regarding the way narratives function in a media text.

story

discourse

Before we continue further with Barthes's theory of narrative, we need to first identify the elements that make up a narrative. These various elements are summarised in Figure 7.6. From a structuralist point of view, all narratives consist of two layers. The first layer is the story, which sets out the content or the chain of events (i.e. the action and happenings) together with the existents (i.e. the characters and setting). The second layer is the discourse, which is the expression, or form, of the story. Chatman (1978:19) explains these components in simple terms when he says 'the story is *the what* in a narrative ... discourse is *the how*'. This distinction between the two layers of a narrative is a synthetic one, as in reality a story cannot exist without a discourse and vice versa.

Narrative Analysis

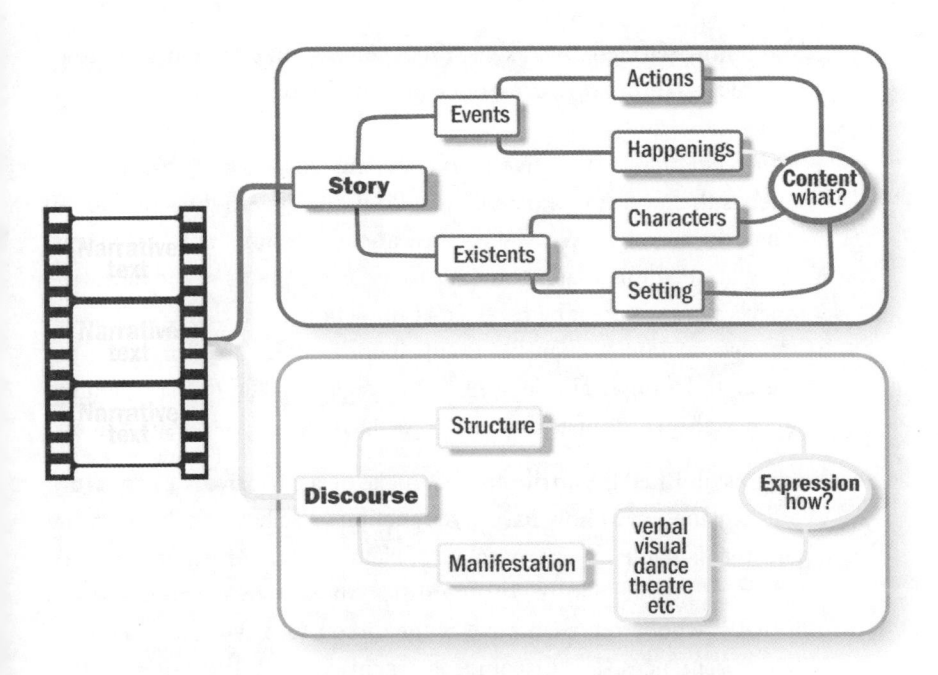

Figure 7.6 A structuralist model of a narrative (adapted from Chatman 1978:26)

Because there is such a clear distinction between story and discourse, we can take the story element of a narrative and easily transpose it onto different media. Thus, as an example, the same Agatha Christie who-done-it narrative can be presented to us as a novel, a film, serialised on radio or presented on the stage as a play. Instead of following the story through words printed in a book, we can alternatively follow that same story through other codes. We can say this because the story element of a narrative is not made up exclusively of words or images, but events and existents that are manifest and signified by words and images. Thus we can say that stories can exist independently of any particular medium (Chatman 1978:20). On the second level we also need to distinguish clearly between the structure of the discourse and the manner in which it is manifest, or presented to us.

Why do we say that narratives are structured? To qualify as a structure, a narrative requires three attributes (Chatman 1978:21). These are as follows:

- *Wholeness*: a narrative is whole because it is made up of distinct elements that differ from what those elements constitute. This attribute is clearly illustrated in Figure 7.6. These elements are not

attributes of a narrative

267

randomly selected, but, as we discuss later in this section, tend to be related in an organised manner and in so doing produce a unique chain of events.
- *Self-regulation*: a narrative maintains and closes itself. This basically means that events or existents that do not belong to the story do not enter the narrative. While the appearance of certain events or existents may not be immediately obvious to us, as recipients of the narrative, their relevance must be revealed at some point in the discourse.
- *Transformation*: to manifest events in a particular medium, the event needs to be physically represented by signs specific to that medium, such as the words in a book. This process is known as transformation.

Having established the attributes that make up a narrative, we can return to our explanation of how narrative functions. We have established that a narrative is made up of a number of elements that are all interrelated and hierarchical in nature. In linguistics, the sentence is the smallest unit that is wholly representative of the discourse. Beyond the sentence are more sentences. The discourse is organised by all the sentences that make up a particular text. Through this discourse, or organisation of sentences, can be seen a message that operates at a higher level than the language in which it was written. The discourse is then made up of a number of units that are fitted together syntagmatically according to specific codes, which in the case of linguistics are the rules of grammar.

This means that if we want to undertake a narrative analysis of a text, it is necessary that we first establish the relationships between the sentences and the discourse, since a formal organisation orders all semiotic systems, whatever their substance and dimension. Structurally, television narratives share the same syntagmatic characteristics as the sentence, except that television narratives make use of different and far more complex signs and signifiers.

elements of a narrative

From linguistics, we have learned that in order to analyse the narrative of a media text we need to make explicit every system of meaning through its organisation. The narrative is not a simple sum of the propositions that constitute the dialogue. In other words, merely retelling the story that makes up the narrative is not a narrative analysis. In order to analyse the narrative we need to begin by classifying the enormous number of elements that make up that narrative. This embodies the concept of a level of description. A sentence can be described hierarchically on several levels: for example, it can be described phonetically, grammatically or contextually. Each of these levels has its own unit and correlation, which require a second description. What Barthes is saying here, is that on its own a unit has no meaning. A unit only takes on meaning if we integrate that unit into a higher level. For instance, in language, syllables give meaning only when we consider them on the higher level of words, and words only give meaning when integrated into a sentence, and so on. In this integrational system of creating meaning we find two types of relationship between the signs we use – distribution, which occurs on the same level, and integration, which occurs on the next higher level.

To follow the unfolding of a story, it is not enough to understand the narrative. We need to project the horizontal links of the narrative onto a vertical axis. To read a narrative means not only moving horizontally from one unit to the next, but also moving vertically from one descriptive level to the next. Barthes (1977a:87) distinguishes three levels of description in a narrative:

- the level of function;
- the level of action of characters;
- the level of narration in the discourse.

These three levels are fully integrated. A function only has meaning in so far as it has a place in the action of a character, and this action in turn receives meaning when it is narrated.

Therefore, to begin a narrative analysis, we need to define the smallest unit that we can find in the narrative. Meaning must be the creation of such a unit. Its contribution to the story makes it a unit and these first-level units are called functions. As Barthes (1977a:89) says, 'the essence of a function is, so to speak, the seed that it sows in the narrative, planting an element that will come to fruition later – on the same level or elsewhere, on another level'. In narrative, everything has a meaning. Every action must contribute to the narrative, and this, rather than the manner in which it is said or done, makes it a functional unit. Some functions can be represented by small units. For example, in a James Bond film, the telephone rings during the night shift at Secret Service headquarters. James Bond picks up one of the four receivers. The four constitutes a functional unit, referring connotatively to a concept necessary to the story, that of a highly developed bureaucratic

| functions

technology. This narrative unit is not the linguistic unit, which is one word – four – but rather the connoted value. This explains how short functional units can be, yet still be an integral part of the discourse. Such units, although incredibly short, extend beyond the level of denotation, and become indexical to a higher order meaning (Barthes 1977a:91).

distribution

integration

At this point, it is necessary that we return to Barthes's concepts of distribution and integration in order to consider the different levels of meaning. Some units correlate to other units on the same level, which is distribution, while others relate to a higher level, which is integration. On the first level, an example of a distributional function in a film or television narrative would be the picking up of a telephone receiver, as this corresponds to the moment of putting it down. On the second level, an example of an integrational function would be the purchase of a revolver, which correlates later in the narrative with the moment it is used. Integrational units also function as indices, since the unit refers not to a complementary and consequential act, but to a more diffuse concept that is necessary to the understanding of the story. The relationship between the unit and its correlate is now no longer distributional. To illustrate this aspect, we take as our example an episode of the action drama series *MacGyver*, titled 'The Lost Amadeus'. The casual integration of an invitation to a 'Roaring 20s Bash' (a theme party) at the beginning of the episode leads to a major setting at the resolution of the narrative in a nightclub known as 'The Speakeasy' (see also Table 7.1 for more detail).

indices

Several indices can refer to the same signified, but the order of their occurrence is not pertinent. For example, from later on in the same episode of *MacGyver*, Lulu agrees to hand over the violin to the villains, Tubbs and Ginko, in a place with a lot of people to ensure her own safety. This function also points towards the 'Roaring 20s Bash' at 'The Speakeasy', but in a different way. In order to understand these indexical units, we have to move to a higher level, that of the characters' actions and narration, for only on this higher level is the index clarified by being given meaning. Unlike functions that refer to a signified, indices become semantic units because of the vertical nature of their relationships. Indexical meanings are paradigmatically confirmed higher up the narrative through integration, while that of their function is confirmed syntagmatically by distribution. Some narratives, like folk tales, tend to be heavily functional, while others, such as psychological thrillers, are mainly indexical.

Narrative Analysis

This simple classification can then be further subdivided. Not all units are of the same importance. Some form hinge points in the narrative. Let us return to our episode of *MacGyver* for an example:

- Having arrived at Izzy's home, which belongs to Lulu's musician boss, MacGyver gets out of the car and refuses a lift home because of Lulu's erratic driving.
- Trying to organise his damaged bicycle, MacGyver drops his newspaper at the front gate and subsequently finds Lulu's invitation to the 'Roaring 20s Bash' lodged inside the newspaper.
- MacGyver goes into the house in order to return the invitation.

In this manner, MacGyver becomes embroiled in the villains' attempt to extort the Amadeus violin out of Izzy and Lulu, who are inside the house at that moment. From this example we can see that hinge points are necessary for the chain effect to occur in order to move the narrative forward.

| hinge points

Other functions act as fillers to merely occupy narrative space between hinge points. Fillers play an important role, particularly in television narratives, where exact timing is essential. A programme has to run for a set time, and fillers provide a convenient way in which the narrative can be expanded, or collapsed, to fit an allotted space of time.

| fillers

Barthes (1977a:93) refers to hinge points as cardinal functions, while fillers are referred to as catalysers because of their complementary nature. To qualify as a cardinal function, the action must have a direct consequence on the development of the story. Between two cardinal functions we can find any number of catalyser functions, which then do not modify the story. This is illustrated graphically in Figure 7.7.

| cardinal functions

| catalysers

The squares represent the position of cardinal functions (or hinge points) in the narrative

The large circle represents the extent of influence of a cardinal function

The dots represent catalyser functions (or fillers) that fill in space between cardinal functions

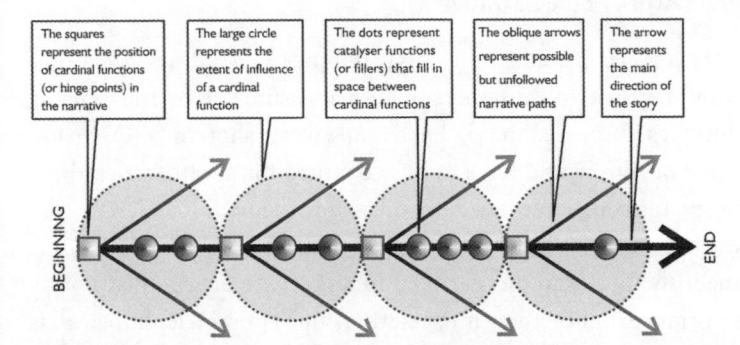

The oblique arrows represent possible but unfollowed narrative paths

The arrow represents the main direction of the story

Figure 7.7 Graphic illustration of the position of cardinal and catalyser functions in a narrative (adapted from Chatman 1978:54)

271

Catalyser functions are consecutive units only, while cardinal functions are both consecutive and consequential – what comes after the unit is caused by that unit. Thus, as shown in Figure 7.7, the first cardinal function is the cause of the second cardinal function, while the second becomes the cause of the third, and so on until the narrative ends. Table 7.1 illustrates the position of the first few cardinal and catalyser functions in 'The Lost Amadeus'. The fact that Lulu insists on taking MacGyver home, after damaging his bicycle, leads directly to MacGyver becoming involved with the villains. Barthes (1977a:94) described catalysers as being parasitic. Their function is merely chronological and they only serve to separate two moments in the story. Cardinal functions have a dual, yet simultaneous, function. They are both chronological and logical. If we were to isolate the cardinal functions in a narrative, as we have done in Table 7.1, we would be left with the structural framework of that narrative. On catalyser and cardinal functions, Barthes (1977a:95) says, 'Cardinal functions are the risky moments of a narrative. Between these points of alternative, these "dispatchers", the catalysers lay out the areas of safety, rests, luxuries.' There are distinct rules that we need to follow when stringing together the different paradigmatic functional units into the narrative syntagm. These rules are as follows:

- Indices always point to a higher level in the narrative.
- Cardinal and catalyser functions link by implication.
- A catalyser function implies the existence of a cardinal function, but not vice versa.
- Catalyser functions (or fillers) can be removed from the narrative, cardinal functions (or hinge points) cannot.
- Cardinal functions are bound together by reciprocity and this defines the framework of the narrative.

In any narrative there can be a large number of cardinal functions, but it would prove too cumbersome to measure all of these using the techniques discussed here. Each and every shot in a television programme or film would have to be accounted for as either a cardinal or catalyser function. We need to make provision for a description that we can use to collectively describe a number of narrative units simultaneously. For example, cardinal functions are determined not by their importance, but by their interrelationship. Thus a telephone call is made up of several functional events: the telephone rings; the receiver is picked up; a conversation takes place; the receiver is put down. These

Narrative Analysis

actions can be grouped together and collectively referred to as sequence, which is a logical succession of units bound together by a relationship. The sequence opens when one of its units has no antecedent and continues until it reaches a unit with no consequence. The sequence can

Table 7.1 Cardinal functions and catalysers found in the *MacGyver* episode entitled 'The Lost Amadeus'

Cardinal functions	Catalysers
	• MacGyver and his friend, Wilt, are out for a Sunday morning bicycle ride.
• MacGyver stops to buy a newspaper.	
• MacGyver meets Lulu when she knocks him over and crushes his bicycle as a result of her erratic driving.	
• Lulu insists on taking MacGyver home …	
	• … but has to fulfil an errand en route for Izzy, her boss.
• A pothole in the road, and Lulu's erratic driving, causes the contents of the glove compartment to spill on to the floor of the car, including an invitation to a 'Roaring 20s Bash'	
	• Lulu stops at a pawnbroker to redeem an item for Izzy, her boss. The pawnbroker's shop is closed because it is Sunday.
• Lulu needs to report back to Izzy	
• MacGyver argues with Lulu about her erratic driving style and, once reaching Izzy's home, refuses to travel any further with her.	
• Lulu enters the house	
• MacGyver turns to leave, but drops his newspaper at the front gate, where the invitation to the 'Roaring 20s Bash' spills out. He returns to the house to give Lulu her invitation back.	

then be labelled as, in the case of our elementary example, a telephone call. If we group the cardinal functions from 'The Lost Amadeus' that we listed in Table 7.1 we find the following sequences:
- hero meets girl;
- girl attempts to influence the hero;
- hero meets villain.

Later on in this chapter you should recognise this particular grouping of functions in Eco's model.

macro level

Barthes's later work focuses more on a macro level, where he considers the structure of the narrative above that of the sentence. Here Barthes examines the macro processes by which meaning is structured into the narrative; where the reader's interpretation becomes an important part of the process (Fiske 1987b:142). It is here where the cultural context – in which a narrative is created and ultimately read – strongly influences the interpretive process. For us to make sense of a narrative, certain conventions are used, which we interpret from our accumulated cultural knowledge (Whitehead 1992:47; Watson 1998:137). In this way we, as the readers of a particular text, not only make sense of the narrative but simultaneously anticipate its development.

To Barthes, behind the apparently fixed and stable structure of beginning, middle and end in a story, lies a process that produces meaning that is extremely unstable. This process is unstable because it is made up of a set of elements with a very loose relationship between them. Within this relationship Barthes identifies a set of five codes that work towards producing meaning. By identifying these codes within a text, and the many links between them, we can determine how a narrative achieves meaning (Palmer 1991:57). Unlike the codes we discussed earlier, these codes are not derived from linguistics. Barthes considers these codes rather as 'the place where there is some form of transfer of meaning, of interaction between signs' (Palmer 1991:58). This is in addition to the meaning derived from the linguistic codes that we discussed earlier in this section. The five codes identified by Barthes are:
- *Hermeneutic or enigma code*: this code sets and resolves the enigmas (a riddle or mystery) of a narrative. The hermeneutic code controls the pace and style of the discourse by controlling the flow of information we receive from the narrative in order to resolve the enigma. An enigma is created at the beginning of the narrative, which is then held

in suspense awaiting final resolution. Various techniques are used to delay resolution of the narrative in order to heighten tension on our part, as readers. Often a number of false clues to the resolution of the mystery are provided. The purpose of this code is to create a tension in the narrative that in turn holds our attention. Resolution is rather important in a narrative, as it brings about closure. Barthes suggests that the hermeneutic code is the motor that drives the narrative and works through 10 stages, in any combination or order. These stages are (Fiske 1987b:143):
- thematisation;
- proposal of the enigma;
- formulation of the enigma;
- request for an answer;
- snare;
- equivocation [use of ambiguity to conceal the truth – author];
- jamming;
- suspended answer;
- partial answer;
- disclosure.
- *Semic code*: this is the way the iconography of existents and events take on a collective symbolic meaning that points to the general theme of the narrative. For example, the way characters are dressed points to a particular lifestyle that forms the theme of the narrative. Other attributes that contribute to the generation of meaning include speech, gestures and actions (Fiske 1987b:142). Semic codes, then, work connotatively within the context of the narrative in order to generate images of characters, objects or places (Whitehead 1992:47–48). To generalise, we can say these are the cultural stereotypes that are created in the narrative, such as the Western cultural expectations for the hero to be physically perfect and the villain to be portrayed as degenerate (Lacey 2000:73). These images are not determined by any needs of the narrative, but rather by the needs of the culture in which the narrative has been created (Fiske 1987b:142).
- *Symbolic code*: these are the fundamental oppositions on which the narrative is based (Fiske 1987b:142). It is through these oppositions that the identity of an individual character is created within the narrative, where existents and events are interpreted symbolically at a connotative level. Lacey (2000:73) suggests a good method of interpreting the symbolic codes in a narrative is to establish the

binary oppositions at work in the narrative. We discuss this aspect in more detail in the next section.
- *Proairetic or action code*: this is the portrayal and sequence of events in the narrative, and is closely related to the cardinal functions we discussed earlier. Todorov's and Propp's models, which we will discuss later, provide us with a method of illustrating the sequence found in a narrative. Proairetic codes can also be a form of shorthand to represent what is not shown. For example, a shot of characters boarding a bus would signify a journey without actually showing that journey.
- *Referential code*: rather than making reference to meanings within the text, referential codes extend meaning beyond the text. In other words, in order for us to understand the text we need to bring a certain body of generalised knowledge to that text. Often this knowledge comprises predetermined stereotypes that we bring to the text. For example, in order to fully contextualise *Doctor Quinn, Medicine Woman*, we need to have some prior understanding of life in frontier America, such as the relationship between the pioneers and American Indians (Native Americans).

Trying to identify these five codes within a text is not a particularly easy task, on one hand because of the closeness between each of the codes, and on the other hand the interdependence in their functioning.

7.4 THE ROLE OF BINARY OPPOSITION IN A NARRATIVE

Claude Lévi-Strauss, considered the father of structuralism, investigated tribal culture by analysing 800 Native American myths. Lévi-Strauss concluded that a single logic underlies all these myths. The myth is a mechanism that deals with irresolvable contradictions by depending on simple and recognisable meanings within a culture that reinforces and challenges social understanding. These contradictions are expressed in terms of oppositional pairs (Fiske 1987b:132). Seemingly different aspects of society, such as art, religion and customs, can all be reduced to oppositional pairs, which produce meaning. These codes operate in all cultures, from the primitive to the most sophisticated.

Lévi-Strauss theorised that 'when two characters are opposed in a binary structure, their symbolic meaning is virtually forced to be both general and easily accessible because of the simplicity of the difference between them' (Bywater & Sobchack 1989:95). Structuralism relies on binary opposition in order to transfer meanings in the easiest way. We make sense of concepts and ideas by contrasting them with their opposites. Thus in a narrative we would, as an example, automatically contrast rich against poor. Berger (1997:29–30) explains 'If everyone has a great deal of money, rich loses its meaning; rich means something only in contrast to poor'. Other examples of binary oppositions are light–dark, virtuous–evil and individual–community. In the Western, as an example of a particular film genre, the contradictions between culture and nature are manifested in an indoors–outdoors opposition and can be associated with other oppositions such as law and order–lawlessness, settler–Indian, humane–inhumane, cowboy–homesteader, and so on.

> So a scene of Indians attacking a white homestead is a concrete metaphorical transformation of the opposition between nature and culture, and the narrative is an argument ... about the characteristics and consequences of this opposition. (Fiske 1987b:132)

In television programmes, we find a deep common structure in each episode that can be shared with similar programmes in the same genre. For example, *Hart to Hart* shares the same deep structure as *Remington Steele*, *The Scarecrow and Mrs King* and, more recently, *Bones*, which all have male–female hero pairs. Fiske (1987b:132) provides a model of the deep structures manifest in *Hart to Hart*, which is illustrated in Figure 7.8.

The opposed values are then given the narrative consequences of successful–unsuccessful. Paralleling this set of oppositions is a deeper second structure of oppositions between the hero pair, which is illustrated below.

masculine	–	*feminine*
active	–	*passive*
thinking	–	*object of look*
controller	–	*controlled*

Characters are therefore also presented as pairs of opposites, with each pair having a different meaning. For example, in the Western genre, Wright (1975) has identified oppositions like the gunfighter–homesteader, which represents a contrast between individual independence and social domesticity. We can also have the homesteader in opposition to the rancher, which forms a binary opposition on a different level. Binary

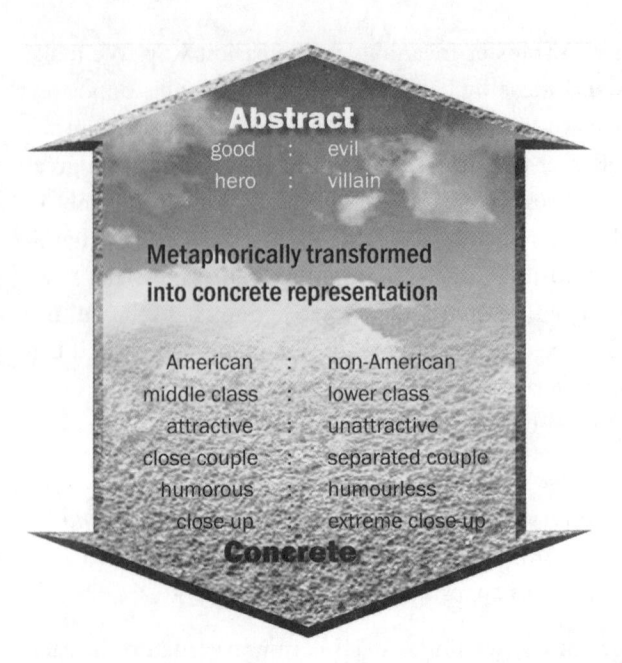

Figure 7.8 Binary oppositions found in *Hart to Hart* (adapted from Fiske 1987b:132)

oppositions are kept fairly general since this allows for complex action to take place in the narrative.

From this description we can see that Lévi-Strauss is not interested in the sequential development of the narrative, but rather in the relationships between the various characters and their settings. Binary opposition then provides us with a means of undertaking a paradigmatic analysis of a text where we can determine these relationships. One way in which binary oppositions reveal themselves in a narrative is through the physical appearance of the characters – the hero is handsome while the villain is ugly (Lacey 2000:66–67). On a more abstract level, binary oppositions can reveal ideological positions in the text. We return to this point later when we discuss Umberto Eco's narrative model.

7.5 TODOROV'S MODEL OF NARRATIVE

The simplest way of explaining a narrative structure is in terms of Todorov's model (see also Chapter 6). Todorov's model functions on two levels (Fiske 1987b:138–139):
- a state of being which is either stable or unstable;
- a causal transformation from one state of being to another via a chain of events.

Narrative Analysis

From these two levels, Todorov determines five steps in the linear progression of the narrative (Lacey 2000:29). These steps are as follows:
- a state of equilibrium;
- a disruption of that equilibrium by some action;
- recognition that there has been a disruption;
- attempts to restore the equilibrium;
- a reinstatement of equilibrium.

The narrative begins with a state of equilibrium or social harmony. This harmony is disrupted by a change agent or villain (see Figure 7.2) early on in the narrative, which then charts the course of the disequilibrium. Matters are finally resolved when the disequilibrium is returned to equilibrium and the narrative draws to a close. However, the second equilibrium differs from the initial equilibrium, in that the action is usually divergent where the characters begin moving off in differing directions and go their separate ways. This is opposed to the convergent nature of the initial equilibrium where the action brings characters together. This interconnectivity of events at the beginning with those at the end and those in between provides the narrative with a temporal axis and causal logic (Young 1990:198). This basic elementary framework supports most narratives.

When analysing a narrative using Todorov's model, we need to define the initial equilibrium, or beginning, in terms of its relationship to the disequilibrium, or middle, and the new equilibrium, or end. This requires us to identify the significant chain of events that brought about the disequilibrium and the restoration of the equilibrium. However, at the beginning of a narrative we cannot be sure of the significance of events, nor of the direction they will take the narrative. To establish the sequence of events in a narrative it is best to work backwards, retracing the sequence that led up to the end in order to arrive at the beginning. A simplified version of Todorov's model is illustrated in Figure 7.9.

To illustrate Todorov's model, we will return to the episode from *MacGyver*, titled 'The Lost Amadeus', that we referred to earlier in this chapter. MacGyver can be considered a superhero as he specialises in the use of clever, self-made, innovative technology and mechanical means to save himself and various victims from a whole range of criminals and their activities. In terms of Todorov's model, the narrative structure for *The Lost Amadeus* is as follows:

- Step 1 – *Initial state of equilibrium*: the initial equilibrium is established in the opening shots where MacGyver is cycling with a friend, Wilt, on a Sunday morning.
- Step 2 – *Disruption* of the initial equilibrium: when MacGyver stops to buy a newspaper, his bicycle is crushed by a car driven by a girl, Lulu. She insists on taking MacGyver home, but stops en route at the home of her employer, Izzy, a concert violinist, after unsuccessfully trying to fulfil an errand for him. It is at this point that we get a second disruption entering the narrative, which changes the direction of the story. Izzy is at that moment being molested by two thugs who are after a special violin, once owned by Mozart. The two thugs then turn their attention to MacGyver and rough him up before rushing out of the house. Following on from this incident we have the beginning of the disequilibrium in this narrative.
- Step 3 – *Recognition of the second disruption*: MacGyver decides to help Lulu and Izzy to retrieve the violin.
- Step 4 – *Attempts to restore the equilibrium*: Izzy is kidnapped by the thugs and his safe return is only guaranteed by payment in the form of the Amadeus violin. The exchange is set to take place at a theme party, where the thugs are double-crossed by Lulu and MacGyver. And so the disequilibrium continues until the villains are apprehended.
- Step 5 – *Reinstatement of the equilibrium*: a new equilibrium is created when the violin is returned to its rightful owner, and MacGyver and Lulu go their separate ways so that MacGyver can be ready for his next adventure in the following episode.

In television narratives, step 1 – establishing the initial equilibrium – is usually very short, or can be omitted altogether, since it is assumed by the producers that we are already familiar with the characters and their setting. Steps 2 and 3 can be presented in combination, with a limited duration of several minutes, so that the rest of the programme can be devoted to step 4. In some instances, step 3 can literally last only a few seconds and as a result is easily missed. The disruption can be identified from the kinesics, such as body language, of actors in addition to the tone or words spoken. Step 5 is also given only a few minutes at the conclusion of the programme. This is a good example of how the organisational requirements of television can influence the development of a narrative (Lacey 2000:33).

7.6 VLADIMIR PROPP'S NARRATIVE MODEL

The structural approach to narrative analysis was initially used by Vladimir Propp, when he analysed hundreds of Russian folk tales in order to find their underlying structure. Before 1928, Russian folk tales were classified along the lines of fairy tales, animal tales, tales of daily life, and so on. Early attempts at classification did not have much success as these categories overlap too much. For instance, an animal tale often makes much the same point as a tale from any other category. Propp searched for some basic content structure underlying the wide variety of themes, actors and settings, which we early referred to as existents. Propp (1968:19–20) presents several folk-tale scenarios, as illustrated in Table 7.2.

Table 7.2 Folk tale scenarios according to Vladimir Propp

• A tsar gives an eagle to a hero.	The eagle carries the hero away to another kingdom.
• An old man gives Súčenko a horse.	The horse carries Súčenko away to another kingdom.
• A sorcerer gives Ivan a little boat.	The boat takes Ivan to another kingdom.
• A princess gives Ivan a ring.	Young men appear out of the ring and carry Ivan away into another kingdom.

From reading these scenarios, it is quite clear that, in spite of the fact that the characters change, all the sequences have something in common. Each scenario has the same action and function: a gift is given to someone, who is then transported to some other place. Because the action is similar in each scenario, Propp labelled these actions as a constant. Different actions may produce identical constants, not on the basis of surface familiarities, but insofar as they fulfil the same function in a sequence of events. On the other hand, the existents – that is, the gift and the transported person, the motives behind the gift, and so on – more often than not differ from scenario to scenario. These differences Propp termed as variables.

constants
existents
variables

Propp was able to compile a sequence of 31 constant functions in the folk tales he analysed. Propp termed these constants 'functions' because he wanted to emphasise that what characters do to advance the narrative is more important that who they are (Fiske 1987b:136). These functions are sequential and common to all folk tales. Although every function identified by Propp need not be part of the narrative, each function

functions

that is present must contribute to the general development of the plot. From his analyses, Propp (1968:21–24) was able to formulate four laws that govern functions in folk tales. These laws are as follows (Kozloff 1992:71):

- The functions of characters serve as stable, constant elements in a tale, independent of how and by whom they are fulfilled. They constitute the fundamental component of a tale.
- The number of functions known to the folk tale is limited.
- The sequence of functions is always identical – in other words, Propp's scheme is chronological and the sequence cannot be varied.
- All folk tales are of one type in regard to their structure.

The functions Propp identified are indicated in Table 7.3. Although the number of functions totals 31, for some unknown reason Propp decided to introduce an extra function following function 8, without adjusting the numbering sequence. The initial sequence is not allocated a number.

Figure 7.9 shows there is a striking similarity between Propp's model and that of Todorov. We need to read Figure 7.9 in conjunction with Table 7.3, which explains the action in each of the numbered functions. Both models are chronological in their structure, using the action of characters to take the narrative forward.

While Propp admittedly limits his analyses to Russian folk tales, the significance of his work extends far beyond the folk tale as such. Any folk tale, whether Russian or any other language, is more than a folk tale,

Figure 7.9 Similarities between the narrative models of Todorov and Propp (based on a discussion by Lacey 2000:48)

Table 7.3 Functions of characters in Russian folk tales according to Vladimir Propp (adapted from Lacey 2000:47; Berger 1997:26)

Preparation		
α	initial situation	Members of the family and hero are introduced
1	absentation	One of the members of a family absents himself and leaves home
2	interdiction	An interdiction is addressed to the hero
3	violation	The interdiction is violated (the villain enters the tale)
4	reconnaissance	The villain makes an attempt at reconnaissance
5	delivery	The villain receives information about his victim
6	trickery	The villain attempts to deceive his victim in order to take possession of him or his belongings
7	complicity	The victim submits to deception, thus unwittingly helping his enemy
Complication		
8	villainy	The villain causes harm or injury to a member of the family
8a	lack	One member of the family either lacks or desires to have something
9	mediation	Misfortune or a lack is made known; the hero is approached with a request or command; he is allowed to go or he is dispatched
10	counteraction	The seeker agrees to or decides upon counteraction
Transference		
11	departure	The hero leaves home
12	1st donor	The hero is tested, interrogated, attacked etc., which prepares the way for his receiving either a magical agent or helper
13	hero's reaction	The hero reacts to the actions of the future donor
14	receipt of agent	The hero acquires the use of a magical agent
15	spatial change	The hero is transferred, delivered or led to the whereabouts of the object of the search
Struggle		
16	struggle	The hero and the villain join in direct combat
17	branding	The hero is branded
18	victory	The villain is defeated
19	liquidation	The initial misfortune or lack is liquidated
Return		
20	return	The hero returns
21	pursuit, chase	The hero is pursued
22	rescue	The hero is rescued from pursuit
23	unrecognised arrival	The hero, unrecognised, arrives home or in another country
24	unfounded claims	A false hero presents unfounded claims
25	difficult task	A difficult task is proposed to the hero
26	solution	The task is resolved
Recognition		
27	recognition	The hero is recognised
28	exposure	The false hero or villain is exposed
29	transfiguration	The hero is given a new appearance
30	punishment	The villain is punished
31	achievement	The hero is married and ascends the throne

it is a narrative. According to Chatman's (1978:26) breakdown of the narrative, which we illustrated in Figure 7.6, the manifestation of a story is not limited to folk tales, but can include any mediated form, such as television programmes, novels, mime, cartoon strips, advertising, films, sports commentaries and news reports. They all contain narrative messages. What Propp did was to identify the narrative character of a particular kind of message and to devise a method of analysis that is applicable not just to the folk tale but to many types of narrative messages, and therefore by implication to most messages found in the media, however they are expressed.

dramatis personae

Although function forms an important part of the narrative structure, it is also necessary to look at the characters, or, as Propp terms them, the *dramatis personae*. Characters set a particular problem for narrative analysis. Without the characters the action simply could not happen, and there is no narrative without any characters. Yet narrative analysis is not concerned with the definition of characters in the psychological terms of 'beings', but rather as participants in the discourse (Barthes 1977a:105–106). Every character can be the agent of a sequence of actions, which then belong to that character. Thus Propp's classification of characters, illustrated in Table 7.4, is concerned more with what the character does to advance the narrative than with whom he or she is as an individual. The characters are defined in terms of the spheres of action assigned to that character by the narrative (extent and nature of action evidenced by a character in the narrative). It is possible that one character can be placed in several categories simultaneously. Propp (1968:78–80) identified seven constantly recurring *dramatis personae*.

recurring character
bit-player

Television characters can easily be classified using Propp's categories of *dramatis personae*. Some examples are illustrated in Table 7.5. In television narratives, new villains and princesses appear regularly in each episode in order to provide the hero with fresh challenges. The donor and false hero have been omitted, as it is rare to find them, especially in American television narratives. Exceptions to the rule can always be noted. In *JAG*, a naval courtroom drama, the hero has two helpers, supported by a legal team, while in *18 Wheels of Justice* we find a recurring character (a character that appears regularly in a narrative) in the form of the arch-villain Jacob Calder, who has a henchman played by a guest star to do his dirty work in each episode. In *Relic Hunter*, the position of the dispatcher is filled by a bit-player (a minor actor in a film or television programme). The interchangeability of the *dramatis personae* is well illustrated by the characters found in *JAG*, where in certain episodes, instead of acting as helpers, Colonel MacKenzie and Lieutenant Roberts are pitted against the hero, Commander Rabb.

Table 7.4 Propp's *dramatis personae* categories (adapted from Tilley 1991:58; Watson 1998:141; and Lacey 2000:51)

Character role	Sphere of action	Purpose	Function
Hero	Departs on search, reacts to demands of donor	Seeks to restore equilibrium	10, 13, 31
Donor	Gives or provides the hero with the magic agent	Sends the object, which helps to restore equilibrium	12, 14
Helper	Moves the hero, makes good a lack, rescues from pursuit, solves difficult tasks, transforms the hero	Aids and moves the action towards resolution	15, 19, 22, 26, 29
Princess	A sought-after person who assigns difficult tasks, brands, exposes and recognises, with her father, who punishes the false hero	Leads to the climax of the narrative by being threatened by the villain	17, 25, 28, 30, 31
Dispatcher	Sends hero on journey/ mission/quest	Sends the subject (hero) on the mission	9
Villain	Fights or struggles with the hero	Blocks the action, so complicating the narrative	8, 16, 21
False Hero	Unfounded claims to hero's sphere of action	Appears as good, but eventually revealed as bad	10, 13, 24

Propp's model, with some adaptation, has a universality about it that can be used to analyse the structure of the narrative in media messages. Look at the elementary examples below by Kozloff (1992:71–72), who made use of Propp's model to analyse the narratives found in television advertisements.

Consider the following:
- Housewife X's sink is clogged. Josephine the plumber suggests Liquid Plumr. The drain cleaner cuts through the clog and the housewife's problem are solved.

- Customer Y has dry, chapped hands from washing dishes. Madge the manicurist suggests Palmolive dishwashing detergent. Customer Y returns to the beauty parlour with restored hands.
- Housewife Z makes bad coffee and husband complains. Mrs Olson recommends Folger's coffee. Housewife Z tried Folger's and wins husband's praise and approval.

In each of the above scenarios, the heroine has a lack or misfortune (Propp's function 8a) that is noticed (function 9). She comes into contact with a donor (function 13), who suggests the use of a magical agent (function 14). The initial misfortune or lack is liquidated (function 19). Often the heroine is then praised and thanked by family members (figuratively function 31).

application to television

Some adaptations have been made here to Propp's model so that we can use it in analysing television narratives. In these examples it is science and technology, in the guise of the product being advertised, that assumes the qualities of the 'magical agent'. We need to keep in mind that the purpose of the 'magical agent' is to effect a transition on the part of the hero and, in so doing, to achieve some or other goal. In example one, the blocked drain is cleared; in example two Customer Y gains beautiful hands; while in example three Housewife Z gains praise and approval, all brought about by using a particular product, or 'magical agent'.

Similarly, it is also rare for contemporary narratives to end with a wedding and ascension to the throne. So this function needs to be seen in allegorical terms of achieving some or other particular goal. Other examples that use Propp's model to analyse narratives include the following:

- Peter Wollen's (1976) analysis of Alfred Hitchcock's film *North by Northwest*;
- Roger Silverstone's analysis of an episode of the British soap opera *Intimate Strangers* (1976) and his analysis of the scientific documentary *Death of the Dinosaurs* (1987) from the *Horizon* series;
- Arthur Berger's (1989) analysis of the pilot episode of the sitcom *Cheers*, which is described in more detail as Case study 7.1;
- Will Wright's (1975) analysis of the structure of the Western as a film genre.

Narrative Analysis

Table 7.5 *Dramatis personae* found in television narratives (adapted from Kozloff 1987:50)

Programme	Hero	Helper	Dispatcher	Villain	Princess
JAG	Commander Harmon Rabb, Jr	Colonel Sarah MacKenzie, Lieutenant Bud Roberts	Admiral AJ Chegwidden	Guest star	Guest star
Relic Hunter	Sydney Fox	Nigel Bailey	Guest star	Guest star	Guest star
MacGyver	Angus MacGyver	Jack Dalton	Pete Thorton	Guest star	Guest star
18 Wheels of Justice	Chance Bowman	Celia 'Cie' Baxter	Burton Hardesty	Jacob Calder Guest star	Guest star

CASE STUDY 7.1: A SYNTAGMATIC ANALYSIS OF THE SITCOM *CHEERS*

This syntagmatic analysis of *Cheers* by Berger (1989) provides us with some indication of how meaning has been generated and conveyed in this popular sitcom television programme. This is achieved by placing the focus on such aspects as signs and codes, binary oppositions from Lévi-Strauss and the chronological structure determined by using Propp's narrative model. This is but a simplified study – the text of *Cheers*, as with all television programmes, is an extremely complex one requiring a deep semiological analysis – the purpose of which is to show how we can analyse a narrative text.

The episode selected by Berger (1989:89–101) for his analysis was the pilot programme, first screened by NBC on 30 September 1982. The series was screened in South Africa by the SABC over many years and still enjoys a number of equally successful re-runs some 20 years after the show's initial debut. The cast for the episode analysed here was Shelley Long as Diane Chambers, Ted Danson as Sam Malone, Rhea Perlman as Carla Tortelli, John Ratzenberger as Cliff, George Wendt as Norm, and Nicholas Colosanto as Coach. Shelley Long left the cast after the 1987 season, to be replaced by Kirstie Alley as Rebecca Howe.

Binary oppositions are a tool by which we can find meaning in a text, based on the simple premise that nothing has meaning in itself. It is through binary oppositions that we come to understand the various characters in the text. As an example, Table 7.6 illustrates the oppositions between the characters of Diane and Carla.

binary oppositions

Table 7.6 Binary opposition of Diane and Carla in the pilot episode of *Cheers* (adapted from Berger 1989:95)

DIANE CHAMBERS	CARLA TORTELLI
tall	short
blonde	dark hair
single (to be married)	was married (now single)
cool and reserved	hot and bitchy
middle class	working class
WASP	ethnic
innocent	experienced
schoolmarm	bar girl

It is apparent that these two characters are opposites in many important ways. While there are many other oppositions between characters found in *Cheers*, let us focus on the oppositions that are crucial to the series: those between the two central characters of Sam Malone and Diane Chambers.

Table 7.7 Binary opposition of main characters from the pilot episode of *Cheers* (adapted from Berger 1989:96)

DIANE CHAMBERS	SAM MALONE
female	male
blonde	dark hair
middle class	working class
education	common sense
vulnerable	worldly
beauty	beast
useless	handy

These oppositions are of central importance in moving the narrative along, not only in this particular episode but in the whole series. The binary oppositions between the two main characters denote the theme of the programme as not only a battle of the sexes but also a battle between the classes. We have to be careful when analysing main characters based on a single episode. Characters tend to be discussed in more stereotypical terms, whereas after viewing a number of episodes, we establish a history for each character and can therefore interpret non-filmic codes with a greater depth of understanding. Thus, says Berger (1989:98), a regular viewer of a series like *Cheers* sees more in a given episode than a casual viewer does.

Narrative Analysis

Berger (1989:89) considers *Cheers* as a modernised fairy tale, based on the fact that the narrative can be analysed in terms of a number of specific functions. Table 7.8 provides a breakdown of the pilot episode of *Cheers* in terms of Propp's narrative functions.

Table 7.8 Proppian functions in the pilot episode of *Cheers* (adapted from Berger 1989:99)

Proppian function		Events in Cheers
α	Initial situation	Sam, Diane and Sumner are introduced
1	Absentation	Sumner leaves the bar to get the ring
2	Interdiction	Sumner tells Diane to stay in the bar
7	The victim submits to deception	Sumner goes to the home of his ex-wife, Barbara; Diane lets him go
8	The villain causes harm	Barbara 'casts a spell' on Sumner
8a	Lack or desire to have something	Diane 'lacks' Sumner and waits for his return
9	Misfortune is made known	Diane discovers Sumner has gone to the Bahamas with Barbara
11	The hero(ine) leaves home	Diane cannot return to Boston University
13	The hero(ine) reacts to the action of a future donor	Diane tells Sam she doesn't talk with bartenders
14	The hero(ine) acquires the use of a magical agent	Various characters sympathise with Diane
19	The initial misfortune of lack is liquidated	Sam offers Diane a job at his bar
29	The hero(ine) is given a new appearance	Diane becomes a waitress and dons a uniform
31	The hero(ine) is married and ascends the throne	Diane starts a relationship with Sam

The algorithm for this particular episode of *Cheers* is:

$$\alpha + 1 + 2 + 7 + 8 + 8a + 9 + 11 + 13 + 14 + 19 + 29 + 31$$

This algorithm represents a highly simplified form of the narrative, which can then be used to compare this episode with other episodes in the same series or with other similar sitcoms. Berger (1989:100) concludes that, although highly camouflaged and modernised, there are elements of the folk tale in our contemporary story forms, which then help to carry important social messages. In this brief synopsis, we illustrate how meaning can be created through the use of symbols, binary oppositions and chronological structures.

Kozloff (1978:49) draws two conclusions from the application of the Propp model to television narrative:
- American television evidences a structure not unlike the Russian folk tale. Certain motifs, situations and characters feature again and again in popular television programmes.
- Television stories are governed by a set of unwritten rules acquired by storytellers and received in much the same way that they acquired the basic rules of grammar; that is, they are culturally determined. This explains the variability, yet consistency, present in television narrative.

Propp's model, as with that of Todorov, provides us with a means of identifying the conventional narrative structure in a text. From this perspective, the model is useful if we want to compare texts (Lacey 2000:53). But to gain deeper insight into the structure of a text, we need to add other analytical devices, such as Lévi-Strauss's binary opposition, as seen in case study 7.1.

7.7 UMBERTO ECO'S NARRATIVE MODEL

The first James Bond novel, Ian Fleming's *Casino Royale*, was published in 1953. Between 1953 and 1965, when the author died, a further 12 novels appeared. It did not take long for Fleming to gain celebrity status as a bestselling author.

This was the problem that Umberto Eco set out to resolve: what were the reasons for the phenomenal success of James Bond? Eventually, Eco concluded that the Bond novels became popular in the Anglo-Saxon world simply because readers could easily identify with the positive and superior way in which Fleming portrayed the British and negatively stereotyped the popular 'enemies' of the time. To achieve this Fleming made use of a series of oppositions with a limited number of permutations. These oppositions and permutations then group and regroup on three distinct levels to make up the narrative. We will look at each level in turn.

7.7.1 Level one: binary oppositions

Eco (1982:245) identified 14 constant binary groups, the first four of which relate to characters, and the remaining 10 to values personified by the four basic characters. These oppositions are indicated in Figure 7.10. For Eco, these binary oppositions are indicative of a specific relationship between the two characters. This relationship is indicated by the secondary oppositions, of which one is illustrated in Figure 7.10. As an example, Fleming saw 'Bond as an absolutely ordinary person' (Eco 1982:246) despite what we may interpret from the books or subsequent film versions thereof. Eco (1982:246) explains that it is only when Bond is placed in opposition to another character that the real stature of Bond 'emerges, endowed with physical attributes, with courage and fast reflexes, without possessing any other quality in excess'. In writing on the Bond–Villain opposition, Eco (1982:247) says:

> In Moonraker, Hugo Drax is six feet tall, with "exceptionally broad" shoulders, has a large and square head, red hair. The right half of his face is shiny and wrinkled from unsuccessful plastic surgery, the right eye different from the left and larger because of a contraction of the skin and eyelashes ... has heavy moustaches, whiskers to the lobes of his ears, and patches of hair on his cheekbones: the moustaches concealed with scant success a prognathous [having a projecting jaw or chin – author] upper jaw with a marked protrusion of his upper teeth.

margin notes: binary groups, characters, values

7.7.2 Level two: play situations

The various oppositional character pairs then combine regularly through the narrative. However suspense is created by the fact that we, as readers of the text, do not know at what point(s) in the narrative these oppositional pairs will meet and interact with each other. These interactions go to make up a prearranged pattern that Eco (1982:253) calls the 'algebra' of the narrative structure, which takes the form of a game: M beats Bond, Bond beats the Villain, the Villain beats the Woman, the Free World beats the Soviet Union, moderation beats excess, and so on. Because of Eco's emphasis on the combination of oppositional pairs according to certain rules the narrative is then established according to a prearranged scheme based on the outcome of the interaction. Eco (1982:254–255)

margin notes: play situations

identified nine moves resultant from the binary interaction, which becomes the invariable scheme, as follows:

- A   M sends Bond on a mission:
- B   The Villain (or someone representing the Villain) acts, and is introduced to Bond;
- C   Bond beats the Villain, or the Villain beats Bond;
- D   Bond meets the Woman;
- E   Bond attempts to seduce the Woman;
- F   The Villain captures Bond (with or without the Woman);
- G   The Villain tortures Bond (with or without the Woman);
- H   Bond finally defeats the Villain (or those representing him) completely;
- I   Bond convalesces with the Woman, whom he will eventually lose.

Primary oppositions

Characters:
1. Bond : M
2. Bond : Villain
3. Villain : Woman
4. Woman : Bond

Values:
5. Free World : Soviet Union
6. Great Britain : Countries not Anglo-Saxon
7. Duty : Sacrifice
8. Cupidity : Ideals
9. Love : Death
10. Chance : Planning
11. Luxury : Discomfort
12. Excess : Moderation
13. Perversion : Innocence
14. Loyalty : Disloyalty

Secondary oppositions

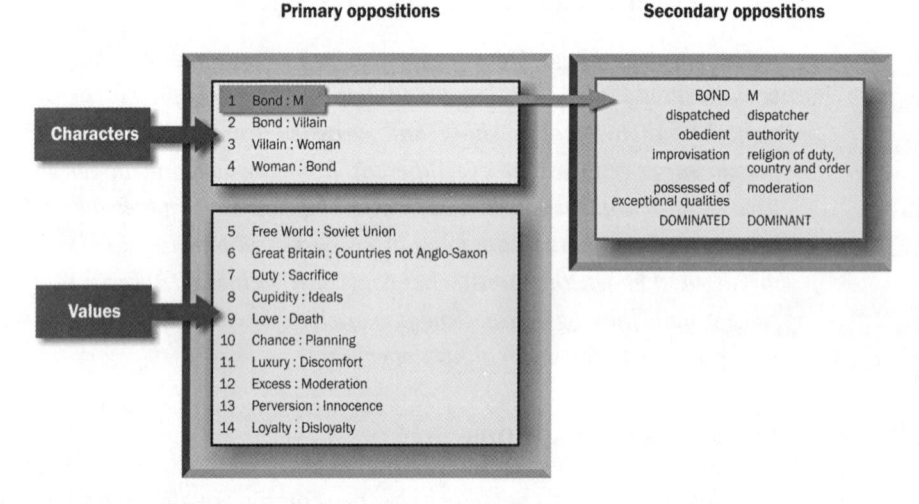

BOND	M
dispatched	dispatcher
obedient	authority
improvisation	religion of duty, country and order
possessed of exceptional qualities	moderation
DOMINATED	DOMINANT

Figure 7.10 Binary oppositions found in Umberto Eco's narrative model

The scheme is invariable in that all the elements are always present in every novel, but are seldom in the same sequence – there are constant variations, with moves either inverted or repeated or both. As an example, for *Dr No* we find the set scheme:

A – B – C – D – E – F – G – H – I

However, for *Goldfinger* we have the following sequence of moves:

B – C – D – E – A – C – D – F – G – H – E – H – I

Here the play begins with 'B' rather than 'A', while 'C', 'D', 'E' and 'H' are repeated twice. Eco (1982:255) terms the pattern made up from the unique play situation as the fundamental scheme. Paralleling this fundamental scheme are numerous side issues, which enrich the narrative but do not alter the fundamental scheme. The function of the fundamental scheme can be likened to that of the cardinal functions of Roland Barthes, discussed earlier in section 7.4, while incidental moves are similar in nature to Barthes's catalysers.

> fundamental scheme

7.7.3 Level three: a Manichean ideology

The action resultant from the oppositional structure established in level one gives us the fundamental moves in level two, but the stereotypical differences between the characters in that opposition provides the ideology in level three. This interaction between the various levels is shown in Figure 7.11. Eco uses the term 'Manichean' here to describe the ideological outcomes of a narrative, as the concept is based on Manicheism, a dualistic religious philosophy that originated in Persia during the 3rd century AD. Simply put, Manicheism holds that the world is not governed by one perfect being, but rather by a balance between the forces of good and evil, where the devil, personifying evil and represented by darkness, is elevated to a position of power comparable to that of God, represented by light. In this way, the existence of evil in a world created by God could be explained.

When studying the Bond novels, it does not take long to realise that Fleming considers the British as superior to the oriental or Mediterranean races, while also being rather anti-Communist. Yet before we accuse Fleming of being a racist, Eco (1982:260) reminds us that Fleming wrote from a popularist perspective, making use of popular opinion in establishing his oppositions. In times of international tension, popular notions such as that of a 'wicked Communist' and the 'Nazi criminal' develop, and Fleming draws on these notions in an uncritical manner. Even the very names of the protagonists suggest a stereotyped image of the character of the person, so building up elementary associations, for example:

> He is working for the Reds? He will be called Red and Grant if he works for money, duly granted. A Korean professional killer by unusually means will be Oddjob, one obsessed with gold, Auric Goldfinger ... (Eco 1982:260)

With this in mind, the narrative then begins to function as a model of the world for the reader, setting out the wider social and cultural forms of organisation and behaviour. From the Bond novels, we then learn how a Communist should look and behave. Transferring this concept to contemporary times, modern novels, films and television programmes provide us with a view of how an Arab terrorist should look and behave.

In this way, the use of binary oppositions in a narrative can reveal political or racist stereotypes that carry ideological implications – in the case of the Bond novels, this is the ideology of the Cold War. While the deep structure of opposing values remains permanently embedded in the text, the specific ideological messages vary in meaning according to historical contexts. For example, if we were to read a Bond novel today, long after the Cold War has ended, our interpretation of that novel would be from a historical perspective rather than from when the events were contemporary at the time of publication some fifty years ago. This point relates back to the definition of structuralism and the relevance of history we considered in section 7.1 of this chapter.

7.7.4 Eco's narrative model and television

Although Eco's model was specifically devised to analyse the Bond novels, it is flexible enough to use, in an adapted form, to analyse the narrative structure of television programmes. However, Eco's model does not work well for all media content, particularly programmes that have an open-ended narrative, such as soap operas and serialised dramas – unless one takes all episodes into consideration. Nor can the model be applied to the sitcom, as it is impossible to establish the four basic characters – we do not normally find a dispatcher, victim and villain in a sitcom. But the model is most effective when applied in a modified form to the closed linear narrative found in action-drama and reality-drama genres.

In order to analyse the narrative of an action-drama programme we do need to make some amendments to Eco's model. As the model stands, it has been specifically developed to analyse the structure of James Bond narratives. Since the four binary oppositions of character refer specifically to Bond by name, we need to make some substitutions in order to establish a generic version of the model. Thus, we can swap the term 'Hero' for 'Bond'. Since it is what a character does that is

Narrative Analysis

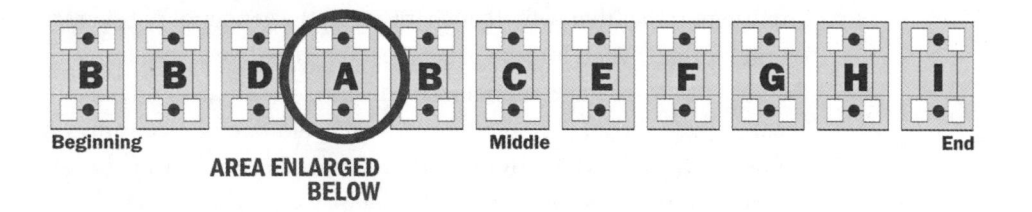

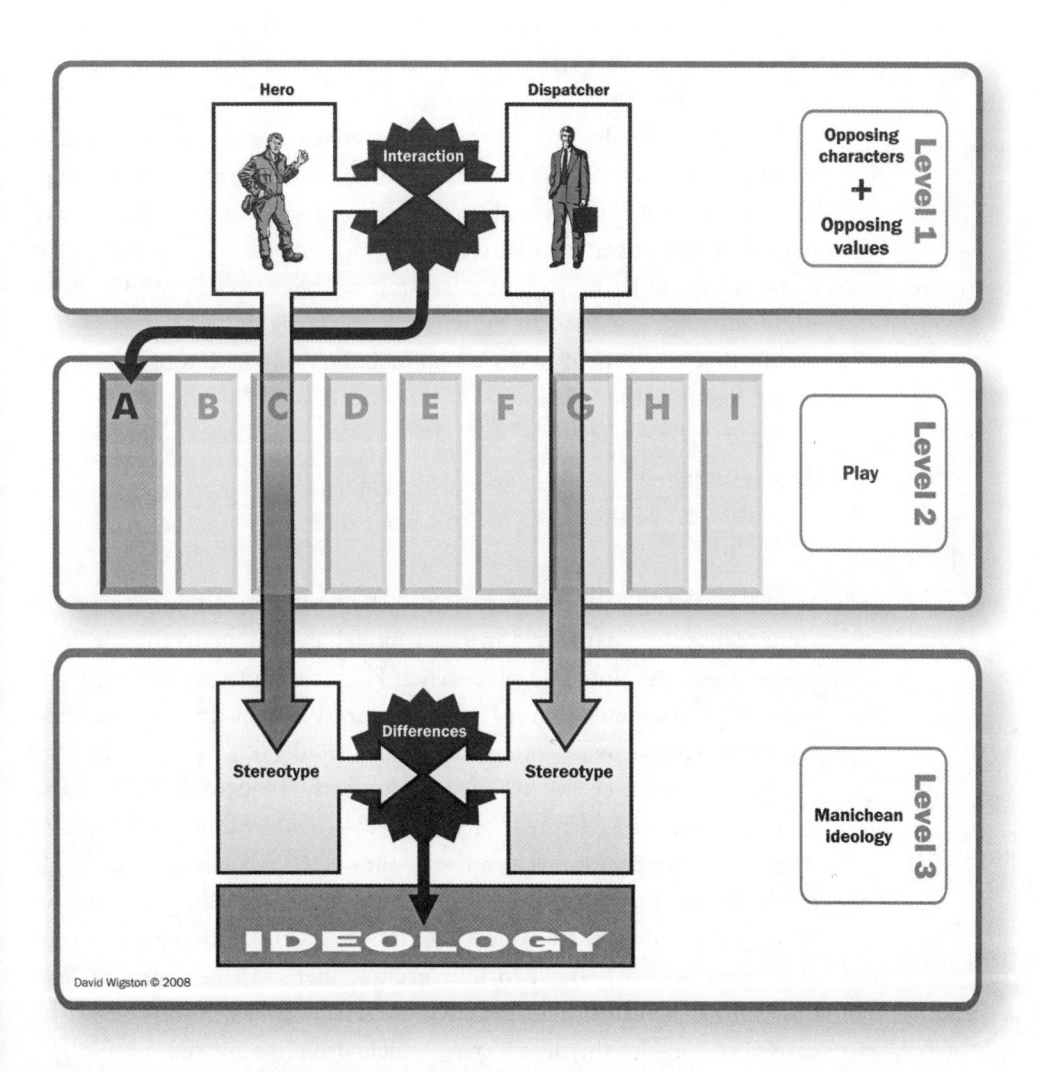

Figure 7.11 A generic overview of Umberto Eco's narrative model, specifically showing the interaction between the three levels for the move labelled 'A'. Each of the nine moves will have a similar interaction.

important, rather than who that character is, the gender of the character is unimportant. Therefore, by using the term 'Hero' we do not imply that the hero has to be male and an individual. As the character descriptors become generic concepts, the term 'Hero' could describe an individual person, or a team, which in turn will produce its own subsidiary set of binary oppositions between the team members.

In Eco's model, 'M' is the character that sends Bond on his various missions. If we go back to Propp's model we will find that this person is referred to as the dispatcher. So we can easily substitute 'Dispatcher" for 'M'. Following the same line of argument, we can substitute 'Woman' with 'Victim'. In film and television narratives, the concept of 'Victim' usually comprises a range of people either as individuals or as a group, such as families, children or the elderly. In the context of film and television narrative, we can define the Victim as being someone or some group subjected to unfair treatment. The concept of the 'Villain' is already a generic version in Eco's model, so we do not have to make any further adjustment here. A generic binary opposition of characters would look like the following:

- Hero – Dispatcher;
- Hero – Villain;
- Villain – Victim;
- Victim – Hero.

We now need to turn our attention to the remaining 10 oppositions of value. The values expressed in Eco's model are unique to the ideology prevailing at the time and place when Fleming wrote the novels. If we try and analyse the value in a contemporary action-drama film, then the *Free World–Soviet Union* dichotomy would not be applicable, as the Soviet Union ceased to exist in the early 1990s. Similarly, if the narrative is set in the United States, then the *Great Britain–Countries not Anglo-Saxon* opposition is also not applicable. Thus, when we use Eco's model we need to substitute the opposing values accordingly, based on those generated by the characters in the text. Unlike the opposition of characters, which is fixed to four groups, there can be more, or less, oppositions of value. The generic character labels will, of course, be carried through to the nine moves, which also remain fixed.

When it comes to identifying the ideology in the text we need to consider the form in which the text has been presented to us. Eco's work was

Narrative Analysis

limited to the original Bond novels, which meant that all he worked with were words. In film and television we have additional codes to consider and need to distinguish between verbal and visual codes. With regard to visual codes we, in turn, need to distinguish between filmic codes (or codes of form – manipulations that occur behind the camera lens) and non-filmic codes (or codes of content – that which occurs in front of the camera lens). As these aspects have been dealt with in Chapter 2, 4 and 5, we will not consider them here.

In conclusion, what then is the value of Eco's model for us today? The model serves as a point of departure for the interpretation of the relationship between the text and its social context. Here we need to distinguish between the context in which the text was made and that in which it was read. This is achieved by allowing us to reveal the deeper underlying ideology of the text. The popularity of that text can then be easily influenced by positive public identification with that ideology, since it forms part of the viewer's greater worldview.

7.8 POSTMODERN NARRATIVE

Postmodernism relates specifically to the criticism of art, literature and culture, as opposed to postmodernity, which refers to social, economic, political and technological developments. Postmodernity is considered to represent a period in which we see the emergence and spread of new media, together with the growth of information transfer and communication technologies that have triggered social change, and is considered to have precipitated globalisation. Of more interest to us, in this chapter, is the rise of a consumer culture, where we see a move from elitist values, which were revealed in the so-called high-art forms, to a fragmentary, shallow consumerism that is lacking moral responsibility to others, such as disadvantaged groups who cannot access the rewards of technological progress. Postmodernism can then be considered as a reaction to elitism by rejecting realism. Strinati (1992:2–3) identifies five characteristics of postmodernism.

postmodernism
postmodernity

- There is a breakdown of the distinction between culture and society, which has come about as a result of the growing importance and power of the mass media and popular culture. The media govern and shape all forms of social relationships and our perceptions of the environment are shaped by mediated cultural representations.
- There is an emphasis of style over substance, as we consume images

characteristics of post-modernism

and performances rather than engage with the written word where we are required to consider and reflect over the content.
- There is a breakdown between the distinction of high art and popular culture, as the media now embraces both art and the popular as one.
- There is confusion between time and space that is brought about by global communication technologies, economics and politics.
- There is a decline of metanarratives, such as Marxism and Christianity, which have lost their meaning for modern society.

7.8.1 The contribution of Jean Baudrillard

Postmodern thought is perhaps best represented by the work of Jean Baudrillard (1929–2007), a French cultural theorist, sociologist and philosopher who taught at the Université de Paris-IX Dauphine. Baudrillard also has a reputation for being controversial as his writings are cryptic and often difficult to understand. For example, Baudrillard makes the seemingly absurd claim that Disneyland is the real America. He puts forward the argument that postmodern societies, which are saturated by media and information technology, have entered an age of simulation, more particularly a third-order simulation (Laughey 2007:148). The distinction between the various orders of simulation is set out in Table 7.9.

Table 7.9 Baudrillard's three orders of simulation (adapted from Laughey 2007:149)

Order of simulation	Type	Description
First order	*Signification* refers to signs that imitate the real thing	Reality is constructed through representation, manifest in objects such as paintings or maps, and so on
Second order	*Reproduction* where signs refer to signs which imitate the real thing	Representations of reality (as in the first order) are reproduced by mechanical technologies such as photography and film
Third order	*Simulation* where signs no longer represent real things but serve to mask the absence of reality	No connection exists between reality and representation, as we now have hyperreality, such as Disneyland

Whereas the first- and second-order simulations maintain a relationship between reality and its representation, third-order simulation refers to a set of signs and symbols that have no relationship at all to reality, but rather function to hide the absence of genuine real things.

Baudrillard cites Disneyland as an example of a third-order simulation, in that Disneyland has become the real America, even though it is a hyperreal phenomenon split from a real America that has vanished from human experience (Laughey 2007:149). The outcome of this simulated reality is termed hyperreality, or what Baudrillard calls simulacra, where there is no distinction between the image and the real. Disneyland is more real than the reality it is supposed to depict, and in this process has become authentic, as it has lost any referential function it might once have had.

hyperreality
simulacra

The key aspect that has, according to Baudrillard, brought about hyperreality and simulation, where signs in the media no longer refer to real things, is their passage through various communication technologies, in particular that of television, which has removed the distinction between the real (the physical) and the metaphysical (knowledge). As a result, we can no longer speak about a distortion of reality as there is nothing against which we can measure the mediated images. Thus we have come to a point where the medium now dictates the narrative. In fact, Baudrillard's theory of media-saturated simulation draws heavily on Marshall McLuhan's concept that the medium is the message, except that now the medium and the message have collapsed into becoming the hyperreal (Laughey 2007:150).

7.8.2 The contribution of Frederic Jameson

Frederic Jameson (1934–), an American literary critic and Marxist political theorist at Duke University, also holds that from as far back as the mid-20th century the distinction between high and commercial art forms has been constantly narrowing, eventually becoming impossible to distinguish between the two. Jameson holds the view that in postmodern culture it is impossible for an individual style still to exist as all styles are determined by the needs of globalism, consumerism and capitalism. Central to Jameson's view of the disappearance of individuality is the concept of pastiche and how it differs from that of parody. Parody is a form of mimicry with the specific intention to mock the original with a humorous outcome, such as in an impersonation or imitation, in order

pastiche

to deliver a critical comment. The important point here is that there has to be an original and real object before it can be impersonated or copied, and the parody has no intention of removing the original form. While parody mocks, it does not threaten.

Pastiche, on the other hand, denies the existence of an original form and therefore lacks the satirical function, as it makes no attempt to distinguish itself from that of an original. For Jameson, pastiche has replaced parody, considering it as 'blank parody'. On this point Laughey (2007:155) comments that 'pastiche is less about comedy and more about plagiarism'. Styles and images are borrowed with no intent to provide any form of critical comment. Instead, images are endlessly recycled for public consumption, becoming nothing more than a succession of perpetual events. As these images lack any referential depth, they are quickly discarded for the next cycle of images. McGuigan (1999:70) is of the opinion that Jameson's hypothesis is that postmodern culture is not meant to be understood as something intellectual or aesthetic and has been brought about by a waning of effect, which McGuigan interprets as a decline in emotional identification and human sympathy. This perspective has the implication that there can be no individualism, even though postmodern advertising attempts to create the illusion of individualism by using images that define specific positions, such as being the one who is desirable, sophisticated, sexy, and so on.

7.8.3 The contribution of Jean-François Lyotard

metanarratives

Unlike Baudrillard and Jameson, Jean-François Lyotard (1924–1998), a French philosopher and literary theorist known for his articulation of postmodernism, does not see the forces of capitalism as the cause of the collapse of high art, but rather as the deligitimisation of scientific knowledge. As high art forms were threatened by the onset of postmodernism, so too, holds Lyotard, is the truth of science threatened, as a direct result of the decline of metanarratives. A metanarrative is an all-embracing narrative that functions to explain or comment on the validity of all other stories (Denning 2004). It is a universal and absolute set of truths, which rise above social, institutions or human limitations. What this basically means is that the outcome of some minor research, or action by an individual, becomes significant only because it reflects or supports a broader metanarrative, such as the pursuit of truth and justice. We will focus further on the decline of two types of metanarrative: the narrative of emancipation and the narrative of speculation.

The narrative of emancipation, or freedom, is a politically related metanarrative which holds that science is a liberating force against older orders. As an example, we can see that the press is losing its credibility when we consider that knowledge production is held in the hands of a few multinational news conglomerates. Previously, knowledge production was either in the hands of the state or a large number of private enterprises. Concentration, together with a decline in the metanarrative of emancipation, has delegitimised knowledge production, replacing it with the logic of mass consumption (Laughey 2007:159).

<aside>narrative of emancipation</aside>

The narrative of speculation seeks to legitimise scientific knowledge. Narratives of speculation differ from those of emancipation by refusing to accept knowledge at face value, while emphasising a holistic approach to learning. Thus we see a combination of the arts with science, whereas narratives of emancipation see art and science as distinct, but separate, entities (Laughey 2007:158). To Lyotard, both of these metanarratives are in decline, losing credibility as a direct result of postmodern culture. Yet Lyotard does not explain how postmodernism has brought about this loss of credibility. He suggests that it is advanced liberal capitalism and its pursuit of consumerism that is the root cause. Lyotard also argues that the growth of technology has impacted on the status of knowledge. The rapid development of communications technologies has resulted in knowledge becoming the principal force of production, and in so doing it threatens the narrative of emancipation produced by nation-states, as knowledge transfer has now become independent of any state intervention. Computerisation and intellectual property rights have become the new battlegrounds for knowledge and power, not between nation-states but multinational corporations in search of lucrative markets.

<aside>narrative of speculation</aside>

<aside>postmodernism</aside>

The commodification of knowledge by means of information-processing technologies is also the cause of the decline of media metanarratives, particularly that of public service broadcasting. Public broadcasters globally, including the SABC, have lost sight of the original values set out by Lord Reith relating to the provision of high culture, education and information. Instead, commercial services, based on consumerist and capitalist values, have undermined the public service broadcaster's

<aside>public service broadcasting</aside>

market forcing the public broadcasters to provide programming that contains more and more popular culture, such as soap operas and reality TV. Laughey (2007:159) sums up the situation neatly by writing that 'the close association between popular aesthetics and postmodernity is no better manifested than in the case of twenty-first century public service broadcasting, which in highly competitive television markets – such as the USA – is diminishing fast'.

In conclusion, then, we can sum up Lyotard's point of view by saying that knowledge, as a way of building minds and creating individuals, is becoming obsolete. Knowledge has become a commodity in a relationship between the supplier and user of knowledge. In other words, knowledge is produced in order to be sold and consumed so that the process can be perpetuated, the ultimate goal of which is simply exchange of money. Knowledge ceases to be an end in itself and as such begins to lose its value.

7.8.4 Postmodern television

We have discovered from the discussion above that television can be considered as one of the main drivers of the postmodern process. This leads us to the question, what does postmodern television look like? Morley (1996:61) provides us with a succinct answer when he writes the following.

> ... it can be characterised as the '3-minute culture' – the culture of the short attention span, where politicians no longer address us in speeches, but in 30-second 'sound bites' and through 'photo opportunities'; a world in which the news comes to us in 90-second bits, each disconnected from the last, in a plethora of little stories and images; where we are all so used to the fast editing of the adverts and the pop promos that the traditional Hollywood film seems so slow as to be almost quaint. It is ... a culture which induces us to graze the TV channels, zapping back and forth whenever our boredom threshold is triggered, rather than watching a programme. It is ... a culture where rarely does anyone do just one thing at a time, in a concentrated way for an extended period; it is ... increasingly a culture catering for people with the attention span of a flea.

Within such conditions, narrative, in the form that we spent much of this chapter discussing, cannot exist; it has simply become a flow of information. Similarly sequence, so very important to the existence of a narrative, has become randomness, while connection is replaced by disconnection. The end result is that everything increasingly becomes the same. Morley (1996:63) explains; 'with the gradual, uniform bombardment of information, all differences of content are cancelled: all that is left is Spectacle, without meaning'.

To sum up, we can identify the following as characteristics of the postmodern narrative:
- The narrative is lacking any conventional plot structure.
- The story is incoherent in terms of its form, structure and traditional conventions of narrative.
- The referents are usually heavily grounded in culture and history, without an understanding of which the text becomes very difficult to follow.
- The narrative rejects and defies meaning as it is full of gaps.
- There is an emphasis on spectacle and image, which takes precedence over the narrative.

A classic example can be found in the television series *Twin Peaks*, which first aired in the United States on 8 April 1990. Despite its initial success and a number of industry awards, the programme only survived two seasons as a result of declining viewer ratings. Viewer interest waned as a result of the resolution of the murder, the main drawing point, in the middle of the second season. Also, the subsequent storylines became more and more obscure and drawn out. Yet the series became entrenched in popular culture, being referred to in other television shows, advertising, video games, films and song lyrics. The initial popularity of *Twin Peaks* led to a merchandising industry ranging from books to audio tapes. *Twin Peaks* is characterised by a structure that is distinctly uncommon in American television. As an example, there are several points in which director David Lynch improvised by incorporating on-set accidents into the story. The most notable of these was when set decorator Frank Silva was accidentally filmed in a mirror. Lynch liked this so much that he kept it in the show.

There are a number of other such programmes that evidence postmodern attributes, such as *Miami Vice, Moonlighting, Max Headroom* and the entire contents of MTV. Film and television can be seen as the pinnacle

Media Studies: Volume 3

of mass-produced cultural products, and many programmes exhibit the postmodern motifs shared by other art forms. Table 7.10 provides a brief description of these themes, with some examples.

Table 7.10 Categories of postmodern motifs found in television programmes

Category	Description	Examples	
Pastiche	Tongue-in-check rehashes and tributes to classic pop culture	• The Simpsons	TV's longest-running sitcom follows a dysfunctional family attempting to live the American Dream
		• Charmed	Three beautiful witches save the world daily in postmodern rehashes of classic fairy tales
		• Buffy the Vampire Slayer	Tongue-in-check horror/comedy that follows a suburban high school student and vampire hunter
		• Xena: Warrior Princess	Camp fantasy adventure that mixes multiple mythologies, time periods and a touch of postmodern feminism
		• Dark Angel	Jessica Alba's leather-clad body is a genetically engineered weapon in another spin on the postmodern feminist superhero
Spectacle	In the ever-competitive battle for an audience, these programmes cater for the basest and shallowest impulses in order to get attention	• Survivor	Postmodern game show that mixes reality TV with the novel Lord of the Flies, as malnourished contestants plot and scheme against one another
		• Married with Children	America's first family of dysfunction, which spawned several sitcom clones
		• South Park	A low-tech animated adult sitcom, providing raunchy parables on the state of current mass culture

Narrative Analysis

Category	Description	Examples	
Faux TV	Self-referential mocku-mentaries, shows about shows, and fake news	• *Seinfeld*	Pseudo-reality sitcom about 'nothing' featuring a comedian with offbeat friends using rampant inside jokes as well as being a show within a show
		• *The Office*	Original British mockumentary on workplace psychology, which follows an incompetent boss and awkward reality TV moments
		• *Da Ali G Show*	Borat and other Sacha Baron Cohen-created characters dupe unsuspecting interviewees into revealing their prejudices
Mystery	Bizarre, eclectic searches for the unknown involving spirituality, philosophy and technology	• *Twin Peaks*	Mind-bending mystery full of twisted plots, self-reference and bizarre events
		• *Lost*	Drama of philosophy and signs where a group of castaways battle 'The Others' amidst flashbacks and a web of connections
		• *The X-Files*	Paranoid and paranormal search through the mysteries of the FBI's unsolved cases involving aliens, myths and legends

In many ways postmodernism is problematic in that it is amorphous in nature. Postmodern narrative is also largely contradictory, in that it is difficult to identify any narrative in a postmodern text. This dichotomous situation arises from the fact that we are trying to analyse postmodern narrative by using structuralist tools, simply because that is all we currently have to hand. Thus the question arises as to whether we can use structuralist tools in order to benchmark postmodern narratives. If we go back to the timeline illustrated in Figure 7.1 we can easily see that structuralism has had a long period in which to evolve and develop when viewed in comparison to postmodernism, which is still relatively embryonic in nature. Given that postmodernism can be seen as a reaction to structuralism, and given the deeply entrenched nature of structuralism, one cannot help but wonder if postmodernism is not just a particular quirky passing phase that will fade as quickly as it appeared?

7.9 AN EVALUATION OF NARRATIVE ANALYSIS

Like all research methods, narrative analysis has its limitations. Kozloff (1987:42–3) sums up these limitations when she says 'Because this field is concerned with general mappings of narrative structure, it is inescapably "formalist" and largely unconcerned with questions about "content"'. Since narrative analysis focuses directly on the text itself, other aspects regarding that text, such as effects on the audience, regulation and organisation of the production industry, are left to other critical methods. Nor is narrative analysis concerned about the audience and any possible effects the message may have. On the limitations of narrative, Barthes (1977a:115–16) says 'Just as linguistics stops at the sentence, so narrative analysis stops at discourse – from there it is necessary to shift to another semiotics'. Beyond that of narrative, fields such as sociology, economy and ideology take over.

value of narrative analysis

What value does narrative theory have for us, then, as scholars of mass communication? Narrative analysis presents us with a critical research tool, which should not be underestimated. Media messages, particularly those found in film and television, are steeped in the culture that created them. The various genres that emerge are obviously narrative in nature as they all basically tell a story, from the news bulletin to the accompanying advertisements. Narration can only receive meaning from the world that creates and makes use of it.

popular culture

It would seem that popular culture, such as evidenced on television, is more rigidly patterned and formulaic than high art forms. Even television programmes that do not outwardly display any element of either Propp or Eco's models still display a recognisable framework. For example, if we take each episode of the *Star Trek* series, the USS *Enterprise* will encounter some form of alien life, members of the crew will become separated from the ship, a crew member will become romantically involved, with either the ship or the crew placed in jeopardy. Kozloff (1987:49) argues that such predictability in television has led to a deficiency in one of the major forces driving narrative, that of suspense. Each event in the narrative should open up a number of possibilities, with the viewer anticipating what should happen next.

Narrative Analysis

Barthes (1977a:119) considers suspense as a privileged form of distortion, created by keeping a sequence open by making use of techniques like delay and renewal, which we now find in the serialised format of many television programmes. However, genuine suspense cannot really occur in television narratives, perhaps with the exception of factual genres such as news and documentaries. In such genres, the narrative is complicated because of the high number of unpredictable turns in the plot, with no guarantee that the good guys will win in the end. For fictional genres, the hero will always be back, if not next week then in the next season. So the narrative is not a question of whether the hero *will* survive the episode, but rather a question of *how* he survives.

To compensate for this lack of suspense, certain television genres develop a proliferation of story lines. Two or more story lines can run simultaneously extended over several episodes. Soap operas can have up to six different story lines, with different characters, at any one time. Each story line carries its own narrative, but they combine, parallel and complement each other in a unique way. Thus we can come to the conclusion that while 'television stories may be formulaic ... the ways in which they are told can vary considerably' (Kozloff 1987:54).

| suspense

SUMMARY

In this chapter we considered two distinct approaches to narrative: structuralism and postmodernism. From a structuralist point of view, we are not concerned with the quality of a text, but rather with how it generates meanings. To discover how meaning is created, we need to look at the structure of the narrative. From Seymour Chatman we learned about the layered structure of a narrative, which we can divide into the story and the discourse. Roland Barthes then provided us with the necessary theoretical understanding of the relationships that exist between the elements that make up a narrative. Every single item present in the narrative has to contribute in some way to the meaning of that narrative. This generation of meaning is achieved either by distribution or integration. Barthes also distinguishes two types of functions: cardinal functions, which are responsible for moving the narrative along, and catalyser functions that simply fill in the gaps. On a macro level, Barthes identified five codes that we use to generate a culturally determined meaning in the narrative.

A key element to our understanding of the deeper meanings in a narrative is that of Claude Lévi-Strauss's binary opposition. Meaning is created through the simple expedient of creating a contrast between two elements in the narrative. This is based on the premise that values, attitudes and characteristics only emerge when contrasted against an equal opposite. Binary oppositions work on abstract as well as concrete levels.

We concluded this section on structuralism narrative analysis by looking at three narrative models. We began with Tzvetan Todorov's elementary model, which explained the construction of a narrative in the simplistic terms of equilibrium–disruption–recognition–disequilibrium–new equilibrium. Vladimir Propp derived his model from an analysis of Russian folk tales, where he identified 31 sequential functions. These functions are determined by what the characters do to advance the narrative. With some adaptation, the models can be used to analyse the narratives found in media texts, particularly that of television. This was demonstrated by means of a case study in which Propp's model was used to analyse the sitcom *Cheers*. Then we considered the paradigmatic model devised by Umberto Eco, which was originally devised to explain the popularity of the James Bond novels. Eco's model consists of three interrelated levels, beginning with a set of four characters that are seen in terms of binary oppositions. The interaction generated by these opposition give rise to nine recurring functions, which Eco terms play situations and which function to move the narrative forward. The values that arise out of the first-level oppositions lead to the third level where stereotypes emerge. From this, the ideology, or the particular view of the world, of the text can be determined.

Following on from the discussion of structuralist narrative analysis we turned our attention to a brief introductory look at postmodern narrative. In many ways postmodernism is problematic to understand because of its amorphous nature. We looked at the contribution made by three scholars. Jean Baudrillard concluded that because of the prevalence of the mass media we have a form of simulation where representation becomes the real, a situation known as hyperreality. Frederic Jameson sees a coalescing between high art forms and popular culture brought about by globalisation and consumerism, which produces a form of pastiche where content is devoid of any real meaning and which leads to a bland sameness for everyone. Jean-François Lyotard was concerned about the decline in metanarratives, which have led to the deligimisation of scientific knowledge brought about by increasing consumerism and capitalism. The end result is a dominance of television as a medium where texts are fractured and difficult to follow, aimed at the lowest common denominator, and where information is treated as a commodity to be sold at the best prices.

LEARNING ACTIVITIES

1. You are training a group of broadcasters for a local community radio station. The students are required, as an assignment, to write and present a short radio talk of two minutes about a meaningful event in their lives. The students' efforts turn out to be exceedingly poor and bland. You then realise that they have no understanding of the importance of narrative to a story. What practical advice concerning narrative would you give these students so that they can improve on their stories?

2. Describe Roland Barthes's contribution to narrative theory and the analysis of television texts with reference to the following concepts:
   - function;
   - catalyser;
   - integration;
   - cardinal function;
   - distribution;
   - indices.

3. Select a single episode of a television soap opera, sitcom and action-drama series. Deconstruct that episode according to Barthes' five codes of narrative, which are:
   - hermeneutic or enigma code;
   - semic code;
   - symbolic code;
   - proairetic or action code;
   - cultural or referential code.

   Compare your findings for each programme genre. How are they similar and how do they differ?

4　Explain the value of Lévi-Strauss's concept of binary opposition to our understanding of the narrative to a text. Demonstrate how we can use binary opposition as an analytical tool by analysing several news items in a televised news bulletin.

5　Select several advertisements aired during prime time on television and analyse these advertisements by identifying the following aspects, based on Propp's narrative model:
- the hero/*subject* whose function is to seek the object that is sought;
- the *donor* of the object;
- the *receiver*, where it is sent;
- the *helper* who aids the action;
- the *villain* who blocks the action.

6　Write a modern short story based on Propp's functions of narrative. Remember to use past tense when writing your story, and to include descriptions and dialogue, and make sure there is action and conflict. Structure your story according to the following functions:
- *Initial situation*: members of the family, hero introduced;
- *Absentation*: one family member absents him- or herself;
- *Interdiction*: interdiction addressed to the hero, or the other way around;
- *Violation*: the interdiction is violated;
- *Villainy*: the villain causes harm to members of the family;
- *Mediation*: a misfortune is made known and the hero is dispatched;
- *Receipt of magical agent*: the hero acquires use of a magical agent;
- *Spatial change*: the hero is led to the object of his search;
- *Struggle*: the hero and villain join in combat;
- *Branding*: the hero is branded;
- *Victory*: the villain is defeated;
- *Unfounded claims*: the false hero is exposed;
- *Wedding*: the hero is 'married' and 'ascends the throne'.

As this is a modern story, you need to adapt some of the functions accordingly. For example, at the end of your story, the hero need not literally marry a princess and ascend the throne. This is the reason why the word 'married' and the phrase 'ascends the throne' are placed

Narrative Analysis

inside inverted commas. When writing your story, you can also use the fuller descriptions of each function given in Table 7.3.

7   Select the first three items that feature in a news bulletin, either on radio or television. List the oppositions that feature in these particular stories. From your list of oppositions, what conclusions can you come to regarding the bias of the news reports you used for this activity?

8   Select an action-drama series that is currently being screened on television. Using Todorov's model, analyse your selected programme(s) in order to establish the structure of the narrative.

FURTHER READING

Barthes, R. 1964. *Elements of semiology*. London: Jonathan Cape.

Berger, A.A. 1997. *Narratives in popular culture, media and everyday life*. Thousand Oaks, Calif: Sage.

Chatman, S. 1978. *Story and discourse: Narrative structure in fiction and film*. Ithaca, New York: Cornell University Press.

Currie, M. 1998. *Postmodern narrative theory*. Basingstoke: Palgrave.

Hawkes, T. 1997. *Structuralism and semiotics*. Revised edition. London: Routledge.

Lacey, N. 2000. *Narrative and genre: Key concepts in media studies*. London: Macmillan.

Mcquillan, M. 2000. *The narrative reader*. London: Routledge.

Nash, C. 1990. *Narrative in culture: The use of storytelling in the sciences, philosophy, and literature*. London: Routledge.

Propp, V. 1968. *Morphology of the folktale*. Austin: University of Texas Press.

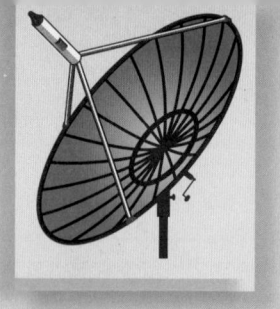

chapter eight

FILM THEORY AND CRITICISM

Pieter J. Fourie

LEARNING OUTCOMES

At the end of this chapter, you should be able to:
- explain film theory and its value and importance;
- give an overview of the key assumptions in classic film theory, with reference to the distinction between expressionism and realism and to the work of key theorists in this period;
- explain the basic tenets of *auteur* and genre theory;
- describe the shift in emphasis between classic film theory and the semiotic approach;
- give an overview of the contribution of film semiotics to our understanding of film;
- apply some of the aspects of film semiotics in an analysis of a film;
- describe the shift in emphasis between film semiotics and contemporary film theory;
- describe and explain the assumptions in ideological criticism;
- apply Lacan's psychoanalytical theory to the viewer's (subject's) experience of film;
- briefly explain the main issue in contemporary film theory;
- view a film critically from:
  - an ideological perspective;
  - a psychoanalytical perspective;
  - a contemporary film theoretical perspective of your choice.

Film Theory and Criticism

THIS CHAPTER

In this chapter, we introduce you to the field of film theory. We begin with the question, what is film theory? We look at different kinds of film theory, the questions asked in film theory and the differences between film history, film criticism, film analysis and film theory. We conclude this part of the chapter with questions about the value of film theory.

In the second part, we discuss classic film theory. The emphasis is on the distinction between expressionism and realism in film art and communication. With reference to the work of a few key theorists, we distinguish between expressionist, formalist and realist film theory and theorists. We conclude this part with a brief discussion of *auteur* theory and genre theory.

This is followed by an introduction to film semiotics. Because you have already studied the basics of semiotics in Chapter 2, we briefly concentrate on a few key aspects in film semiotics, such as film as a sign, denotation and connotation in film, film codes, the paradigmatic and syntagmatic nature of film, levels of meaning in film and the communicative functions of film.

The last part of the chapter deals with contemporary film theory up to ideological criticism, feminist criticism and the psychoanalytical approach.

8.1 INTRODUCTION

A director requires no knowledge of film theory to produce a film. Indeed, until recently people working in the field showed no interest in film theory. The argument was that film directors instinctively knew (or did not know) what to do. The gradual growth and rise of film as an art form or form of communication has, however, brought theory and practice closer together. Nowadays, the leading directors are thoroughly conversant with film theory. In other words, the work of the most prominent modern directors has a specific theoretical basis.

Consider the work of well-known directors such as Woody Allen (*Annie Hall*, 1977), Steven Spielberg (*Jaws*, 1975), David Lynch (*Blue Velvet*, 1986), Wim Wenders (*Paris, Texas*, 1984), Ingmar Bergman (*Fanny and Alexander*, 1982), Martin Scorsese (*Taxi Driver*, 1976), Francis Ford Coppola (*Apocalypse Now*, 1979) Robert Altman (*Short Cuts*,

1993) Quentin Tarantino (*Pulp Fiction*, 1994), Pedro Almodovar (*All About My Mother*, 1998) and Majid Majidi (*Children of Heaven*, 1997), to mention a few.

The above does not include the classic work, now forming the canon of filmmaking, of directors such as Eisenstein, Pudovkin, Griffith, Murnau, Hitchcock, Wiene, Hawks, Welles, Kazan, Ford, Fellini, Buñuel, etc.

Initially the argument was that the 'Hollywood style', which today still largely governs cinematic style, was not underpinned by any theory of what a film is or can be. Nevertheless, ever since films began to be produced, certain theoretical ideas have been current. Think, for example, of the view of one of the first American directors, D.W. Griffith (whose films stimulated a considerable number of theoretical views), that for film to succeed, the tempo should essentially be in tune with the average human heartbeat, which, of course, increases in rapidity under influences of excitement, and almost stops in moments of pregnant suspense (cf. Monaco 1984:323).

Many of the first casual theoretical comments, such as the one above, show an underlying need to elevate the film medium, which was originally viewed as popular entertainment for the masses, to the level of art, and to place it on the same level as the other art forms. The need to command respect for an art form may therefore be seen as one of the chief reasons for the development of theories about films. But what is film theory?

8.2 WHAT IS FILM THEORY?

Film theory is an intellectual and critical activity dealing with divergent questions about the nature of the film as a phenomenon. Answering these questions leads to insight and a better understanding of the phenomenon. The questions and answers are probably not essential to the viewer's pleasurable experience of the film, or the producer's potential financial gain. Yet the insight gained from the questions asked and the answers sought is vitally important to critics, film actors and viewers because it contributes to their understanding of, approach to and experience of the film medium.

Just as theories, philosophies and history of art enrich our experience and practice of art, so film theory enriches our experience and practice of film(s) as a form of art and communication.

8.2.1 Establishment, medium and close-up theories

Based on the questions that are and may be asked in film theory, the Russian director Sergei Eisenstein (1898–1948), one of the first and most eminent of the film theorists, distinguished (in film terminology) between three types of film theories:
- total-shot (establishing-shot) theories;
- medium-shot theories;
- close-up theories.

In *establishing-shot theories* (an establishing shot provides us with an overall picture of a scene), the emphasis is on the social context of a film and/or the social context in which films are made. In *medium-shot theories* (the demarcation of a specific aspect of a scene, but still not detail) the emphasis is on the relationship between a film and its public (or films and their publics) and human relationships in the film as such. In the *close-up theories* (focus on detail), the emphasis is on the different components of a film and the ways in which the film conveys meaning, as in the semiotics of the film. Typical contemporary questions that might be asked in each of these approaches are the following:

establishing-shot theories

medium-shot theories

close-up theories

Establishing-shot theories
- What effect did apartheid have on the content and form of South African films?
- What effect did apartheid have on the South African film industry as a whole?
- How are films affected by a social institution, such as censorship?
- How does the public's literacy level influence films?
- How are films influenced by religion?
- How is religion influenced by films?
- How are the contents of films influenced by the American culture and way of life?
- What effect does the economy have on films?
- How do politics affect films?
- How are films affected by technology?

Medium-shot theories
- How are people depicted in films?
- What kind of human relationships are depicted in films?

Media Studies: Volume 3

- How are groups, or a group, such as Jews, women, gays, blacks, Afrikaners, and so on, depicted in films?
- How does the viewer experience a film?

Close-up theories
- What is a film?
- What does a film consist of?
- What are the hidden components of a film?
- How do films create and convey meaning?

The above questions are a few examples of the type of questions asked in film theory. In short, they amount to a consideration of the classical distinction between *form*, *content* and *function*. Questions about what a film is and how it comes into being are related to its *form*. Questions concerning what the film depicts are related to *content*. Questions regarding the effect of films on viewers and society, and how social factors influence films and the producers/directors of films, are related to the *functions* of films.

Form is the way in which a film depicts something – it consists of the codes and techniques and the way the film gives shape to the content. Content is the actual content of the film – what the viewer sees. It

Figure 8.1 The Russian director and film theorist, Sergei Eisenstein, directs a scene from his film *October*, 1928.

comprises the theme and narrative and the way the actors portray the theme and narrative. Function is the value of the film for the producer and director, other film artists – in short, the film communicator – and for the viewer or recipients.

8.2.2 Normative and descriptive film theory

A further distinction between different kinds of film theory is made between *normative* and *descriptive* film theory (cf. Monaco 1984:322–3).

The approach to the above questions is mainly normative and/or descriptive. *Normative theories* are concerned with idealistic views on what film as a phenomenon can and ought to be. Normative theory operates inductively, that is, it starts by creating a set of values or rules with which, ideally, films should comply and then proceeds to apply these rules to a film in order to determine its value. If a film does not comply with these rules (norms), it is a failure. Normative theory is essentially a qualitative judgement.

<small>normative theory</small>

Descriptive theory adopts the deductive method: the theorist first collects data on the entire field of film activity and only then arrives at preliminary findings on the nature of a film.

<small>descriptive theory</small>

The following is a practical example: if normative theory were used to assess a South African film, that is, if it were evaluated inductively, then the theorist/critic would apply generally valid rules/norms and assess the film accordingly. If operating descriptively, the critic would take into account the circumstances, including the economic, political, production and social circumstances surrounding the production of the South African film (the field of film activity), and probably arrive at the conclusion that for economic reasons it is impossible to judge the South African film by the standards which apply to large internationally produced films.

8.2.3 Film history, film criticism, film analysis and film theory

From the above, it appears that film theory is concerned with a comprehensive view of film as an art medium and a communication medium (symbolic form of expression), as an industry that manufactures a commercial product (entertainment), as an ideological instrument, with the place, function and value of film in society, with its history and with film makers and viewers. Because it is so encompassing, it is clear that, for the purposes of scientific study, a clearer definition of the field of film theory needs to be made.

To make this delineation possible, the discipline of film study is divided into two subdisciplines: *film history* and *film theory*. Film theory further differentiates *film critique, film analysis* and *film theory*.

As a discipline, film art strives towards the scientific and thus objective delineation, organisation and definition of film, as well as the development of scientific methods in order to answer questions on every aspect of film (cf. Hommel 1991:41–9). Such questions include enquiries into film production and the film industry, namely, enquiries about the communicators, including producers, directors, artists (e.g. actors and scriptwriters); questions on the techniques of film writing; on film as an art and communication form (the message of film, then, as a form of symbolic expression); questions concerning the relationship between the film and its viewers (the recipients) and concerning the relationship between film and society (state, education, church, economy, politics, etc.).

For posing questions and developing appropriate scientific methods, film theory is characterised by an intensive interaction between diverging disciplines that study the phenomenon of film from different angles: linguistics, for example, film semiotics or semiotic methods (in which the emphasis falls on the study of film as a unique language); art history (the study of film as a unique art form that has a unique substantive form of content); literature (the study of the narrative nature and structure(s) of film, or narratology as method); communication science (the study of film as a mass communication medium, e.g. rhetoric as method); film as an industry (economical analysis as method); and as a political philosophy (the study of film as an ideological instrument). These angles, together with the principle of ordering or organising, find employment in the two most important subdisciplines of film art, namely, film history and film theory.

| film history |

Film historians organise the questions concerning *film history* along a *diachronic* axis. Hommel (1991:45) explains that film historians attempt to explain a film phenomenon (e.g. a certain film in a certain time period) in a chronological order. They do not only ask why something happens in film history and try to describe this, but also attempt to

Film Theory and Criticism

fathom why something occurs in a certain way and not in any other; why certain changes in film history occur and how these changes affect the nature of film in a certain time period.

In this way, film historians reconstruct, for example, the complicated production history (e.g. developments in technology and the development of the Hollywood industry) underlying a film such as *Gone with the Wind* (Fleming 1939). Or they try to understand the origin and meaning of a certain movement, such as the Italian *neo-realism* of the 1940s, or the French *new wave* of the 1950s, against the background of developments in social, political, economic, art, media and existential spheres.

Film history is thus concerned with the context in which the film phenomenon (e.g. a specific film or movement) originates and develops. The investigation can focus on the production or the reception of the film (or group of films). The most important factor is that the investigator looks at the film from an historical perspective. What does a film such as *Pulp Fiction* (1994) and its maker (Quentin Tarantino) say about late 20th-century society, for example, or about violence, humankind, production techniques and the influence of something such as postmodernism on technique and narrative structure? What do Tarantino and his films say about the film industry as such, about viewers and what they like or don't like, and why? How do all these things influence the eventual form and content of a film such as *Pulp Fiction*?

Based on the work of Allen and Gomery (1985), four forms of film historiography (or film history writing) are generally distinguished today:
- aesthetic film historiography;
- technological film historiography;
- economic film historiography;
- social film historiography.

Aesthetic film historiography deals with the historian's definition and description of how certain codes are aesthetically employed at a certain point in the history of film, for example, in a certain time period, or in the work of a certain director, to convey a specific effect. For example, how is direction, composition, lighting, and so on, handled in order to create a certain impression in the French new wave, Italian neo-realism or in *film noir*. What were the reasons for using these and related

aesthetic film historiography

codes in that specific manner, and how did this usage relate to similar applications in other art forms, social trends at that stage, the economy of the entertainment industry, political trends in society, and so on? In short, the emphasis falls on aesthetic style.

A good example is *film noir*. The concept '*film noir*' was used by French critics to describe a characteristic dark (*noir* = black) dramatic thriller that was fashionable especially during the period of the Second World War, and which is today still a stylistic characteristic of certain films. Historians of *film noir* attempt to discover why the films made at this time and in this style were 'dark', and what techniques were used to visualise this 'darkness'. Can this darkness be traced back to German expressionism in painting, and how does it relate to the artist's need to visualise people's psychic anguish during the Second World War? How does this compare with the 19-century British tradition in thriller fiction? Today, we recognise stylistic elements of *film noir* (dark lighting, dark streets, misty and smoky scenes, rain, shots fired from behind barred windows, etc.) in films such as *Pulp Fiction* (1994), *Basic Instinct* (1992), *Natural Born Killers* (1994), etc. The historian would try to learn why there is a tendency for contemporary directors to return to this style. Does this say something about the era in which we live?

technological film historiography

Technological film historiography deals with the history of film technology. The origin and development of various sorts of film material (8mm, 16mm, Cinerama, synchronised sound and image), cameras, projectors, production studios, animation, special effects, the influence of television and video on film and vice versa, sound equipment, etc.) is described and investigated historically. This kind of historiography reveals a close relationship between the history of film and related technological developments at a given stage in history. Also examined is how this technology dictated and still dictates the form and content of film. Would Spielberg have made *E.T.* (1982), for example, if he had not had the technology to do so?

economic film historiography

Economic film historiography is concerned with the questions of who provides the money for the production of films, and why and how they do so. In short, it is the history of production companies and the motion picture business or separate film businesses in various countries. How did Hollywood, as the leading manufacturer of films, originate, and what is the influence of Hollywood around the world? How is it run

Film Theory and Criticism

economically, and why is it successful as a business? In South Africa, the focus would be on the history of the South African film industry. How did it begin, why has the film industry produced only flashes-in-the-pan, and why has it been unsuccessful up until now? Good examples of economic historiography in the South African economy (although also categorised as social film historiography) is Thelma Gutsche's (1972) classic work *The history and social significance of motion pictures in South Africa: 1895–1940* and Keyan Tomaselli's (1979) *The South African film industry*. How are film industries in various countries financed, and how does film regulation (including censorship) and film policy influence this? (See Part 1 in Volume 2 of this book for a discussion of media and communication policy.)

Allen and Gomery (1985) (see also Hommel 1991:129) describe *social film historiography* in terms of:

- who makes film and why?
- who watches films, how and why?
- what was showing at given stages in the history of film, how and why?

> social film historiography

Social film historiography investigates film in a historical–social context, as a social phenomenon, among other social phenomena, in a specific time period and environment.

For example, who began making films in South Africa, when and why? How do some of the first South African films, such as *Sarie Marais* (1931) and *Moedertjie* (1931), relate to the Afrikaner as poor white and the urbanisation of the Afrikaner during the 1930s? How does *Hans en die Rooinek* (1961) by Jamie Uys, doyen of the South African film industry, relate to the Boer/Brit relationship in South Africa, and how do films such as *Die Bou van 'n Nasie* (1939) relate to the rise of Afrikaner nationalism? Who went to see films in those days, and, in that time period, how were the bioscope theatres influenced by this: who built them, and who was responsible for the distribution of films at that time? Why did South African films show such promise in the 1960s, and why did critical questions on apartheid begin to crop up in films such as Jans Rautenbach's *Katrina* (1969)? Why did this movement fade? Was it as a result of apartheid censorship? Why did black South Africans still not truly join the production of South African films, and why can we still not talk of a unique South African film style? Is it a result of apartheid? These are the questions that are addressed in social film historiography. A good example of South African film historiography is Keyan Tomaselli's (1989) *The cinema of apartheid: race and class in South African cinema*; see also Gutsche (1972), cited above, and Botha and Van Aswegen's (1992) *Beelde van Suid Afrika: 'n alternatiewe rolprentoplewing*.

<small>classical and revisionistic film historiography</small>

Along with the abovementioned forms and/or methods of film historiography, we differentiate between *classical* and *revisionistic* film historiography. The former is a chronological documentation of films and the work of directors and artists (e.g. actors) since the beginning of film up until today, or of a specific period, or of the work of a specific director or film artist. This often appears as a list of films, directors, actors, scriptwriters and other film artists, margin notes on the production as such, the date of production and usually a short summary of the plot of the film. It may be generally typified as an overview.

<small>macro and micro history</small>

Hommel (1991:149) believes that classical film historiography, which was the dominant form of film historiography up until the 1970s especially, is a *macrohistory*. It attempts to present a chronologically holistic picture of the development of film in general, of a period, a genre, or of the work of a specific artist. In contrast to this, revisionistic film historiography is a *microhistory*. It looks in greater detail at a certain aspect of a film, or at a director or other film artist's work, and places it in historical perspective: for example, the relationship between the music of a specific pop group and its use in films of a certain historical period; the relationship between the themes of a film and the particular spirit of the era, and so on. Revisionistic historiography *revises* classical (macro-) historiography, and focuses in on more detail. It thus usually considers a work from an aesthetic, social, technological or economic viewpoint.

<small>film theory</small>

Unlike film history, *film theory* investigates the film phenomenon along a *synchronic* axis. Film theorists view a film apart from its historical links and purely as a manifestation of film art and as the exploitation of film as a communication medium. The angle is not the historical perspective, but the nature and function of film art or aspects of this. *Gone with the Wind* is thus not important because it reflects something of Hollywood or even American history, but because it says something of the *nature* and *possibility* of film as art and communication. The result is, according to Hommel (1991:45), a view in which abstract characteristics and functions of film are explained according to examples. Whereas original film theory concentrated chiefly on film or a film as such, the recent emphasis has fallen on the position of the viewer and what the viewer does with that film.

As mentioned above, we further divide the subdiscipline film theory into criticism, analysis and theory.

The most important function of *criticism* is to educate viewers in terms of a specific film. De Putter (1991:166) distinguishes between two kinds of criticism: film criticism that focuses on the story of a film and film criticism that looks at technical aspects (production aspects such as camera use, lighting, sound, and so on). The former is what we usually find in newspaper reviews, while the latter is a more advanced form of criticism, and is usually found in film and academic journals.

> film criticism

Another distinction is made by Bordwell (1989), who distinguishes between film criticism that is directed towards the interpretation of a film, and film criticism that focuses on the discovery of the hidden meanings of a film. In both cases, it is the critic's aim to explain the film to readers, and to establish links with other films and literary works, to expose the relationship of the film to reality and to describe the deeper, underlying meanings of a film in terms of this.

In summary, film criticism aims to describe a specific film against the background of knowledge of the medium of film, and on the basis of this to develop a set of criteria and to deliver a value judgement. Usually, the success of a film for the majority of (newspaper) reviews depends on whether or not the story is told in a logical, consistent manner. Newspaper reviews seldom contain the ideal form of criticism, namely, a combination of:
- information on a film (the story, actors, director);
- opinions on the technical and artistic construction of a film (the success of the film as art and communication that is dependent on the use of the camera, direction and lighting);
- interpretation and establishment of relationships.

Where a report merely provides information and discusses the plot, we talk of a 'review'. Where this is coupled with an evaluation of the artistic quality of a film and an explanation and interpretation of a film, we refer to film criticism.

film analysis

In contrast to film criticism, which is chiefly a personal description and value judgement, *film analysis* is an exact and rational description of the role of the *filmic medium* in bringing about meaning in a film. In other words, a careful inventory is made of how the depiction of a story derives meaning through the actors, decor, lighting, sound, camera shots and direction (this is the filmic medium); what this meaning is; what the plot construction is and how it plays on the (un)consciousness of the viewer (cf. De Putter 1991:167).

The analysis may be undertaken from a single or many viewpoints: for example, a feminist, ideological, psychoanalytical perspective, and so on. In film art, several analytical methods exist that may be employed in this analysis, such as narratology (to systematically describe and analyse the plot), ideology criticism (to describe and analyse the ideological meaning of a film), semiotics (to describe and analyse the meaning construction of a film, and film as a unique grammar), rhetorical analysis (to analyse the rhetorical workings of a film), content analysis (making a quantitative analysis of the incidence of certain aspects, e.g. violence), psychoanalysis (to analyse how film plays on the (un)conscious of the viewer), and so on.

film theory

Film theory includes both film criticism and film analysis and places the opinions expressed in film criticism and the findings of film analysis in a broader context. It especially examines the social, political and philosophical implications of criticism and analysis, and how film differs from other arts and communication forms, on the basis of what is unique to the medium. Whereas film criticism is practical, film theory operates on a more abstract level.

Here, the consideration is the difference between criticism (practice) and theory (ideal). As was done earlier, it is on these grounds, too, that we make a distinction between descriptive and normative theory (cf. Monaco 1984:322–3).

In film theory's often abstract association with the meaning, value and function of the phenomenon of film, several different perspectives may be currently distinguished. Originally, film theory dealt with the difference between realism and expressionism (expressionism is often also referred to formalism in film theory). Since then, the emphasis has shifted to film as a unique 'language' – film semiotics. After this, the ideological workings of film were emphasised. At present, the viewer's experience of film is the focal point of film theory. In the following section, an overview of these film theories is presented.

To conclude: we differentiate between film history and film theory for academic purposes, and distinguish criticism, analysis and theory within the field of film theory. However, keep in mind that, in practice, these fields converge, overlap and link up with each other; indeed, not one of these fields could exist without the others.

8.2.4 Why film theory?

Against the background of the above, it may appear as if film theory occupies itself on an abstract level with things that most people experience as commonplace; that it abstracts, rather than explains, the phenomenon of film. This is in fact not the case. What film theory tries to convey is that:
- film is a unique and complex form of art and communication;
- various factors play a role in the production and experience of a film;
- a film is always created from a certain perspective;
- we always look at a film from a certain perspective, or experience it from within a certain context.

Film theory concentrates on four subjects in different ways and from different perspectives:
- the fundamental nature and properties of film as an art and communication medium;
- the film artist and communicator;
- the film viewer/audience;
- the wider context of the medium – the social, political, economic and ideological implications of film.

Film theory organises all the views and opinions on the above and at the same time develops new ideas on film by always posing new questions on these issues.

Film theory is thus a scientific process of organising, through which we learn to be disciplined and as objective as possible in our judgements about films. As such, it is a complete academic discipline that delineates its field of investigation in much the same way as other disciplines, and which poses questions based on the uniqueness of this field of investigation (film, film artists and communicators, film viewers and film in general). These questions then open up new perspectives. Film theory further develops analytical instruments for the investigation of these questions. Although many of these instruments (such as semiotics, psychoanalysis, ideology criticism, feminist criticism and analysis, plot analysis, reception theory, and so on) link up with and originate from disciplines such as linguistics and literary science, they are revised and adapted for this unique field of study (film) for application to the subject of investigation. In this way, film theory also contributes to the development of the methodology and paradigmatic trends that relate to studies in the human sciences on symbolic forms and humankind's understanding of these.

SUMMARY

In the preceding pages, we looked at some of the questions asked in film theory. On the basis of these questions we identified film theory, which is concerned with the role and function of film, the properties of film, film artists, communicators and audiences. We also distinguished between film history and descriptive film theory. Regarding the nature of film studies as an academic discipline, we distinguished between film history, together with the different kinds of film historiography, and film theory, which includes film criticism and film analysis. We concluded by defining film theory, its value and our reasons for studying it, and discovered that it provides us with perspectives that allow us to order our observations and experiences concerning the properties of film, its producers, its audiences and its wider contexts. In the process of answering the questions posed in and by film theory, film theory develops and tests different methodologies. As such, it not only improves our knowledge of film as an object of study, but also contributes to the epistemology of the human sciences in our endeavour to understand the human mind and its symbols.

8.3   CLASSIC FILM THEORY

8.3.1 Introduction

representation

Classic film theory was mainly concerned with film's representation of reality and whether this should be realistic or expressionistic/formalistic. The dichotomy between *expressionism/formalism* and *realism* in classic film theory (from about 1915) can be traced back to the ideas of the Greek philosophers Plato (427–347 BC) and Aristotle (384–322 BC) on the nature and purpose of art and their respective interpretations of *mimesis* (imitation or *representation*).

Plato saw art largely as an inferior copy or replica of reality. In his view of art, the *copyist* (artist, communicator) contributed no individual creative vision and, since a copy can never possess all the attributes of the original, the product was merely a feeble imitation (mimesis) of the real thing or nature.

| Plato

Compared to Plato, Aristotle regarded mimesis as a unique process, entailing more than just a copy or replica of nature. Art, although an imitation of reality, is not inferior but requires the craftsmanship of an artist.

The history of painting – from the early Renaissance works of the Italian painter Giotto (1267–1337) to the French impressionist painter Claude Monet (1840–1926) – supports the Aristotelian conception of art. The 19th-century French and Russian novelists Honoré de Balzac (1799–1850) and Leo Tolstoy (1883–1945) achieved a more accurate, realistic reproduction of reality than anything produced previously in the history of literature. The Norwegian and Russian dramatists Henrik Ibsen (1828–1906) and Anton Chekhov (1860–1904) perfected realism in the theatre, which portrayed life and reality in a naturalistic, realistic manner.

| painting

The period from the late Middle Ages to the end of the 19th century could be described as the *age of naturalism*. During this period Western art strove to depict reality as faithfully as possible. True, the romantics of the late 18th century, and in due course the impressionists as well, departed somewhat from the naturalist view of art. Thus the impressionists set greater store by beauty than by realism and introduced unconventional uses of line and colour. Nevertheless the overriding view was naturalistic: art was seen as a life-like rendering of reality, a mimesis.

| naturalism

After World War I, these realistic approaches underwent a radical change. One factor that put paid to this tradition was the emergence of photography, which helped to trigger a revolution in the arts. After all, if photography reproduced reality mimetically (imitatively), what remained for the other art forms?

| photography

The quest for solutions to this problem gave rise to expressionism, cubism, abstraction, conceptualism, surrealism and other trends in the fine arts. In theatre, there were forms such as happenings, street theatre and theatre of the absurd. These new forms all suggested that artists should not merely imitate reality but should express their own feelings about the world, interpreting, idealising and/or distorting it. The accent was on emotion and the capacity of the creative person to give unique form and stature to reality, thus investing it with new meaning.

The expressionists rejected illusions about reality. They consciously distorted natural objects and did not attempt to reproduce reality. The movement from realism to expressionism (leaving photography, film and later television to imitate reality mimetically) meant that photographic media were not and could not be viewed as art forms. This led to reflection on whether film (and television) as a technical medium could and should be confined to realistic imitation, or whether – as in the arts – the director could use photographic media to interpret reality expressionistically.

This debate crystallised in the film theories of Sergei Eisenstein (1898–1948), André Bazin (1919–1958), Rudolf Arnheim, V.I. Pudovkin (1893–1953), Siegfried Kracauer (1989–1966) and others. Before long, a clear distinction was made between realism and expressionism in filmic art. The controversy was conducted between adherents of Russian formalism and supporters of the French cinema journal *Cahiers du cinéma*. It profoundly influenced filmmakers and was reflected in such movements as Russian social realism, German expressionism, the French new wave and Italian neo-realism. Particularly in our time, the productions of what are known as *auteur* directors show clear evidence of these theoretical considerations.

SOME DEFINITIONS

Expressionism and formalism: In film theory the concepts 'expressionism' and 'formalism' are often used interchangeably to refer to views distinct from realism. Expressionism also refers to a specific period during the 1920s in theatre, art and film, especially in Germany. An outstanding characteristic of expressionism is its emotionalism and the desire of the artist (whether writers, painters or filmmakers) to experiment with the form (techniques) of his or her medium in order to give a new meaning to the content of the work and thus to the topic of the expression. In painting, the work of the painter Van Gogh is a good example of expressionism; and in film the work of the Russian directors Sergei Eisenstein and V.I. Pudovkin. Expressionism presents physical reality on the screen as a projection, or expression, of the subjective world, generally of a character in the film (cf. Konigsberg 1987:108).

Formalism refers to a cultural revival, especially in literature and film, in Russia during the 1920s. There is a small but nevertheless important difference between formalism and expressionism. Expressionism represents the global and theoretical idea of film as a unique form of artistic expression and communication – unique in the sense that film is capable of interpreting reality or an aspect thereof in specific ways. Formalism is more exact and pronounced in its description(s) of how film is capable of doing this. It gives a more concrete and 'scientific' description of film's codes (techniques), enabling film to be a unique form of expression. A good example of formalism is early narrative analysis (see Chapters 6 and 7) and formalist semiotics (see the later discussion in this chapter).

Realism refers to art (symbolic forms in general) that tries to imitate reality as closely as possible. The artist's techniques and methods disappear into the background and the reader/viewer (subject) becomes so involved with the content of the work that he or she is hardly aware of the artist's own interpretation and techniques. Apart from this form of realism, which is known as psychological realism, we also distinguish aesthetic realism. Aesthetic realism has as its goal the true expression of emotion or an emotional quality. Realism in film refers to a direct and truthful view of the real world through the presentation of characters and their physical surroundings with minimal distortion from either the filmmaker's point of view or from filmic techniques. In this respect, film realism is related to the traditional mimetic school of criticism in literature and painting, which argues that art should be a representation of reality, heightening our consciousness about the world that surrounds us (cf. Konigsberg 1987:285).

Reality: When we use the concept 'reality' in this chapter, we do not refer to reality in the sense of what is real or in terms of documenting something that is real, for instance in documentary films or in the news. We refer to the *representation* of something, and by doing so creating the impression of reality and/or imitating reality or an aspect thereof, for instance in feature films. In feature films (dramatic films) the film artist(s) creates something that imitates reality, for instance a love affair or a crime. The artist gives form to this by using actors, sets and the numerous techniques of the film medium.

What we as viewers eventually see on the screen is not reality, but an imitation thereof. This imitation can be of a realistic or expressionistic nature.

Raw material: Depending on the context in which it is used, *raw material* can either refer to the subject matter of a film, that is, the topic, or to the film stock – that is, the kind of film used: for instance, 16 or 35 mm, colour or black and white.

8.3.2 Expressionist film theory

Introduction

expressionism

The cardinal argument of expressionist film theory is that film, like all art, should introduce structure and order into the chaos and meaninglessness of the world around us. It holds that the camera and editing techniques should be used to add something to reality. A feature film should not simply imitate real life or some scene from it; through imitation of the real-life scenes the director should say something about the world and human existence. Hence the film should present a fresh angle on reality through the expressive use of cinematography and editing.

Expressionist directors prefer to use the camera subjectively and concentrate on individual interpretation and self-expression as opposed to literal renditions of reality. The camera is consciously and deliberately used to interpret reality rather than merely to record and reproduce it.

On expressionism, Gianetti (1972:186) says the following:

> Expressionists show a marked preference for form over content, for subjectivity and self-expression over factuality and literalness. The camera is used in a self-conscious manner to interpret reality, not only to record it. Expressionists are concerned with inner and psychological truths, which they feel can be captured by distorting the outer surfaces on the natural world.

Technically this emphasis is achieved through the number of stylised techniques: symbolic and artificial lighting, fragmentary editing techniques, nonsynchronous sound, extreme angles, and special-effects cinematography.

In the following sections, we focus on the theories of some of the theorists labelled as expressionists/formalists.

Vachel Lindsay

The expressionist tradition in film theory dates roughly to the period 1915–35. In *The art of the moving picture* (1932), Vachel Lindsay advocates the acceptance of the film as a *synthesis* of the arts. Soon after the publication of this book, a movement arose in France which concentrated exclusively on the parallels between film and music and film and poetry. The surrealist and experimental films of such French directors as Germain Dulac (*La Souriant Madame Beudet*, 1923), Jean Epstein (*Coeur Fidèle*, 1923) and Abel Gance (*Napoleon vu par Abel Gance*, 1927) demonstrated that film, like music, could *cast reality into a particular form*. Like poetry, it offered human beings a dream experience.

> Lindsay — film as synthesis

At about the same time the expressionist movement arose in Germany. In this movement the emphasis was placed on the portrayal of people's *inner experience*, that is, of the invisible and the abstract.

Hugo Münsterberg

Hugo Münsterberg, one of the first expressionist film theorists, believed that the art of filmmaking lay not in its technology but in people's aesthetic experience of the medium. A Kantian disciple and a thoroughgoing aesthete, he maintained that the art object (including the film) has a purpose but no function. It (film) is *distinct* and *separate* from reality and all other human experience. In experiencing a film, human beings are cut off from all other events. In the process both the human mind and the art object are liberated to a new experience, in which the viewer is not interested in relating the art object and the experience of it to anything else, or even in evaluating it. The art object and the experience of it become ends in themselves.

> Münsterberg — aesthetic experience as purpose

Rudolf Arnheim

In line with this view, Rudolf Arnheim formulated his film theory in his book, *Film as art* (1933). Like Münsterberg, he was a Gestalt psychologist who maintained that the purpose of the film (as of all art) is to express human existence. In normal perception human beings are chiefly observing the material world. The aim of a film is not to present a mirror image of material reality, but to alienate reality to the extent that its *metaphysical meaning* will address the viewer. Arnheim claimed that

> Arnheim — metaphysical meaning

photography and film cannot imitate or reflect reality as it is, but can only reproduce a part of it. In this sense they are essentially abstractions of reality. Because of their very limitation, the electronic and mechanival visual media are art forms.

Arnheim's theory can be summarised as follows:
- A work of art (and film as art) has value to the extent that the artist *manipulates* his material (both content and form).
- The artistic potential of a medium is enriched by its very *limitations*.

In Arnheim's view, the main limitations of film (and hence its artistic potential) reside in the *difference* between *normal human perception* of reality and *human perception of images*, or of reality through the lens of a camera.

These differences include the fact that human perception of reality is not demarcated by, and confined to, the boundaries of frames. By contrast, the vista of reality afforded by images is a limited perception from a given perspective (angle), confined to the image frame. The film viewer can do nothing about this perspective on reality. The spatiotemporal continuum of ordinary perception is delimited, in contrast to film images that have no boundaries of time and space. This difference between normal perception and perception of images formed the basis of the expressionist principle of *viewer manipulation*.

At the same time, visual communication is the crux of the problem in reception aesthetics. The images perceived by film viewers are not their own experience but a *representation* of reality as experienced and interpreted by the director. The director's choices and presentations in fact assign meanings to reality on behalf of the viewer, leaving the latter defenceless against the director's unlimited power. The director has full command of all the techniques of the visual medium in order to impose a given image of nature on the viewer.

8.3.3 Formalist film theory

Formalist film theory is related to expressionism in the sense that both emphasise that film should not merely imitate events as they occur in real life, but should produce an expressionistically edited version of nature. The Russian directors Sergei M. Eisenstein and V.I. Pudovkin, are seen to be the most prominent formalist film theorists.

Film Theory and Criticism

Figure 8.2 Expressionism: a scene from the 'Odessa Steps' sequence in Sergei Eisenstein's film, *The Battleship Potemkin*, 1925

Sergei Eisenstein

Eisenstein regarded the *single camera shot* as the primary semantic chapter of the film. In addition, he emphasised the meanings that originate from the combination and *juxtaposition* of single shots by means of editing or *montage*.

Eisenstein — montage

Eisenstein's ideas on film were influenced and shaped by the following art forms, movements and theories:
- Japanese Kabuki theatre, characterised by stylised acting and a succession of emotions.
- Italian futurism, launched by Filippo Tommaso Marinetti around 1907. This movement was a revolt against convention and traditionalism in the arts.
- Russian formalism, which developed mainly among literary critics in the 1920s and spread to the other arts. The formalists held that a work of art is characterised by certain universal formal properties. These, rather than its other qualities, determine its artistic merit.

- The American director David Wark Griffith, still regarded as one of the outstanding figures in film history. He was the first Western director to experiment with such techniques as cross-fading (or mixing), changing camera perspective within single shots and close-ups. As a result, the film medium began to move away from the static, theatrical style that had characterised the early films. He also helped to shape the style of narrative films (i.e. the way in which stories are narrated in films). His best-known films were *The Birth of a Nation* (1915) and *Intolerance* (1916).
- Intellectually, Eisenstein was influenced mainly by Hegelian dialectical philosophy, which formed the basis of his montage technique. Hegel's theory boiled down to the unity of all intellectual, spiritual, historical and political experiences and activities. The various spheres of human life contained divergent and contrasting elements, which, on closer analysis, are linked in polarised relations. These are seen as *thesis* and *antithesis*, with the whole of reality as a *synthesis* between the various polarities. In other words, unity is seen as the product or aggregate of divergent elements and relations within a given subject. Conflict develops when these disparate elements cannot be synthesised.

This last principle underlies Eisenstein's approach to both his theory about *conflict* in the single shot and montage. Montage consists of organic relations between the different elements both within single shots and between separate shots that are combined. In brief, Eisenstein's montage theory, which influences filmmaking even today, can be summarised as follows:

The single shot (shot A) is comparable to a cell in which various forms of conflict are operative. This conflict forms the basis of the conjunction of shot A with a subsequent shot (shot B), which is likewise torn by inner conflict. The combination of shot A with shot B is not simply an arbitrary concatenation of shots. The two are antithetical. This is the crux of film communication – the idea and meaning created by the combination of shot A with shot B.

Eisenstein distinguishes between the following real and potential conflicts, both within single shots and between different shots that are combined.

Conflict montage within a *single shot*
- *Graphic conflict*: the eye is confronted with contrasting lines, and therefore with opposing trends within the same shot.

| conflict montage |

Film Theory and Criticism

- *Conflict of planes*: by way of example he cites his production of *The Battleship Potemkin*. In one single shot the foreground is filled with a large group of active soldiers shooting at the solitary figure of a mother to the right, beyond the centre plane of the shot.
- *Conflict of volume*: a single shot containing objects of varying volume and magnitude.
- *Spatial conflict*: the screen space is filled by several shapes that together form a composition, guiding the eye to a focal point towards the back of the shot.
- *Conflict of lighting*: some objects in the shot are brightly illuminated – even overlit – whereas others are underlit.
- *Conflict in tempo*: the movement of objects within the single shot conflicts with the tempo of the camera movement and/or musical accompaniment.
- *Camera-created conflict*: This refers to spatial distortion created by camera point of view, as well as optical distortion by the camera lens. The conflict is caused because these effects are not in keeping with normal human perception.
- *Conflict created by the frame*: conflict is created by activities within the frame of a single shot which is too confined to accommodate all the activities. In other words, the viewer senses that the activities are too much (or too great) for the parameters of the frame of the single shot, and that they may well continue beyond the shot.

Conflict montage between *different shots*
- *Attraction montage*: in its simplest form, this type of montage (or combination of single shots) amounts to a shock effect on the viewer, created by the succession of images and the idea or meaning this may generate. A well-known example from Eisenstein's film *Strike* is the images of strikers who are pursued and shot down by soldiers. These images alternate with images of oxen being slaughtered at an abattoir. Eisenstein feels that this kind of montage is made meaningful by the *idea* that it conveys – in this case that the workers are being slaughtered like animals. He uses images that, in respect of content, have nothing to do with the events being portrayed. The conflict between two images which form an emotional rather than an intellectual association gives rise to new *meaning*.
- *Metric montage*: here the criterion is the duration of single shots, which are combined on this basis according to a scheme that matches

the beat of the musical accompaniment. Metric montage has a physiological effect in that it constitutes the pulse/*beat* of a film.
- *Rhythmic montage*: the content of the shot determines its duration and its combination with other shots.
- *Tonal montage*: the lighting contrasts and colour in one shot form the basis for its combination with the next shot.
- *High-tone montage*: this refers to the aggregate of the conflicts discussed under conflict montage in a single shot. The composition, lines, colours, lighting and the like provide a basis for the combination with other shots.

Eisenstein therefore used montage techniques to 'edit' reality in a premeditated way. Apart from dialectical philosophy, the basis of his montage theory may be traced to the view that realism effects an artistic experience which lulls the recipients: they can feel like heroes or martyrs without actually doing anything about it. Who will bother to perform heroic acts if one can share in and experience the glorification of one's ideals in the cinema? Eisenstein sought to analyse and fully control the power that art exercises over the beholder, so as to harness art (images) in the advancement of a cause.

V.I. Pudovkin

Pudovkin — construction montage

The theories of Eisenstein's fellow Russian, V.I. Pudovkin, were not fundamentally different. Pudovkin formulated a carefully considered theory of montage, which greatly influenced film directors in the 1920s and 1930s. He propagated a theory of *construction montage*: the viewer should be shown only what is essential and constructive. Details are components constituting the whole. By concentrating on detail, an idea and meaning are shaped and communicated.

Whereas Eisenstein's attraction montage used shots which, content-wise, had nothing to do with the events he was portraying, Pudovkin's construction montage concentrated exclusively on the content of the events portrayed. His premise was that *the camera lens replaces the eye of the viewer and therefore has to imitate the latter's 'normal perception'*.

He uses the following example. A horse-drawn carriage is trundling along a muddy road. The driver is impatient. Inside the carriage is a passenger donning a military coat to protect himself against a cold wind. They pass a pedestrian. The driver asks him the distance to the next town (written subtitle). The pedestrian points with his hand. The carriage proceeds jerkily. The pedestrian follows its progress with his eyes.

Pudovkin maintains that these events should not be shown in a single shot, but should emerge step by step in several detailed shots: (1) the wheels of the carriage; (2) the mud; (3) the wheels in the mud; (4) the driver's face; (5) the passenger; (6) the coat; (7) the passenger putting on the coat; (8) the dismal winter landscape; (9) the pedestrian; etc. *From the characteristic detail the whole can be construed.*

Figure 8.3 Expressionism: Vera Baranovskaia and Nikolai Batalov in V.I. Pudovkin's *Mother*, 1926

D.W. Griffith likewise believed that details were the constituents of a whole, but he used them to build suspense or to present the viewer with a consistently 'ideal' image. To Pudovkin, construction montage was a means of constructing a sphere, an overall impression, and to portray the cognitive content of a scene.

His assumption of what constitutes, or ought to constitute, the viewer's normal perception is, in terms of expressionist tradition, a denial of the individuality and freedom of the viewer. Like Eisenstein, he *guides the viewer* to perceive what he (the communicator) wishes or expects his viewers to see. As will be seen in due course, this is in direct contrast to André Bazin's view concerning sequence shots and depth focus.

Béla Balázs

> Balázs –
> viewer
> identification

In his *Theory of film: character and growth of a new art* (1970), Béla Balázs considers how the techniques of visual media may be harnessed to guide the viewer to *identify* with the content.

Balázs maintains that the viewer sees the world through the eyes of the communicator and has no personal viewpoint or perspective. The viewer can, and must be, guided to identify with the content of the image. This is done by deploying the *formal elements* of the image to this end. Accordingly, Balázs is one of the few theorists who discusses the formal elements in detail. He elaborates on close-ups, variations of camera point of view and montage and identification techniques. In his view the expressive value of the various camera movements and punctuation techniques, such as fading and cross-fading, is to guide the viewer towards identification.

FILMS TO VIEW

The viewing of the following films should help the reader towards a better understanding of the above discusssed assumptions in expressionist and formalist film theory discussed above:

Expressionism/formalism
V.I. Pudovkin: *Mother* (1926); *The End of St Petersburg* (1927); *Storm over Asia* (1928); *Deserter* (1933)
Sergei Eisenstein: *The Battleship Potemkin* (1925); *October* (1927/28); *Old and New* (1929); *Alexander Nevsky* (1938); *Ivan the Terrible* (Part I, 1944)

German expressionism
Paul Wegener: *Der Golem* (1914)
Robert Wiene: *Das Kabinett des Dr Caligari* (1919)
Fritz Lang: *Der Müde Tod* (1921)
Friedrich Murnau: *Nosferatu* (1922)

Film Theory and Criticism

Figure 8.4 Expressionism: Max Schreck as the vampire Nosferatu in Friderich Murnau's film *Nosferatu*, 1922

SUMMARY

The purpose of the above discussion has been to illustrate how expressionist and formalist theorists were all concerned with 'the belief that the art of cinema is possible precisely because a movie is unlike everday reality' (Giannetti 1990:374) and '... how they were all concerned with patterns and methods of restructuring reality into aesthetically appealing designs' (Giannetti 1990:377). Underlying their work was the need to show that film does not only imitate reality or provide us with iconic representations reality or an aspect thereof, but that it inherently provides us with an expressionistic interpretation and evaluation of reality. As such, it is an art similar to all other recognised forms of art.

8.3.4 Realist film theory

Realist film theorists are primarily concerned with the raw material – that is, reality itself. They argue in favour of film that reproduces reality undiluted, *imitating* it as closely as possible. The director

| realism

(communicator) and film techniques should not interfere with the viewer's own interpretation of the events.

Realist theorists advocate a relatively conservative use of the camera, which is seen as an instrument that should objectively record the events enacted. Film should reproduce life very much as it is physically rather than create a world of its own. Technically this is achieved by using natural environments rather than decor and sets. *Natural lighting* is preferred, as well as *long shots, sequence shots* and *depth focus*. On the whole realist films stay clear of special effects.

Realist theorists are concerned with the capacity of film to convey reality intact to the recipients, thus giving them a new awareness of life (reality or a piece of reality as [re-]presented by film). Film should not impose an interpretation of something on the viewer, but should lead the viewer to interpret reality or an aspect thereof and thus bring the viewer in closer contact with reality.

Realist theory is the best illustrated by the work of Italian neo-realist directors such as Visconti, Rossellini, de Sica and Fellini.

Italian neo-realism, and thus the techniques favoured by realist theorists, is characterised by:
- a predilection for neutral, objective renditions of the ordinary life of ordinary people;
- a democratic spirit, with emphasis on the values of ordinary people like labourers, peasants and factory workers;
- a refusal to make moral judgements;
- an emphasis on emotion rather than abstract ideas;
- an avoidance of neatly plotted stories in favour of loose, episodic structures that evolve from the situations of the characters;
- a documentary visual style;
- the use of actual locations, usually exteriors, rather than studio sets;
- the use of nonprofessional actors (or unknown actors);
- an avoidance of literary dialogue in favour of conversational speech, including dialects;
- an avoidance of artifice in the editing, camerawork and lighting in favour of a simple style.

The camera work and editing are not poetic or abstract, and the viewer is seldom aware of aesthetic image compositions. The camera is objective

Film Theory and Criticism

Figure 8.5 (Neo)realism: a scene from Vittorio de Sica's film *Miracle in Milan*, 1950.

and the viewer rarely perceives the action subjectively 'through the eyes of the character' (cf. Giannetti 1990:369).

The aim of the neo-realists was to expose anew the details that always form part of real life and to make the viewer aware of them.

The above are also characteristic of most contemporary European (especially French and Italian) films, compared to most American films, which tend to be more expressionist.

If manipulation of viewer perception is the key to expressionist film theory, then *neutrality* and *objectivity* are the keys to realist theories. The art of the film consists in its ability to present an imitation of reality. The camera should record the existing reality.

Siegfried Kracauer and André Bazin distinguish between two types of film communicators: those who use the medium to *amplify the meaning* of reality, and those who render reality *purely for its own sake*. The second type does not impose a particular, interpreted version of the world on the viewer but merely sensitises the latter to reality. A film should put viewers in touch with reality and make them perceive aspects of it that they might otherwise have overlooked.

Siegfried Kracauer

Kracauer – meaning of reality

The German theorist Siegfried Kracauer was less concerned with producing a realistic portrayal and recording reality than with using film to convey the *meaning* of reality, or an aspect of it, realistically. Thus a director may use an unrealistic film portrayal or recording of a scene or an action to convey the untrammelled meaning of that reality to the recipient.

The sole purpose of the film is to put the recipient in touch with reality and with real human beings. Kracauer maintained that 20th-century technology and science have alienated people from real life, and that the film can serve to make them aware of its true meaning once more. The camera should therefore be an instrument to record *unstaged reality – nature caught in the act*.

Giannetti (1990:371–2) lists the following key aspects that illustrate Kracauer's argument for realism in film:
- The subject matter must give the illusion that it has been found rather than arranged – in other words, the narrative structure, and the fact that the film is telling a story, must be hidden. The viewer should not constantly be aware that he or she is looking at a story.
- With the expression 'nature caught in the act', Kracauer means that film is best suited to recording events and objects that might be overlooked in life. The realistic cinema is a cinema of 'found moments' and poignant revelations of humanity (cf. Giannetti 1990:371).
- To be realistic a film should suggest endlessness. It must imply a slice-of-life, a fragment of a larger reality rather than a self-contained whole. By refusing to tie up all the loose ends at the conclusion of the movie, the filmmaker can suggest the limitlessness of reality (Giannetti 1990:371).
- Stylistic self-consciousness, best illustrated in film adaptations of literary and dramatic works, historical films and fantasies, stands in the way of film realism and is, according to Kracauer, uncinematic.

André Bazin

Bazin – ambiguity and multiple meanings

In his discussion of the ontology of film, André Bazin makes a clear distinction between film and reality, subordinating the former to the latter. Nevertheless, the film is a unique phenomenon in that it is freed from spatiotemporal constraints.

To Bazin, the outstanding quality of reality is its *ambiguity* or the *multiple meanings* of everything. In his opinion, the expressionist approach, particularly its use of montage, eclipses this ambiguity. Montage does not permit the viewer to observe the multiple meanings of reality, offering instead a synthetic reality in and through which truth is corrupted: it only generates images, unconnected in the real world, with the result that we, as viewers, are denied the active intellectual potential of choice to make the connections within the image which we view (Bazin 1967:15).

Instead of montage, he advocates *sequence shots* and *depth perspective*, arguing that by these means one can emphasise the union of humanity and reality, their interdependence and the *multiple meanings* of things. Awareness of the multiple meanings of reality is the essence of people's aesthetic experience of films.

In support of his arguments concerning sequence shots and depth perspective, he refers specifically to the films of Orson Welles, Robert Flaherty, Jean Renoir, William Wyler, the Italian neo-realists and directors of the French new wave.

On the American director Flaherty's classic film, *Nanook of the North* (1922), Bazin, for instance, says:

> The camera cannot see everything at once but at least it tries not to miss anything of what it has chosen to see. For Flaherty, the important thing to show when Nanook hunts the seal is the relationship between the man and the animal and the true proportions of Nanook's lying in wait. Editing could have suggested the passage of time; Flaherty is content to show the waiting, and the duration of the hunt becomes the very substance and object of the image. In the film this episode consists of a single shot. Can anyone deny that it is in this way much more moving than "editing by attraction" would have been? (Bazin 1967: 29)

To illustrate his argument concerning sequence shots, Bazin (1967:39) says the following of Orson Welles's *The Magnificent Ambersons* (1942):

> Anyone who can use his eyes must realize that Welles' sequence shots in The Magnificent Ambersons are by no means the passive "recording" of an action photographed within a single frame, but

> *that on the contrary this reluctance to break up an event or analyse its dramatic reverberations within time is a positive technique which produces better results than a classical breakdown [like in construction of conflict montage – author] of shots could ever have done.*

He concedes that because of the emphasis on sequence shots and depth perspective, as opposed to montage, the communicator has to omit certain things that could have helped viewers to understand the message – that is, understand it in the way the communicator wants them to understand it. He calls these omissions the ellipses in film communication, the things which are not shown. These ellipses are not defects but in fact an acknowledgment of the potential multiple meanings of reality and the intelligence and experience of the viewer:

> *... the empty gaps, the white spaces, parts of the event that we are not given, are themselves of a concrete nature. It is the same in life: we do not know everything that happens to others.* (Bazin 1967:66)

The viewers themselves have to supply the omissions on the basis of their knowledge and experience of reality.

To Eisenstein, the essence of film communication is the combination of shot A with shot B to constitute shot C. To Bazin, on the other hand, the single shot has its own phenomenological integrity.

Bazin believes that the communicator should not interfere with reality, but should render or recreate it intact on film. The sole aim of the film is to bring the recipients *closer to reality*, to make them *aware* of it *anew*. Film should not recreate reality analytically and in the process interpret it to the viewers: they should be left to do their own interpretation.

Giannetti (1990:144–53) notes the following as some of the key issues in Bazin's theory:
- Influenced by the philosophical movement called Personalism, Bazin emphasised the individualistic and pluralistic nature of truth. Therefore film should not try to impose a reality, interpretation of reality or a truth on the viewer. The viewer will decide for him/herself what the truth is. In film there are many ways of portraying the real. The essence of reality lies in its ambiguity. To capture this ambiguity,

the filmmaker must be modest and self-effacing, a patient observer willing to follow where reality leads (cf. Giannetti 1990:144).
- Thematic editing violates the complexities of reality. Montage superimposes a simplistic ideology over infinite variability of actual life.
- Being aware that cinema, like all art, involves a certain amount of selectivity, organisation and interpretation, and thus distortion, Bazin did not advocate a simple-minded theory of realism (cf. Giannetti 1990:147). The values of the filmmaker will always influence the manner in which reality is perceived. However, the filmmaker must try to keep in balance his personal vision with the objective nature of the medium. Certain aspects of reality must be sacrificed for the sake of artistic coherence, but Bazin felt that abstraction and artifice ought to be kept to a minimum. The materials should be allowed to speak for themselves (cf. Giannetti 1990:147). This the filmmaker can do by including all the dramatic variables within the same frame – that is, by exploiting the resources of the long shot, the lengthy take, deep focus and widescreen. He or she can preserve actual time and space by panning, craning, tilting or tracking rather than cutting (montage) to individual shots (cf. Giannetti 1990:148).

The summarise Bazin's theory, Giannetti (1990:144) writes:

> *Bazin's realist aesthetic is based on his belief that photography, TV and cinema, unlike the traditional arts, produce images of reality automatically, with a minimum of human interference. This technological objectivity connects the moving image with the observable physical world. A novelist or a painter must represent reality by re-presenting it in another medium – through language [prose and poetry – author] and color pigments [painting – author]. The filmmaker's image, on the other hand, is essentially an objective recording of what actually exists. No other art, Bazin felt, can be as comprehensive in the presentation of the physical world. No other art can be as realistic, in the most elementary sense of the word.*

Media Studies: Volume 3

Figure 8.6 Realism: Orson Welles as Kane in his film *Citizen Kane*, 1941

Jean-Luc Godard

Godard – film as inner experience

Although the names of Jean-Luc Godard and Bazin are usually linked as representative of the realistic and neo-realistic approach to films, they differ in their *evaluations* of montage – Godard's view being positive (cf. Monaco 1984:343–52).

Godard developed a *synthesis of montage and mise-en-scène*. In the first place, he maintains that if a director is dishonest in his choice of images recorded in sequence shots and depth focus (mise-en-scène), it could distort reality in the same way that montage does. The very choice of certain images (and image content) is an act of abstraction.

Secondly, he argues that montage does not have to entail a distortion of reality, nor does it necessarily imply dishonesty on the part of the communicator. Although he agrees with Bazin that reality is better rendered by mise-en-scène than by montage, he gives a broader definition of realism. Unlike Bazin, Godard does not see it purely as the communicator's untrammelled rendering of reality. Neither does he, like Kracauer, concern himself with the psychological realism that the director creates for the viewer with the aid of montage. To Godard, realism resides, not in the content and form of the images, but in the *intellectual reality* that the director creates with his message – the *dialogue* that he conducts with the viewer. Is this dialogue conducted in good faith? If so, the film is realistic. Is the director *sincere*, does he address the recipient directly, or does he try to manipulate the viewer?

Eisenstein sees montage preeminently as the means used by the director to alienate reality for the sake of reconceptualising it. Bazin sees mise-en-scène (including sequence shots and depth perspective) as the communicator's cardinal technique for showing the recipient an unstaged reproduction of reality. Godard, by contrast, does not favour either of these techniques: he takes both for granted as basic filmic codes. To his mind, film communication should aim at a *particular effect*, at creating a *lasting impression* on the viewer. (*Effect* and *impression* here refer to the meaning a film has for the viewer rather than its emotional impact.)

The effect of a film resides in what it reveals about people's *inner experience* and their *relation* with and to reality. For this reason Godard's theory and films are described as *human-centred cinema*.

Film techniques are employed for the sake of *emotion*. The creative and expressive plane is that of emotional truth. The aim is not simply to present a plausible rendering of reality or some situation, but to render the complete emotional experience of human beings, the emotional quality of events. This should be done in such a way that the images radiate this truth. They should portray the *spirit* of a nation, of human beings, of an individual. Art is not a replica of what we see and hear around us. It should strive to visualise that which is not perceptible to the human senses.

To the director, says Godard, the film is a means of self-expression. In and through this medium, the viewer discovers the world, *humanity*, him/herself. It makes the viewer aware of *beauty*, but also of the evil that threatens beauty. In and through the film, the viewer elevates the essence of his or her conviction to a symbol, thus giving reality new meaning and form.

To the viewers, the film offers a *new perspective* on reality. It is for them to accept or reject it. Either way, the very awareness of a different perspective on life and the world helps to shape their minds and enrich their knowledge, understanding and experience of life.

To Godard, then, film, like theatre, is essentially emotional. The effectiveness of film depends on rhythm, phrasing and intensity. At every level the communicator constructs the film *theatrically* by means of dialogue, mise-en-scène, camera point of view and the like, in order to achieve the desired emotional impact.

FILMS TO VIEW

The viewing of the following films should help the reader towards a better understanding of the assumptions of realist film theory discussed above:

Luchino Visconti: *Obsessions* (1942), *La Terra Trema* (1948), *Senso* (1954)
Roberto Rossellini: *Rome, Open City* (1945), *Paisa* (1946), *Germania, Anno Zero* (1947)
Jean Renoir: *La Grande Illusion* (1937)
Jean-Luc Godard: *Une Femme est une Femme* (1961), *Le Gai Savoir* (1968)
D.W. Griffith: *The Birth of a Nation* (1915); *Intolerance* (1916)
Orson Welles: *Citizen Kane* (1941)
Robert Flaherty: *Nanook of the North* (1922)

Figure 8.7 Realism: a scene from D.W. Griffith's film, *The Birth of a Nation*, 1915

348

Film Theory and Criticism

SUMMARY

The purpose of the above discussion is simply to introduce you to some of the ideas of some of the realist theorists and their emphasis on film's ability to record and reflect reality; that

> ... cinema is essentially an extension of photography and shares with it a pronounced affinity for recording the visible world around us ... [that] unlike other art forms, photography and cinema tend to leave the raw material of reality more or less intact. (Giannetti 1990:368)

8.3.5 Auteur theory

The early realist film theories of Bazin and Godard were the direct precursor of, and impetus for, the development of the *auteur* theory. In this theory it is postulated that the relation between the image and reality can only be described in terms of a specific director's individual interpretation of reality: how this individual discloses, describes, experiences and ultimately visualises reality in the image. In this sense *auteur* theory is related to existentialist philosophy and should be studied against that background.

auteur

The film theorist Alexander Astruc initially used the term *caméra stylo* (camera pen) to refer to a director whose work is thematically and stylistically recognisable. Although this term never caught on, the term *auteur* – from the influential French cinema journal *Cahiers du cinéma* – is its equivalent. *Auteur theory* places the emphasis on the director (the communicator), who is equated with the serious writer, the artist whose personality is *inscribed* in the work of art. The most eminent exponents of auteur criticism were the cinema journals *Cahiers du cinéma* in France, *Movie* in Britain and the critic Andrew Sarris in the USA.

One of the factors that contributed to the origin and development of this theory was, like in the debate between expressionist and realists, the controversy about the film as an art form. By placing directors on a par with great writers, and by applying to their productions the same analytical methods used for literature, *auteur* theory indicated that the director could be an artist. The emphasis on the director as an *auteur* relates to the romantic view that art cannot be the result of a collective production process. Despite the collective character of film production, auteur criticism shows that it is possible to isolate an individual artist in the electronic pictorial media.

Although film production is a collective activity, a film only has value if it is essentially a communication by a director. The presence of a director (who is actually an artist, an *auteur*) will permeate the film with that individual personality. This personality can be traced, both *thematically* and *stylistically*, in virtually all the work of a specific director. On this basis, it is possible to distinguish between an *auteur* and a *metteur en scène* (a French term for 'director'). The auteur is 'consistently expressing his own unique obsessions, the other [is] a competent, even highly competent, filmmaker, but lacking the consistency which betrays the profound involvement of a personality' (Caughie 1981:9).

auteur theory

Originally the emphasis in *auteur theory* was on those Hollywood directors working in the *studio system* who were still able to leave their distinguishable trademarks or signatures on the films they directed: for instance, directors such as Alfred Hitchcock, Charles Chaplin, John Ford, Howard Hawks and Orson Welles.

A good example of *auteur* criticism is the work of the American critic Andrew Sarris. He used the *auteur* philosophy to rank American directors according to their *technical competence* (a basic requirement) and on two other levels: their *identity as stylists*, and their ability to convey their *own interpretation* of the material, reflecting some personal vision or outlook on the world. These criteria were also followed in Europe, where directors such as Ingmar Bergman, Federico Fellini and Luis Buñuel have been elevated to the rank of *auteurs*.

At its most basic level, *auteur* criticism provides a means of classification and analysis according to the characteristics common to many films directed by the same filmmaker. It is based on the assumption that any one film can be better understood and appreciated by considering it in relation to the qualities and concerns evident in the other films made by the same director.

The value of the theory is that it is a means for identifying and understanding the basic components of style and structure in a director's work. It functions as a systematic but flexible means of placing a film within a class and some historical context.

Auteur theory should not be seen as an aggrandisement of the director and his/her power over the recipient – rather as if the director is the sublime creator using various techniques to 'play' with reality. The emphasis is wholly on the director's mental world and the way this is communicated. When analysing a director's work, one should not concentrate on the techniques used, but on his or her description of his or her chosen theme and the images he or she chooses to present to his or her viewers. This is where one can discern a director's attitude to reality. By determining what images a director has chosen 'we can talk about reality as it is filtered through the consciousness of the authors' (Caughie 1981:84).

The main criticism, from prominent film critics such as Pauline Kael and Dwight Macdonald, is that *auteur* theory tends to grade art and the work of an individual artist. This kind of grading is impossible in art. Art is an individual and subjective expression of the artist. This makes the grading of art or a work of art impossible. Structuralists have condemned it as conservative and neo-romantic. They question the notion that an individual director can somehow avoid or transcend the deep structures of society by virtue of his or her intense creative inner visions. The director always remains part of society. Furthermore, *auteur* theory and criticism can become a cult of personality, in which poor films made by recognised *auteurs* are preferred to better films made by directors not afforded *auteur* status (cf. Stromgren & Norden 1984:260–62).

To summarise: in our brief discussion of the *auteur* theory we referred to the relation between the *auteur* theory and realist film theory, the origin of the theory, concern about the collective nature of film production and how this was an impetus for the auteur theory, the theory's emphasis on the theme and style in a director's work, Sarris's ranking of directors, the value of the theory and criticism of the theory.

8.3.6 Genre theory

Closely related to auteur theory, with its emphasis on the director and the style and content of a director's work, is genre theory, with its emphasis on the kind of film we are dealing with or are watching. The word 'genre' comes from the Latin word *genus*, meaning 'kind'. Genre theory in film originated from the study of literary genres that has its origins, at least in the West, in the third book of Plato's *Republic*. In this work, Socrates suggested a tripartite division of literary forms based on their manner of presentation. This division consists of the distinction between tragedy

| genre

and comedy, way of recital (presentation), for instance a Greek chorus (dithyramb), and the mixture of the two (tragedy and comedy) as well as different forms of presentation, also referred to as an epic. This distinction or categorisation was followed up by Aristotle in his *Poetics*. In this work, it is proposed that different kinds of poetry exist and each kind should be understood in terms of its unique qualities. Aristotle suggested that these qualities could be explained by distinguishing between the medium of representation, the object represented in a literary work, and the mode of representation. Stam (2000:13) explains how Aristotle's definition of tragedy contains criteria in terms of which genres can be defined: kinds of events portrayed (or story/theme), types of characters (and their social ranks), ethics of characters, narrative structure and audience effects (or how audiences are going to react to a work). This early discussion about different kinds of literary works has been much debated, both by literary theorists and film theorists.

defining genre

Theoretically, the question is how to define a genre. Bosma (1991:322), for instance, defines genre as a collection of films with common characteristics as far as narratives and visual style are concerned, and which are recognised by the viewers as such. He continues that part of the film theorist's most important work is to draw up a taxonomy of styles, themes, and so on, in order to assist the viewer in understanding a film – in other words, to categorise films based on a number of parameters. Obviously, there are also many other definitions. However, most conclude that genre can be defined based on a description of the repetitive nature of, inter alia, one or more of the following distinguishing characteristics related to:
- theme and subject matter;
- setting (or milieu or iconography);
- style or the use of codes of content and form and conventions in a particular way (see the discussion of codes in Chapter 2);
- emotional quality or mood (e.g. comedy, tragedy, drama, melodrama, action);
- technology (the distinguished use of film technology, as in, for instance, science fiction and animation);
- audience expectations and recognition;
- substance (black and white, widescreen, Cinemascope, video, etc.).

Film Theory and Criticism

Obviously, the description of a genre and of the above characteristics can be done from different theoretical perspectives. For instance, Will Wright, in his classic work, *Sixguns and Society* (1975), used structuralist methods to describe the Western ('cowboys and crook movies') as a genre. By focusing on the analysis of myth (see Chapter 5 in Volume 1 of this book, Fourie (2007: 251–6)), and by drawing on Propp's distinction of the function(s) of plot and character types in folk tales (see chapters 6 and 7). Wright identified 16 functions of the hero character that can be recognised in almost all Westerns, and, as such, can be used to characterise the Western as a particular genre. Broadly, the 16 functions deal with the way(s) in which the hero(s) is/are accepted in a group (society), their goals or missions based on their values, their opposition(s) to the villain(s) and the villain's values, their actions to eliminate or overpower the villain(s) and restore and safeguard the group/community/society's values.

| structuralist perspective |

Many of the (narrative) functions of the hero, as applied by Wright to the Western movie, can today also be applied to modern television genres such as the soap opera, the situation comedy, the hospital or court drama, cops and robbers dramas, etc., if not to all popular or mass-mediated forms of symbolic expression. In this regard, also see the discussion of rhetorical motives in television entertainment in Chapter 3 of Volume 1 of this book (Fourie 2007: 216–19). Fourie wrote that television (and film) content has certain intrinsic rhetorical motifs (functions) related to:

- knowledge about *identity*: by seeking to answer questions related to the individual's relation with and to others, including his or her role, place and function in society, in a group, in a relationship, etc.;
- knowledge about *ability*: by trying to demonstrate possibilities and emphasising the hero/group/society/individual's ability to achieve something;
- knowledge about *survival*: by making the viewer aware of eternal values (e.g. love, friendship, generosity and fellowship);
- knowledge about and an *understanding of reality*: by trying to shed new light on reality or an aspect thereof.

When one watches even a simple and/or hilarious situation comedy or an episode of a soap opera, it is usually possible to identify these motifs (and functions) in the programmes and to ask yourself how the

353

programme has contributed to your knowledge about identity, ability, survival and an understanding of the world and its people.

Still from a structuralist perspective and also analysing the Western, Edward Buscombe focused our attention on the *visual elements or iconography* as a criterion for describing a genre. Doing this, he draw attention to the underlying meanings of the open landscapes, lonely trees, wide-brimmed hats, saloons, guns, prostitutes' bodices, covered wagons, and so on, and how these visual elements related to social and cultural values and mores.

<small>poststructuralist perspective</small>

Writing from a more poststructuralist perspective, Steven Neal draws our attention to the audience as a criterion for analysing and describing a genre. In the context of poststructuralism (compared to, for instance, Wright), Neal actually moved beyond the content and form of film and focused more on the political economy of the film industry. He argued, for instance, that genres were 'systems of orientations, expectations and conventions that circulate between industry, text and subject' (Stam 2000:127). A genre is what an audience, or a member of an audience, expects (based on publicity) a specific film to be. If a film is advertised as a horror movie, then you expect to experience tension and even anxiety, as that is what a horror film is supposed to achieve according to its nature as a genre (its specific techniques, settings, plots, themes, characters). Usually, the film production industry promotes a film as a specific genre because they know from experience that a specific genre, such as horror, draws or is more likely to draw bigger audiences than a war drama or a so-called art movie. For instance, the recent 'art movie' *Revolutionary Road* (2008) was promoted as a *family drama* and the recent blockbuster *No Country for Old Men* (2007) as a *crime* movie.

<small>postmodern perspective</small>

Lately, the postmodern perspective has become dominant. In this perspective, the concept of *genre mixing* and the *submerged nature* of genre is emphasised, which makes the categorisation of a film in one particular genre difficult. From this perspective also stems the criticism against genre theory and criticism. Such criticism (cf. Stam 2000:128–30) mainly centres on problems related to *extensionism*, *normativism* and the *monolithic* nature of genre theory and criticism. It is emphasised that generic labels are too broad. For instance, what is comedy and what is tragedy? Comedy can also be tragedy, and vice versa. Genre criticism may also be plagued by *a priori* ideas about what a film should be or why and how it could be categorised as being or belonging to a specific genre. Again, a so-called horror film can also be a romantic love drama. Also, and again this is emphasised in postmodern critique of genre theory, the categorisation of a film in a particular genre may not take account of the underlying meanings of a film. On the surface, a film may seem to belong to a specific genre while on a deeper level it may be something else. This is often the case with so-called art movies and lately also with many mainstream movies in the film industry. How, for instance, does one classify a film such as *Revolutionary Road* (2008), which is mainly shown in art-movie houses, or *No Country for Old Men* (2007), which was one of the big award winners in 2008? As mentioned above, the first was advertised as a family drama and the second as a crime movie. Both can also be categorised and classified as being intense psychological and existential human dramas. The postmodern concept of *genre mixing* thus becomes very relevant in contemporary genre discussions.

To summarise: as *auteur* theory can be described as a typology of films based on the *nature* and *style* of a specific director's work, genre theory is a typology of kinds of films based mainly on the story or theme of a film, which may lead a viewer to recognise a film as, for instance, a war film, a spy film, a musical, a crime film, and so on. Apart from story or theme, a film also has other properties or characteristics on the basis of which it can be described and/or catalogued as a specific genre. This can include characterisation (the types of characters in film), settings, visual elements or iconography, time or period (for instance a historic or period movie), the format (e.g. comedy or tragedy), technology and raw material. The role of the audience in recognising and categorising a particular genre is increasingly recognised, as is the concept of *genre mixing*.

8.4 FILM SEMIOTICS

After 'classic' film theory and aesthetics, with their emphasis on expressionism and realism, followed *auteur* and genre theory and criticism as dominant paradigms in film theory and analysis. The next major movement was semiotics. (For an overview, definition and discussion of semiotics, see Chapter 2).

The main figure in *film semiotics* was the French theorist Christian Metz. In his book *Film language: a semiotics of the cinema* (1974), he used semiotics as a systematic and scientific method to analyse the ways in which films produce meaning. This development in film theory is in line with the so-called structuralist movement in linguistics and literature studies during the 1960s and 1970s (cf. Fourie 1996).

Originally, Christian Metz (1974), Peter Wollen (1972), Roland Barthes (1977) and Umberto Eco (1979) argued that film communicates according to a specific set of *grammatical* rules. The accent was on the nature of the image as an iconic sign, the ways in which camera and editing codes produce meaning, paradigmatic and syntagmatic structures in visual communication, and the way in which film creates different kinds of meaning.

Apart from the theory underlying film semiotics, which also concerns the relationship between film and reality, or the relation between film as signifier, reality and signified, semiotic theory and analysis also provided us with the analytical tools to analyse the working of film (moving images) as a *signifying practice*. Some of the key insights gained through semiotics in the nature of film as a signifying practice are summarised here in a more general way.

8.4.1 Film as a sign

sign

A *sign* is never the real object. It is not reality, but represents and serves as a means of referring to reality. In their daily communication, people use linguistic signs in order to refer to things, to express their feelings, their desires, their thoughts and attitudes. How could one refer to something like a dog, for example, unless one knew the linguistic sign D-O-G? One could draw a dog, but that would simply be to use a pictorial or iconic sign as opposed to a linguistic one. In the same way, film uses images (pictorial signs) to refer to reality. Film is never reality but a semiotic representation of reality. Nevertheless people readily experience film as real – hence the *credibility* of film.

Film is both iconic and indexical. Here the signifier (the image) resembles the signifier. An image (the signifier) of a dog looks like a dog. It is immediately recognisable and the recipient does not need any special knowledge to interpret the sign. Because of the directly identifiable resemblance between an iconic sign and reality, it is possible that the recipient will treat the iconic sign as the real thing. This can explain the persuasive power of film.

Film is indexical in the sense that the image as an effect of a photochemical process (the celluloid strip projected on a screen) is caused by what it represents (the prefilmic signifier in reality) (cf. Easthope 1993:7).

8.4.2 Film, denotation and connotation

Film (all photographic and moving images) does not only denote a literal meaning. The image is iconic, indexical and symbolic in the sense that the interpretation and meaning of an image is not untouched by cultural and social codes. In order to understand a film or an image, viewers fill it with their own knowledge, which cannot be separated from their own cultural and ideological background. Thus, apart from the image being or containing iconic, indexical and symbolic features, the viewer and what the viewer does with the image must be kept in mind. An image of a cow (although iconic, symbolic and indexical) will/can portray different meanings in, for instance, Western and Eastern cultures. The image is both denotative and connotative.

_{denotation and connotation}

In addition, there is in film a distinction between *paradigmatic connotation* and *syntagmatic connotation*. Paradigmatic connotation refers to the connotative meanings that viewers attach to an image on the basis of their own experience of various objects in the image and the resultant associations. A dog shown with a boy may remind a viewer of his or her childhood, and he or she might associate it connotatively with carefreeness. Advertisements afford good examples of paradigmatic connotation. Advertising agencies usually trade on the possibility that viewers will form pleasant associations with the objects shown in advertisements. The combination of a bottle of suntan lotion next to a bathing beauty lying on an idyllic beach is used to prompt an association with health, pleasure, gratification, carefreeness and sexuality.

_{paradigmatic connotation}

Syntagmatic connotation refers to the semantic associations formed by the *interrelationship* of various shots. For example:

_{syntagmatic connotation}

> Shot 1: soldiers being shot in battle;
> Shot 2: cattle being shot at an abattoir.

This combination of shots may give rise to a syntagmatic connotation that people are shot like animals.

8.4.3 Codes in film

codes of content

codes of form

Semiotics – and this is especially valuable for the purpose of film analysis – emphasises the difference between *codes of content* and *codes of form*. Codes of content refer to what the viewer perceives (sees and hears) in an image: the theme, the story, the mise-en-scène (decor, costumes, props), lighting, music, sound effects, acting and the like.

Consequently, we can distinguish between narrative codes, thematic codes, codes of the mise-en-scène, acting codes, production codes, lighting codes and so forth. Consider, for example, the various lighting codes used in a film in order to create a certain atmosphere and convey a particular meaning. What role does colour (e.g. in the costumes and decor) play in the communication of meaning? What is the contribution of the actor's performance, the style of production, the presentation style of the newsreader, composition and so forth?

nonfilmic and filmic codes

These codes are not peculiar to film (and television or the internet). Film in a sense inherited them from literature (narrative codes), the theatre (lighting codes, costume codes, decor codes), painting, architecture and the other arts. Consequently these codes are also referred to as *nonfilmic* codes. These techniques, although 'borrowed' from other media, are nonetheless vital for the transmission of meaning in film.

Codes of form are the actual *filmic* or *visio-linguistic* codes – specifically those of the *camera point of view* and *editing*. These are the distinctive codes of film (and television), in the sense that they impart meaning to images in a unique manner.

In the case of camera point of view (cf. Peters 1974:16–19), the following *theoretical* possibilities can be distinguished:
- active and passive camera point of view;
- the camera as a point of view and as a mere reflection of reality;
- objective and subjective camera point of view.

In the case of active and subjective camera points of view, as well as that of the camera as a point of view, the scene enacted before the camera is seen from a specific perspective (chosen by the director). In the case of the passive, objective use of the camera, as well as that of the camera as the reflector of reality, a purely mimetic version of the scene is produced – the camera merely records.

In the first case, the use of the camera expresses how the communicator (director) perceives and interprets the events enacted. In the second case, the camera serves to reproduce a realistic version of those events.

In the case of the camera as point of view and subjective and active camera points of view, the codes used include varying camera distances (close-ups, long shots, zoom shots) and camera movements (panning, dolly, crane, lens changes, filters, camera heights). In the case of camera point of view as mere reproduction, the camera remains predominantly static. In the first case, the camera is used to impart *form* to the events enacted; in the second, the main concern is with the *content* of those events.

When describing, interpreting and evaluating film from a semiotic perspective, one has to ask how these codes contribute to the meaning of the message conveyed. Does the difference between a long shot and a close-up signify something in terms of the meaning conveyed? If the camera-person takes a shot from below, thus producing an unflattering image of, say, a politician, does it affect the meaning (interpretation) that recipients attach to that image and, ultimately, their image of the politician?

Among *codes of form* one could also list *optic-acoustic* effects. These make up the *substance* of the image. Does the choice of film or video type, the choice between black-and-white or colour film, or between synchronised or nonsynchronised sound, influence the meaning that the communicator conveys? Could the substance influence the meaning that viewers will attach to an image and the nature of their aesthetic experience?

8.4.4 The paradigmatic-syntagmatic nature of film

A *paradigm* represents the choices at the communicator's disposal when formulating a message. The *syntagm* is the formulated message/statement/film shot. In language, the smallest semantic chapter is the word (actually, the word can be broken down into morphemes). To be able to conduct a conversation, words have to be combined into sentences according to certain grammatical rules. Sentences are in turn combined into larger chapters to form paragraphs, and so on.

<aside>paradigmatic-syntagmatic structure</aside>

In film the smallest chapter of meaning is the (single) shot. In order to tell a story, single shots are combined into scenes and scenes into sequences by means of editing techniques to tell the eventual story. The single shot, as the smallest semantic chapter, is only one component of a series of semantic chapters that convey the eventual meaning of the film. In 'formulating' a shot, the director has a choice of paradigms offering different options. The director who wants to take a shot of a man walking down a street has such options as the following: camera distance (e.g. a close-up, a medium shot, a long shot), camera movement (e.g. panning, crane, dolly), filter and speed.

Choice is therefore a key factor, without which communication would not be possible. In people's daily spoken and written communication they are constantly choosing, albeit often unwittingly. Depending on their communication need(s) (to inform, tell a story, persuade, express emotions, etc.), they choose among a range of words and syntactic constructions. The same thing happens in film, where the communicator's means of expression include not only words but also images.

In film we can furthermore distinguish between three paradigmatic articulations of meaning:
- *first articulation of meaning*: the director's choice of what to represent (the eventual *content* of the image);
- *second articulation of meaning*: the way the director presents or portrays the chosen content (camera point of view as a means of creating *form*);
- *third articulation of meaning*: the way in which the director combines single shots into sequences and scenes (editing as a means of creating *form*).

The decisions at each of these levels of articulation influence and determine the eventual meaning conveyed in and by an image.

Levels of meaning

For purposes of analysis, film semiotics distinguishes between five levels of meaning in film (cf. Peters 1974):
- topic, theme and story;
- presentation of topic, theme and story;
- filming and editing of topic, theme, story;
- sound;
- optic-acoustic level.

Together, these five levels constitute the meaning that is conveyed. The

Film Theory and Criticism

level of the *topic/theme/story* is concerned exclusively with the narrative and/or subject and the narrative structures it contains. Here one would look at literary factors such as exposition, crisis, climax, denouement, characterisation and the like. *Presentation* relates to the previously mentioned nonfilmic codes, such as director's style, acting, costuming, lighting and composition. *Filming and editing* concern filmic codes – camera point of view and editing. At the level of sound, there are, for instance, music and sound effects to reinforce a particular meaning. The *optic-acoustic* level has to do with the substance of the image (the material of which it is composed, e.g. type of film stock, colour, synchronised sound, etc.) and the way this contributes to the overall meaning conveyed.

8.4.5 Communicative possibilities of film

On the strength of the qualities outlined above, film has the following *communicative possibilities* (cf. Peters 1974):

- It portrays and represents.
- It acts for both the communicator and the recipient (viewer) as a means of observation and experience.
- It acts for both the communicator and the recipient as a means of expression and visualisation.

communicative possibilities

Film can portray and represent reality both factually (documentary) and fictionally (feature films). In the second case, a reality first has to be created before it can be presented, filmed and structured with the aid of the camera and editing techniques. Because directors have certain techniques at their disposal (such as close-ups and microscopic techniques), they can show things that people cannot observe with the naked eye, such as the germination of a seed. In this sense, the electronic image is a means of observation.

At the same time, film enables people to observe events that they could not have witnessed personally – a bomb explosion in London, a demonstration in Soweto, a sporting event in Cape Town. Feature films, again, offer people experiences that they could never have in their own lives. In this sense, film and television are a means of experience.

As a means of expression and visualisation, images in the first place permit communicators to express themselves through images rather than through verbal (linguistic) signs. Consequently film – like the plastic arts, music, literature and the theatre – are art forms that require the communicator to have some expertise in handling the medium. As a means of visualisation, images can, through editing techniques, express abstractions.

8.4.6 Communication functions in an image

communication functions

Another aspect emphasised in film semiotics is the linguist Roman Jakobson's (1960) six communication functions. These were first applied to film by the Dutch linguist J.M. Peters (1974). The functions are as follows:
- a *referential function*;
- a *phatic function*;
- an *expressive function*;
- a *conative function*;
- a *poetic function*;
- a *metalinguistic function*.

Referential functions of the messsage are those that refer to the theme or subject of the communication. They concern the content or subject matter of the image – people, fauna, flora, objects and the like.

The phatic functions are those that seek to establish contact by capturing the attention and fascinating the recipient. It could include the size of the object portrayed, colour, composition or a dramatic camera point of view.

The communicator expresses each message in a distinctive way. That is, the subject matter or content of the message is formulated in a particular way. The expressive functions refer to this formulation, which, in the case of film and television, entails camera work and editing.

Conative functions of an image are those that are designed to persuade the recipient to accept and share the communicator's point of view – in effect, those things that make an impression on the viewer. These could include anything from the subject and the story to the acting, camera work and mise-en-scène.

If the aesthetic qualities of an image emerge clearly, the poetic functions will address the recipient. The viewer is explicitly conscious of the formulation (the way the communicator uses the camera and editing techniques).

A message is always formulated and conveyed by means of various sign systems. A newspaper predominantly uses written language, although it also contains photographs. Film and television do not rely exclusively on images to convey their messages but also make use of spoken and even written language (consider the use of subtitles). Dialogue comprises not only spoken language but also gestures, facial expressions, eye contact and the like. In the case of newspapers, the photographs represent the metalinguistic functions of the message; in pictorial communication these are the language and in dialogue the nonverbal behaviour. We could describe metalinguistic functions as those *things* used by the communicator to communicate more intelligibly.

None of these functions occur in isolation. They overlap and can only be separated for analytical purposes.

SUMMARY

The above aspects of film semiotics have been dealt with by different authors in different ways, ranging from practical applications and intricate analyses, to abstract treatments on theoretical and philosphical levels. What they all have in common is a concern about the formal qualities of film. What constitutes a film and how does this enable a film to produce and convey meaning?

The main value of semiotic activity in film theory is that it succeeded in '... pushing film theory beyond the naturalist [realist – author] fallacy' (Easthope 1993:7). The one thing film semiotics made clear is that film, although it might be a mechanical and electronic reproduction of reality and although it is by its very nature iconic, is also symbolic and thus arbitrary. Although its raw material (reality and the selection of images from reality) is iconic, film as a sign is constructed by its communicators. Such constructions always imply interpretation against the background of the communicator's culture, experience and knowledge. In the same way the viewer interprets and understands film against the background of his or her culture, knowledge and experience. The signifier is never closed in the sense of having a fixed meaning. The signifier (image) is open to many interpretations and possibilities. Thus the notion of film as a realistic portrayal of either physical or mental reality is a fallacy.

8.5 CONTEMPORARY FILM THEORY

8.5.1 Introduction

Whereas in classic film theory the emphasis was on the relationship between film and reality, and in the first phase of film semiotics on the formal qualities of film, the emphasis in contemporary theory is on the role of the *subject* (viewer) and on film as an ideological practice.

According to Lapsley and Westlake (1988:32–66), film semiotics is no longer concerned with the formal qualities of an image or even with the nature of film as an iconic sign, but with Lacan's conception of meaning as produced in the exchange between subject and a set of signifiers. In the tradition of poststructuralism, film semiotics has also accepted that meaning is not at all the stable relationship between signifier and signified presumed by Saussure. What fixes meaning is the punctuation of the signifying chain by the action of the subject.

| subject

This 'new' insight, based on the linguist Emile Benveniste's contention that the analysis of discourse can no longer afford to ignore the role of the subject within signification (because language is deeply marked by subjectivity), has, according to Lapsley and Westlake (1988), forced film semioticians like Christian Metz (1974), Umberto Eco (1979) and Stephen Heath (1981) to re-evaluate their former writings on the nature of film as a language, and to follow Julia Kristeva (1974) in her call for a theory of the speaking subject constituted within language. The emphasis is thus on the *relation* between the viewer and film, between *text* and *subject* and the text's power to determine the subject's response.

Watching a film necessarily entails adopting the viewer position that is inscribed in the text, in other words, the position the communicator (producer/director) wants the subject to take on a specific topic. In accordance with this dictum, 'new' film semiotics is, according to Lapsley and Westlake (1988), concerned with the following question: how do the codes in a film (especially the use of the camera and montage) position the subject to take a specific view on a topic, for instance on romance, corruption, crime, sex, etc.?

To answer this question, semiotic analysis has shifted away from the text as a system (the analysis of specific aspects in a text, such as signs) towards the text as a process; away from the '*object cinema*' towards the '*operation cinema*' and into a theoretical discussion and analysis of the ideological nature and role of film. This new phase in film semiotics continues in many forms and disguises, be it psychoanalysis, postmodern, postcolonial, Third Cinema, and/or queer cinema theory, despite the reference to Lapsley and Westlake's 1988 work. In all these new branches of film theory the emphasis always moves in the direction of the viewer/spectator.

According to Lapsley and Westlake (1988), semiotics has, in its fixation on the formal attributes of texts, risked blocking an understanding of how cinema is related to other practices as well as the more general relations between signification, ideology and history. Semiotics itself ran the risk of becoming an obstacle rather than the road to the analysis of the text's political functioning. To circumvent this danger, a conception of film as a specific *signifying practice* was proposed.

Signifying indicates the recognition of film as a system or series of systems of meaning, of film as an articulation of a specific meaning. The term *practice* entails that film is not some neutral medium transmitting a given ideology, but is the active production of meaning. The term also carries the further implication that, since film produces meanings, the question of the positioning of the viewer enters into the analysis of film.

> signifying practice

As a specific signifying practice, film is now studied not in terms of *langue* and *parole* but of *discourse*, thereby implying a subject. Under such a conception, cinema is furthermore viewed as one of a number of 'machines' generating ideology; rather, through its mechanism

> ... the viewer is moved, and related as subject in the process and images of that movement. (Lapsley & Westlake 1988:33)

Film is seen as a work of *semiosis*, meaning a work that produces effects of meaning and perception, self-images and subject positions for all those involved, makers and viewers (cf. Lapsley & Westlake 1988:33–66).

It is against this background that the film theories related to film as ideology, feminist criticism, psychoanalytical, queer, race, postcolonial, postmodern and post-cinema theory are briefly introduced in the paragraphs below. The emphasis is mainly on ideology and psychoanalysis.

For the purpose of this discussion we only summarise some of the assumptions of these approaches in contemporary film theory. We mainly rely on the works of Lapsley and Westlake (1988), Easthope (1993) and Stam (2000).

8.5.2 Ideological criticism

The fact that film is a construction against the background of the culture, experience and knowledge of both the communicator (producer/ director/artists) and the subject (viewer), places it within the realm of ideology and *ideological criticism*. Our culture, experience and knowledge underlie our view of life, of reality and of humanity, and cannot be separated from existential and political beliefs and orientations. In this sense, each and every film can be viewed as an ideological construct.

Although this may be a deterministic argument, every film, whether it is a drama, a thriller, a war movie, a comedy or even a musical, embodies the communicator's interpretation of the theme, topic and content against the background of his or her culture, knowledge and experience, and thus ideology (the way in which we see and understand something).

In the same way, the meaning(s) ascribed to a film by a viewer are ideological in the sense that the viewer brings to the movie an understanding based on his or her culture, knowledge and experience.

With this as a point of departure, central questions in contemporary film theory and analysis emphasising ideology are as follows:
- How does *mainstream cinema* contribute to maintaining the existing social structure?
- What is the appropriate form for an *oppositional cinema* that will break the ideological hold of mainstream cinema and transform film from a commodity to an instrument for social change?

Mainstream cinema is usually associated with, and seen as, the products of a dominant production industry in a society, such as for instance the productions of Hollywood. Oppositional cinema sets itself the goal of analysing and interpreting dominant ideology.

For instance, in South Africa, film production was for decades dominated by apartheid and the ideology underlying the practices of apartheid, also in the film industry. Beginning in the 1980s, a few directors questioned this dominant ideology. This gave rise to the so-called oppositional cinema. With films such as *Jobman* and *Taxi to Soweto*, the *ideology of apartheid* was increasingly questioned. Today, after liberation, new structures and policies are in place in the South African film industry. New role players both in industry management and ownership and in production, represent South Africa's black majority. The 'new' industry has already contributed to the production of world-famous South African films such as *Tsotsi*, *U-Carmen eKhayelitsha* and *Yesterday*. The question is, which ideology does the new South African film support, and how do its audiences react to it?

SOME DEFINITIONS

Ideology: according to its popular definition, ideology refers to ideas, attitudes, values, belief systems or interpretive and conceptual frameworks held by members of a particular social group or culture (cf. Geuss 1981:5). Significantly, our own ideology is seldom if ever recognised as being ideological. Ideology is thus used to describe a system of beliefs held by others (not by ourselves or those agreeing with us), which are regarded as fundamentally untrue. Ideology thus refers to the assumptions through which groups or societies conceptualise the values and beliefs that enable them to operate effectively (cf. Dupre 1983:240), and can be broadly defined as the total system of beliefs, which selectively provide limited perceptions of reality. In this sense, every human group, society or culture has an ideology (cf. Lemon 1991).

Mainstream cinema: by mainstream cinema we mean (1) films produced by the big studios, (2) the so-called big box-office movies and thus popular films, and (3) films produced against the background of capitalist considerations, thus with the emphasis on commercial success.

Oppositional cinema: this refers to those films that challenge the underlying ideology of mainstream cinema. Ideology here means both production practices as well as the political and existential content of films. For years in South Africa, the majority of films were part of the hegemony of apartheid, and reflected this ideology in both content and form. Whereas these films were produced by a few so-called big production houses, oppositional South African film (also referred to as alternative film) began to question this ideology.

Subject: the concept 'subject' can have a political meaning, a grammatical meaning or a philosophical meaning, implying the thinking recipient. We use the concept in terms of the latter meaning. The political meaning relates to the citizen as a subject of the state. It implies, within the context of Marxist ideology, the subject's lack of freedom in the state. The grammatical meaning refers to the subject of a sentence (as in subject–verb–predicate). The notion of the thinking subject is the site of the consciousness. Against the background of poststructuralism, the recipient (viewer/reader) is no longer seen as passive, but uses all his or her senses in the interpretation of a text.

Suffice to say that ideology theory (see also the chapters on ideology in volumes 1 and 2 of this book) has resulted in numerous theoretical studies on the ideological nature of film. It has also produced numerous analyses of specific films with the aim of showing how the political-economic structure of a given society, at a given point in time, determines to a large extend the form and content of that society's films. Every film can be interpreted as an ideological statement, because it was determined by, and hence reflects, the dominant ideology of the society that produced it.

For instance, in South Africa a number of studies were done to show how apartheid influenced South African film and how apartheid (as an ideology) determined the content and form of films. Even the so-called *alternative films* of the late 1980s and early 1990s, such as *Taxi to Soweto* (1991), have been analysed as ideological constructs of apartheid ideology (cf. Tomaselli 1989; Botha & Van Aswegen 1992).

Against this theoretical background, the ideological analysis of film sets itself the goal of analysing the relationship between a given film, its society and the ideology of that society, en route to determining the specific ways that the film either supports or attacks the dominant ideology of the society that produced it. For instance, critics claim that Hollywood presented, and still presents, an incredible, distorted view of the world, masquerading as truth. Most Hollywood films, they assert, do not prompt the audience to question what it is perceiving, or even to think about it. Instead, the audience is encouraged to react passively and lose itself in the story of the film or television production, while concomitantly accepting the purveyed capitalist and conservative dogma. Hollywood is not about to question the society of which it is a part, because it is an industry that literally profits heavily from that very specific society (cf. Stromgren & Norden 1984:266–7).

Film Theory and Criticism

The main criticism against ideological film criticism and theory is that it tends to be biased and subjective. The very nature of ideological criticism is to downplay or ignore the artistic and technical aspects of film, the multiplicity of meanings a film may have and its polysemic nature, the complexity of the political economy of the film industry, the complexities of film production, and the complexities and multidimensionality of film's audiences. All this is too easily pushed into the background in order to focus on directors' and producers' ideological stance.

| pluralism

Film theorists, critics and analysts who emphasise the ideological nature and content of films want to warn the public that film is not an innocent form of entertainment. To the contrary, the fact that films are usually produced by big production studios operating in terms of capitalist market criteria and values, or otherwise produced and/or subsidised by government-controlled agencies with the purpose of propagating certain political ideas and values, makes film a powerful ideological instrument. In terms of Althusser's vocabulary, it is a powerful ideological state apparatus.

The danger with emphasising ideology is its heavy-handedness and polemical simplification, with a simplistic application of the concept of 'power' to a work of art (film) (cf. Konigsberg 1987:204).

To conclude, it must however be said that ideological film criticism as explained above has lost much of its vigour since the 1990s and the emergence of the emphasis on the role of the spectator (viewer) in deciding the meaning of film. Furthermore, Hollywood is no longer the bastion of capitalist film production and with that the dominant purveyor of capitalist and bourgeois ideology, hegemony and power. There are also other role players, and globalisation has contributed to the availability and distribution of more (filmic and artistic) voices and a plurality of film production and distribution outlets. Even more so, Hollywood itself has become increasingly aware of the need to express the human condition as a victim of ideological power.

8.5.3 Psychoanalysis

Introduction

The psychoanalytical theories on the *subject/object* relationship (object = in this case a film) in film communication originate from the French theorist Jacques Lacan's adaptation of Sigmund Freud's theory on the

| psychoanalysis

unconscious psychological structures that operate in humankind. These structures are said to characterise the acquisition of the self-image and motivate behaviour. (For a complete overview of Lacan and Freud's psychoanalytical theory and its application in film theory, see Lapsley & Westlake 1988:67–104. See also the discussion on psychoanalysis in Chapter 13 of this volume.)

The Freudian and Lacanian view on the workings of the unconscious, the acquisition of a self-image and the enquiry into the symbolic opened up new perspectives on the subject/object relationship in film communication. In other words, the psychoanalytical approach heavily influenced future film theory, in which the emphasis moved away from a focus on content, form and technique (e.g. realism, expressionism, *auteurism*, genre and even ideology) to focus on the role of the viewer/subject in understanding film (a film) and applying meaning to it.

> imaginary signifier

In the first place, psychoanalysis makes a meaningful shift from the formalistic study of film as a discrete entity on the screen to a deep contemplation of the relationship between the film (object) and the viewer (subject). In this regard, there is an important emphasis on the concept '*absence*' and the idea that the filmic signifier is an absent signifier, and therefore an *imaginary* signifier.

Imaginary signifier means, among other things, that besides the fact that a motion picture, especially, is a product of the imagination for the imagination, what one sees on the screen is essentially absent (thus, the signifier is absent). In other words, the actors and events – in short, the depicted content – is physically absent and exists merely as light and sound on celluloid; it exists only in and through the camera and projector signals, which are themselves empty forms that have no existence outside of the total *filmic apparatus*.

> filmic apparatus

In the second place, the psychoanalytic perspective initiates inspection, albeit of a speculative nature, into the unconscious processes in play during the perception of a film, and upon which the filmic apparatus focuses. Put differently: the filmic apparatus directs itself towards imitating processes of the human unconscious.

Filmic apparatus refers to a complex interwoven structure, of which the viewer forms a central part, and which includes the following:
- the technical nature of film communication, including the effects

that may be obtained with the camera, editing, sound, lighting, projection, and so on (the filmic design that is implemented with technical apparatus);
- the conditions for the showing of a film (dark theatre, filmic circumstances of the viewer, size of screen, projector, etc.);
- the image in itself (or the image as text) and its inherent quality, for example, the iconic and mimetic nature of the image that leads to the illusion of reality;
- the mental processes of the viewer.

In the third place, the psychoanalytical approach ascribes the viewer's enjoyment (and therefore the popularity of film as a mass communication medium) to the fact that it succeeds in, and is tuned into, reactivating the deep and universal structural processes of the human psyche in an enjoyable way.

filmic enjoyment

To clarify this assumption, psychoanalytical film theory theorises about, among other things, approximately five explanations for the viewer's enjoyment of film, and how the filmic apparatus is tuned into bringing about this enjoyment through identification. The explanations are as follows:
- The persons in the film identify with their action of perception.
- The persons in the film identify with imagined emotions.
- There is a correspondence between people's experience of a film and a dream experience.
- There is a correspondence between the perception of a film and voyeurism.
- The viewing of a film is a form of fetishism.

These five explanations are discussed more fully below.

SOME DEFINITIONS

Fetish: a pathological and sexually determined attachment to objects associated with a sexual object.

Voyeur: a person who obtains sexual gratification from observing others' sexual actions or organs.

Psychoanalysis: a therapeutic method of treating mental disorders by investigating the interaction of conscious and unconscious elements in the mind and bringing repressed fears and conflicts into the conscious mind (cf. Allen 1990).

Oedipus: in Greek mythology Oedipus was the son of Laius, king of Thebes, and of Jocasta. Laius was warned by an oracle that he would perish at the hands of his son. Oedipus was brought up in Corinth. When he had grown up Oedipus was told by the Delphic oracle not to return home, as he must inevitably be the murderer of his father. He consequently fled from Corinth, and on his way to Thebes slew Laius in a quarrel, being ignorant of Laius's identity. Oedipus then delivered the country from the Sphinx and was rewarded with the hand of Jocasta (his mother), by whom he had four children. As a punishment for this incest Thebes was devastated by a plague. The oracle declared that the country could only by saved if the murderer of Laius was expelled. Oedipus made inquiries and discovered to his horror that he was the guilty man. His mother/wife Jocasta hanged herself and Oedipus, having put out his eyes, left Thebes. The story of Oedipus is the topic of many dramas and was set forth by the classic Greek dramatists Euripides, Aeschylus and Sophocles.

Oedipus complex: the Austrian psychoanalyst Sigmund Freud believed that the causes of psychoneurotic disorders are generally found to lie in early emotional relationships with the parents. The typical form of this relationship is called the *Oedipus complex* in the case of men and the *Electra complex* in the case of women, and concerns the strong emotional attachment to the parent of the opposite sex and jealousy and hatred of the parent of the same sex. Both the love and the hate are normally unconscious and the conscious attitudes may be very different. The unwillingness of a patient to recognise this source of his or her troubles is attributed by Freud to repression, the active banishment of the underlying cause for psychoneurotic behaviour from the conscious mind into the region of the unconscious. The cure depends on the removal of this repression and the consequent emergence of the repressed into the conscious mind, where it can be dealt with in a rational manner.

Identification with the action of perception

perception and identification

Film presents images of something that is absent. Instead of the presence of actual actors, décor, sets, theatrical property, etc., as one would find in a theatre, the film screen confronts the viewer with a world that is physically absent and exists merely through light and noise impressions (cf. Lapsley & Westlake 1988:81).

The outstanding quality of film is therefore *absence*. This implies that the filmic signifier (what a person looks at on the screen, e.g. a man or woman performing an action) is not there; only the light and sound impressions, and the things projected by the mechanisms of a projector, are present. Film thus involves the viewer in a play of absence/presence.

The *presence* of a rich visual image on the screen and the *absence* of what the image refers to or conveys defines the fundamental nature of film communication.

The question is now, as the signifier is merely an imaginary signifier, what does the viewer *identify* with during the showing of a film? The French film semiologist Christian Metz (1982) argues that although the viewer identifies with the fictional character(s) or star(s), and although such an identification is part of the enjoyment of the film, it is a *secondary identification*. Prior to this secondary identification, however, *primary identification* must occur. This enables the viewer to identify with the projected image on the screen.

Metz argues that viewers identify with their action of perception. His explanation (cf. also Lapsley & Westlake 1988:83) is as follows:
- Firstly, viewers are always aware that they are in a theatre and in the presence of something that is imaginary and absent.
- Secondly, viewers are also aware of their own absence on the screen, that they find themselves outside that screen in a position of *all-seeing mastery*.
- Thirdly, viewers are aware of the conditions for the viewing of a film, namely, that the film has no existence outside of the viewer as a present, seeing, hearing subject in the auditorium or in front of the television screen.

This consciousness of absence, of all-seeing mastery and of the non-existence of the film outside of the viewer constitutes primary identification and enables viewers to identify with their own actions of seeing and hearing as an act of perception – as a kind of *transcendental subject* that precedes all that happens on the screen.

Stephen Heath (1981:120) states it perhaps more simply by saying that

> ... the apparatus of look and identification institutes the viewer in the totalising security of looking at looking. (own emphasis)

while John Ellis (1984:44) adds that

> identification with the cinematic apparatus involves the fantasy of self as a pure perceiving being. (own emphasis)

Primary identification (that is, identification with the action of perception) is powerfully *reinforced* by the viewer's simultaneous identification with the camera, whose monocular perspective approaches the quality of almost godlike omniscience. The *viewer is the camera* who actively directs his or her vision towards certain objects, but who at the same time passively receives the results of this perception.

Identification with imagined emotions

A second reason for viewers' enjoyment, according to the psychoanalytical perspective, is that they do not experience real emotions with which they may identify, but rather experience and identify with *imagined emotions*.

Viewers' experience of film shows clearly that they are or can be moved by it: they can, for example, feel sexual arousal, aggression, compassion, heartache, joy, and so on. But are these emotions genuine? It is also a fact that viewers can indeed watch films where they are confronted with unpleasant experiences like grief, death, disappointment and failure. The question is, is the viewer's grief, anxiety, hate and anguish real?

The French philosopher Jean-Paul Sartre (1969:237), who was also concerned with the relationship between emotions and imagination, reasons that an object that exists only in and for the imagination is incapable of evoking genuine emotion. The imagined object (such as a film) is unreal and can therefore not be the cause of a real effect. If someone presents you with a delicious meal, he argues, and your mouth begins to water, it is not the suggestion of the food that prompts the secretion in the mouth, but the already existing feeling of hunger. If a 'pin-up' picture sexually arouses a viewer, it is not the pin-up that leads to the arousal, but an already existing feeling of sexual desire.

The world of film, too, is an unreal world (imagined signifier) that is given 'life' by viewers themselves, with their own feelings. Furthermore, the imagined characters, things and events on the screen resemble so closely real people, things and events – real people do in fact appear in front of the camera – that viewers can easily conceive that these imagined people, things and events touch them emotionally.

In reality, then, the process runs in two stages:
- Viewers colour the images with their own subjective feelings, or project themselves into the image.

Film Theory and Criticism

- Because these images so closely resemble real objects, they impress themselves on viewers, who can identify with the feelings that the images portray.

However, this identification is also an identification with imagined emotions. Viewers do not actually experience grief over a dying heroine, for example, but imagine sorrow within themselves. In other words, viewers pretend that they are filled with grief. In short, although viewers make believe that the actions on the screen are real, they know throughout that this is not reality.

Although viewers get emotionally involved, they are aware that theirs' is a limited experience and that, should they wish it, they can distance themselves from the events unfolding on the screen. Viewers know that they will not be seriously hurt by the emotions that they feel during this time (e.g. lingering heartache and pain) nor sustain persisting feelings of happiness or enjoyment. The crux of the experience is that viewers, although they may become emotionally involved, nevertheless retain a distance.

This *distance* between the viewer and the events on the screen means that viewers never become completely part of the action – they remain, so to speak, safe. The film provides the chance for viewers to acknowledge the loves and heartbreaks of the characters and the events in which they find themselves *outside* of themselves and others. This always occurs outside of the self, and the viewer is never a participant, but always an observer – essentially a spy, a quasi-voyeur. For the voyeur, to spy or peep means enjoyment, satisfaction and the experience of a sublime state.

Dream experience

A third reason for viewers' enjoyment is that the perception of a film corresponds to people's 'perception' and experience of their own dreams. In both dream and film, viewers have no hold on the image itself.

As in film, the imaginary world of the dream offers viewers no perceptual freedom. Dreamers, in an imaginary world of danger, cannot think 'do I have a gun with me?', for as soon as the thought appears, the gun is immediately there. Sartre (1969) calls this the *fatality* of dream events. In film, events have the same fatality – viewers cannot do anything to change them, and they are not free in terms of what is shown to them. Another similarity between the dream and the film is that viewers can

dream experience

see the imagined events from a different standpoint (albeit the director's chosen standpoint): the all-seeing or all-knowing outsider who perceives events from an external position, and from the perspective of the subject who performs the actions. A typical example is as follows:

> *In a dream, I arrive just too late at the station to catch the last train. Rather distraught, I ask the stationmaster if there are any more trains leaving that evening – I have to be at my destination the following morning. The stationmaster answers that there are no more trains as it is New Year's Eve, and very few trains are running. 'Oh, yes', I answer, 'I didn't think of that'.*

The significance of this is that I, who am myself the maker of the dream, am also the subject in the dream who is not aware that there are fewer trains running because it is New Year's Eve; however, the stationmaster, who is also the product of *my* dream, is aware of this (cf. Peters 1976:12).

The same occurs in the film experience. For example, viewers see the murderer carefully turn the doorknob; next they see the unsuspecting victim in the bed. Both the murderer and the victim know less than the viewers. But now the man in the bed wakes up; he heard a noise; he grabs his revolver and creeps to the door where he takes up his position. He waits tensely; the viewers wait anxiously with him (and identify with the victim's tension). Consequently, the viewers do not see that in the meantime the murderer has come in through the window. They do not see because they, with the victim, feel for that moment of tension like the victim – and yet viewers do see it as well because they, as viewers and as outsiders, can adopt an all-seeing viewpoint.

The alternation of neutral and subjective camera positions reinforces the character of a film experience. In our example, then, viewers see the victim through the keyhole together with the murderer. However, viewers (as the murderer) do not see that a policeman has appeared behind the murderer, while as neutral spectators they can indeed see this. The continual displacement or interchange of the viewers' perspective, and the fact that they constantly share an emotional life with other characters, accentuates the association between dream and film.

In spite of this illusion of *all-knowingness* and *omniscience*, or rather because of it, viewers are caught up in a process of alienation and distancing, a process that shows correlations with *voyeurism* and *fetishism*, as mentioned above.

Voyeurism

From a psychoanalytic perspective, Metz (1982) relates the preceding arguments to voyeurism and fetishism. He also uses the imagined signifier as a point of departure in this regard. Metz begins with the notion that viewers' experience of film images can be related to two basic needs: *scopophilia*, or the need to see, and the need to hear.

| voyeurism

These two drives are distinguished from other human drives by their reliance on absence, not only in the sense that these drives give rise to a fruitless desire to see and hear that (the original completed self-image) which can never be regained, but also in the sense that these needs can only be satisfied if there is a distance between the subject and the object.

Although maintaining distance is a diagnostic characteristic of all the arts, film differs from the other arts in that the object from which the distance is maintained is effectively absent. In drama, opera and ballet, the physical togetherness ensures a sort of assumed complicity in what is happening on the stage: the viewer's voyeurism is paired with the artist's exhibitionism. Contrary to this, the artist in film communication is present (during the making of a film) while the viewer is absent; and the viewer is present (during the screening) when the artist is absent. The reciprocal recognition of the existence of the other is less clear, even absent: a characteristic of film communication that is further strengthened by the fact that film actors seldom look directly into the camera, an act that would confront viewers with their own voyeurism.

This voyeurism involves looking at something that allows itself to be looked at without presenting itself to be seen. Metz (1982) believes that the enjoyment that viewers obtain from this is related to people's unconscious yet fundamental observation of their parents' copulation, which determines the nature and structure of voyeurism as such, and which shows clear correlations with the viewer's situation and the act of looking. Various characteristics of film communication emphasise this relationship: the viewer sits in the dark in front of a lighted screen – a situation that is nearly like peeping through a keyhole; although viewers are part of an audience, they retain their individuality and separateness;

actors are neither aware of nor acknowledge the viewer's existence; and, finally, the events of the film unfold in a place where viewers are both closed in and inaccessible. All these characteristics make the experience of voyeurism in the film theatre one of 'trangression'.

Fetishism

In the last reason (for the purposes of this discussion) provided by Metz (1982) for the enjoyment experience, fetishism is the topic discussed. Like the filmic signifier itself, this mental process is related to the interaction between absence and presence.

Psychoanalytically, fetishism is defined as follows: anxiety is created due to the child's becoming conscious of sexual differences and the accompanying awareness that the mother does not possess a phallus. To ward off this anxiety and the threat that it presents, the child rejects the existence of sexual differences and so with it the mother's 'defect'. The result is a contradiction: 'I know a lot, but nevertheless ...' The child replaces this 'defect' with another object, one that both fills the gap created by that loss and denies that anything is missing – but which, by its very presence, acknowledges this absence. When this happens, rejection takes the form of fetishism.

Metz (1982) argues that something similar occurs in the viewer (subject)/film (object) relationship. Viewers know that what they watch is fiction, but they nevertheless believe that it is real – indeed, their enjoyment depends on this belief. Film communication thus depends on the fact that viewers know one thing and, at the same time, completely believe the opposite. This is the exact structure of rejection and fetishism. Further, as the fetishist rejects an object and yet in so doing acknowledges its existence, so the film apparatus, in this case the camera viewfinder, becomes in itself a kind of substitute for the absence of the filmic signifier. The camera shot confirms the presence of that which is absent and, in so doing, emphasises the fact of its absence. The technical ingenuity of the film lies precisely in the fact that the absent is made convincingly present so that the viewer's absence is almost, but never completely, forgotten.

If an awareness of absence is not maintained, viewers cannot appreciate what is present. Viewers' enjoyment depends, as in classical fetishism, on a simultaneous awareness of what is absent and what is present. The

Film Theory and Criticism

fetishist derives enjoyment from the object that replaces the rejected thing; the viewer finds enjoyment in the awareness of the gap that exists between imagined presence and actual absence.

To summarise, the question 'how does film produce enjoyment and the desire for more?' is answered according to a psychoanalytical perspective as follows: in film communication, attribution of meaning is based on and is ascribed to a process of absence. The image, which is in itself an imagined signifier (impulses in light and sound), steps forward to fill this absence, but cannot ever completely succeed in doing this. The viewer unconsciously experiences this gap between absence and presence as a constant defect, which evokes a continual need to see more.

Film theory moving through phases

From the above it should be clear that there has been movement in film theory and aesthetics in their endeavour to understand and explain film as a means of communication.

phases in film theory

In the preceding sections, we introduced classic film theory, with its emphasis on realism and expressionism. From there the emphasis moved to the artist or film *auteur* and then to the classification and categorisation of films in genres, arguing that such classification contributes to the viewers' understanding and enjoyment of film and that it gives theorists themselves and the industry a grip on film as a phenomenon.

Film semiotics developed as the second phase in film theory and aesthetics. The main purpose was to understand film as a unique language of visual signs, symbols, metaphors, codes, paradigms, syntagms, etc. Departing from linguistic knowledge about human language, theorists set out to describe the relationships between film as a signifier (of meaning) and the understanding of film's processes of signification and with it its interpretations of reality. From this *formalistic* approach to film as a language, developed an awareness of film not only as the maker and dispenser of fixed meanings, but also and mainly of social meanings and understandings of the world. This was the beginning of social semiotics (see Chapter 2) in film theory, which signalled a movement away from formalist semiotics to an awareness of the multiplicity of meanings a film may have and produce – film as a 'floating' or 'open' signifier. From here on, it was a short step to focusing on the ideological nature and meanings of film. This again opened film theory to the investigation of the political economy of the film industry, and by so doing to Marxist and neo-Marxist perspectives.

All of the above theory, one may argue, has dealt with its topics in the context of structuralism. (See Chapter 2 for an explanation of structuralism and poststructuralism). Theory was primarily concerned with the building blocks of film as a communication medium, its form, technique and content.

As in the study of art, literature, society (sociology), psychology and communication, the next phase or major paradigm in film theory was poststructuralism and deconstruction. The emphasis moved to the subject as the creator of meaning. In the case of film, we entered the stage of psychoanalytical theory (as discussed above) with its explanation of the act of viewing, and motivations for why people view (and enjoy) movies.

Apart from ideological criticism and psychoanalysis (as examples of contemporary film theory and within the second phase of film theory, with its emphasis on the viewer) there are a number of additional approaches in contemporary film theory that can be summarised under the heading of *film theory and identity*.

8.5.4 Film theory and identity: feminist criticism, queer theory, film and race, postcolonial theory

| Deleuze |

It can be argued that the focus on the relationship between film and identity started with Gilles Deleuze's 'destruction' (Stam 2000:256) of two major pillars of film theory: film semiotics and psychoanalysis, or Saussure and Lacan. For Deleuze, the purpose of film theory should no longer be to seek and describe signs and codes as signifying practices similar to linguistic language. Nor should the purpose of film theory be to extrapolate the 'Oedipus story as a mechanism of repression …' (op cit.:256) and as such use it as a basis for explaining film communication. Rather, film theory is a philosophy (of life) and should have the purpose to discover film as a 'philosophical instrument for the generator of concepts and a producer of texts which render thought in audiovisual terms … (op cit.:258). Cinema is philosophy (and philosophy is cinema which can be enriched with cinema). As a philosophy, cinema triggers new ways of thinking about time, space and humanity itself.

Film Theory and Criticism

It can be argued that Deleuze's emphasis on cinema and/as humanity is the foundation of movements such as feminist criticism, queer theory, a focus on film and race, and film and postcolonialism. All of these movements are in one or another way concerned with representation, and more so with the stereotypical representations of films. All of these movements concern human identity, how humanity arrives at identities and the role of film in identity formation. All of them are concerned with identity politics.

For an overview and explanation of postmodernism and the theories of some postmodern authors such as Baudrillard, see, for instance, Chapter 3 in Volume 1 of this book, (Fourie 2007:157–77.) Also see this chapter for an introduction to postcolonialism. On the topic of identity and how it forms a key issue in contemporary media studies, including film studies, see Part 3 of Volume 2 of this book, on representation. In this part of the book we introduce theory related to media and identity, media and race, media and gender, and media and sexual orientation. It can be argued that the discussions in these chapters can form the theoretical foundation for any deliberation about the nature of film's depictions of identities and groups. In this regard, the reader may also find it valuable to return to the part on stereotypes and stereotyping as explained by Fourie in Volume 1 of this book (Fourie 2007:247–64.)

We start with a brief introduction to feminist criticism, in order to illustrate contemporary film theory's engagement with identity formation and identity politics.

Related to ideological film theory and criticism, the key assumptions in *feminist criticism* are that films are products of a sexist society, and that they frequently present biased and stereotyped depictions of women's roles.

> feminist criticism

In general feminist critics are concerned with three broad areas:
- the ways women have been depicted and treated in films throughout the years;
- the qualities and concerns of films made by women;
- the ways that women in society have been affected by the (sex) roles presented in film.

One of the main critiques is that men are often presented in films as the people in and of history, who shape the destinies of both their own lives and the societies they inhabit. Women, on the other hand, are typically in supportive roles, and they are presented as eternal, unchanging and without much historical significance.

Following these fundamental assumptions, feminist critics classify women appearing in, for instance, American films up to the mid-1930s into one or more of the following categories:
- the *Mother* (whose nurturing, selfless image offends many feminist critics);
- the *Virginal*, unworldly woman;
- the streetwise *Whore* or *Vamp*;
- for lack of a better term, *Window Dressing*.

Most women appearing in the immediate postwar period of American cinema could generally be classified as one of two types: the *male-hungry* woman who desired nothing more than marriage, children and a clean suburban home; and the *strong-willed*, independent woman who by the end of the film was shown to be neurotic, psychotic or both (cf. Stromgren & Norden 1984:267–8).

According to feminist critics, it is clear that Hollywood, along with many other postwar American institutions, sought to discourage women from acting in an independent fashion. Little changed until the 1970s, when women began to be portrayed as more aggressive.

Although Hollywood as such may have changed and may have adopted a more liberalised and balanced view of and about women, and although feminist film theory has been broadened to include additional topics and the cinema industry in general, the same kind of assumptions and concerns still exist about discriminatory, prejudiced and biased views of women. Moreover, the same kind of assumptions and concerns are raised about film representations of black people, minority groups, ethnicities, gays and lesbians and the colonised. These assumptions and concerns now form the core of gay and lesbian film criticism (or queer theory), theories about film and race, and theories about postcolonialism and film, including so-called Third Cinema. However, this, as well as the impact of the new digital and computerised media (such as the internet) on film (or, as Stam (2000:314) calls it, 'post cinema') will have to form the topic of another publication.

Film Theory and Criticism

LEARNING ACTIVITIES

1. Summarise the following theories and describe the differences between them:
   - establishing-shot theories;
   - medium-shot theories;
   - close-up theories;
   - normative theory;
   - descriptive theory.
2. Formulate on the basis of the difference between the theories and the questions asked in them, five of your own questions about the nature, content and form of film and its relation with reality. Apply the questions you have formulated to a recent film you have seen, either on television or in a film theatre.
3. Explain the difference between each of the following areas of film study:
   - aesthetic film historiography (history writing);
   - technological film historiography;
   - economic film historiography;
   - social film historiography;
   - classic film historiography;
   - revisionist film historiography.
4. Explain the difference between:
   - film criticism;
   - film analysis;
   - film theory.
5. Design a critical framework for your future viewing of films. Base your framework on the discussion of what film theory is, the different kinds of theories and the distinction between film history and film theory. Your framework should consist of at least five points or parameters. For example, are you, in future, going to concentrate in your viewing on one or more of the following:
   - the relation between film and social reality;
   - the content of a film;
   - the form of a film;
   - the portrayal of a specific group;
   - the industry responsible for the production of the film and the influence of this industry on the content and form of the film;

- any of the other topics and/or parameters discussed in the preceding pages.
6. Write an essay in which you give an overview of the expressionist and formalist film theories. Apply the underlying assumptions to a film you have seen recently and which you would describe as expressionist in terms of the underlying assumptions of expressionist film theory. Explain in detail, and with reference to his theory of conflict montage, Eisenstein's formalist film theory.
7. Explain V.I. Pudovkin's theory of construction montage.
8. Write an essay on realist film theory. Substantiate your discussion with examples from a recent film you have seen and which you would describe as realist in terms of the underlying assumptions of realist film theory.
9. Summarise the *auteur* theory in terms of the following: its relation to realist film theory; the origin of the theory; concerns about the collective nature of film production; its emphasis on the theme and style in a director's work; Sarris's ranking of directors; the value of the theory and criticism against the theory.
10. Design a framework for the analysis of the work of a director of your choice. Base your framework on Sarris's distinction between the technical competence of a director, his or her identity as a stylist and the director's ability to convey an own interpretation.
11. Explain with examples the different ways of defining and categorising genre.
12. Explain with your own examples taken from a film(s) the following semiotic concepts:
    - film as a sign;
    - denotation and connotation in film;
    - codes in film;
    - the levels of meaning in film;
    - the communicative functions of film.
13. Describe the assumptions of ideological criticism. Apply them to a film of your choice.
14. Summarise the psychoanalytical approach to the questions why and how people experience film as a pleasure. Pay attention to the following:
    - identification with the act of perception;
    - identification with imagined emotions;

- film and dream experience;
- the comparison of the film experience and voyeurism;
- the comparison of the film experience and fetishism.

15 Briefly explain the different phases of film theory and the emphasis in contemporary film theory.

FURTHER READING

The following general 'classic' works, or any later editions thereof, are recommended:

Andrew, D. 1984. *Concepts in film theory.* Oxford: Oxford University Press.

Bordwell, D. & Thompson, K. 1997. *Film art: An introduction.* New York: McGraw-Hill.

Easthope, A. (ed) 1993. *Contemporary film theory.* London: Longman.

Giannetti, L. 1972. *Understanding movies.* Englewood Cliffs, New Jersey: Prentice Hall.

Lapsley, R. & Westlake, M. 1988. *Film theory: An introduction.* Manchester: Manchester University Press.

Mast, G. & Cohen, M. 1985. *Film theory and criticism. Introductory readings.* New York: Oxford University Press.

Monaco, J. 1977. *How to read a film. The art, technology, language, history and theory of film and media.* New York: Oxford University Press.

Nelmes, J. (ed) 1996. *An introduction to film studies.* London: Routledge.

Nichols, B. 1976. *Movies and methods. An anthology.* Berkeley: University of California Press.

Stam, R. 2000. *Film theory: An introduction.* Malden, Mass: Blackwell Publishers.

Wollen, P. 1974. *Signs and meaning in the cinema.* London: Secker and Warburg.

See also the preceding volumes of this book:

Fourie, P.J. (ed) 2007. *Media Studies. Volume 1: Media history, media and society.* 2nd edition. Cape Town: Juta.

Fourie, P.J. (ed) 2008. *Media Studies. Volume 2: Policy, management and media representation.* 2nd edition. Cape Town: Juta.

PART 2
Media Audiences

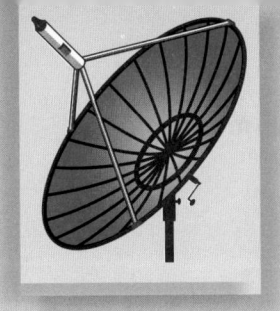

chapter nine

MEDIA AUDIENCE THEORY

Magriet Pitout

LEARNING OUTCOMES

At the end of this chapter, you should be able to:
- discuss the importance of audience-centred theories;
- describe and explain the underlying assumptions of the uses and gratifications theory, reception theory and ethnography;
- critically evaluate these theories.

THIS CHAPTER

Theorising about audiences is a critical and intellectual activity that provides different questions about the nature of audiences, their needs, how they interpret media messages (that is, for instance, newspaper stories, television and radio programmes, internet sites, films, and so on) and about the social and cultural contexts of media consumption. Audiences are those people for whom media messages are intended. Without the study of audiences the basic communication process of communicator, message and recipient is not complete. In this chapter, we focus on the uses and gratifications theory, reception theory and ethnography as three of the most popular and prominent audience theories in media studies.

9.1 INTRODUCTION

Since the first appearance of mass communication media, many effect theories have been formulated to explain how people use media messages and the possible effects media messages may have on audiences. Although theorising about media effects remains a hotly debated area, this does not mean that we should discontinue the search for theoretical explanations of how audiences are affected by the mass media and the relationship between audiences and mass media texts. On the contrary, we should continue to find answers to questions that may lead to insight and a better understanding of why audiences are important to media studies.

In this chapter we give an overview of the uses and gratifications theory, reception theory and ethnography. We also look at the assumptions, characteristics as well as the strengths and weaknesses of each theory.

9.2 THE ACTIVE AUDIENCE PARADIGM

bullet effects
active audience paradigm

The first scientific audience studies were done within the behaviourist tradition, which is based on the assumption of passive audiences who have no resistance against the all-powerful 'bullet' effects of media. The passive audience concept however, was first challenged by the uses and gratifications theory. Although generally regarded as behaviourist, the uses and gratifications theory sees audiences as actively engaged in media messages to satisfy specific needs (see section 9.3.2 below). And from this assumption originated a paradigm that is characterised by a

Media Audience Theory

shift in ideology from a passive to an active audience. But what do we mean with active audience?

When researching the 'active audience' concept, academics attempt to learn more about how audiences interact with and respond to what they see, hear and read before making a judgment on the power and influence of the media (Williams 2003:192). Roscoe, Marshall and Gleeson (1995:88) expand on the active audience concept by saying that within the active audience paradigm researchers examine how audiences actively ascribe meaningful interpretations to media messages, however within the boundaries of the messages being presented. That is, the agenda-setting function of the media should also be considered because the media do indeed have the power to highlight important issues while excluding others. But instead of perceiving audiences as passive – being told how and what to think – audiences are active in their media consumption. This active engagement however, takes place within the boundaries and parameters set by media texts. For example, we do not expect to be entertained by the news because the main function of news is to provide us with information. The same applies to us watching/reading a comedy; the aim of this genre (comedy) is to entertain and not to provide information.

9.3 THE USES AND GRATIFICATIONS THEORY

A popular and influential audience theory is the uses and gratifications theory (sometimes called needs and gratifications theory), a spin-off from the functionalist paradigm in the social sciences. This approach focuses on media audiences who actively select media to satisfy particular needs. As already mentioned, this view is contrary to the media effects tradition, which assumes a homogeneous passive mass audience who are at the mercy of the strong influence of media. In other words, the uses and gratifications theory is part of a broader trend amongst media researchers that is more concerned with how people use the media, allowing for a variety of audience responses to and interpretations of media messages. By redefining media audiences from passive to active, the major research question asked by uses and gratifications theory is, 'what do people do with media?' instead of the effects tradition's question of 'what do media do to people?' (Schroder 1999:39).

active selection of media messages

what do people do with the media?

Uses and gratifications research was first conducted in the 1940s to determine the reasons why housewives listened to radio soap operas.

During the 1970s and 1980s this approach underwent a revival when Blumler and Katz (1974) formulated some basic theoretical assumptions to increase its value and status as a theory.

9.3.1 Theoretical assumptions

- Media use is defined in terms of the way the media satisfy (or gratify) individual media users' social and/or psychological needs (see typology of needs below).
- Media users are actively and purposefully involved in selecting media to satisfy specific needs, of which they (media users) are aware and which they are able to articulate verbally. In other words, media users consciously select specific media to adequately fulfil their needs. However, although the initiative lies with the audience to link the gratification of a need(s) to specific media, it cannot be denied that media use is sometimes coincidental. For example, a media user may select the news to satisfy information needs but is also entertained at the same time by a human-interest story.
- Different media sources exist to gratify needs that may lead to direct competition between the media: for example, choosing between newspapers, television, the internet or radio as a source(s) of news. However, gratification can also be obtained from media content (watching specific programmes), and from familiarity with genre conventions of a programme (sitcoms, science fiction, soap operas etc.). The degree to which the mass media per se and media content satisfy needs varies because they can only satisfy a small portion of the wide range of human needs.

The degree of gratifications being satisfied will determine media choices and experiences in future.

On the basis of these assumptions, Blumler and Katz (1974) formulated a typology of needs, which was reaffirmed and adjusted by McQuail (1987b:73).

9.3.2 Typology (categories) of needs

Cognitive needs

These needs, also called information/surveillance needs, include:
- seeking information about relevant events in immediate surroundings, society at large and the world;

Media Audience Theory

- looking for advice on practical matters such as decision-making choices;
- learning about important topics and self-improvement;
- gaining a sense of security through knowledge in the media (the reassurance function of the media).

For example, should we need detailed information about our immediate surroundings, like municipal elections in our city/town and political representatives in our suburbs, we may consult our local newspaper (i.e. *Pretoria East* newspaper); for national and international news regarding international events, like the political crisis in Zimbabwe, we may consult national newspapers (*The Star, Sunday Times, Rapport*) and international internet sources such as Sky News, BBC and Google. Furthermore, newspapers, television documentary programmes, talk shows (i.e. 3 *Talk with Noeleen* on SABC3, *Oprah*) and magazines provide us with medical advice, the correct dress code for specific events, and how to improve ourselves to have a better quality of life. Consulting the media about the satisfaction of such needs gives us a sense of security/reassurance that we are informed citizens who can make informed choices.

Affective needs

These needs refer to the emotions we experience when interacting with the media, for example:
- escape from daily and/or personal problems;
- relax (for example, after a hard day's work);
- provide and strengthen aesthetic experiences and enjoyment;
- fill time because of boredom and/or nothing else to do;
- provide emotional release from pent-up anger, disappointment, and so on;
- get sexually aroused.

These needs deal mainly with the emotions that we experience when using the media. For example, instead of dealing with problems in real life (i.e. relational problems) we watch/read a television programme or magazine to escape from or avoid the problem. After a hard day's work, we switch on the television/computer/radio to relax. Sometimes we watch television because we are bored or have nothing else to do – then we may use the remote control to hop between channels. We often watch a good film to provide us with an aesthetic experience, which may include an appreciation for the script, the actors' portrayal of characters in the film, the filmmaker's style and the technical aspects of the film. Sometimes we watch television violence or play violent video games to get rid of pent-up anger or frustration (the cathartic function of the media). Many people have a need for sexual arousal and therefore access pornographic websites. This may be the reason why these websites are the most popular on the internet. Pornographic magazines are also popular sources to satisfy sexual needs.

Social integrative needs

The desire for affiliation and social contact falls under social integrative needs and includes:
- getting insight into circumstances of others and developing social empathy with them;
- fulfilling a sense of belonging to a group;
- finding topics for conversation for social interaction;
- finding substitute experiences for real-life companionship by, for example, getting involved in a para-social relationship with media personalities and characters. This relationship is also called 'intimacy at a distance', where media users talk to television characters is if they are real people of flesh and blood.

For example, people use cyberspace to make friends, and become members of a selected group with the same interests (photography, art, films, sport etc.). In other words, by means of internet chat rooms, social networking websites (e.g. Facebook, YouTube), dating sites and the websites of particular television programmes, newspapers, films and magazines, people become members of cyber-communities, which to a great extent fulfil people's needs for belonging to a group and allow them to get insight into the circumstances of others. Many cyberspace users find their soulmates and spouses on internet dating sites.

The mass media also provide us with a wide range of topics for conversation. Just think of gossip in the media about the scandals of politicians, film, television and sport stars, which people just love to talk about. And for the lonely – whatever their circumstances – the media create opportunities to get involved in pseudo-relationships, that is, substitute experiences for real-life companionship (see section 9.4.4 of this chapter for a discussion of para-social interaction).

Media Audience Theory

Personal integrative needs
This category refers to needs that relate to:
- finding reinforcement for personal values;
- identifying with valued others (role models in the media, or significant other);
- gaining insight into oneself and to improve self-esteem.

Applied to the media, we see that people often use the media to confirm or reinforce personal values. For example, we may read books, magazines and watch television programmes that strengthen core values such as honesty, integrity, caring for others and selflessness. We often identify with prominent political and sport figures who then become our role models. For example, many young children and adults identified with the late cricketer Hansie Cronje, who was the captain of the Proteas in South Africa and an excellent leader. When it became public that Cronje was involved in match-fixing, his fans were devastated by his dishonesty. Valued others (significant others) thus help us to understand ourselves better, and by identifying with core values they represent, give us self-confidence and allow us to expand our life-world.

From the preceding discussion we deduce that in general people turn to the media to satisfy certain basic needs, such as to be informed, to learn more about themselves, to socialise, to be entertained and to escape. However, merely to identify and empirically test these needs does not explain to what extent (if at all) the media satisfy these needs.

To strengthen the explanatory value of the uses and gratifications theory, another dimension was introduced by distinguishing between 'gratifications sought'. before exposure to the media and its content, and the expected 'gratifications obtained', after exposure is completed (Bryant & Heath 2000:363; Penzhorn & Pitout 2006).

distinction between gratifications sought and gratifications obtained

9.3.3 The dimension of 'gratifications sought and obtained'
Palmgreen, Wenner and Rayburn (1980) did ground-breaking research when they empirically investigated the relationship between 'gratifications sought' and 'gratifications obtained' when viewers watch television news. The results indicate that individual 'gratifications sought' are moderately to strongly related to the expected 'gratifications obtained'. The lack of a perfect match between expectations and perceived gratifications therefore suggests that not every need (gratification) will necessarily

be satisfied. Another example: to relax, we may read a detective novel about a crime that has been committed in Tibet. While reading, we may learn more about Tibet and Tibetan culture, customs, practices, religion and rituals. In this case, the relation between 'gratifications sought' and 'gratifications obtained' is not perfect because the need for information may now become more important than the need to be entertained. This may lead to consulting additional sources, like the internet, to get more information on Tibetan culture.

However, in spite of the lack of a perfect match it cannot be denied that the distinction between gratifications media users sought and the eventual gratifications thereof added value to uses and gratifications as a theory.

expectations influence search for gratifications

Further research studies (see Pitout 1989) also proved that expectations and perceptions media users have about media do influence their motivation to search for that gratification, which ultimately impacts on audiences' media consumption. What then happens is that future media consumption will influence the perception of gratifications obtained and will either reinforce or challenge existing expectations and perceptions about the ability of a specific media source to satisfy specific needs. For example, viewers who seek information about a specific topic will most probably watch a documentary or an educational programme on television. Viewers thus expect that these programmes will contain the necessary information to answer their questions and to add value to their existing knowledge. Should these programmes meet the expectations of viewers, their belief is confirmed that educational programmes and/or documentaries provide the necessary information. However, should these programmes not provide the expected information, viewers will turn to other channels, such as the internet, newspapers or radio, to satisfy their information needs.

9.3.4 Ritualised and instrumental media use

ritualised and instrumental media use

In addition to the research regarding 'gratifications sought and obtained', Rubin and Perse (1987:59) researched the level of audience activity when using different media and media content. They distinguished between ritualised (habitual) media use – for example, to pass the time or to relax – and instrumental use, where media users actively select media content to satisfy specific information needs. Rubin and Perse concluded that the degree of audience activity is an important variable when studying media uses and effects – ritualised media users are more inclined to be affected by the media than instrumental media users.

To summarise: the uses and gratifications theory has made a valuable contribution to media studies and the understanding of the active audience. The birth of this theory in the 1960s was a turning point in the history of effect studies because of its basic assumption that audience members are actively involved in selecting messages to gratify individual needs, such as to relax, to be entertained, to escape from daily routine or worry, to be informed about the immediate and more distant world and to obtain advice about how to deal with personal problems. The active-recipient assumption thus nullified the assumptions of the great influence of the media on assumed 'helpless', 'mindless' audiences.

An important contribution towards the development of the uses and gratifications theory is the distinction between audiences' gratifications sought and the gratifications they perceive to have obtained. 'Gratifications sought' refers to audience member's motives for using mass media to satisfy specific needs while 'gratifications obtained' indicates the probability or ability/inability of a mass medium (or programme content), to satisfy those needs. This distinction addresses the criticism of the tautological nature of the uses and gratifications theory – that media use necessarily leads to the gratification of needs.

Apart from being tautological, this theory is also criticised for the claim that the media has very little influence on people because they can decide for themselves whether or not they want to be influenced. That is, the uses and gratification theory overemphasises freedom of choice without taking into account the influence of the social and cultural contexts within which media use takes place. And this is nothing but a pure form of individualism that completely ignores the notion of contextualisation, says Reimer (1998:137).

| cognitive needs |
| cultural and social contexts |

This means that the uses and gratifications theory offers little understanding of the connection between our individual psychological and cognitive needs and the influence of cultural and social contexts on how we use and interpret the media. Although uses and gratification research helps us to investigate media functions on a macro level, it is not sensitive enough to explain and investigate micro processes such as interpretation. As a result, an interpretive tradition has arisen primarily from cultural and critical studies approaches.

9.4 RECEPTION THEORY

influence of social-cultural circumstances on interpretation

Extending the concept of an active audience still further, in the 1980s and 1990s audience researchers conducted research on the way individuals received and interpreted a text, and how their individual circumstances (gender, class, age, ethnicity) affected their reading (interpretation). This came to be known as reception theory and/or reception analysis. Reception theory argues that texts can be interpreted in different ways depending on cultural circumstances and how audiences decode (interpret) media messages. Furthermore, reception theory also rejects the notion of a single, objective truth, as we explained in the discussion of the assumptions of this theory.

process of interpretation

negotiation between readers and texts

The concept of reception in media audience studies means that we are interested in the way readers interpret media texts. Therefore, we use reception theory to investigate theoretically and empirically the process of interpretation (sense-making). Against this background, we can define interpretation as the result of the process of negotiation between texts and readers (audience members) situated within specific social and cultural contexts. (When applying reception theory to studying mass media and audiences, we substitute the concept 'reader' for user, audience or viewer, while the term 'texts' refers to newspapers, television programmes, radio or any other mass medium.)

negotiation

Of central concern to reception theory is the process of negotiation. We all understand that we negotiate or bargain with people, but is it possible to negotiate with apparently 'lifeless' texts? We explain the process of negotiation by looking at some of the basic assumptions of reception theory. (See Eagleton 1989 and Iser 1978 for a detailed discussion.)

9.4.1 Assumptions of reception theory

internalise messages

When readers interpret messages there is interaction between them and the text (message). Georges Poulet (1969:54), a phenomenologist, describes the relationship between readers and a text as '… (y)ou are inside it (the text); it is inside you; there is no longer either inside or outside'. Although this may sound somewhat far-fetched and ethereal (airy-fairy), it is not so because few messages are self-explanatory and transparent; we must engage with or act upon a text to produce meaning. That is, we must internalise and appropriate a message in order to make it our own.

Media Audience Theory

For example, when watching the film *Titanic*, we are transferred to the time (1912) the ship was built, the luxurious first-class accommodation on the ship, the elegantly dressed people and the two lovers who met by chance. We get a visual presentation of the history of the *Titanic*, the horrific way the ship sank, and the gruesome way many of the passengers died in the icy waters of the Atlantic. We get engrossed with the happenings in the film to the extent that we loose track of time (objective time ceases to exist) and we become 'one' with the text as we experience the plight of the passengers and the two young lovers. The same kind of involvement occurs most of the time when we read a newspaper or magazine article, watch a television programme, listen to a radio programme, etc.

A text always contains blanks (gaps) that only readers can fill. Therefore, the act of interpretation requires that we fill these blanks with our knowledge, our private and public experiences and our frame of reference, which is an unescapable part of our social and cultural life-world. During the act of reading – that is, when we appropriate messages – there is a fusion or encounter between our own 'historical horizon' and the alien 'horizon' of the text itself (Eagleton 1989:433–4). Think, for example, of how your historical and cultural circumstances influence your interpretation of a topic – a new university course – you have little knowledge of and how your alien horizon expands with new knowledge about that topic.

| blanks in texts |
| expansion of horizons |

Wolfgang Iser (1978), one of the main exponents of reception theory (also called reception aesthetics), adds to our understanding of the interaction/confrontation between a text and reader by means of concepts such as wandering viewpoint, protension and retention.

| wandering viewpoint |

Wandering viewpoint means that we can hardly experience and understand a text as a whole while reading it because we wander inside the flow of the text. Iser uses the metaphor of a traveller to explain wandering viewpoint: while within a moving vehicle, the traveller can never experience the journey as a whole. In the same way, the reader is always inside the flow of the story and can at no time have a complete or total view of that journey. Therefore, we can only experience and understand a text in full after reading it.

To further explain wandering viewpoint Iser distinguishes between *protension* and *retention*; whilst 'travelling' through a text, we

| protension and retention |

399

continuously alternate between these two dimensions. Protension means that we have certain expectations about how a story or plotline is going to develop. These expectations are based on our retention – that what we remember of characters and events in the story we are reading. Our viewpoints constantly 'wander' backwards (retention) and forwards (protension) between different story lines, sequences and chapters.

<small>dialectical interaction</small>

This dialectical interaction between protension and retention encourages us to form links and to fill the gaps in the text with our own imagination based on our social and cultural background. For example, when we read a 'whodunit' thriller (that is, we do not know the identity of the killer until the last chapter) we wander backwards and forwards in the text to find clues about who the real murderer is. After many red herrings (how often do we suspect the wrong person!) the killer is brought to book and receives the punishment he or she deserves. The norms of society are upheld because justice has been done.

<small>syntagmatic and para-digmatic levels</small>

Iser's theory of active reading is also based on a semiotic distinction between syntagmatic and paradigmatic levels of a text. The *syntagmatic* level of a text refers to the horizontal arrangements of story elements. For example, the syntagmatic elements of a plot or story line lead us from exposition (how the story begins), to the rising action to the climax, then downwards to the resolution when the conflict is resolved (the ending) (Schrag & Rosenfeld 1987:363).

The way these elements are arranged allows us to make a *paradigmatic* connection between them. That is, when we read or look (watch a film, television, look at a photo) or listen (to radio or someone telling us a something), we only see or hear the syntagmatic combinations (the different story lines and their relating scenes); therefore we have to fill in the paradigmatic connections ourselves by means of protension and retention. As indicated above, a narrative (be it television, a film, a newspaper story, and so on) consists of many paradigmatic teasers or unresolved questions, which 'force' us to move through the text in order to find answers. By looking/searching for answers and resolutions, we remain involved while reading a text. After many interruptions, apparent confusions and red herrings, the solution finally unfolds and all enigmas and problems are resolved. We can now see that the paradigmatic structure of a text together with protension and retention, invite readers to become actively involved with a text.

Horizons of expectations also influence readers' involvement with, and interpretation of, texts. For example, as readers we have certain expectations about ways television programmes, newspaper articles (or any other mass media message, for that matter) will develop. We then interpret the content based on our experience of the same types (genres) of programmes in the past. Horizons of knowledge and expectations enable us to recognise things as familiar in this world, says Wilson (1993). In soap operas, for instance, we know that a story line may stretch over several months before reaching a climax, and that the content is to a great extent melodramatic (tears, pain and suffering), which is especially apparent in story lines dealing with love relationships. Viewers will therefore not expect a great deal of humor in soaps because funniness and laughter are associated with comedies. On the other hand, when we watch a documentary we expect and accept that it is based on the truth. Thus, the horizons of expectation generated by the documentary genre imply that we will accept its claim as being an authentic and truthful depiction (Harindranath 1998:285). Take as an example a documentary on the mistreatment of the Tuli elephants by their owners: we will accept the plight of the elephants as the truth, especially if the claims of the battered elephants are supported by pictures in newspapers and on television.

horizons of expectation

fusion of horizons

The fusion of horizons (those of the reader and those horizons being presented by a text) makes *identification* possible. To identify with a character in a text, we must appropriate a character's social role, together with the rules of behaviour governing that role. Jauss (1982:40, 161) says that identification with a character – the hero, for instance – affords the reader the opportunity to take part in the actions and emotional life of that character.

identification

From the discussion of these assumptions, it becomes clear that reception theory rejects ideas of passive viewers being dominated by powerful texts or the opposite – powerful viewers having complete control over obscure texts. Reception theory provides us with a theoretical basis that media use is a process of negotiation between readers and texts.

9.4.2 Application of reception theory to popular culture: the soap opera genre

viewers involvement

soap opera's lack of narrative closure

Although Iser's version of reception theory deals mainly with the interaction between readers and literary texts, we can also use this theory to explain the relationship between mass-media messages (texts) and audiences (readers). We use the television soap opera genre as an example to illustrate how elements in a text enhance viewers' involvement and pleasure. Soap operas are also especially suitable for reception analysis because of the absence of any formal narrative closure in a specific episode. That is, an episode of this genre does not comply with the classic narrative structure of beginning → disruption → climax → denouement → resolution. But what exactly is the soap opera genre?

SOAP OPERA

The soap opera genre may be defined as a serialised drama that appears regularly during the week in a specific time slot on television or the radio. Soaps are open narratives that resist narrative closure and therefore stretch over years to build up a large loyal audience. Most story lines in soaps centre round the melodramatic portrayal of family life and its problems, romance and tragedy.

The first soaps were broadcast on radio in the early 1920s in the United States and were sponsored by producers of soap products like Procter & Gamble. Because of its association with soap products this genre became known as the 'soap opera'. Today these serialised dramas (soaps) appear regularly on our television screens and on radio because of their popularity with media users.

Now what is it that makes soaps so enjoyable (for so many people)? Is it the lack of narrative solution and closure that generates pleasures and extended gratifications? What pleasures are generated by watching soaps? Robert Allen (1987), renowned professor of cultural studies in the US, did ground-breaking work on the formal qualities of soaps by developing an analytical model – which he called a 'reader-oriented poetics model'– to analyse soap operas. With this model he brought some of the insights of contemporary reception theory, especially those of Iser, into the arena of popular culture.

After an extensive literature review of the characteristics of soaps and viewers' interpretation of soaps by this author (Pitout 1996) and the contributions of Allen (1987), we developed the following structural model to explain viewers' involvement in soaps.

9.4.3 Structural model for the analysis of the soap opera genre

The analysis of the television soap opera within the analytical framework of reception theory indicates that the conventions (characteristics) of the soap opera provide us with ample opportunities and positions from which we can create meanings and get actively involved in the process of reading (interpretation). These conventions are outlined below.

narrative conventions

Regular exposure to soaps: scheduling

Daily soaps are broadcast in regular time slots, usually five times a week. For soap fans, viewing soaps becomes a ritual because they habitually watch at a specific time of day, usually after 4:00 pm. And many viewers rush home from the workplace so as not to miss out on an episode of their favourite soap(s). During focus groups conducted with regular female viewers of the South African soap *Egoli*, participants emphatically said that soap time was their own private space, and they did not want to be interrupted by telephones, visitors, their children or even the deacon of the church.

scheduling

Strategic interruptions

An episode of a soap usually consists of three to four story lines, and to secure viewers' interest, there is continuous cutting between story lines – just when viewers' attention has been captured by the characters and circumstances of a given story line, the camera cuts to another story line with its related set of characters and plot. Put another way, there are usually three to five nonlinear story lines unfolding in an episode, which creates gaps that ensure viewers' involvement. Viewers thus constantly wander between the different story lines. Viewers familiar with the structure of the soap opera text know that in any soap the various story lines can stretch over months or even years. Guessing and second-hand guessing about the outcomes of story lines keeps viewers clued to the screen.

interruptions

For example, viewers may speculate about the identity of a serial killer on the rampage, and it can take months before the scriptwriters reveal the identity of the murderer. Or when two lovers break up, viewers hold their breath to find out whether they will make up again. Such story lines, (and subsidiary ones) ensure viewers' involvement by 'forcing' them to watch each episode in case they miss out on possible resolutions. As the results of focus group interviews revealed, soap fans get involved with the happenings in a soap to the extent that when they miss an episode, they ask co-viewers to fill them in and together they speculate about possible outcomes of story lines. No wonder viewers get hooked on a particular soap; they cannot but keep on watching faithfully even if a soap stretches over years. In fact, the longer viewers watch a soap(s), the better it gets!

Codes of form: camera shots, camera movements, editing techniques and the cliffhanger

<small>codes of form</small>

The use of the dramatic close-up camera shot plays an important role in captivating viewers' attention because it draws viewers nearer and nearer the action and gives them an intimate view of the characters' emotions (fear, sadness, a mean smile) and inner conflicts. To further enhance viewers' involvement, each episode ends with a cliffhanger to keep the audience in suspense and to ensure that viewers watch forthcoming episodes in order to follow the development and ending of story lines.

Flash-forwards and flashbacks are frequently used to ensure viewer involvement. Some soap operas offer flash-forwards to whet viewers' appetite for the forthcoming action. For instance, prior to transmission of an episode of the soap *Generations* (a popular South-African produced soap) snippets of major events in that episode are shown on television during the week. Flashbacks may also be used to orientate and bring the viewer up to date with what has been happening over the past days, weeks and even years. In *Egoli*, for example, Jane is haunted by memories of how she mistreated her children and nearly killed them. These memories are shown by means of flashbacks to remind viewers what happened in the past but in such a way that they cannot say for sure whether she really attempted murder or hired someone else to do her dirty work. In this way another opportunity is created for viewers to get involved with the story line and to fill in the gaps with their own imagination (did she or did she not poison the food?).

Media Audience Theory

Gap filling: paradigmatic and syntagmatic organisation

As already discussed, the soap opera is a relatively open text in serial format that works against narrative closure because of the cutting between nonlinear story lines.

| gap filling

Gap filling relies on paradigmatic and syntagmatic organisation, and this is especially true for the soap opera genre. As already indicated, the paradigmatic and syntagmatic components in the soap opera are different from narrative scheme of the sitcom, police/detective and hospital genres. In these genres, the syntagmatic elements of a story (that which we see on the screen) leads us from exposition (the beginning of a story), up the rising action to a climax and then down the falling action to the resolution (ending) of the story (narrative).

The soap opera, on the other hand, concentrates more on paradigmatic complexity, that is, the range of possible choices available to the viewer expressed through the interrelationship between characters rather than on the syntagmatic juxtaposition of two or more plot lines in an episode. The paradigmatic complexity of characters' relationships encourages the viewer to imagine all sorts of possible connections. For example, viewers may speculate about when Ingrid will find out about the true nature of At. When will it be revealed that he killed his daughter by means of a deadly injection? Many questions can thus be asked about the story lines unfolding over months before a solution or answer is found. In other words, successful soaps have several interconnected plots, which develop in any number of directions to keep viewers glued to the screen to find out how a story line(s) will unfold.

| soap opera and paradigmatic complexity

Longevity of soap operas and archetypical characters

Soaps are open narratives that stretch over years to build up a large loyal audience – we can also talk of the longevity of soaps – who daily come into contact with a regular group of archetypical characters. These are found in almost all soap operas, for example:

| longevity

- *The young, vulnerable romantic heroine*: this character is very popular with viewers. She is pretty though naive and trusts men too readily. She is vulnerable, gets hurt quite often and therefore has a history of relationships with men that came to naught. Soars (1979:59) says that viewers see this coming and that is where the hand-wringing comes in 'and it is not all done on the screen ...'. In *Egoli* Lynette was an example of the romantic heroine: her husband died in a car accident and she had disastrous relationships with Adriaan and Chris Edwards, a married man.

- *The romantic hero (Mr Right)*: he has all the qualities that make him the ideal husband – he is hardworking, shows upward mobility and has a good job. He is tall, good-looking, a romantic at heart and a gentleman. He is the kind of man every mother would like to have as a son-in-law. In *Egoli*, Johan is a good example of the romantic hero. He is the managing director of the mine, attractive and always smartly and neatly dressed. While he and Esther lived together, he treated her with respect and spoiled her by taking her on romantic outings.
- *The female antagonist (super-bitch)*: this female character destroys people's lives without thinking twice. She is selfish and loves men, especially older wealthy men. These men are usually married, which makes her a natural opponent for 'good' female characters. Cherel in the South African soap *Isidingo* is the archetypical lying, conniving antagonist, who toys with men without showing any remorse. Even murder is not beyond her.
- *The arch-villains*: these male characters hurt and blackmail people, tell lies and are guilty of the most unforgivable sin in soaps, namely pure and premeditated selfishness (Soares 1978:61). Barker Haines in *Isidingo* is one such bad character; he did not hesitate to murder and blackmail people.
- *The loving, caring mother/grandmother*: these women have had their fair share of hardship in life. Therefore, they have great understanding of the problems of others. They believe in marriage as a social institution and the family as a core unit. They are caring, loving mothers and grandmothers. Nenna in *Egoli* and Agnes in *Isidingo* are examples of the archetypical mother/grandmother who shows great commitment to ensure the well-being of their families.
- *The meddling and sometimes mean mothers*: Yvonne in the South African soap *Binnelanders* is the archetype of the meddling mother. She is always interfering with Gideon (her son) and the decisions he makes regarding his occupation and the girl (Stephanie) in his life. She is a troublemaker who loves to gossip, especially about her own family and people working in the hospital.
- *The Cinderella clone*: in this category, we find the beautiful, talented daughters of low social standing who marry older, super-rich men

who live in mansions and maintain a jetset lifestyle. Brooke in *The Bold and the Beautiful* and Louwna in *Egoli* are examples of Cinderella clones. As children they were poor, and out of determination, however, not to remain miserable and poor, both married wealthy and powerful men.
- *The family man/patriarch*: this character is kind but strict. He is a combination of idealism and pragmatism. Although he may have a roving eye, he puts the interests of his family first. Eric Forrester in *The Bold and the Beautiful* can be regarded as a patriarch: although he has been involved with many women (even with his daughter-in-law), he is a caring and loving father. His children and wife regard him as the head of the family.

In sum, the application of reception theory to the soap opera genre shows that this genre provides ample opportunity for viewers to get actively involved with the events on the screen. This active involvement is heightened by textual gaps, strategic interruptions, and the paradigmatic and syntagmatic aspects of the soap opera text. The never-ending story lines keep soap fans glued to the screen and eventually fans become so intimately involved with characters that they 'bond' with them to the extent that the characters become like best friends.

Although we have focused mainly on the soap opera genre, we may with a few adjustments also use reception theory to analyse other types of media and television genres. For example, in a hospital drama, whether on television or the radio or in a magazine, a seriously wounded patient may be saved by the skills of the hero, the famous surgeon. Yet the central problem, which deals with illness, suffering and death in society, is not resolved and the mystery – a problem related to health – is carried over from week to week.

Furthermore, reception theory can also be applied to other traditional media (newspapers, magazines) and electronic media such as the internet. For example, in 2008 South African followed the unfolding of the political drama in the ANC government regarding the appointment of a new President. This major news event was covered by all media over months, and we, the media audience, waited with bated breath to see who was going to be appointed as the President. It is thus not only television soaps that provide us with ample opportunities to get actively involved with the text but also news events in the media. Like the soap opera, other media messages contribute to our active involvement as we move through the text. Our involvement is further heightened by textual gaps, strategic interruptions and the paradigmatic and syntagmatic aspects of a news event, which keep us guessing and speculating on what is going to happen next.

In the next section we discuss the social and cultural contexts of television viewing and the influence these contexts have on viewers' interaction and interpretation of media messages. This is an attempt to address criticism levelled against the uses and gratifications theory for its lack of attention to the social and cultural contexts of media use.

9.4.4 Viewers' pleasures: rituals and the social dimension of television viewing

Because of the never-ending story lines, soap opera viewing becomes a ritual: year after year, every week day, at the same time, fans gather in front of the television set; they disconnect the phone and the doorbell, pour a drink and sit back to escape for half an hour into a fantasy world of the soap community. One woman in a focus group interview said that when she watches *Egoli* she switches off the phone and doesn't answer the doorbell; her children know not to interrupt while she is watching *Egoli* (Pitout 1996).

The social dimension of television can be divided into the following categories: interpretive communities, para-social and social interaction and identification.

Interpretive communities

Interpretation includes the process of negotiation within specific social and cultural circumstances. Although we generally accept that television viewing is primarily a family activity, the social context in which television viewing takes place is not only limited to the immediate family setting – our social group memberships (or the interpretive communities to which we belong) also influence our interpretation of messages.

> social positionings

We can therefore argue that viewers will draw on knowledge as informed by various 'social positionings', whether in a family setting or the workplace (Roscoe et al. 1995:90). In other words, because interpretation is also a social process, different social contexts may influence the process of interpretation. For example, in one family different 'interpretive communities' may exist; the husband may be addicted to sports programmes while the wife prefers to watch something else. He will then have to turn to another 'interpretive community' to share his experience of that programme. The same applies to watching soaps: the mother and her daughter may love soaps while the males in the family may frown upon, and criticise, them for watching programmes that they regard as frivolous and in bad taste. (See the discussion of entertainment as a value judgement in Fourie 2007:224.)

Para-social interaction

The para-social and social dimensions of television viewing explain why we get involved with television characters and how we make imaginary friends with them. Focus-group results have shown that viewers built up a para-social relationship with soap characters whom they regard as their friends, friends they can talk to and share in their daily joy and hardship. It is this daily encounter with soap characters that feeds the imaginary relationship between viewers and characters (Pitout 1998). The same happens when we watch sport. How often do we insult the referee or the opposition aloud and in no uncertain terms?

Furthermore, participants also indicated that they recognise aspects of a character similar to those of an important person – also called the 'significant other' – in their own lives and then engage in para-social interaction, which leads to 'intimacy at a distance'. This means that viewers interact with characters as if they are real people – people of flesh and blood. Para-social interaction is thus based on a process of recognition. That is, there are similarities between the everyday lives of viewers and the reality presented in the soap opera. In this way, viewers enter the fantasy world of the soaps by playing opposite a character who resembles someone they know in real life.

> significant other
>
> process of recognition

Social interaction

Para-social interaction spills over to social interaction, that is, when participants discuss soaps with family members, friends and colleagues. Because television programmes are popular topics for discussion, they serve as a cultural forum for social discourse about aspects of the represented reality in these programmes. The results of the research by Pitout further indicates that a group of working women find it rewarding to discuss their favourite soap, *Egoli*, with their colleagues. This has led

> social interaction
>
> soap opera culture

to soap opera culture at the workplace. Furthermore, the participants admit that they discuss *Egoli* during office hours, usually during tea and lunch breaks. And, it is often social issues and humour in *Egoli* that stimulate discussion. From the results of this study, it is evident that the participants successfully combine the private sphere of their lives with their everyday life at the workplace. Their conversations often take the form of gossip sessions and the participants succeed in convincing the uninitiated or non-viewers to start watching *Egoli*.

Identification

> imitation
> role modelling

Identification with television characters is especially true for those viewers who watch serials (soaps) and series (sitcoms, detective programmes etc.) over years. These characters are important because they mediate the different effects of television through processes such as identification, imitation, role modelling and para-social interaction. The nature of the relationship we build up with characters over the years is quite intense – we may identify with a particular character by putting ourselves in that character's shoes or we may regard characters as role models and imitate their behaviour. Role models however, are not limited to entertainment programmes; television sports programmes are also very popular; through watching tennis, cricket, soccer and rugby, sports stars become role models, and fans often imitate their heroes' dress and mannerisms.

> identification with themes

As viewers, we can identify with many of the themes in television programmes because in real life we are confronted with the same problems – divorce, loss of friendship and death, to name but a few. Identification with television characters and their problems heightens our involvement with them and contributes to the pleasure we derive from watching television. In terms of reception theory, identification with television themes and characters carries us into an imaginary world that is far superior to dreary everyday existence. On the other hand, television viewing also has a reassuring function in the sense that we realise that we are not the only ones with problems – television characters also have their fair share of pain and disappointments. Television programmes may thus enable us to get a new perspective on life. (See Fourie 2007:216–24 for a detailed discussion of rhetorical motifs and identification.)

In brief, although reception theory acknowledges the active role assumed by audiences and the influence of social contexts, it does not study audiences over a long term. Most reception studies are of short duration and amount to qualitative focus groups and in-depth interviews that last not longer than two to three hours. Another theoretical approach, one which studies the way people 'live' their culture and the mass media as part of that culture, is ethnography.

9.5 ETHNOGRAPHY

A third main theory and/or theoretical approach to the study of media audiences (that is, also apart from the empirical methods discussed in chapters 10 and 12) is ethnography.

<aside>describing a culture</aside>

Ethnography has its roots in the fields of anthropology and sociology and 'literally means "a portrait of a people"' (Harris & Johnson 2000, in Genzuk 2001). Ethnography aims to investigate and describe a particular culture – its beliefs, customs and behaviour – by means of intensive fieldwork where the anthropologist/ethnographer closely observes, records and engages in the daily life of a cultural group. An investigation of a foreign culture (one that differs from that of the ethnographer) should take place in the natural environment where the action or behaviour occurs. Thus to fully understand the cultural practices of foreign cultures and/or subcultures the researcher should spend lengthy periods of time, at least two years and longer, amongst such groups.

Traditionally, anthropologists have undertaken ethnographic research in small communities with relatively few inhabitants; for example, one of the best-known ethnographic researchers in the social sciences, Margaret Mead, spent many years living amongst Samoan villagers (Terre Blanche et al. 2005:320). Mead might have been the first, or among the first, non-native to visit a particular part of the world. It usually takes researchers a year or more in the native field to gain the language skills necessary for communication before becoming able to fashion appropriate guiding questions. These long stretches away from their homelands must have been very stressful. (See also http://www.sas.upenn.edu/anthro/CPIA/METHODS/Ethnography.html accessed on 2008/12/01.)

<aside>exotic cultures</aside>

Today, however, field sites are no longer limited to 'exotic' cultures but can be nearly anywhere; for example, ethnography is also increasingly taking place in urban locations and in the native language of the ethnographic researcher. Furthermore, sometimes the 'culture' we want to study is not limited to one location, or the field of observation may be a workplace (such as a newspaper), a school environment (like a school hostel) or even a chat room in cyberspace.

> definition: ethnography

In view of the above, we agree with Massey (1998) that it is notoriously difficult to find a uniform, clear definition of ethnography because it is often used interchangeably with qualitative, naturalistic, and anthropological research, which reminds us of its anthropological roots. These roots are reflected in the theoretical assumptions of both classic and audience ethnography (Lindlof & Taylor 2001; Deacon et al. 1998).

Massey further contends that for a study to be called 'ethnographic proper' it should consists of at least seven elements: study of a culture; application of multiple research methods; long-term engagement; researcher as an instrument; multiple perspectives; cycle of hypothesis and theory building; intention and outcome. These requirements become apparent in the summary of the assumptions of ethnography.

9.5.1 Assumptions of ethnography

The assumptions of ethnography are firmly imbedded in the interpretive paradigm and overlap with hermeneutic philosophy, phenomenology and German idealist philosophy, amongst others (Lindlof & Taylor 2001:11–12). Ethnography as applied by audience researchers, especially those belonging to the cultural studies approach, has lost a great deal of the precision it once had (see Chapter 11). The claim to ethnographic status in studying media audiences does, however, remind us of ethnography's anthropological roots as we discuss below.

- Ethnographers are concerned with the epistemological assumption (shared views about suitable methods to gather knowledge about reality) that social reality can only be revealed in natural settings – that is, where things are happening or lived out. Therefore ethnographers should become part of that social reality to experience it from the native point of view, that is from the viewpoint of the cultural group(s)/community/group being observed.
- Knowledge of social realities emerges from the interdependence of the observer (the researcher) and the culture being observed. Lindlof and Taylor (2001:11) even claim that the researcher does not need to use methodological instruments (e.g. questionnaires) because

'the researcher is the instrument'. In other words, the researcher personally gathers information – by means of participant observation and in-depth interviews – about a topic by actively participating with the cultural group being observed.
- Evidence for claims about social action should be recorded as truthfully as possible. Although the researcher must keep an open mind about what is happening in the field, it does not mean 'anything goes'. After all, one begins fieldwork with a problem statement that implies at least some assumptions informed by existing theories to guide and inform the observation. However, because ethnographers are expected to be culturally open-minded from the start of the observation, they should be prepared to challenge their assumptions, theories and understanding, constantly testing them against their observations. Furthermore, Gold (in Massey 1998:4) advises that instead of relying on a fixed framework for gathering and analysing data, ethnographers should use their interactions with participants to discover and create analytical frameworks, frameworks that are based in the intimate interaction with the empirical world grounded in the actual experiences of participants. The openness of ethnographic fieldwork means that the ethnographer should be prepared to modify hypotheses and theories in the light of further data, which Gold describes as the ongoing 'interaction between formulating and testing and reformulating and retesting'.
- When interpreting the results of ethnographic observation, the aim is not to generalise the findings beyond the case itself because statistical random sampling and generalisation seldom feature in ethnographic research. As with all other qualitative research, ethnography aims at getting a better understanding of a specific cultural group. In describing that culture (the outcomes of the research) a kind of narrative or storytelling format should be used because ethnography deals with descriptions of local places, human lives and relationships, thoughts, feelings, rules, triumphs and disasters. At the end of all this, the ethnographer, through a combination of empirical experience, systematic activity and appropriate theory, tries to construct a coherent story that may lead to a deeper understanding of the people who have been studied (Massey 1998:5).

In the case study below, we apply the above assumptions to a hypothetical example of media ethnography.

CASE STUDY: APPLIED ETHNOGRAPHIC ASSUMPTIONS

The aim of our observation is to establish students' use of the electronic media – computers and the internet – at the Unisa library on main campus. As researchers, we go to the primary venue (the library) where the action is taking place, and ask permission from the relevant authorities to observe first hand the research problem (students' electronic media use). After observing the students for a week we may begin to notice certain trends and then break down the research problem into research questions:
- Why do students use the library's computer facilities?
- Are they from disadvantaged communities?
- For which courses are the students who use the facilities registered?
- What are their computer skills (how computer-literate are they)?
- What suggestions do they have to make more computer facilities available to students who do not have access to computers and the internet at home or venues near the place where they live?
- Do the students work alone on a computer or do they work in groups on one computer?
- Do they have to book in advance to use a computer?

During our observation we may notice that not all students who visit the library use computer and internet facilities. We may then decide to observe and talk to those students as well, and find out the reasons why they do not use these facilities. We can now see how our initial planning may change as we observe other behaviour that we did not initially set out to study.

To gather our data, we may use a combination of research methods (techniques) such as participant observation, in-depth interviews and focus group interviews (see Chapter 11 for a detailed application of these methods). Applied to our example, we may observe what the students are doing at the computer centre in the library. For example, do they stand in rows to use the computer? Do they have to make bookings in advance to use the computer facilities? How much time are they allowed to work on the computer – half an hour, one hour or more? As we gradually build up a relationship of trust with the students, we may ask them if we can sit with them while they are working on the computer. In this manner we will obtain firsthand information on what computer and internet facilities they use most often.

We may supplement our participant observation by using focus group and in-depth interviews, that is, one-on-one interviews. (See Chapter 11 for examples of these interviews.)

We should also record our observations and interviews with students, for example by means of note-taking, tape recorders and a video camera. We should first ask the students for permission to use these devices. Note-taking should be done as unobtrusively as possible because feverish note-taking can be distracting and hinder the building-up of a relationship of trust.

As far as theoretical understanding is concerned, we may find information in our literature study that the use of electronic media in Third World countries is lower than that in First World countries. In the literature, we may also find different theoretical views – or schools of thought – on the use of electronic media. For example, one school offers a utopian vision of the future, that is, all media users will have unlimited access to computer networks and will become part of the electronic information highway.

On the other hand, we may find theories with a negative view of the influence of electronic media. Such theories, for example, offer a dystopian vision of the future in which an increase in choices of electronic media implies higher costs that will inevitably produce greater inequalities in access to electronic information between nations as well as individuals (McQueen 1998:211). In other words, the gap between the 'haves and the have-nots' will increase, because only a small elite will be able to afford access to new electronic media. These theories may also help us to structure or research questions further and to assist us in our interpretation of the research results. For example, how do the students perceive assumptions about the gap between the information-rich and information-poor sections of society? Do they have optimistic/pessimistic views of the consequences of the electronic superhighway? This information may help us to understand the students' cultural and social circumstances and the influence these have on their use of electronic media.

As we discuss in Chapter 11, the analysis of data consists mainly of filing and analysing the content of our field notes and recorded interviews. Filing involves the arranging of transcriptions of interviews and our field notes in an orderly way: for example, by using categories. The types of categories will depend on the research problem and type of data we have collected. In our example of Unisa students' use of computers and the

internet in the library, we can use the following categories based on our research questions:
- primary users (students who only have access to computers in the library), secondary users (those students who have access to computers in other venues and only occasionally use computers in the library) and non-users;
- computer and internet facilities used most often;
- positive/negotiated/negative views on and attitudes towards the gap between the information-rich and the information-poor countries and members of society;
- suggestions of how to make more computers available to students.

ethnography: subjective and interpretive

To conclude, media ethnography does not claim to be objective and empirical (as is the case with positivism – see Fourie 2007, Volume 1). One of the reasons is that ethnography is subjective and interpretive because it is undertaken by human beings (ethnographers) who have their own identities, cultural frameworks and social backgrounds. All these will have an influence on the questions ethnographers ask as well as to what an extent the participants allow researchers to become part of their lives.

validity and reliability of ethnographic data

Does not 'being objective' question the validity and reliability (the ethnographic authority) of ethnographic data and ethnographic insights into the cultures being investigated? Ethnographers have seriously considered these questions and have come up with the following answers (Abu-Lughod 1993; Clifford & Marcus 1986):

cultural relativism

- Anthropologists generally subscribe to some form of cultural relativism, because there is no one standpoint from which to judge all cultures and ways of being in the world. Because of this, ethnographers look at the world through different theoretical perspectives and the things they learn in the field are seen as 'partial truths' (Clifford & Marcus 1986). Therefore, there is no single truth to be uncovered in a research situation – there are many.

reflexitivity

- Ethnographers adhere to the principle of reflexivity, which means that they should provide a clear picture (description) of how the research was conducted and how they as researchers have been affected by what they brought to the research situation.

- To enhance the validity and reliability of research results, ethnographers use triangulation, which means that researchers have more than one way to show how they arrived at the conclusions of their research. That is, ethnographers should use a variety of data collection methods, such as field notes, document analysis, in-depth interviews and the focus group interview, which all work together to support research results (see Chapter 11).
- Ethnographic research takes place over a long period of time often months or years for professional ethnographers. Ethnographic conclusions are, therefore, arrived at only after extended consideration.

> validity and reliability

When we apply the above answers to our case study of computer use by students in the Unisa library on main campus, we discussed two theories to help us understand and explain students' media electronic use, namely the utopian and dystopian view of the electronic superhighway and the implications of the increasing gap between the information-rich and information-poor countries and sections of society. We may also use other theoretical points of departure, such as cultural studies, with its emphasis on the process of meaning-making, which allows researchers to study the different reading positions (dominant reading, negotiated reading and oppositional reading; see Fourie 2007:281–2) individuals may occupy when they interact with texts (media messages) and how they make sense of these messages from their own perspectives and against their social and cultural circumstances.

Ethnographic researchers plan and conduct their research in a coherent fashion. For example, as researchers we negotiate access to the locations and people we want to observe. Furthermore, ethnographers must work within a well-constructed and flexible plan; otherwise they will drift into confusion. (We discuss the planning of research techniques in detail in Chapter 11.) As we can deduce from the application of our example of Unisa students' electronic media use, we may use different research techniques (methods) – participant observation, in-depth interviews and the focus group interviews – to cross-validate our research results. That is, we use triangulation to increase the validity and reliability of the research results.

In ethnography researchers remain in the field for extended periods of time (we may stay at the library for a period of three months and longer) to allow them to use the research methods in a scientific way. When interpreting the results, we should also keep in mind how we and the participants have been affected by what we brought to the research situation. For example, did our status as researchers perhaps hinder the establishment of a relationship of trust with the students? If we are from a minority ethnic or racial group, did this affect our interaction with the students? Thus, all characteristics that may have an effect on the way we conduct our research should be considered.

SUMMARY

We started this chapter by explaining the importance of theorising about media audiences. We introduced you to three popular audience-centred theories from the active-audience paradigm, each with its own set of assumptions about social reality, human beings and methodological points of departure. Although all three theories adhere to the 'active audience' principle, they differ in terms of methodological points of departure (cf. Chapter 11).

In the literature, confusion exists about the difference between reception research and audience ethnography. For example, Schroder (1999:42) says that the contemporary ethnographic approach to studying media audiences includes both reception research and more genuinely ethnographic approaches. Unfortunately, this is an oversimplified and perhaps incorrect assumption, especially against the background of the basic requirement of ethnography that communication researchers must spend at least a few months in the field (the primary site) with the group they want to observe.

In Chapter 11 we discuss the methodology of ethnography and reception research and suggest a hybridisation of qualitative field research methods to investigate the complex issue of active audiences situated against their social and cultural circumstances.

Media Audience Theory

LEARNING ACTIVITIES

1. You are invited to address second-year communication science students on the importance of audience communication theories. Prepare a lecture of ten pages in which you summarise the basic assumptions and points of departure of the uses and gratifications theory, reception theory and ethnography, and illustrate with media examples.
2. Summarise and compare the advantages and shortcomings of the uses and gratifications theory, reception theory and ethnography.
3. Compare the basic assumptions of the uses and gratifications theory, reception theory and ethnography, and discuss the differences and similarities between these assumptions.
4. You are asked by a broadcasting television station to provide them with a research proposal on how to determine the reasons why people watch entertainment programmes, television news and documentaries. Write a proposal in which you suggest and give reasons why you regard a particular theory (or theories) as the most suitable to determine reasons for watching these programmes.
5. How has reception theory been adjusted to explain the interaction between media texts and audiences? To illustrate your explanation, choose one of your favourite soaps, sitcoms or detective series, or a news event covered by the traditional and/or electronic media, over a period of a week or longer. Use the structural model in your analysis and explain how reception theory overlaps with this model.
6. Answer the following questions and illustrate your answers with examples from your own viewing/reading experiences:
    - Do you belong to an 'interpretive community' that differs from the one your parents/partner/children/family/friends belong to?
    - Do you get involved in para-social interaction with characters while watching a television programme(s) or using other media?
    - Do you discuss television programmes/news events/gossip news about famous people with other people?
    - Do you have role models based on your experience with media characters?
    - Have you ever imitated behaviour and/or dress codes of people you have seen on television or any other mass media?
7. Explain in your own words how ethnographers address the problem of objectivity versus subjectivity in ethnography.

FURTHER READING

Alasuutari, P. (ed). 1999. *The media audience.* London: Sage.

Geertz, C. 1988. *Works and lives: The anthropologist as author.* Palo Alto, Calif: Stanford University Press.

Genzuk, M. 2003. *A synthesis of ethnographic research.* Occasional Papers Series. Center for Multilingual, Multicultural Research (eds). Center for Multilingual, Multicultural Research, Rossier School of Education, University of Southern California. Los Angeles.

Hammersley M. & Atkins P. 1995. *Ethnography: Principles in practice.* 2nd edition. London: Routledge.

Harris, M. & Johnson, O. 2000. *Cultural anthropology.* 5th edition. Needham Heights, Mass: Allyn & Bacon.

Iser, W. 1978. *The act of reading. A theory of aesthetic response.* London: Routledge & Kegan Paul.

Lindlof, T.R. & Taylor, B.C. 2002. *Qualitative communication research methods.* 2nd edition. Thousand Oaks, Calif: Sage.

Patton, M. 2002. *Qualitative research and evaluation methods.* 3rd edition. London: Sage.

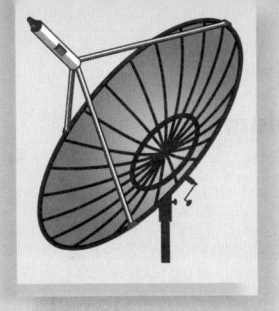

chapter ten

QUESTIONNAIRE SURVEYS IN MEDIA RESEARCH

Elirea Bornman

LEARNING OUTCOMES

At the end of this chapter, you should be able to:
- discern whether a questionnaire survey is appropriate to investigate a particular media-related research problem or issue, or not;
- make an informed choice of sampling design appropriate for investigating a particular media-related problem or issue;
- draw various probability and nonprobability samples;
- make an informed choice of a type of survey appropriate for investigating a particular media-related problem or issue;
- design a questionnaire to investigate a particular media-related problem or issue;
- critically evaluate questionnaire survey studies;
- conduct a questionnaire survey of your own on a limited scale.

Media Studies: Volume 3

THIS CHAPTER

This chapter gives an overview of the theory and practices associated with questionnaire surveys as a quantitative methodology, with specific reference to the ways in which surveys are used in media research. An application of how questionnaire surveys are used in audience research is illustrated by a case study. The most important topics dealt with in the chapter are the following:

- historical development of the use of questionnaire surveys in the social sciences and other applied disciplines;
- research topics appropriate for questionnaire surveys;
- steps in questionnaire surveys;
- probability and nonprobability sampling;
- types of surveys;
- designing of questionnaires;
- reliability and validity as yardsticks of quality for questionnaire surveys;
- sources of error in questionnaire surveys.

10.1 INTRODUCTION

Most of us are accustomed to questionnaire surveys. At some or other time each of us has been confronted by a fieldworker or a letter (with a questionnaire attached to it) with a request to answer some questions. A questionnaire could be included in your study material for a course in media studies. One of the questions could read as follows: 'What is your opinion of your textbook on media audiences? Do you think it is (a) an excellent book; (b) a good book; (c) an average book; (d) not such a good book; or (e) a poor book?'

You would probably not be ruffled by such a request, as you have encountered questionnaires before. The reason is that the questionnaire survey is one of the most widely used research methodologies in the social sciences as well as in the marketing industries and other applied fields (Babbie 1990; Neuman 2006). However, the popularity of surveys might be misleading. It might appear to a layperson that surveys are a quick and easy option to obtain information about a topic. A poorly conducted survey could, however, easily yield misleading or worthless results. Good surveys are complex endeavours that require a lot of thought, effort and dedication. In this chapter, you will learn more about the ingredients of good surveys as well as the strengths and limitations of questionnaire surveys as a research methodology.

10.2 BRIEF HISTORICAL OVERVIEW OF SURVEY RESEARCH

The survey is a very old technique. It can be traced back to ancient forms of the census. The aim of a census is usually to count people and/or to obtain information on the characteristics of the entire population of a particular territory (Babbie 1990; Neuman 2006).

survey research

In the Old Testament, Moses instructed Eleazar, the son of Aaron, to take a census of all the people of Israel. King David also conducted a census of all the people in his kingdom. Jesus was born when Joseph and Mary went to their ancestral town to be counted. Ancient Egyptian leaders conducted censuses to assist them in administering their domains. The *Domesday Book* represents a famous census of England conducted from 1085 to 1086 by William the Conqueror. Particularly in early censuses, the aim was to assess the potential income or property available for taxation or the number of young men available for military service. The power of ancient leaders was also established by the number of their subjects.

Over time, surveys also acquired other political functions. Babbie (2001:238) gives the example of a little-known survey that was conducted in 1880. A German socialist mailed approximately 25,000 questionnaires to French workers. The rather lengthy questionnaire contained intricate questions such as the following: 'Does your employer or his representative resort to trickery in order to defraud you of a part of your earnings?' The survey researcher in this case was none other than the socialist theorist, Karl Marx.

The development of representative democracy as a form of government has added to the importance of both censuses and surveys (Babbie 1990; Neuman 2006). Nowadays, censuses are, among others, used to assign the number of parliamentary representatives for a particular group or region. Census bureaus have also made important contributions to the development of various aspects of surveying. Opinion polls have furthermore become part and parcel of modern elections. Today, very few democratic elections take place without research organisations conducting polls in an attempt to predict the outcome. Commercial research organisations have furthermore played an important role in expanding the use of surveys to marketing research (especially during periods when no elections are conducted).

The refinement of questionnaire surveys as a respectable 'scientific' research methodology in the social sciences started at universities in the United States and the United Kingdom. Babbie (1990) mentions two individuals in this regard, namely Samuel A. Stouffer and Paul Lazersfeld. Stouffer did pioneering work by employing survey methods to investigate social problems such as the effects of the Depression in the US and the status of black Americans during the 1930s. Paul Lazersfeld, who came from a European intellectual background, applied rigorous survey techniques in studying phenomena such as communications, leadership and economic behaviour. The use of questionnaire surveys in academia was furthermore stimulated by the quest of social scientists to model themselves after natural scientists and to become more professional, objective and nonpolitical.

World War II served as a further important incentive for the development and refinement of survey research techniques (Neuman 2006). The war also promoted cooperation between academic social researchers and marketing practitioners who joined forces in the war effort by studying morale, enemy propaganda, production capacity, and so forth. In doing so, they learnt from each other and gained experience in conducting large-scale surveys. Academic researchers helped practitioners to appreciate precise measurement, sampling and advanced methods of statistical analysis. Practitioners, on the other hand, introduced academic researchers to the practical side of organising and conducting the fieldwork in large-scale surveys. Many of these researchers joined universities after the war, where they promoted the use of survey methods in social research. Despite the fact that some university researchers were initially sceptical of a research technique that had been used predominantly by politicians and the marketing industry, survey research has constantly grown in use within academia.

Nowadays, survey research is widely used in both academic research as well as applied areas (Neuman 2006). Researchers in many social science disciplines (for example, communication, education, sociology, political science and social psychology) conduct surveys to expand the knowledge base within their respective fields. Quantitative survey research has furthermore become a major industry. Many applied fields rely heavily on surveys. Governments all over the world regularly conduct surveys to inform policy decisions. Surveys have, in particular, become indispensable in media industries, where broadcasting, print and other industries make use of surveys to obtain information about

Questionnaire Surveys in Media Research

media audiences (see Chapter 12). Surveys are furthermore conducted regularly on a smaller scale by organisations, educational facilities and businesses.

Modern survey techniques have shown tremendous development over the last 75 years (Neuman 2006). Technological development, such as computers, have facilitated survey research by making data capturing, data storage and statistical analysis easier and quicker. In recent decades, researchers have started to develop theories and to conduct research into aspects of the survey process itself, such as the communication–interaction processes associated with survey interviews, the effectiveness of visual clues, the impact of question wording and ordering, and the reasons for respondent cooperation and refusal. As such, this kind of metatheoretical research to enhance the validity of surveys has become an exciting field of scientific enquiry in itself.

10.3 WHAT IS A SURVEY?

Survey research has developed within the positivist paradigm of social research. The data produced by a survey are inherently statistical in nature. Robert Groves (1996:389) calls surveys 'quantitative beasts'. Although it is possible to include open-ended questions in a questionnaire, which can yield data of a more qualitative nature (see section 10.8.1), survey research is predominantly a quantitative methodology and the data are reported in the form of tables, graphs and statistics such as frequencies, means, standard deviations, t and F values, correlation coefficients, and so forth. In most cases, even the responses on open-ended questions are coded in such a way that the results can be reported in the form of statistics.

social research

A further important characteristic of survey research is that it is essentially a self-report methodology (Neuman 2006). The term 'self-report' refers to the fact that we ask people – called respondents – questions when conducting a survey. Respondents are requested to provide information regarding themselves and/or to describe their own behaviour, attitudes, opinions, and so forth.

When studying surveys as a methodology, you need to keep in mind that survey research is just one of a range of research methodologies available to the social researcher (Babbie 1990). Whereas the questionnaire survey is a versatile methodology that can be applied in a variety of contexts to investigate a multitude of topics, it is not appropriate to many research topics, and might not be the best approach to study some of the topics to which it is sometimes applied.

10.4 RESEARCH TOPICS APPROPRIATE FOR QUESTIONNAIRE SURVEYS

As surveys involve self-reporting, it is an appropriate methodology to investigate research questions dealing with topics on which we can ask questions which people will be able to answer. Questions can be asked on the following issues (Neuman 2006):

- *Characteristics* – We can ask people questions on their demographic characteristics, such as their age, gender, race, language, educational qualifications, income, marital status, and so forth.
- *Behaviour or behavioural intentions* – People can answer questions on what they did in the past, what they usually do and/or what they intend to do: did you watch *Generations* last night? Do you listen to the radio in the mornings? To which radio stations do you listen? How many hours do you watch television during weekends? Do you subscribe to satellite television? Do you intend to subscribe to satellite television in the near future?
- *Self-classification* – People can be asked to classify themselves into various groups: into which social class would you categorise your family? Do you consider yourself to be a heavy television viewer, moderate television viewer, or light television viewer? Would you call yourself a soap opera addict?
- *Preferences* – People can voice their preferences: which radio programmes do you prefer? If you have a choice, would you rather watch a rugby game or a soccer match?
- *Attitudes/beliefs/opinions* – Surveys are, *par excellence*, appropriate to question people about their attitudes, beliefs and/or opinions on almost any topic: what kind of job do you think the SABC Board is doing? Do you think that the media in South Africa are really free? What is the most important factor threatening press freedom in Africa?
- *Expectations* – People can answer questions on what they expect to happen: who do you think will become the new chairman of the SABC Council? Do you think that press freedom will improve, stay the same or deteriorate in Africa?

- *Knowledge or awareness* – People can be asked questions to establish their knowledge or awareness of certain issues: do we have commercial television stations in South Africa? If yes, name them. Which soap operas are broadcast on the television channels of the SABC?

When conducting survey research, it is important to remember that respondents can only provide reliable and valid answers on questions pertaining to themselves. Questionnaire surveys are therefore a very personal research method. Respondents cannot answer questions on behalf of other people. In audience research, parents are sometimes requested to provide information on the television viewing behaviour of their children (see Chapter 12). However, research has proven the results of such studies to be less reliable as parents tend to underestimate their children's television viewing (Webster, Phalen & Lichty 2006). Sometimes a representative is requested to complete a questionnaire on behalf of the organisation or group. In such a case, only specific information pertaining to the characteristics of the organisation or group can be answered. The representative cannot, for example, provide information on the attitudes or opinions of individual employees.

Questionnaire surveys are also not a good option to provide answers on 'why' questions, that is, research questions dealing with the reasons for particular trends or phenomena (Neuman 2006). It is, for example, not possible to establish by means of survey research the reasons why many South African learners watch television during school hours. A particular learner can, however, be asked about his or her own behaviour, that is, whether he or she watches television during school hours. People can also be asked for their opinions regarding such behaviour or what they think are the reasons for a particular trend or phenomenon. Researchers can also ask respondents what they think are the reasons for the lack of discipline in South African schools. They can also ask respondents whether they think that television plays a role. The responses will, however, represent nothing more than opinions, namely respondents' subjective understanding of the issue at hand. Few respondents will have the expertise to be fully aware of the complexity of factors that shape a particular phenomenon, such as undisciplined behaviour among children.

Survey research is also not a good option to investigate 'how' questions. The results of survey research can assist policy-makers in identifying potential problem areas with regard to a particular phenomenon and could thus form the basis for deriving strategies to address problem areas. However, the results of a survey can only provide information on how respondents behave and/or what they think or feel should be done, that is, information on behaviour, perceptions, opinions and/or attitudes. Few respondents would, however, have the insight into the complexity of a particular phenomenon to make informed proposals to address problem areas.

In media research, surveys are also inappropriate where questions regarding the contents of media products are investigated. Surveys can, for example, not answer questions on the foreign and/or local contents of television schedules or the violent contents of particular programmes. Again, survey research can only provide information on respondents' behaviour (for example, whether they watch particular programmes or not), opinions and/or attitudes on such phenomena.

10.5 STEPS IN SURVEY RESEARCH

research steps

The steps in survey research are discussed here in order to indicate the complex nature of the decisions that have to be taken at each stage. The steps are, however, not necessarily in chronological order. The following basic steps are followed in most questionnaire surveys (Neuman 2006; Van Vuuren, Maree & De Beer 1998):

- *Formulate the research question or problem, sub-problems and/ or hypotheses* – In survey research, a deductive approach is usually followed (Neuman 2006). This means that the researcher begins with a research question and/or problem and ends with empirical measurement and data analysis. Research questions usually follow from an idea that requires research. Especially in academic environments, the idea could represent a personal preference or interest of a researcher. Experienced researchers in a particular field usually have such a proliferation of research ideas that they cannot research them all. In the end, the curiosity and creativity of the researcher play an important role in identifying research ideas. In institutional and marketing research environments, the research problem is usually predetermined by the needs of an institution or particular clients. In audience measurement, for example, the research questions are determined by the needs of the media and marketing industries. Whatever the case, the research question is the rudder that steers the boat and determines the nature of the journey. Every single step in a survey is determined by the aim of a study, as represented by the research question or problem, sub-problems and/or hypotheses. This means that, in the absence of absolute clarity on the aim of a survey study, the researcher(s) will fumble in making the crucial decisions involved with each of the other steps.

- *Answer the question: is a survey a viable and/or the most appropriate methodology to investigate the research problem?* – Again, at this stage the researcher must seriously consider whether the research question indeed addresses one or more of the aspects that can be investigated by means of survey research as discussed in section 10.4. If not, it should be considered whether an alternative methodology would not be more appropriate.
- *Study the literature* – Now the researcher has turned his or her research idea into an acceptable research question, problem, sub-problem(s) and/or hypotheses. The researcher has also established that survey research is indeed a viable method to provide answers on these. What now? How does one start? Before starting with the real business of conducting a survey, the wise and sensible researcher will have a look at what other researchers have done in the field. This is done by doing a thorough review of the available literature. Reading of the available literature should be both extensive and intensive. Students often say that they could find nothing in the literature relating to their study. That usually means that they did not search hard enough, did not make use of modern technology available for literature searches or did not use the available facilities correctly. Even in the case of experienced researchers, it is wise to seek the assistance of a subject librarian. The survey researcher, in particular, should search for articles and/or reports that describe other survey studies that have been done on the same topic or related topics. How did these researchers approach the topic(s)? Which questions did they ask, and how did they ask questions on relevant issues? In doing so, the researcher will get a good idea on what has worked for other researchers and what has not.
- *Do some homework and investigative research* – Apart from studying the literature, it is also a good idea to talk with experts and/or experienced researchers in the field. There are some tricks of the trade that are not written in textbooks, articles or reports. Many researchers also conduct investigative research, usually of a qualitative nature

(see Chapter 11). Interviews can be conducted with people who can offer insight into the topic and/or problem under investigation. Focus group interviews with people representative of the population could furthermore help the survey researcher to get a grasp on the problem area or the variety of issues at stake. Such research will help the researcher to set relevant questions in the questionnaire (Bailey 1987).

- *Identify the target population and accessible populations* – The nature of the population is another factor determining most of the other steps and decisions in the process of survey research. The nature of the population should also be taken into account in the construction of the questionnaire and the formulation of questions. It is therefore imperative to identify and describe the target and accessible populations clearly and unambiguously (see section 10.6.1).

- *Decide on the type of questionnaire survey to be employed, and when, where and how the survey will be conducted* – The aim of the study and the nature of the population should be considered when decisions on the nature of the survey are made. In addition, all kinds of practical considerations, such as the time factor and the availability of financial and other resources, should be taken into account in order to ensure the success of the survey. Various types of surveys as well as their strengths and limitations are discussed in section 10.7.

- *Decide on the sample size, the type of sampling and the procedure of sampling to be employed* – Sampling is pertinent to questionnaire surveys. Both the reliability and validity of a survey depend largely on the type and procedure of sampling employed, and on the size of the sample. The survey researcher should therefore have a thorough knowledge of both the techniques of survey research, and the theory of sampling. Once again, in the case of complex populations, the researcher should not hesitate to obtain the service of sampling experts (usually statisticians who specialise in sampling). Sampling is further discussed in section 10.6.

- *Draw the sample* – After deciding on the sample size, and the type and procedure of sampling, the procedure should be applied meticulously in every step of drawing the sample. No shortcuts should be taken; otherwise both the reliability and validity of the survey could suffer (see section 10.9).

- *Construct the questionnaire* – The quality and usefulness of the data obtained will depend largely on the quality of the questionnaire. The questionnaire is the survey researcher's methodological instrument, just as the scalpel is the instrument of the surgeon. It is imperative that this instrument should be sharp and effective. The researcher should therefore carefully consider the issues to be covered in the questionnaire, the wording and format of each question, the logical order of questions, and so forth. More information on questionnaire construction is provided in section 10.8.

- *Pilot-test the questionnaire; obtain the opinions of experts* – As already indicated, no questionnaire researcher should ever depend solely on his or her own insight, knowledge and/or expertise when constructing a questionnaire. Other experts on questionnaire construction and experts within the field of investigation should be consulted. Even after the insight and advice of such experts has been obtained, the questionnaire should be pilot-tested, and adjusted according to the insights yielded by pilot-testing, before the final layout and printing are done. No changes can be made to a questionnaire once it has been printed or copied. Care is therefore necessary to ensure that data obtained by means of the final questionnaire will indeed meet the expectations of the researcher and other stakeholders. One of the techniques of pilot-testing is to ask a small number of people who are representative of the population to complete the draft questionnaire. After having done so, the researcher conducts interviews with the respondents in order to establish whether they experienced any problems with the questionnaire, whether there were any instructions, questions, words and/or phrases that they did not understand, and so forth. In doing so, potential problems with the questionnaire can be identified and rectified before the printing of the final questionnaire.
- *Do the layout of the questionnaire* – The technical layout of a questionnaire should be carefully done, as the electronic capturing of the data depends on the correct layout. Researchers are advised to consult with the persons who will be responsible for data capturing in order to ensure that the layout meets their requirements.
- *Train interviewers and conduct the survey* – Once the questionnaire has been finalised and printed or copied, the researcher reaches the stage where the actual survey can be conducted. If the type of survey requires the involvement of interviewers, thorough training of interviewers is imperative to ensure that the interviewers will follow the sampling instructions meticulously and conduct the interviews according to the requirements of the researcher.

- *Code open-ended questions* – Once all the questionnaires have been completed and returned, open-ended questions have to be coded in order to allow for the electronic capturing of the data. (Closed or structured questions are usually presented in coded format in the questionnaire.) Principles similar to those for the thematic coding of text in content analysis are followed (see Cooper & Schindler (2001:424–34) for guidelines on the coding of questions).
- *Capture the data in electronic format* – After the coding of open-ended questions, the data can be captured electronically. Most statistical packages nowadays have a program that enables researchers to capture the data themselves. However, mistakes in the capturing of data imply faulty data, from which wrong conclusions could be drawn. The capturing of data should therefore be meticulously controlled in order to ensure that each respondent's answers are captured correctly. If fairly large samples are involved, it is usually too time-consuming for the individual researcher to capture the data. In such cases, researchers make use of professional data-capturing services.
- *Do the statistical analysis of the data* – This is the stage to which all survey researchers look forward! Finally, the researcher will be able to see what answers the data yield on the research question(s). As already mentioned, questionnaire data are essentially statistical in nature. Statistical analysis enables the researcher to summarise the data and draw relations between variables. Nowadays, a number of user-friendly statistical packages, such as the Statistical Analysis System (SAS) and Statistical Software for the Social Sciences (SPSS), are available. Analysing the data themselves is usually an immensely fulfilling experience for researchers who have been involved in the project from the beginning. However, the user-friendliness of statistical packages can be misleading. Researchers should have a sound background in the underlying assumptions and premises of the statistical techniques that they use. If they do not have the knowledge or expertise to do the data analysis, a statistician should be consulted.
- *Interpret the statistics and draw conclusions* – Whereas the statistical analysis of the data can be done by a statistician, it is the responsibility and privilege of the researcher (sometimes with the help of a statistician) to interpret the data and draw conclusions in the light of the initial aim of the study.

- *Disseminate the findings* – The final stage of the research venture is perhaps the most important. All the trouble taken with the previous steps will be in vain if the research findings are not appropriately disseminated and applied in decision-making. The form in which the findings will be reported will depend on the aims of the study and the stakeholders involved. Academic research is usually reported in the form of dissertations, theses, conference papers and articles published in academic journals. In commercial settings, concise executive summaries of the most important findings are often preferred. Oral presentations, which allow the researchers to interact with groups of stakeholders on the findings, represent another popular form of dissemination. A researcher should always be ready to adapt the reporting of findings according to the needs of particular stakeholders.

Again, it needs to be emphasised that the steps as discussed in this section do not necessarily need to be followed in the same order. Although it is, for example, essential to develop a questionnaire before there can be any question of data gathering, the sample-drawing procedure and the development of the questionnaire could quite feasibly proceed simultaneously. After the pilot-testing of the questionnaire, the researcher will probably go back to the questionnaire development phase to address problems that have been identified in the pilot-testing. And this does not mean – nor is it advisable – that the researcher should take full responsibility for each phase. Good questionnaire surveys are usually a team effort rather than a solo flight. Few researchers have the expertise and capacity to conduct every step in survey research successfully on their own. A survey researcher should therefore not hesitate to seek the advice and assistance of experts when needed.

10.6 SAMPLING

If you go for a blood test, the nurse will take only a sample of your blood. As your blood is exactly the same throughout your body, the sample will be sufficient to provide information on the state of your health. More or less the same principle applies to sampling in questionnaire surveys. If, for example, you want to study the radio listening behaviour of the South African public, it is hardly possible to interview every member of the public. You will therefore have to take a so-called sample of the South African public.

sampling

The main motivations for sampling in survey research are time and cost. Theoretically, it might be possible to interview every member of the sector of society that you are interested in. For example, in the population censuses that are conducted at regular intervals in South Africa, the underlying principle is to obtain information about every person who sleeps within the borders of South Africa on a particular night. Unfortunately, surveys where you interview every member of the population are in most cases too expensive and time-consuming and just not practically possible. Survey researchers therefore make use of sampling methods to select a subgroup of the population, the members of which are then interviewed. Sampling as practised in survey research is, however, more complex than taking a blood test. Unlike the blood in your body, the members of most societies are not the same throughout, but tend to differ from one another in a variety of characteristics. Societal variety and heterogeneity are indeed some of the most difficult problems that sampling practitioners have to deal with.

10.6.1 Important concepts in sampling

Before we discuss methods of sampling in greater detail, you should acquaint yourself with the vocabulary used when sampling methods are discussed (Babbie 2001; Neuman 2006).

Unit of analysis

units of analysis

A sample is drawn from a larger pool of cases or elements. The sampling elements are called units of analysis. In media research, the units of analysis are usually individuals as most media researchers are interested in people's media behaviour, media consumption or reactions towards the media. The units of analysis could, however, also be organisations. A researcher can, for example, be interested in how various newspapers deal with race-related issues. Here, the focus of interest is not the opinions of individual journalists that work for a particular newspaper, but the official policy of the newspaper itself. The questionnaire will therefore be sent to the offices of newspapers. The questionnaire can be completed by the editor or any other person with the expertise to answer the questions. Only a single questionnaire will be completed for each newspaper. The unit of analysis will therefore be newspapers. In content analysis, the units of analysis are often newspaper articles, television programmes, policy documents, television schedules, and so forth.

Population or universe

The larger pool, from which a sample is drawn, is called the population. The term 'universe' is often used interchangeably with 'population'. The term 'population' as used in sampling should not be confused with the general way the term is used in the layman's world. In sampling, it is imperative to define the population very precisely. In the case of the All Media and Products Survey (AMPS) conducted by the South African Advertising Research Foundation (SAARF), the population is all members of the South African public of 16 years or older (SAARF sa). Three aspects are usually specified in the definition of the population:

- The units of analysis – in the example of AMPS, the units of analysis are individual members of the society.
- Geographic location – in AMPS, only people residing in South Africa are included in the population.
- Temporal or other boundaries – in AMPS, the population is limited to individuals of 16 years or older, that is, persons born before a specific date.

In delineating the population of a study, vague terms such as 'adults' or 'teenagers' should be precisely defined by specifying age limits. When a term such as 'university students' is used, it should, for example, be indicated whether both full-time and part-time students, undergraduate and postgraduate students, university students and/or students of technical colleges, and so forth, are considered. In short, there should be no ambiguity or uncertainty about who is included in the population (or universe) and who is excluded.

Target and accessible population

Apart from the terms 'sample' and 'population', a distinction is sometimes drawn between the target and the accessible population. Whereas the *target population* refers to the total pool or section of society that we are interested in, the *accessible population* refers to that section to which we have access in order to draw a sample. Let us take the example of the researcher who wants to study the opinions of the South African public on the SABC. The target population in this case is all adult members of the South African public of 16 years or older. However, because of time and cost constraints, the researcher decides to draw a sample from the readily available address list of South Africans who pay television licences. In this case, the accessible population is all the members of the public whose names appear on this address list.

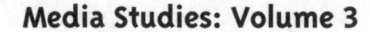

The definitions of the target and accessible populations have serious implications for the generalisation of the results of a study and therefore the impact and applicability of the results (Du Plooy 2001). For example, if you draw a sample only from the names on the address list of people who pay television licences, you will only be able to generalise the findings to the people on the list.

Sampling frame

sampling frame

A sampling frame is the list, or quasi-list, that closely approximates all the elements or units of analysis from the population (Neuman 2006). If a sample is, for example, drawn from the address list of people who pay television licences, this list of addresses represents the sampling frame. The sampling frame plays a cardinal role in drawing probability samples. Examples of sampling frames are telephone directories, tax records, lists of the students registered at a particular university, the list of employees of an organisation, and so forth. Most techniques in probability sampling depend on the availability of a sampling frame. It is furthermore only possible to draw generalisations about the population represented by the sampling frame. A good sampling frame is therefore vital to good sampling. A mismatch between the conceptually defined population and the sampling frame can give rise to invalid sampling and sampling error.

Sampling ratio and sampling interval

sampling ratio and interval

The sampling ratio is the sample size to the size of the population, that is the number of names on the sampling frame (Neuman 2006). For example, if the population consists of 50,000 people and a researcher draws a sample of 1000, the sampling ratio is 1:50. Thus the sampling ratio is the number of elements in the population divided by the number of elements in the sample. The sampling interval represents the standard distance between the elements selected for a sample. Given a sampling ratio of 1:50, every 50th element in the sampling frame will be selected. The sampling interval is therefore 50. The sampling ratio and sampling interval play an important role in probability sampling techniques such as systematic sampling.

Sample size

A common worry among questionnaire researchers is how large a sample should be in order to conduct a reasonably good survey (Nardi 2003). There is no simple answer to this question. Some textbooks offer formulae to calculate the desirable sample size. It is, however, the experience of this author that such formulae are seldom used in practice. Decisions on sample size are rather determined by practical considerations such as financial, manpower and time constraints. The type of survey is also an important factor. As internet, postal and self-administered surveys are relatively simple and cost-effective, it is possible to involve relatively large samples. Face-to-face interviews are, however, expensive and labour-intensive endeavours, and financial and manpower considerations will play an important role in decisions on sample size (see section 10.7).

There are a number of considerations to keep in mind. The first is rather simple: the larger the sample, the better. Sampling error is bigger when generalising from a small sample to the population (see section 10.10). According to Kerlinger (1986:119), probability sampling techniques require that the sample should be sufficiently large to give the principles of randomisation 'a chance to "work"' (see section 10.6.2). Larger samples also have greater statistical power in the testing of hypotheses. However, if nonprobability sampling techniques are used, the sample size does not matter as much (see section 10.6.3). A large sample size will not correct the bias inherent to nonprobability sampling. Regardless of the sample size, generalisation to the population will not be possible (Nardi 2003).

The nature of the population that is being studied should also be kept in mind (Nardi 2003). When a population is relatively homogeneous, a smaller sample can be acceptable. Also, if it is expected that all members of the population think or behave more or less the same, that is, when there is not large variation in the phenomena being studied, a smaller sample could sufficiently reflect the population. However, larger samples are required for heterogeneous populations (for example, the South African population) and where large variations in the phenomena being studied are expected.

Another important consideration is the kind of statistical analyses you are planning to do. A smaller sample size can restrict the choice of statistical analyses that can be conducted. If you are planning to compare subgroups, such as gender, age or racial groups, the sample size should be big enough to ensure a sufficient representation of these subgroups. A minimum sample size is also required to conduct more sophisticated statistical analyses such as factor analyses. In order to prevent later disappointment, it is therefore recommended that a statistician should be consulted in making decisions on sample size.

10.6.2 Probability sampling

In survey research, we distinguish between two types of sampling, namely probability and non-probability sampling (Babbie 2001; Neuman 2006). The terms 'random' and 'non-random' sampling are also used. The term 'random' refers to a mathematical process that yields a mathematically random result, that is, an outcome with no distinctive pattern. In a true random sampling process, each element or unit of analysis in the population has an equal chance of being selected for the sample.

random and non-random sampling

In most cases, random or probability samples require more work and effort than non-random samples (or non-probability samples). Some of the most tiresome tasks are to acquire or compile a sampling frame and to reach each of the elements selected for the sample to complete the questionnaire. However, probability samples are in most cases superior to and preferred above non-probability samples. Firstly, probability sampling avoids a researcher's or fieldworker's conscious or unconscious bias in selecting respondents. It is consequently more likely to generate a sample that will be truly representative of the population. Probability sampling furthermore enables the researcher to use powerful statistical techniques in the analysis of the data and to generalise the findings to the population. Several options are available for drawing a probability sample.

Census-type sampling

census-type sampling

When the pool from which elements are drawn is relatively small, the researcher can consider including all the elements in the study. Such studies are called census-type studies (Kotzé 2004). For example, if a researcher investigates the internet-usage behaviour of the employees of a small organisation, all employees can be asked to complete the questionnaire. (Of course, it will seldom be possible to involve each and every employee. Some might be sick or on leave during the period when the study is conducted, while others might simply refuse to participate.) As a rule of thumb, a census-type study should be considered when the population has 500 or less elements. In the case of larger populations, a census-type study can be considered when the manpower and financial resources are available and one of the easier methods of interviewing, such as self-administration, is employed.

Simple random sampling

Simple random sampling is exactly what the term indicates. It represents the simplest way of drawing a probability sample (Babbie 2001; Neuman 2006). For this form of probability sampling an accurate sampling frame needs to be obtained, whereafter elements listed in the sampling frame are selected according to a mathematically random procedure. The simplest procedure is to throw all the names into a hat or other container, shuffle the names and draw elements for the sample one by one. More advanced techniques require that each name in the sampling frame is numbered. If there are 100 names on the list, 100 numbers are required. A table of random numbers is then used to draw the sample. Tables of random numbers and exact descriptions of the sample drawing procedure can be found in most general research and statistical handbooks (see the list of recommended books). If the sampling frame is available in a form that can be read by a computer program (for example a computer database, a DVD or CD or any other form of computer disc), a simple random sample can be drawn by means of a computer program. In practice, the computer program numbers all the elements in the sampling frame, generates its own list of random numbers and prints out the list of elements selected. Although simple random sampling is the purest form, on which all other forms of probability sampling are based, it is often not practical to implement.

simple random sampling

Systematic sampling

Instead of relying on random numbers, researchers often use systematic sampling when a list of elements (a sampling frame) is available. In systematic sampling, the sampling interval serves as a basis for selecting elements (Babbie 2001; Neuman 2006). Every kth element in the total list is selected. For example, if the list contains 10,000 elements and a sample of 1000 is required, every 10th element would be chosen. The sampling will start with any random number between 1 and 10. In order

systematic sampling

to avoid any human bias, it is important to select the first element at random. In order to select a random starting point between 1 and k, the person responsible for drawing the sample often closes his or her eyes and points (with closed eyes) to a number between 1 and k. The element having that number is included in the sample and from there on every kth element is selected.

In most cases, simple random sampling and probability sampling will yield similar results. However, systematic sampling is sometimes not desirable where there is a cyclical pattern in the way elements are listed in the sampling frame. Babbie (2001) quotes in this regard the example of a classic study conducted during World War II, in which every 10th soldier was selected from unit rosters. The rosters were, however, arranged squad by squad, with the sergeants first, then corporals and then privates. Each squad had 10 members. The end result was that the systematic sample contained only sergeants. If another random starting point was used, the sample could – for the same reasons – have contained no sergeants at all, which is also not desirable. When a systematic sample is considered, the sampling frame should therefore be examined carefully. If the elements are arranged in a specific order, the researcher should ask the question whether the order would bias the sample in any way.

However, Babbie (2001) regards systematic sampling not only as more convenient but also as superior to simple random sampling in most cases. Systematic sampling is furthermore often used in combination with other forms of sampling – see, in this regard, the discussions of stratified sampling and multi-stage cluster sampling.

Stratified sampling

Stratified sampling is a different but effective approach to probability sampling (Neuman 2006; Rosnow & Rosenthal 1996). The researcher firstly divides the population into subpopulations (also called substrata) on the basis of supplementary information on the population. After dividing the population into relevant strata, a random sample is drawn from each stratum – usually by means of systematic sampling. In doing so, the researcher controls the relative representation of each stratum in the final sample instead of allowing random processes to do it. The result is a more representative sample of the population than would normally be yielded by means of simple random sampling. However, prior knowledge of the population is required.

A simple example is a population of 10,000 that consists of 55% males and 45% females. If a sample of 1000 is required, a proportion of 550 (55%) will be drawn randomly from the male elements and 450 (45%) from the female elements. If a simple random sample is drawn, the composition of the final sample could deviate from the true gender ratio in the population.

Stratified sampling is, among other things, used when the researcher has reason to believe that a certain group (or stratum) of interest could differ from others with regard to the topic under investigation. The researcher could, for example, believe that the media behaviour of rural people differs from that of urban people. Stratified sampling is also used when certain strata are relatively small in number in comparison with others. When drawing a simple random sample, the smaller strata could be 'missed' altogether by the random procedures. For example, a researcher investigates the media attitudes of students of the Department of Communication Science at Unisa. However, as master's and doctoral students form only a very small portion of the total number of students, it could happen that no students from this stratum could be included in the final sample if simple random sampling is applied. Stratification could ensure a fair representation of this group.

Multi-stage cluster sampling

Multi-stage cluster sampling is a complex form of sampling usually employed for diverse and geographically dispersed populations where no sampling frame is available (Neuman 2006; Pitout & Du Plooy 2001). This form of sampling is mostly employed in large-scale surveys of a whole country or a particular region. As the term indicates, the sampling process involves various steps or stages.

multi-stage cluster sampling

Cluster sampling closely resembles stratified sampling in the sense that the population is divided into 'blocks' or 'clusters' in the first stages. The difference, however, is that the clusters are treated temporarily similar to elements in a population. A sampling frame of clusters – and not of individual elements – is therefore required. In national or regional surveys, the existing official division of the country into census enumerator areas is often employed for clustering purposes.

In a second stage, the clusters – which are still treated similar to individual elements – could be stratified according to relevant substrata.

In South Africa, clusters are usually stratified according to the various provinces as well as rural and urban areas. Racial group membership could furthermore serve as a basis for stratification. Once stratification of the clusters has been done, a certain number of clusters is drawn randomly – usually by means of systematic sampling – for each substratum, similar to the process of stratified sampling.

In the next step or stage, a number of households is systematically drawn within each of the clusters selected for the sample. The exact number of households to be drawn will depend on a number of factors such as the sample size, the number of households that can be comfortably completed by a single fieldworker or a team of fieldworkers during the survey period, and so forth. In the end, the households can be seen as smaller clusters within the larger clusters usually represented by census enumerator areas.

The last stage involves selection of one of the household members within each selected household. The question here is who to choose. The instinct of a fieldworker could be to select the first person he or she encounters, such as the person that opens the door. This could, however, lead to sample bias as certain household members are less likely to be at home during certain hours. Working people are, for example, not likely to be at home during daytime. A random procedure for within-household sampling therefore needs to be followed. There are various techniques available to do so. In most South African surveys a selection grid is used. Household members that fulfil the sample requirements are listed from the eldest to the youngest (or the other way round) and a number is allocated to each one. A specific number (representing a household member) is then selected on the basis of the number allocated to the household according to the order in which households have been selected or visited in the larger cluster. Other techniques of simple random sampling can also be employed.

Cluster sampling is less expensive than simple random sampling for large and geographically dispersed populations. The reason is that the individual elements within a cluster are physically close to each other. If a simple random sample is drawn and the elements are widely dispersed over a large geographical area, it would be very expensive to travel to each selected respondent. Multi-stage cluster sampling is, however, less accurate than the other techniques of probability sampling. Sampling

Questionnaire Surveys in Media Research

error can occur in any of the different stages. It is nevertheless the sampling method used in most large-scale surveys. A complex method of multi-stage cluster sampling is, for example, followed in the AMPS studies conducted by SAARF (see section 10.11 – SAARF sa).

Overall, random sampling involves much more work than the techniques for non-probability sampling. A probability sample is, however, usually preferable above a non-probability sample because it enhances the reliability and validity of the findings (see section 10.9), it enables the researcher to use powerful statistical techniques in the analysis of the data and to generalise the findings to the population. The best possible sample for a particular study is usually well worth the time, cost and effort.

10.6.3 Non-probability sampling

Despite the advantages of probability sampling, some research studies are conducted in circumstances that do not allow for random selection of elements. In some studies probability sampling is also inappropriate. Suppose you want to study the information needs and media usage patterns of migrant workers. Probability sampling will not be possible as no list of migrant workers exists. Such cases call for non-probability sampling.

Quota sampling

Quota sampling is often used in audience and marketing research (Babbie 2001; Mytton 1999). Of all the non-probability sampling techniques, quota sampling shows the closest resemblance to probability sampling as it is modelled on the principles of stratified sampling. It is, however, not a true probability sampling technique. Quota sampling is used when interviewers need to look for fixed numbers of respondents of different categories or types. The variables involved are typically gender, age, housing type, social class, housing type or ethnicity. Quotas (the number of respondents to be interviewed for each category) are calculated for each category of each variable that are regarded as relevant for the particular study. One interviewer may, for example, be instructed to interview 10 male respondents in the age group 18 to 25 years that fall in the high socioeconomic group. Another may be given the task to interview 10 female respondents of the same age and socioeconomic group.

quota sampling

443

The sampling process usually starts with a matrix or table of variables important to the study, as well as information on the distribution of the population with regard to these variables. If a researcher wants to study the cellphone-usage behaviour of teenagers from 12 to 18 years old, there are various characteristics that could be important, such as socioeconomic background, age and gender. On the basis of the population proportions of each cell in the matrix representing these variables, a quota of the sample (a decision on the size of the sample should be made beforehand) is allocated to each cell of the matrix. That means that the researcher will need to know, for example, what percentage of the population is 12 years old, male and belongs to the higher socioeconomic group. Information on proportional distributions is necessary for all possible combinations of the variables at stake, that is, for all cells in the matrix.

Quota samples generally take less time and are cheaper than probability samples (Mytton 1999). Interviewers in surveys using quota sampling also complete many more interviews per day than when they need to seek specific individuals according to a random sampling plan. For these reasons, quota sampling is used in many commercial and marketing surveys. Interviewers are often seen with clipboards in shopping malls searching for respondents that fulfil their quota requirements. Often, when a respondent does not meet these requirements, the interview is politely ended.

Despite its resemblance to stratified sampling, there are several problems inherent to quota sampling. It is firstly, as already mentioned, difficult to obtain information on relative population proportions. It is therefore difficult to compile quota frames (the matrix with proportions for different cells) that represent a population correctly. The selection of sample elements could furthermore be biased even if correct information on cell proportions can be obtained. Fieldworkers instructed to find respondents fulfilling a complex set of characteristics could introduce bias in several ways. They could select and interview respondents that are easily available, such as family members, friends, people in their neighbourhood, church, and so forth. Fieldworkers will also tend to avoid people in places difficult to reach (for example, people living in high-rise buildings) and those living in remote areas. If those people that are more accessible differ with regard to the topic of the study from those living in difficult-to-reach places, the findings could be biased.

Questionnaire Surveys in Media Research

Interviewers can furthermore refrain from approaching people who look unfriendly or seem too busy. A further source of bias is the places where selections are made. Quota sampling done in shopping malls, for example, will be biased towards people who tend to spend more time in these malls.

There are, however, techniques that can be used to reduce the bias associated with quota sampling. The researcher can, for example, vary the places where respondents are sought. Some people can be selected at homes and others at places of work. In recent years, quota sampling has often been combined with probability sampling techniques such as cluster or systematic sampling. Fieldworkers are, for example, instructed to systematically visit homes in particular selected residential areas where they should attempt to find respondents fulfilling their quota requirements. The problem, however, is that it is difficult to estimate the representativeness of such hybrid sampling designs. At the same time, the logic of quota sampling can be applied to other research designs. When studying an organisation, representatives of different levels of management as well as employees can be interviewed, both men and women, and so forth.

Random-digit dialing (RDD)

The telephone has become an important tool in audience and marketing research. Random-digit dialing (RDD) is a sampling technique used for projects where the general public is interviewed by means of telephone interviews (see section 10.7.6 – Mytton 1999; Neuman 2006). Although telephone directories can serve as sampling frames, a number of groups are missed when telephone directories are used: people without telephones; people who have recently moved; people with unlisted numbers; people in hostels; people who only have cellphones; and so forth. People without telephones are perhaps the most important group in this regard because they represent the poor, the uneducated, the transient. These people would be difficult to reach in any telephone survey. However, in most developing countries ownership of mobile phones is more widespread than landline telephones.

| random-digit dialing (RDD)

When using RDD, the focus is on telephone numbers and not on directories. In South Africa, landline telephone numbers have three components: a three-digit area code (municipal area); a three-digit residential area code; and a four-digit number. Similar to landline numbers, cellphone numbers also have 10 digits. A computer program is used to randomly generate telephone numbers: landline numbers, cellphone numbers or both. A problem is that the program can select any number. This means that some selected numbers would be out of service, disconnected, payphones or numbers of businesses. Until an interviewer calls a particular number, it is not possible to know whether it really is what the researcher wants, namely the number of an individual or household. This can mean that a lot of time and money is spent on making calls to numbers that do not yield any interviews. Some research organisations make use of a computer program that dials the numbers automatically. However, it is still necessary for a human to listen to find out which numbers are individual or residential numbers.

As mentioned already, the sampling element in RDD is telephone numbers and not individuals. As in the case of multi-stage cluster sampling, interviewing in all cases the person who answers the telephone would give rise to sample bias. A secondary stage of within-household sampling is consequently necessary to select the person to be interviewed.

When landline numbers are drawn, it is possible to stratify the sample according to municipal areas and/or residential areas. Stratification is, however, generally not possible in the case of cellphone numbers. The most important reason why RDD cannot be regarded as a true probability sampling technique is, however, the fact that both landline and cellphone penetration is often low among the poor and in far-off rural areas – particularly in developing countries. That means that some degree of sample bias is almost inevitable.

Haphazard, accidental or convenience sampling: reliance on available subjects

convenience sampling

Many survey studies rely on available subjects, such as stopping people visiting a shopping centre, at street corners or in other locations, interviewing members of clubs or other organisations, and so forth. University lecturers, for example, frequently request students enrolled in their classes to complete questionnaires (Babbie 2001; Neuman 2006).

The ease and inexpensiveness of such selection techniques explains their popularity. However, these techniques do not allow any control over the representativeness of the sample. It is consequently not possible to generalise the findings to the population and to establish the general value of the data. Available subjects could be selected to pre-test questionnaires. Although studies based on available subjects could yield valuable insights, care should be taken not to over-generalise the findings.

Purposive or judgmental sampling

Purposive or judgemental sampling implies that elements are selected on the basis of knowledge of the population and the aims of the study (Babbie 2001). For example, a researcher wants to study the role of opinion leaders in a society. It would be difficult to identify all opinion leaders in order to compile a sampling frame. However, the researcher could decide to focus on the most visible leaders voicing opinions during community meetings and through the media. In doing so, sufficient data for the purposes of the study could be collected. Some researchers might also be particularly interested in deviant cases that do not fit regular patterns of attitudes and behaviour. A researcher might, for example, be interested to study the reasons why some South African children watch television during school hours (see Chapter 12). In order to provide in-depth information on the phenomenon, it would be necessary to search for and select children involved in this form of deviant behaviour. Selecting such deviant cases represents a form of purposive sampling.

| purposive sampling

Snowball sampling

Snowball sampling is appropriate when the members of a special population are difficult to locate: for example, homeless people, migrant workers or undocumented immigrants (Babbie 2001). In snowball sampling, the researcher first interviews those individuals that he or she is able to locate. These members are then requested to provide information on or to locate other members of the population that they happen to know. The term 'snowball' refers to the process of accumulating respondents as each located respondent suggests other potential respondents. The representativeness of such samples is, however, also questionable and the technique should only be used in exploratory studies.

| snowball sampling

Volunteer sampling

Some researchers call for volunteers to participate in their research (Rosnow & Rosenthal 1996). For example, ethical guidelines at

| volunteer sampling

universities sometimes prohibit lecturers from pressurising students to participate in research projects, and they therefore make an appeal on students to volunteer to participate in a study.

In recent years, researchers have come to know a great deal about the differences between typical volunteers and non-volunteers in research studies. Rosnow and Rosenthal (1996:204) name the following:
- Volunteers tend to have higher levels of education than non-volunteers.
- Volunteers tend to have a higher social status than non-volunteers.
- Volunteers tend to be more intelligent than non-volunteers.
- Volunteers tend to have a higher need for social approval than non-volunteers.
- Volunteers tend to be more arousal-seeking than is the case with non-volunteers.
- Volunteers tend to be more unconventional than non-volunteers.
- Women are more likely to volunteer than men.
- Volunteers tend to be less authoritarian than non-volunteers.

The differences between typical volunteers and non-volunteers imply that sampling bias is virtually inevitable when making use of volunteers. Apart from the general differences between volunteers and non-volunteers, it is furthermore difficult for a researcher to establish whether there are important differences between the two groups with regard to the topic of a study. For example, if a researcher makes use of volunteers to investigate students' attitudes towards soap operas, the volunteers might be predominantly soap-opera addicts, while students not really interested in soap operas could refrain from participating. If that is indeed the case, the use of volunteers can give rise to biased findings and conclusions. Of all the non-probability sampling techniques, volunteer sampling is probably the least desirable. It should be avoided if possible.

In conclusion, it can be said that non-probability sampling has its uses for certain research projects within particular contexts (Babbie 2001). However, researchers should at all times be aware of and acknowledge the shortcomings of non-probability sampling techniques especially with regard to the accurate and precise representation of the population.

10.7 TYPES OF QUESTIONNAIRE SURVEYS

Since survey research is used for a wide variety of purposes in a multitude of contexts, various types of interviewing may be used. Each of the interviewing types has particular advantages and disadvantages. The choice of a type of survey will depend on several factors, such as the aim of the study, the geographical distribution and characteristics of the population, the financial, human, technological and other resources available, and so forth. A sound knowledge of the advantages and disadvantages of each type is a prerequisite for making informed choices.

10.7.1 Self-administered surveys

In this type of survey, questionnaires are usually handed directly to respondents. The respondents have to read the instructions and complete the questionnaires by themselves – usually in their own time and at their convenience. They can also check personal records if necessary (Babbie 2001; Neuman 2006). The advantages of self-administered surveys are the following:

self-administered surveys

- Self-administered surveys are by far the cheapest and easiest way of conducting surveys. As self-administered surveys are also relatively simple to organise, they can be conducted by a single researcher. These considerations are usually important for poorly funded students and university lecturers.
- The response rates may also be high for well-educated populations who have a strong interest in the topic of a survey.
- Respondents might furthermore be more willing to respond to questions on sensitive issues in self-administered surveys than when they are interviewed.

Self-administered surveys hold, however, several important disadvantages:

- Self-administered surveys are not really appropriate for populations where relatively large numbers of people are illiterate or semi-literate. In order to complete a questionnaire, a person needs to be able to read and comprehend both the instructions and questions. Open-ended questions furthermore require a person to express his or thoughts in words and to be able to write these down. If a person has not reached a sufficient level of literacy, his or her responses could be unreliable.

- Self-administered surveys are not a good option for surveys with complex questionnaires.
- Where questionnaires are completed in private, the researcher has no control over the conditions under which questionnaires are completed, and does not know who really completed the questionnaire. A respondent could, for example, complete the questionnaire in a noisy bar where fellow drinkers may also render their inputs on the questions asked. A respondent can also assume a bogus identity in the questionnaire.
- Nobody is available to clarify questions or to provide assistance when needed.
- Poor questionnaire completion, where some questions are not answered, is another serious problem. Poorly completed questionnaires are regarded as a source of non-response error. Where completed questionnaires are picked up individually by the researcher or a fieldworker, the questionnaires can, however, be checked for full completion before they are received back.

10.7.2 Postal surveys

Postal surveys constitute a specific form of a self-administered survey. The questionnaires are posted to the respondents, who have to complete the questionnaires and return them to the researcher. A stamped and addressed envelope is usually included for posting the completed questionnaire back to the organisers (Babbie 2001; Neuman 2006; Van Vuuren & Maree 1999).

Postal surveys hold the same advantages as other forms of self-administered surveys. Particular advantages to postal surveys are the following:

- It is probably the cheapest form of surveying. For the price of an envelope and two stamps, a questionnaire can be sent to any address in the country.
- Questionnaires can be distributed over a wide geographical area.
- A postal survey is particularly convenient where an address list of the population is available.
- Postal surveys furthermore offer anonymity and avoid interviewer bias.

However, apart from the disadvantages associated with self-administered surveys in general (see section 10.7.1), a major problem with postal surveys is that response rates are usually very low. Questionnaires can furthermore trickle in over a long period of time. For these reasons, postal surveys are rarely used in market and audience research (Van Vuuren & Maree 1999).

Several techniques can, however, be employed by researchers in an attempt to raise response rates. A number of reminder letters are usually sent out, but add to the cost of the survey. Various incentives can also be offered to encourage respondents to complete and return questionnaires. Sometimes respondents are promised that their names will be entered into a prize draw once their questionnaire has been returned. An ingenious form of incentive was offered in a recent survey conducted on behalf of Elsevier Publishers among authors who had published articles in Elsevier journals. The publisher undertook to donate a particular amount to a charity on behalf of the respondent if he or she completed and returned the questionnaire. The respondent could even make a choice between three charities. In this way, an appeal was made to the conscience of the respondent to make sure that a charity of his or her choice did not lose an amount of money due to the fact that he or she had not completed and returned the questionnaire.

10.7.3 Group-administered surveys

The group-administered survey is yet another form of self-administered survey. Respondents are gathered in a group, questionnaires are handed out to each and the questionnaires are completed within the group situation. This form of surveying is particularly appropriate where the population lives or works closely together or gathers regularly for other reasons. It is often used by university lecturers, who can ask students attending a class to complete a questionnaire during class time.

group-administered surveys

There are several advantages to this form of surveying:
- A large number of questionnaires can be completed within a relatively short period of time with a limited amount of effort.
- The researcher can furthermore control the circumstances under which the questionnaires are completed.
- The researcher or a fieldworker is also available to clarify instructions or questions and to render assistance where needed.

The presence of the researcher or a fieldworker could, however, be intimidating and make respondents feel that their anonymity is threatened. They could therefore feel less free to express their true opinions and feelings. This type of survey is therefore not appropriate for investigating sensitive issues. Interviewer bias could also result from the presence of the researcher or fieldworker.

10.7.4 Computer surveys

computer surveys

The development of computer technology has opened new ways for conducting questionnaire surveys. In this form of self-administered surveying, the questionnaires are sent to the respondents via e-mail. After completion, the questionnaire is usually also sent back via e-mail. An important prerequisite for internet surveys is that all elements in the population should have internet access and a list of the e-mail addresses of the population should be available.

The technology that has been playing a major role in establishing international information highways – the internet – has indeed made global surveys possible. Questionnaires can be distributed with relative ease and speed to any e-mail address in the world. However, as a form of self-administered survey, internet surveys hold the same disadvantages as discussed in section 10.7.1. Like postal surveys, response rates can also be low for internet surveys, and special measures should be taken to encourage the full completion and return of questionnaires.

10.7.5 Face-to-face interviews

face-to-face interviews

Face-to-face interviews are the original way of collecting survey data, and are still used extensively today – particularly in media and marketing research (Van Vuuren & Maree 1999). Face-to-face interviews in questionnaire surveys should, however, be distinguished from qualitative, in-depth individual interviewing. Whereas it is possible to deviate from the interview schedule and to do probing in in-depth interviews, the interview in questionnaire surveys is usually focused on the completion of the questionnaire. Interviews are usually conducted at the homes of respondents by trained interviewers. The interviewer will assist the respondent to complete the questionnaire by asking the questions and recording the responses on a standardised interview schedule. Only the responses on the questionnaire are recorded. Additional information such as facial expressions is generally not important.

Although this method of questionnaire interviewing is probably the

most expensive, it is in most cases superior to all the other types of surveying for the following reasons (Babbie 2001; Neuman 2006; Van Vuuren & Maree 1999):
- It is the most appropriate method in situations where members of the population are illiterate or semi-literate. In developing countries like South Africa, it is the only option for surveys that include, for example, rural areas where illiteracy is still prevalent.
- It allows the completion of relatively long and complex questionnaires.
- Visual prompts and other aids can be used.
- The circumstances under which questionnaires are completed are closely controlled. Fieldworkers can also verify the most important demographic details of respondents.
- The interviewer can provide clarification – in rural areas of South Africa, interviewers often need to explain questions in vernacular languages.
- The presence of an interviewer usually constrains 'don't know' and other kinds of irrelevant responses.
- Poorly completed questionnaires are limited, as interviewers are instructed that all questions should be completed for each respondent. In most cases, interviewers are only paid for fully and correctly completed questionnaires.
- Response rates are usually high as interviewers are instructed and paid to implement the sampling plan and to complete the required number of interviews. Properly executed interview surveys usually achieve response rates of 80% or higher.

The disadvantages of face-to-face interviews include the following:
- The high costs involved in the recruiting, training and paying of interviewers and covering their travelling expenses; due to these costs, this kind of survey can seldom be afforded by individual researchers.
- A very important disadvantage is that the interviewer may influence the responses, especially in cases where sensitive or highly politicised issues are covered.

The interviewers are, indeed, a very important factor in face-to-face surveys (Babbie 2001). In large-scale surveys, a relatively large number of interviewers are usually involved. They are usually paid per completed questionnaire, while their travelling and other expenses are also covered. Where a number of interviewers are involved, their efforts need to be controlled and a number of supervisors also need to be recruited, trained and paid. Both interviewers and controllers need to be properly trained in order to ensure that the sampling plan will be implemented correctly and that the questionnaires are completed in a way that will ensure the survey yields data of a high quality. The interviewers also need to be sensitised to the fact that they should not act in a way that will influence or pressurise respondents to respond in a certain way.

Another golden rule is that interviewers – notwithstanding their position in society – should never be trusted completely even when they have been trained intensively. Survey interviewing is hard work and the temptation to cut corners is often irresistible. When seasoned survey researchers come together, stories abound on how they have been taken in by interviewers. The following incident is but one example. A researcher once conducted a survey in the Gauteng area among adults of 18 years older on issues related to social identification. In one census-enumerator area selected for the study, a secondary school teacher was recruited as interviewer. This interviewer should have visited a number of selected households in the area and conducted one face-to-face interview per household. Instead, she handed the questionnaires out to the grade 10 learners in one of her classes and asked them to complete the questionnaires at home. This roguery was discovered when one of the learner's parents phoned the researcher to complain about the nature of the questions, which she did not think were appropriate for children (the telephone number of the researcher was given in the introductory letter to the questionnaire).

In order to avoid tricks like these and to ensure the integrity of the data, a telephone number and address is usually obtained for each completed questionnaire. Survey organisers usually go back to about 10% of the households where questionnaires were completed to ensure that the correct respondent was selected by means of the within-household sampling process, that an interview really took place, to control the correctness of demographic details, and so forth. However, to ensure the anonymity of respondents, the telephone numbers and addresses of respondents are usually not captured in the final data set.

10.7.6 Telephone interviews

telephone interviews

Telephone interviews are another form of personal interviewing. However, in this instance, the interviewers conduct the interviews per telephone. In the developed world where telephone penetration is high, telephone surveys are often conducted as a cost-effective alternative to face-to-face interviews (Van Vuuren & Maree 1999). Telephone directories can serve as sampling frames or random telephone numbers can be generated by means of RDD (see section 10.6). However, due to the relatively low penetration of both landline and cellular phones, in particular in rural areas, telephone interviews are less useful in developing countries.

The advantages of telephone surveys are the following (Neuman 2006; Van Vuuren & Maree 1999):

- Telephone surveys are a quick and easy way of surveying, as a staff of interviewers can conduct a large number of interviews in a relatively short period of time.
- A wide geographical area can be covered. Although the costs of an interviewer and a long-distance call will be more than the costs of the stamps required for a postal survey, telephone interviews avoid the disadvantages such as low return rates of postal surveys.
- As already indicated, telephone interviews have a high response rate, especially for short interviews.
- Telephone surveys work well for surveys on sensitive issues as a sense of anonymity is better retained than in face-to-face interviews.

The disadvantages of telephone surveys are the following:

- The amount and complexity of information that can be gathered is limited due to resistance to long telephone interviews. Telephone questionnaires should therefore be relatively short, simple and straightforward.
- Visual aids such as those employed in readership surveys cannot be used (see Chapter 12).
- Long-distance calls can be expensive, but the costs are usually less than for face-to-face interviews.
- The main drawback is, however, that sampling bias is almost inevitable where significant sections of the population do not have access to telephones. However, even in developing countries, telephone interviews can be used for populations with high telephone penetration such as urban populations.

10.7.7 New technological developments and survey interviewing

technological developments

As we have already seen in the discussion of internet surveys, many of the new technological developments that influence people's lives have also opened new possibilities for survey research. Recent innovations in computer technology in particular are making not only the work of interviewers easier, but also the completion of questionnaires in the case of self-administered surveys. Some of these techniques are the following (Babbie 2001:265):

- *CAPI (computer-assisted personal interviewing)* – As discussed in Chapter 12, interviewers carry laptop computers with them and a respondent's responses are recorded on the computer.
- *CATI (computer-assisted telephone interviewing)* – This technique is basically the same as CAPI, but the interviews are conducted per telephone.
- *CASI (computer-assisted self-interviewing)* – A research worker brings a computer to the respondent's home and the respondent reads the questions and enters his or her responses on the computer.
- *CSAQ (computerised self-administered questionnaires)* – The respondent receives the questionnaire on a computer disc or any other means, runs the software which asks the questions and accepts the respondent's responses. The data file is then returned to a research worker or the research organisation.
- *TDE (touchtone data entry)* – The respondent needs to initiate the process by calling a number given by the research organisation. The call prompts a series of computerised questions which the respondent answers by pushing buttons on the telephone keypad.
- *VR (voice recognition)* – Instead of using the telephone keypad, as in TDE, the system is enabled to accept and record spoken responses.
- *Personal digital assistants (PDAs)* – PDAs are electronic devices often used in media research (see Chapter 12). They are pre-loaded with questionnaires and distributed to respondents. Respondents are required to carry the PDAs with them. At various times throughout the day the devices ring, asking the respondents to complete a short questionnaire. After a pre-determined period, the devices are returned to the research organisation for the off-loading of the data (Webster et al. 2006).

According to Babbie (2001), research has indicated that these devices are generally more efficient than conventional methods such as the traditional pen-and-paper method of completing questionnaires. It furthermore does not appear that their usage gives rise to a reduction in the quality of data. Some of these techniques such as CAPI are nowadays used in audience measurement surveys such as AMPS (see Chapter 12). However, as most of these techniques are relatively new, more research needs to be done to determine their impact on questionnaire surveying.

10.8 QUESTIONNAIRE DESIGN: THE ART OF ASKING QUESTIONS

There is an English saying: 'if you ask a silly question, you get a silly answer' (Mytton 1999:37). This is nowhere more true than in the construction of questionnaires. As already mentioned, the questionnaire is the basic data-gathering instrument of the survey. No matter how much care has been taken with all the other steps in survey research, if the questionnaire is not well-constructed, the data will be spoiled. Asking questions is therefore a crucial skill that survey researchers need to develop. It is unfortunately not a skill that is quick and easy to acquire. There is, however, a logic to questionnaire construction that can be learned with time, practice, experience and dedication.

questionnaire design

The problem that questionnaire researchers have to deal with is that human behaviour is wonderfully varied and complex (Mytton 1999). No two people are exactly the same. They differ in their media consumption behaviour, opinions and ways of thinking about issues. The media researcher, on the other hand, wants to summarise and generalise with regard to the varied opinions, attitudes and behaviour of individuals and to categorise media consumers into categories that make a variety of forms of analysis possible. In doing so, a complex reality is simplified and distorted in a certain way. However, as it is too time-consuming to describe in detail the media behaviour of each individual in a population, some degree of summarising, aggregation and/or generalisation is inevitable in media research. The questionnaire is the main instrument that makes this possible. We put the same questions to each individual included in a sample. Their combined responses provide a picture of the whole.

However, just as individuals differ with regard to almost anything, they also differ with regard to the way that they interpret and respond to any question put to them. Questionnaire questions consequently differ distinctively from questions habitually asked in everyday conversations (Mytton 1999). For example, you may ask a friend: 'which television channels do you watch?' Your friend may mention one or two channels. However, your friend may assume that you mean 'which television channel do you watch the most' or even 'which programme do you like the most?' Your friend's answer will depend on the way that he or she interprets your question. If you put the question to somebody else, it might be interpreted quite differently. In order to avoid such variation, questionnaire questions should be precise; vagueness and ambiguity need to be avoided. Mytton proposes the following questions that need to be asked by survey researchers for every question that is included in a questionnaire:

- *Will all respondents understand the question in the same way and give similar (not the same) responses?* Vague, imprecise questions should be replaced by precise, unambiguous wording. A question such as 'which television channel do you watch most frequently?' is, for example, more precise and will yield more consistent responses, that is, it can be expected that everyone will understand the question in the same way. A question such as 'have you watched *Generations* in the past two weeks?' is also a better option and will yield more reliable responses regarding habitual watching behaviour than merely asking 'do you watch *Generations*?' In the latter case, a respondent can answer 'yes' even if he or she has watched the programme only once a year or two ago.
- *Can it be reasonably expected that respondents will know the answer or be able to answer the question?* This question is of paramount importance for media research. We often ask people questions about their media behaviour – for example, the radio stations they listen to, the television channels they watched and/or the newspapers they read the previous day, week, two weeks or even a longer period back. However, will they be able to remember? Questions asking people in great detail about behaviour that took place too far in the past might be a waste of time. Considerations like these have given rise to the development of an array of audience measurement practices, as discussed in Chapter 12. In many questionnaires, people are also requested to give information on their household income. However, only the head(s) of a household will probably be able to provide such information.
- *Can it be reasonably expected, even if a respondent knows the answer,*

that he or she will tell the truth? Even when people know the answer to a question, they may be hesitant to reveal the correct information. Despite assurances of confidentiality, people might, for example, be reluctant to reveal their income as they could fear that the government, taxman – or even family members – might get hold of the information. One solution is not to request precise information, but to show a range of income categories from which respondents have to make a choice. The socioeconomic status of a household can also be established by considering other factors such as ownership of items such as radios, television sets, cars, and so forth, as is being done by means of the SAARF Universal Living Standards Measure (SAARF LSMTM) (SAARF sa). People might also be afraid or hesitant to reveal sensitive or controversial behaviour, such as visiting pornographic websites.

- *Will the question, as stated, provide the information that you want?* The dilemmas associated with question wording have already been touched on in the introduction to this section. It needs furthermore to be considered that there is not a single question format that will suit all the researcher's information needs. The wording and format of questions should be varied according to particular information needs. Question format and wording will be discussed further in the following sections.

10.8.1 Open-ended versus closed-ended questions

There are basically two types of questions in a questionnaire, namely open-ended and closed-ended questions (Babbie 1991). In open-ended questions, respondents are asked to formulate and write down their own answers to a question, for example:

For what purposes do you use the internet?

_____

_____

_____

In closed-ended questions, respondents are requested to select their answer from a list of response options that are provided, for example:

For which of the following purposes do you use the internet? Tick off the functions that you use:

> open-ended and close-ended questions

E-mail   _____

Internet banking   _____

Internet shopping   _____

Seeking information   _____

Visiting chatrooms   _____

One can also combine the two methods by adding 'Other' to the response options in the abovementioned example. Under the 'Other' category, individual respondents are free to describe, in their own words, any additional purposes not mentioned in the list of response options.

Both open-ended and closed-ended questions have distinct advantages and disadvantages (Mytton 1999; Neuman 2006; Rosnow & Rosenthal 1996). The advantages of open-ended questions lie in the fact that they:
- offer opportunities to express feelings and experiences spontaneously;
- do not lead respondents by suggesting specific answers;
- provide exploratory, unanticipated or novel findings;
- allow respondents to answer in their own language, thus increasing rapport;
- permit creativity and self-expression;
- can provide rich detail on a complex issue or an issue with which the researcher is not very familiar.

The disadvantages of open-ended questions are the following:
- time-consuming for the researcher (who has to analyse and code each response) as well as for the respondents and interviewer;
- often invite off-the-mark or rambling responses;
- difficult to assess the reliability of open-ended questions;
- comparisons and statistical analyses are difficult;
- articulate, highly educated respondents and respondents with strong viewpoints on the issues at hand have an advantage;
- language plays an important role – in other words, respondents who have difficulty in expressing themselves in a particular language are at a disadvantage.

The advantages of closed-ended questions tend to be the complete opposite of the disadvantages of open-ended questions:
- easier and quicker for respondents to answer closed-ended questions, thus the work of interviewers becomes easier;

- much easier and quicker to code, capture and analyse than open-ended questions;
- direct comparisons between the responses of individual respondents, groups of respondents and across surveys are possible;
- closed-ended questions force respondents to reply according to the dimensions that are of interest to the researcher;
- the categories of closed-ended questions help to explain what is wanted to the respondent;
- irrelevant responses are reduced;
- closed-ended questions make it easier for respondents to answer sensitive questions;
- less articulate or less literate respondents are not at a disadvantage.

Again, the disadvantages of closed-ended questions are almost the complete opposite of the advantages of open-ended questions:
- the response categories provided by the researcher could miss the point altogether or important issues could be left out;
- closed-ended questions could suggest ideas and elicit responses that the respondent would not otherwise have given;
- closed-ended questions could enforce simplistic answers to complex issues;
- clerical mistakes (or marking the wrong response) are possible.

It is up to the researcher to decide whether a closed-ended or open-ended question is the most appropriate in a particular case. However, novice questionnaire researchers tend to prefer (and overuse) open-ended questions – probably because open-ended questions are easier to construct. However, one of the most important disadvantages of open-ended questions is that they are extremely time-consuming and difficult to analyse and report (Mytton 1999). Consequently, the questionnaires for large-scale surveys involving relatively large samples usually consist predominantly of closed-ended questions, while open-ended questions are used only in exceptional cases where the researcher wants to explore a new or relatively unknown phenomenon or field. In most large-scale surveys, the number of open-ended questions is restricted to no more than two or three per questionnaire.

10.8.2 Compiling closed-ended questions

Although most questionnaires consist predominantly of closed-ended questions, compiling closed-ended questions requires knowledge, skill and expertise. Closed-ended questions should meet the following requirements (Babbie 2001; Mytton 1999; Neuman 2006):

- *The response options should be exhaustive, that is, the options should cover all possibilities.* Although it is possible to add an 'Other' category to make provision for aspects not covered in the existing options, the coding and analysis of responses to an 'Other' category are time-consuming and difficult – similar to open-ended questions.
- *The response options should be mutually exclusive.* That means options should not overlap and the same meaning should not be reflected in more than one option. For example, when using – as in the following example – categories to determine age, a particular person's age should not fall in more than one category:

	WRONG	MORE CORRECT	
Age:	16 to 25 years	16 to 25 years	1
	25 to 35 years	26 to 35 years	2
	35 to 45 years	36 to 45 years	3
	45 to 55 years	46 to 55 years	4
	55 to 65 years	56 to 65 years	5
	65 years +	66 years and older	6

- *Items/questions should not be leading and should not pressurise respondents in a particular direction.* Mytton (1999:39) gives the following example of a statement that was used in India in a survey on the newly introduced cable television channel (CTV):

WRONG

Some of the CTV feature films contain sex/violence, which affects the minds of children. What is your opinion about this aspect of CTV?

The statement already indicates what respondents should think about the issue. A statement should rather be formulated in such a way that it gives respondents the freedom to agree or disagree, for example:

MORE CORRECT

Films containing sex could affect the minds of children negatively. To what extent do you agree or disagree with this statement?

- *Items/questions should be as simple, straightforward and short as possible.* Long and complex statements should be avoided. The following excessively long and complex statement was also used in the abovementioned survey in India (Doordarshan is the state television channel – Mytton 1999:39):

WRONG

It is generally believed that the indiscreet showing of foreign films on CTV without removing objectionable scenes/dialogues (unlike Doordarshan, which shows only classical/award-winning foreign films and even removes objectionable scenes) is a direct invasion of our culture. What is your opinion about this?

Apart from the fact that the statement is also leading, it is almost self-evident that respondents would be lost halfway through the statement and that they would have difficulty in grasping the meaning. A simpler and more straightforward wording would be the following:

MORE CORRECT

Films containing scenes involving sexual behaviour should be edited before screening on television. To what extent do you agree or disagree?

- *The wording should be such that confusion, vagueness or ambiguity is avoided.* Language that could mean different things to different people should not be used. Consider the following question:

WRONG

How much time do you spend watching television?

A great deal	1
A moderate amount	2
Not a lot	3
No time at all	4

Only the last response option has a definite meaning. With the other options only subjective opinions are measured on the amount of time watching television. For a businessman, an hour might be 'a great deal', while for a teenager it might be 'not a lot'.

- *Questions and statements should be unidimensional.* Double-barrelled items – usually characterised by the use of 'or' and 'and' – such as in the following example should be avoided:

WRONG

Do you eat breakfast and read your newspaper in the mornings when listening to the radio?

In this case it will be unclear whether a 'yes' response applies to eating breakfast, listening to the radio or to both. The same applies to a 'no' response. It will be better to use two separate unidimensional questions, namely:

MORE CORRECT

Do you eat breakfast when listening to the radio in the morning?

Do you read your newspaper when listening to the radio in the morning?

- *Instructions should be clear.* It should, for example, be indicated clearly whether respondents should choose only one response option or whether they are allowed to choose more than one.
- *The question format should be appropriate to the kind of information that is needed.* There is no single format that can fulfil all the researcher's information needs. The skilled survey researcher will vary the format of questions for different information needs. Some of the frequently used formats are discussed in the following sections.

10.8.3 Quantity questions

quantity questions

The response to a quantity question involves a number – exact or an approximation – in response to a question to give information in numerical form. Information on a respondent's age, the number of people living in a household, the number of television or radio sets, can be recorded in the form of numbers, for example:

Age: ……….. years

10.8.4 Multichoice type and checklist questions

multichoice-type questions
checklist questions

In multichoice-type questions, respondents need to make a choice between response options that are mutually exclusive (Mytton 1999). Sometimes only one response option can be chosen; at other times more than one option can be chosen. This type of question is very versatile. It

Questionnaire Surveys in Media Research

is most often used to obtain demographic information, but is also used for a range of other purposes, as illustrated by the following examples:

Gender:

Male   1

Female   2

Do you have access to television?

Yes   1

No   2

How often do you watch Generations?

Almost every day   1

A few times per week   2

A few times per month   3

Less than once or twice per month   4

Almost never   5

Checklist questions are very similar to multichoice-type questions. In this type of question format, respondents are often allowed to choose more than one response option, but should be instructed that they can do so, as in the following example:

Which of the following television soap operas have you watched in the past two weeks? You can mark more than one.

Generations   1

Isidingo   2

Sewende Laan   3

Binnelanders   4

Villa Rosa   5

10.8.5 Contingency questions

Contingency questions – also called screening questions or skip questions – are used in order to avoid asking questions that are irrelevant for a | contingency questions particular respondent (Neuman 2006). A contingency question is a two- (or more) part question in which the first question determines which question(s) the respondent needs to answer next. In other words, on the basis of the respondent's response to the first question, the respondent can be instructed to skip one or more questions, for example:

1. Does your household currently subscribe to satellite television?

   Yes   1

   No   2

   If you answered 'Yes' to question 1, please skip question 2 and move to question 3.

   If you answered 'No', please answer question 2.

2. What are the most important reasons why your household does not subscribe to satellite television?

10.8.6 Rank–order questions

rank–order questions

Rank–order questions are one way of measuring opinions and attitudes (Mytton 1999). In this type of question, respondents are asked to put possible answers in a rank order of importance or desirability. Some detail might be provided to help respondents to make informed choices. Respondents might be asked to order their preferences of radio or television programmes, stations or channels, as illustrated in the following examples:

Here is a list of various types of television programmes. Please rank them in order of your preference. Put a 1 next to the type of programme that you like the best; a 2 next to the type of programme that you like the second best, and so on.

_____ News programmes

_____ Sports programmes

_____ Soap operas

_____ Documentaries

_____ Talk shows

_____ Comedies

The television channels of the SABC regularly broadcast the following sports:

rugby, tennis, soccer, boxing, athletics, hockey and netball. Please indicate which of these broadcasts you like best (first choice), second best (second choice) and third best (third choice):

First choice:

Second choice:

Third choice:

Rank–order questions can also be used to establish the popularity of presenters. This type of question can furthermore be used for more serious purposes (Mytton 1999). Suppose you want to know how young mothers in rural areas would like to get information about child health. You might ask a question like the following:

The following are possible ways in which information about child health can be made available to mothers in your area. Please rank them in order of your own preference. Give your first choice the number 1, the next choice the number 2, and so on, up to the number 5 for the information source which is the least important to you.

Personal information sessions with a clinic sister

Radio programmes

Television programmes

Information pamphlets distributed at clinics

Posters at clinics and hospitals

Other – please state _____

10.8.7 Intensity measures

Opinions, attitudes and feelings cannot easily be categorised in a dichotomous way, as reflected in questions with a simple 'yes'/'no' or 'agree'/'disagree' format (Nardi 2003). Although people might have clear preferences, most people feel more or less strongly about most issues. For example, you might feel extremely strongly in favour of greater press freedom and the freedom of the individual to express his

| intensity measures

or her feelings freely. However, although you might also be in favour of the availability of more television channels in South Africa, you might not feel as strongly about the latter as about the former issues. In other words, it is often not enough to have respondents choose between two opposing categories such as 'yes' or 'no' or 'agree' or 'disagree'. They also need to indicate the intensity of their feelings, that is how strongly they 'agree' or 'disagree'. People's attitudes, opinions and feelings are consequently often measured by means of intensity measures such as Likert-type or semantic differential scales.

Likert-type scales

The Likert-type scale is a closed-ended scale appropriate *par excellence* for measuring attitudes or opinions (Rosnow & Rosenthal 1996). It represents a numerical scale in which numbers are associated with different responses. In most cases, the response options reflect varying degrees of agreement or disagreement. Likert-type scales often consist of statements to which respondents should indicate the extent to which they agree or disagree. However, as can be deduced from the following examples, the Likert-type format is extremely versatile and can take a variety of formats. Neuman (2006:296) gives a list of potential response formats that can be used when compiling Likert-type scales. The following are some examples of Likert-type scales that can be used in media research:

Television programmes often contain scenes that I find offensive.

Strongly agree	1
Agree	2
Neither agree nor disagree	3
Disagree	4
Strongly disagree	5

Indicate to what extent you are interested in documentary crime programmes:

Very interested	1
Interested	2
Neutral	3

Not interested   4

Not interested at all   5

What is your opinion of the programmes offered by SABC3?

Very good   1

Reasonably good   2

Neither good nor bad   3

Bad   4

Very bad   5

In the above examples, five-point scales have been used. There is, however, no rule against a greater or smaller scale size. However, Mytton (1999) holds that four or five options yield the most easily analysed results. It is generally agreed that a neutral option (for example, 'neither agree nor disagree') should be provided to enable the respondent to indicate that he or she does not agree or disagree with any of the other response options that are offered. However, some researchers prefer to exclude the neutral option in order to get a clear indication of opinion. The implications of forcing a respondent to take a stand with regard to a particular issue should, however, be considered.

Of particular importance is the order of the response options. The options should follow a logical order: for example, from positive to negative, large to small or vice versa, with the neutral option always in the middle. Response options should never be scattered in an illogical order.

A Likert-type scale should also be well-balanced. The following scale was used some years ago by a South African airline to establish opinions on the food served on board:

WRONG

How would you rate the food served on this flight?

Good   1

Very good   2

Excellent   3

The problem with this scale is that respondents are not allowed to indicate that they did not like the food. A more appropriate scale would have the same number of positive and negative options such as in the following example:

MORE CORRECT

How would you rate the food served on this flight?

Very good   1

Good   2

Cannot say   3

Bad   4

Very bad   5

Matrix questions

matrix questions

In order to enhance the reliability of measurements (see section 10.9), a set of items is sometimes compiled to evaluate opinions or attitudes towards a particular subject or issue (Neuman 2006). In matrix questions the scales are listed in a compact form where the response categories for all the questions are the same. The responses on the various scales are usually summated in order to obtain a single measure of attitudes or opinions towards the object or issue at stake.

Indicate to what extent you agree or disagree with the following statements regarding the news programmes of the SABC:

SA   A   N   D   SD

The news programmes are politically neutral.

The news programmes give preference to particular political parties.

The news programmes are objective in presenting political events.

The contents of news programmes are controlled by the ruling party.

Questionnaire Surveys in Media Research

Semantic differential scales

According to Rosnow and Rosenthal (1996), the semantic differential was developed for the measurement of the connotative meaning – as opposed to the denotative meaning – of things in everyday life. The term *denotative* refers to the assigned meaning of an object or subject as reflected in dictionaries, while *connotative* refers to the representational meaning, that is, one's own subjective associations. The inventors of this question format, Osgood, Suci and Tannenbaum (1957), argue that most things in life (for example, dogs, flowers, individuals, ethnic groups, presenters, programmes) are perceived in terms of three primary dimensions of subjective meaning, namely *evaluation*, *potency* and *activity*. Osgood et al. developed the method of using bipolar cue words to tap all three dimensions of connotative meanings.

semantic differential scales

In media and marketing research, semantic differentials are often used to evaluate products, programmes, persons, groups, and so forth. The semantic differential can also be employed to make comparisons. Suppose you are interested in comparing the two presenters of an early morning radio programme in terms of their connotative meaning for regular listeners to the programme. Listeners can then be requested to evaluate the two presenters on the same semantic differential scale. To tap the evaluative dimensions associated with the two presenters, the following bipolar anchors can be used:

Bad	1	2	3	4	5	Good
Unpleasant	1	2	3	4	5	Pleasant
Dull	1	2	3	4	5	Sharp
Polite	1	2	3	4	5	Rude

The numbers represent dimensions of a continuous scale and can be explained for the first scale in the following fashion: 'extremely bad' (1); 'quite bad' (2); 'neutral' (3); 'quite good' (4) and 'extremely good' (5). An example is usually discussed in the instructions for a semantic differential scale in order to help the respondents to understand the significance of the various dimensions of the scales.

Please note that the poles of the scale should represent direct opposites. It is furthermore important to note that no particular order is followed in ordering the positive or negative poles of the scales. In varying the order, that is, whether the positive or negative pole is given first or last, recency effects can be avoided. Recency effects refer to the effect that occurs when respondents tend to pursue with their last response offered rather than considering each question or item seriously (Neuman 2006). For example, a respondent who marked '2' on the first semantic differential scale, can tend to proceed in a similar way by marking '2' for all the other scales also.

10.8.8 Overall structure of a questionnaire

A questionnaire usually consists of the following sections:

A Letter of introduction

The letter of introduction is an important part of the questionnaire, in which the researcher should do the following:
- introduce himself or herself and give information on the people, institutions or organisations involved in the study;
- give an indication of the reason(s) for or aims of the study;
- motivate the respondents to participate in the study;
- assure the respondents of the confidentiality and anonymity of their responses;
- give contact details of the researcher(s).

B Demographic or other relevant details

This section could follow directly after the letter of introduction or could be placed at the end of the questionnaire. In most large-scale surveys, demographic questions follow directly after the letter of introduction due to their vital importance in the analysis of the data. However, whatever its position in the questionnaire, the section should contain questions on the demographic details relevant to the field of study. Most questionnaires contain questions on gender and age. Other details that might be relevant are race, marital status, highest level of education, personal income, socioeconomic status of household, occupation and/or home language. In intra-organisational studies, other variables such as division or rank might be relevant, while details like occupation and income might be superfluous as information on these might already be reflected in the rank of an employee. In all cases, the researcher should decide which demographic variables are relevant to a particular study, and only those variables should be covered in the questionnaire.

C Questions related to field/topic of investigation

This section contains the questions aimed at investigating the research problem(s) or issue. The order of questions within a section needs to be considered carefully (Mytton 1999:53). Here a funnel structure is mostly used. Funnelling refers to the ordering of questions from the general to the more specific. For example, if you ask 'have you read the *Sowetan* in the past seven days?', your respondent might be startled. It is better to start with a general question on newspaper reading patterns such as 'I want to ask you some questions about newspapers. Do you ever read any newspapers? If yes, which newspaper do you read the most?' From these general questions, you can proceed to more specific questions regarding the reading of particular newspapers.

Another important issue is the length of the questionnaire. The questions included in a questionnaire are determined by the purpose of the study (Mytton 1999:41). The designer of a questionnaire should, however, retain a balance between the number of the questions to be included and the overall length of the questionnaire. If the questions included are too few to explore the research issue(s) sufficiently, the project will fail. The project will, however, also fail if the questionnaire is so long that it wearies out the respondent, the fieldworker, or both. It is therefore not a good idea to 'play it safe' and include everything that might be of relevance. The real skill is to reduce the questionnaire to those questions that are absolutely essential to meet the research objectives. As a general principle, Mytton holds that questionnaires that take longer than a maximum of 45 minutes to administer should be avoided.

10.9 QUALITY MEASURES FOR EVALUATING SURVEYS: RELIABILITY AND VALIDITY

Reliability and validity are central issues in research (Neuman 2006). They represent the yardsticks with which the quality of all kinds of research – quantitative, qualitative or participatory – are evaluated. Discussions on reliability and validity in most textbooks are, however, often more applicable to measuring scales (for example, a number of items measuring the same construct) than to survey studies in general. For instance, it is not practically possible to repeat a questionnaire survey on the same sample to determine the test–retest reliability of a survey study. The following sections contain some notes on reliability and validity pertaining more specifically to questionnaire surveys.

reliability and validity

10.9.1 Reliability

A variety of definitions of reliability can be found in textbooks on research methodology. Neuman (2006) defines reliability simply as dependability or consistency. It suggests that the same measurement or response will be obtained under identical or similar conditions. For example, you get on to your bathroom scale and read your weight. If you get off and get on again a number of times, it should give approximately the same weight each time – assuming, of course, that you have not eaten or drunk anything or changed your clothing. If the measurements are consistent, the bathroom scale can be regarded as a reliable measuring instrument. If not, it is unreliable. All researchers want their measuring instruments (for example, the questions included in a questionnaire), to be reliable and valid. However, it needs to be kept in mind that perfect reliability – as well as perfect validity – is not possible.

Neuman (2006) distinguishes three forms of reliability that are relevant for survey research, namely:
- Stability reliability: does a particular question or item give the same results over time?
- Representative reliability: does a particular question or item give the same results when applied to different groups/samples?
- Equivalence reliability: does a particular question or item give the same results as other indicators measuring the same construct or variable?

Mytton (1999) holds the reliability of a questionnaire survey to be the extent to which a questionnaire yields similar results on different occasions. A question that yields one response from a respondent on one occasion, but a different response from the same respondent on another occasion, might be unreliable. (It needs, however, to be kept in mind that a person's attitudes, for example, could change.) The reliability of a questionnaire survey depends mainly on the rigour of the research design; that is, the sampling procedures, the way that the questionnaires are applied and the wording of questions. Neuman (2006) suggests the following ways in which the reliability of surveys can be enhanced:
- Clearly conceptualise all constructs – each question should address one and only one concept, which implies that ambiguous, clear theoretical definitions should be developed for all issues to be measured.
- Use precise levels of measurement – this principle also implies that

all ambiguity and vagueness in the wording of questions and/or response options should be avoided.
- Use multiple indicators of a variable – for example, a number of items measuring the same construct, such as a matrix scale containing a number of items to measure attitudes towards a country's public broadcaster.
- Use pre-tests and pilot studies to identify defects such as problems with the wording of questions or items.
- Use a probability sampling design to enhance the representative reliability of a survey.
- Ensure that interviewers are thoroughly trained.

There are various ways, some very complex, to test reliability (Mytton 1999). One can use a number of items to measure a particular concept. One can also test a question on the same respondent on different occasions. The problem is, however, that the person can remember what his or her previous answer was. If he or she gives the same response, it could be the result of a good memory rather than the reliability of the question at stake. It is rather through experience that survey researchers learn which questions are likely to yield reliable results. Pilot testing is, however, one of the most important ways in which the reliability of survey questions can be improved.

10.9.2 Validity

Consistency of results, as reflected in reliability, is not enough. A questionnaire can be highly reliable, but still be invalid. Mytton (1999) defines the validity of a survey as that quality of a questionnaire that ensures that what is measured reflects reality. Neuman (2006), on the other hand, relates validity to a specific purpose or definition. A question, scale or questionnaire might be valid for a particular purpose but less valid or invalid for other purposes. In this sense validity also refers to our theoretical and operational definitions of concepts. For example, if a researcher is interested in the public's opinion on violence on television, the theoretical definition of violence will determine how the concept 'violence' is operationalised in the questionnaire. Neuman holds that it is more difficult to achieve validity than reliability.

Five forms of validity as distinguished by Neuman (2006) are particularly relevant to survey research:
- Construct validity: does a question, item or scale measure the construct or issue that it is supposed to measure?

- Face validity: does the question appear to measure the (theoretical or operational) construct or issue that it is supposed to measure?
- Expert validity: do experts within the field agree that the question appears to measure the (theoretical or operational) content or issue that it is supposed to measure?
- Content validity: do I measure the 'full content' of what I should measure: for example, do the response options of a question consider all possible responses to the question? Does a questionnaire measure all areas relevant to the research issue?
- External validity: can I generalise the results to the population?

The validity of survey research can be improved in the following ways (Neuman 2006):

- Do your homework in order to ensure that you cover the issues that are relevant to providing the answers to a particular research problem; study the literature.
- Do explorative research.
- Use a variety of research methods (triangulation), such as focus groups, to assist you with the development of a questionnaire.
- Make use of the judgement of experts, colleagues, peers and/or representatives of the population that you intend to study as you develop your questionnaire.
- Conduct pre-testing and pilot studies.
- Make sure that you take into consideration the particular (cultural) context in which your study will be conducted.
- Use probability sampling designs to enhance the external validity of the survey.

According to Mytton (1999), audience researchers are faced with various validity problems. In measuring radio audiences, for example, different results can be obtained by means of questionnaire surveys and diaries. The question then arises: which is valid, that is, which measurements best reflect reality? It is doubtful that audience researchers will ever be able to answer all the questions related to the validity of various measures obtained by different instruments. It is furthermore highly likely that all measurements are distorted in some or other way. It may, however, not matter too much given that we consistently use the same method of measurement for investigating a particular issue or problem. The distortions will then at least remain consistent over time. That brings us back to Neuman's (2006) definition of validity in terms of

Questionnaire Surveys in Media Research

10.10 SOURCES OF ERROR OR BIAS IN QUESTIONNAIRE SURVEYS

From everyday life we know that, despite careful planning, few things ever operate perfectly (Mytton 1999). This is also true of survey research. All surveys are susceptible to a multitude of sources of error that can lead to distortions or bias in the results. Here we need to repeat what is covered in Chapter 12, namely that the concept 'error' as used in research has a different meaning from the understanding of mistakes in everyday life (Webster et al. 2006). Error as used in social science research refers to the extent to which measurements obtained by means of survey research fail to reflect reality. The concept of 'bias' is often used in conjunction with error. Bias refers to a misrepresentation in what is being measured in a particular direction (Babbie 2001:G1). In the following section we discuss some of the sources of error or bias associated with questionnaire surveys.

error and bias

10.10.1 Sampling error

Sampling error is the degree of error associated with a particular sampling design. It is usually used in connection with the notion of probability sampling designs (Babbie 2001; Nardi 2003). Discussions of sampling error usually refer to so-called 'population parameters' or the exact value of a particular measurement for a particular population: for example, the exact number of the adult South African population that watches a particular television programme. If we could draw a perfect probability sample, we should theoretically be able to calculate the population parameter from the responses to the questionnaire. However, the notion of a perfect probability sample is in practice a mere fiction (Tredoux 2002). In most practical research situations, even the most carefully drawn probability samples are distorted and imperfect reflections of the populations they are supposed to represent. There will consequently almost always be a difference between the true population parameters and the estimations of these parameters obtained from a sample. This difference is called sampling error.

There are, however, ways in which researchers attempt to reduce sampling error and/or to correct for it. Sampling error can be reduced by applying the principles of probability sampling in drawing and executing a sampling design (Nardi 2003). It is furthermore assumed that sampling error is smaller for larger than for smaller samples. Non-response should also be reduced (see section 10.10.2). Researchers sometimes also correct for sampling error by reporting confidence intervals instead of or in addition to the exact values obtained from the sample (see Babbie 2001:193).

10.10.2 Non-response error

The failure to get a valid response on each question in a questionnaire from every selected respondent, that is, non-response error, weakens a questionnaire survey (Neuman 2006). Several sources of nonresponse error can be identified. Sometimes respondents may refuse to answer questions on sensitive issues such as, for example, their monthly income or questions on visiting pornographic websites. Sometimes respondents can simply neglect to complete a questionnaire fully. The consequence can be misleading findings. Other major sources of non-response are associated with the practical implementation of sampling plans. Sometimes a sampled respondent cannot be found; a respondent is not at home or cannot be reached after several attempts; a respondent can be reached but does not fulfil the requirements (for example, age requirement) of the survey; and/or a respondent can refuse to participate in the survey. In South Africa, non-response has become a serious problem, as it is becoming increasingly difficult for fieldworkers to gain entrance to households in higher socioeconomic areas due to security measures such as gated communities, high walls and electrified gates. The magnitude of non-response error in a survey can be estimated by comparing the realised sample size to the sample size in the initial sampling plan and/or inspecting the response rates to specific questions.

Several measures can be taken to reduce non-response error (see Neuman 2006:295-299). Careful consideration should be given to the formulation of questions and response options to sensitive issues. Researchers should furthermore put measures in place to ensure that respondents complete questionnaires fully. A system for replacement should be devised and implemented when a selected respondent cannot be found, does not fulfil the survey requirements or refuses to participate. In household surveys, for example, a household can be replaced with the household to its immediate right or left if an eligible respondent cannot be found at the household initially selected. Respondents may also be more willing to participate if a fieldworker represents their cultural group and is able to speak their home language. Refusals can also be reduced by sending a letter or calling a respondent in advance. The initial contact between the respondent and fieldworker is also important. Delivering a questionnaire personally, instead of leaving it on the doorstep or in a postbox, can also enhance participation. The use of incentives, particularly in postal surveys, can furthermore raise participation rates.

10.10.3 Interviewer effects

The interviewer's tone of voice, body language, posture and the relationship he or she is able to establish with a respondent, especially in the initial contact phase, are all factors that can influence the responses to the questions in a questionnaire. An interviewer can, for example, introduce bias in a survey by introducing his or her own expectations on what the responses to particular question(s) should be or attitudes towards particular issues in a questionnaire interview. Mytton (1999) suggests two ways in which interviewer bias can be reduced. Firstly, the wording of questions should be as neutral as possible to avoid giving the fieldworker, and also the respondent, the impression that certain responses are expected. Fieldworkers should furthermore be thoroughly trained to maintain a critical self-awareness of the dangers of influencing respondents and/or a subjective interpretation of responses. Interviewers should furthermore be trained to treat every respondent with politeness, care and respect despite possible cultural, class or caste differences.

10.10.4 Response bias

Some respondents are prone to responding in a particular way (response set), to give socially desirable responses (the responses that they think the researcher wants), to exaggerate the truth or simply provide false information (Nardi 2003). There are several ways in which a researcher can attempt to avoid response bias in a questionnaire survey. We have already referred to recency effects and the need to vary the order of positive and negative cue words when compiling semantic differential scales (see section 10.8.7). The tendency to lie or to give socially desirable responses can be detected by including so-called 'trap' questions. For example, when asking a question on the newspapers that respondents read, the name of a fictitious newspaper – that is, a newspaper that does not exist – can be included in the list. The same information can also be obtained in different ways. For example, information on the newspapers that respondents read can be obtained by a checklist question as well as by a question with a 'yes'/'no' format. When definite signs of response bias are detected in a number of questionnaires, the researcher can opt to exclude these questionnaires from the overall analysis or to analyse them separately.

10.11 CASE STUDY

The most well-known media survey in South Africa is the All Media and Products Study (AMPS® survey), conducted by the South African Advertising Research Foundation (SAARF). Whereas the nature of this survey is discussed in more detail in section 12.9.1 of Chapter 12 we discuss the SAARF AMPS® here as an example of a large-scale survey that employs complex multi-stage cluster sampling to draw a sample of the heterogeneous and geographically dispersed South African population.

For the 2007A SAARF AMPS®, a total countrywide sample of 24,812 respondents of 16 years or older were interviewed (SAARF sa). All metropolitan and urban areas with a population of 100,000 or more were included in the sample. Within each province, metropolitan areas were listed alphabetically in five strata (or categories) reflecting population size – 40,000 to 99,999; 8000 to 39,999; 4000 to 7999; 500 to 7999 and less than 500 – with their cumulative populations also listed. From each stratum a sample of communities (or clusters) was drawn using systematic sampling, with a standard random starting point and fixed interval technique.

The sample required for rural areas was proportionally allocated to the various provinces and, within each province, to magisterial districts proportional to population size as indicated in the 2006 population estimates (also an example of stratification).

The Nielsen GeoFrame served as the main sampling frame for the selection of households. The Nielsen GeoFrame lists the residential addresses in most (but not all) metropolitan areas and contains 5,983,703 addresses that are arranged alphabetically by suburb and, within each suburb, by streetname. For communities listed in the Nielsen Geoframe, a method of systematic sampling was again followed, by starting from a random start in the sampling frame of addresses in each of the clusters drawn and drawing addresses on the basis of a fixed interval. To simplify fieldwork, one other address was then drawn in the immediate vicinity of each address drawn, to form clusters of two.

For areas not covered in the Nielsen GeoFrame, GPS coordinates were employed to draw households. Within a chosen (drawn) community or magisterial district, a grid was overlaid electronically and coordinates selected on a random basis. These coordinates were provided to the fieldworkers who used GPS devices to guide them to the specific point indicated by the randomly selected coordinates. Clusters of two were again formed by instructing fieldworkers to move three dwellings to the right to select the second respondent to form clusters of two. The final coordinates were captured and used to control for the accuracy of the sample selection.

Each address/household that formed part of the designated sample, was predesignated to provide either a male or a female respondent – in equal proportions. Exceptions were mines, hostels and domestics, where the points were allocated to either males or females. The equal gender proportions are reflected in the final realised sample that consisted of 12,405 male and 12,407 female respondents.

At each selected address, within-household sampling was done by means of a random grid where adults of the designated gender in each household were listed according to their age order. Fieldworkers were instructed to interview the selected individual irrespective of language.

The sampling plan also made provision for replacement or substitution in the case of non-response. Substitution was allowed after a number of unsuccessful calls at a particular address. Alternatively, an individual at the address to right or the left of the address originally selected had to be interviewed. At the substituted address, an individual of 16 years or older had also to be selected by means of the random grid of the same gender as the originally designated respondent.

This sampling plan of the AMPS® survey represents an application of some of the best practices employed in the organisation of large-scale surveys in the rest of the world. However, it also illustrates the unique challenges presented by the complexity of the South African

Media Studies: Volume 3

population and how the sampling plan needed to be adapted to cover both metropolitan and far-off rural areas.

Questionnaires are completed by means of face-to-face interviews in which the responses of respondents are recorded by means of CAPI (see sections 10.7.5 and 10.7.7). Visual prompts in the form of shuffle cards that display the mastheads and logos of newspapers and magazines are furthermore used in the investigation of readership patterns.

SUMMARY

At this stage it should be clear why survey research is not for the fainthearted. Every step of questionnaire surveys presents unique challenges to the researcher. The questionnaire survey is nevertheless a highly versatile tool in the hands of the skilled social science researcher. Most of the skills associated with questionnaire surveys can also be developed by experience and practice. However, questionnaire surveys do not present the final answer for all the research problems and topics in media studies. Questionnaire surveys, for example, cannot offer an in-depth understanding of the unique experiences of individuals and communities of the media. In order to obtain an in-depth and multi-faceted understanding of the relationship between people and the media, the results of questionnaire surveys should be supplemented with the results of other research methods, such as in-depth interviews, ethnography as well as quantitative and qualitative content analysis.

LEARNING ACTIVITIES

1. Formulate five research questions related to your field of interest in media studies that can be investigated by means of survey research.
2. Choose any one of the research questions that you formulated in activity 1. Compile a questionnaire to investigate the research question.
3. Conduct a pilot study to investigate the research question that you chose in activity 2. Follow the following steps:
   - Define the population.
   - Select an availability sample of five respondents to participate in the pilot survey.

- Conduct a self-administered survey among the selected respondents.
- Conduct interviews with the five respondents. Try to determine whether they experienced any problems with the questionnaire.
- Adapt your questionnaire in response to the feedback that you received from respondents in the pilot study.
- Analyse the results of the pilot study by making use of simple frequency tables and graphs.
- Critically evaluate your study.

FURTHER READING

Babbie, E. 1990. *Survey research methods*. Belmont, Calif: Wadsworth.

Babbie, E. 2001. *The practice of social research*. 9th edition. Belmont, Calif: Wadsworth.

Du Plooy, G.M. 2001. *Communication research: Techniques, methods and applications*. Lansdowne: Juta.

Mytton, G. 1999. *Handbook on radio and television audience research*. London: UNICEF and UNESCO.

Neuman, W.L. 2006. *Social research methods: Qualitative and quantitative approaches* (6th edition). Boston: Pearson Education.

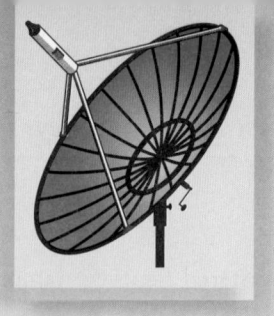

chapter eleven

FIELD RESEARCH IN MEDIA STUDIES

Magriet Pitout

LEARNING OUTCOMES

At the end of this chapter, you should be able to:
- plan and conduct an ethnographic field audience research study by using participant observation, the in-depth interview and document analysis;
- plan and conduct reception research by using the focus-group interview;
- explain the difference between ethnographic and reception research.

THIS CHAPTER

In this chapter, the focus is on field research as one of the main research methods used in media studies to study media audiences, be it television and film viewers, radio listeners, internet users, newspaper and magazine readers, etc. We specifically look at ethnographic research and reception research as two of the main sorts of field research.

Ethnography is one of the fundamental research methods of cultural anthropology and seeks to answer central anthropological questions concerning the ways of life (cultural practices) of human beings. Ethnographic questions generally concern the link between culture and behaviour and/or how cultural processes develop over time. The database for ethnographies is usually extensive description of the details of social life or cultural practices of people, and the data is gathered by means of participant observation, the in-depth interview, focus group interviews and document analysis. Reception research, which also claims to be 'ethnographic', offers an alternative to the long-scale, intensive observation of classic ethnography.

11.1 INTRODUCTION

Field research in media studies falls under the qualitative research paradigm. In this chapter, we discuss ethnography and reception research as qualitative field research methods used in media studies to investigate the relationship between media texts (media messages) and readers (media users) and their understanding and interpretation of messages. 'Qualitative' may also be substituted for 'interpretive', 'critical', 'phenomenological' and 'naturalistic'.

As we discussed in Chapter 9, there exists confusion in the literature about the difference between audience ethnography and reception theory/research. Schroder (1999:42) for example, says that the contemporary ethnographic paradigm to studying media audiences includes both reception research and more genuinely ethnographic approaches. Alasuutari (1999:4) goes even further and claims that a few reception studies (see examples in section 11.4 of this chapter) paved the way for a gradual shift away from the audience reception paradigm to the new audience ethnography paradigm. In addition, Wimmer and Dominick (1997:106) refer to ethnography as a special kind of qualitative research where a variety of qualitative research techniques – field observation (participant observation), in-depth and focus group interviews and case studies – are utilised.

Ethnography as applied by audience reception researchers, especially those belonging to the cultural studies approach, has lost a great deal of the precision it once had. However, its claim to ethnographic status in studying media audiences reminds us of its anthropological roots. These roots are reflected in the assumptions of both classic ethnography and reception research (see Chapter 9). To summarise these assumptions: the researcher goes to the field where the action is happening and spends considerable time with the group he or she wants to observe. Researchers strive to see events in the field through the viewpoint or frame of reference of the people being observed and they (the researchers) use qualitative research techniques to record the data. Although reception researchers do not live for *long periods of time with the culture being observed* we regard reception research as a qualitative research method that, like 'classic' ethnography, uses field research techniques, as we discuss in the next section.

11.2 FIELD RESEARCH TECHNIQUES

The most important field research techniques used in media ethnography and reception research are participant observation, the in-depth interview, document analysis and the focus group interview. Although the focus group interview has not initially been used in the first long-scale studies of ethnography, we include this interview as a field research technique because of its popularity with reception researchers and its increased use in ethnography.

Let us explain the application of these field research techniques by means of the following example: you want to research the 2008 management crisis in the SABC, when Group CEO of the SABC, Dali Mpofu, dismissed Snuki Zikalala, group executive of news and current affairs in May 2008. Mpofu claimed that Zikalala was responsible for leaking sensitive documents to the personnel of the SABC. The following day, Mpofu was himself suspended by the SABC board with immediate effect because he failed to implement decisions made by the board (Sapa, 2008). Let us say you are commissioned to investigate this crisis using field research techniques. First of all, you will have to get permission from top management (the gatekeepers) to observe (participant observation) for a period of time how the SABC board functions according to internal

Field Research in Media Studies

and external policies, the rules and regulations guiding the composition of the board, what the procedures are to fire members of the board, the CEO and the executive of news programmes. You may also conduct in-depth interviews with Mpofu and Zikalala, and individual members of the board. To get the necessary information to guide your participant observation and to conduct your in-depth interviews, relevant bills and documents could also be analysed. You may also conduct focus group interviews with the personnel of the SABC to determine how they feel about the dismissal of Zikalala and Mpofu and the actions of the SABC board.

In the next section, we discuss the planning of participant observation in more detail.

11.2.1 Participant observation

Like all forms of research, participant observation needs careful and flexible planning because without a well-constructed plan of what our research entails we will soon drift into confusion. Firstly, we have to state our research problem/question and define the audience (group) we want to observe.

Step 1: Formulating the research problem/question

Formulating the research problem/question will help us to focus on what we want to achieve. Although the research question may change as the research progresses – and this happens often – this may lead to insightful breakthroughs in research. Guiding research questions are aimed at the basic point of ethnography: gaining the world-view of a group of people. To guide the formulation of a research question/ research problem, we may ask: what do we want to find out? Who are the people we need to observe and talk to?

> research problem/ research question

A good example of how to formulate a research problem is case study 11.1, where Lemish (1985) conducted an ethnographic investigation, over a period of more than nine months, of the soap-opera viewing patterns of college students at Ohio State University in the United States. The aim of her study was to examine a particular subaudience (or a subcultural group) of soap viewers in specific viewing situations, namely college students who view soaps in public college locations (context of viewing).

Ethnographers may also choose a field site first and then make a guiding question appropriate to the site. Or start with a question about a certain cultural process and find a site where that question might be appropriate. Both approaches for setting up a project can work, as long as the site and the research problem/question are relevant to one another. Let us look again at the example of Lemish's problem formulation: she conducted her investigation at Ohio State University to observe students' soap-opera viewing patterns in public college venues, as she stated in the research problem.

Step 2: Entry to research site

The first traditional anthropological research took place in small villages (research sites) where ethnographers lived among the village's relatively few inhabitants. Under these circumstances, a lack of knowledge of the native language could initially be a barrier – think, for example, of the problems a Tswana- or English-speaking researcher may encounter when he or she observes Zulu-speaking people living in a remote village, to determine media usage patterns like cellular phones, radio, television, and so on. However, today field sites can be nearly anywhere and participant observation increasingly takes place in urban locations and in the mother tongue of the researcher (observer). In other words, the group whom we want to observe does not necessarily have to live in one location (a township, a suburb, a village etc.). Therefore our main site could be the workplace (like a bank, or a factory) or a religious centre (like a church) or a school, family home, or even in cyberspace (like a chatroom). For instance, if we want to study the group dynamics involved when journalists select news items for their newspaper, we will have to go to the place – the newsroom – where the actual selection usually takes place. In the case of Lemish (case study 11.1) she observed the students in the sport lounge and recreation centre where the actual television viewing – soap-opera viewing – took place.

| open and closed locations

To get entry to a research site, we distinguish between *open* and *closed* locations. Open locations can usually be entered by the public: for example, shopping malls, sports events, restaurants, cinemas, theatres, and so on. And we usually do not have to ask permission to enter these public venues. For example, if we want to study the cellphone use of teenagers in public places – such as a restaurant or shopping centre – we can merely take the role of a 'fly on the wall' (see step 3 below).

Field Research in Media Studies

That is, we observe without asking for permission to do so and without participating actively.

Closed locations, on the other hand, imply conditional entry because we must first ask permission to enter. For example, when a researcher wants to investigate the electronic media usage patterns of schoolchildren in a hostel or at home, he or she first has to ask permission from the relevant authorities and gatekeepers to access these venues over a period of time. We must explain the purpose of our research, what access we require and who or what we want to observe, the time we anticipate we will spend on location and possible disturbances our research may cause. No matter which location we need to enter, we must be honest and open about our objectives as well as the possibility of the inconvenience our research may engender.

<small>closed locations: negotiate entry with gatekeepers</small>

Deacon et al. (1999) quite correctly observe that it is indeed ironic that the majority of the elements of mass communication (from the production of media messages to the consumption thereof by audiences) that need to be studied by means of ethnography are closed for observation. Therefore, we must negotiate entry to these premises. Even if we want to do observations at discos and cinemas, which in principle are open to the public, an entrance fee must be paid and not all researchers – especially when there is a big age gap – can easily remain inconspicuous in a teenage disco crowd. The next step is to decide which roles we shall take as observers.

Step 3: Decide on roles of observers: overt and covert

When we enter premises, we must decide whether we will adopt an overt or covert role. When we adopt an overt (open) role, the people being observed are aware of our status as researchers and the purpose of our study. Alternatively we can observe under cover or as a 'fly on the wall' – then our roles as researchers are covert (our identities remain a secret) and the participants do not know that they are being observed.

<small>overt roles

covert roles – 'fly on the wall'</small>

We have already said that conducting research in public places does not pose any problems with regard to entrance. However, public places do not really have much use for communication researchers, because very few of the communication activities we want to investigate are in public places. Yes, we can indeed observe nonverbal behaviour in a queue, or teenagers' behaviour at rave parties, but if we do not have a very good reason for doing so, it becomes 'so what' research. Merely observing teenagers' behaviour will not give us enough information about the reasons they attend rave parties, for example, or why they prefer certain music genres (e.g. hard rock, kwaito) or why and how they use MXit on their cellular phones. We will thus have to combine our covert role with follow-up studies of participant observation, in-depth interviews and focus groups at the primary site – the home, school or wherever they use their cellphones.

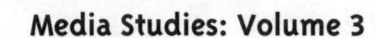

concealed observation

Although the most common type of ethnographic observation is *overt research* in *closed locations*, we do find examples of ethnographic research (mainly in disciplines such as the social sciences) that have in the past been conducted under cover (covert research). Such instances occur because researchers have established over the years that one way to understand a 'problematic' cultural sub-unit (e.g. street children, prostitutes, those involved with Satanism) is to go to the places where cultural groups live, or that they frequent. One of the main problems is to gain entry to subcultural groups because if we reveal our identity as researchers, group members may become distrustful.

undercover research

Furthermore, certain contexts are dangerous to enter. In such cases, we can enter the premises under cover, that is, we conceal our roles as researchers, become a member of the group and participate actively in their daily activities.

An example of undercover observation is where the researcher wants to investigate the professional practices of journalists. The researcher can pretend to be a journalist (with permission of the editor) to experience the research problem first-hand. After gathering sufficient information the researcher should then debrief the journalists. That is, the researcher tells the journalists that they have been observed for research purposes and asks their permission to use the results for publication in a research journal. Undercover observation involves the following ethical issues.

Ethical issues in undercover field observation

debriefing interview

Undercover research has major ethical implications because researchers are faced with a dilemma – is it ethical to deceive people we are studying? One way out is to use a debriefing interview. *Debriefing* means that we inform participants that they have been observed without their knowledge; we explain the importance of our study and ask their permission to use the data for research purposes. We should also give the participants the assurance that they are entitled to have access to the outcomes of the research project.

Another ethical issue is that although participant observation allows us to build up a relationship of trust, which then enables us to obtain first-hand information, we should be careful that we do not intrude on people's privacy – peering over people's shoulders, or perching on their desks, workspaces or when they perform rituals, asking embarrassing questions that can make group members uncomfortable. Unfortunately there are no hard-and-fast rules about how to handle such problems. The golden rule is to 'read the situation' and be sensitive; to back off when we observe that people are becoming embarrassed (Deacon et al. 1999:248).

Variation in observation: full participant or onlooker?

We have mentioned several times that the researcher must become actively involved in participant observation. But is it always possible and necessary? This brings us to the degree of involvement of the researcher. According to Genzuk (2000), the extent to which it is possible for a researcher to become a full participant in an observation will depend partly on the nature of the setting being observed. For example, in the observation of how children interact and react to child educational television programmes, it is not possible for the researcher to become a learner and therefore experience the setting as a child; it may be possible, however, for the research observer to participate as a parent, volunteer or staff person in such a setting and thereby develop the perspective of an insider in one of these adult roles. Experiencing an environment as an insider is what necessitates the participant part of participant observation. At the same time, however, there is clearly an observer side to this process. The challenge is to combine participation and partial observation so as to become capable of understanding the experience as an insider while describing the experience for outsiders. With reference to the above example (how children experience and interpret educational television programmes), the researcher will have to observe the situation for at least three months to make sure that other variables do not play a role: for instance, fatigue, absence from school for a period of time, or first or second language use, which may influence the children's comprehension of messages.

degrees of involvement

Sampling

sampling

Sampling in participant observation is more ambiguous than in any other of the field research approaches (Wimmer & Dominick 1997:93–4). The main problems are, firstly, how many people or groups to observe, and secondly, what behaviour should be observed. The researcher cannot be everywhere and see everything. We may choose from different forms of non-probability sampling to recruit participants (see section 11.2.4, step 2 for discussion of non-probability sampling in field research). According to Wimmer and Dominick (1997) purposive sampling is used most often in field observation because researchers' knowledge is based on their familiarity with the subjects, and they then sample only the appropriate behaviour or events to be observed. For example, when observing newsroom decision-making processes, staff meetings are important components of the decision-making process. However, other important informal places where decisions are made are the lounge, tea room and even the hallways – all these should also be considered and observed.

Once researchers have passed the hurdle of sampling and getting into the field of observation they must become involved in group activities to become part of the group's inner circle, which will help them to understand the group.

Inside the field we must decide what forms of data collection techniques/devices (field notes, tape recorders, video cameras) we will use to record data. We discuss these techniques below, and illustrate them with examples from media research.

Step 4: Data collection techniques

Field notes

One of the most important data collection techniques in participant observation (in fact, all audience field research techniques) is field notes. Therefore we must learn how to take useful and reliable field notes to assist our field observation because these notes make up a major part of the data on which later conclusions will be based. First-hand information implies immediacy. When we are at the primary research site, we actually witness events happening and therefore cannot rely on our memories – we know how fallible memories of events can be! Notes should thus be written down soon after leaving the field site – immediately, if possible. In the case of observing the newsroom decision-making processes, the researcher may take discreet notes while attending staff room meetings because note-taking is quite natural when attending meetings. However, when listening to what journalists say and discuss in informal settings like the hallway, staff room or wherever they hang out, the researcher has to listen carefully and go to a private place – empty office, rest room – to jot down impressions and summarise conversations.

Chiseri-Strater and Sunstein (1997) have developed a list of what should be included in all field notes:

WRITING FIELD NOTES

- Date, time, and place of observation
- Sensory impressions: sights, sounds, textures, smells, tastes
- Jottings: keep a notebook and pen with you at all times. Jot down noteworthy interactions and quotes when possible. Jottings are intended to help you to remember things you want to include when you write the full-fledged notes. While not all research situations are appropriate for writing jottings all the time, they do help a great deal when sitting down to write afterwards.
- Note-taking should be done as unobtrusively as possible because feverish note-taking can be distracting.
- Make descriptions of everything you can remember about the incidence you are writing about – a meal, a ritual, a meeting, a sequence of events, etc. While it is useful to focus primarily on things you did or observed that relate to the guiding question, some general information may also help to link related phenomena to one another or to point out useful research directions later.
- Type up a detailed version of your notes for future analysis. Fill in the gaps in your field notes by reading the keywords and fully explaining the situation you observed. Use code names for the people you observed to protect their identities.
- Analyse what you have learned in the setting regarding your guiding research question and other related points. For example: what themes can you begin to identify regarding your guiding question? What questions do you have to help focus your observation on subsequent visits? Can you begin to draw preliminary connections or potential conclusions based on what you learned?

- Reflect on what you have learned of a personal nature. For example, what was it like for you to be doing this research? What felt comfortable for you about being in this site and what felt uncomfortable? In what ways did you connect with informants, and in what ways didn't you? While this is extremely important information, be especially careful to separate it from analysis.

Tape recorders and video cameras

recording devices

In addition to field notes, we may use recording devices such as tape recorders and video cameras; however, we should first ask the participants' permission to use these devices. In case of a tape recorder, we should use it as unobtrusively as possible in order not to disturb the natural flow of a conversation. Before starting with the interview we must make sure that the tape recorder works and that we exactly know how to use it. Say, for example, we want to record in-depth interviews with journalists, managers or any other person involved; we should first ask their permission to use a tape recorder. Video cameras also provide additional information regarding our research topic. For example, using video cameras can highlight facial expressions and body language (nonverbal communication), which will add another dimension and interpretation of verbal expressions.

Step 5: Data analysis

(See section 11.3 for a discussion of data analysis of field research.)

To supplement our participant observation, we may also use in-depth interviews, the analysis of various documents and the focus group interview.

11.2.2 In-depth interview

in-depth interview

The in-depth interview (also called the intensive and qualitative interview) is used frequently in field research. When using this interview, we talk with separate participants on a one-to-one basis. If, for example, we need extra information of a personal nature, such as why a person is not participating in the decision-making process when selecting news in the newsroom, we may conduct an in-depth interview. Being alone with the researcher creates an atmosphere of trust where the respondent can elaborate on personal feelings, recollections and opinions. Because

Field Research in Media Studies

building up a relationship of trust may be very time-consuming, researchers should allow for enough time to conduct the interview, which may last for longer than two hours. Researchers should also make sure that the setting is conducive for an uninterrupted interview. Nothing is more disturbing and disruptive than people popping in or telephones ringing. For instance, should we conduct an in-depth interview with one of the journalists involved in the decision-making process we may conduct the interview in a private place, such as an empty office or restaurant, to limit interruptions.

Usually no standard questions are compiled beforehand, because each individual is unique and researchers base their questions on the answer of each participant. However, the main research problem/question should be kept in mind and be probed further. Hake (2003:35–6), for example, investigated the way five-year-olds reconstruct and interpret a television story. After showing the children the television programme, Hake conducted qualitative (in-depth) interviews with each child by asking them questions, such as, 'tell me about the story you have just watched. What is it all about?' By asking open-ended questions the children were allowed to freely reconstruct the story. This enabled Hake to uncover children's fascination with the story.

The following are some guidelines when conducting an in-depth interview (see Patton 1987; Terre Blanche et al. 2006).

GUIDELINES FOR IN-DEPTH INTERVIEWING

- Start the interview with a summary of what the interview is about – but it should be short. And do not start with sensitive questions.
- Throughout all phases of interviewing, from planning through data collection to analysis, the purpose of the ethnographic research should guide the interviewing process.
- The fundamental principle of in-depth interviewing is to provide a safe and trusting environment within which participants can express their own understandings in their own terms.
- Be aware of the different kinds of information one can collect through interviews: behavioural data, opinions, feelings, knowledge and background information.
- Ask truly open-ended questions.

Media Studies: Volume 3

- Questions should be clear and unambiguous, using appropriate and understandable language.
- Ask one question at a time and allow the participant to formulate his or her answer.
- Do not interrupt the interviewee when he or she is giving an answer.
- Use probes and follow-up questions to solicit depth and detail.
- Avoid leading questions and communicate clearly what information is desired, why that information is important, and let the interviewee know how the interview is progressing.
- Listen attentively and respond appropriately to let the person know he or she is being heard.
- Know the difference between an in-depth interview and an interrogation. Ethnographers conduct in-depth interviews while members of the police conduct interrogations!
- Establish personal rapport and a sense of mutual interest. However, remain neutral towards the content and the answers of the interviewee – you are conducting an interview to collect information, not to make judgements
- Observe while interviewing. Be aware of, and sensitive to, how the person is affected by and responds to different questions. Jot down notes about nonverbal reactions such as hand movements, dry mouth, smile, tears or any other nonverbal reactions that could shed light on verbal answers.
- Make sure that you are in control of the interview. Should the interviewee wander off, steer him or her discreetly back to the topic under discussion.
- Tolerate silences – sometimes interviewees need time to think about their answers.
- Tape record whenever possible to capture full and exact quotations for analysis and reporting.
- Take discreet notes to capture and highlight major points as the interview progresses.
- As soon as possible after the interview, check the recording for malfunctions; review notes for clarity; elaborate where necessary; and record observations.
- Take whatever steps are appropriate and necessary to gather valid and reliable information.
- Treat the person being interviewed with respect. Keep in mind that it is a privilege and responsibility to peer into another person's experience.
- Practise interviewing. Develop your skills.

Field Research in Media Studies

- 'Enjoy interviewing. Take the time along the way to stop and "hear" the roses.' (Patton 1987)

Apart from gathering data by means of field notes and the in-depth interview, we can also analyse various documents related to the research problem.

11.2.3 Document analysis

When available, documents can add additional insight or information to projects. There are two types of documents available – public and private. Public documents include advertisements, budgets, work descriptions, annual reports, memos, brochures, teaching materials, newsletters, websites, contracts, records of court proceedings, posters, minutes of meetings, laws, policy documents, and so on. Private documents may include life stories of participants, diaries, home movies, appointment books and faxes (Wimmer & Dominick 1997:95–6). Hammersley and Atkins (1995) refer to an example of how Jhuma Chaudhuri used *official (public) documents* – posters, brochures – to supplement her ethnographic study of how an organisation portrays and creates awareness of HIV and Aids: Chaudhuri took note of the variety of posters in the office that portrayed messages about the HIV virus and people suffering from Aids. She also collected informational brochures distributed but not produced by the organisation, as well as a questionnaire produced by agency staff regarding quality-of-life issues for local HIV-positive individuals. These documents added to her understanding of what she learned through participant observation and in-depth interviews with regard to her main interest: how the organisation socially constructs HIV and Aids.

document analysis

The use of the analysis of *private documents* is illustrated by the reception research of Pitout (1995) who analysed letters (private documents) written by soap fans to the *Egoli* fan club. This analysis enabled Pitout to identify themes related to the research problem of how viewers interpret the messages in *Egoli*, a popular multicultural soap in South Africa. The themes identified were identification, romantic association, para-social interaction, social interaction and *Egoli* as a cultural forum for the portrayal of South African realities. She used themes to guide the focus group interviews she conducted with selected participants (viewers of *Egoli*).

When doing field research, we should keep in mind that privacy or

497

copyright issues may apply to some of the public documents we gather. It is therefore important to enquire about this when we use official documents. Should we receive permission to publish these documents they should be acknowledged and included in the bibliography of the final paper (Hammersley & Atkins 1995).

11.2.4 The focus group interview

focus groups

The focus group is becoming an increasingly popular tool in the study of media audiences: for example, to determine a group of viewers attitudes and perceptions of South African television news programmes, such as *e.tv*, in comparison to the presentation of news on SABC channels; or how different cultural groups perceive and interpret locally produced South African drama series; or to determine listeners, attitudes and perceptions of the change in programme format of a radio station; or to determine the popularity of Facebook on the internet.

Where the in-depth interview allows us to understand the subjective experience of a participant, focus group interviews allow us to gain access to intersubjective experiences of a group of people of a community (Terre Blanche et al. 2005:304). The focus group interview thus allows us to interview a group of people – typically composed of six to 12 members – who are selected because they have certain characteristics in common that relate to the topic of investigation. The focus group is led by a moderator (discussion leader) who promotes interaction between members and makes sure that the discussion remains on the topic of interest (Krueger 1994; Stewart & Shamdasani 1990).

Focus groups are particularly useful when we conduct exploratory research where little is known about our topic of interest: for example, when

- identifying problems that media audience members have with the content of a particular newspaper or problems employees may have with communication channels in the organisations they are working for, or the popularity of television programmes (e.g. soaps) and the role this genre plays in soap fans' lives;
- determining why children play video games and the possible effect of video games on them;
- determining media audience members' attitudes, perceptions, frames of reference and media usage (viewing, reading, listening) patterns.

Guidelines on how to design a focus group study

The following five steps are involved when designing a focus group interview:

Step 1: Determine the number and composition of a focus group interview

To compose a group, we should keep in mind that a focus group is characterised by homogeneity, but with sufficient variation among the members of the group to elicit contrasting opinions. In general, we look for homogeneity in terms of variables such as age, gender, education, family characteristics, or use of a particular mass medium. The guiding principle in the composition of a group is the degree to which the above variables will influence participation within the group discussion. Research findings indicate that certain combinations do not work well, and we must therefore exercise care when combining these groups (Krueger 1994:77–8; Stewart & Shamdasani 1990:51–2):

- Individuals from different lifestyles and life stages should be carefully considered because combining, for example, young working women with mature homemakers who have never been employed outside the home might create problems. However, if the topic or research problem clearly cuts across these lifestyles and life stages, then these two groups can be combined. For instance, when we want to determine views about advertisements of household products (e.g. soap powder), we may combine working women with homemakers because the majority of women use soap powder to do their washing. Because of changing roles of gender, men may also be included to evaluate soap powder. In the case of using focus groups in ethnography, one should carefully consider the role of seniority in the cultural group being investigated.
- The mixing of gender in focus groups can sometimes create problems, especially if the topic is experienced differently by each gender. Furthermore, there is a tendency for some men to speak more frequently and with more authority when in the company of women. This is called the 'peacock effect', and can irritate the women in the group, which in turn can have a negative effect on the research. Again, we should be culturally sensitive towards gender roles in a cultural group being investigated.
- The combination of husband and wife in the same focus group does not

work well because there is a tendency for one spouse to dominate the discussion while the other remains silent or is reluctant to comment even when such comments are solicited from the discussion leader (moderator).
- A group composed of parents and children will produce a different type of discussion than one group of parents and a separate group of children. The same applies to combining highly skilled people with novices; or technically skilled with non-technical people – the presence of skilled people may inhibit the participation of the rest of the group.

The above discussion may create the impression that different genders, ages, occupations or family members should not be combined in a group discussion. Though these variables should always be taken into consideration, in some situations it is desirable to use a group made up of a mixture of people, such as viewers of a television channel and the programme managers of that channel, or readers and non-readers of a particular newspaper. The way we compose our focus groups will be determined by the purpose, main problem and subproblems of our research, for example:
- To determine employees' communication channel preferences, will it be necessary to conduct separate focus groups with male and female employees?
- Should we distinguish between race and age when determining communication channel preferences?

pilot study

If we are in doubt regarding the membership of a focus group, we should first conduct a pilot study and take the preliminary findings as guidelines to determine the selection and composition of focus group members. A pilot study refers to the pre-testing or pre-study of a topic, which allows us to identify mistakes and problems which can be rectified before we begin with our actual research.

We can follow the same procedure when we want to determine the opinions and feelings of people about sensitive issues, such as radio programmes and newspaper articles dealing with the prevention of Aids. In such cases, we should, for example, take cultural differences into consideration. However, to test the assumption that different cultural, gender and age groups also differ in their perception of Aids, we must first conduct a pilot focus group interview consisting of one cultural

Field Research in Media Studies

group (e.g. consisting of only men or women or blacks or whites) and ask them if they would mind taking part in a focus group interview that will be composed of different cultural, gender and age groups. If we notice that people are hesitant to talk about sensitive issues, we may then consider the in-depth interview where responses are more private.

To summarise, the kind of questions we are faced with include: do we have to take into consideration variables such as age, income, living conditions, race or differences in language preferences? We should remember that composition of groups is not a haphazard exercise. We must therefore anticipate (or determine by means of pilot studies) the impact of the way a group is composed before recruiting participants. Furthermore, we should take care that the characteristics of members of any given focus group are consistent with the objective of the study. This implies that the objective, main problem and subproblems to be investigated must be established clearly and at a very early stage of the research project.

After the population parameters (characteristics such as age, gender, etc.) have been established for the composition of each group, the next step in focus group research is to sample the target population, that is, to recruit participants.

Step 2: Recruit participants (sampling)

Because focus groups consist of a small number of participants per group (between six and 12 participants) we need to define a narrow audience for the study, keeping in mind that data gathered by means of focus groups cannot be generalised beyond the members of the groups to a larger population. Therefore, Stewart and Shamdasani (1990:20) suggest that the sample needs only be a good approximation of the population of interest: for example, people (e.g. members of a rural community) who have access only to a specific form of mass communication (e.g. the radio) or elderly people living in old-age homes, who have access to one communal television set and cannot exercise a choice of programme selection.

sampling

Possible forms of non-probability sampling to recruit participants are as follows:

non-probability sampling

- *Available sampling* (also called convenience sampling) is used when we collect respondents amongst a readily accessible group of people. For example, we want to determine the viability of a new radio music programme for teenagers. We can go to a high school that is conveniently situated near our offices, and recruit learners (with permission from the relevant authorities) of that school until our sample reaches the desired size, that is, until we have enough respondents to make up two or three focus groups (6–12 respondents per group).

- We use *volunteer sampling* when we ask people to participate voluntarily in a research project. For instance, if we want readers to evaluate an article in a newspaper containing explicit portrayal of victims of violent crime, we can place an advertisement in the newspaper and ask for volunteers who have read the article to participate in our research project. We may then use the first 24 respondents and divide them in two to three focus groups.
- When using *purposive sampling*, we base our selection on respondents who share specific characteristics or qualities and eliminate those who do not fulfil the requirements (Wimmer & Dominick 1997). Suppose we want to determine how Indians (18 to 35 years of age) in South Africa perceive media messages dealing with the prevention of Aids, we select only Indians (and no other cultural group) between 18 and 35 years old. Because of the reasons mentioned above (for instance, the influence of gender), we should conduct separate focus groups with Indian men and women, except of course if we can establish beforehand (e.g. by means of a pilot study) whether female respondents will not be inhibited by the presence of their male counterparts.

Step 3: Determine the location

location

When using the focus group interview, we may conduct the interview where the actions are happening or at locations close to the participants' workplaces or homes because then they are more likely to participate. Say, for example, we want to determine employees' attitudes towards the use of e-mails instead of circulars in the communication of decisions taken by top management, focus group interviews may be conducted during office hours at the workplace. On the other hand, if we want to determine newspaper readers' opinions about the way a specific newspaper reports on political events, we may consider conducting the interviews over a weekend in a community centre or any other venue that is convenient for the participants (respondents).

Step 4: Prepare the study mechanisms and focus group material

This step includes decisions regarding the type of recording apparatus to be used and the remuneration that participants will receive for their participation. Say, for example, you want to question a group of newspaper readers about a newspaper's reportage on crime in South Africa. You could offer to pay each participant a certain amount of money (say R200 per session) or present them with a gift (a bottle of whisky or whatever) and also provide lunch and refreshments.

recording apparatus

Guidelines to help us in our planning before conducting the actual focus group interviews are as follows:
- decide which recording devices will be used: for example, field notes, tape recorders, pen and paper and/or video cameras;
- prepare a pre-group questionnaire that participants are required to complete before the start of the focus group interview;
- prepare a moderator (interview) guide that contains the topics to be addressed during the focus group interview. For example, when we want to research which radio station listeners prefer to be informed about important community matters, we can make a list of all the possible radio stations and ask the participants to evaluate and discuss each.

The existence of a moderator guide does not mean that we cannot ask questions that are not in the guide. One advantage of focus groups is that this method allows us to deviate from the guide, as groups sometimes take on lives of their own. In such instances, the agendas are dictated by the natural flow of the discussions. A moderator guide is just that – a guide to address issues pertaining to the research problem. The moderator and group members should be allowed to modify the agenda if it proves desirable to resolving the initial problem.

For example, when the moderator observes that employees of a company are not in favour of e-mail messages, he or she can probe for further information. By means of probing, the moderator can, for instance, establish that the main reason why e-mail is not regarded as a suitable communication channel is that it is being used by colleagues and management as a vehicle to fight personal battles. Consequently, employees ignore e-mail messages and therefore miss out on important messages about managerial decisions.

Step 5: Conducting the focus group session

_{conducting interviews}

We always begin the actual focus group interview with an explanation of the purpose of the research project. To put the participants at ease and to create a warm, friendly atmosphere, we can explain the following points: that there are no right or wrong answers; that they (the participants) may differ from one another in their views regarding a topic; that the session is being recorded and ask their permission for recording the data; that they should regard the discussion as an informal gathering and they should not hesitate to speak without being invited (Wimmer & Dominick 1997).

When we act as moderators, we should exercise self-discipline. For instance, we must withhold our personal opinions and refrain from being sarcastic towards, or critical of, participants. The latter is particularly important if we are faced with participants such as the

- *expert* – some people in a group consider themselves experts because they have considerable experience about the topic under discussion;
- *dominant talker* – people in a group who regard themselves as experts, with more experiences, or who have a higher educational qualification and who tend to answer on behalf of other participants;
- *rambler* – participants who never get to the point and drone on and on, wasting valuable time.

For the novice moderator (which no doubt applies to the majority of us), conducting a focus group may seem a daunting task. Fortunately, interviewing improves with practice and experience. We can, for instance, practise on a group of friends, fellow students or even family members.

In the next section, we discuss the transcription, analysis and interpretation of data when using field research techniques such as focus groups, in-depth interviews and participant observation.

11.3 TRANSCRIBING, ANALYSING AND INTERPRETING FIELD RESEARCH DATA

_{transcription}

Field research produces an overwhelming amount of data. For example, a single focus group and in-depth interview could produce 10 to 15 pages of field notes combined with 30 to 60 pages of transcripts. The question is, how do we analyse and interpret this data? First we look at the different strategies that can be used to transcribe in-depth and focus group interviews.

- *Transcript-based strategy.* The first strategy is to transcribe the entire interview. A complete transcription not only provides us with a basis for further analysis, but also establishes a permanent record of the interviews (focus group and in-depth) that can be shared with other interested parties. The transcriptions may be edited to increase readability. For example, half-finished sentences, nonsensical thoughts or inaudible voices on the tape may be omitted. However, it is important that the character of participants' answers be maintained – even if they sound confused or use poor sentence construction and grammar. Since one of the aims of a focus group and in-depth interview is to learn how people talk and think about a topic, too much editing of a transcript should be avoided.
- *Tape-based strategy.* This type of strategy means that we transcribe an interview in its entirety (just like transcript-based analysis) but summarise the transcriptions for further analysis. Thus, instead of using participants own words, we summarise the main points and present the results in the form of summaries of the main themes.
- *Note-based strategy.* With this strategy we do not tape-record the interviews but make notes of conversations during the sessions. In the case of a focus group interview, we may ask someone (a colleague or friend) to assist with note-taking because it is sometimes difficult to make meaningful notes and to conduct or guide the interviews at the same time, especially when a group consists of more than six participants.
- *Memory-based strategy.* This strategy means that we do not tape-record or make notes of the interviews but rely solely on our memories. After the completion of the focus group and in-depth interviews, the researcher writes a summary of the main findings. However, this strategy can only be used if we have excellent memories! And we all know how fallible memory can be. Therefore, this analytical strategy should not be attempted, especially by novice moderators.

Once the transcriptions have been completed (irrespective of the strategy being used) we can analyse the data further. The analysis of field data consists mainly of filing and analysing the content of our field notes and recorded interviews. Filing involves the arranging of transcriptions of interviews and our field notes in an orderly way: for example, by using categories. The types of categories will depend on the research problem and the type of data we have collected. Lemish, for example, used the

content analysis

following categories to analyse her data (case study 11.1): needs being satisfied by watching soaps (entertainment, relaxation, excitement); and social context of television with emphasis on social group formation (leaders, followers, observers and challengers). Another example is Hake (2003:37–8), whose research illustrates the use of the following categories to analyse the data regarding the way children interpret television stories: *focus* (most important aspects of story children focus on); *understanding* (children describing the main flow of the story line and understanding cause–effect relationships between events); *identification* (the events and persons who arouse emotional involvement and emotional identification).

data analysis

The following hints may also be useful to arrange and interpret ethnographic data analytically (Hammersley & Atkins 1995; Pitout 1996; Wimmer & Dominick 1997; Terre Blanche et al. 2003. Also compare these suggestions with case study 11.1):

- Study field notes, interview notes, interview transcripts, selected documents, or any other data that has been gathered a number of times. The more familiar we become with the information, the easier it will be to analyse and categorise the data.
- Be on the lookout for patterns, connections and similarities. Mark the data and take notes on any patterns, connections, similarities and contradictions. All these will help to establish categories for analysis.
- To help the coding process, Hammersley and Atkins (1995) advise using a computer-assisted data analysis program like Nud/ist or Ethnograph. We should see the computer lab TA for assistance in getting started. But in the end we must look for local categories of meaning in the data. Do the participants have local terms for things? Can we identify certain ritualistic behaviour? Is it possible to identify certain themes even if the participants cannot? We should always keep the main aim of ethnography in mind, which is to elicit the 'native points of view'; these 'local categories' are the components of the ways of life of those being observed.
- Also look at different theoretical perspectives to come up with explanations of patterns of behaviour; for example reception theory (see Chapter 9); uses and gratifications theory (see case study 11.1); Roland Barthes's narrative theory, to study children's acquaintance with the narrative codes of television (Rydin 2003:77–8), and so on.
- To enhance the validity and reliability of ethnographic data, we may

use triangulation among the different various forms of data gathered; that is, if an explanation or point appears repeatedly across the results of different methods you have used. If, for example, a point can be supported by in-depth and focus group interviews, field notes and documents, then you can be confident that you have found something fundamental to contribute to your understanding of the research problem/question. See for example how Lemish (case study 11.1) used triangulation to increase the validity of her research.

To interpret the results, we may summarise the most important findings under the different categories we have identified. Hake (2001:39), for instance, summarises the category *Focus* as follows:

> *In the reconstruction of both programmes (television programmes, Beethoven and Spot – author) a clear majority of the children focused explicitly on themes such as problem solving, coping, succeeding and working hard to be competent ... (T)he children identified with the Spot character as the hero; he succeeds. Spot finds solutions before the adults manage to do so, and he receives praise. Beethoven wins and gets his way. ... Beethoven ... is a story about solidarity, friendship and helpfulness in a difficult situation ...*

In the last section of this chapter we briefly discuss the evolution of reception research, and the differences and similarities between classic ethnographic and reception research.

11.4 RECEPTION RESEARCH AND MEDIA ETHNOGRAPHY

In section 11.1 we referred to the debate about whether reception research is indeed 'ethnographic', as many supporters of reception research claim. Historically, the first reception research was done on the popularity of romantic serials, such as the soap opera genre (Hobson 1991; Liebes & Katz 1990; Ang 1985). These studies became known as qualitative, or first generation, audience reception studies. During this phase, researchers mainly conducted focus group interviews to determine how particular audiences interpret popular television programmes, such as soaps and sitcoms.

These small-scale first generation reception studies paved the way for the ethnographic turn in audience research, or, as Alasuutari (1999:4) puts it, there was a gradual shift away from the audience reception paradigm to the new audience ethnography paradigm. This paradigm requires first-hand experience over a long period of time in the culture being observed. However, the first audience ethnographic (reception) research shows that these studies differ vastly from classic ethnography: for example, the studies by Hobson (1991) and Tulloch (1991).

SOME ETHNOGRAPHIC STUDIES

Dorothy Hobson (1991) investigated the way television soap operas fitted into the cultural environment of the workplace (office). She conducted focus group interviews over a period of one week with six women working in the same department and who watched the same soaps. She met with the six women at a restaurant during their lunch break and conducted focus group interviews to determine how soaps fitted into their workplace. Hobson tape-recorded these interviews while her secretary took notes, and at a later stage transcribed the tapes.

John Tulloch (1991) studied a group of elderly viewers' television viewing habits and their interaction with and interpretation of television soaps. Tulloch conducted his research in two phases: he first analysed the letters elderly fans wrote to the fan club and to producers of soap operas. The analysis of these public discourses (fan mail) provided insight into the elderly people's feelings about an interaction with soap operas.

The second phase of his research was to conduct interviews with the elderly in their home environment. Tulloch's uncle, who lived in an old-age home in Bournemouth, England, arranged the interviews among 20 people he knew in the home. The first set of interviews took place in November 1985 in the flats (apartments) of the participants. During these interviews, Tulloch discussed with them their television likes and dislikes, their viewing habits, daily routines and a little of their past background.

During the second series of interviews Tulloch sat with each set of participants for a couple of hours on a Wednesday evening in November 1986, writing down their reaction to television shows (especially Dallas, because at the time of the investigation it was the most popular soap opera and also the focus of most reception research), their conversations and their choices of programmes.

As we can deduce from the above examples – especially the research of Hobson – they are not the same as the lengthy periods of participant observation carried out by pioneers of classic ethnographic research; for example, Malinowski lived for three years amongst the Trobriand Islanders (Moores 1993:4). Alasuutari (1999:5) further notes that some of these studies were not even conducted in the natural context where the action occurred.

Although Hobson (1991) and Tulloch (1991) worked with extremely small non-random samples, and did not comply with all the requirements of 'ethnography proper' research, we can assume that both researchers attempted to deal with questions of how viewers create meaning within specific social contexts. After all, one of the underlying assumptions of audience ethnography is to determine how audiences make sense of, and derive pleasure from, their daily interaction with their favourite media, television programmes and television characters (see Chapter 9).

There are of course valid and practical reasons why researchers nowadays cannot spend lengthy periods of time in the (native) field where the action is happening: it is expensive, time consuming and sometimes difficult to get entry to the primary group researchers want to observe. At this stage, suffice to say that, in spite of criticism, much of the early audience research has played an important role in promoting a greater sensitivity for the potential of ethnography in media studies.

We need to mention that reception research is still an option available for qualitative field researchers. In fact, reception research is very much alive and has been used by many qualitative researchers, for example:

- Biltereyst (1995) investigated Belgian audiences' interpretation of locally produced television programmes.
- Liebes and Katz's (1990) well-known research studied foreign cultures' interpretations of the American soap opera *Dallas*.
- Pitout (1996) conducted reception research to determine how female viewers from different cultures in South Africa interpreted the portrayal of South African realities in the locally produced soap *Egoli: Place of Gold*.
- Penzhorn (see Penzhorn & Pitout 2006) conducted a reception study on the interactive nature of reality television.
- Rydin (2003) applied qualitative methods (techniques), such as ethnographic observations (participant observation) and in-depth interviews, to capture children's and teenagers' conceptions and dispositions in relation to media texts.

The majority of the above studies used focus group discussions to gather data about audiences' interpretation of messages. The above also mainly applies to television research. Obviously, there are also many examples of reception research related to other media, such as radio listeners, newspaper and magazine readers, internet users, and so on.

11.5 CASE STUDY: AUDIENCE ETHNOGRAPHIC RESEARCH

Although Daphna Lemish (1985) refers to her study as 'naturalistic', we equate 'naturalistic' with 'ethnographic' because her research complies with all the requirements of ethnographic research.

Lemish conducted a naturalistic (ethnographic) investigation of the soap-opera viewing patterns of college students at Ohio State University in the United States. The aim of her study was to examine a particular sub-audience (or a subcultural group) of soap viewers in specific viewing situations, namely college students who view soaps in public college locations (context of viewing). Because these locations were open to the public, Lemish had no problem entering the premises. The students were observed in two locations, the sports lounge and the recreational centre on campus, where access to these locations was free to all students. At 3:55 each afternoon these two locations were filled with students who wanted to enjoy a break from schoolwork and to watch their favourite soap, *General Hospital*. According to Lemish, viewing soaps was an established pastime for students, involving both females and males, and undergraduate and postgraduate students. The viewing of *General Hospital* thus had become a ritual.

The following research questions guided Lemish's research:
- Why do students watch soap operas?
- Which kinds of needs do soap operas satisfy?
- What role does the social context play in the viewing of soap operas?

Lemish's study was based on the following theoretical assumptions:
- Viewers actively select media content and show a definite preference for particular programmes.
- Exposure to the medium fulfils certain needs such as those of entertainment, relaxation and excitement.
- The social context of media use (e.g. television viewing) plays an important role in the lives of viewers.

Field Research in Media Studies

This research was a longitudinal study, which means that Lemish studied the students' soap viewing patterns over a period of nine months. This observation resulted in a total of 55 note-taking hours that took place in the two locations, the sports lounge and the recreational centre on campus.

Lemish used ethnographic field research techniques such as participant observation, in-depth and focus group interviewing during the nine months that her field study lasted. The students she interviewed were aware that Lemish was conducting research. She used a concealed tape recorder for the recording of spontaneous conversations. These interviews enabled Lemish to draw conclusions about students as social groups: for example, to identify different types of viewers, such as leaders, followers, observers and challengers:

- *Leaders* were regular viewers, well versed in the story lines and plot and always prepared to share their knowledge with enthusiasm. They were always surrounded by other viewers who, by then, had become acquaintances.
- *Followers* were identified by their attentiveness about what leaders had to say. Although followers were familiar with the story lines, they usually asked questions which were answered by the leaders. Leaders thus influenced other viewers' interpretation of soaps.
- *Observers* were often situated in a secondary viewing situation, were quiet and did not initiate conversation. Although observers did watch *General Hospital*, they told Lemish that it was more fun to watch other viewers' reactions, such as shouting and cheering in response to what occurred on screen.
- *Challengers* made challenging, disapproving and negative remarks and could not understand why viewers become addicted to soaps. During the interviews, however, it became clear that challengers were quite familiar with story lines and characters in *General Hospital*.

As far as the social context of soap viewing is concerned, the results indicate that student viewers did form a social collective group, as short-lived as it was, with a shared group spirit; for example, viewers shared information, opinions and personal feelings with strangers. Together they laughed, giggled, clapped hands and cheered. They gathered around leaders, and passed essential information around the room. In some cases, lasting friendships were formed and soap viewing served to cement the friendship. The results thus reveal that the social context (viewing in public places) does play an important role in viewing soap operas.

Many of the students admitted that they did not watch with the same intensity and involvement when watching alone or at home. Lemish came to the conclusion that when watching television programmes in public places with peers, students discovered a new interactive, social dimension of television viewing. The research results also provided additional information about the role that leaders play in group dynamics.

The results of the research also indicated that the following needs were satisfied by soaps: to relax, to be entertained and to escape from daily routine or anxiety.

To test the validity of the study, Lemish used triangulation: she used different research techniques to gather data (field notes, intensive (in-depth) interviews and focus group interviews), which she followed up with a series of post-research interviews with participants and informants. These interviews generally confirmed her conclusions and provided additional validity to the research results.

SUMMARY

In this chapter we introduced you to field research techniques used in ethnographic and reception research, namely participant observation, the in-depth interview, document analysis and the focus group interview. These are the main methods of field research in media studies. We provided you with the steps to plan field research as well as the necessary devices and techniques – field notes, tape recorders, video cameras – to gather data. To analyse data, we suggested the use of categories to systemise and present the data in an orderly way. We concluded this chapter with an explanation of the differences between ethnography and reception research and suggested solutions of how to bridge the gap between the two. We should keep in mind that few researchers have the luxury of time and money required to spend months or even years in the (native) field where the action or phenomenon is happening and thus to conduct 'true' or 'classic' ethnographic research.

Field Research in Media Studies

LEARNING ACTIVITIES

1. Define participant observation, the in-depth interview and the focus-group interview.
2. Select a research topic suitable to be investigated by means of field research techniques such as participant observation, in-depth interviews and document analysis. Consider the following topics: people's attitudes towards and interpretation of Aids awareness messages in the media (you may select radio, newspapers, magazines, television, the internet); the role of the media in creating awareness of family planning; eating disorders related to media portrayals (role models); the uses of and interpretations of computer games or chatrooms on the internet. Then apply the following steps:
   - formulate the research problem/question;
   - discuss and apply the steps to be followed in participant observation; in-depth interviews and document analysis as well as data-gathering techniques;
   - explain how you will analyse and interpret the data.
3. After studying the case study by Lemish (1985), answer the following questions:
   - Would you describe the students' location as open or closed?
   - Which role did Lemish adopt – overt or concealed?
   - What was the main research problem of the study?
   - What theory did Lemish use to formulate the theoretical assumptions of her study?
   - Did she formulate a hypothesis and/or research questions?
   - Was the study short-term or longitudinal? Give reasons for your answer.
   - Which research techniques did she use to gather field data?
   - How did Lemish record the data?
   - What were her main findings and how did she present the results?
4. Explain how you feel about concealed observation in participant observation. Make a list of three topics related to the field of media studies that you think should be studied by concealing your identity. Give reasons why you think these topics should be studied undercover.

5   Design a focus-group interview about a topic in the field of media studies. Take the following into consideration:
    - formulation of the research problem/question;
    - recruitment of participants;
    - venue to conduct focus-group interview(s);
    - recording, analysing and interpreting results.
6   Discuss the main differences between classical ethnography and reception research.

FURTHER READING

Chiseri-Strater, E. & Sunstein, B.S. 1997. *Fieldnotes*. [O] Available: http://www.sas.upenn.edu/anthro/CPIA/METHODS/Fieldnotes.html Accessed on 2008/12/01.

Deacon, D., Pickering, M., Golding, P. & Murdock, G. (eds) 1999. *Researching communications: A practical guide to methods in media and cultural analysis*. London: Arnold.

Genzuk, M. 2003. *A synthesis of ethnographic research*. Occasional Papers Series. Center for Multilingual, Multicultural Research (eds). Center for Multilingual, Multicultural Research, Rossier School of Education, University of Southern California, Los Angeles.

Hammersley, M. & Atkins, P. 1995. *Ethnography: Principles in practice*. 2nd edition. London: Routledge.

Penzhorn, H. & Pitout, M. 2006. The interactive nature of reality television: An audience analysis. *Communicare* 25(5):85–103.

Methods ... What is ethnography? [O] Available: http://www.sas.upenn.edu/anthro/CPIA/METHODS/Ethnography.html Accessed on 2008/12/01.

Wimmer, R.D. & Dominick, J.R. 1997. *Mass media research: An introduction*. 5th edition. Belmont, Calif: Wadsworth.

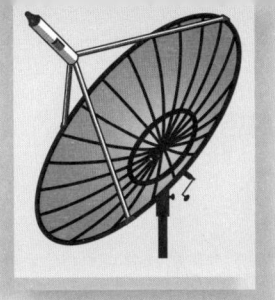

chapter twelve

MEASURING MEDIA AUDIENCES

Elirea Bornman

LEARNING OUTCOMES

At the end of this chapter, you should be able to:
- understand important concepts in audience measurement;
- understand and interpret audience measurement statistics and data;
- critically reflect on various audience measurement practices;
- plan and conduct limited audience measurement studies.

THIS CHAPTER

This chapter is about some of the practices of audience research and, in particular, the methodologies and techniques employed in measuring the audiences of different broadcasting, print and outdoor media, the cinema as well as new media such as the internet. It also gives attention to audience measurement in South Africa and gives a glimpse of some of the problems associated with, and criticism on, audience measurement. The relevance of audience measurement for academic researchers is illustrated by means of a case study.

The most important topics dealt with in this chapter are:
- reasons for audience measurement;
- key concepts in audience measurement;
- research questions in audience measurement;
- methodologies and techniques in measuring audiences for broadcasting media (radio and television), print and outdoor media, the cinema as well as new media such as the internet;
- audience measurement in South Africa;
- problems associated with, and criticism on, audience measurement.

12.1 INTRODUCTION

Imagine that a newspaper, radio station or television channel has no audience. Does it deliver its message? Does it matter at all whether there is an audience or not? Of course it matters! All activities of the media – both content-related and market-related – are focused on the audience (Webster, Phalen & Lichty 2006). Without the audience, all media-related activities become completely senseless.

The problem with media audiences, however, is that they are very hard to find. Audiences are mostly elusive, geographically dispersed and hidden away in homes, businesses and/or motor vehicles. They remain largely unseen for those involved in the business of the media. It is only through research that the audience becomes visible (Webster et al. 2006). A former director-general of the BBC, Michael Checkland (in Van Vuuren 1994:120), comments: 'In the absence of research we know nothing about our customers. Maybe this is something unique to broadcasting. All we do is send invisible signals out into the ether. How do we know whether anyone receives them? The answer is audience research.'

However, audience research – and audience measurement in particular – has become much more than merely satisfying the curiosity of broadcasters about their unseen audiences (Webster et al. 2006). As early as the 1920s, AT&T in the United States (US) started to charge clients a toll to make announcements over their station and found it to be an effective way to fund their medium. 'Toll broadcasting' as this practice was initially called, led to the spread of commercial television, not only in the US, but all over the world (Fourie 2003; Gane 1994). Public service broadcasting systems primarily regulated and funded by governments have been widely replaced by the dual system of the US, which entails a combination of both public service and commercial broadcasting. Deregulation and the dominance of the market-orientated paradigm has resulted in increasing pressure on both commercial and public service-oriented broadcasting media, as well as the print and other forms of mass media, to cover costs and/or to increase income by means of advertising revenue. Currently, most media rely to a larger or smaller extent on sponsorship and/or advertising as a source of revenue. The media and marketing worlds have consequently become inextricably intertwined.

The need for audience measurement is currently largely a function of this changing media environment (Fourie 2003; Gane 1994). In the marketing industry, increased competition due to factors such as product deluge and saturated markets has created the need for more precise identification of market segments in order to target advertising to designated segments more efficiently (Buzzard 2002). The same efficiency is nowadays also sought in the media industry. Blanket targeting of undifferentiated mass audiences with the hope that somehow, somewhere, some media products will be acceptable for some or most people, is no longer possible. Precise targeting of products – also media products – has become essential for success. Media networks are consequently shifting away from the traditional idea of the mass audience – known as the lowest common denominator for programming – towards smaller targeted audiences. This process of targeting precisely defined audiences is known as narrowcasting.

Audience research – empirical research aimed at uncovering the mysteries of the audience and its behaviour and distilling it into hard data – has thus become of crucial interest to all of those involved in the media (Abelman & Atkin 2002). Audience measurement has furthermore become a complex and highly specialised industry in which huge sums of money are spent on an annual basis all over the world. Technological innovation is furthermore constantly transforming the possibilities for and practices of audience measurement.

Whatever your personal career goals in the media, you will need to achieve a theoretical as well as practical knowledge and understanding of audience research (Webster et al. 2006). In this chapter, we explore the practices of audience measurement (sometimes also called ratings research).

12.2 WHO NEEDS INFORMATION ON AUDIENCES?

Various groups of people and/or institutions require detailed information about audience size and structure, as well as audience use of and/or attitudes towards the media (Kent 1994):

- Programme and film producers, broadcast schedulers and newspaper and magazine editors all need to address a potential audience or 'market' for their products with a suitable marketing mix. This means that product design, contents and specification (e.g. programme planning and development), pricing (e.g. charge for advertising slots), promotional activities as well as coverage (e.g. the area of broadcasting or physical distribution) need to be matched not only with the opportunities that exist in the market, but also with the organisation's capabilities and limitations. The same principle as for all kinds of human communication applies here (Mytton 1999). We speak differently, for example, to toddlers than to secondary school learners. Similarly, all aspects of media programming have to be matched to the target audience. This process of matching cannot take place without basic information on the size and structure of the audience as a whole, as well as for individual channels, stations, programmes, newspapers or magazines. Programme schedulers furthermore need information on certain aspects of consumer behaviour (e.g. channel switching behaviour) and preferences for and attitudes towards particular programmes and/or contents.
- Media owners – Media owners typically operate in two different markets: the market of audiences for their particular media products, on the one hand, and the market of advertisers on the other, to whom they hope to sell advertising opportunities for communicating with potential customers. In dealing with advertisers, they need

to convince them that a particular medium will reach a particular audience in terms of both size and composition. In order to do that, detailed information on the audience is needed.
- Similarly, advertisers and sponsors, that is the buyers of opportunities in the media to market their products, need information in order to select media or a combination of media in which to advertise; the specific channel(s), station(s), newspaper(s) and/or magazine(s) to use; what type of messages or content to convey; and the best time, frequency and/or methodology to convey their messages.
- Advertising agencies, media consultants and/or market research agencies usually act on behalf of advertisers or sponsors. In order to provide specialist advice to their clients, they also need detailed information on audiences for all the media.
- Last, but hopefully not the least, are academic researchers and analysts. In the end, research on media audiences is necessary in order to test and develop theories on audience behaviour and media consumption.

12.3 WHICH QUESTIONS ARE ADDRESSED IN AUDIENCE RESEARCH?

From the preceding section the conclusion can be drawn that audience research today needs to address a variety of complex information needs of a wide range of interested parties with different motivations, interests and levels of sophistication. The following key research questions form the basis of most audience measurement endeavours (Webster et al. 2006:31–9):

12.3.1 How many people are there in the audience?

This single factor – the size of the audience – mostly determines the value of a programme, station, channel, newspaper and/or website to the media as well as advertisers. The measures of *coverage*, *audience share* and/or *audience ratings* are mainly used when referring to audience size (see section 12.4).

12.3.2 How often do people show up in the audience?

This factor relates to audience behaviour, which underlies the size of the audience. It is necessary to obtain information on how individuals use the media over time. Firstly, it is, for example, necessary to establish whether two television soap operas with similar ratings are viewed by the same group of people or completely different groups of people (audience duplication). Advertisers also want to know how many different people are exposed to their message. *Coverage* (see section 12.4) is the measure most often employed in this regard. Another key factor is the frequency of exposure, namely the number of times that members of an audience see or hear a particular programme, read a particular newspaper or magazine or visit the cinema or a particular website. The frequency of exposure will determine, in the end, the number of times individuals are exposed to a particular message. The measure of *frequency* is used in this regard (see section 12.4).

12.3.3 Who are the members of the audience?

We emphasise in the introduction that the audience can no longer be regarded as a faceless mass (Ivala 2007). Nowadays most messages and programmes are targeting a specific kind of audience – a strategy called market segmentation or narrowcasting. The need for information on the composition of the audience consequently does not lag far behind information on audience size. Audiences are usually segmented according to particular traits and characteristics. Researchers usually refer to these traits as *variables*. The SAARF Living Standard Measure (LSM) is for, example, widely used in South Africa for market segmentation (see section 12.9). According to Webster et al. (2006), audience attributes can be grouped into the following categories:

- *Demographic variables* – Demographics most commonly reported in audience data are race, ethnicity, age, gender, income, education, marital status and/or occupation. Of these, age and gender are perhaps the most important. Broadcasters and advertisers, for example, often sell or buy programmes directed at pre-school children, teenagers, women or the whole family.
- *Geographic variables* – Just as people differ with regard to demographic attributes, they also differ in terms of where they live. Geographic variables often used in audience research are country of residence, province, residential area as well as rural versus urban areas. Newspapers, radio stations, television channels and other media are often directed at specific geographical areas. Living in particular residential areas can furthermore reflect a person's income, lifestyle and/or station in life. One can assume, for example, that people living in Waterkloof in Pretoria will have a relatively high

Measuring Media Audiences

income, fill important posts in government or the private sector and consequently pursue a particular lifestyle.
- *Behavioural variables* – Behavioural variables distinguish between people on the basis of particular behavioural patterns. It is, for example, important to know whether people listen to or watch particular channels, stations and/or programmes, read particular newspapers and/or magazines or visit particular websites, and how often they do so. Other behavioural variables important to advertisers, in particular, are product-purchase variables. As most advertisers want to reach the audience members that are most likely to buy their products, audiences are often also segmented into buyer-graphics.
- *Psychographics* – Psychographics draw distinctions between people on the basis of particular psychological characteristics such as values, attitudes, motivations and/or preferences. According to Webster et al. (2006), psychographic variables that have caught attention recently are audience loyalty, involvement and/or engagement. It has become important for media professionals as well as advertisers to know who are the people that are particularly loyal and/or committed to particular media products. It has, for example, been found that the fans of a particular programme will also be more attentive to the advertisements contained within it.

It can be concluded that the media – and all those involved – are complex institutions that use information in a variety of ways and for a multitude of purposes. With regard to academic research into the media, audience measurement can yield important insights into media consumption as well as the power and potential effects of the media.

12.4 KEY CONCEPTS IN AUDIENCE MEASUREMENT

The following concepts are fundamental to all aspects of audience measurement:

12.4.1 The concepts of 'watching', 'listening', 'reading' and/or 'visiting'

At a glance it does not seem that there is much to ponder about these concepts (Kent 1994). However, there are two questions that both researchers as well as practitioners should consider:

| watching, listening, reading and/or visiting |

- Precisely what kind of behaviour is involved in the activities 'watching', 'listening', 'reading' and/or 'visiting' (an internet website)?

- How long is it necessary to pursue with these activities in order to be considered, for example, to have 'watched', to have 'listened', to have 'read' a newspaper, book or magazine and/or to have 'visited' an internet website?

With regard to television audiences, 'watching' may simply mean being in a room where a television set is switched on. Alternatively, it may entail claiming in a questionnaire or diary that watching has taken place. Where electronic devices such as peoplemeters are used (see section 12.7.3), the definition may change from mere presence in the room where a television set is switched on or to facing a television set. Similarly, the concept of 'listening' can refer to claims to have listened to a particular programme for a particular period (sometimes a period is not even indicated). The possibilities of defining the 'reading' of a newspaper or 'visiting' an internet website are even more difficult.

Currently, most methods and techniques of audience measurement rely on respondents' own subjective definitions and whether they themselves believe that watching, listening, reading and/or visiting has taken place (Kent 1994; Van Vuuren 1994). However, variations in the definitions of these concepts make comparisons of audience sizes across methods, techniques and instruments extremely difficult, if not impossible. In the end, all audience measures are dependent on the underlying definitions of these activities and audience measurements will vary accordingly.

12.4.2 Coverage or reach

coverage

As mentioned in section 12.3, coverage is an important indicator of audience size. Kent (1994) defines *coverage* – known in the US as *reach* – as the proportion of the total number of unduplicated individuals or households reached by a particular medium or item of communication (e.g. a television or radio programme, newspaper report or advertisement). According to Du Plooy (2001), coverage is usually calculated as a percentage of the population. For example, if 600 households within a given target population of 1000 are exposed to a particular radio programme, the reach is 60%.

Firstly, coverage is dependent on the definitions of the activities of 'watching', 'listening', 'reading' and/or 'visiting'. Secondly, coverage is determined by who is included in the definition of the total potential audience of interest – the so-called universe or population. Webster et al.

(2006) point out that measurements of coverage are commonly based on the entire potential audience (or universe) for a particular medium. For one of the television channels of the SABC, the total population would be the numbers of households in South Africa with one or more television sets – it does not matter whether those sets are switched on or not. For M-Net, the population would be the total number of subscribers. In the case of regional channels, the population would be those households in a particular region that have television sets.

It has furthermore to be borne in mind that populations can be composed of different building blocks or units of analysis. Whereas households equipped with television sets are commonly used as units of analysis in estimating television audiences, individual readers, radio listeners or individuals visiting an internet website are taken into account when newspaper, radio or internet audiences are estimated. However, television channels might also use individuals as units of analysis when different groups of people are considered. Television ratings might, for example, draw a difference between men and women or different age groups. Depending on the definition of the population, it may or may not, for example, include children. Children, on the other hand, may be defined differently according to specific age ranges (e.g. 0–5 years or 10–16 years of age).

Coverage furthermore takes on various forms for various media. The coverage of a television programme is, for example, determined by the size of its audience expressed as a percentage of the relevant population. For the print media, coverage is normally expressed as the average issue readership. In advertising, coverage is often measured in terms of the proportion of the population seeing at least one spot of an advertising campaign. With regard to the electronic media, coverage can also be attached to a particular time frame. The coverage of a television channel can, for example, be defined in terms of the percentage of the population watching the channel in a particular minute.

12.4.3 Audience share

The term 'audience share' usually refers to radio and, in particular, to television programmes. A programme's share refers to the percentage of total *viewing* or *listening* households within the universe whose sets are tuned to that programme. Audience share consequently refers to a particular programme as well as to the programmes broadcast

| audience share

during a particular time slot, such as prime time. For the calculation of share, the population (or universe) is therefore not the total number of households in a particular country, but the total number of households who actually watch television or listen to the radio during a particular time slot (the time slot when a programme of interest is broadcast). It is therefore necessary to have information on the total number of viewing or listening households in a particular population during particular time slots. Statistics on audience share are normally not used to sell advertising time, but play an important role in decisions on scheduling (Blumenthal & Goodenough 2006).

12.4.4 Audience ratings

The term 'ratings' is closely related to coverage or reach (Webster et al. 2006). Audience ratings have become so common and popular that the term 'ratings research' is often used as an umbrella term or shorthand title for audience measurement in general. However, it is important to keep in mind that the rating of programmes is only one of a series of statistical summaries that can be derived from the data obtained through the data-gathering instruments and procedures that we discuss in this chapter.

Similar to 'share', the term 'ratings' represents a description of audience size (Webster et al. 2006). Blumenthal and Goodenough (2006) define the ratings of a television programme as the percentage of total number of households in an area that have television sets that were tuned to the particular programme. Whereas audience share compares the appeal of all programmes broadcast within a particular time slot, audience ratings are used to compare all programmes broadcast in a more or less equal way. It is assumed that programmes that are likely to draw a large audience will be broadcast during more popular time slots.

According to Beville (1988), audience ratings are a powerful force within the media industry that determines the price of a particular programme and the payment that performers will receive. They are furthermore an important factor determining the price that advertisers will be willing to pay for advertising time in and around the time that the programme is broadcast. Ratings also determine the rank order of stations or channels in a particular market as well as their monetary value if and when they are put up for sale. The compensation of key executives and their job security, as well as their chances of being promoted or demoted, can also be affected by the ratings. In the end, the simple push of a button – as members of the audience switch on their sets or tune from one station or channel to another – provides the single most important piece of information regarding audience behaviour.

Especially in the US, audience ratings are the most visible component of audience research, and hold a unique place in industry practice as well as in the public consciousness (Webster et al. 2006). Audience ratings have virtually become part and parcel of popular culture. The Nielsen ratings in the US are famous – or infamous – for serving as the 'bullets' that killed programmes like *Star Trek* and *Twin Peaks*. However, the

Table 12.1 South African programme ratings: average from 1 January 2008 to 22 May 2008 (SAARF TAMS®)

Position	Programme	Channel	AMR%
1	Generations	SABC1	22.0
2	Zone 14	SABC1	19.7
3	SAMA Awards 2008	SABC1	18.6
4	A drink in the passage	SABC1	16.9
5	Shakespeare: Entabeni	SABC1	16.8
6	Shakespeare: Izingane Zobaba	SABC1	16.6
7	Hopeville Mansions	SABC1	16.5
8	MTN African Cup of Nations Ghana – South Africa vs Senegal	SABC1	16.1
9	Unsindiso	SABC1	10.6
10	The Vice Chancellor, the Chicken & the Mayor	SABC1	10.5
11	Stars of Mzansi Awards	SABC1	14.9
12	Zulu news	SABC1	14.9
13	The Fast and the Furious	e.TV	14.9
14	Twins of the Rain Forest	SABC1	14.1
10	Xhosa news	SABC1	13.7
16	The Basikol	SABC1	13.7
17	Zola 7	SABC1	13.7
18	The Rundown	e.TV	13.6
19	Jika ma jika	SABC1	13.6
20	MTN African Cup of Nations Ghana – Cote d'Ivoire vs Nigeria	SABC1	13.5

Source: Milne (2008)

influence of ratings on the culture, content and business of television stretches much further than the mere power to stop the broadcasting of shows.

Notwithstanding the dominating role of ratings in the television industry, it has always to be borne in mind that audience research entails much more than mere ratings analysis. Some of the rich detail of audience research should emerge from the contents of this chapter, but also from the other chapters on audience research.

12.4.5 Frequency

frequency

As already discussed in section 12.3, it is not only important what proportion of the population have been reached by a particular medium or communication item. In most cases, it is also important to know how often people 'watch', 'listen', 'read' and/or 'visit'. The concept *frequency* also has different meanings. *Frequency* may indicate the number of times an individual has watched a particular programme within a particular period (e.g. a two-week period) or the number of times an individual has seen a particular advertisement. Frequency multiplied by coverage gives the total number of possibilities and/or opportunities for a particular programme to have been watched or an advertisement to have been seen. In combination, coverage and frequency form the yardsticks with which the media industry evaluates its successes and failures. It furthermore represents the 'currency' on which negotiations for the buying and selling of advertising opportunities are waged. Measurements of coverage and frequency are consequently one of the main aims of audience measurement endeavours.

12.5 ESTIMATING THE AUDIENCE

population versus sample

When researchers conduct research into media audiences, they are usually interested in an entire population or universe (Kent 1994; Webster et al. 2006). The nature of the population can differ from study to study. Most audience research endeavours in South Africa are interested in the entire South African population. However, as discussed in section 12.4, definitions of the population can vary from study to study and measure to measure. In most cases, however, it is logistically impossible to interview or to obtain data from every single member of the population. Researchers therefore need to *estimate* the audience from a subset that is called a *sample*. Sampling is widely used in scientific research in the social sciences. Audience measurement endeavours are often criticised, however, due to the fact that the audience estimates that they produce are based on samples and not the whole population. However, without sampling, audience measurement becomes virtually impossible. The founder of one of the world's largest audience-research organisations, Arthur Nielsen, was fond to respond to criticism on the practise of sampling by saying: 'If you don't believe in sampling, the next time you have a blood test, ask them to take it all out' (Webster et al. 2006:113).

In the end, it is the quality of a sample that has a tremendous influence on the accuracy of the audience measures obtained (Kent 1994; Mytton 1999; Webster et al. 2006). Issues of sampling are discussed in more detail in Chapter 10. Here it is sufficient to point to the two big classes into which all samples are divided, namely probability (also called random samples) and non-probability (or non-random) samples. The difference between these two classes lies in the way researchers identify and select members of the population to participate in the research. Probability samples make use of methods and techniques in which every member of the population has an equal or known chance of being selected. In contrast, non-probability samples depend on happenstance or convenience in selecting participants (or respondents). In comparison to non-probability samples, probability samples are usually extraordinarily expensive and time-consuming to construct and execute. However, researchers have much more confidence in data obtained from probability samples. Furthermore, probability samples allow for generalisation or expanding the results to the population as a whole, while that is not the case with non-probability samples.

Generally, audience measures will only be trusted and accepted if they are based on a probability sample – or a good approximation thereof. All trustworthy research organisations involved in audience measurement therefore strive towards employing probability sampling in their research endeavours. Their research and technical reports are also laced with the vocabulary related to probability sampling. In order to make sense of these reports, you will need to become familiar with the principles and terminology of probability sampling as discussed in Chapter 10.

12.6 SOURCES OF ERROR IN AUDIENCE MEASUREMENT

A great concern for both the producers and users of audience research is the potential of error in the data. According to Webster et al. (2006), the concept 'error' as used in research should be understood differently from the normal understanding of mistakes being made. It rather refers to the extent to which the audience measures estimated on the basis of samples fail to reflect what is really happening in the population. Error therefore refers to the difference between what audience estimates hold audience measures to be, and what the measures really are. Sophisticated users of audience data need to understand the potential sources of error and how audience-research organisations deal, or do not deal, with these.

The following sources of error are of particular relevance to audience measurement (Kent 1994; Webster et al. 2006):

12.6.1 Sampling error

sampling error

Sampling error is perhaps the most abstract of all the sources of error. Basically, it recognises the fact that as long as we try to estimate what is true for a population from something that is less than the population, namely a sample, the chance exists that we may miss the mark. Even when we use large probability samples that are perfectly executed, these might fail to accurately represent the population from which they were drawn. This potential is inherent in the process of sampling. Sampling error is discussed in more depth in Chapter 10.

12.6.2 Non-response error

non-response error

There are furthermore sources of error associated with the process of executing sampling designs. One of the most important is non-response error. Non-response error occurs because not everybody selected to participate in a study will respond or cooperate. The possibility exists that a sample can become biased if those who do respond or participate differ from those who do not want to, or fail to, participate. Some research designs are more prone to non-response error than others. Non-response error is also discussed in greater detail in Chapter 10. When studying audience measurement reports, non-response error can be detected by comparing the original sampling design with the final realised sample. Research organisations involved in audience measurement should also report on the reasons for non-response and indicate the procedures that they followed to prevent or correct non-response error.

12.6.3 Response error

Other sources of error are related to the research process itself. When asking people about their watching, listening, reading or visiting behaviour, their responses are based on their memory recall of their own behaviour. Memory is, however, subject to failure, which can give rise to incorrect or incomplete responses. Problems related to memory recall, and the steps that research organisations take to prevent it, will be addressed in the discussion of the methods and techniques employed in audience measurement. Response error can also occur when respondents and/or participants misunderstand instructions or questions (see the section on questionnaire design in Chapter 10). When push-button metering systems are used, panellists can forget to push their buttons to register their own viewing or push the wrong buttons. Participants can furthermore be plainly dishonest or cheat intentionally.

response error

12.6.4 Interviewer error

Interviewers can make mistakes when recording the responses of respondents and/or participants. The way in which interviewers understand or approach questions can also influence respondents/participants to respond in a certain way and result in biased responses. The training of interviewers is also discussed in Chapter 10.

interviewer error

12.6.5 Sources of error external to the research process

Measures can be biased by unusual promotional and publicity efforts on the parts of the media in order to raise their audience levels during measurement periods. For example, newspapers can run competitions offering exciting prizes that require readers to buy the newspapers every day during the period that audience surveys are conducted. There is little that researchers can do to address biased measures due to such efforts. However, measurements that are done on a continuous basis, such as in the case of peoplemeters, are less prone to such sources of error (see section 12.7).

external sources of error

Although professionals in the media and advertising industries are often aware of the potential sources of error and bias in measurement data, these limitations are seldom considered in practice (Kent 1994). The daily pressures of running media and advertising businesses usually require some kind of yardstick in the form of audience data on which important decisions can be made. It is often assumed that, provided errors are relatively constant, that the figures provide a relatively balanced reflection of the situation as it really is. The fact that all audience measures, in the end, are mere estimates of the 'truth' is often conveniently overlooked.

12.7 INSTRUMENTS FOR CAPTURING DATA ON AUDIENCES

In the early years of the development of the mass media no systematic audience research was done (Mytton 1999). The likes and dislikes of editors, media owners, channel managers and/or sponsors most often determined the contents of the media. However, it soon became clear that information was needed that was independent of their own views or opinions. Some of the early forms of audience measurement entailed the counting of letters elicited by particular reports, articles or programmes. Other forms of 'measurement' were no more reliable. In an attempt to determine audience size, broadcasters would draw a circle on a map with a radius reflecting what they thought the reach of the station to be and determined the number of people living in the area. However, these measures were meaningless as it was not a given fact that all these people were indeed members of the audience. A number of things, such as transmitter power, local geography, station programming, wavelengths and other factors are known to influence the size of the audience.

As the limitations of these ad hoc methods of audience measurement have been realised, audience research has developed as a formal and systematic enterprise. The applications of audience data are endless (Mytton 1999): it is used to assist in the creative process of writing and/or programme-making; it provides a scientific basis for programming, policy and marketing decisions; it can be used to maximise the efficient and cost-effective use of scarce resources; and it can be employed to determine the effectiveness of public advocacy campaigns. In the end, large amounts of money are spent on the basis of decisions informed by audience research and millions of lives are affected by these decisions (Webster et al. 2006).

The high stakes in audience measurement imply that it not only needs to fulfil a wide variety of complex information needs, but also

Measuring Media Audiences

has to provide highly accurate and precise information. Although the practice of audience measurement is constantly changing, a number of instruments for capturing audience data have stood the test of time. Each of these instruments has unique applications within the media world, and each has certain advantages and limitations, which should become clear in the following sections.

12.7.1 Social surveys

Questionnaires are probably one of the oldest and best-known ways of investigating social phenomena, such as media behaviour (Ivala 2007; Kent 1994; Mytton 1999; Webster et al. 2006). Questionnaire surveys as a research methodology in media research are discussed in detail in Chapter 10. Here it is sufficient to explain briefly how surveys are employed in audience measurement.

> surveys

A questionnaire is a self-reporting method, and information can be gathered on any aspect on which questions can be asked to a respondent. Data can thus be gathered on demographic characteristics, print and electronic media usage patterns, lifestyle, values, attitudes and opinions, as well as the products and services that people buy and use. These responses can provide a treasure trove of information to media researchers, practitioners and advertisers, as particular demographics, media usage patterns, values, attitudes and opinions can be linked to particular patterns of product purchase and usage of particular services. The idea of a questionnaire is, in the end, that the questions put to each respondent are standardised so that exactly the same questions are put in a similar way to each respondent. These responses can then be counted up and/or compared.

Whether questionnaires are self-administered or completed by means of interviewers (see Chapter 10), the conventional paper-and-pen method is most widely used in the media industry for completing questionnaires. Technological advances have, however, stimulated the development of new forms of surveying (Greenberg et al. 2005). In conducting the All Media Products Survey (AMPS – see section 12.9.2), the South African Advertising Research Foundation (SAARF) replaced the traditional pen-and-paper methodology with computer-assisted personal interviewing (CAPI) where fieldworkers capture responses by means of laptop computers that they carry with them (SAARF sa). Webster et al. (2006) furthermore mention the advent of personal digital assistants (PDAs), which are pre-loaded with questionnaires and distributed to respondents. Respondents are required to carry the PDAs with them. At various times throughout the day the devices ring, asking people to complete a short questionnaire. People can be asked to report their mood, where they are and to report on the media and/or promotions within the particular location (e.g. at work, in the car, in a store, and so forth). After a couple of days the researchers reclaim the devices and the data can be read, captured and analysed. Online data gathering by means of web-based surveys is another new innovation available to media researchers.

Telephone interviews have also been widely employed in media research, but have particular limitations especially in developing countries such as South Africa with low telephone densities (see Chapter 10). However, two techniques associated with telephone surveys are of particular relevance to audience measurement (Webster et al. 2006):

- *Telephone recalls* – Respondents are contacted by telephone and requested to report on what they have seen or heard over a particular period of time. However, the quality of recalled information will be influenced by how far back a person is required to remember. The further certain events are removed from the present, the more the recalled information is subject to memory error. The salience of the behaviour in question, that is, the relative importance or unimportance, also has an influence on the quality of responses. Important or regularly occurring patterns are more clearly recalled than trivial or sporadic events.

- *Telephone coincidentals* can overcome some of the problems of memory associated with telephone recalls. In these surveys, people are asked questions about what they are seeing or listening to at the moment of the telephone call. As respondents can be expected to verify who is using what media at the particular time, problems of memory can be overcome and be reduced to a minimum. Thus telephone coincidentals have often been used as the yardstick against which other methods of audience measurement are evaluated. However, although telephone coincidentals are still being used in quality evaluations of other measures (see section 12.8), they are no longer routinely employed in audience research. The problem is that this type of survey only provides a momentary glimpse of media usage. Thus, although it offers high-quality information, it does not provide quantity of information on audience behavioural patterns over time. There are also practical limitations on where and when calls can be made. Much radio listening, for example, is done in cars where people cannot be reached by regular landline telephones. Also, while much television viewing is done late at night, it is regarded as inappropriate to call people at late hours.

Whatever the method being employed, social surveys offer the media researcher opportunities to investigate a wide range of issues – probably a larger variety of issues than any of the other methodologies or techniques employed in audience measurement. However, some of the disadvantages of social surveys have already been highlighted in the discussion of the methods of telephone recall and telephone coincidentals. The most important disadvantage is the relatively low accuracy in the reporting of actual behavioural patterns, such as listening, viewing, reading or visiting websites (Wind & Lerner 1979). This lack of accuracy can be ascribed to a variety of sources of error related to respondents (e.g. poor memory, forgetting, deliberate falsification of information, low awareness of the importance of particular information, reporting errors, etc.), the nature of the questionnaire (e.g. ambiguous question formats) as well as other aspects of the procedure (e.g. fieldworker/interviewer bias).

Due to the problems associated with memory error, in particular, social surveys on their own are no longer regarded as sufficient to provide high-quality and precise information on audience behaviour for broadcast media. However, due to the versatility of social surveys, they are still widely used in combination with other measuring instruments and/or techniques.

12.7.2 Diaries

The diary is another self-reporting method widely employed in measuring audiences in an attempt to overcome the lack of accuracy associated with social surveys. Diaries are distinguished by the fact that they capture data on audience behaviour on an individual basis over a period of time (Kent 1994). In most cases, respondents are instructed to record a particular form of behaviour (e.g. listening to the radio and/or watching television) every time that it occurs within a given period – often a week, two weeks or longer. Thus diaries record behaviour that is normally repeated at frequent intervals and which is difficult to recall correctly in a

diaries

Media Studies: Volume 3

questionnaire survey. The focus of diaries is predominantly on behaviour – and the frequency of behaviour – and not on attitudes and/or other variables of interest. One of the reasons why attitudes are not measured in a diary is the fear that the mere act of recording one's attitudes could influence behaviour. If a respondent, for example, records a negative attitude towards a particular programme, he or she can stop watching the programme and/or switch channels or stations.

Diaries may be sent to the respondent by post or delivered personally by an interviewer. At the end of the designated period, they can be collected personally or sent back to the organisers of the research by post. As already mentioned, diaries are usually completed by individuals who record their own behaviour. However, it is also possible that a particular person (e.g. the housewife) is made responsible for recording the behaviour of the members of a household as a whole. This is particularly the case when researchers are interested in the media behaviour of young children who are not able to complete a diary by themselves.

Diaries can differ to the extent to which they are fully structured or pre-coded, semi-structured or unstructured. Structured diaries usually include lists

Figure 12.1 Section of the diary employed by SAARF

Source: The Nielson Company

534

of all the channels, stations and/or even programmes that can be received within a particular area. This implies, however, that a number of versions of the diary will have to be devised to make provision for regional differences within a country. Also, if programmes are pre-listed, last-minute schedule changes may be overlooked. In the case of unstructured diaries, respondents have to write in the names of channels, stations and/or programmes. In such a case, one version of a diary can be used for the whole country, but more effort is required from the respondent in completing the diary. It furthermore implies the post-coding of diary entries that could add considerably to the time and effort of researchers.

Diaries used to record listening or watching behaviour usually arrange entries by time segment on a daily basis, often in 10-minute or 30-minute periods. The time segments are usually indicated down the left side of the page, while channels, stations or programmes will be listed or entered across the width of the page. The respondent is requested to indicate all segments in which listening or watching takes place. Diaries for the print media resemble more of a product diary, where a list of newspapers and/or magazines is provided and respondents mark off those that they have read. Alternatively, respondents could write in the names of newspapers or magazines that they had read on a particular day. Diaries can also include additional aspects, such as questions on household composition, region, stations and/or channels that can be received, and so forth.

According to Kent (1994) diaries act as a type of 'reminder' to respondents that enhances the completeness and accurateness of reporting. The following potential sources of error have, however, to be kept in mind when employing diaries in audience research (Kent 1994; Webster et al. 2006):

- The completion of diaries requires a certain level of literacy from respondents.
- Respondents can forget to record viewing, listening or reading behaviour – this could be a result of failing to complete diaries as they go along and trying to recall behaviour after a couple of days or even at the end of the period just before they need to submit the completed diaries. To the extent that diary entries are delayed, memory errors are more likely.

- The respondent can record behaviour, but make a mistake on the details due to faulty memory or erroneous recording.
- There is evidence that diary-keepers are more diligent at the beginning of the recording period than towards the end. This so-called diary fatigue might depress viewing or listening levels at the end of the period. Viewing/listening late at night, of short duration and/or of less well-known programmes as well as viewing/listening of secondary sets (e.g. in the bedroom) also tends to be underreported.
- False information can deliberately be provided, either by omission of some media use or making imaginary entries. However, Webster et al. (2006) report that most people have a sense of the importance of audience research and the way it can affect programming decisions and will therefore refrain from deliberately providing false information. On the other hand, some people might regard the completion of a diary as an opportunity to 'vote' for particular programmes whether they are actually a member of the audience or not.
- When a housewife (or other household member) has to complete the diary on behalf of other household members, the person can be unaware of some media usage patterns of other members of the household (e.g. children can watch television without their parents being aware that they watch). It is consequently a known tendency that audiences of children's programmes are usually underestimated in diary measures (Friedman & Ayer 1989).
- The increasing complexity of the media environment, as well as audience fragmentation, has made diary-based measurement problematic in recent years (Webster et al. 2006; Friedman & Ayer 1989). For example, a person watching a movie recorded by means of a video recorder (VCR) might find it difficult to remember on which channel the movie was originally broadcast. Also, if a person 'jumped' about 40 channels before finally watching a programme, it would also be difficult to remember in the end which channel he or she finally really 'watched'. It is also easy to confuse channels, such as the various international news channels. It is for these reasons believed that diaries usually under-report the audience for satellite and cable television or independent radio stations/television channels.
- Lastly, Friedman and Ayer (1989) hold that the more entrenched a particular station or channel or other medium is in the minds of diary-keepers, the more likely it is that it will be remembered when the diary keepers fill out their diaries.

These sources of error can be influenced by a number of factors: the type of programme, newspaper or magazine; the frequency of media use; the position of a page in the diary; the position and prominence of the entry on a particular page; the complexity of the layout; the overall length of the diary; the workload involved in completing the diary, and the method of, and nature of, contact between the respondent and the researchers.

Despite the abovementioned limitations, diaries hold several advantages (Webster et al. 2006):
- One of the most important advantages is that they are a relatively cheap method of data collection. Taking into account the wealth of information that can be obtained by properly completed diaries, no other method is as cost-effective.
- Diaries hold the potential for the collection of very detailed information, including demographics.
- Diaries are a non-intrusive method of data collection. They can be completed at respondents' convenience.

Similar to social surveys, diaries are nowadays often used in combination with other methods of audience research, such as the more expensive metering techniques.

12.7.3 Metering devices

In recent decades, the drive towards obtaining precise audience data of a high quality has resulted in audience measurement being dominated by technological advances and, in particular, by the development of electronic metering devices (Buzzard 2002; Gill 2000; Webster et al. 2006).

Set or household meters

Household meters have become one of the alternatives to diary-based audience measurement. The well-known Nielsen Audimeter was one of the first electronic devices that were installed in homes to monitor radio listening. The next generation of meters – known as household or set meters – were developed for television. These are essentially small computers, attached to one or all of the television sets in a home, that record automatically whether a set is on or off and to which channel it is tuned. The information is stored in a special unit and can be retrieved via a telephone line and downloaded to a central computer. For years,

| set meters

set meters represented the full scope of electronic metering activity. As such, they had particular advantages over diary measurement of media usage patterns. Meters eliminated human memory error, as viewing was recorded as it occurred. Even brief exposures could be detected. Respondents did not need to be literate and 'respondent fatigue' did not play a role. In fact, respondents did not need to do anything at all. As information was captured electronically, it could also be captured and processed much faster than pen-and-paper questionnaires and diaries.

However, there were certain disadvantages to set meters. Firstly, they were expensive. It cost a lot to manufacture, install and maintain the electronic hardware to make the system work. According to Webster et al. (2006), this limitation holds true for all types of electronic metering. Due to the costs involved, electronic media metering is only viable for relatively large media markets (such as a country) and not for local and/or regional markets. The most important disadvantage is, however, that set meters provide no information on the composition of the audience, that is, the people watching, save from the known household characteristics. The lack of precise information on the nature of the audience that has become so vitally important to media people and advertisers caused set meters to be largely abandoned in favour of so-called peoplemeters, as we know them today. However, Webster et al. point to the fact that set meters are not completely a thing of the past. Nowadays, digital video recorders (DVRs) have the ability to record exactly the activity on television sets on a moment-to-moment basis. The equipment used to receive pay television in homes can also track tuning. The implication is that in the near future a set meter can be placed in virtually every home with a television set. This could provide a broad database of television activity. However, information on the exact nature of the audience would still be lacking.

Peoplemeters

peoplemeters

Peoplemeters are currently the only electronic device that measures exactly who in a household is viewing a particular set. In the early 1980s, the London-based research group AGB Research, nowadays known as Taylor Nelson Sofres (TNS), developed the first meters to gather information on who was viewing (Gill 2000). Thus the modern peoplemeter was born. The peoplemeter replaces the diary-keeping activity of recording television viewing behaviour with the simple push

Measuring Media Audiences

of a button on a special handset whenever a person enters or leaves a room where a television set is switched on.

Basically, the device consists of a handset that consists of a number of push buttons. Every member of a household is assigned a number that corresponds with one of the push buttons on the handset. When a particular member of the household starts viewing, he or she is supposed to press the pre-assigned button on the handset and to press the button again when he or she leaves the room. The hand-held sets are more or less the size of other remote control devices. As in the case of household meters, data are retrieved via a telephone line. Most peoplemeters also include a display unit that shows which household members are registered to be watching. The display unit can also be used to prompt household members to check whether buttons have been pushed correctly.

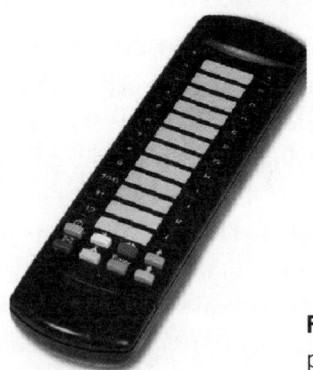

Figure 12.2 Handset and display unit of a peoplemeter used in South Africa

Source: AGB Nielsen Media Research

Peoplemeters hold the following advantages over other methods of audience measurement:
- The most important reason for the widespread acceptance of the peoplemeter is that it is widely accepted that peoplemeters provide highly accurate information on audiences and their television usage patterns that are not subject to the deficiencies of diary-keeping and questionnaires (Gill 2000). Trust in the quality of information provided by peoplemeters is based on coincidental surveys that have become the

standardised method of assessing the accuracy of peoplemeter data in most countries. This technique involves telephoning a sample of panel homes and enquiring who is watching television at the time of the call. The information obtained by means of the telephone coincidentals are then compared with the household viewing status as recorded by the peoplemeter at the time of the call. The results obtained by telephone recalls tend to be remarkably consistent indicating a push-button accuracy of around 90%. That means that around 90% of people who were said to be viewing at the time of the call indeed registered their viewing on the peoplemeter. Also, approximately 90% of the people who indicated they were not viewing at the time of the call were also not registered on the peoplemeter.

- No literacy is required to participate in peoplemeter panels. Illiterate people as well as small children can therefore record their own viewing.
- Continuous measurement of viewing activity means that even short periods of viewing can be registered.
- The demographic data of household members are available and can be used in the analysis of the data.

However, high levels of accuracy in peoplemeter data are not a given fact. To achieve these levels of accuracy usually involves a considerable amount of effort from the organisation that conducts the peoplemeter research. Gill (2000) cites the following factors that can influence the quality of peoplemeter data:

- *Motivation of panel members* – It is firstly necessary to motivate the household to become members of a panel. As peoplemeters are usually installed in a household for several years, it is imperative to continuously motivate household members to keep pushing their buttons meticulously whenever they watch television. Incentives that can take a variety of forms, such as cash payments and shopping vouchers, can play an important role. However, incentives are seldom sufficient to keep panel members motivated. Ongoing contact between the organisers and panel members is essential, and a communication strategy for interaction between the research organisation and panel members should be in place. Becoming a member of a panel is usually presented as becoming a member of a club. Newsletters, personalised mail, phone calls and visits from technicians and representatives of the panel operators all form part of the research strategy. In addition,

panel members who are suspected of poor performance should be targeted more specifically to establish whether there is a problem that can be rectified and then to remind the household members to perform their button-pushing tasks.
- There exist a number of quality control checks that organisations can employ to detect households whose button-pushing activity is not satisfactory. Some of these are the following:
  - nil viewing, that is when no viewing is recorded in a household for several days;
  - uncovered set tuning, where unexpected large amounts of set tuning are registered, while nobody is registered to be viewing;
  - long viewing sessions, where particular household members are registered as viewing for suspiciously long, unbroken periods;
  - low cover, where cover analysis reveals that some household members are registered to be watching considerably less than what could be expected from that type of household.
- *The design of the handset* – Response from household members is optimised when the response mechanism – that is the push-button handset as well as the display unit – is simple and easy to understand and use. It is, in reality, through ease of use that peoplemeters have become the most important instrument for the capturing of television viewing. Most peoplemeter handsets contain the following:
  - a button dedicated to each household member – most handsets can register up to eight household members;
  - button(s) for guests – nowadays most handsets have one or more buttons to make provision for the registering of the television viewing of guests;
  - holiday – buttons are assigned to inform panel operators that household members are going away;
  - audience appreciation – in some countries (e.g. the Netherlands and Denmark) buttons are assigned to allow household members to register their views and/or appreciation of particular programmes. This is done by prompting panel members who are viewing at a particular time to score the programme they are viewing. However, there are several concerns about measuring appreciation in addition to viewing patterns. It is felt that the need to indicate appreciation adds to the task load of panel members and could affect their willingness to cooperate. It could also raise

their awareness of their own viewing and, in the end, affect their viewing patterns. However, research has indicated that the task of providing views on programmes could serve as a motivational force that could encourage participation in the panel.
- The display unit as well as the prompt to remind viewers to push their buttons correctly should not intimidate panel members and/or disrupt their viewing. It should be kept in mind that panel members will be subjected to these prompts for several years. Various techniques are employed to make prompts relevant to panel members, such as the use of a home language and personalised messages using a panel member's name.

Peoplemeter data are, however, not perfect. The following disadvantages and potential sources of error are associated with peoplemeters (Gill 2000; Webster et al. 2006):
- As already mentioned, peoplemeters are expensive to manufacture, install and maintain.
- Although peoplemeters do not require literacy, analysts feel that they do require a degree of technological literacy.
- Similar to diaries, peoplemeters are believed to under-represent the television viewing of children. It turns out that young children especially are not conscientious button-pushers.
- As peoplemeters are installed in households for several years, there are concerns about button-pushing fatigue. As previously discussed, ongoing contact between the panel-operating organisation and panel members is essential to keep household members motivated.
- The potential of button-pushing fatigue implies that panel samples should be changed frequently. Whereas peoplememters used to be installed in US households for five years, doubts about the long-term diligence of panel households has resulted in Nielsen (the operating agency) changing their turnover of households to two years.
- Although methods of random sampling are employed in selecting panel households, participation in a panel remains voluntary. The question can be asked whether households that refuse to become members of a peoplemeter panel differ with regard to important characteristics from those who are willing to participate in such a panel.
- Peoplemeters focus on the household – the nuclear family – as the unit of analysis. Household peoplemeters are, however, unable to register individual viewing such as viewing in bedrooms and viewing

at out-of-home venues (e.g. at work, at the homes of friends, in bars or cafeterias). Household measures are also increasingly becoming inadequate to meet the needs of the emerging media and marketing arenas. As such, researchers were looking for instruments to obtain individualised information about the audience.
- Peoplemeters are currently mainly restricted to measuring television audiences.

The above shortcomings indicate that, although peoplemeters can be regarded as an improvement on questionnaires and diaries in measuring audience behaviour, they do not offer a complete solution to all the needs for audience measurement. The technology of metering devices is, however, continuously developing in the quest for more precise information.

Portable personal meters (PPMs)

One of the most recent developments is that of portable personal meters (PPMs), which overcome the housebound limitations of peoplemeters (Gill 2000; Smit 2006; Webster et al. 2006). These individualised systems have the advantage that they can capture media usage away from home and can be employed to measure both television and radio usage. PPMs depend on the cooperation of broadcasters, who need to embed an inaudible code in the audio portion of their broadcasts. Each person selected for the sample or panel is requested to carry a pager-size device that is capable of capturing these audio codes. (In Switzerland PPMs take the form of wristwatches.) Whenever the person is within earshot of a particular broadcast, the metering device 'hears' it and credits the person to be a member of the audience. At the end of a predetermined period, the panel members need to take their devices to docking stations, where the data are automatically retrieved via telephone lines. PPMs have several advantages above household peoplemeters (Gill 2000; Webster et al. 2006):

- No literacy is required.
- PPMs do not require any button-pushing. Once a panel member has remembered to carry the PPM with him or her for the day, there are no other tasks to perform.
- PPMs can detect any television or radio content that emits the prearranged code. They can therefore track exposure to media with great precision.

portable personal meters (PPMs)

- PPMs can capture out-of-home media use.
- PPS can capture multimedia. They could even be enabled to capture print media if these media could insert some kind of radio frequency device in their publications.
- PPMs are cheaper than household peoplemeters as technicians do not need to visit a household to install them. The necessary hardware, that is, the metering device, can simply be posted to members of the participating panel.
- Continuous measurement enables the capturing of very brief instances of exposure to media.
- The demographic characteristics of the participating panel are available.

However, PPMs also do not offer the final answer to audience measurement, for the following reasons:
- The PPM devices are also expensive to manufacture.
- PPMs can easily be lost or stolen (under the misperception that it is a real watch, cellphone or other usable device). Due to the risk of theft, PPMs are currently not regarded as suitable for use in South Africa.
- PPMs require cooperation from the media to embed the identifying codes.
- PPM samples need a higher turnover than household peoplemeter samples.
- PPMs may pick up signals from adjacent venues.

Furthermore, an important question that needs to be asked is whether it can be assumed that viewing, listening and/or reading really takes place when a person comes within earshot of the audio code detected by the PPM. In the case of questionnaires, diaries and peoplemeters, people have to consciously register and/or identify themselves as members of the audience. This is not the case with PPMs. The quality and intensity of audience-related behaviour can therefore not be established.

What does the future hold?

passive meters

The 'holy grail', to which all organisations, researchers and engineers involved in audience measurement strive, is the development of a so-called *passive peoplemeter*. Passive peoplemeters would require no effort from people. Although PPMs come close, people still need to carry them around and need to remember to do so. The ideal passive peoplemeter would be unobtrusive and able to detect exactly which people are in the audience.

Several attempts have already been made towards the development of passive meters (Buzzard 2002). In April 1998, R.D. Percy announced his peoplemeter service in the US. This involved a passive infrared device that could detect how many people were in a room at a given time, thus passively registering viewers. Percy's research focused on commercials, and his ratings confirmed the worst fears of advertisers. He found that commercials were watched 17% less than the programmes during which they are aired because of channel switching and people leaving the room during the broadcasting of commercials. However, Percy's device met with resistance, as the idea of an electronic peeper in people's homes invoked privacy issues. It was also pointed out that the device needed further validation to eliminate the possibility that household pets might be counted as members of the audience. It was also felt that the presence of such an electronic peeper could cause people to alter their behaviour.

Other house-bound technologies have also been developed (Webster et al. 2006). One of these involves a computerised 'face recognition' device. This device translates a person's facial image into a set of distinguishing features that are stored in a data bank. The device then scans a particular field, such as that in front of a television set and compares the objects discerned with the features stored in the data bank. In this way family members are recognised and registered as members of the audience. However, like Percy's passive meter, this device is probably too intrusive.

Gill (2000) predicts that the future will probably see significant changes and innovative developments in the electronic measurement of listening and viewing behaviour. Buzzard (2002) uses the term 'peoplemeter wars' to depict the fierce competition in the peoplemeter market to come up with ever more advanced devices that will no longer rely on human memory and/or actions to provide precise audience information.

12.8 MEASURING THE AUDIENCES FOR PARTICULAR MEDIA
12.8.1 Measuring television audiences

television audiences

As already mentioned in the introduction to this chapter, the television industry has changed drastically with the introduction of commercial channels, which are heavily dependent on advertising sales. This has changed the television airtime market to one based on supply and demand. In these circumstances, the need for much more detailed and precise audience measurements has arisen.

The measurement of television audiences has graduated from the conventional and relatively simple methods of surveys and diaries to metering (Kent 1994). The technical characteristics of the television medium make it ideally suited to the use of meters. Meters furthermore have the potential to supply both the detail and the precision required in the commercialised television industry. Thus peoplemeter panels have become the universal standard method for measuring television audiences in more than 70 countries (Gill 2000; Webster et al. 2006).

Panel research is a longitudinal research design in which a sample of units – households in the case of peoplemeters – are studied over an extended period of time (Danaher & Balnaves 2002; Kent 1994; Mytton 1999). According to Danaher and Balnaves (2002), there are two elements to peoplemeter panels: the peoplemeter and the panel. Peoplemeters are installed in a panel of households for a number of years. Panels offer the potential for more sophisticated data capturing than in the case of once-off interviews (as is the case for questionnaire surveys), because they measure television viewing behaviour over time among the same people. Trends and changes in viewing behaviour can be recorded on the same continuous sample over time, in contrast with the disruptive effect of using different samples in a number of cross-sectional studies. It is furthermore possible to observe several aspects of viewing (e.g. exposure and frequency of viewing and changes in television viewing behaviour) for individual respondents over time. Peoplemeters furthermore make the collection of continuous minute-by-minute data possible. With regard to the composition of peoplemeter panels, it is important that methods of probability sampling should be employed to ensure that a panel is representative of the television viewing public.

However, due to technological advancement in recent years, the well-established practice of metering television viewing by means of peoplemeter panels is facing a number of important challenges. These are outlined below.

Improving cooperation and compliance in a world of deteriorating response rates

In recent years, it has become a well-known fact that the willingness to participate in questionnaire surveys has been constantly declining and will probably continue to do so (Garland 2002). The same applies to participation in peoplemeter panels. New techniques have therefore to be developed to recruit new panel members and to manage and maintain those households that are already participating in panels. Research into the development of passive meters is being pursued to minimise the button-pushing burden on panel members (see section 12.7.3).

Measuring analogue versus digital signals

The capturing of the tuning of television channels has always been the most basic measurement function of metering devices (Garland 2002). With the advent of digital signals, the current basic technology is, however, no longer sufficient. Nielsen Media Research, one of the leading global audience measurement agencies, has therefore been establishing links with the leading digital-standards organisations all over the world to ensure that digital broadcast standards will include channel and programme identification details that can be detected by means of peoplemeter technology. However, it can be assumed that analogue and digital television will coexist for a long time and that some television operators will fail to embed an identification signal in their broadcasts. Nielsen has consequently embarked on one of the world's most comprehensive approaches to channel detection. Where a broadcaster agrees to cooperate, Nielsen will take the initiative to place an invisible or inaudible signal in the channel's video or audio stream to permit the measurement of the broadcasts. Even when no active code is embedded, digital broadcasts can be identified by taking the video or audio signatures collected by meters and matching them to a reference database of all possible signatures. This combined methodology, patented worldwide by Nielsen, makes possible the identification of channel-specific viewing within an analogue, digital or mixed analogue-digital environment, even without the cooperation of operators.

Measuring increasing fragmented viewing

As the number of channels available has steadily increased, the number of channels watched by an individual has also been increasing, but at a much slower rate. Currently, the average individual watches 10 to 15 channels per month (Danaher & Balnaves 2002; Garland 2002). However, the limitations of sample sizes have made the measurement of the audiences for small-share and niche channels less precise. In order to compensate for this problem, a range of low-cost metering technologies are being developed that can be used in large-scale samples or smaller customised samples for more specific applications. In future, these metering devices could make it possible for pay-television services to conduct their own metering independent of national peoplemeter panels.

Time-shift viewing

Video recorders (VCRs) have been in use for more than two decades. When firstly introduced, VCRs presented audience researchers with one of the most complex measurement problems (Danaher & Balnaves 2002; Garland 2002). These problems were initially ignored, with the result that television viewing was underestimated. However, the more sophisticated modern peoplemeter can now pick up the fingerprinting of programmes that are recorded. When these are played back, the peoplemeter can register the date, time and channel. In doing so, the additional audience for programmes and commercials is registered.

Another problem that confronts media researchers is the possibility of 'channel switching' made possible by remote control devices and the practices of 'zapping' (fast-forwarding advertisements when watching recorded programmes) and 'time shifting' (the possibility to move back to the beginning of a programme while it is broadcast) enabled by personal video recorder (PVR) satellite decoders. Although PVR penetration is currently relatively low, it is believed that their use will grow rapidly when they are delivered as integral components of digital decoders. Agreements between the operators of PVR technology and major audience measurement organisations are, however, already in place to ensure that time-shift activities could be captured from PVR devices.

The enhanced viewer

Digital television platforms allow viewers to enrich their television experience through features such as interactive television games (e.g. trying to answer quiz questions before the participants in the studio) or obtaining further information on programme or commercial contents (e.g. particular information about a rugby or soccer player or details about a new car). Broadcasters and platform operators are still learning how these capabilities can engage the television viewer (Garland 2002). It is believed that an engaged viewer will spend more time with a programme or channel. However, in order to understand interactive behaviour, it is necessary to be able to collect interactive data by means of peoplemeter technology. In order to do so, research organisations need access to decoder technology. Cooperation with the manufacturers of digital decoders for a particular country is thus necessary to ensure that it will be possible to identify and capture interactive television activity.

The conclusion can be drawn that, with the advent of a variety of digital television platforms, it will not be possible to achieve comprehensive measurement of television audiences in the 21st century without significant investment in measurement science, measurement technology and industry partnerships (Garland 2002). It furthermore needs to be kept in mind that metering technologies on their own cannot provide all the information needed by the television and advertising industries. As already indicated, meters can seldom provide information on attitudes and psychographics. Therefore most countries currently use a combination of peoplemeter methodology with more traditional methods, such as surveys, to obtain a wide spectrum of information on television audiences. The discussion of media measurement in South Africa should shed more light on how methodologies are combined.

12.8.2 Measuring radio audiences

The unique nature of the radio as a broadcast medium presents problems of audience research that are in many ways, not only different to researching television audiences, but also relatively more complex and difficult (Twyman 1994). It is, in fact, the advantages of radio as a medium – the fact that the medium is mobile and allows people to go on with their daily activities instead of requiring everything to come to a standstill – that make it difficult to measure radio listening:

- The way memory works makes it difficult to recall radio listening.

radio audiences

Normally, past events are retrieved from memory more easily if they are linked with some kind of association. These associations (also called 'codes' or 'labelling') link to the time and place that the event occurred, the uniqueness of the event and habitual behaviour. However, as radio listeners are often mobile, and listening is often more casual than habitual, and as radio programmes are often of an ongoing nature and not unique (e.g. the morning and late afternoon programmes), it becomes difficult for people to code and thus to retrieve radio listening.
- It is also more difficult to identify the radio station listened to. Radio stations therefore need to establish a particular identity over and above their programme material and to repeat the name and/or identity of the station at regular intervals to ensure that people realise to which station they are listening.
- Radio listening often serves as a type of 'companion' to other concurrent activities, such as performing household tasks, driving to work, doing homework, and so forth. This is in stark contrast to other media, such as television, film and print, where media behaviour is much more purposive (e.g. a person plans to watch a particular television programme, goes to the cinema deliberately to see a particular film or buys a particular newspaper to read), involves being in the right place at the right time (sitting in front of television when a programme is broadcast and/or being at a cinema when a film is showing) as well as abandoning all other activities. Defining 'listening' in the case of the radio consequently becomes very subjective. In the absence of clear defining criteria, people can exclude certain categories of radio listening. Research indicates, for example, that respondents tend NOT to report radio listening if they were doing something else at the time, were not paying full attention and/or when they themselves did not control tuning decisions (e.g. somebody else turned the radio set on).
- As radio is a mobile medium, a lot of listening happens outside the home. It is consequently not really feasible to capture radio listening by means of household meters.

The following techniques are employed in measuring radio audiences (Twyman 1994):
- systematic recalls and coincidentals, as discussed in section 12.7.1;
- surveys in which respondents are questioned with regard to what they

usually listen to, when they usually listen and how often they listen to particular programmes, namely their radio listening habits;
- diaries, as discussed in section 12.7.2;
- metering – as already indicated, audio metering was introduced before its applications for television. However, the growth in radio mobility (e.g. the development of car radios, the explosion in the availability of small portables) and the rise of multi-set ownership led to the demise of these systems of radio metering. PPMs, on the other hand, could be employed in metering radio listening.

Various studies have been conducted to compare different techniques in measuring radio audiences. In most of these studies, data obtained by means of coincidentals were taken as the standard to which the quality of data obtained by means of other techniques were compared (see section 12.7.1). A series of North American studies indicated that the exact way in which these techniques are applied, in interaction with local conditions, determines the levels of listening reported. An overview of research studies brings Twyman (1994) to the conclusion that levels of reported radio listening are depressed (lower) when compared to the standard, where:
- there is sole reliance on memory and recall techniques such as in questionnaire surveys and systematic recalls;
- the reporting of radio listening needs to compete with other media – due to the purposive nature of other media such as television, radio listening is often overlooked when it happens parallel with other activities, is accidental or imposed by other people. If diaries are used to record radio listening, it is consequently better not to include other media also.
- there is less intensive questioning. In research conducted in Germany, as reported by Franz (in Twyman 1994), recall techniques yielded similar results to diaries when respondents were required to reconstruct their previous day in great detail, recalling all activities and not only radio listening. This study demonstrates that if sufficient care is taken to reconstruct memory by means of intensive interviewing, then the responses on recalls can match the levels obtained by diaries and/or coincidentals.
- questioning focuses on 'usual habits'. The problem is that radio listening is often casual and not based on habit to the same degree as television, where people often follow a series or serials.

The conclusion can be drawn that the strength of radio as a broadcast medium – of being receivable in a variety of contexts – makes research difficult. Researchers therefore need to work harder and probably need to use a variety of methods, such as intensive interviewing and diaries designed especially for radio, to measure radio audiences. The potential of new technological developments, such as PPMs that can recognise radio signals, still needs to be fully explored and researched.

12.8.3 Measuring the audience of print media: newspapers and magazines

print audiences

Similar to most other media industries, editors and organisations involved in the publication of newspapers and magazines operate in two markets. The first is the market for the selling of copies. With regard to this market, readership data provide editors and circulation departments with information on the relative 'success' of the publication in attracting the size and profile of the target audience. The second is the market for selling advertising space. As much as 70% of the revenue of newspapers and magazines might rely on selling advertisement space. Here also, readership estimates have become the 'currency' for the trading of advertising. There is consequently similar pressure on the print industry, as on the broadcasting industries, for detailed, valid and reliable readership data.

Most readership research focuses on two issues (Brown 1994):
- The audience size of a newspaper or magazine is usually measured in terms of the *average issue readership*, that is, the number of different people that reads a particular issue averaged across issues (coverage). Here it is important to point out that each copy of a particular issue could potentially have several readers.
- It is, however, insufficient to categorise people either as readers or non-readers of a particular newspaper or magazine. It is also necessary to establish the regularity or frequency of their reading (frequency). Frequency is usually indicated by the *probability* of contact with a particular issue. Frequency will usually correlate with other features of the audience. It will, for example, be more likely that people who purchase or subscribe to a particular newspaper or magazine would be regular readers. Frequent readers are furthermore more likely to read the contents more thoroughly and intensively – an important reason why frequency is often given more weight in estimating readership.

Readership research is confronted with a number of unique problems related to the nature of the medium (Brown 1994):
- More than for any other medium, defining 'reading' is difficult, highly controversial and often differs from method to method and from study to study. Reading can vary along a wide spectrum, from a cursory glance taking notice of headlines to thorough perusal of a publication that takes a considerable period of time and leads to the transfer of the contents to the reader's mind. Readership estimates are heavily dependent on the operational definition of reading. The tighter the definition (i.e. the higher the intensity of reading required), the lower reader estimates would probably be.
- There are a number of factors that can be measured which are predictive of the intensity of reading: the source of a copy (bought copies would probably be consumed more intensely than copies passed on or casually encountered); the context of reading (in-home reading may be more intense than reading while commuting, at a hairdresser, a doctor's consulting rooms, etc.); the time and circumstances of reading (reading during lunch hour may differ from reading in bed at night); total time spent with an issue; the total number of times an issue is picked up; and/or the proportion of the issue which is read or looked at.
- In estimating print media audiences, the focus falls predominantly on an *issue* or issues of a particular newspaper or magazine and not on particular sections of the contents, such as the editorial page or an advertisement. When readership estimates therefore speak of 'issue readership', this does not necessarily imply thorough reading of particular sections or taking notice of a particular advertisement. Readership data is mostly also not concerned with communication effectiveness with regard to any sections of the contents.
- Many reading events are casual and not particularly memorable. That is particularly the case with publications that are read infrequently, irregularly and/or accidentally. Most people can recall habitual behaviour very well: for example, the name of the newspaper delivered to their doorstep that they read every morning. It is, however, more difficult to remember the name of a magazine read at a hairdresser that one does not usually buy and/or read.
- Whereas coincidentals usually serve as yardstick or standard against which other television and radio audience estimates are compared, no such yardsticks exist for evaluating the quality of readership data.

It is important to note that circulation figures can never be used to represent the total audience as many copies would have multiple readers.

In the absence of electronic metering devices for measuring readership, readership research is mostly dependent on more traditional research methodologies and techniques (Brown 1994):

- *Face-to-face interviews* – both qualitative and quantitative interviews are employed in readership research. However, it is seldom possible to involve adequately representative samples in the case of qualitative interviews. Structured questionnaire interviews are consequently employed to obtain comparative national data for the most important publications published in a particular country. Personal interviewing conducted by fieldworkers – whether qualitative and/or quantitative – holds several advantages in readership research. As it is sometimes difficult for respondents to identify correctly the publications that they read, a personal interviewer can prompt a respondent visually by carrying the necessary field materials (e.g. copies of the publications, pictures of mastheads, and so forth) around with them.
- *Questionnaire surveys* – as already indicated, various types of surveys have become commonplace in readership research. Although telephone surveys are widely used in the US and Europe, they have limitations in developing countries (see Chapter 10). With regard to the question formats in surveys, it is important to remember that completely unstructured, open-ended questions such as 'what do you read?' generally lead to considerable under-reporting of reading. It is therefore common practice to prompt respondents by providing a list of the publications to be covered or by showing illustrations of their logos or mastheads, examples of their covers or even complete issues (where a limited number of publications are covered). Brown (1994) regards the aids used to prompt readers as critical to the quality of data obtained in readership interviews. However, when readers have to self-complete questionnaires, there can be no guarantee that each of the newspapers/magazines on the list will be given balanced and equal attention.
- Readership surveys are associated with a number of techniques, namely:
    - 'Through-the-book' (TTB) – this is one of the oldest techniques, but is currently in limited use. The technique involves interviewers

showing respondents a particular issue of a newspaper or magazine, taking them through it page by page and prompting them as to whether they have read particular key articles. The original technique has undergone some changes. Due to the need to cover multiple publications, interviewers nowadays often use 'skeleton' issues containing only a small portion of the full issue. Also, filtering has been added. Typically, a respondent is given reproductions of the logos of publications on small cards that need to be sorted into groups comprising the ones they have or have not read in the past year.
- 'Recent reading' (RR) – this technique is different from TTB in the sense that it relies on respondents recalling having read any issue of a particular publication rather than on the recognition of a particular issue. Respondents are prompted for each of a number of newspapers or magazines, either by naming them or, generally, by using visual material displaying their logos or mastheads. A key question or series of questions is repeated for each publication to establish when the respondent last read or looked at any issue.
- 'First reading yesterday' (FRY) – respondents are questioned on the newspapers and magazines that they saw 'yesterday', that is, the day before the interview. In follow-up questions, respondents can be asked whether the newspapers and/or magazines encountered on the particular day were seen or read for the first time and/or whether they are seen/read regularly.
- Where media research has to cover a large number of publications, such as in national surveys, the media lists can contain tens or even hundreds of publications. In such cases 'order effects' could become a source of error. Publications higher on the list will have a greater chance of being chosen than those lower on the list. This problem is conventionally addressed by administering a readership questionnaire in a number of different, balanced orders amongst different sub-samples.
- Many newspapers and magazines conduct readership surveys by enclosing a questionnaire in one or particular issues of the publication. Although such surveys cannot be employed to estimate general readership estimates, they can be useful to establish the reading and/or appreciation of particular sections of the publication. However, the problem is that such questionnaires are generally completed by

the person who originally 'owns' the copy, that is, the person who bought or subscribed to the publication. Little or no information will be obtained from additional readers to whom the copy is passed on, although they might represent a sizable portion of the readership.
- *Readership diaries* – similar than for radio and television, a sample of respondents can be requested to maintain day-by-day records on which publications they saw and/or read. The strength of diaries is that they provide a longitudinal record of a person's reading over a continuous period of time. Regularity and frequency of contact with particular publications may thus be estimated with greater accuracy than when recall techniques are used.

Similar to the quest for a passive peoplemeter, readership researchers are contemplating the idea of 'passive' systems of measurement that will not require respondents' voluntary cooperation and will make researchers independent of the veracity of data offered by respondents (Brown 1994). The analogous system for readership research would be one that could 'sense' proximity to a particular title or issue and capture the data. Such systems have already been proposed to the industry and have proved to be workable. All of them involve the insertion of a microchip or radio frequency device in the pages of publications. However, in order to be effective in measuring comparative readership figures for a country, the microchips need to be inserted in each and every copy of each publication printed in the country. The flexing of pages when a publication is read, would then produce an ultrasonic signal that could be picked up by electronic metering devices similar to PPMs. However, although the designs and patents already exist, the funding for such projects is generally still lacking. Here also, questions can be asked regarding the quality and intensity of reading that will be picked up by electronic devices.

12.8.4 Measuring cinema audiences

cinema audiences

Since its emergence as a commercial medium at the beginning of the 20th century, cinema has captured the hearts of audiences all over the world (Chilton & Butler 1994). However, whereas going to the cinema used to be the social event of the week, cinema lost its grip on audiences with the advent of television in the 1950s. Since the mid-1980s, however, cinema has regained some of its popularity due to sustained efforts to produce quality films and investment in new and refurbished cinema venues.

This revival has also boosted cinema advertising revenue. This is good for advertisers, as research has indicated that recall of advertisements is better for cinema than for television.

Chilton and Butler (1994) list the following industry sectors that are interested in data on cinema audiences: cinema advertising contractors and their clients (cinema advertising time can be sold only if information on the audience is provided); cinema distributors (when launching a new film, information on the audience of other similar films is helpful; they also want to track the progress of new films); cinema exhibitors (who need to know how a particular venue and films are doing); video distributors (the popularity of films at the cinema will probably also determine their popularity as videos and/or DVD releases). One can also assume that the managers of television channels would also be interested as the popularity of films at the cinema, as well as the composition of audiences for particular films, would also determine decisions on the broadcasting of films.

The following methods and techniques are employed in measuring cinema audiences (Chilton & Butler 1994):

- *Cinema admissions* – cinema is in the fortunate position that measuring exposure to it is much easier than for most other media. People actively choose to go to the cinema and need to purchase an admission ticket. It is therefore possible to obtain exact admissions data, that is, information on the size of the audience. However, admissions data provide information on how many people go to the cinema, but not on the composition of the audience – that is, the demographic characteristics of cinema audiences.
- *Audience composition* – questionnaire surveys are the acknowledged method to conduct research on the composition of cinema audiences. Questions on cinema-going are usually included in large-scale national surveys, and focus on the following: frequency and recency of cinema-going, as well as information on the particular films that respondents recently saw.
- *Audience by film* – apart from information on the composition of cinema audiences in general, information on the audiences of particular films is also needed by both the advertising and cinema industries. There are manifold reasons for this need: child audiences are, for example, more important and more active during school holidays; advertising packages are planned for particular audiences;

and advertisements for alcoholic drinks and cigarettes are, for example, not included where it is anticipated that more than 25% of the audience will be under the age of 18 years. Again, social surveys are the preferred method for obtaining information on audiences per film. Respondents can be requested, in an open-ended question, to provide details on the films they have seen recently. A list of films can also be provided; for each film, respondents can be probed whether they saw it or not.

The conclusion can be drawn that cinema is in many ways a unique medium (Chilton & Butler 1994). Cinema-going has, for example, a sense of occasion that is different from the habitual listening/viewing associated with radio and television. Indications are that the impact of cinema – and therefore also the impact of advertising that accompanies the showing of a film – could differ from the other media. Cinema is therefore not only important for the recreation industry, but could also play an important role in information and advertising campaigns. Research into cinema audiences should therefore take its rightful place next to the other media.

12.8.5 Measuring outdoor media

outdoor media

Outdoor posters and/or billboards are seldom included when the mass media are considered. However, Bloom (1994) points out that outdoor media are not all about advertising, but also play an important role in governmental and other information campaigns (for example the *Living positively* campaign against HIV/Aids). The number of large poster panels along major urban roads is but one indication that outdoor media still have an important role in communication with the public. However, as outdoor posters are not embedded within entertainment media, people's contact with them is usually casual and unintentional. As they are also not consciously used like other media, people often have difficulties to recall the posters that they have seen. Research on outdoor media is furthermore complicated by the fact that posters can be scattered over numerous – even hundreds and/or thousands – of locations all over a building, city and/or country. However, major agencies involved in information and advertising campaigns do have the need for a scientific approach towards estimating poster audiences to provide a scientific basis for campaign planning.

According to Bloom (1994), poster audience research differs from country to country due to the funds available and the research tradition that developed in a particular country. In many European countries, audiences for posters are measured in terms of the number and frequency of people that pass the sites where posters are displayed, as well as whether posters are well-positioned for visibility to create opportunities for passersby to see them. Cover and frequency are often estimated, based on information about the travel habits of a probability sample of inhabitants. The geographical area involved may be a town, city and/or larger area, even a country as a whole. Typically, respondents are questioned about their journeys in the recent past – the previous day, the last few days or the previous week. Certain kinds of prompts, such as street maps or illustrations of places, can be used. Alternatively, respondents can be requested to record their journeys in a diary format. The technique can be applied for a particular campaign, or for all posters displayed in a particular area in general. It has to be borne in mind that the longer the period, the larger the strain on the memory. Also, the larger the area, the more difficult to apply the technique. The findings are matched with major poster sites, and in this way the potential audiences for posters are estimated.

The Outdoor Site Classification and Audience Research programme (OSCAR) in the United Kingdom focuses on individual poster sites and poster panels (Bloom 1994). The programme has three elements: (a) a complete listing all important poster sites in the UK based on a detailed census and a classification of each site based on a number of site characteristics; (b) a visibility measure for all poster panels, also based on a list of characteristics; (c) a model for estimating the vehicular and/or pedestrian audiences for each location. Audience measures are calculated by means of advanced statistical models. The variables that are considered are the number of people passing by a site on foot or per vehicle based on official traffic counts and the characteristics of a site, as well as the visibility measures of a particular poster panel obtained by fieldworker estimates. Similar studies have been done in the Netherlands. In Sweden, audience estimates are done on the basis of respondent claims in a postal survey of sites passed. In the United States, measures of cover and frequency are also calculated on the basis of national surveys, in which people have to indicate the average number of urban miles travelled per week in the recent past. Additionally, people are asked to trace their journeys on street/road maps. Official traffic counts are also regularly done for major roads and streets. In countries such as Canada, Italy and France, audience measures are also mainly based on official traffic counts, while both surveys and traffic counts are taken into account in Ireland.

Research in various countries has revealed some enduring characteristics of poster audiences: men are more exposed to posters than women, and the employed more than the unemployed. These findings reflect the extent to which different groups move about the streets – employed people are more likely to leave their homes and move about the streets, and men are more likely to be employed than women. It has furthermore been found that posters are particularly good in reaching light television viewers. It seems to indicate that people who do not watch a lot of television move more around road systems than do heavy television viewers.

With regard to the current state and future of poster audience research, Bloom (1994) points to the fact that in some countries surveys play an important role, while only traffic counts are considered in others. Bloom holds the opinion that hybrid systems, as used in the UK and Ireland, are to be preferred above single-method systems. Traffic counts on their own can, for example, give an indication of potential audience size, but do not provide any information on audience composition. It is, however, difficult to integrate the information obtained from very different sources such as traffic counts, questionnaire surveys and/or fieldworker estimates. Elaborate multivariate systems such as OSCAR are also very expensive. Geographic information systems (GIS) could simplify the mapping of poster sites and also hold the potential of accurately tracking the routes travelled by respondents. In doing so, the interview load on respondents can be reduced. More fundamental research should, however, be done on visibility – that is, the ability of pedestrians, drivers and passengers to see designs on poster panels. In summary, the conclusion can be drawn that although outdoor media are probably the 'black sheep' when mass media are considered, research into poster audiences is nevertheless an exciting and challenging field.

12.8.6 Measuring internet audiences

internet audiences

According to Webster and Lin (2002), the visiting of an internet website can be thought of as a kind of mass media behaviour similar to reading a particular newspaper, choosing a particular television programme to watch and/or listening to a particular radio station. The internet is, indeed, a mass medium. As such, measures of audience size and audience duplication are also relevant. Similar to the broadcasting and print media, the internet also depends on audience ratings and indicators of audience size to sustain its operating costs. Sheer audience size is furthermore an indicator of the medium's cultural significance and its potential effects on society. Audience duplication, on the other hand, indicates a form of cumulative behaviour that reflects aspects such as frequency of exposure, audience flow and audience loyalty. These are furthermore indicative of patterns of exposure in the longer term, as well as the intensity with which people use different websites. Both measures are important to both programmers and advertisers – the more so as the divisions between the internet, broadcasting and print media are fast diminishing due to media convergence.

According to Danaher and Balnaves (2002), there are currently two converging approaches to the measurement of internet audiences: a site-centric and a user-centric approach. In the site-centric approach, all internet traffic going through a particular server is monitored. For example, in the case of a university website, every time somebody goes to view it, the call to the server is logged and counted. It seems very simple. However, apart from the fact that this method does not provide any information on audience composition, there is a lot of bogus internet traffic out there. So-called 'web crawlers', 'web spiders' or 'web robots' are put out by search engines to trawl the internet to find information on any new pages that appear on the internet or the price of products on particular sites. These are, of course, not real people. There are also other tricks that are employed by webmasters to manipulate the number of hits to their pages. When a website contains a lot of graphics, the downloading of each graphic counts as a call. If two graphics are downloaded, for example, two calls are registered.

In the user-centric approach, major global ratings companies are currently using internet measurement software as a data collection method (Danaher & Balnaves 2002; Webster et al. 2006). This system is predominantly home-based. A selected panel of respondents – usually very large panels with several thousand respondents – are requested to download software to monitor online web and other internet activities. When a panellist accesses their internet browser, a drop-down menu comes up with the name of each member of the household aged two or older. The panellist needs to click his or her name off before he or she can start browsing the internet. This system is able to generate an overwhelming amount of information on website visits. A further advantage is that the demographic characteristics of household members are available.

The user-centric approach holds, however, some disadvantages. Privacy is a major concern, as every instance of web and/or internet activity is monitored with great precision. The software can only be installed on a computer with the approval of the owner(s). Many people may be reluctant to do so. In the end, there is a great chance that those who do agree to have the software installed may differ from those who do not wish it to be done. Furthermore, the presence of the monitor technology on computers might influence the choices that respondents make. Another problem is that a great volume of internet activity takes place at work. If companies are not willing to have the software installed, then truly random samples of internet users are not possible. There is furthermore such an overwhelming number of websites available that even for samples of several thousand people only the most popular sites such as yahoo.com and msn.com will receive a substantial number of visits.

Thus, the measurement of internet audiences is a minefield fraught with difficulties and pitfalls – perhaps more so than for any other medium. However, as more and more money is spent on internet advertising, pressure is mounting on ratings agencies not only to provide reliable measures of internet audiences for planning and decision-making purposes, but also to allow external auditing of their research processes to ensure the quality of their data (Klaaste sa). It can be assumed that the field of measuring internet audiences will be one of the most important growth and development areas in future.

12.9 AUDIENCE MEASUREMENT IN SOUTH AFRICA

It should have become clear from the previous sections that research into media audiences involves complex and expensive endeavours – the more so as research has to be conducted on an ongoing basis (Kent 1994). The high levels of precision and accuracy required by the interested parties also mean that audience research needs to be conducted according to the highest scientific standards. Research of this nature is so expensive that very few organisations are able to afford it on their own. Also, if a number of organisations were able to conduct research on their own, there would be a lot of duplication and the public might become research-saturated.

Accordingly, the common practice in most countries – including South Africa – is to set up joint research bodies that are responsible for commissioning, coordinating and overseeing research for interested parties in the media and advertising industries (Kent 1994). Such a joint research body holds several advantages. It creates generally acceptable and commonly acknowledged data on media audiences that can inform decision-making and be used as 'currency' in negotiations between interested parties. It furthermore avoids unnecessary competition between various research organisations as well as arguments about the merits and demerits of competing methodologies and measures. There could, however, be disadvantages to such an approach: for example, it could be difficult to bring about change and to get new ideas and/or practices accepted.

In South Africa, broadcasting research goes as far back as 1945, when the research report *Report on Radio Listening in South Africa* was published (SAARF sa; Smit 2006; Van Vuuren 1994). This report focused on listening patterns of the radio services of the SABC at the time. The research was conducted by a private research organisation, South African Research Services. This report was followed by sporadic attempts to report on the readership of newspapers and magazines by way of surveys, mostly commissioned by the publishers themselves. These included some National Readership Surveys. The SABC also conducted, at its own cost, regular studies into radio audiences. When the introduction of television became imminent in the early 1970s, a small group of far-sighted people from the marketing, media and advertising industries realised the need for a comprehensive, unbiased, reliable, regular and technically excellent research service into South African media audiences. Thus a joint research structure was created for measuring media audiences in South Africa, and the South African Advertising Research Foundation (SAARF) was born.

12.9.1 The South African Advertising Research Foundation (SAARF)

SAARF was created on 4 December 1974 with the aim of providing an overarching research service to the media and marketing industries in South Africa (SAARF 2004; Van Vuuren & Maree 1999). Basically, SAARF provides a service to the media and advertising industries by conducting, promoting and sponsoring regular, comprehensive and continuous media audience and product usage surveys. SAARF is responsible for conducting SAARF AMPS®, RAMS® and OHMS and also produces SAARF TAMS® reports. It strives towards continuously improving standards and methods in media and marketing research and to evaluate and validate existing and new methods in order to ensure the reliability, validity and credibility of the research results obtained by their various research initiatives. Additionally, it conducts training to improve the effective use of the research results obtained by SAARF projects. In order to ensure that media and marketing research in South Africa keeps up to date with what is happening in the rest of the world, contact is maintained with international organisations involved in media and marketing research.

Among the founder members of SAARF are the most important media, advertising and marketing organisations in South Africa: the South African Broadcasting Corporation (SABC); the National Association of Broadcasters; Print Media South Africa (PMSA); Out of Home Media South Africa; Cinemark; the Marketing Federation of South Africa; the Association for Communication and Advertising (ACA, formerly AAA) and the Advertising Media Forum. Individuals, institutions, companies and corporations can apply for membership.

SAARF receives an annual endowment from two sources, a levy-collecting agency as well as the PMSA. These bodies also support another important industry body, the Advertising Standards Authority (ASA). The bulk of its financing is obtained from an industry levy on advertising expenditure. This levy is collected by media owners on behalf of the industry.

SAARF is governed by a board of directors. The research projects conducted by SAARF are guided and overseen by a series of councils, while the Advisory Council is involved with all aspects of SAARF's work. The Advisory Council consists of representatives of all the full members of SAARF, as well as a number of research experts. The mandate of the Council is to advise the SAARF board on what research should be undertaken and, when a research project has been approved, on the details of the study. Ad hoc committees and study groups are formed when needed to perform specific tasks and/or to investigate particular issues. The actual research work is contracted out to independent marketing research organisations. SAARF itself operates with a limited number of permanent staff members.

Due to the coordinated research endeavours of SAARF, South Africa currently has a well-developed market and media research industry that endorses standards of best practice comparable to those in the rest of the world (Van Vuuren & Maree 1999). SAARF is also a founder member of the global forum for joint industry committees (JICs). South Africa can be proud of the fact that SAARF was depicted as a model JIC for the rest of the world at the founding meeting of the global organisation. The objectives of this forum are to exchange ideas, to learn from one another's successes and failures and to promote the formation of JICs in as many countries as possible.

12.9.2 SAARF All Media and Products Survey (SAARF AMPS®)

The best-known product of SAARF is the All Media and Products Survey (AMPS®). SAARF (2004) depicts this survey as one of the most comprehensive single-source surveys in the world. The concept 'single source' implies that all media are covered in a single survey (Smit 2006). The AMPS® questionnaire not only covers media (television, radio, newspapers and magazines, cinema, outdoor advertising and the internet), but also products, services (e.g. usage patterns of financial and insurance services) and activities (e.g. activities to lose weight, exercise, buying patterns, travelling, etc.) as well as demographic variables (e.g. age, education level, income, etc.) and social attitudes. In its current format, the survey yields extensive information on characteristics of users of the media and media consumption, as well as data on their usage and purchasing behaviour regarding certain products, brands and services.

SAARF AMPS®

The AMPS® questionnaires are completed by means of personal interviews that are conducted at the homes of respondents, making use of computer-assisted personal interviewing (CAPI – see Chapter 10). South Africa is only the third country in the world to make use of this method in audience measurement surveys. It is estimated that the first component of the questionnaire takes about 50–60 minutes to complete (Milne 2008). The second component consists of a self-completion questionnaire that interviewers leave behind. This component was added due to the fact that the measurement of products and brands had been neglected due to the time constraints imposed by a relatively long questionnaire. This component is also called Branded AMPS, as the questions deal mainly with preferences for particular brands as well as numerous activities and interests. The fact that the second component involves self-completion makes the questionnaire more cost-effective and reduces the time of interviews. However, SAARF (sa) emphasises that Branded AMPS is not a separate survey, but an integral part of the regular AMPS® survey.

In 2008, SAARF AMPS® was conducted in two waves (Milne 2008). The first wave, conducted from mid-January to June, involved a national sample of 12,400 respondents of 16 years or older from urban, semi-urban and rural areas. The second wave, conducted from July to December, involved a sample of 8600 respondents from urban and semi-urban areas (including large towns). In total, 21,000 respondents were interviewed. SAARF plans to conduct two full waves of 12,400 respondents each from 2009 – a total of 25,000 respondents will thus be involved. Both waves will include urban, semi-urban and rural areas. A method of multistage area (cluster) stratified probability sampling is employed for the AMPS® surveys . The sample is pre-stratified by province (nine strata), community size (four strata), gender (two categories) and age (four categories). One respondent is selected at every address, using gender and age to ensure a proportionate sample by these two variables. Inhabitants at mines and hostels and domestic workers are sampled differently, in accordance with their gender composition.

The first AMPS® survey was conducted in 1975 (SAARF sa). Over the years this survey has changed and grown from a fairly modest endeavour to a comprehensive and highly sophisticated product. Although sometimes criticised when compared to similar surveys throughout the world, SAARF AMPS® is still of the highest quality. In 2007 the survey was audited by an independent international consultant, Erhard Meier, who found the study to be a well-designed and well-executed survey that compares well with international standards (Research 10 2008). The results of SAARF AMPS® serve as the official currency for the print media industry and plays an important role in decision-making in the other media industries.

12.9.3 SAARF Radio Audience Measurement Survey (SAARF RAMS®)

The SAARF AMPS® surveys can only ask about radio listening in very general terms. However, users of audience data need to know for each station, for each day of the week, and for each quarter hour of the day, how many people were listening and what their demographics were (SAARF sa; Smit 2006). SAARF RAMS® is designed to fulfil this need for more precise information on radio listening patterns. The survey makes use of radio diaries to provide detailed information on radio listening behaviour, in addition to the information provided by SAARF AMPS®. The following aspects are covered (Research 10 2008):

- radio stations listened to during the period of seven days;
- times listened to each station for each day of the week, for each quarter of an hour, for the 24 hours of each of seven consecutive days;
- radio stations listened to in the past four weeks;
- three most preferred radio stations (in order of preference) – this is done because people are sometimes forced to submit to the radio listening choices of other family members, especially in poorer households with only one radio set (Milne 2008);
- non-listeners – Milne (2008) points to the fact that information on non-listeners is also important, and it is therefore included.

The same sample of respondents used for SAARF AMPS® is also used for SAARF RAMS®. However, a new procedure called 'flooding' was introduced in 2004, whereby all household members of 16 years and older – in addition to the one selected for the SAARF AMPS® interview – are requested to keep a SAARF RAMS® diary for one week (seven days). This procedure more than doubles the diary sample. The SAARF RAMS® diary is left with the household members at the end of the SAARF AMPS® interview and collected a week later. Where some members of the family are illiterate or semi-literate, other family members and neighbours are requested to help them to complete the diary. However, according to Milne (2008), the SAARF RAMS® diary does not require a high level of literacy to complete. Results are published every two months, six times a year, and every reporting period covers the most recent two fieldwork periods on a rolling basis.

Critics point to the fact that the SAARF RAMS® data currently do not include information on the place of listening or mode of listening (Research 10 2008). So there is no indication whether people listen in their homes, in their cars or elsewhere. Likewise, there is no indication whether listening takes place via radio, the internet, a cellphone or any other mode. As there is an increasing need for this kind of information in the digital age, these shortcomings should receive consideration in future.

12.9.4 SAARF Television Audience Measurement Survey (SAARF TAMS®)

SAARF TAMS®

Besides the information provided by SAARF AMPS®, peoplemeters have been employed in South Africa since the late 1980s to measure television viewing (SAARF sa; Smit 2006). SAARF TAMS® is able to measure the second-by-second television viewing of a representative sample of households with television and mains electricity in which TAMS® peoplemeters are installed. The SAARF TAMS® peoplemeters automatically register everything that occurs on one or more television sets and other equipment, such as VCRs or M-Net decoders, that may be attached to them. From 2001, digital satellite transmissions were also metered. The handsets make provision not only for the registering of the viewing of household members, but also for visitors.

Peoplemeters installed in a representative panel of approximately 1600 households across the country measure the television viewing behaviour of about 5000 individuals (Research 10 2008; Milne 2008). The panel sample is modelled according to the population (universe) of people in South Africa who have working television sets and mains electricity as indicated by the SAARF AMPS® data. In 2008, the panel included 387 households subscribing to DStv and an additional 120 households subscribing to M-Net. The data are automatically transferred during the night from panel homes to a central computer every 24 hours via landline telephonic or other electronic links.

During the first years of SAARF TAMS®, large sections of the black population who lived in rural areas did not have access to electricity or landline telephones. Measurement of television viewing in these areas was consequently limited. By 2000, Eskom had expanded electricity supply to almost 80 percent of the country. In addition, technological developments have also made it possible to transfer peoplemeter data by means of radio frequency, GSM cellular phones or via Fastnet, which transfers the data signal to a neighbouring house with a landline telephone from where the data is then uploaded to the central computer. These developments made possible the expansion of the SAARF TAMS° panel to rural areas.

SAARF TAMS° measures the television viewing behaviour of all panel household members from seven years and older (Milne 2008). Currently, SAARF is piloting a project where children from the age of four years are included. As there is no forced rotation, households can stay on the panel as long as they want to. There is, however, a natural attrition rate of about 25 percent per annum. That means that approximately 25 percent of the panel households need to be replaced each year. AGB Nielsen Media Research is the private research organisation responsible for the organisation and upkeep of the SAARF TAMS° panel. Households are continuously monitored to ensure full compliance of all household members. If necessary, they are counselled either by telephone or in person. Telephone coincidentals are furthermore undertaken from time to time to evaluate the quality of the data.

According to Chris Eyre, the executive director of AGB Nielsen Media Research, who manages the SAARF TAMS° panel, they have a policy never to use incentives to recruit households to join the panel (Milne 2008). The reasons are that when a household joins the panel because of the incentives offered, they will tend to take advantage of the incentives, get what they need and then leave fairly quickly. In other words, they will not be committed to participating in the panel. When households are requested to join the panel, an appeal is made to the prospective household to help broadcasters in their choice of programming. They are told that their programme choices will in the end influence programme decisions. It appears that this line of reasoning is accepted well by panel households. A once-off payment of R100 is made to a household when they join the panel. However, as this amount has not changed over the last six years, it could hardly serve as the dominant incentive for joining the panel. (An annual amount of R1140 is paid to DStv households because it is difficult to recruit up-market households.) The names of panel members are, however, entered into prize draws from time to time. SAARF furthermore undertakes to fix any television viewing equipment of panel households if these break down, to a maximum of R400. This is done because broken equipment implies that the data from the particular household will be lost for a particular period of time.

12.9.5 SAARF Out of Home Media Survey (SAARF OHMS)

SAARF OHMS

In addition to the AMPS® data on outdoor media, SAARF OHMS represents an attempt to provide the media, advertising and marketing industries with data comparable to the peoplemeter data for television to plan outdoor campaigns (Milne 2008; SAARF 2008). SAARF worked with Nielsen Media Research in the US and South Africa to become the first JIC to pilot a new methodology that could evolve into an international currency for outdoor advertising.

The OHMS device, called the Npod, is a pocket-size device for the measurement of outdoor media. It makes use of GPS satellite methodology to track not only outdoor media passed, but also the speed at which the respondent is travelling as well as the route taken. The device also measures 'opportunity to see' defined by the pre-defined visibility zone of each outdoor media site. It can be installed on the dashboard of a vehicle or carried around by pedestrians. A sample drawn from adults with mains electricity – a subsample of the AMPS® sample – has to take the device everywhere with them for a period of nine days. The data is stored on a memory card and downloaded electronically. At the end of each of the nine days the respondents also need to complete a questionnaire in which they have to indicate, for each day, whether they left their homes, how much time they spent travelling and whether they took the Npod with them. The data is overlaid with data on outdoor media sites obtained from Out of Home Media South Africa (OHMSA) in order to measure the audience size for various sites.

Since its roll-out in Gauteng and KwaZulu-Natal in 2006, the Npod device has also been tested in Frankfurt, Germany and is also in use in the US. The first South African results were released in January 2008. The data indicated strong year-on-year growth in exposure to outdoor media. The conclusion can be drawn that the importance of outdoor media, and therefore also the measurement of exposure to outdoor media, is increasing in importance.

12.9.6 SAARF Universal Living Standards Measure (SAARF LSM™)

During the 1980s, audience researchers and marketers used to categorise the population into rural and urban segments (Research 10 2008). However, it became evident that the differences between rural and urban markets were fast disappearing, and the need for a new segmentation tool became clear. SAARF consequently embarked on a project to develop a combined measure that would be able to distinguish between respondents on the basis of their living standards rather than any single demographic characteristic (SAARF 2004). By using advanced multivariate statistical techniques, such a measure was developed in 1988 and fine-tuned in 1989 – the SAARF LSM™. This measure was again reviewed on the basis of the SAARF AMPS® 2000A data in order to test a number of new variables included in the survey. The result was that 4 of the initial list of 20 variables used in the construction of the SAARF LSM™ were dropped and replaced by new variables. However, in order to make the SAARF LSM™ more useful, a new SAARF Universal LSM™ was developed from the AMPS® 2001A data. This new index is based entirely on household variables that were expanded to a list of 29 variables. These variables are statistically ranked according to their discriminatory power. The SAARF LSM™ groups were also expanded from 8 to 10 SU-LSM® groups – 1 (lowest) to 10 (highest). Currently the variables indicated in Table 12.2 are employed in distinguishing between the 10 SU-LSM® groups.

The SAARF Universal LSM® represents a unique means of market segmentation in South Africa for both the media and advertising industries. It cuts across race and other ways of categorising people on the basis of single demographic variables. As it is a multivariate segmentation tool constructed from 29 individual variables, it is a much stronger differentiator than any single demographic variable, such as gender or race. Particular kinds of media, goods and services are used by the various SU-LSM® groups (Van Vuuren & Maree 1999). The SU-LSM® groups are also increasingly employed for the segmentation of media audiences.

Most marketing campaigns are aimed at SU-LSM® groups 7 to 10 as these are relatively wealthy people with money to spend on consumer goods (Van Vuuren & Maree 1999). However, a politician wishing to convince people to vote for his party will need to take special notice of SU-LSM® group 1. This category comprises the poorest of the poor – about 4.5 million people. Research shows that none of these people have appliances such as stoves or geysers, but about 82% have access to a

Table 12.2 Variables included in development of SAARF LSM™ groups

1	Hot running water	16	Less than two radio sets in household
2	Fridge/freezer	17	Hi-fi/music centre
3	Microwave oven	18	Rural outside Gauteng/Western Cape
4	Flush toilet in/outside house	19	Built-in kitchen sink
5	No domestic in household	20	Home security service
6	VCR	21	Deep freezer
7	Vacuum cleaner/floor polisher	22	Water in home/on plot
8	No cellphone in household	23	M-Net/DStv subscription
9	Traditional hut	24	Dishwasher
10	Washing machine	25	Electricity
11	PC in home	26	Sewing machine
12	Electric stove	27	Gauteng
13	TV set	28	Western Cape
14	Tumble dryer	29	Motor vehicle in household
10	Home telephone		

Source: SAARF sa

radio. Their top four needs are access to clean drinking water, electricity, roads and job opportunities. Any communication campaign to reach this group will need to take these factors into account.

SAARF was awarded the prestigious AAA 'Media Innovator of the Year' award in 1993 for the development of the SAARF LSM groupings and the contribution that this measure has made toward market segmentation in South Africa. The SU-LSM® measure has furthermore been implemented in some African countries, as well as in India and Russia. The SU-LSM® measure is re-calculated on a continuous basis to make provision for change. An illustration of the use of the SAARF LSM groupings in media research is found in the case study discussed in section 12.10.

12.9.7 The SAARF Media Groups Measure (SAARF MGM)

The SAARF MGM was developed as a segmentation tool to be used in addition to the SAARF SU-LSM® (Research 10 2008). A major reason behind the initiative for developing the MGM was the realisation that when the SAARF SU-LSM® is used for media scheduling, without taking media-related variables into account, there is an existing risk

Measuring Media Audiences

that potential consumers could be excluded. A broader approach than using merely the SAARF SU-LSM® was consequently required. A further motivation was the desire expressed by the government to be able to reach as many people in the entire population and across the whole country in the most cost-effective manner, and the need to identify media that could optimally achieve this objective. Thus the SAARF MGM aims to assist people to identify the best media to reach large groups of people. The measure comprises the following eight groups (Research 10 2008:32):

- MGM1 – extensive exposure to radio (particularly public service broadcasting) and some exposure to television, outdoor media in stores and on billboards and, to a lesser extent, on buses and taxis.
- MGM2 – high exposure to radio, though lower in comparison with MGM1 as other media come into play, such as increased exposure to television; outdoor media follows a similar pattern.
- MGM3 – limited average issue readership (AIR) of newspapers and magazines; radio listening is at a high level; greater exposure to television; exposure to all forms of outdoor media, but limited exposure to posters on taxis and buses.
- MGM4 – similar exposure to radio, television and outdoor media as MGM3, but improvement in the readership of newspapers and magazines.
- MGM5 – exposure to radio and television shows a further increase; readership shows a considerable increase; also extended exposure to outdoor media.
- MGM6 – high exposure to radio and television; growing interest in print, culminating in enhanced reading of weekly and monthly magazines; increasing levels of urbanisation result in inclusion of moving outdoor media (buses, trailers and trucks).
- MGM7 – evidence of some cinema and internet consumption; print media rises further; exposure to radio and television remains high; continued growth of all types of outdoor media.
- MGM8 – exposure to television is at its highest and exposure to radio at its second highest (next to MGM1); more exposure to outdoor media as a result of greater mobility; higher income and discretionary spending give access to the full range of media options; cinema and internet consumption at its peak.

12.10 CASE STUDY: PEOPLEMETERS DETECT POTENTIAL DISCIPLINARY PROBLEMS IN SOUTH AFRICAN SCHOOLS

The relevance of audience measurement data for academic researchers, as well as for disciplines outside the media and marketing industries, is illustrated by a study conducted by Van Vuuren and Gouws (2007) in which they made use of the SAARF TAMS® data obtained by means of peoplemeters for March 2006. In analysing the SAARF TAMS® data for 2005, they found that an estimated 145,640 South African children between the ages of seven and ten years were watching television during school hours. In follow-up analyses in 2006, even higher figures were recorded. The average AR for weekdays from 6 to 26 March 2006 during the time slot of 07:30 to 13:30 was 6.3. Extrapolated to the population of South African children between the ages of seven and 10 years of age, an estimated 243,054 were to be found in front of their television sets during school hours (1 AR accounted for 23,580 children).

It can be assumed that a portion of the children who watched television during school hours had legitimate reasons for not being at school such as illness. However, this portion should be relatively small, not more than 2.5 ARs. Van Vuuren and Gouws (2007:11) provide the following demographic data from children watching television during school hours:

Demographic variable	%
Gender	
Male	60
Female	40
Age	
7–12 years	67
13–10 years	33
Language	
Afrikaans	21
English	14
Nguni language group: (Swazi, Ndebele, Xhosa, Zulu)	43
Sotho language group: (South Sotho, Northern Sotho, West Sotho)	22
SAARF LSM™ groups	
1–4	8
5–6	60
7–10	32

The following observations can be made:
- More male than female children watched during the mornings.
- The younger age group represented about two thirds of the children watching during the mornings.
- The children were spread over all the language groups, but the largest percentage belonged to Nguni-speaking groups.
- A relatively low percentage of children from the low socioeconomic groups were found to be watching in the mornings. The largest percentage came from the middle socioeconomic groups, while the high socioeconomic groups were also fairly represented. Due to the fact that the majority were from the middle and higher socioeconomic groups, the conclusion can be drawn that more of them were living in urban rather than in rural areas.

Further analyses indicated that Mondays and Tuesdays were particularly problematic, as the highest 'absenteeism' figures were recorded for these days. Figures for Wednesdays were the lowest, but they started to build up again from Thursdays to Fridays. It was furthermore found that the children predominantly watched SABC1 and SABC2 during school hours and, in particular, the repeat broadcasts of three soapies: *The Bold and the Beautiful, Generations* and *Isidingo*, and, somewhat later, the repeat of *7de Laan*.

Although the SAARF TAMS® data give a strong indication that there is a problem, the data cannot explain why the children were not at school. Van Vuuren and Gouws (2007) speculate that rapid urbanisation, the disintegration of traditional family systems and the existence of many single-parent families are some of the factors that could play a role in the disciplinary problems indicated by the data. African children could also feel alienated in the overwhelmingly Western culture of most public schools, and especially in private and former Model 'C' schools. Many township schools are also not functioning optimally. Due to the fact that parents work long hours, children also have little contact with their parents. Soapies might fulfil an important role in the lives of these children. They might be avoiding school due to poor performance and the soapies serve as escapist tools – the soapies create an imaginary world of warmth and friendship, that is a 'virtual' reality that is much nicer than the actual reality of the children's lives.

This study illustrates some of the strengths as well as some of the limitations of audience measurement. The data obtained by means of peoplemeters could identify the trend that unacceptably large numbers of South African children of a school-going age are watching television during school hours. However, the data do not offer any explanations for this trend. Van Vuuren and Gouws (2007) can only speculate on possible reasons for the problem. Further research is needed to investigate the problem in depth and to come up with possible solutions.

12.11 PROBLEMS, LIMITATIONS AND CRITICISM OF AUDIENCE MEASUREMENT

The discussions in this chapter indicate that audience measurement has become a highly sophisticated industry with an impressive arsenal of methodologies, technologies and techniques at its disposal. However, audience researchers are continuously confronted with new problems and challenges due to the ever-changing media environment. The practice of audience measurement is also widely criticised, especially within academia (Ivala 2007).

Firstly, the nature of the audience is becoming increasingly complex. Not so long ago, most families had only one television and one radio set (Kent 1994). Today, many households have more than one or several of each. Whereas listening and watching have traditionally been family or group-related activities, these activities are increasingly becoming more individualised. People – and especially children – have, for example, television and radio sets in their rooms. Technological innovation is also having a huge impact on the audience. Radio listening has been expanded by car radios and personal radio/cassette players, while VCRs, PVRs and CD players have promoted control over television watching. Cable and satellite television, as well as the deregulation and commercialisation of the media, have furthermore extended the available choice of stations and/or channels. As mobile telephony and the internet have been added to the media mix, individuals can make use of web newspapers, web radio or web television, thus intensifying media layering. People are also actively contributing to this complexity by mixing and integrating media, media sources and media activities. A person can, for example, read a newspaper, book or magazine while listening to the radio or an MP3 track, casually following a cricket game on television and/or answering a call on his or her mobile phone. The question can be asked whether separate measurements of the audiences of various media still offer a realistic picture of media audience practices in the 21st century.

Continuous technological innovation has, however, succeeded in keeping audience research organisations abreast of some of the transformations in the media environment (Danaher & Balnaves 2002; Garland 2002; Kent 1994). PPMs, for example, can provide for the need for measuring the increasing individualisation of media behaviour. Peoplemeter technology has developed to capture multiple equipment per household and to be able to register cable, satellite and digital television. However, one of the most vexing problems that confronts audience researchers today is the highly fragmented and rapidly expanding choice of radio stations and television channels (Kent 1994). In some countries, hundreds of stations and/or channels are available. The financial size and 'footprint' of a typical regional radio station is, for example, relatively small. This serves to restrict the sample sizes of listeners to particular regional stations in national surveys and makes it difficult to draw conclusions regarding their listenership. Thus regional stations are hampered in competing for advertising revenue. The same problem applies to the multiple television channels available through cable and satellite broadcasting such as DStv. Although developments in inexpensive technology could make the independent metering of pay television possible, the impact for national audience measurement initiatives needs to be reckoned if some services or channels do their own measurement.

The controversy regarding the conceptualisation of watching, listening, reading and/or visiting is also continuing (Ivala 2007), the more so as devices such as PPMs no longer require respondents to consciously indicate that any of these activities have taken place. It is legitimate to ask whether it can be assumed that hearing has really has taken place if a person moves into the vicinity of a radio set that is switched on and the audio code is picked up by a PPM.

In academic circles, audience measurement is sharply criticised, in particular within the cultural studies and critical traditions. Critics hold that audience measurement practices lead to the creation of oversimplified, limited and static quantitative pictures of audiences, in which averages, regularities and generalisable patterns are emphasised, while particularities, idiosyncracies and surprising exceptions are ignored (Ang 1991; Ivala 2007). The audience measurement industry is also accused of being insensitive to alternative viewpoints of audiencehood. Audience measurement is furthermore accused of failing to highlight the vibrancy of audience behaviour and the variety of practices involved in being a member of the audience, as well as the experiences of actual members of the audience and how meaning is produced through processes of media consumption. Audience measurement furthermore focuses on the media behaviour of individuals, while ignoring the cultural and social contexts in which individuals are integrated. In summary, audience measurement is accused of creating a limited and shallow view of the complexity of audiences and of being uncritical of the notions of audiencehood that it portrays.

SUMMARY AND CONCLUSIONS

The conclusion can be drawn that, notwithstanding the rather impressive arsenal of methodologies and techniques that have developed over the years to capture audience behaviour, audience researchers are continuously confronted with new problems and challenges due to technological developments and an ever-changing media environment. Criticism of audience measurement practices furthermore points to the fact that the results of audience measurement endeavours can never be regarded as the full and final answer to the quest for knowledge about media audiences. Knowledge produced through audience measurement practices should be enriched by being embedded within theoretical paradigms. Knowledge of media audiences should furthermore be expanded and deepened by research within alternative paradigms, in which qualitative and participative methodologies are employed.

LEARNING ACTIVITIES

1 You are the manager of the campus radio station of your university. Devise a diary that can be used to investigate the radio listening patterns of students. Ask five students to complete the diary for seven days. Analyse the results and write a report to the management committee in which you make recommendations for the future operation of the station on the basis of the results of your study.

2 Plan an information campaign on child health aimed at young

> mothers of the SAARF MGM groups 1 and 2. Your campaign should aim to reach as many people as possible.
> 3 You are a research consultant for your campus newspaper. Develop a research plan for a readership study for the newspaper.

FURTHER READING

Beville, H.M. (Jr). 1988. *Audience ratings: Radio, television, and cable* (revised edition). Hillsdale, New Jersey: Lawrence Erlbaum Associates.
Kent, R. (ed) 1994. *Measuring media audiences*. London: Routledge.
Mytton, G. 1999. *Handbook on radio and television audience research*. London: UNICEF and UNESCO.
Van Vuuren, D. & Maree, A. 1999. Survey methods in market and media research, in *Research in practice: Applied methods for the social sciences*. Cape Town: University of Cape Town Press:269–86.
Van Vuuren, D., Maree, A. & De Beer, A. 1998. Mass media research: The quest for certain knowledge, in *Mass media: Towards the millennium*, edited by A. de Beer. Pretoria: JL van Schaik:391–422
Webster, J.G., Phalen, P.F. & Lichty, L.W. 2006. *Rating analysis: The theory and practice of audience research*. Mahwah, New Jersey: Lawrence Erlbaum.

ACKNOWLEGEMENTS

The author wishes to thank the following persons for their assistance in the writing this chapter:
Dr Daan van Vuuren – former Head of Research at SABC
Piet Smit – former Chief Technical Officer, SAARF
Michelle Boehme – Technical Manager, SAARF
Claire Milne – Technical Support Executive, SAARF

chapter thirteen

PSYCHOANALYSIS AND TELEVISION

Stefan Sonderling

LEARNING OUTCOMES

At the end of this chapter, you should be able to:
- provide a definition of psychoanalysis;
- explain the role of the image, language and society in constructing the human mind;
- describe the conscious and unconscious structures of the human mind;
- recognise the main assumptions of psychoanalytical theories and their relevance to the study of film and television;
- identify the main stages in the experience of film and television viewing;
- apply a model of psychoanalysis to describe the interaction between the viewer and television texts.

Psychoanalysis and Television

THIS CHAPTER

The aim of this chapter is to provide you with an awareness of the psychological process experienced by film and television viewers. The chapter thus seeks to explain psychoanalysis as a way of understanding the viewer's experience of film and television viewing. The psychological development of the human mind, and its conscious and unconscious structures, is applied from a psychoanalytical perspective to the understanding of the viewing experience of film and television. In short, psychoanalysis as a way of describing and evaluating the interaction between the viewer and the film and television programmes, is explained.

13.1 INTRODUCTION

The popularity of television viewing, as well as that of film, indicates that these media must somehow have affinity with their audiences' frames of mind. Watching films and television programmes is both meaningful and pleasurable, and implies that the viewer is involved and engrossed in these texts, in a 'pleasure–meaning–commodity complex' (cf. Heath 1985:200). However, traditional film and television theories have largely ignored the spectator's experience and focused on the structure of the film or television programmes as 'text' or examined the intention, personality or genius of the author/producer, forgetting that films and television programmes are made for the viewer. In fact, film and television as industries, and artistic and cultural forms, could not exist without the viewer.

The psychoanalytic approach to the study of film and television corrects this and provides an insight into the viewer's conscious and unconscious interaction with film and television texts. The filmic/televisual *text* refers to the organisation of language (visual and oral), codes and signifying systems produced to create meaning, and the viewer may be considered as the reader or interpreter. Both text and reader are products of culture and history (cf. Kaplan 1990:11). Psychoanalysis explains the link between the pleasures and desires of the spectator *for*, and the fantasies and desires represented *in*, film and television texts.

| psychoanalytic approach |

The application of psychoanalysis to film and television is based on the assumption that film and television viewing resemble a state of dreaming. Watching film and television activates conscious and unconscious mechanisms of the viewer's mind and gratifies repressed desires (cf. Flitterman-Lewis 1987:179).

film theory

Indeed, there is a long tradition in film theory, dating as far back as 1916 – to Hugo Münsterberg's psychological study – that suggests that films, like dreams, project the spectator's imagination on the screen. Subsequent generations of critics followed the film–dream analogy and considered Hollywood, the major producer of popular feature films, to be the 'dream factory' (cf. Altman 1977:264–5). Likewise, the popularity of television may be related to its dream-like quality: in its form and content, television projects the dream-life of a whole society (cf. Wood 1982) performing a 'ritual condensation' – giving abstract ideas visible material form (cf. Fiske & Hartley 1982:89–90).

viewing and dreaming

Considering film and television viewing as analogous to dreaming also means that it is no longer possible to regard these media in terms of either a 'window' that displays objects in the world or a 'frame' that shapes and constructs the meaning of images appearing within its space. They are rather seen as a 'mirror' reflecting the viewer's inner mental states (cf. Altman 1977:260; Andrew 1984:134).

Psychoanalysis as a cultural theory and method of analysis contributes to the understanding of art, literature, film and television, and explains how the conscious and unconscious mental processes function in the production and understanding of works of art (cf. Wright 1984:9). The application of psychoanalysis to the study of film and television may be considered as an extension of structuralism. Structuralism attempts to uncover some coherent unity that underlies and makes meaningful the surface manifestation of diverse cultural phenomena. Freud's theory of the unconscious is similar to the structuralist project: the unconscious and its link to sexuality and the primordial Oedipal drama provide the hidden structure that animates human conscious behaviour. Psychoanalytic methods involve the interpretation of dream narratives, and uncovering their hidden meaning may be described as a form of structuralist textual analysis. Psychoanalysis applied to film and television is a critical discourse that explains the various levels of the viewing process and the way the viewer and text interact.

Readers do not only work on texts, but texts work on readers, and this involves a complex double dialectic of two bodies inscribed in language (Wright 1984:17).

Although the application of psychoanalysis to the study of art, literature and film is by now a well-established intellectual enterprise, and dates back to Freud's own work on art and literature, its application to the study of television is still a new and problematic field. Some theorists object to the direct application to television of psychoanalytic methods developed in film studies because of differences between these media (cf. Flitterman-Lewis 1987). However, it must be remembered that similar objections, based on the formal differences between film and dreams, were raised against the application of psychoanalysis to the study of film (cf. Altman 1977:265). The objection to the application of psychoanalysis to television may be based on the elitist stance of scholars who still consider television as a vulgar form of popular culture and an unsuitable object of study to be included among 'high culture' products such as literature and film (cf. Petro 1986).

While it must be acknowledged that film and television are two different and distinct media, they share many similarities, making it possible to apply psychoanalytic methods developed in film studies to the study of television fictional programmes, such as the soap opera (cf. Butler 1986; Flitterman-Lewis 1987), and to the study of news and actuality programmes (cf. Stam 1983). Television and film may be considered as 'two technologically and social distinct versions of a single language': the language of the cinema underlies both these media (cf. Hall & Metz in Heath & Skirrow 1977:7). Furthermore, in contemporary society, film and television exist in a symbiotic relationship: television has taken over most of the conventions of mainstream narrative film, and film, in turn, is influenced by and incorporates televisual conventions (cf. Barker 1988:50; Ellis 1984:237–9; Hilmes 1985). Like the film, television is 'an imaginary signifier in its own right' (Flitterman 1985:58).

In order to understand the application of the psychoanalytical method to film and television, the basic concepts of psychoanalysis as developed by Sigmund Freud and Jacques Lacan must be outlined.

13.2 PSYCHOANALYTIC THEORY: FREUD AND LACAN

Psychoanalysis is the name Sigmund Freud gave in 1896 to a scientific theory of the human mind and personality and a therapeutic method of investigating unconscious mental processes. Freud also used psychoanalysis as a tool for the analysis of literary texts (cf. Kaplan 1990:12).

| Freud

For Freud, the human personality is the product of the relationship between inner, biologically determined drives or urges and the external constraints of the physical world and society. The human mind may be considered as analogous to an iceberg: beneath conscious activities lies hidden an unconscious element, and any proper understanding of conscious activities must also take into account the unconscious. The human being is born with powerful sexual instincts or drives, which demand gratification. However, human existence is characterised by a harsh struggle for physical survival. In order to survive, basic needs must be provided by toil and labour undertaken in social association with other people. The basic necessity to work and cooperate with others means that man (human male) must repress his natural tendencies to seek pleasure and gratification. Thus, human society and culture are built on a principle of repression, and man finds himself in permanent conflict between the fundamental motivation to avoid pain and seek pleasure and social demands for self-control, delayed gratification and sublimation of desires towards more valued social ends.

Oedipus complex

According to Freud, happiness has no cultural value; renunciation and delay in satisfaction of desires are a prerequisite for social progress (cf. Marcuse 1973:23). Every human being must undergo repression of the 'pleasure principle' by the 'reality principle' to become a member of society (cf. Eagleton 1983:151). The mechanism by which the individual is socialised is the *Oedipus complex*. The Oedipus complex is based on the Greek myth of a son's act of patricide and his incestuous relationship with the mother. Freud considers the myth of Oedipus as symbolic of the basic desire of the son to sexually possess his mother and kill his father and which every male child entering social relationships must overcome.

In the pre-Oedipal stage, the child has a close relationship with his mother and depends on her for the satisfaction of his physical needs for survival. Through the satisfaction of physical needs, such as sucking the mother's breast, the child discovers that performing this essentially biological activity is also pleasurable. This is the beginning of sexuality, which develops through various stages when different parts of the infant's body become the centres of sexual pleasure.

During the development of sexuality, the child also experiences libidinal desires for the mother. This close, incestuous relationship between the child and the mother is shattered when he becomes aware of the father. The father is seen as posing a threat to the child's sexual desires for the mother and becomes a rival for love and affection. The threat that the child experiences is of punishment by castration. Because of this threat and fear of castration, the child detaches himself from the mother and identifies with the father and takes on a position of a gendered subject in society. The father's prohibition of incest is symbolic of all other higher authority in society, which he will experience later in life. The child's forbidden sexual desires for the mother are repressed into the unconscious. The unconscious is in fact created in the process of repression. The result of this massive repression creates an individual who is split between two levels of existence: a person who has a conscious life as member of society and an unconscious life of repressed sexual desires.

The repressed sexual desires lodged in the unconscious manifest themselves in dreams and artistic and linguistic expressions (cf. Wright 1982:113). Dreams are considered as the symbolic fulfilment of unconscious wishes; these wishes manifest themselves in symbolism because direct expression of the material could be shocking and disturbing to the individual. The unconscious softens and distorts the true erotic meaning of these desires through a process Freud terms *the dream work*. The dream work projects the *latent content* (repressed desires) into coded and distorted *manifest content*. In order to understand the 'true' meaning of the dream the manifest contents have to be interpreted. The unconscious 'speaks' its distorted messages through various processes (cf. Eagleton 1983:157; Wood 1982:519):

marginal note: unconscious processes

- *condensation* – by which latent elements are compressed, combined and fragmented into one single manifest image;
- *displacement* – by which a latent element is replaced by a more remote or obscure image and the meaning of one object is displaced onto another somehow associated with it;
- *inversion* – 'regressive translation of thought into images'; these images contain ambiguity and contradiction;
- *dramatisation* – the latent thoughts are given some continuous dramatic forms.

The operation of the unconscious, especially through condensation and displacement, can be compared with the two primary operations of language: *metaphor*, which implies condensing meaning together; and *metonymy*, which implies displacing one meaning for another.

> Lacan

This analogy is what motivates French psychoanalyst Jacques Lacan to claim that the unconscious is structured like language. For Lacan, the unconscious is not a biological residence for drives and instincts but a linguistic and cultural construction. Lacan points to the fact that any understanding of the unconscious demands understanding of language.

> language

Indeed, language and the unconscious have other close similarities. Ferdinand de Saussure describes language as a system or structure (*langue*) that can be distinguished from actual speech (*parole*). Language as a system is in the unconscious of every speaker, of whom the speech act is only meaningful in relation to the unconscious structure (cf. Archard 1984:60). The unconscious element is also in operation in the linguistic sign – the sign is divided into *signifier*, the sound-image, and *signified*, the concept conjured up by the signifier (cf. Fourie 1988:29); thus the signified is always indirectly and imaginatively invoked from the unconscious.

While Freud provides a theory of human development, it is incomplete without consideration of language. Lacan reinterprets Freud's theory in the light of structural linguistics. Language is an important element in human development as without it no social relationship can be imagined. In fact, human life is life in a 'symbolic universe' of language and meaning (see Chapter 3).

> social construction

According to Lacan, the individual is socially constructed in two stages:
- the mirror stage, at the age of six months, during which the child becomes aware of his or her image;
- the symbolic stage, at the age of 18 months, when 'the child enters into society and society's language enters into the child' (Harland 1988:38–9).

> mirror stage

According to Lacan, the early pre-Oedipal and pre-linguistic stages of the child's development process are the realm of the '*imaginary*'. At this stage, the child cannot distinguish between itself and the outside world and exists in an amorphous and genderless state, which Lacan, using a pun, calls '*l'hommelette*' – meaning the 'little man' and 'omelette' (cf. Wright 1984:107–8). The child develops a sense of self through perceptual identification with its image in a mirror. Lacan terms this the '*mirror stage*'. The concept of the mirror coined by Lacan should not be taken literally, as what is meant is that the child either sees an image of itself reflected in the mirror or another *image*, such as its mother's face, which it mistakes to be itself and with which it can identify (cf. Eagleton 1983:165). The child's identification with a mirror image (primary identification), which it takes to be a unified concept of itself, is a misrecognition, as the child mistakes an image for a more perfect whole than it actually is. The misrecognised image is then projected outside itself and considered as ideal. Later, this is again internalised and a desire to identify with others begins (cf. Greenberg & Gabbard 1990:100).

Freud's Oedipus complex is seen by Lacan as an entry into the *symbolic order* (or stage) of language and culture and the acquisition of sexual identity. The figure of the father, which according to Freud signifies the threat of castration and prohibits the total unity of the child with the mother, is seen by Lacan as signifying the introduction of the child to language and the wider social order. For Lacan, the father is symbolic of the laws of the patriarchal society that repress the libidinal drives in the child and his incestuous identification with the mother. The acquisition of language occurs simultaneously with the primal repression that constitutes the unconscious (cf. Lemarie 1982:53). In order to overcome his painful separation from the mother, the child develops linguistic skills to represent the mother's absence, to represent his sexual desires and represent his identification with the role of the father (secondary identification). Not being able to express his desires directly, language becomes a symbolic substitute, always standing between desires and the objects of desires. Thus begins life in the symbolic order.

| symbolic stage |

Language is a primary medium for symbolic identification as it essentially provides a point of reference for man to constitute himself as subject. Language provides 'empty forms', which each speaker can appropriate for himself and relate to his personal identity, defining himself as 'I' and the partner to discourse as 'you' (cf. Benveniste in Morse 1985:2). The 'I' and 'you' are only understood in relation to the existing social relations in society. The concept of 'self' or 'individuality' is not a natural phenomenon nor is it a unified and concrete 'personality' but an elusive construction through social and linguistic processes.

The entry of the individual into society and language also means that he enters into the ideological framework provided by language. Ideology is a system of representations – images, discourse, myths – that explain and make meaningful the social conditions in which people live, reflecting the meanings of these conditions as interpreted by dominant social classes. Ideology is part of the unconscious; it is the taken-for-granted assumptions about the way things are.

ideology

Ideology is *inscribed in* discourse in the sense that it is literally written or spoken *in it*; it is not a separate element that exists independently in some free-floating realm of 'ideas' and is subsequently embodied in words, but a way of thinking, speaking, experiencing (Belsey 1986:5).

Through the acquisition of language, humans can make sense of themselves and their world. Conversely, understanding humans and human society is made possible by the scientific study of language.

Because all the practices that make up a social totality take place in language, it becomes possible to consider language as the place in which the social individual is constructed. In other words, humans can be seen *as language*, as the intersection of the social, historical and individual (Coward & Ellis 1986:1).

From a psychoanalytic perspective, human beings are the product of biologically determined sexual drives, culture and language. The concept of a human's identity as a gendered subject has been internalised during the formative years of the Oedipal drama of infancy. With language and the media, such as film and television, the primal processes are reinforced.

13.3 PSYCHOANALYSIS AND THE STUDY OF TELEVISION

audience

Television as a medium of communication and a cultural and commercial institution could not exist without its *audience*; after all, television programmes are made for the viewer, or, as stated by Godard, 'television doesn't make programmes – it makes viewers' (Flitterman 1983:95). For the viewer, watching television is a *pleasurable* and meaningful experience: no one is forced to watch television, yet large numbers of people turn on their television sets day and night and find the experience enjoyable. The pleasure of television viewing is not limited to the traditional entertainment genres, such as drama, fictional feature films or the soap opera, but also includes the viewing of documentary and news broadcasts (cf. Stam 1983:23).

The pleasure of film and television viewing is found in the characteristic features of these media. Television is a highly visual medium that

Psychoanalysis and Television

combines images and sound to tell stories or fictional narratives. Thus, the pleasure of the viewer is derived from a combination of *looking* and *listening* to *narratives*.

Television and film are 'story-telling machines', technologies utilised to tell tales and satisfy a human desire for narratives (cf. Andrew 1984:143). Thus, like the film, television can be described as a 'technique of the imaginary' (cf. Metz 1982:3):
- consisting of *imaginative* or fictional narratives, creating a world of fantasy in their texts;
- consisting of *imagery* or iconic images, telling their narratives audiovisually;
- '*imaginary*' in Lacan's distinction between the *imaginary* order and the *symbolic*.

As most films and popular television programmes are fictional narratives represented visually, they resemble *dreams*. Thus, viewing a film or a television programme can be compared to the act of dreaming; the audiovisual text of these media mobilises the conscious and unconscious of the viewer. The film or television text lures the viewer to enter the world of fiction, and to suspend his or her belief or disbelief in the unreality of the text.

| dreams

The similarities between television and dreams are outlined as follows (cf. Wood 1982:514–16):
- television and dreams have a highly visual quality;
- television and dreams are highly symbolic;
- television and dreams have a high degree of wish fulfilment;
- television and dreams appear to contain much that is disjointed and trivial;
- television and dreams have powerful content, most of which is readily and thoroughly forgotten;
- television and dreams make use of material drawn from recent experience.

The viewer as a dreamer is positioned and engaged by a whole complex structure of television technology and social institutions. The television institution is not merely the industry that produces programmes, but it is also the mental machinery of the viewers accustomed to television (cf. Stam 1983:38). This complex institution may be termed (to borrow

| cinema/
| television
| apparatus

589

from psychoanalytic film theory's concept of the *cinema apparatus*) the *television apparatus*, consisting of the following elements (cf. Flitterman-Lewis 1987:181):

- the technical base, such as the camera, film, video, light and the projection of the images on the screen;
- the condition of viewing, in the home and familial setting;
- the television 'text' itself, the way it is constructed in order to present visual continuity, illusion of space and illusion of reality;
- the mental machinery of the viewer, and his conscious and unconscious processes.

The television apparatus thus positions the viewer in such a way that he or she has an illusion of being the actual producer of, and the main character in, the text. The viewer considers the television text as his or her own fantasy designed to fulfil his or her desires. It is obvious that the viewer is an important and central part of the whole complex television apparatus. The television apparatus both invites and makes place for and positions the viewer for participation and experience. The viewer's experience and involvement may be represented as a complex process.

To analyse the viewer's involvement with television, the following model can serve as a guideline.

13.4 MODEL FOR THE ANALYSIS OF THE TELEVISION VIEWER'S INVOLVEMENT

The interaction between the viewer and the text in the televisual apparatus centres on a number of elements: *desire, pleasure, regression, identification* and the *mode of enunciation* (cf. Flitterman-Lewis 1987). In other words, the viewer regresses to a dream-like state where he or she takes the images on the screen as his or her own dreams; in this dream-state, he or she is able to identify with images and views presented on the screen. Regression and identification are induced by the quality of the text itself, techniques through which the text is constructed and its mode of addressing the viewer.

13.4.1 Desire and pleasure

desire and pleasure

The imaginative narrative is pleasurable in itself. Eidsvik (1978:6) suggests that all narratives, regardless of their medium, invoke the viewer's imagination by initially asking the viewer or reader an implicit question, 'what if ...?', that can only be answered imaginatively in the narrative. The viewer's imaginary participation in narrative fantasy is cathartic and pleasurable because it relieves the pressure of frustration, both conscious and unconscious (cf. Fourie 1988:78). The pleasure and catharsis are derived from re-experience of the Oedipus complex that motivates all narratives. Because all narrative plots follow an Oedipal structure, the protagonist's desire and the text itself originate in the primordial desire for the mother and the search for the father. In a more complex sense, the text may be considered as a signifier of deeper basic psychosexual structuring processes associated with the Oedipus complex (cf. Altman 1977:258–59). Thus, the narrative is an endless return to the primal scene. Freud's Oedipus is essentially a 'family romance', re-enacted in every film or narrative of television soap opera.

The narrative itself, in its formal structure and fantasy, is also a source of sexual pleasure. The pleasure of the narrative text is derived from its resemblance to sexual intercourse, with its orgasmic rhythm of tensions and resolutions, culminating in a climax (cf. De Lauretis 1984:108).

In addition to the pleasure of narratives, the pleasure of film and television is based largely on perception. According to Lacan (cf. Metz 1982:58), the desire to see (*scopophilia* and voyeurism) and the desire to hear are major components of the sexual drive and thus sources of pleasure. Film and television viewing satisfy the erotic pleasure of perception itself, as well as the pleasure of looking at images of the human form that are erotically stimulating.

13.4.2 Regression

Viewing a film or television entails a mental process of *denial* or *disavowal*, a double suspension of belief or disbelief – believing and not believing simultaneously – in the reality of the fiction and regression to the pleasures of the imaginary stage. Film and television construct their fictional narrative by the use of iconic images, creating an illusion of reality. The power of these media is derived from their ability to convince the viewer that the unreal has been realised (cf. Metz 1974:5). Film and television and their photographic/video iconic images stage their effect with the presence of images (signifiers) that point to the absence of the original object – a play of shadow, referential illusion, or a play of signifiers that leads Metz (1982) to term the cinema as the 'imaginary signifier'. The viewer knows that he or she is seeing a

regression

fictional narrative but suspends this knowledge in order to remain in the state of the illusion and the dream-like state (cf. Metz 1982:69–78). The quality of the visual image reduces the viewer's awareness of his or her actual distance from the real object. The viewer feels as if he or she were not in the presence of a signifier but that of the signified or the object itself. The image has iconic visual similarity to the world it records and is also an index of this world, as it is an imprint left behind by the real object. The viewing situation and mental machinery allow the viewer to suspend his or her belief and enter the dream-like state. He or she has already been prepared by the primordial experience of the mirror stage. Thus, the viewer in front of the screen is like the infant in front of the primordial mirror, fascinated by the images. The viewer's regression and entry into the imaginary world of the narrative have also been prepared by knowledge and experience of other cultural forms of narrative, such as art and literature (cf. August 1981:417).

The viewing situation in the cinema – for example, the dark theatre, the reduced physical activity of the viewer, the comfortable seats, anonymity, the withdrawal from everyday reality – resembles the situation of the helpless infant and is considered to induce a dream-like state. Television viewed in the privacy of the home, with its domestic distraction, may superficially seem to exclude regression. It is claimed that television has a quality of 'immediacy', that it is a 'live medium' bringing the events of the world to the viewer as they happen. However, the liveliness and immediacy of television is rather a myth.

In fact, much of what we think of as 'television' originates on film; filmed series have predominated over live television since the mid-1950s. Yet we still speak of television's 'immediacy', 'spontaneity', 'intimacy'. These terms originated in the early 1950s in reference to truly 'live', unrecorded television; the fact that they have lived on for 30 years after its demise points past technology to ideology (Hilmes 1985:30).

Television modes of address, especially its news, documentaries and talk shows, seem to address the viewer directly, as if he or she were a partner in discourse, and shatter the voyeuristic illusion. However, its audience does not experience television as real. Television is a 'new mode of fiction', because the viewer does not consider the television images on the screen as being truly present or partners to a discourse, but rather as quasi-subjects. Television offers an illusion of discourse: 'we know that elsewhere discourse may be "real", but in our living room that same discourse is imaginary' (Morse 1985:3). Therefore, the viewer is able to regress to an imaginary stage and enter the fictional world of soap operas, televised films, commercials, talk shows and news programmes, and take pleasure in them. The pleasure of the television viewer's identification is derived from his or her experience and participation as subjects in the multiple discourses that make the social reality. However, Freudian and Lacanian psychoanalytic theories' fixation with the over-determination of the Oedipal construction of the subject have neglected other discursive influences that construct the individual beyond the infantile stage.

13.4.3 Mirror identification

The experience of viewing television may be compared to Lacan's mirror stage, where the child identifies itself in an image. Viewing a film or television is pleasurable to the viewer precisely because he or she has experience of this in infancy. In viewing the viewer identifies with his or her own act of looking, and the look itself is termed *primary identification*. The viewer's identification with his or her own look is a source of narcissistic pleasure. Primary identification in television coincides with the look of the camera, and offers the viewer an unlimited camera view and possibilities of identification (cf. Stam 1983:24). Through the primary identification the viewer experiences *secondary identifications* with the perceived human and non-human characters on the screen. Television offers endless sources of secondary identification – characters both imaginary and real – with which the viewer can identify (cf. Stam 1983:27).

<mark>mirror identification</mark>

The pleasure of perception and identification positions the viewer as an ideal *voyeur*, looking on the 'private world' represented by the images and gratifying his sexual desires. The position of the voyeur also gives the viewer a sensation of power, as he can look on the action and be unobserved. The pleasure of perception of film and television is theorised as that of the male viewer. According to this perspective the traditional Hollywood film and contemporary television reflect the dominant patriarchal ideology and produce filmic/televisual texts that satisfy the male unconscious (films are made by male producers for male viewers). The dominant ideology is communicated through the use of a complex series of cinematic and televisual 'looks', in which the viewer is implicated as a male subject: (1) the look of camera to the filmic event, among others; (2) from the male viewer to the screen; and (3) the interplay of looks exchanged between the characters on the screen (cf. Flitterman 1981:243). The structure of the reverse shot and matching view shots increase the illusion of participation as the viewer always has a certain subjective view from the position of one of the characters with whom he may imaginatively identify. The pleasure and fascination of film and television reinforce pre-existing patterns of fascination already at work within the viewer. According to feminist theories, film and television images reveal and play on socially established sexual differences, thus the female form in most narratives becomes a centre of attraction and is displayed for the benefit of the predominantly male audience. In this way, dominant cultural ideology is reflected and reinforced (cf. Mulvey 1985:307). However, the feminist view cannot explain why women viewers find film and television pleasurable. Television programmes such as sport represent both male and female bodies for display, while other fictional programmes present images of male sexuality that both men and women may identify with, for example a figure such as a sexy detective hero: 'far from repressing the erotics of the gaze, the structures of fascination in looking at the male body are utilised to permit this signifying articulation' (Flitterman 1985:43).

13.4.4 Modes of enunciation

enunciation

The regression and entry to the imaginary are helped by the 'modes of enunciation' or the specific structure of the text and use of production techniques that create the illusion in the viewer that he is observing his own fantasies. The term 'enunciation' is derived from structural linguistics and refers to both the 'said' and the act of 'saying' – in other words, a distinction between a *story* (as 'his-story' and 'history'), which refers to the content, and *discourse*, or the way the content is communicated. In film and television theory, enunciation attempts to describe the way the cinematic/televisual text is organised and how this act of organisation is distinctively concealed, creating a specific form of address to the viewer constituting him as a subject.

A discourse implies the position from which the various subjects speak and address each other as you and I. Each of the participants is aware of the other person and his own position. A story is experienced in a more oblique way, according to Barthes:

... as soon as a fact is narrated no longer with a view to acting directly on reality but intransitively, that is to say, finally outside of any function other than that of the very practice of the symbol itself ... the voice loses its origin. (Barthes 1984:143)

For the film and television text to be taken by the viewer as if it were his own dream fantasy, all the marks of construction, and the fact that it is a discourse, should be eliminated. Every film and television programme has a place of enunciation from which it proceeds, or a point of view from which the representations are organised and made meaningful. This point of view is occupied by the director or author of the film/television programme and coincides with the view of the camera recording the film/television programme.

The same point of view must then be given to the viewer who can imagine that he can see his own desires visualised on the screen (cf. Flitterman-Lewis 1987:185). Thus, the experience of film and television is based on the disappearance of the producer, who leaves his place empty for the viewer to take over the production of the discourse. The position of the viewer is considered as an *empty space*, which can be filled by any viewer. The viewer can occupy this empty position as he was already prepared for it through the acquisition of language. In classical Hollywood film, the effacement of the marks of enunciation are produced by the smooth editing of various scenes and combining matching camera shots, all creating a feeling of continuity and coherence of narrative, distracting attention from the fact that a film consists of various shots and sequences that are cut and joined together. The concealment of the marks of enunciation transforms the film from a *discourse* to that of a *story* as if told by no one, and is a mere fact from the viewer's own unconscious story (cf. Flitterman-Lewis 1987:186).

Television has incorporated the conventions of film to conceal its modes of enunciation (cf. Hilmes 1985). However, television also uses its own specific technique to provide unity and coherence to its text, and allows the viewer to imagine that he hears his language and society speaking. Because he has internalised language and ideology, it is the viewer's own story of repressed desires that is narrated.

Television consists of diverse programmes, genres and commercials (advertising), which superficially may seem fragmentary. However, television is experienced by the viewer as a unified whole that 'flows' continuously (cf. Williams 1974:95). The texts of television receive their unity from the commercials that seemingly break programmes, but in fact provide the undercurrent ideology of the consumer society, performing a 'condensation of values and aspirations with commodities' (cf. Flitterman 1983:95). The diverse texts on television are also united by self-referential advertising and the cross-programme references by which characters from one show appear on another, creating a *metatext* of the self-enclosed world of television. The unity of fictional and non-fictional programmes is 'brought together as part of a larger, continuous imaginary world ... which addresses the spectator-as-ideal-subject across temporal, spatial, and narrative diversity' (White 1986:62). Thus, rather than evaluating television according to its live programmes, such as news and talk shows, these programmes should be evaluated according to the fictional and imaginary nature of television.

The unity of television provides a general ideological framework, a 'continuous story' for the viewer's perception of his society. However, the continuous story of television as a metatext is unique and characterised by its 'unity of contradiction' and reflects the viewer's own complexity. Thus, television may be termed a 'postmodern' medium. However, while the viewer and text can exist happily in contradiction, traditional Freudian and Lacanian psychoanalysis is inadequate to explain the viewer's experience and should be supplemented with poststructuralist insight.

13.5 CRITICAL EVALUATION

Freudian and Lacanian psychoanalysis as applied to film and television is not free from criticism. Psychoanalysis is based on Freud's biological behaviourism, which resembles a stimulus–response model. The overemphasis on the determinism of the Oedipus complex of the human personality during the infant years is reductionist and does not consider other important stages of human development. The importance of the Oedipus complex in Freud's theory is a reduction and a rewriting of the whole rich and random multiple realities of concrete everyday experience into the contained, strategically pre-limited terms of the family narrative – whether this be seen as myth, Greek tragedy or 'family romance' (Jameson 1983:21–2).

| bourgeois family |

Thus, psychoanalysis attempts to interpret all human phenomena as manifestation of a single myth of the bourgeois family. When this is applied to film and television, the interpretive activity is reduced to the endless search for the characters in the Oedipal drama. Critics of structuralism and psychoanalysis, such as Michel Foucault, provide the insight that the individual is not constructed merely by a single episode in infancy but is continuously constructed as a subject in and through the interplay of the numerous discourses that constitute the social totality. The subject thus gains experience of multiple forms of identification and competence to assume various positions required of him by the social discourses.

It is a subject that exists *as* a multiplicity of particular subjectivities, among codes, conventions, and sets of symbols by which the 'real' is imagined (Deming 1985:48).

Thus, the viewer's encounter with television reflects the sum of his experience as a discursive subject and his ability to assume different positions required by the various discourses of television. Thus, the subject's involvement with television is not merely a passive, but an interactive encounter (cf. Deming 1985).

Psychoanalytic film theory acknowledges the complexity of the viewer and the importance of the pre-linguistic stage. However, it traditionally privileges the symbolic dimension; thus 'manifest content of images as well as formal structures tend to get read as signs of a symbolic order implicit in the materiality of the images' (cf. Koch 1985:147). The analysis of film tends to be limited to the symbolic and linguistic experience. However, the symbolic is preceded by a pre-linguistic imaginary stage unmediated by language and the experience of film is not only symbolic but also involves the re-experience of the pre-social pre-linguistic realm that is unmediated by language (cf. Koch 1985:147). | symbolic emphasis

Psychoanalytic film and television theorists also do not draw the proper conclusion from the structuralist theory of enunciation. Enunciation implies the removal or 'death' of the author and the birth of the reader. However, psychoanalytic critics perpetuate the 'auteur' theory in an attempt to discover a 'real' person as the producer and source of the textual truth and meaning. However, Foucault (1981) points out the author is merely a name and social function whose existence is of no relevance because the text does not depend on its author for existence and meaning. According to Barthes (1984:146), a text does not convey a 'message' from an author but it is a multidimensional space in which | 'death' of the author a variety of writings, none of them original, blend and clash. The text is a tissue of quotations drawn from the innumerable centres of culture (Barthes 1984:146).

The unity of any text does not lie in its origin but rather in the destination or its viewer (cf. Barthes 1984:148). The reader or viewer is highly complex and an articulated subject whose unity is imaginary. Thus, the viewer's pleasure is derived from his likeness to the highly complex and articulated texts of film and television. He can enjoy the multiple identifications and contradictions offered by the text because these reflect his experience of the discursive, symbolic and pre-linguistic experience of the imaginary.

The experience of viewing film and television is gratifying because it is complex and contradictory. The images and narratives of television may be experienced as unified and mediated by the symbolic sphere and simultaneously as discontinuous dreams.

> heterogeneous system

Because television is a heterogeneous system of representation, 'a site of textual intersection and coexistence of varying narratives, genres, appeals and modes of address' (White 1989:161), the viewer's experience is 'at once dispersed and distracted while at the same time intensely preoccupied and absorbed' (Petro 1986:18). Roland Barthes's pertinent description of the reader of the (postmodern) text may serve as descriptive of the later day postmodern television viewer:

> *Imagine someone (a kind of Monsieur Taste in reverse) who abolishes within himself all barriers, all classes, all exclusions, not by syncretism but by simple discard of that old spectre: logical contradiction; who mixes every language, even those said to be incompatible; who silently accepts every charge of illogicality, of incongruity; who remains passive in the face of Socratic irony (leading the interlocutor to the supreme disgrace: self-contradiction) and legal terrorism (how much penal evidence is based on psychology of consistency!). Such a man would be the mockery of our society: court, school, asylum, polite conversation would cast him out: who endures contradiction without shame? Now this anti-hero exists: he is the reader of the text at the moment he takes his pleasure.* (Barthes 1986:3)

FURTHER READING

Bywater, T. & Sobchack, T. 1989. *Introduction to film criticism: Major critical approaches to narrative film*. New York: Longman.

Flitterman-Lewis, S. 1987. Psychoanalysis, film, and television, in: *Channels of discourse*, edited by R.C. Allen. London: Methuen.

Kaplan, E.A. (ed) 1990. *Psychoanalysis and cinema*. New York: Routledge/American Film Institute.

Rose, G. 2001. *Visual methodologies*. London: Sage.

Stam, R. 1983. Television news and its spectator, in: *Regarding television – critical approaches: An anthology*, edited by E.A. Kaplan. Frederick, Maryland: University Publications of America.

Wright, E. 1982. Modern psychoanalytic criticism, in: *Modern literary theory*, edited by A. Jefferson and D. Robey. London: Batsford.

References

Abelman, R. & Atkin, D.J. 2002. *The televiewing audience: The art & science of watching TV*. Creskill, New Jersey: Hampton Press.

Abu-Lughod, L. 1993. *Writing women's worlds: Bedouin stories*. Berkeley: University of California Press.

Alasuutari, P. (ed) 1999. *The media audience*. London: Sage.

Allen, R. (ed) 1990. *The concise Oxford dictionary of current English*. 8th edition. Oxford: Clarendon Press.

Allen, R. & Gomery, D. 1985. *Film history: Theory and practice*. New York: Knopf.

Allen, R.C. 1987. Reader-oriented criticism, in: *Channels of discourse*, edited by R.C. Allen. London: Methuen.

Altheide, D.L. 1991. The impact of television news formats on social policy. *Journal of Broadcasting and Electronic Media*, 35(1):3–21.

Althusser, L. 1971. *Lenin and philosophy and other essays*. Translated by B. Brewster, New York: Monthly Review.

Altman, C.F. 1977. Psychoanalysis and cinema: The imaginary discourse. *Quarterly Review of Film Studies*, 2(3):257–72.

Andrew, D. 1976. *The major film theories: An introduction*. London: Oxford University Press.

Andrew, D. 1984. *Concepts in film theory*. Oxford: Oxford University Press.

Ang, I. 1985. *Watching Dallas: soap opera and the melodramatic imagination*. London: Routledge.

Ang, I. 1991. *Desperately seeking the audience*. London: Routledge.

Archard, D. 1984. *Consciousness and the unconscious*. London: Hutchinson.

Arnheim, R. 1957. *Film as art*. Berkeley: University of California Press.

Arnheim, R. 1969. *Visual thinking*. Berkeley: University of California Press.

Asmal, K. 1998. A second look: Squeals from the free speech symphony. *Mail & Guardian*, 14(31): 7–13 August:28.

Asp, K. 2007. Fairness, informativeness and scrutiny. *Nordicom Review, Jubilee Issue*, 28:31–49. Göteborg: Nordic Information Centre for Media and Communication Research.

Aufderheide, P. (ed) 1993. *Media literacy: A report of the national leadership conference on media literacy*. Aspen, Colorado: Aspen Institute.

August, B. 1981. The lure of psychoanalysis in film theory, in: *Cinematographic apparatus: Selected writings*, edited by T. Hak Kyunk Cha. New York: Tanam Press.

References

Austin, J.L. 1984. *How to do things with words*. 2nd edition. New York: Oxford University Press.
Babbie, E. 1989. *The practice of social research*. 5th edition. Belmont, Calif: Wadsworth.
Babbie, E. 1990. *Survey research methods*. 2nd edition. Belmont, Calif: Wadsworth.
Babbie, E. 1992. *Practicing social research: Guided activities to accompany the practice of social research*. 6th edition. Belmont, Calif: Wadsworth.
Babbie, E. 2001. *The practice of social research*. 9th edition. Belmont, Calif: Wadsworth.
Bagnara, S., Simion, F., Tagliabue, M.E. & Ultima, C. 1988. Comparison processes on visual mental images. *Memory & Cognition,* 16(2):138–46.
Bailey, K.D. 1987. *Methods of social research*. 3rd edition. New York: The Free Press.
Balázs, B. 1970. *Theory of film: Character and growth of a new art*. New York: Dover.
Banks, A. 1992. Frontstage/backstage: Loss of control in real-time coverage of the war in the Gulf. *Communication,* 13(2):111–119.
Barbatsis, G. & Guy, Y. 1991. Analyzing meaning in form: Soap opera's compositional construction of 'realness'. *Journal of Broadcasting & Electronic Media,* 35(1):59–74.
Barker, D. 1988. 'It has been real': Forms of television representation. *Critical Studies in Mass Communication,* 5(1):42–56.
Barnhurst, K.G. 1994. *Seeing the newspaper*. New York: St Martin's Press.
Barthes, R. 1964. *Elements of semiology*. London: Jonathan Cape.
Barthes, R. 1967. *Elements of semiology*. New York: Hill & Wang.
Barthes, R. 1972. *Mythologies*. London: Paladin.
Barthes, R. 1977a. An introduction to the structural analysis of narratives, in: *Image music text*, edited by S. Heath. London: Fontana/Collins.
Barthes, R. 1977b. *Image, music, text*. London: Fontana/Collins.
Barthes, R. 1982a. *Image, music, text*. London: Fontana/Collins.
Barthes, R. 1982b. *Selected writings*. London: Fontana/Collins.
Barthes, R. 1984a. *Image, music, text*. London: Fontana/Collins.
Barthes, R. 1984b. *Writing degree zero & elements of semiology*. London: Jonathan Cape.
Barthes, R. 1986. *The pleasure of the text*. New York: Hill and Wang.
Barthes, R. 1999. Rhetoric of the image, in: *Visual culture: The reader,* edited by J. Evans & S. Hall. London: Sage, in association with the Open University.

Baudry, J.-L. 1975. Ideological effects of the basic cinematographic apparatus. *Film Quarterly*, 28(2):39–47.

Bauman, R. 1986. *Story, performance, and event: Contextual studies of oral narrative*. Cambridge: Cambridge University Press.

Bayart, J.-F. 2005. *The illusion of cultural identity*. London: Hurst & Company.

Bazin, A. 1967. *What is cinema?* Translated by H. Gray. Berkeley: University of California Press.

Bell, A. 1991. *The language of news media*. Oxford: Blackwell.

Bell, D.V.J. 1975. *Power, influence, and authority: An essay in political linguistics*. New York: Oxford University Press.

Belsey, C. 1986. *Critical practice*. London: Methuen.

Bennett, W.L. 1990. Toward a theory of press–state relations in the United States. *Journal of Communication*, 40(2):103–25.

Berelson, B. 1952. *Content analysis in communication research*. Glencoe, Illinois: Free Press.

Berg, B.L. 1989. *Qualitative research methods for the social sciences*. Boston: Allyn & Bacon.

Berger, A.A. 1989. "He's everything you're not…": A semiological analysis of "Cheers", in *Television studies, textual analysis*, edited by G. Burns & J. Thompson. New York: Praeger, 89–101.

Berger, A.A. 1991. *Media analysis techniques*. Revised edition. Newbury Park, Calif: Sage.

Berger, A.A. 1997. *Narratives in popular culture, media and everyday life*. Thousand Oaks, Calif: Sage.

Berger, J. 1972. *Ways of seeing*. New York: Penguin.

Berger, P.L. 1980. *Invitation to sociology: A humanistic perspective*. Harmondsworth: Penguin.

Berman Brown, R. & Saunders, M. 2008. *Dealing with statistics. What you need to know*. Maidenhead: Open University Press.

Best, S. & Kellner, D. 1991. *Postmodern theory: Critical interrogation*. New York: Guilford.

Beville, H.M. (Jr) 1988. *Audience ratings: Radio, television, and cable*. Revised edition. Hillsdale, New Jersey: Lawrence Erlbaum Associates.

Biltereyst, D. 1995. *Hollywood in het avondland*. Brussel: Vubpress.

Bitzer, L.F. 1981. Political rhetoric, in: *Handbook of political communication*, edited by D.D. Nimmo & K.R. Sanders. London: Sage.

Bloom, D. 1994. The audience to outdoor posters, in: *Measuring media audiences*, edited by R Kent. London: Routledge, 146–176.

Blumenthal, H.J. & Goodenough, O.R. 2006. *This business of television: The standard guide to the television industry.* 3rd edition. New York: Billboard Books.

Blumler J.G. & Katz, E. 1974. *The uses of mass communications: Current perspectives on gratifications research.* Beverly Hills, Calif: Sage.

Borchers, T. 2006. *Rhetorical theory: An introduction.* Belmont, Calif.: Thomson Wadsworth.

Bordwell, D. & Thompson, K. 1980. *Film art: An introduction.* Reading, Mass: Addison-Wesley.

Bordwell, D. & Thompson, K. 1986. *Film art: An introduction.* 2nd edition. New York: Knopf.

Bordwell, D. 1989. *Making meaning. Inference and rhetoric in the interpretation of cinema.* Cambridge: Harvard University Press.

Bosma, P. (ed) 1991. *Filmkunde. Een inleiding.* Heerlen: Open Universiteit.

Botha, M. & Van Aswegen, A. 1992. *Beelde van Suid-Afrika: 'n alternatiewe rolprentoplewing.* Pretoria: Raad vir Geesteswetenskaplike Navorsing.

Botha, P.J.J. 1991. Orality, literacy and worldview: exploring the interaction. *Communicatio,* 17(2):2–15.

Bourdieu, P. 1984. *Distinction: A social critique of the judgement of taste.* Cambridge, Mass: Harvard University Press.

Bourdieu, P. 1992. *Language and symbolic power.* Cambridge: Polity Press.

Braham, P. 1982. How the media report race, in: *Culture, society and the media,* edited by M. Gurevitch, T. Bennett, J Curran, & J. Woollacott. London: Methuen.

Brand, R. 1996. Verdict on constitution could usher in new era of democracy – or more political wrangling. *The Star,* 5 September:3.

Brown, M. 1994. Estimating newspaper and magazine readership, in: *Measuring media audiences,* edited by R. Kent. London: Routledge, 105–45.

Bruner, J. 1986. *Actual minds, possible worlds.* Cambridge, Mass: Harvard University Press.

Bryant, J. & Heath, R.L. 2000. *Human communication and theory and research: Contexts and challenges.* Hillsdale, New Jersey: Lawrence Erlbaum Associates.

Burnett, R. 2004. *How images think.* Cambridge, Mass: MIT Press.

Burrows, T.D., Wood, D.N. & Gross, L.S. 1989. *Television production: Disciplines and techniques.* 4th edition. Dubuque, IA: Wm. C. Brown.

Burton, S. 1987. Ideology on the beat: labour and the English-language press, in: *Narrating the crisis: hegemony and the South African press,* edited by K. Tomaselli R. Tomaselli & J. Muller. Johannesburg: Richard Lyon.

Butler, J.G. 1986. Notes on the soap opera apparatus: Televisual style and 'As the World Turns'. *Cinema Journal,* 25(3):53–70.

Butler, J.O. 1994. *Television: Critical methods and applications.* Belmont, Calif: Wadsworth.

Buyssens, E. 1967. *La communication et l'articulation linguistique.* Paris-Bruxelles: PUF.

Buzzard, K.S.F. 2002. The peoplemeter wars: A case study of technological innovation and diffusion in the ratings industry. *Journal of Media Economics,* 10(4):273-91.

Bywater, T. & Sobchack, T. 1989. *Introduction to film criticism: Major critical approaches to narrative film.* New York: Longman.

Cardwell-Gardner, T. & Bennett, J.A. 1999. Television advertising to young children: An exploratory study. *Communicare,* 19(1):44-60.

Carlsson, U. 2007. Media and mass communication research. Past, present and future. *Nordicom Review, Jubilee Issue,* 28:223-9. Göteborg: Nordic Information Centre for Media and Communication Research.

Carlsson, U. & Helland, K. (eds) 2007. Media structures and practices. As time goes by ... *Nordicom Review, Jubilee Issue,* 28. Göteborg: Nordic Information Centre for Media and Communication Research.

Caughie, J. (ed) 1981. *Theories of authorship: A reader.* London: Routledge & Kegan Paul.

Chandler, D. 2002. Semiotics: The basis. London: Routledge.

Chandler, D. 2008. Semiotics for beginners. D.I.Y. semiotic analysis: Advice to my own students. [O] Available: http://www.aber.ac.uk/media/Documents/S4B/sem12.html. Accessed 2008/10/03.

Chatman, S.B. 1978. *Story and discourse: Narrative structure in fiction and film.* Ithaca, NY: Cornell University Press.

Chilton, P. (ed) 1985. *Language and the nuclear arms debate: Nukespeak today.* London: Pinter.

Chilton, P. & Ilyin, M. 1993. Metaphor in political discourse: The case of the 'common European house'. *Discourse and Society,* 4(1):7-31.

Chilton, R. & Butler, P. 1994. Measuring cinema audiences, in: *Measuring media audiences,* edited by R. Kent. London: Routledge: 177-95.

Chiseri-Strater E. & Sunstein, B.S. 1997. Fieldnotes. [O] Available: http:/www.sas.upenn.edu/anthro/CPIA/METHODS/Fieldnotes.html Accessed 2008/03/03.

Clarke, S., Seidler, V.J., McDonnel, K., Robins, K. & Lovell, T. 1980. *One-dimensional Marxism. Althusser and the politics of culture.* London: Allison & Busby.

Clifford, J. & Marcus, G.E. (eds). 1986. *Writing culture: the poetics and politics of ethnography.* Berkeley: University of California Press.

References

Comstock, G. 1978. *Trends in the study of incidental learning from television viewing.* Syracuse, NY: Syracuse University Press.

Connolly, W.E. 1983. *The terms of political discourse*, 2nd edition. Oxford: Robertson.

Cook, P. (ed) 1985. *The cinema book.* London: British Film Institute.

Cooper, R.D. & Schindler, D.R. 2001. *Business research methods.* Singapore: McGraw-Hill.

Corcoran, P.E. 1979. *Political language and rhetoric.* Austin: University of Texas Press.

Coward, R. & Ellis, J. 1986. *Language and materialism: Developments in semiology and the theory of the subject.* London: Routledge & Kegan Paul.

Craig, R.L. 1992. Advertising as visual communication. *Communication*, 13(3):165–79.

Crystal, D. 1974. *Linguistics.* Harmondsworth: Penguin.

Culler, J. 1976. *Saussure.* Glasgow: Fontana.

Danaher, P. & Balnaves, M. 2002. The future of ratings measurement. *Media International Australia,* 105, November:40–8.

Davie, D. 2008. Zero to hero. *Mail & Guardian,* 5–11 September:61.

Davis, D. 1974. *The grammar of television production.* 3rd edition. London: Barrie and Jenkins.

Davis, H. & Walton, P. (eds) 1984. *Language, image, media.* Oxford: Blackwell.

Deacon, D., Pickering, M., Golding, P. & Murdock, G. (eds) 1999. *Researching communications: A practical guide to methods in media and cultural analysis.* London: Arnold.

Deal, T.E. 1985. The symbolism of effective schools. *Elementary School Journal,* 95(5):601–20.

Debes, J.L. 1969. The loom of visual literacy. *Audiovisual Instruction,* 14(8):25–7.

De Lauretis, T. 1984. *Alice doesn't: Feminism, semiotics, cinema.* London: Macmillan.

Deming, C.J. 1985. *Hill Street Blues* as narrative. *Critical Studies in Mass Communication,* 2(1):1–22.

Deming, R.H. 1985. The television spectator-subject. *Journal of Film and Video,* 37(3):48–63.

Denning, S. 2004 Storytelling and post-modernism: Jean-François Lyotard. [O] Available: http://www.stevedenning.com/postmodern.html Accessed 2007/05/07.

De Putter, J. 1991. Theorievorming rond de filmkritiek, in: *Filmkunde. Een inleiding,* edited by P. Bosma. Heerlen: Open Universiteit.

Dethier, H. 1985. *Semiologie*. Kursusteks: Vrije Universiteit van Brussel. Brussel: VUB.

Dethier, H. 1993. *Het gesicht en het raadsel. Profielen van Plato tot Derrida*. Brussel: VUB.

Dixon, P. 1971. *Rhetoric*. London: Methuen.

Dondis, D.A. 1973. *A primer of visual literacy*. Cambridge: Mass Institute of Technology.

Du Plooy, G.M. 1981. The use of music as communication code in television. MA dissertation, University of South Africa, Pretoria.

Du Plooy, G.M. 1995. The role of formative research and supportive communication in affirmative action. *Communitas*, 2:21–33.

Du Plooy, G.M. 2001. *Communication research: Techniques, methods and applications*. Lansdowne: Juta.

Dupre, L. 1983. *Marx's social critique of culture*. New Haven, CT: Yale University Press.

Eagleton, T. 1983. *Literary theory: An introduction*. Oxford: Basil Blackwell.

Eagleton, T. 1989. *Reading theory. International encyclopaedia of communication*. Volume 4, edited by B.E. Barnow, G. Gerbner, W. Schramm, T. Worth & L. Gross. New York: Oxford.

Easthope, A. (ed) 1993. *Contemporary film theory*. London: Longman.

Eaton, B.C. & Dominick, J.R. 1991. Product-related programming and children's TV: a content analysis. *Journalism Quarterly*, 68(1/2):67–75.

Eberwein, R. 1979. *A viewer's guide to film theory and criticism*. Metuchen, New Jersey: Scarecrow.

Eco, U. 1979. *A theory of semiotics*. Bloomington: Indiana University Press.

Eco, U. 1982. Critique of the image. in: *Thinking photography*, edited by V. Burgin. London: Macmillan.

Edelman, M. 1974. The political language of the helping professions. *Politics and Society*, 4(3):295–310.

Edelman, M.J. 1977. *Political language: Words that succeed and policies that fail*. New York: Academic Press.

Edelman, M.J. 2001. *The politics of misinformation*. Cambridge: Cambridge University Press.

Eidsvik, C. 1978. *Cineliteracy. Film among the arts*. New York: Random House.

Eisenstein, S.M. 1949. *Film form: Essays in film theory*. Edited and translated by J. Leyda. New York: Harcourt Brace.

Elam, K. 1980. *The semiotics of theatre and drama*. New York: Methuen.

Ellis, D.G. 1992. *From language to communication*. Hillsdale, New Jersey: Erlbaum.

References

Ellis, J. 1984. *Visible fictions: Cinema, television, video*. London: Routledge & Kegan Paul.

Evans, J. & Hall, S. (eds) 1999. *Visual culture: The reader*. London: Sage, in association with the Open University.

Fairclough, N. & Wodak, R. 1997. Critical discourse analysis, in: *Discourse as social interaction, discourse studies: A multidisciplinary introduction, Volume 2*, edited by T. van Dijk. London: Sage.

Fairclough, N. 1990. *Language and power*. London: Longman.

Fairclough, N. 1992a. *Discourse and social change*. Cambridge: Polity.

Fairclough, N. (ed) 1992b. *Critical language awareness*. London: Longman.

Farb, P. 1977. *Word play: What happens when people talk*. London: Coronet Books.

Finegan, E. 1994. *Language: Its structure and use*. 2nd edition. Orlando, FL: Harcourt Brace College Publishers.

Fiske, J. 1982. *Introduction to communication studies*. London: Methuen.

Fiske, J. 1987a. British cultural studies and television, in: *Channels of discourse. Television and contemporary criticism*, edited by R.C. Allen. London: Methuen.

Fiske, J. 1987b. *Television culture*. London: Routledge.

Fiske, J. & Hartley, J. 1978. *Reading television*. London: Methuen.

Fiske, J. & Hartley, J. 1982. *Reading television*. London: Methuen.

Flew, A. (ed) 1984. *A dictionary of philosophy*. 2nd revised edition. London: Pan/Macmillan.

Flitterman, S. 1981. Women, desire, and the look: Feminism and the enunciative apparatus in cinema, in: *Theories of authorship: A reader*, edited by J. Caughie. London: Routledge & Kegan Paul/British Film Institute.

Flitterman, S. 1983. The real soap opera: TV commercials, in: *Regarding television – critical approaches: An anthology*, edited by E.A. Kaplan. Frederick, Maryland: University Publications of America.

Flitterman, S. 1985. Thighs and whiskers: The fascination of 'Magnum, P.I.' *Screen*, 26(2):42–58.

Flitterman-Lewis, S. 1987. Psychoanalysis, film and television, in: *Channels of discourse. Television and contemporary criticism*, edited by R.C. Allen. London: Methuen.

Foucault, M. 1980. *Power/knowledge: Selected interviews and other writings 1972–1977*. New York: Pantheon.

Foucault, M. 1981. What is an author?, in: *Theories of authorship: A reader*, edited by J. Caughie. London: Routledge & Kegan Paul/British Film Institute.

Foucault, M. 1986. *The archaeology of knowledge*. London: Tavistock.

Foucault, M. 1988. *Politics, philosophy, culture: Interviews and other writings 1977–1984*. New York: Routledge.
Fourie, P.J. 1983. *Beeldkommunikasie. Kultuurkritiek, ideologiese kritiek en 'n inleiding tot die beeldsemiologie*. Johannesburg: McGraw-Hill.
Fourie, P.J. 1985. Betekenis en betekeniskonstruksie in beeldkommunikasie. *Communicare*, 4(1):33–40.
Fourie, P.J. 1988. *Aspects of film and television communication*. Cape Town: Juta.
Fourie, P.J. (ed) 1991. *Critical television analyses: An introduction*. Cape Town: Juta.
Fourie, P.J. 1991. Media, mites, metafore en die kommunikasie van apartheid. *Communicatio*, 17(1):2–6.
Fourie, P.J. 1992. Diskoersontleding as 'n metode in die sosiale wetenskappe. *Communicatio*, 18(1):19–29.
Fourie, P.J. (ed) 1996. *Introduction to communication – course book 3: Communication and the production of meaning*. Cape Town: Juta.
Fourie, P.J. (ed) 1997. *Introduction to communication – course book 6: Film and television studies*. Cape Town: Juta.
Fourie, P.J. (ed) 2001. *Media studies. Volume 2: Content, audiences and production*. Cape Town: Juta.
Fourie, P.J. 2003. The future of public broadcasting in South Africa: The need to return to basic principles. *Communicatio* 29(1&2):148–81.
Fourie, P.J. (ed) 2007. *Media studies. Volume 1: Media history, media and society*. 2nd edition. Cape Town: Juta.
Fourie, P.J. (ed) 2008. *Media studies. Volume 2: Policy, management and media representation*. 2nd edition. Cape Town: Juta.
Fowler, R. 1991. *Language in the news: Discourse and ideology in the press*. London: Routledge.
Francis, S., Dugmore, H. & Schacherl, R. 2000. *The madams are restless. A new Madam & Eve collection*. Johannesburg: Rapid Phase.
Frankfurt, H.G. 2005. *On Bullshit*. Princeton, New Jersey: Princeton University Press.
Frey, L.R., Botan, C.H., Friedman, P.G. & Kreps, G.L. 1992. *Interpreting communication research: A case study approach*. Englewood Cliffs, New Jersey: Prentice Hall.
Friedman L. & Ayer, N.C. 1989. How good is the seven-day TV diary now? *Journal of Advertising Research*, 29(4):RC3–5.
Friedman, S. 2007. Uncaring core of Mbeki's message. *Business Day*, 22 August. [O] Available: http://www.businessday.co.za/articles/topstories.aspx?ID=BD4A545102 Accessed 2007/22/08.

References

Gane, R. 1994. Television audience measurement systems in Europe: A review and comparison, in: *Measuring media audiences*, edited by R. Kent. London: Routledge, 22–41.

Garland, I. 2002. The future of television audience measurement: Nielsen Media Research's view. *Media International Australia*, 105, November:49–54.

Geertz, C. 1988. *Works and lives: The anthropologist as author*. Palo Alto, Calif: Stanford University Press.

Genzuk, M. 2003. *A synthesis of ethnographic research*. Occasional Papers Series. Center for Multilingual, Multicultural Research (eds). Center for Multilingual, Multicultural Research, Rossier School of Education, University of Southern California. Los Angeles.

Georgakopoulou, A. & Goutsos, D. 1997. *Discourse analysis: An introduction*. Edinburgh: University of Edinburgh Press.

Gerbner, G., Gross, L., Morgan, M. & Signorielli, N. 1980. Aging with television: Images on television and conceptions of social reality. *Journal of Communication*, 30(1):37–47.

Geuss, R. 1981. *The idea of a critical theory. Habermas and the Frankfurt School*. Cambridge: Cambridge University Press.

Giannetti, L. 1972. *Understanding movies*. Englewood Cliffs, New Jersey: Prentice Hall.

Giannetti, L. 1990. *Understanding movies*. 5th edition. Englewood Cliffs, New Jersey: Prentice Hall.

Gibson, J.J. 1982. *Reasons for realism: Selected essays of James J. Gibson*. Hillsdale, New Jersey: Lawrence Erlbaum.

Gill, J. 2000. Managing the capture of individual viewing within a peoplemeter service. *International Journal of Market Research*, 42(4):431–8.

Gillespie, M. 2006. Narrative analysis, in: *Analysing media texts*, edited by M. Gillespie & J. Toynbee. Maidenhead: Open University, 77–117.

Gledhill, C. 1997. Genre and gender: The case of soap opera, in: *Representation: Cultural representations and signifying practices*, edited by S. Hall. London: Sage, 337–87.

Gold, R. 1997. The ethnographic method in sociology. *Qualitative Enquiry*, 3(4):387–402.

Gombrich, E.H. 1982. *The image and eye*. Ithaca, NY: Cornell University Press.

Gombrich, E.H. 1986. *Art and illusion: A study in the psychology of pictorial representation*. Oxford: Phaidon Press.

Graber, D.A. 1976. *Verbal behaviour and politics*. Champaign: University of Illinois Press.

Graber, D.A. 1981. Political language, in: *Handbook of political communication*, edited by D.D. Nimmo & K.R. Sanders. London: Sage.

Greenberg, B.S., Eastin, M.S., Skalski, P., Cooper, L., Levy M. & Lachlan, K. 2005. Comparing survey and diary measures of Internet and traditional media use. *Communication Reports,* 18(1):1–8.

Greenberg, H.R. & Gabbard, K. 1990. Reel significations: An anatomy of psychoanalytic film criticism. *Psychoanalytic Review,* 77(1):89–110.

Griffin, M. (ed) 1992. Visual communication studies in mass media research: Parts I and II (Special double issue). *Communication,* 13:2–3.

Griffin, M. 2001. Camera as witness, image as sign: The study of visual communication in communication research, in: *Communication Yearbook 24,* edited by W.B. Gudykunst. Thousand Oaks, Calif: Sage Publications, 433–463.

Grimes, T. 1990. Encoding TV news messages into memory. *Journalism Quarterly,* 67(4):757–66.

Gripsrud, J. 2006. Semiotics: Signs, codes and cultures, in: *Analysing media texts,* edited by M. Gillespie & J. Toynbee. Berkshire: Open University Press, 9–41.

Groves, R. 1996. How do we know what we think they think is really what they think?, in: *Answering questions,* edited by N. Schwartz & S. Sudman. San Francisco: Jossey-Bass, 389–402.

Guiraud, P. 1971. *Semiology.* London: Routledge & Kegan Paul.

Gumede, W.M. 1998. Alliance fallout puts spotlight on ANC's tug-o'-war. *The Sunday Independent,* 5 July:5.

Gurevitch, M., Bennett, T., Curran, J. & Woollacott, J. (eds) 1982. *Culture, society and the media.* London: Methuen.

Gusfield, J. 1976. The literary rhetoric of science: Comedy and pathos in drinking driver research. *American Sociological Review,* 41(1):16–34.

Gutsche, T. 1972. *The history and social significance of motion pictures in South Africa: 1895–1940.* Cape Town: Howard Timmins.

Habermas, J. 1972. *Toward a rational society: Student protest, science and politics.* London: Heinemann.

Hake, K. 2003. Five-year-olds' fascination for television. A comparative study, in: *Media fascinations. Perspectives on young people's meaning making,* edited by Ingegerd Rydin. Göteberg: Nordicom.

Hall, S. 1973. *Encoding and decoding in television discourse.* Birmingham: University of Birminghan Centre for Contemporary Cultural Studies.

Hall, S. 1977. Culture, the media and the ideological effect, in: *Mass communication and society,* edited by J. Curran, M. Gurevitch & J. Woollacot. London: Edward Arnold, 315–48.

Hall, S. 1982. The rediscovery of ideology: The return of the repressed in media studies, in: *Culture, society and the media,* edited by M. Gurevitch, T. Bennett, J. Curran, & J Woollacott. London: Methuen, 56–90.

References

Hall, S. (ed) 1997. *Representation: Cultural representations and signifying practices.* London: Sage.

Hammersley, M. & Atkins, P. 1995. *Ethnography: Principles in practice.* 2nd edition. London: Routledge.

Hardy, W.G. 1978. *Language, thought, and experience: A tapestry of the dimensions of meaning.* Baltimore, Maryland: University Park Press.

Harland, R. 1988. *Superstructuralism: The philosophy of structuralism and post-structuralism.* London: Routledge.

Harré, R. 1985. Persuasion and manipulation, in: *Discourse and communication*, edited by T.A. Van Dijk. New York: De Gruyter.

Harindranath, R. 1998. Documentary meaning and interpretive contexts, in: *Approaches to audiences: A reader*, edited by R. Dickinson, R. Harindranath, & O. Linne. London: Hodder Arnold.

Harris, M. & Johnson, O. 2000. *Cultural anthropology.* 5th edition. Needham Heights, Mass: Allyn & Bacon.

Hartley, J. 1982. *Understanding news.* London: Methuen.

Hawkes, T. 1985. *Structuralism and semiotics.* London: Methuen.

Hayakawa, S.I. 1973. *Language in thought and action.* 2nd edition. London: Allen & Unwin.

Heath, S. & Skirrow, G. 1977. Television: A world in action. *Screen*, 18(2):7–59.

Heath, S. 1981. *Questions of cinema.* London: Macmillan.

Heath, S. 1985. Jaws, ideology and film theory, in: *Popular television and film*, edited by T. Bennett, S. Boyd-Bowman, C. Mercer & J. Woollacott. London: British Film Institute.

Hebdige, D. 1979. *Subculture: The meaning of style.* London: Methuen.

Hervey, S. 1982. *Semiotic perspectives.* London: Allen & Unwin.

Hilmes, M. 1985. The television apparatus: Direct address. *Journal of Film and Video*, 37(4):27–36.

Hobbs, R. 1998. Teaching with and about film and television. Integrating media literacy concepts into management education. *Journal of Management Development*, 17(4):259–72.

Hobson, D. 1991. Soap operas at work, in: *Remote control: Television, audiences, & cultural power*, edited by E. Seiter, H. Borchers, G. Kreutzner & E. Warth. Paperback edition. London: Routledge.

Hodge, R. & Kress, G. 1988. *Social semiotics.* Cambridge: Polity Press.

Hogarth. 2007. Mere bagatelle for 'advanced ubuntu'. *Sunday Times.* [O] Available: http://www.sundaytimes.co.za/Columnists/Article.aspx?id=565351 Accessed 2007/15/09.

Hoijer, B. 1992. Socio-cognitive structures and television reception. *Media, Culture & Society*, 14:583–603.

Hollingdale, R.J. 1978. Appendices, in: *Twilight of the idols and the Anti-Christ*, by F. Nietzsche, translated by R.J. Hollingdale. Harmondsworth: Penguin.

Holsti, O.R. 1969. *Content analysis for the social sciences and humanities*. Reading, Mass: Addison-Wesley.

Holub, R.C. 1984. *Reception theory: A critical introduction*. London: Methuen.

Hommel, M. 1991. Hartstocht voor film, in: *Filmkunde. Een inleiding*, edited by P. Bosma, Heerlen: Open Universiteit.

Hospers, J. 1992. *An introduction to philosophical analysis*. 3rd edition. London: Routledge & Kegan Paul.

Houston, B. 1984. Viewing television: The metapsychology of endless consumption. *Quarterly Review of Film Studies*, 9(3):183–95.

Howells, R. 2003. *Visual culture*. Cambridge: Polity Press, in association with Blackwell Publishers Ltd.

Hunter, J.E. 1976. Images of woman. *Journal of Social Issues*, 32(3):7–17.

Iser, W. 1978. *The act of reading. A theory of aesthetic response*. London: Routledge & Kegan Paul.

Ivala, E. 2007. Television audience research revisited: Early television audience research and the more recent developments in television audience research. *Communicatio*, 33(1):26–41.

Jakobson, R. 1964. Concluding statement: Linguistics and poetics, in: *Style in language*, edited by T.A. Sebeok, Cambridge: Massachusetts Institute of Technology.

Jameson, F. 1983. *The political unconscious: Narrative as a socially symbolic act*. London: Methuen.

Janks, H. & Ivanič, R. 1992. CLA and emancipatory discourse, in: *Critical language awareness*, edited by N. Fairclough. London: Longman.

Janks, H. 1997. Critical discourse analysis as a research tool. *Discourse: Studies in the cultural politics of education*, 18(3):329–42.

Jauss, H.R. 1982. *Towards an aesthetic of reception*. Brighton: Harvester.

Johnson, R. 1986. What is cultural studies anyway? *Social Text (Theory/Culture/Ideology)*, 16(Winter):38–80.

Journalism.com. (sa) http://www.journalism.co.za/blaps

Kaplan, E.A. (ed) 1990. *Psychoanalysis and cinema*. New York: Routledge/American Film Institute.

Kassin, S.M. & McNall, K. 1991. Police interrogation and confessions: Communicating promises and threats by pragmatic implication. *Law and Human Behavior*, 15(3):233–51.

Kent, R. 1994. Measuring media audiences: An overview, in: *Measuring media audiences*, edited by R. Kent. London: Routledge, 1–21.

References

Kepplinger, H.M. & Köcher, R. 1990. Professionalism in the media world? *European Journal of Communication*, 5(2/3):285-311.

Kerlinger, F.N. 1986. *Foundations of behavioral research*. 3rd edition. Fort Worth, Texas: Holt, Rinehart & Winston.

Khumalo, F. 2008. The green and gold in black and white. *Sunday Times*, 7 September:17.

Koch, G. 1982. Why women go to the movies. *Jump Cut*, 27:51-3.

Koch, G. 1985. Ex-changing the gaze: re-visioning feminist film theory. *New German Critique*, 34:139-53.

Kochman, T. 1974. Orality and literacy as factors of 'black' and 'white' communicative behavior. *International Journal of the Sociology of Language*, 3:91-115.

Konigsberg, I. 1987. *The complete film dictionary*. New York: Penguin.

Kotzé, G. 2004. Quantitative research in the social sciences. Seminar presented at the Annual Winter school for MA and Doctoral Students conducted by the Department of Communication Science, Unisa, Pretoria.

Kozloff, S.R. 1987. Narrative theory and television, in: *Channels of discourse: Television and contemporary criticism*, edited by R.C. Allen. London: Routledge, 42-73.

Kozloff, S.R. 1992. Narrative theory and television, in: *Channels of discourse, reassembled: Television and contemporary criticism*. 2nd edition. Edited by R.C. Allen. London: Routledge, 67-100.

Kracauer, S. 1960. *Theory of film*. New York: Oxford University Press.

Kress, G. 1983. Media analysis and the study of discourse. *Media Information Australia*, 28:3-17.

Kress, G. 1984. Linguistic and ideological transformation in news reporting, in: *Language, image, media*, edited by H. Davis & P. Walton. Oxford: Blackwell.

Kress, G. (ed) 1988. *Communication and culture: An introduction*. Kensington: New South Wales University Press.

Kress, G. & Hodge, R. 1979. *Language as ideology*. London: Routledge & Kegan Paul.

Kress, G. & Van Leeuwen, T. 2000. *Reading images. The grammar of visual design*. London: Routledge.

Kristeva, J. 1974. The system and the speaking subject. *The Times Literary Supplement*, 12 October: 1249.

Krueger, R.A. 1994. *Focus groups: A practical guide for applied research*. 2nd edition. Thousand Oaks & London: Sage.

Kubey, R. (ed) 1997. *Media literacy in the information age: Current perspectives*. New Brunswick, New Jersey: Transaction.

Lacey, N. 2000. *Narrative and genre: Key concepts in media studies.* London: Macmillan.

Lakoff, G. & Johnson, M. 1980. *Metaphors we live by.* Chicago: University of Chicago Press.

Laplanche, J. & Pontalis, J.-B. 1973. *The language of psycho-analysis.* London: The Hogarth Press.

Lapsley R. & Westlake, M. 1988. *Film theory: An introduction.* Manchester: Manchester University Press.

Laughey, D. 2007. *Key themes in media theory.* Maidenhead: Open University Press.

Leech, G. 1974. *Semantics.* Harmondsworth: Penguin.

Leeds-Hurwitz, W. 1993. *Semiotics and communication. Signs, codes, cultures.* Hillsdale, New Jersey: Lawrence Erlbaum.

Leedy, P. D. 1980. *Practical research.* New York: Macmillan.

Lemarie, A. 1982. *Jacques Lacan.* London: Routledge & Kegan Paul.

Lemert, J.B. 1989. *Criticizing the media: Empirical approaches.* Newberry, Calif: Sage.

Lemish, D. 1985. Soap opera viewing in college: A naturalistic enquiry. *Journal of Broadcasting & Electronic Media,* 29(3):275–93.

Lemon, J. 1991. Ideological criticism and analyses, in: *Critical television analyses: An introduction,* edited by P.J. Fourie. Cape Town: Juta.

Lester, P.M. 1995. *Visual communication: Images with messages.* Belmont, Calif: Wadsworth.

Lewis, G & Slade C. 1994. *Critical communication.* Sydney: Prentice-Hall.

Liebes, T. & Katz, E. 1990. *The export of meaning: Cross-cultural readings of Dallas.* New York: Oxford University Press.

Lindlof, T.R. & Taylor, B.C. 2002. *Qualitative communication research methods.* 2nd edition. Thousand Oaks, Calif: Sage.

Lindsay, V. 1932. *The art of the moving picture.* New York: Liveright.

Linton, J.M. 1992. Documentary film research's unrealized potential in the communication field. *Communication,* 13(2):85–93.

Loucharf, S. & Aylett, R. 2004. Narrative theory and emergent interactive narrative. *International Journal of Continuing Engineering Education and Lifelong Learning,* 14(6):506–18.

Lull, J. 1991. *China turned on. Television, reform and resistance.* London: Routledge.

Lyons, J. 1977a. *Introduction to theoretical linguistics.* Cambridge: Cambridge University Press.

Lyons, J. 1977b. *Semantics I.* London: Cambridge University Press.

Lyotard, J.-F. 1984. *The postmodern condition: A report on knowledge.* Manchester: Manchester University Press.

References

MacCabe, C. 1978/79. The discursive and the ideological in film – notes on the conditions of political intervention. *Screen*, 19(4):35–48.

MacDougall, C.D. 1969. *Interpretative reporting*. 5th edition. New York: Macmillan.

Mail & Guardian. 1998. Cracking down on critical allies. 3–9 July, 14(26):24.

Manghani, S., Piper, A. & Simons, J. 2006. *Images: A reader*. London: Sage.

Marcuse, H. 1970. *One-dimensional man*. London: Sphere Books.

Marcuse, H. 1973. *Eros and civilization*. London: Abacus/Sphere Books.

Martinez-de-Toda, J. 2002. Six dimensions of media education. *Communicator*, 37(1):12–26.

Massey, A. 1998. *The way we do things around here: The culture of ethnography*. Paper presented at the Ethnography and Education Conference, Oxford University, United Kingdom. http:website//www.geocities. com/Tokyo/2961waywedo.htm.1998

Mast, G. & Cohen, M. 1985. *Film theory and criticism: Introductory readings*. New York: Oxford University Press.

Masterman, L. 1985. *Teaching the media*. London: Routledge.

Mbeki, T. 2007. Who are our heroes and heroines? *ANC Today: Online voice of the African National Congress*. 7(32). 17–23 August. [O] Available: http://www.anc.org.za/ancdocs/anctoday/2007/at32.htm#preslet Accessed 2007/17/08

McDermott, J. s.a. The magic of vision. *Topic*, 166:32–9.

McGuigan, J. 1999. *Modernity and postmodern culture*. Buckingham: Open University Press.

McLuhan, M. 1969. *Understanding media*. London: Sphere Books.

McMillan, S.J. 2000. The microscope and the moving target: The challenge of applying content analysis to the World Wide Web. *Journalism & Mass Communication Quarterly*, 77(1):80–98.

McNeil, T. 2006. Roland Barthes: Mythologies (1957). [O] Available: http://orac.sund.ac.uk/~os0tmc/myth.htm Accessed 2006/05/31.

McQuail, D. 1980. *Communication*. London: Longman.

McQuail, D. 1987a. *Mass communication: An introduction*. London: Sage.

McQuail D. 1987b. *Theories of mass communication*. 2nd edition. London: Sage.

McQueen, D. 1998. *Television: a media student's guide*. London: Arnold.

Melander, I. 2007. Web search for bomb recipes should be blocked: EU. [O] Available: http://www.reuters.com/article/internetNews/idUSL1055133420070910 Accessed 2008/10/09.

Merriam, A.P. 1964. *The anthropology of music*. Evanston, Illinois: Northwestern University Press.

Messaris, P. 1992. Visual manipulation: Visual means of affecting responses to images. *Communication*, 13(3):181–95.

Messaris, P. 1994. *Visual 'literacy'. Image, mind and reality*. Boulder, Colorado: Westview.

Messaris, P. 1997. *Visual persuasion: The role of images in advertising*. Thousand Oaks, Calif: Sage.

Messaris, P. 1998. Visual aspects of media literacy. *Journal of Communication*, 48(1):96–108.

Metallinos, N. 1996. *Television aesthetics*. Mahwah, New Jersey: Lawrence Erlbaum

Methods ... What is ethnography? [O] Available: http://www.sas.upenn.edu/anthro/CPIA/METHODS/Ethnography.html Accessed on 2008/12/01.

Metz, C. 1974. *Film language: A semiotics of the cinema*. New York: Oxford University Press.

Metz, C. 1982. *The imaginary signifier: Psychoanalysis and the cinema*. Bloomington: Indiana University Press.

Mey, J. 1985. *Whose language? A study in linguistic pragmatics*. Amsterdam: John Benjamins.

Meyrowitz, J. 1998. Multiple media literacies. *Journal of Communication*, 48(1):96–108.

Mills, C.W. 1978. *The sociological imagination*. Harmondsworth: Penguin.

Milne, C., Technical Support Executive, South African Advertising Research Foundation. 2008. Interview by author. [Transcript]. 23 May, Bryanston.

Modleski, T. 1979. The search for tomorrow in today's soap operas. *Film Quarterly*, 33(1):12–21.

Modleski, T. 1983. The rhythms of reception: Daytime television and women's work, in: *Regarding Television – critical approaches: An anthology*, edited by E.A. Kaplan. Frederick, Maryland: University Publications of America.

Monaco, J. 1977. *How to read a film. The art, technology, language, history and theory of film and media*. New York: Oxford University Press.

Monaco, J. 1984. *Film. Taal, techniek, geschiedenis*. Translated by M. Seton & A. van den Bogaard, Antwerpen: Standaard.

Montgomery, M. 1986. *An introduction to language and society*. London: Methuen.

Moore, B., Nuttall, D. & Willmott, A. 1974. *Data collection*. Bletchley: Open University Press.

Morley, D. 1992. *Television, audiences and cultural studies*. London: Routledge.

Morley, D. 1996. Postmodernism: The rough guide, in: *Cultural studies and communications*, edited by J. Curran, D. Morley & V. Walkerdine. London: Arnold.

References

Morse, M. 1985. Talk, talk, talk. *Screen*, 26(2):2–15.

Mounin, G. 1970. *Introduction à la sémiologie*. Paris: Minuit.

Mulvey, L. 1975. Visual pleasure and narrative cinema. *Screen*, 16(3):6–18.

Mulvey, L. 1985. Visual pleasure and narrative cinema, in: *Movies and methods: An anthology*. Volume 2, edited by B. Nichols. Berkeley: University of California Press.

Münsterberg, H. 1970. *The film: A psychological study*. New York: Dover.

Mytton, G. 1999. *Handbook on radio and television audience research*. London: UNICEF and UNESCO.

Nardi, P.M. 2003. *Doing survey research: A guide to quantitative methods*. Boston: Pearson Education.

Ndaba, D. 2008. Bargain hunting. *Creamer Media's Engineering News*, 28(33):11.

Nelson, N.L. 1990. Metaphor and the media, in: *Studies in communication*. Volume 4, edited by S. Thomas. Norwood, New Jersey: Ablex.

Neuman, W.L. 2006. *Social research methods: Qualitative and quantitative approaches*. 6th edition. Boston: Pearson Education.

Nichols, B. 1994. *Blurred boundaries. Questions of meaning in contemporary culture*. Bloomington: Indiana University Press.

Niebuhr, R. 1960. *Moral man and immoral society. A study in ethics and politics*. New York: Scribner.

Nietzsche, F. 1978. *Twilight of the idols and the Anti-Christ*. Translated by R.J. Hollingdale. Harmondsworth: Penguin.

O'Sullivan, T., Hartley, J., Saunders, D., Montgomery, M. & Fiske, J. 1994. *Key concepts in communication and cultural studies*. 2nd edition. London: Routledge.

Ong, W.J. 1982. *Orality and literacy: The technologizing of the word*. London: Methuen.

Orwell, G. 1975. *Inside the whale and other stories*. Harmondsworth: Penguin.

Osgood, C.E., Suci, G.J. & Tannenbaum, P.H. 1957. *The measurement of meaning*. Champaign: University of Illinois Press.

Palmer, J. 1991. *Potboilers: Methods, concepts and case studies in popular fiction*. London: Routledge.

Palmgreen, P., Wenner, L.A. & Rayburn II, J.D. 1980. Relations between gratifications sought and obtained: a study of television news. *Communication research* 7(2): 161–192.

Pateman, T. 2005. Structuralism and narrative. [O] Available: http://www.selectedworks.co.uk/structuralism.html Accessed 2008/08/26.

Paton, C. 1998a. Battered SACP retreats after Mbeki onslaught. *Sunday Times*, 5 July:1.

Paton, C. 1998b. Waving a red rag to the ANC. *Sunday Times,* 5 July:4.

Patton, M.Q. 1987. *How to use qualitative methods in evaluation.* Newbury Park, Calif: Sage Publications.

Patton M.Q. 2002. *Qualitative research and evaluation methods.* 3rd edition. London: Sage.

Peirce, C. 1960. *Collected papers of Charles Sanders Peirce.* Cambridge, Mass: Harvard University Press.

Peirce, C.S. 1931-58. The icon, index and symbol, in: *Collected works. 8 volumes*, edited by C. Hartshorne & P. Weiss. Cambridge, Mass: Harvard University Press.

Penzhorn, H. & Pitout, M. 2006. The interactive nature of reality television: an audience analysis. *Communicare.* 25(5):85-103.

Peters, J.M. 1972. *Theorie van de audiovisuele communicatie.* Groningen: H.D. Tjeenk Willink.

Peters, J.M. 1974. *Principes van beeldcommunicatie.* Groningen: H.D. Tjeenk Willink.

Peters, J.M. 1976. *Fictioneel beeldamusement. Het amusementskarakter van de bioscoop en televisiefilm.* Leuven: Centrum voor Communicatie-wetenschappen.

Peters, J.M. 1977. *Pictorial communication.* Revised and translated by M. Coombes. Cape Town: David Philip.

Peters, J.M. 1978. *Semiotiek van de beeld.* Leuven: Centrum voor Communicatie Wetenschappen.

Petro, P. 1986. Mass culture and the feminine: the 'place' of television in film studies. *Cinema Journal,* 25(3):5-21.

Philips, L. & Jorgensen, M. 2002. *Discourse analysis as theory and method.* London: Sage.

Pitout, M. 1989. Die gebruike- en bevredigingsbenadering in televisienavorsing: 'n kritiese evaluering van die teorie en metode. Ongepubliseerde MA-verhandeling. Pretoria: Unisa.

Pitout, M. 1996. Televisie en resepsiestudie: 'n analise van kykersinterpretasie van die seep-opera Egoli: *Plek van Goud.* Ongepubliseerde doktorale proefskrif. Pretoria: Universiteit van Suid-Afrika.

Pitout, M. 1998. Reception analysis: a qualitative investigation of the parasocial and social dimensions of soap opera viewing. *Communicatio,* 24(2):39-47.

Pitout, M. & Du Plooy, G.M. 2001. Audience research, in: *Media studies. Volume 2: Content, audiences and production,* edited by P.J. Fourie. Cape Town: Juta, 301-20.

Posel, D. 1989. A 'battlefield of perceptions': State discourse on political violence,

1985-1988, in: *War and society: The militarisation of South Africa*, edited by J. Cock & L. Nathan. Cape Town: David Philip.

Poster, M. 1990. *The mode of information: Poststructuralism and social context.* Cambridge: Polity.

Poster, M. 1994. The mode of information and postmodernity, in: *Communication theory today*, edited by D. Crowley & D. Mitchell. Cambridge: Polity.

Potter, W.J. 1991. The linearity assumption in cultivation research. *Human Communication Research*, 17:562–83.

Poulet, G. 1969. Phenomenology of reading. *New Literary History*, 1(1):53–68.

Pretoria News. 1994. Politics sneaks into council meeting. 31 March:3.

Pretoria News. 1995. Content always overshadows accent. 22 April:1.

Pretoria News. 1995. Shot runner back in city. 19 April:1.

Pretoria News. 1996. End the circus. 18 September:11.

Pretoria News. 1996. Stop the war of words and talk. 9 October:11.

Pretoria News. 1998. Madiba gets tough with SACP. 2 July:1.

Propp, V. 1968. *Morphology of the folktale.* 2nd edition. Translated by L. Scott. Austin: University of Texas Press.

Pudovkin, V.I. 1954 (1926). *Film technique and film acting.* Translated by I. Montagu. London: Vision.

Ramaprasad, J. & Hasegawa, K. 1990. An analysis of Japanese television commercials. *Journalism Quarterly*, 67(4):1025–33.

Reimer, B. 1998. Crisis? What crisis? Analysing audience studies. *Nordicom Review*, 19(1):35–145.

Research 10. *MarketingMix*, 26(3/4):24–32.

Rhodes Journalism Review. 1997. Tough talk from the president. Extract from a meeting of Sanef editors and Nelson Mandela, November, 15:34.

Richardson, J. 2007. *Analysing newspapers. An approach from critical discourse analysis.* Basingstoke: Palgrave Macmillan.

Ricoeur, P. 1979. Structure, word, event, in: *The conflict of interpretations: Essays in hermeneutics*, edited by D. Ihde. Evanston, Illinois: Northwestern University Press.

Ricoeur, P. 1986. *Lectures on ideology and utopia.* New York: Columbia University.

Roelofse, J.J. 1983. *Towards rational discourse: An analysis of the report of the Steyn Commission of Inquiry into the Media.* Pretoria: Van Schaik.

Roscoe, J., Marshall, H. & Gleeson, K. 1995. The television audience: A reconsideration of the taken-for-granted terms 'active', 'social', and 'critical'. *European Journal of Communication*, 10(1): 87–108.

Rosengren, K.E., Wenner, L.A. & Palmgreen, P. 1985. *Media gratifications research: Current perspectives.* Beverly Hills: Sage.

Rosnow, R.L. & Rosenthal, R. 1996. *Beginning behavioural research: A conceptual primer*. Englewood Cliffs, New Jersey: Prentice Hall.

Rossi-Landi, F. 1990. *Marxism and ideology*. Oxford: Oxford University Press.

Rubin, A.M. & Perse, E.M. 1987. Audience activity and television news gratifications. *Communication Research*, 14(1):58–84.

Russell, T. & Verrill, G. 1986. *Otto Kleppner's advertising procedure*. 9th edition. Englewood Cliffs, New Jersey: Prentice Hall.

Rydin, I. 2003. Children's television reception. Perspectives on media literacy, identification and gender, in: *Media fascinations. Perspectives on young people's meaning making*, edited by Ingegerd Rydin. Göteberg: Nordicom.

SABC Education. 2008. Magic cellar. [O] Available: http://www.sabceducation.co.za/magiccellar/Cellar.html Accessed 2008/07/11.

Salomon, G. 1974. Internalization of filmic schematic operations in interaction with learners' aptitudes. *Journal of Educational Psychology*, 66:499–511.

Sammur, G.B. 1990. Selected bibliography of research on programming at the Children's Television Workshop. *Educational Technology Research and Design*, 38(4):81–92.

Sapa. 2008. Mpofu, Zikalala suspended. [O] Available: http://news.iafrica.com/sa/886686.htm Accessed 2008/15/09.

Sapir, E. 1957. *Culture, language and personality: Selected essays*. Berkeley: University of California Press.

Sartre, J.-P. 1969. *Het imaginaire: fenomenologische psychologie van de verbeelding*. Amsterdam: Meppel.

Saussure, F. de 1916. *Cours de linguistique générale*. Paris: Payot.

Saussure, F. de 1959. *A course in general linguistics*. New York: Philosophical Library.

Saussure, F. de 1981. *Course in general linguistics*. London: Fontana/Collins.

Schiller, H.A. 1976. The deepening nature of visual literacy. *AECT Newsletter*, 5:5–6.

Schrag, R.L. & Rosenfeld, L.B. 1987. Assessing the soap opera frame: Audience perceptions of value structures in soap opera and prime-time serial dramas. *The Southern Speech Communication Journal*, 52(4):362–76.

Schroder, K.C. 1999. The best of both worlds? Media audience research between two rival paradigms, in: *Rethinking the media audience*, edited by P. Alasuutari. London: Sage.

Schudson, M. 1997. Why conversation is not the soul of democracy. *Critical Studies in Mass Communication*, 14(4):297–309.

Schwartz, D. 1992. To tell the truth. Codes of objectivity in photojournalism. *Communication*, 13(2):95–109.

References

Sebeok, T.A 1991a. *A sign is just a sign*. Bloomington: Indiana University Press.
Sebeok, T.A. 1991b. *Semiotics in the United States*. Bloomington: Indiana University Press.
Seiter, E., Borchers, H., Kreutzner, G. & Warth E. (eds) 1991. *Remote control: Television, audiences, & cultural power*. Paperback edition. London: Routledge.
Shapiro, J. (Zapiro) 2007. *Take two veg and call me in the morning*. Auckland Park: Jacana Media.
Shoemaker, P.J. & Reese, S.D. 1996. *Mediating the message: Theories of influences on mass media content*. White Plains, NY: Longman.
Silverstone, R. 1976. An approach to the structural analysis of the television message. *Screen*, 17(2):9–40.
Silverstone, R. 1981. *The message of television: Myth and narrative in contemporary culture*. London: Heinemann.
Silverstone, R. 1987. Narrative strategies in television science, in: *Impacts and influences: Essays on media power in the twentieth century*, edited by J. Curran, A. Smith & P. Wingate. London: Methuen, 291–330.
Silverstone, R. 1988. Television myth and culture, in: *Media, myths and narratives: Television and the press*, edited by J.W. Carey. Newbury Park, Calif: Sage, 20–47.
Silverstone, R. 1999. *Why study the media?* London: Sage.
Singer, B. 1988. Film, photography, and fetish: The analyses of Christian Metz. *Cinema Journal*, 27(4):4–22.
Singletary, M.W. & Stone, G. 1988. *Communication theory and research application*. Ames: Iowa State University Press.
Singleton, R., Straits, B.C., Straits, M.M. & McAllister, R.J. 1988. *Approaches to social research*. New York: Oxford University Press.
Sjoberg, U. 2003. Making sense of screen-based media. The uses and readings of television, computer games and internet among Swedish young people, in: *Media fascinations. Perspectives on young people's meaning making*, edited by Ingegerd Rydin. Göteberg: Nordicom.
Slack, J.M. 1983. Imagery effects and semantic similarity in sentence recognition memory. *Memory & Cognition*, 11(6):631–40.
Smit, P., Technical Support Executive, South African Advertising Research Foundation (SAARF). 2006. Interview by author. [Transcript]. 10 August, Bryanston.
Smith, M.J. 1988. *Contemporary communication research methods*. Belmont, Calif: Wadsworth.

So, C.Y.K. 1987. The summit as war: How journalists use metaphors. *Journalism Quarterly*, 64(2/3):623–6.

Sonderling, S. 1991. Psychoanalysis and television, in: *Critical television analyses: an introduction*, edited by P.J. Fourie. Cape Town: Juta, 141–62.

Sonderling, S. 1992. Murder of the combi-taxi industry by the mass media: Perceptions and realities of road safety. *Communicatio: South African Journal for Communication Theory and Research*, 18(2):57–63.

Sonderling, S. 1993. Power of discourse and the discourse of power in making an issue of sexual abuse in South Africa: The rise and fall of social problems. *Critical Arts*, 6(2):1–26.

Sonderling, S. 1994. An exploration of poststructuralist discursive critique and its implication for the study of communication. *Communicatio: South African Journal for Communication Theory and Research*, 20(2):9–24.

Sonderling, S. 1996. Language, in: *Introduction to communication – course book 3: Communication and the production of meaning*, edited by P.J. Fourie. Juta: Cape Town, 88–111.

Sonderling, S. 1997. Psychoanalysis and television, in: *Introduction to communication – course book 6: Film and television studies*, edited by P.J. Fourie. Cape Town: Juta, 237–50.

Sontag, S. 1977. *On photography*. New York: Farrar, Strauss & Giroux.

Sorlin, P. 1980. *The film history: Restaging the past*. Oxford: Blackwell.

South African Advertising Research Foundation (SAARF). 2004. *SAARF trends 1999–2003*. Bryanston: SAARF.

South African Advertising Research Foundation (SAARF). 2008. *SAARF stakeholders report*. Bryanston: SAARF.

South African Advertising Research Foundation (SAARF) s.a. *Sampling method*. [O] Available: http://www.saarf.co.za/AMPS Accessed 2008/09/25.

South African Advertising Research Foundation (SAARF). *South African Advertising Research Foundation*. [O] Available: http://www.saarf.co.za/ Accessed 2007/04/19.

Spender, D. 1980. *Man made language*. London: Routledge.

Spindler, G. & Spindler, L. 1992. Cultural process and ethnography: An anthropological perspective, in: *The handbook of qualitative research in education*. London/New York: CBS Publishing.

Stacks, D.W. & Hickson, M. 1991. The communication investigator: Teaching research methods to undergraduates. *Communication Quarterly*, 39(4):351–7.

Stacks, D.W. & Hocking, J.E. 1992. *Essentials of communication research*. New York: HarperCollins.

References

Stam, R. 1983. Television news and its spectator, in: *Regarding Television – critical approaches: An anthology*, edited by E.A. Kaplan. Frederick, Maryland: University Publications of America.

Stam, R. 2000. *Film theory: An introduction*. Malden, Mass: Blackwell Publishers.

Starck, K. & Villanueva, E. 1993. Foreign correspondents and cultural framing. *Ecquid Novi*, 14(1):3–35.

Stempel, G.M. & Westley, B.H. (eds) 1989. *Research methods in mass communication*. 2nd edition. Engelwood Cliffs, N.J: Prentice-Hall.

Stewart, D.W. & Shamdasani, P.N. 1990. *Focus groups. Theory and practice*. Newbury Park, Calif: Sage.

Stillar, G.F. 1998. *Analyzing everyday texts. Discourse, rhetoric and social perspectives*. London: Sage.

Stout, P.A, Leckenby, J.D. & Hecker, S. 1990. Viewer reactions to music in television commercials. *Journalism Quarterly*, 67(4):887–98.

Strinati, D. 1992. Postmodernism and popular culture. *Sociology Review*, April:2–7.

Stromgren, R. & Norden, M. 1984. *Movies: A language in light*. Englewood Cliffs, New Jersey: Prentice Hall.

Sturrock, J. 1979. *Structuralism and since. From Lévi-Strauss to Derrida*. Oxford: Oxford University Press.

Sunday Times. 1994. We can all reap fruits of democracy. 18 December:24.

Sunday Times. 1998. Watershed speech has changed our politics. 5 July:18.

Terre Blanche, M., Durrheim, K. & Painter, D. 2006. *Research in practice. Applied methods for the social sciences*. 2nd edition. Cape Town: University of Cape Town Press.

The Star. 1996. Battle marked by accusations, verbal brawls. 7 November:23.

Thompson, J.B. 1990a. *Ideology and modern culture. Critical social theory in the era of mass communication*. Palo Alto, Calif: Stanford University Press.

Thompson, J.B. 1990b. *Studies in the theory of ideology*. Cambridge: Polity.

Thompson, J.B. 1992. *Ideology and modern culture*. Cambridge: Polity.

Tilley, A. 1991. Narrative, in: *The media studies book*, edited by D. Lusted. London: Routledge, 53–79.

Tomaselli, K. 1979. *The South African film industry*. Johannesburg: University of the Witwatersrand.

Tomaselli, K. 1989. *The cinema of apartheid: Race and class in South African film*. Sandton: Radix.

Tomaselli, R. & Tomaselli K. 1987. The political economy of the South African press, in: *Narrating the crisis: Hegemony and the South African press*, edited by K. Tomaselli, R. Tomaselli & J. Muller. Johannesburg: Richard Lyon.

Torfing, J. 1999. *New theories of discourse: Laclau, Mouffe and Zizek.* Oxford: Blackwell

Tredoux, C. 2002. Meta-analysis, in: *Numbers, hypotheses & conclusions: A course in statistics for the social sciences,* edited by C. Tredoux & K. Durrheim. Cape Town: University of Cape Town Press, 402-22.

Tulloch, J. 1991. Approaching the audience: the elderly, in *Remote control: television audiences, & cultural power,* edited by E. Seiter, H. Borchers, G. Kreutzner & E. Warth. Paperback edition. London: Routledge.

Turner, G. 1988. *Film as social practice.* London: Routledge.

Twyman, T. 1994. Measuring audiences to radio, in: *Measuring media audiences,* edited by R. Kent. London: Routledge.

Van Dijk, T. 1988. *News analysis: Case studies of international and national news in the press.* Hillsdale, NJ: Lawrence Erlbaum.

Van Dijk T. (ed) 1999. *Discourse as social interaction, discourse studies: A multidisciplinary introduction.* Volume 2. London: Sage.

Van Leeuwen, T. 1991. Conjunctive structure in documentary film and television. *Continuum,* 5(1):76-113.

Van Vuuren, D. & Maree, A. 1999. Survey methods in market and media research, in: *Research in practice: Applied methods for the social sciences,* edited by M. Terre Blanche & K. Durrheim. Cape Town: University of Cape Town Press, 269-86.

Van Vuuren, D., Maree, A. & De Beer, A. 1998. Mass media research: The quest for certain knowledge, in: *Mass media: Towards the millennium,* edited by A. de Beer. Pretoria: JL van Schaik, 391-422.

Van Vuuren, D.P. & Gouws, P. 2007. The possible interaction between television viewing and problems with discipline in South African schools. Conference proceedings of the International Conference on Learner Discipline: Perspectives on Learner Conduct, April.

Van Vuuren, D.P. 1994. Die SAUK se televisiedienste, in: *Televisie - skyn en werklikheid,* onder redakteurskap van J.B. du Toit. Kaapstad: Tafelberg, 108-27.

Van Zoest, A. 1978. *Semiotiek. Over tekens, hoe ze werken en wat we ermee doen.* Baarn: Basisboeken.

Van Zoonen, L. 1994. *Feminist media studies.* London: Sage.

Watson, J. 1998. *Media communication: An introduction to theory and process.* Houndsmill: Macmillan.

Watson, J. 2003. *Media communication. An introduction to theory and process.* 2nd edition. Basingstoke: Palgrave Macmillan.

Weare, C. & Lin, W.-Y. 2000. Content analysis of the World Wide Web. *Social Science Computer Review,* 18(3):272-92.

References

Webster, J.G. & Lin, S.F. 2002. The internet audience: Web use as mass behaviour. *Journal of Broadcasting & Electronic Media*, 46(1):1–12.

Webster, J.G., Phalen, P.F. & Lichty, L.W. 2006. *Rating analysis: The theory and practice of audience research*. Mahwah, New Jersey: Lawrence Erlbaum.

Weedon, C. 1987. *Feminist practice and poststructuralist theory*. Oxford: Blackwell.

Whatmough, J. 1957. *Language: A modern synthesis*. New York: Mentor.

White, M. 1986. Crossing wavelengths: The diegetic and referential imaginary of American commercial television. *Cinema Journal*, 25(2):51–64.

White, M. 1987. Ideological analysis and television, in: *Channels of discourse. Television and contemporary criticism*, edited by R.C. Allen. London: Routledge.

Whitehead, F. 1992. Roland Barthes's narratology. *Cambridge Quarterly*, 21(1):41–64.

Wigston, D.J. 2001. Narrative analysis, in: *Media studies: Volume 2. Content, audiences and production*, edited by P.J. Fourie. Cape Town: Juta, 150–82.

Wigston, D.J. 1987. Radio Highveld and Radio 702: a comparative analysis of their news services. *Communicatio*, 13(1):37–67.

Willemen, P. 1978. Notes on subjectivity – on reading 'Subjectivity under siege'. *Screen*, 19(1):45–69.

Williams, K. 2003. *Understanding media theory*. London: Wiley.

Williams, R. 1965. *The long revolution*. Harmondsworth: Penguin.

Williams, R. 1974. *Television: Technology and cultural form*. London: Fontana/Collins.

Williams, R. 1985. *Marxism and literature*. Oxford: Oxford University Press.

Williams, R. 1993. Texts and discourses, in: *Mass media for the nineties: The South African handbook of mass communication*, edited by A.S. de Beer. Pretoria: Van Schaik.

Williamson, J. 1978. *Decoding advertisements*. London: Marion Boyars.

Wilson, T. 1993. *Watching television: Hermeneutics, reception and popular culture*. Cambridge: Polity.

Wimmer, R.D. & Dominick, J.R. 1994. *Mass media research: An introduction*. 4th edition. Belmont, Calif: Wadsworth.

Wimmer, R.D. & Dominick, J.R. 1997. *Mass media research: An introduction*. 5th edition. Belmont, Calif: Wadsworth.

Wind, Y. & Lerner, D. 1979. On the measurement of purchase data: Surveys versus purchase diaries. *Journal of Marketing Research*, XVI:39–47.

Winn, W. 1982. Visualization in learning and instruction: A cognive approach. *Educational communication and Technology Journal*, 30(1):3–25.

Wodak, R. & Chilton, P. 2005. *A new agenda in (critical) discourse analysis: Theory, methodology and interdisciplinarity*. Philadelphia: John Benjamins.

Wollen, P. 1972. *Signs and meaning in the cinema*. London: Secker & Warburg.

Wollen, P. 1982. *Readings and writings: Semiotic counter-strategies*. London: Verso.

Wollen, R. 1976. North by Northwest: A morphological analysis. *Film Forum*, 1(1):19–34.

Wood, P.H. 1982. Television as dream, in: *Television: The critical view*, edited by H. Newcomb. 3rd edition. New York: Oxford University Press.

Worth, S. 1981. *Studying visual communication*. Philadelphia: University of Pennsylvania Press.

Wright, E. 1982. Modern psychoanalytic criticism, in: *Modern literary theory*, edited by A. Jefferson & D. Robey. London: Batsford.

Wright, E. 1984. *Psychoanalytic criticism: Theory in practice*. London: Methuen.

Wright, W. 1975. *Six guns and society: A structural study of the Western*. Berkeley: University of California Press.

Wurtzel, A. 1985. Review of procedures used in content analysis, in: *Broadcasting research methods*, edited by J.R. Dominick & J.E. Fletcher. Boston: Allyn & Bacon.

Young K. 1999. Narratives of indeterminacy: Breaking the medical body into its discourses; breaking the discursive body out of postmodernism, in: *Narratologies: New perspectives on narrative analysis*, edited by O. Herman. Columbus: Ohio State University Press, 197–217.

Zelizer, B. 1993. American journalists and the death of Lee Harvey Oswald: Narratives of self-legitimation, in: *Narrative and social control: Critical perspectives*, edited by D. Mumby. London: Sage, 189–206.

Zettl, H. 1990. *Sight, sound, motion: Applied media aesthetics*. 2nd edition. Belmont, Calif: Wadsworth.

Zettl, H. 1998. Contextual media aesthetics as the basis for media literacy. *Journal of Communication*, 48(1):81–95.

Zettl, H. 2008. *Sight, sound, motion: Applied media aesthetics*. 5th edition. Belmont, Calif: Thomson Wadsworth.

Index

18 Wheels of Justice 284
19th Century social science 43
3D charts 29
3-minute culture 302
7de Laan 575

A

aberrant coding 130
absence, consciousness of 373
absent nature of film 370, 372-374
accessible population 430, 435-436
accidental sampling, *see* convenience sampling
action codes 276
active audience paradigm 390-391
active audiences 68-69
active interpretation 68-69
active selection of media messages 391-392
activity, in semantic differential scales 471
address, types of 187-188
advertisements 54-55
advertising 259, 518
Advertising Media Forum 564
Advertising Standards Authority 564
aerial perspective 164
aesthetic appreciation of film 330
aesthetic codes 61
aesthetic film historiography 319-320
aesthetic realism 329
affective meaning 66
affective needs 393-394
African identity, issues of 241
African National Congress 237
African renaissance 241
African traditional medical discourse 207
African, being 210-211
AGB Nielsen Media Research 538, 569
Alasuutari, P 485, 507, 509
alienation 127
All About My Mother 314
Allen, Robert 319, 402
Allen, Woody 313
Almodovar, Pedro 314
alternative film 367
Althusser, Louis 73, 369
Altman, Robert 313
ambiguity of realist film 343
All Media and Products Survey (AMPS) 435, 480-482, 531, 564, 565-567, 568
 case study 480-482
analogue codes 59, 131, 201
analysis, strategies of 196
analytical montage 179
animal tracks as indexical signs 128-129
Annie Hall 313
anonymity in surveys 451
anthropology 44

apartheid 60, 64, 366-367
 it's influence on SA films 321-322, 368
apartheid, SA films about 242
Apocalypse Now 313
application of argument 248-250
applied ethnographic assumptions, case study 414-418
applied media aesthetics, *see* media aesthetics
arbitrary vs motivated signs 120
archetypal characters in soap operas 405-407
architectural structures 134
argument is a dance metaphor 113
argument is war metaphor 97-98
argumentation 206, 243-250
arguments 101-102
 as narrative 250-252
 by analogy 247, 248
 of causal relationships 247, 248
 rules of 244
Aristotle 243, 244, 245, 246, 258, 263, 326-327, 352
Arnheim, Rudolf 136, 331-332, 328
arbitrary signs 51-52
art movies, rebranding of 354
art of other cultures 120
art styles 328
articulation of meaning 360
artificial lighting 150
Asp, K 137
aspect ratios 200
 as codes of form 165
 of TV and film 190
as-seen-on-TV syndrome 256
associations 132
Astruc, Alexander 349
asymmetry of shots 155-156, 199
Atkins, P 497, 506
attitude 20, 426
attraction montage 335, 336
attraction of mass 154, 158, 162, 199
audience activity 396
audience appreciation, measurement of by peoplemeters 541
audience ethnographic research, case study 510-512
audience measurement
 future developments in 544-545
 in SA 562-673
 for particular media 546-562
 limitations of 576
audience metering devices 537-545
audience ratings 519, 524-526
audience research 422
 questions to address in 519-521
audience share 519, 523-524
audiences 205

composition of in cinemas 557
data-capturing instruments for 530-545
estimating 526-527
need for information on 518-519
size of 561
targeting of specific 517
audiovisual codes 126, 186
audiovisual combinations and variations 194
audiovisual Gestalt, ways of creating 193-194
auditory and visual codes of film, integrated nature of 191
auditory codes 186-190
functions of 191-193
auditory variations and typical associations 186-187
Aufderheide, P 137
Austin, John 106
auteur theory 349-351, 355
auteurs 328
personal vision of 350
authoritive sources, use of in news 112-113
authority 208, 212
of sources 246
available sampling, *see* convenience sampling
average issue readership 523, 552
awareness 127, 142, 427
Ayer, NC 135

B
Babbie, E 7, 13, 21, 424, 456-457
balance 200
as a content code 162
Balázs, Béla 338
Balnaves, M 546, 561
Balzac, Honoré de 327
Banks, A 136
bar charts 25, 27
bargain hunting case study 223, 242
Barnhurst, KG 136
Barthe's narrative theory 266-276, 506
Barthes, Roland 46, 49, 50, 68, 73-75, 86, 195, 196, 214, 255, 256, 258, 265, 269, 270, 271, 272, 274, 275, 293, 307, 356, 594-595, 597, 598
Basic Instinct 320
Batman and Robin 227
battle scene example 61-62
Battleship Potemkin 335
Baudrillard, Jean 50, 298-299, 300, 308, 381
Bauman, Richard 214
Bazin, André 136, 179, 328, 338, 341, 342-345, 349
Bazin's realist aesthetic 345
BBC 393
behaviour 426
behavioural codes 58
behavioural variables of audiences 521
behaviourism 39, 391
beliefs 426
Benveniste, Emile 364
Berg, BL 33
Berger, Arthur 17, 130, 277, 286, 287, 288, 289

Bergman, Ingmar 313, 350
Beville, HM 524
bias 121, 448
ideological 122
in responses 479-480
in samples 446
in sourcing quotes for news stories 113
interviewer 452, 453
interviewer 479
sources of in questionnaires 479-480
Big Brother 230
bildungsroman tales 226-227
billboards 558
Bilteryst, D 509
binary oppositions 55, 215, 236-237, 241, 251, 276, 308
application of 238-238-242
in *Cheers* 287-290
in James Bond stories 291-294
in narrative 276-278
of character for generic heroes 294-297
Binnelanders 406
biological determinism 207
birds-eye view 164, 172
Birth of a Nation 334
blanks in text 399
Bloom, D 558, 560
Blue Velvet 313
Blumenthal, HJ 524
Blumler, J 392
Bold and the Beautiful, the 407, 575
Bones 277
Bordwell, D 323
Bornman, Elirea xxiv
Bosma, P 352
Botha, M 322
boundaries between documentary and fiction, blurring of 250
Bourdieu, Pierre 46, 50, 211-212
bourgeois family, myth of 596-597
Bowling for Columbine 248
branded amps 566
bridging function of audiovisual codes 192-193
Bruner, J 214
buddy movies 227
Buffy the Vampire Slayer 304
Bulger, James 248
bullet effects of media 390-391
Buñuel, Luis 350
bureaucratic language 96
Burke 212, 243
Business Day 8
Buyssens, E 49
Buzzard, KSF 545

C
Cagney & Lacey 227
Cahiers du cinema 328, 349
cameo lighting 151-152
camera angle 359
as codes of form 172

Index

camera lens, replacing the eye of the viewer 336
camera level 171-172
camera movement 175
camera positions 376
camera shots 180, 181-182, 200
   as codes of form 169-170
camera viewpoints 200
   as codes of form 170-173
computer assisted personal interview (CAPI) 482, 531, 565
capitalism 299
captions 56
cardinal functions 271-274, 276, 293, 307
Carlsson, U 143
cartoon characters 188-189
cartoon strips 14, 24
cartoons, toy-linked 12
catalyser functions 271-274, 293, 307
categories 16, 19, 24
   defining 32
   value-laden 237-238
cathartic function of media 394
causal relationships between variables 35
causality, in narrative 218, 261
census-type sampling 438-439
Centre for Contemporary Culture Studies (University of Birmingham) 197
chain effect, three elements of 260-263
challenging the down-diagonal 155-156, 174, 199
Chandler, Daniel 69, 73, 75
Chaplin, Charles 350
character functions 225
characters, physical appearance of 278
Charmed 304
charts 25-29
chat rooms 394
Chatman, Seymour 255, 258, 265, 266, 284, 307
Chaudhuri, Jhuma 497
Checkland, Michael 516
checklist questions 464-465
Cheers (sitcom) 286, 308
   a syntagmatic analysis of 287-290
Chekhov, Anton 327
chiaroscuro lighting 150, 151-152
Children of Heaven 314
children watching TV in school hours, case study 574-576
children, advertising to 29-30
children's fiction 251
Chiseri-Strater, E 493
choice in communication 65, 360
Christian symbols, their use by Satanists 64
Christianity, decline of 298
Christie, Agatha 267
chronological sequence 231, 261-262
Cicero 243
cineliteracy 118
cinema admissions 557
Cinemark 564
circuit of culture 205
Citizen Kane 346

class 237
class conflict in *Cheers* 288
classic film theory 326-355, 364
cliffhangers 265
   in soap operas 404
climax 265
   in narrative 264
closed location for research 489
closed-ended questions 459-461
   compiling of 461-464
   requirements of 462-464
close-up theory of film 314, 315-316
closure 265, 275
clothing as a sign system 41
Coca Cola film ad 193
code names, use of in participant observation studies 493
code typology 58-62
codes 41, 47, 49, 50, 57-65, 75, 126, 127, 148, 287
   changing nature of 64-65
   characteristics of 62-65
   in film 358-359
   the way they are used 62-63
codes of content 61-62, 122, 184-185, 263, 297, 358-359
codes of form 61-62, 122, 165-173, 297, 358-359
   in soap operas 404
codes of form and content combined 166-168, 169
coding 19-20
   of print news 20
coding scheme 18, 24
cognitive approach to visual communication 128, 132-135
cognitive coherence 214
cognitive development 127
cognitive knowledge 126
cognitive meaning 66
cognitive needs 392
   of audiences 397
coincidence 22
Collected Papers of Charles Sanders Peirce 45, 48
collective unconsciousness 44, 45
collision 183-184
collocative meaning 67
colour 123, 199
   as a code of content 152-153
Columbine massacre 248
commercial broadcasting, origins of 517
communication, concept of 84
communication semiology 49
communicative value of signs 67
community newspapers 142
comparison and collision 182-183
compatibility, rule of 47
competing sets of representation 210
complexity editing 177, 178-184
comprehension of the world, approaches to 49
computer programmes 26
computer surveys 452
conative function of images 362

conative function of language 106
concept testing 133
concepts 24
conceptual meaning 66, 67
conclusions, drawing of 29-30
condensed codes 131, 132, 201
　in dreams 585
confidence intervals 478
conflict montage between different shots 335-336
conflict montage within a single shot 334-335
conflict, creation of by editing 181
congregation 212
conjunctions 101
Connor, John 69
connotative functions of signs 54-55
connotative meaning 66, 67-68, 124, 129, 200, 357, 471
connotative semiotics 49
constants 281
construct validity 475
construction montage 336-338
consumerism 297, 299, 301,308
contact, establishing 55-56
contemporary film theory 364-382
content 54, 360
content analysis 21, 324
　advantages of 33-34
　an evaluation of 33-35
　cost effectiveness of 34
　definition of 5-6
　its position in the communication process 7
　of field research data 505-506
　of internet content 30-33
　steps in 10-30
　uses of 6-10
content and form 55
content codes 150-165
content validity 476
contexts 34
contexts of media messages 259
contextual variables 194-195
contextualising research 11-12
contingency questions 465-466
continuing vectors 159-160
continuity 158, 178
continuity editing 177-178
convenience sampling 446-447, 501-502
conventions 126, 127
convergence 178
converging vectors 160
Coppola, Francis Ford 313
Corel Presentations 26
correlation coefficients 22
Cosmopolitan 8
counter-hegemonic reading 70
Course de Linguistique Genérale 45, 48
coverage 519, 520, 522-523, 559
　vs ratings 524
covert messages 121
covert observation 489, 490
　ethical issues of 490-491

Craig, RL 136
crane movement 175
credence 246
crime fiction in SA 242
criminalisation of legitimate activities 96
critical analysis 91, 205
　aims of 127
critical media studies, reasons for xxv-xxvi
Critical School 258
Cronje, Hansie 395
Cross, L 195
cross-cutting 177-178
cultural contexts 194, 205
　of codes 63
　of media consumption 397
cultural expectations of narrative 275
cultural influences 134
cultural relativism 416
cultural values, transformative value of 139
cultures, describing of 411

D
Da Ali G Show 305
Daily Sun 246
Dallas (soap opera) 508, 509
Danahar, P 546, 561
Dark Angel 304
dark continent metaphor 98
data analysis 33, 432
data capture 432
data collection techniques in participant observation 492-494
data interpretation 24-25
De Putter, J 323
de Sica, Vittorio 341
Deacon, D 489
deaf MP addressing National Assembly 107
death of the author, birth of the reader 597
Death of the Dinosaurs 286
Debes, John L 118
debriefing interview of observed participants 490-491
decoding 10, 63, 68-70
deductive arguments 247
deep structures 20, 44-45
Deleuze, Gilles, 380-381
deliberative arguments 244, 245, 246, 248, 249
demographic characteristics 426
demographic details on questionnaires 472
demographic variables of audiences 520
demonstrative arguments, *see* epideictic arguments
denotative level of meaning 200
denotative meaning 66, 67-68, 124, 129, 357, 471
denouement 265
depth as a content code 162-165
depth factors, graphic 185
depth of understanding, *see* insight
Derrida, Jacques 50, 68, 259
descriptive film theory 317
descriptive research 7, 8

Index

descriptive sound effects 188-189
desire in TV watching 590-591
Dethier, H 55
deviance 97
diachronic axis 318
diachronic semiotic analysis 65
diachronism, rule of 47
dialectic principle, in montage 183
dialectical interaction 400
dialectical philosophy 336
dialectics 334
dialects 102
dialogue 187-188
   of film director with viewer 347
   vs movement in TV 190
diaries, use of to record audience behaviour 533-537
diary fatique 535
Dickens, Charles 227
Die Bou van 'n Nasie 321
digital codes 59
direct address 187
direct focus 160-161
directions in photos, *see* main directions
disaster vs opportunity 242
disbelief, suspension of 589
discourse 73, 75, 90, 92, 206-209, 210, 243, 268, 365
   analysis of 364
   as social interaction 105-107
   of capital 219, 221
   of helping professions 95-97
   of science 100-101
   orders of 91, 110-111
discursive nature of texts 206
discursive practices 90, 92, 94, 100, 102-105, 106, 110
   social hierarchy of 111
discursive work, *see* discourse
disequilibrium (narrative stage) 217, 221
disharmony 221
Disneyland is the real America 298, 299
dispatcher 227, 239-240
displaced codes 131
displacement, in dreams 585
displacement, rule of 47
disruption 242
   in narrative 219, 221
dissemination of research findings 433
dissonance 134
distance between viewers and screen 375
distribution 269, 270
divergence 178
diverging vectors 160, 161
Dixon, P 245
Doctor Quinn, Medicine Woman 276
docudramas 143
document analysis 486, 497-498
dolly tracking 175-176
dominant reading 69
domination 209-210

Dominick, JR 18, 492, 584
Dondis, DA 119
donor 227, 239-240
double temporal tension 173
down-diagonal 155, 199
dramatic tension 261
dramatis personae 284-286, 287
dramatisation, in dreams 585
dream-like state 592
dreams 585
   awareness in 376
   similarity to film 331, 375-377
dress style, as a sign system 57
DStv 577
Du Plooy, Trudie M xxi
dual hero function 227
duplication (of audiences) 31, 520, 561

E
E.T. 320
e.tv 498
Eco, Umberto 49, 70, 195, 255, 274, 306, 308, 356
Eco's 10 oppositions of value 296-297
Eco's narrative model, *see* Umberto Eco's narrative model
economic film historiography 319, 321
economic implications of film 325
economics 17-18, 44
economy of detail 218
Edelman, MJ 95, 107, 109
editing 176-177
   as a level of meaning 360, 361
editorial opinion vs news 105
edutainment 143
effective communication 135
effective relations 48
effectiveness, measurement of 126
Egoli 404, 405, 406, 407, 408, 409, 509
Egoli fan club 497
Eichenbaum 45
Eidsvik, C 590
Eisenstein, Sergei 136, 179, 314, 328, 329, 332, 333-336, 344, 347
elaborated codes 60
Elam, K 188-189
electricity, as a limiting factor for TAMS 568-569
electronic media, use of 414, 415, 417
electronic superhighway 415, 416-418
elements of a message as units of analysis 15
elephants, Tuli 401
ellipses in film communication 344
Ellis, John 373
emotional coherence 214
emotional nature of film 347-348
emphasis of human voice 187
encoding 9, 63, 68-70
   basic elements of 122-124
   characteristics 125
   effective use of 124
   techniques of 180
English in postcolonial societies 87-88

enigma code 274
enjoyment, as function of media 393
enjoyment, of film 371-379
environmental issues 23-24
epideictic arguments 244, 245, 246, 248, 249
epistemology 110, 126-127, 135, 136, 143
equilibrium (narrative stage) 217
equivalence 18
equivalence reliability 474
errors
   in use of diaries 535-536
     sources of in audience measurement 528-530
     sources of in questionnaires 477-480
escapism 575
   as function of media 393
establishment theory of film 314
ethics in research 35-36
ethnocentricism 194
ethnographic fieldwork, openness of 413
ethnographic studies, examples of 508
ethnography 390, 411-418, 482, 485, 486, 507-512
   definition of 412
   subjective use of 416
ethos (arguer) 245, 246, 248
evaluating surveys 473-477
evaluation, in semantic differential scales 471
Evans, J 120
exhaustivity 18
existentialism 45
existents 281
expansive semiotics 50
expectations 426
experiential nature of film and TV 361
experimental research 141
expert validity 476
explanatory research 7, 8-10
exposition, in narrative 264
expressionism 324, 326, 327, 328, 355
   definition of 328
expressionist film theory 330-332
expressive function of images 362
expressive function of language 106
expressive function of signs 53, 54, 55
extensionism 354
external sources of error 529-530
external validity 476
eye level position
Eyre, Chris 569

F
face validity 476
Facebook 198, 394
face-to-face interviews 452-454, 554
factual representation of reality 361
Fairlady 8
false hero 227
fan mail, as public discourse 508
Fanny and Alexander 313
Faux TV 305
Fellini, Federico 350
feminism 210

feminist film criticism 380, 381-382
feminist perspective on film analysis 324
feminist theories, of film and TV 594
fetish, definition of 371
fetishism 371, 378-379
fictional representation of reality 361
field forces 181, 199
   within shots 182
field notes 492-494
field research data
   analysing of 505-507
   interpreting 507
   processing of 504-507
   transcribing of 504
field research techniques 486-504
figure-ground perception 156-157, 162, 185, 199
filling in gaps, *see* psychological closure
film 41
   as a sign 356-357
   as a sign system 57
   as a signifying practice 365-366
   as an art form 313-314, 331, 349
   as an ideological practice 364
   as an ideological statement 368
   communicative possibilities of 361-362
   theatrical construct of 348
film analysis 317, 324
film criticism 317, 323
film historiography, forms of 319-322
film history 317, 318-322
   vs film theory 325
Film Language: a semiotics of the cinema 355-356
film noir 319, 320
film reviews vs film criticism 323
film semiotics 318, 324, 355-363, 364, 380
film shots, field forces within 153-161
film theory 317, 322-323, 582
   as opposed to film history 322-323
   definition of 314
   phases of 379-380
   reasons for 325-326
film-dream analogy 582
filmic apparatus 370-371
filmic art 328
filmic codes 297, 358
filmic signifiers 372
filters (codes) 63
findings 24-29
first reading yesterday 555
firstness 49
Fiske, John 58, 63, 141, 195, 196, 197, 214, 215, 216
five levels of meaning in film 360-361
five-point Likert-type scales 469
flags 129
Flaherty, Robert 343, 348
flashbacks 262
   in soap operas 404
flash-forwards 262
   in soap operas 404
Fleming, Ian 290, 291

Index

Fletcher, Jessica 16
floating signifier 68
flooding 567
fly on the wall 488, 489
focus 200
   as a code of form 166-169
   as metaphor 168-169
focus groups, 414, 498-504, 510, 511, 512
   conducting sessions with 504
   designing study of 499-401
   interviews with 430, 486, 507
   recruiting participants for 501-502
folk tales, indexical nature of 270
Ford, John 350
forensic arguments 244-245, 246, 248, 249
form 55
form and content, distinction between 197
formal balance 172
formalism 49
   definition of 329
   vs expressionism 328-329
formalist film theory 332-339
formalist semiotics 68
Foucault, Michel 46, 50, 109, 110, 210, 211, 259, 597
Foucault's concept of discourse 206
Fourie, Pieter J xx, xxii, 58, 150
fourth estate 71
fragmented viewing, measuring of 548
Frankfurt, Harry 109
freedom of choice of audiences 397
French new wave 319, 328, 343
frequency 8, 526, 552, 559
   of audiences 520
   of media events 262
Freud, Sigmund 45, 369, 370, 582, 583, 586, 593, 596
Friedman, L 536
functional units of narrative 269-270
functioning, rule of 47
functions of signs, *see* sign functions
functions, four laws that govern 282
funnel structuring 473

G
gatekeepers 489
gender 207, 210, 237
   and status 110-111
   conflict between in *Cheers* 288
   equality of 208
   in focus groups 499
   roles 140
General Hospital (soap opera) 510
general theory of signs 48
general to specific (questions) 473
Generations 404, 575
genre mixing 354, 355
genre theory 351-355, 355
genres 8, 121, 124, 188, 242-243, 265, 401
   criteria with which to define them 352
   distinguishing characteristics of 352

Genzuk, M 491
geographic information systems 560
geographic variables of audiences 520-521
Gerbner, G 195
German expressionism 328
Gestalt principle 157, 179, 183, 331
Gianetti, L 330, 342, 344
Gibson, JJ 196
Gill, J 545
Gleeson, K 391
global forum for joint industry committees 565
globalisation 125, 297, 299, 308, 369
Godard, Jean-Luc 346-348, 349
golden ratio 172-173
Gombrich, EH 126, 195
Gomery, D 319
Gone with the Wind 319, 322
good and evil in James Bond stories 293
Goodenough, OR 524
Google 393
Gouws, P 574
GPS coordinates 481
grammar 98-101
   its effect on meaning 99-101
   of acting 119
   vs meaning 98-99
graphic depth factors 163-165
graphic depth vectors 200
graphic vectors 158-159, 160, 178, 185
gratification, through the media 395-396
Great Expectations 227
Greece, ancient 258
grid of possibilities 266
Griffin, M 136, 139, 143, 198
Griffith 348
Griffith, DW 314, 334, 337
Grimes, T 191
group-administered surveys 451-452
Gutsche, Thelma 321, 322

H
habituation 133
Hake, K 495, 506, 507
Hall, Stuart 68, 69, 121, 196
Hammersley, M 497, 506
handicapped people 63
Hans en die Rooinek 321
haphazard sampling, *see* convenience sampling
haptics 134
Hart to Hart 277, 278
Hartley, J 195
hate speech 86
Hawks, Howard 350
Hawthorne effect 33
headline size 23
Heath, Stephen 364, 373
Hebdige, D 195
Hecker, S 193
Hegel, GWF 334
hegemonic reading 69
hegemony 127, 197

633

helper 227
hermeneutic code 274
   ten stages of 275
hero 219, 227, 275
   always wins 258
   as seeker 226
   functions of in westerns 353
   identity of 221
   repeated testing of 230
high-tone montage 336
Hill Street Blues 265
hinge points 271
hippies 64
Hitchcock, Alfred 231, 286, 350
Hobbs, R 255, 260
Hobson, Dorothy 508, 509
Hocking, JE 35
Hoijer, B 195
Hollywood 319, 366, 368, 593
   origins of 320
   style 314
Holsti, OR 6, 21
Hommel, M 318, 322-323
horizons of expectation 399, 400
horizons, expansion of 399
horizons, fusion of 401
household meters 537-538
Howells, R 139
human factor in news 112
human voice 186, 187-188, 190, 191, 192
human-centred cinema 347
hyperreality 299, 308
hypotheses 12, 428

I

I am a man campaign 246
Ibsen, Hendrik 327
iconic nature of film 356, 357
iconic signs 51, 52, 128
iconography 354
idea-associative montage 182
idealism 42
ideational metafunctions 125
identification signals in media broadcasts 547
identification with themes on TV 410-411
identification with TV characters 410-411
ideological content, unintended 140
ideological criticism 366-369
ideological film criticism, subjective nature of 369
ideological implications of binary oppositions in
   James Bond stories 294
ideological implications of film 325
ideological meaning 67, 68, 70-71, 79
ideological perspective on film analysis 324
ideological positioning 236
ideology 206, 209-211
   as constructed by mass media 141
   as part of the unconscious 588
   challenging of 210
   critical conceptions of 209
   definition of 367

interpretation of 71
   its status as common sense 111
   of mass communication 127
idiosyncratic communication 134
illusion of depth 163
illusory reality 74
image vs substance of politicians 109-110
images, communication functions of 362
Images: a reader 49
imaginary relationship with TV characters 409
imagined emotions, identification with 374-375
imitation of TV characters 410
immanence, rule of 46
impressionism 327
in group 238
in media res 264
incentives, uses of in surveys 479, 569
in-depth interviews 414, 486, 494-497, 511, 512
index vectors 158-159, 160, 161, 178, 185,
   200-201
indexical nature of film, 356-357
indexical signs 51, 52, 128-129, 200-210
indexical units 270-274
indirect address 187-188
indirect focus 160-161
individualism, illusion of 300
inductive arguments 247-248
ineffective relations 48
inferences 10
informal balance 172
information level of signs 74
informing functions of auditory codes 191-192
infotainment 143
initial equilibrium, omission of in TV 280
inkblot, *see* Rorschach test
insight 21
instantaneous editing 176
institutional contexts 211
instrumental media use 396-397
integration 269, 270
intellectual property rights 301
intensity measures, in questionnaires 467-468
intensive interview, *see* in-depth interview
intention 6, 7
interactive TV viewing
intercultural conflicts 87
intercultural misunderstandings 87
internet 30-33, 125, 197, 576
   measuring audiences of 560-562
   use of 414-416
internet dating sites 394
Internet Protocol Television (IPTV) 198
internet surveys 456
interpersonal metafunctions 125
interpretation 7
   of data 29-30, 33
   reader's vs author's 73-74
interpretive character 51
interpretive communities 408-409
interpretive process of narrative 274
interpretive research 141

Index

intertextuality 79
   of codes 63
interval level 21
interview error 529
interviewer effects 479
interviewers, training of 431
interviewers, untrustworthiness of 454
Intolerance 334
intonation 187
introduction letter to questionnaire 472
inversion, in dreams 585
inverted pyramid 92
Iser, Wolfgang 399, 402
Isidingo 406, 575
Italian futurism, its effect on Eisenstein 333
Italian neo-realism 319, 328, 340, 343

J

JAG 284-285
Jakobsen, Roman 46, 53, 105, 106
Jakobsen's six function classification 54, 56, 68, 362
James Bond stories 230, 269, 308
   Eco's analysis of 290-297
Jameson, Frederic 299-300, 308
Japanese Kabuki, its effect on Eisenstein 333
jargon 94-97
Jauss, HR 401
Jaws 313
jingles 190
Jobman (film) 366
Johnson, M 97
joint research bodies 563
journalism, as a discursive practice 103, 104-105
Joyce, James 88
judgemental sampling 447
judicial arguments 244-245
juxtaposition 182-183, 333
   to construct implied meaning 196

K

Kael, Pauline 351
Kant, Immanuel 42
Katrina 321
Katz, E 392, 509
Kerliger, EN 437
kinaesthetic sense 57, 177
kinesics 174-175, 181, 280
knowledge 427
   commodification of 301, 308
Kochman, T 87
Kozloff, SR 285, 306
Kracauer, Seigfried 136, 341, 342, 328, 346
Kress, G 125, 138
Kristeva, Julia 50, 72, 364

L

lables 94
Lacan, Jacques 46, 364, 369, 370, 583, 586, 591, 593 596
Lakof, G 97

landline phones, as a limiting factor for TAMS 568-569
Lang, Fritz 338
language 41, 53, 84
   analysis and study of 88-91
   and political discourse 107-110
   and the unconscious 586
   as a matter of life and death 85
   as a sign system 57
   as a social phenomenon 89
   as political activity 109
   as social activity 106-107
   functions of, 105-107
   in society 85-88
   its relationship with power and ideology 111-113
   its use to classify people 93
   perceived prestige of 110
langue 44, 73, 365, 586
Lapsley, R 364, 365, 370, 373
latent coding 20-21
latent content, in dreams 585
Laughey, D 300, 302
Lazersfled, Paul 424
leading questions 462
Leckenby, JD 193
Leedy, PD 12
left to right reading 155, 175
leitmotiv 192
Lemish, Daphna 487-488, 489, 505-506, 507, 510-512
lenses 200
   as codes of form 166-169
Lester, PM 128, 157
levels of communication 74
levels of description, in a narrative 269-270
levels of meaning 88
levels of signification 74
Lévi-Strauss, Claude 46, 215, 231, 235-238, 238-242, 255, 258, 276, 278, 287, 308
Lewis 89
Liebes, T 509
life-long learning 126
light and dark, proportions of 150
lighting 123, 199
   as a content code 150-152
Likert-type scales 468-470
   neutral option in 469
limitations of content analysis 34=35
Lin, SF 560
Lindlof, TR 412
Lindsay, Vachel 331
line charts 25,
linear cause-effect relationship, *see* chain effect
linear perspective 164
linguistic goods 85
linguistic signs 48-49, 89
linguistics 48, 260, 266
linkage, rule of 47
Linton, JM 136
listening 521-522, 577

635

literacy, meaning of 120
literal sounds 188
literary communication 84
literary theory 46
literate mentality 87
literature reviews 12, 13, 16, 429
Living Positively campaign 558
living standards measure (LSM) 459, 520, 571-573
location, for focus groups 502
logetic arguments 247
logic of the concrete 237
logical codes 61
logos (argument) 245, 246, 248
longevity of soap operas 405
looking at looking 373
looking room, *see* nose room
Lord of the Flies 304
Lost 305
lost luggage letter example 98-99
Lynch, David 303, 313
Lyotard, Jean-François 300-302, 308
lyrics 190

M
Macbeth 266
Macdonald, Dwight 351
MacGyver, 270-274
   narrative structure of after Todorov 279-280
macrohistory of film 322
Madam & Eve 130
Madlala-Routledge, Nozizwe 107
magic agent 225, 230, 286
Magic Cellar 251
magic, use of language in 88
magnetic pull 154
magnetism of the frame 154-155, 162, 184, 185, 199
Mail & Guardian 226
main direction in photos 153-154, 162, 199
mainstream cinema 367
   its contribution to maintaining existing social structure 366
Majidi, Majid 314
male unconscious 593-594
Mandela, Nelson 8, 246
Manichean ideology of James Bond stories 293-294
manifest coding 20-21
manifest content, in dreams 585
manipulation by media 126
markers (codes) 64
market forces 259
market segmentation 520
Marketing Federation of South Africa 564
marks of construction, elimination of in film 595
Married with Children 304
Marshall, H 391
Martinez-de-Toda, J 137
Marx, Karl 45, 423
Marxism, decline of 298

mass culture 74
mass media, as subjective presentation 124
mass media, as systems 141
mass media, future developments of 137-139
Massey, A 412
mathematics, 61
   as a sign system 57
matrix questions 470, 475
Max Headroom 303
Mbeki, Thabo 107, 237
Mcguigan, J 300
McLuhan, Marshall 87, 299
McMillan, SJ 30, 31, 33
Mead, Margaret 411
meaning 41, 50,58, 66-75, 75, 79-80
   amplification of in realist films 341
   assigned by viewers to signs 68
   construction of 47, 89, 122, 127, 149, 195-196, 199
      awareness of 126
      in films 356
   creation of 182
   in media texts, negotiated by individuals 259
   rules that produce construction of 236
measuring analogue vs digital signals 547
measuring cinema audiences 556-558
measuring internet audiences 560-562
measuring outdoor media 558-559
measuring print media audiences 552-556
measuring radio audiences 549-552
   techniques for 550-552
measuring TV audiences 546-549
mechanics of mediation 213
media aesthetics 148,
media audiences, invisibility of 516
media
   as social institution 71
   as symbolic form 71
   as ideological instrument 71
   competition between 392
media content 44
   as sign 40
   reasons for studying 4
media content literacy 121-122, 149
media convergence 561
media effects tradition 391
media environment 30
media ethnography, *see* ethnography
media grammar literacy 122-124, 149
media groups measure 572-573
media layering 576
media literacy 117
   meanings of 118-121
   three types of 121
Media Literacy National Leadership Conference 137
media messages, as construction 259
media research 422
media semiotics 128
   definition of 40
media studies 44
   definition of xviii

Index

three main areas of xxiii
media texts
  as deliberate actions 206
  as mediations 205
  organisation of 212-214
media-linguistic literacy 118
media-saturated simulation 299
mediated content 197
mediated cultural representations 297
mediated experiences 139
mediated images 135
mediated visual codes 149-150
mediating functions of discourse 211
mediation 211-212
medical discourses 110
medium literacy 124-125, 149
medium theory of film 314,
Meier, Erhard 566
melody 189, 190
mental illness, discourse of 95-97
Merriam, AP 189
messages, internalising of 398-399
Messaris, P 120, 136, 196
metafunctions 125
meta-genres 213
metalinguistic functions 79
  of images 362, 363
  of language 106
  of signs 53, 54, 56
  decline of 298
metaphors 97-98, 124, 131, 201
  in dreams 585
metaphysical meaning 331-332
metatext, of the closed world of TV 596
metatheoretical research 425
method 13-24
metonyms 124, 130-131, 201
  in dreams 585
metric montage 179, 335-336
metteur en scène 350
Metz, Christian 179, 355-356, 364, 373, 377, 378, 591
Meyrowitz, J 120, 121, 124
Miami Vice 303
microhistory of film 322
mimesis 327
mimetic school of critics 329
Miracle in Milan 341
mirror nature of film 582
mise-en-scène 123, 150, 195, 347, 348
mobile technology 197
mobile telephones 576
mode (music) 189-190
modern semiotics, *see* semiotics
modes of enunciation 594-595
modes of persuasion 246
Moedertjie 321
moment of decoding 69
moment of encoding 69
Monaco, J 120
Monet, Claude 327

monolithic nature of genre theory 354
montage 124, 177, 178-184, 333, 345
  synthesis with *mise-en-scène* 346
  vs depth perspective 343, 344
  vs sequence shots 343, 344
mood, creation of by music 193
Moonlighting 303
Moore, Michael 248
Morgan, M 195
Morley, D 196, 302, 303
morphemes 93
Morse code 61
motion vectors 159, 160, 174, 178
Mounin, Preito 49
movement in film and TV 173-185
Movie (journal) 349
Mpofu, Dali 486-487
MS Word 26
MTV 303
Münsterberg, Hugo 136, 330, 582
multichoice questions 464-465
multiple bar charts 25,
multiple conceptual meaning 66-67
multiple indicators of variables 475
multiple line charts 25,
multiple meanings of reality 343
multiple non-linear story lines on TV 307, 403-404, 405
multiple plots 265
multiple readers of print media 554
multi-stage cluster sampling 441-442, 446, 480
Muppets 174-175
Murder, She Wrote 16
Murnau, Friedrich 338
music 186, 189-190
  emotional effect of 192, 193
  use of in SA TV programmes 190-191
musical clichés
mutual exclusivity 18
MySpace 198
mythical meanings 129-130
myths 127, 215, 276
Mytton, G 474, 476, 479

N

names as language 86
Nanook of the North 343
narration 187-188
narrative analysis 4, 46
  an evaluation of 306-307
  nature of 265-266
  postmodern 257
narrative development 263
narrative format of ethnography 413
narrative functions 224-230
narrative paradigm, basic 260-266
narrative stages 217
  Propp's vs Todorov's 232
narrative structure 214
  characteristics of 265
narrative syntagm, rules of 272

sequence 273-274
narrative theory 258
narratives 130, 242-243
   as arguments 250-252
   attributes of 267
   causal nature of 216, 217
   construction of 255
   deeper structure of 236
   elements of 266-269
   how they function 268
   human desire for 589
   in literary texts 266
   of emancipation 301
   of labour 219
   of speculation 301
   reasons for 213-215
   structuralist model of 267
narratology 324
narrowcasting 517, 520
National Association of Broadcasters 564
Natural Born Killers 320
natural signs 52
naturalism 327
Navajo Filmmakers Project 196
Nazis 64
Ndaba, Dennis 223
Ndebele art 64
Neal, Steven 354
need to hear 377
need to see, *see* scopophilia
needs and gratification theory, *see* uses and gratification
needs, typology of 392-395
negative comparison 183
negative space 162-163
negotiated reading 69, 398, 401
Neuman, WL 474, 476
new media technologies 30, 197
Newhoudt-Druchen, Wilma 107
news reporting style 92-93, 229-230
news values 104
news, nature of 219, 221
Newspeak 86
Nichols, B 250
Nielsen 542
Nielsen Audimeter 537
Nielsen Media Research 547,, 570
Nielsen ratings 525
NielsenGeoFrame 480-481
Nietzsche, Friedrich 109
No Country for Old Men 354, 355
noise 188
Nokwe, Jongi 226
nominal level 21
non-filmic codes 297, 358
non-linear narrative 262
non-probability sampling 14, 32, 437, 443-449, 492, 501-502, 527
non-racist language 85
non-response error 450, 478-479, 528-529
non-sexist language 85

non-verbal communication 41, 60
normative film theory 317
normative principles 137-138
normativism 354
North by Northwest 231, 286
nose room 154, 170
notan lighting 150-151, 165, 199
Npod 570
Ntini, Makhaya 226

O
object media vs operation media 72
objective camera 170
   in neorealist films 340-341
objective nature of content analysis 5
objective time 173-174
objective truth, rejection of 398
objectivity of language 93
objectivity vs subjectivity 5
observation, degrees of involvement in 491
observers, roles of 489-490
obtuse meaning 74, 75
Oedipus 380
   story of 372
Oedipus complex 584-585, 587, 591, 593, 596, 597
   definition of 372
omnipotence of the media 255-256
ontology 110, 119, 126-127, 135, 136, 142-143
   of film 342
open locations for research 488-489
open narrative 265
open-ended questions 495
   coding of 432
   vs closed-ended questions 459-461
operational definitions 16-17
opinion polls 423
opinions 426
oppositional cinema 366
   definition of 367
oppositional reading 70
Oprah 393
optic-acoustic effect 359, 360, 361
optical centre 172
oral communication 84
   vs literate communication 102
orality 87
order effects 555
order, in narrative 261
ordinal level 21
orgasmic rhythm of narrative text 591
Orwell, George 86, 103, 109
OSCAR 559, 560
Osgood, CE 471
others category 18, 460, 462
Out of Home Media South Africa 564, 570
Outdoor advertising 559- 560
Outdoor Site Classification and Audience Research programme, *see* OSCAR
overt messages 121
overt observation 489 490

Index

P

pacing function of audiovisual codes 192
painting, history of 327
Palmgreen, P 395
panning 175
paradigmatic analysis of narrative 215
paradigmatic complexity of soap operas 405, 407
paradigmatic connotation 357
paradigmatic selection 176
paradigmatic-syntagmatic nature of film 359-360
paradigmatic-syntagmatic systems 65-66
paradigmatic systems 77-79
paradigmatic theories 235-242
paradigms 65
paralanguage 187
parallel action 177-178
para-social interaction with TV characters 409, 410
Paris, Texas 313
Parisian structuralism 46
parody 299-300
parole 44, 73, 365, 586
participant observation 414, 486, 487-494, 511
passive peoplemeters 544-545, 551, 552
passive reading measurement 556
passive voice, its use in science 100-101
pastiche 299-300, 304
Pateman, T 258, 259
pathotic arguments 246-247
pathos (audience) 245, 246, 248, 249
patriarchal discourse 207-208, 209, 238, 251
patriarchal ideology 593
patriarchal society 587
patterns 30
peacock effect 499
peculiarity, rule of 46
Peirce, Charles Sanders 45, 47, 48, 49, 50
Peircean typology of signs 158
Penzhorn, H 509
peoplemeter panels 546
peoplemeters 529, 538-543
    and truancy in SA, case study 574-576
    advantages of 539-540
    ease of use of 541-542
    motivation for users of 540
    quality control checks for users of 540-541
    sources of errors with 542-543
    use in SA 568, 569
perception 127-128
    identification with the action of 372-374
    influence of culture on 135
    structure of by words 94
Percy, RD 544
permanence, rule of 46
Perse, EM 396
personal digital assistants (PDA) 456, 532
personal integrative needs 395
personal narratives 214
personal video recorders (PVRs) 548, 576
personality cults 351
perspective 123

persuasion 101-102
persuasive functions of discourse 211
phallic symbols 131
phatic function of images 362
phatic function of language 106
phatic functions of signs 54, 55-56
phonemes 93
photographs, field forces within 153-161
photography 327
    art or science 135-136
    as a sign system 57
physical movement, as a sign system 57
pictorial codes in film shots and photos 149-173
pie charts 25, 26
pilot studies 18-20, 22, 431, 475, 476
    for focus groups 500-501
pitch 186
    of human voice 187
Pitout, Magriet xxiii, xxiv, 497, 509
pizza ad, case study 139-142
Plato 258, 326-327, 351
play situations in James Bond stories 291-292, 308
pleasurable nature of narratives 590
pleasure of film and TV viewing 582, 588-589, 590-591
plurality of distribution outlets 369
plurality of film production 369
poetic function of images 362
poetic function of language 106
poetic functions of signs 53, 54, 55
Poetics 263, 352
point of view 348, 358, 360, 361
political cartoons 8
political contexts 205
political correctness 85-86
political discourse 107-110
political implications of jargon 95
political rally, case study 198-201
political speeches 20-21
politicians, inactivity of 107-110
polysemy 88
population 435
    establishing of 12
    vs sample 526-527
population parameters 477
population sampling 13
pornography 394
portable personal meters (PPMs) 543-544, PPMs 577
position of articles 24
positive volume 162-163
positivist research 141
postal surveys 450-451, 479
postcolonial film theory 380, 382
postmodern narrative 297-306
    contradictory nature of 305
postmodern perspective on genres 354-355
postmodern TV 302-306
postmodernism 259, 301, 308
    five characteristics of 297-298

poststructural approaches to narrative 237
poststructuralism 596
potency, in semantic differential scales 471
Potter, WJ 195
Poulet, Georges 398
power 211
power dimensions, implicit 214
power of the text 72
power relations 207, 209, 213
pragmatics 89, 90, 91
Prague Circle, the 46
preferences 426
pre-Oedipal stages 586-587
presentational codes 59-60
president, appointing of a new in 2008 407
pretension 399-400
pre-testing 475, 476
Pretoria East 393
primary identification 374, 587, 593
primary movement 174-175
princess role 227
Prinsloo, Jeanne xxi
Print Media South Africa 564
privacy issues with passive peoplemeters 545
privacy, invasion of 36
proairetic codes, *see* action codes
probability sampling 14, 31, 436, 440, 475, 477, 527, 546
problem statement, example of 11-12
production 205
production history 319
programming planning 518
projection 374
 as a research technique 133
property market, narrative example 222-223
proportional distributions 444
Propp, Vladimir 46, 215, 217, 223-231, 235, 236, 255, 258, 290, 306, 308
Propp's 31 narrative functions 224-230, 281-283, 289
 applied to UCT ad case study 234-235
 six stages of 228-229
Propp's narrative model 276, 281-287
Proppian characters 239-240
proxemics 57, 134
proximity 158
pseudo relationships 394
psychoanalysis 44, 324, 365, 380
 and the study of TV 588-590
 as applied to film and TV 596-598
 definition of 371
 of film 369-380
 theory of 583-585
psychoanalytical perspective on film analysis 324
psychographics of audiences 521, 157-158, 162, 179, 180, 185, 200, 201, 216, 399
psychological needs of audiences 397
psychological realism 329, 346
psychological thrillers, indexical nature of 270
psychological time 174
public service broadcasting 301

publication-specific readership surveys 555-556
Pudovkin, VI 136, 179, 328, 329, 332, 336-338
Pulp Fiction 314, 319, 320
purposive sampling 447, 492, 502

Q
qualitative analysis 122
qualitative content analysis 4-5, 198-201, 482
 vs quantitative content analysis 5
qualitative field research 485
qualitative interview, *see* in depth interview
quantification of data 21
quantitative analysis 122
quantitative content analysis, 5-6, 25, 482
quantitative survey research, early days of 424-425
quantity questions 464
queer film theory 380, 382
quest (narrative stage) 217, 219, 226
quest narrative, sequence of 229
questionnaire surveys 554, 557, 558
 appropriate topics for 426-427
 inappropriate topics for 427-428
 types of 449-457
questionnaires
 construction of 430-431
 design of 457-473
 for audience measuring 531-532
 layout of 431
 length of 473
 overall structure of 472-473
 validity of 138
questions, interpretation of 458
questions, order of 473
quota sampling 443-445
 problems inherent in 444

R
race 210, 237
racism 122, 212
 in James Bond stories 293
racist discourse 208, 211
Radio 702 9
radio audiences, measuring of 549-552, 564, 567-568
Radio Audience Measuring Survey (RAMS) 564, 567-568
Radio Highveld 9
Radio Pretoria 8
Radio Sonder Grense 8
random meanings 134
random numbers, table of 439
random sampling 527
 simple 439, 440
rank-order questions 466-467
rap song in UCT ad 238
Rapport 393
ratings for SA programmes 525
ratings research 518
Rautenbach, Jans 321
raw data 19

Index

raw material, definition of 330
Rayburn, II JD 395
random digit dialling 445-446, 455
reach, *see* coverage
reaction in the absence of action 180
read, use of the term 260
readers 148
   active roles of 196-197
   sophisticated nature of 197
   their changing relationships with
      communicators 197-198
   their expectations of conventions 197
readership diaries 556
readership surveys 554-555
reading 577
   between the lines 201
   concept of 521-522
   of print media, defining of 553
reading events, casual nature of 553
realism 324, 326, 355
   definition of 329
realist film theory 339-349
realist theorists 136
reality 42
   definition of 329-330
reality TV 143, 230
recency effects 472, 479
recent reading 555
reception analysis, *see* reception theory
reception research 485, 486, 509
reception theory 390, 398-411
reception theory 506
recognition of disruption (narrative stage) 217
recording devices, their use with focus groups 503
recording devices, use of in participant
     observation 494
recurring characters 284
recycled images 300
re-equilibrium (narrative stage) 127
referent 43, 52
referential function of images 362
referential function of language 105-106
referential function of signs 53, 54
reflective meaning 66-67
reflexivity in ethnography 416
regression 591-593, 594
Reimer, B 397
relaxation, as function of media 393
reliability 20, 21-24
   of surveys 473, 474-475
religious relics 53
Rembrandt lighting 151-152
Remington Steele 277
Renoir, Jean 348
representation 205, 332
representational codes 59-60
representative character 51
representative reliability 474
repressed desires, gratification of by TV and film 582
repression 584, 585

research boundaries 13
research design 474
research issues 136-137
research method, *see* method
research problem, *see* research question
research process 10
research purpose 16
research questions 11-12, 15, 16, 24, 31, 121, 135, 138, 428, 429, 495, 507
   formulating 487-488
research site, entry to 488-489
research surveys, history of 423-425
resolution, in narrative 264
response errors 529
response rates in audience measurement,
     improving 547
response rates to postal surveys 451
restoration of equilibrium (narrative stage) 217
restricted codes 60
retention 399-400
Revolutionary Road 354, 355
rhetoric 109, 211-212, 243, 244
rhetorical analysis 324
rhetorical devices 101-102
rhetorical motifs of film and TV 353
rhetorical practice, kinds of 244
rhetorical triangle 244, 246, 248
rhetorical tropes 79
rhythmic montage 336
Richardson, John 213, 243
ritual nature of soap opera viewing 510
ritualised media use 396-397
rituals of TV viewing 408
role models 410
   in media 395
romanticism 327
Rorschach tests 133
Roscoe, J 391
Rosenthal, R 471
Rosnow, RL 470
Rosselini, Roberto 348
Rousseau's Enlightenment construct of childhood 211
Rubin, AM 396
Rugby World Cup, France 128
running time 173
Russian folk tales 223
   forms of 224
   similarity of to fiction films 230-231
Russian formalism 45, 328
   its effect on Eisenstein 333
Russian social realism 328
Rwanda 247, 248
Rydin, I 509

S

SA film industry 367
SA Advertising Research Foundation (SAARF) 480-482, 520, 531, 564-565, 567-568,
   origins of 563
SABC 9, 486-487, 498, 564

Media Studies: Volume 3

salience 134
sample 24
    selection of 13-14, 31-33
sample size 437-438
sampling 430, 433-448, 626-527
    elements of 446
    in participant observation studies 492
sampling bias, *see* bias
sampling error 442-443, 477-478, 528
sampling frame 436, 439, 455
sampling interval 436
sampling procedures 474
Sapir, Edward 86, 87
Sapir-Whorf hypothesis 87
Sarie Marais 321
Sarris, Andrew 349, 350
Sartre, Jean-Paul 374, 375
Saussure, Ferdinand de 43, 45, 47, 48, 49, 72, 93, 119, 195, 364, 586
scatter charts 25, 28, 29
scenes 173, 359-360
school shooting 248
Schwartz, D 136
scientific knowledge, deligitimisation of 300
scientific method 4
scientific writing, as a discursive practice 103
scientisation of politics 96
scopophilia 377, 591
Scorsese, Martin 313
Scott's pi index 22
screen event density 190
screening questions, *see* contingency questions
search engines 31
Searle, John 106
Sebeok, Thomas 195
secondary identification 593
secondary movement 175-176
secondness 49
sectional analytical montage 180-182
seeing is believing 52
see-saw principle 172-173
segregation 212
Seinfield 305
selective focus 166-169
selective perception 133
selectivity 345
self-administered surveys 449-450, 451, 452
self-classification 426
self-expression through film 347
self-regulation, in narrative 268
self-reporting nature of surveys 425
semantic differential scales 468, 471-472, 479
semantic units 65
semantics 89, 90
semiological analysis 4, 287
semiosis 73, 365
semiotic analysis 65, 364
    a basic guide to 75-80
    of an ad, case study 139-142
semiotic approach to media aesthetics 149
semiotic approach to visual communication 128-132
semiotic systems 125
semiotics 40, 47-50, 89, 90, 93, 195, 205, 324
    history of 42
sensation 127
sentences 98-101
sequence time 173
sequences 173, 359-360
sequential analytic montage 179
Sesame Street, *see* Takalani Sesame
set meters 537-538
settings, as metaphors 194-195
seven stages of semiotic analysis 75-80
sexism 122, 212
shadows, use of to create depth 165
Shamdasani, PN501
shared meaning 134
Short Cuts 313
shot time 173
sign functions 53-57
sign systems 40, 41, 45, 47, 50, 52, 57, 58
sign values 149
significance 74
signification 48, 84, 89
signifieds 43, 48,58, 93, 119, 586
signifiers 43, 48, 58, 93, 119, 268, 586
    imaginary 591-592
signifying codes 58-59
signifying practice 72-73, 356
Signorielli, N 195
signs 41, 43, 49, 47, 48, 50-57, 75, 124, 268, 269, 287
    and meanings, relationship between 129-130
    characteristics of 50-51
    components of 51
    continuum of motivation of 120
    kinds of 51-53
    used as codes 130-131
silent films 179
silhouette lighting 152
Silverstone, Roger 213, 231, 243, 286
similarity 158
similes 131
similitude 149
simulacra 299
simulation, three orders of 298
simultaneity 177-178
single shots 359-360
sitcoms 141
site-centric internet measurement 561-562
Sixguns and Society 353
size of visualised objects as codes of form 165-166
skip questions, *see* contingency questions
Sklovskij, V 45
Sky News 393
Slade, C 89
slang 102
slapstick 17
SmartDraw 26
snowball sampling 447
soap operas 401, 402-408

642

Index

analysis of 403-408
culture of 410
difficulty in analysing 263
lack of narrative closure in 402
regular scheduling of 403
viewing case study 510-512
social codes 61
social construction of individuals 586
social contexts 90, 91, 205, 237
of media consumption 397
of soap opera viewing 511-512
social Darwinism 208, 211
social dimension of TV viewing 408-411
social film historiography 319, 321-322
social forces 125
social hierarchies 211-212
social identity 141
social implications of film 325
social integrative needs 394
social interaction around TV 409-410
social justice 209-210
social networking 198, 394
social orders of discourse 105-107
social research 425
social science police 97
social sciences 90
social semiotics 71-75, 79-80
social surveys, for audience measuring 531-533
society in language 85-88
society, medical and psychiatric programming of 96
sociolinguistics 90
sociology 44
Socrates 351
soliloquy 187-188
Sonderling, Stefan xx-xxi, xxiv
sound 123
sound bites 302
sound effects 186, 188-189, 192, 193
as signs 188-189
South Park 304
space, in narrative 263
space-time image 173
speaking by elites 109
speaking subject 72
special effects, their absence in realist films 340
specificity 21
spectacle 304
speech act 106-107
speech, clarity of 188
Spielberg, Steven 313, 320
spoken language 87
spot time 173
stability reliability 474
stacked bar charts 25, 27
Stacks, DW 35
Stam, R 382
standardised coding forms 22
Star Trek 306, 525
Starck, K 194
static balance 172

statistical analyses 25
statistics, interpretation of 432
Stempel, GM 18
stereotypes 63-64, 121, 122, 124, 130, 194, 247, 276, 308, 381,
in *Cheers* 288
in James Bond stories 293, 294
Stewart, DW 501
stories, being unconsciously surrounded by 256
story time 173
story vs plot 216
story, as a rhetorical and discursive act 251
Stouffer, Samual A 424
Stout, PA 193
strategic interruption in soap operas 403-404, 407
stratified sampling 440-441, 443
strike action, TV coverage of 4
Strinati, D 297
structural codes, *see* codes of form
structural perspectives on genres 353, 354
structural philosophy 47
structuralism 42-47, 258, 582
ahistorical nature of 258-259
as a method 45-47
rules of 46-47
structuralist approach to narrative 214-215
style over substance 297-298
stylistic meaning 66
subject and object 99
subject, definition of 367-368
subjective camera 170-171
subjective meaning 67
subjective meaning, primary dimensions of 471
subjective time 173-174
substitution (in sampling) 481
Suci, JG 471
Sun 4
Sunday Times 393
Sunstein, BS 493
survey interviewing 456-457
survey research, steps in 428-433
survey type, deciding on 430
survey, characteristics of 425-426
Survivor 230, 304
suspense, lack of in TV narrative 306
symbolic codes of narrative 275-276
symbolic dimensions of psychoanalytic film theory 597
symbolic forms 34
symbolic level of signs 74
symbolic meanings 141
symbolic nature of film 357
symbolic signs 51, 52, 129, 201
symbolic universe 86
symbolic universe of language and meaning 586, 587
symbolic violence 111
symbolism, in dreams 585
symbols 124
symptomatic arguments 247
synchronic axis 322

synchronic semiotic analysis 65
synchronism, rule of 47
synecdoche 130, 169, 201
syntactical units of TV and film 119
syntagmatic approach to narrative 223
syntagmatic combinations 177-178
    and field forces 182
    to heighten suspense 180
syntagmatic connotation 357
syntagmatic dimension of Propp's six stages 229
syntagmatic organisation in soap operas 405, 407
syntagmatic sequencing 176
syntagmatic systems 77-79
syntagmatic theories of narrative 215-235
syntax of visual language 119
systematic nature of content analysis 5
systematic sampling 436, 439-440
    disadvantages of 440

T
Table Mountain 238
tables 25
tables, symbolic meaning of in TV 129
Takalani Sesame 174-175
Talk with Noeleen 393
Tannenbaum, PH 471
Tarantino, Quentin 314, 319
target audiences 518
target population 31
    identifying 430, 435-436
Taxi Driver 313
Taxi to Soweto 366, 368
taxonomy of styles 352
Taylor Nelson Sofres 538
Taylor, BC 412
tea leaves, reading of 133
teamwork 19
technical language 87-88
technical terminology, *see* jargon
technological developments in survey interviewing 456-457
technological film historiography 319, 320
technology, its impact on the status of knowledge 301
technology, *see* new media technologies
telephone coincidental 532-533
telephone interviews 454-455, 532-533
telephone recalls 532
television
    and Eco's narrative model 294-297
    as a sign system 41, 57
    dominant cultural messages of 195
    its influence on the development of narrative 280
    modes of address of 592
    offering an illusion of discourse 592-593
    watching habits 255
television ads 12, 190
    analysed by Propp's model
    narrative function of 225
Television Audience Measuring Survey 564, 568-570
television drama 230
television literacy 118
tempo 186, 192
temporal chain-effect 255
tension, in narrative 264
tertiary movement 176-185
text 90
    as mediations 218
    definitions of 148
    language of 91-102
    origin of the word 91-92
    structure of 101
    use of the term 260
    viewed as weaving 211
    syntagmatic and paradigmatic levels of 400-401
text analysis 121, 137, 187, 205-206, 210, 212, 244
    audiovisual 193-194
    in fact and fiction 213
    of music 190
textual gaps in soap operas 404, 405, 407
textual metafunctions 125
The Association for Communication and Advertising (ACA) 564
The Birth of a Nation 348
The cinema of apartheid: race and class in South African cinemas 322
The history and social significance of motion pictures in South Africa:1895-1940 321
The Magnificent Ambersons 343-344
The Office 305
The Republic 351
The Scarecrow and Mrs King 277
The Simpsons 304
The Star 4, 8,393
the western movie genre 353-354
The X-Files 305
thematic editing 345
thematic meaning 67
themes 101
    of content 122
Theory of film: character and growth of a new art 338
Third Cinema 382
thirdness 49
Thompson, JB 209
Thompson, K 216
three-act dramatic structure 263
through-the book surveys 554-555
tilting 175
timbre 186
time 4
    in film 173-174
    in narrative 261-262
time frame 13
time-shift viewing, measuring of 548
Timoshenko 179
Titanic 399
Todorov, Tsvetan 215, 217-223, 235, 236, 255, 282, 290

Index

Todorov's Five Step Model of Narrative 217-218, 221, 229, 242, 276, 278-280, 282, 308
    applied to UCT ad case study 233
Tolstoy, Leo 327
Tomasjevskij 45
tonal montage 336
Toulmin's model 101
Toyota ad 101
track, *see* dolly
traffic code 63
traffic signs, as a sign system 57
transcodification 188-189
transformation 139
    in narrative 218, 268
    nature of 219
trap questions 479
trend line 29
triangulation 476, 507, 512
Tropical Heat 17
trust 495
truth 207-208, 211, 251
truthfulness of survey respondents 458-459
Tshabalala-Msimang, Manto 107
Tsotsi 367
Tulloch, John 508, 509
Tutu, Archbishop Desmond 246
Twin Peaks 303, 305, 525
Twyman, T 551

U

U-Carmen eKhayalitsha 367
Umberto Eco's narrative model 278, 290-297
unambiguous wording of questions 458
unconscious 370
unconscious processes 582, 585
undercover field observation, *see* covert observation
underlying structures affecting society 44
understanding, *see* insight
unemployment 96
unidimensional questions 464
Unisa internet use, case study 413
units of analysis 14-15, 16, 19, 434, 435, 523
    coding of 32-33
universal living standards measure, *see* living standards measure
universe, *see* population
University of Cape Town ad, case study 231233-235
up-diagonal 155
user-centric internet measurement 561-562
uses and gratification theory 390, 391-397, 408-411, 506

V

validity 23
    of surveys 473, 475-477
van Aswegen, A 322
Van Gogh, Vincent 328-329
Van Leeuwen, T 125, 138
Van Vuuren, DP 574

Van Zoest, A 53
van Zoonen, L 212
vanishing point 164
variables 28, 29, 281
    comparisons between 8
    included in LSM measurements 572
VCRs 576
vectors 200
    as content codes 158-161, 162
verbal acts 107
verbal aggression 86
verbal communication 84
verbal messages 89-90
verbal nonsense, as spoken by politicians 109
verbal signs, arbitrary nature of 119-120
verbalisation 48
victim hero 226
video recorders 548
Vietnam, US films about 242
viewer identification 338
viewer involvement density 190
viewer manipulation 332
viewers, interaction with 125
villains 227
    in James Bond stories, appearance of 291
Villanueva, E 194
violence 5, 121
    on TV 16-17
    state, justification of 97
virtual realism 139
Visconti, Luchino 348
visiting 577
    concept of 521-522
viso-linguistic codes 358
visual and media literacy, levels of 121-125
visual codes 142, 198-200
visual communication 117, 120, 126
    in society 138-139
    perceptual approach to 127-135, 149
visual conjunction 179
visual conventions 119
visual elements 119
visual language vs verbal language 118-121
visual literacy 142
    innate nature of 126
    meanings of 118-121
visual media, cultural power of 196
visual narrative structure 123
visual perception 196
    cognitive approach to 149
    semiotic approach to 149
    subjective nature of 132
visual signs 198-199
visualisation 48
vocabulary 94-97
voice, active vs passive 67, 99-101
voice-over commentary 188
volume (of sound) 186
volume 181
    content codes 162-165
volume duality 162-163, 200

volunteer sampling 447-448, 502
voyeur, definition of 371
voyeurism 371, 375, 377-378, 591, 593

W

wage dispute, narrative example 219-221
wandering viewpoint 399
war metaphor 98
watching 577
   concept of 521-522
Webster 531
Webster, JG 521, 522, 531, 560
Wegener, Paul 338
Welles 348
Welles, Orson 343, 346, 348, 350
Wenders, Wim 313
Wenner, LA 395
western genre 286
Western medical discourse 207
Westlake, M 364, 365, 370, 373
Westley, BH 18
what if ... 591
wholeness, of a narrative 267-268
Wiene, Robert 338
Wigston, David xx, xxii
Williams, Raymond 136, 195
Wilson, T 401
Wimmer, RD 18, 485, 492
windows vs mirrors 136
within-household sampling 481
Wollen, Peter 231, 286, 356
women, portrayal of 5, 140, 382
   in ads 130
women, their role in society 64

words 94-97
   and meanings 86
World War II 424, 440
world wide web 33, 125
worms-eye view 164, 172
Wright, Will 286, 353
writing, as a form of mediation 94
written language 87
Wyler, William 343

X

X-axis 153, 174
Xena: Warrior Princess 304
xenophobia 247
X-Files 227

Y

Y-axis 153, 174
Yesterday (film) 367
you, as hero 250
   in UCT ad 238, 240
YouTube 198, 394

Z

Zapiro 130
Z-axis 162, 174, 174-175
Zelizer, B 213
Zettl, H 120, 122, 125, 148, 150, 155, 158, 173, 176, 177
Zikalala, Snuki 486-487
zooming in or out 175
Zuma, Jacob 237
   rape trial of 230